Emanuel Swedenborg

The Delights of Wisdom Pertaining to Conjugial Love,

to which is added the pleasures of insanity pertaining to scortatory love

Emanuel Swedenborg

The Delights of Wisdom Pertaining to Conjugial Love,
to which is added the pleasures of insanity pertaining to scortatory love

ISBN/EAN: 9783337251451

Printed in Europe, USA, Canada, Australia, Japan

Cover: Foto ©Thomas Meinert / pixelio.de

More available books at **www.hansebooks.com**

𝔗𝔥𝔢 𝔇𝔢𝔩𝔦𝔤𝔥𝔱𝔰 of 𝔚𝔦𝔰𝔡𝔬𝔪

PERTAINING TO

CONJUGIAL LOVE

TO WHICH IS ADDED

𝔗𝔥𝔢 ℌ𝔩𝔢𝔞𝔰𝔲𝔯𝔢𝔰 of 𝔍𝔫𝔰𝔞𝔫𝔦𝔱𝔶

PERTAINING TO

SCORTATORY LOVE

BY

EMANUEL SWEDENBORG
A Swede

Being a translation of his work
"DELITIÆ SAPIENTIÆ DE AMORE CONJUGIALI; POST QUAS SEQUUNTUR VOLUPTATES INSANIÆ DE AMORE SCORTATORIO" (Amstelodami 1768)

NEW YORK
AMERICAN SWEDENBORG PRINTING AND PUBLISHING SOCIETY
20 COOPER UNION

1 8 8 5

Published by THE AMERICAN SWEDENBORG PRINTING AND PUBLISHING SOCIETY, *organized for the purpose of Stereotyping, Printing, and Publishing Uniform Editions of the Theological Writings of* EMANUEL SWEDENBORG, *and incorporated in the State of New York,* A. D. 1850.

CONJUGIAL LOVE

AND ITS

CHASTE DELIGHTS.

PRELIMINARY RELATIONS RESPECTING THE JOYS OF HEAVEN
AND NUPTIALS THERE.

1. "I AM aware that many who read the following pages and the MEMORABLE RELATIONS annexed to the chapters, will believe that they are fictions of the imagination; but I solemnly declare they are not fictions, but were truly done and seen; and that I saw them, not in any state of the mind asleep, but in a state of perfect wakefulness: for it has pleased the Lord to manifest himself to me, and to send me to teach the things relating to the New Church, which is meant by the NEW JERUSALEM in the Revelation: for which purpose he has opened the interiors of my mind and spirit; by virtue of which privilege it has been granted me to be in the spiritual world with angels, and at the same time in the natural world with men, and this now [1768] for twenty-five years."

2. On a certain time there appeared to me an angel flying beneath the eastern heaven, with a trumpet in his hand, which he held to his mouth, and sounded towards the north, the west, and the south. He was clothed in a robe, which waved behind him as he flew along, and was girt about the waist with a band that shone like fire and glittered with carbuncles, and sapphires: he flew with his face downwards, and alighted gently on the ground, near where I was standing. As soon as he touched the ground with his feet, he stood erect, and walked to and fro: and on seeing me he directed his steps towards me. I was in the spirit, and was standing in that state on a little eminence in the southern quarter of the spiritual world. When he came near, I addressed him and asked him his errand, telling him that I had heard the sound of his trumpet, and had observed his descent through the air. He replied, "My commission is to

call together such of the inhabitants of this part of the spiritual world, as have come hither from the various kingdoms of christendom, and have been most distinguished for their learning, their ingenuity, and their wisdom, to assemble on this little eminence where you are now standing, and to declare their real sentiments, as to what they had thought, understood, and inwardly perceived, while in the natural world, respecting HEAVENLY JOY and ETERNAL HAPPINESS. The occasion of my commission is this: several who have lately come from the natural world, and have been admitted into our heavenly society, which is in the east, have informed us, that there is not a single person throughout the whole Christian world that is acquainted with the true nature of heavenly joy and eternal happiness; consequently that not a single person is acquainted with the nature of heaven. This information greatly surprised my brethren and companions; and they said to me, 'Go down, call together and assemble those who are most eminent for wisdom in the world of spirits, (where all men are first collected after their departure out of the natural world,) so that we may know of a certainty, from the testimony of many, whether it be true that such thick darkness, or dense ignorance, respecting a future life, prevails among Christians.'" The angel then said to me, "Wait awhile, and you will see several companies of the wise ones flocking together to this place, and the Lord will prepare them a house of assembly." I waited, and lo! in the space of half an hour, I saw two companies from the north, two from the west, and two from the south; and as they came near, they were introduced by the angel that blew the trumpet into the house of assembly prepared for them, where they took their places in the order of the quarters from which they came. There were six groups or companies, and a seventh from the east, which, from its superior light, was not visible to the rest. When they were all assembled, the angel explained to them the reason of their meeting, and desired that each company in order would declare their sentiments respecting HEAVENLY JOY and ETERNAL HAPPINESS. Then each company formed themselves into a ring, with their faces turned one towards another, that they might recall the ideas they had entertained upon the subject in the natural world, and after examination and deliberation might declare their sentiments.

3. After some deliberation, the FIRST COMPANY, which was from the north, declared their opinion, that heavenly joy and eternal happiness constitute the very life of heaven; so much so that whoever enters heaven, enters, in regard to his life, into its festivities, just as a person admitted to a marriage enters into all the festivities of a marriage. "Is not heaven," they argued, "before our eyes in a particular place above us? and is there not there and nowhere else a constant succession of satisfactions

and pleasures? When a man therefore is admitted into heaven, he is also admitted into the full enjoyment of all these satisfactions and pleasures, both as to mental perception and bodily sensation. Of course heavenly happiness, which is also eternal happiness, consists solely in admission into heaven, and that depends purely on the divine mercy and favor." They having concluded, the SECOND COMPANY from the north, according to the measure of the wisdom with which they were endowed, next declared their sentiments as follows: "Heavenly joy and eternal happiness consist solely in the enjoyment of the company of angels, and in holding sweet communications with them, so that the countenance is kept continually expanded with joy; while the smiles of mirth and pleasure, arising from cheerful and entertaining conversation, continually enliven the faces of the company. What else can constitute heavenly joys, but the variations of such pleasures to eternity?" The THIRD COMPANY, which was the first of the wise ones from the western quarter, next declared their sentiments according to the ideas which flowed from their affections: "In what else," said they, " do heavenly joy and eternal happiness consist but in feasting with Abraham, Isaac, and Jacob; at whose tables there will be an abundance of rich and delicate food, with the finest and most generous wines, which will be succeeded by sports and dances of virgins and young men, to the tunes of various musical instruments, enlivened by the most melodious singing of sweet songs; the evening to conclude with dramatic exhibitions, and this again to be followed by feasting, and so on to eternity?" When they had ended, the FOURTH COMPANY, which was the second from the western quarter, declared their sentiments to the following purpose: "We have entertained," said they, "many ideas respecting heavenly joy and eternal happiness; and we have examined a variety of joys, and compared them one with another, and have at length come to the conclusion, that heavenly joys are paradisiacal joys: for what is heaven but a paradise extended from the east to the west, and from the south to the north, wherein are trees laden with fruit, and all kinds of beautiful flowers, and in the midst the magnificent tree of life, around which the blessed will take their seats, and feed on fruits most delicious to the taste, being adorned with garlands of the sweetest smelling flowers? In this paradise there will be a perpetual spring; so that the fruits and flowers will be renewed every day with an infinite variety, and by their continual growth and freshness, added to the vernal temperature of the atmosphere, the souls of the blessed will be daily fitted to receive and taste new joys, till they shall be restored to the flower of their age, and finally to their primitive state, in which Adam and his wife were created, and thus recover their paradise, which has been transplanted from earth to heaven." The FIFTH COMPANY, which was the first of the ingenious spirits from the southern quarter, next delivered their opinion: "Heavenly joys and eternal happiness," said they, "consist solely in exalted power and dignity, and in abundance of wealth, joined with more than princely magnificence and splendor. That the joys of heaven, and their continual fruition, which is eternal happiness, consist in these things, is plain to us from the examples of such persons as enjoyed them in the former world; and also from this circumstance, that the blessed in heaven are to reign with the Lord, and to become kings and princes; for they are the sons of him who is King of kings and Lord of lords, and they are to sit on thrones and be ministered to by angels. Moreover, the magnificence of heaven is plainly made known to us by the description given of the New Jerusalem, wherein is represented the glory of heaven; that it is to have gates, each of which shall consist of a single pearl, and streets of pure gold, and a wall with foundations of precious stones; consequently, every one that is received into heaven will have a palace of his own, glittering with gold and other costly materials, and will enjoy dignity and dominion, each according to his quality and station: and since we find by experience, that the joys and happiness arising from such things are natural, and as it were, innate in us, and since the promises of God cannot fail, we therefore conclude that the most happy state of heavenly life can be derived from no other source than this." After this, the SIXTH COMPANY, which was the second from the southern quarter, with a loud voice spoke as follows: "The joy of heaven and its eternal happiness consist solely in the perpetual glorification of God, in a never-ceasing festival of praise and thanksgiving, and in the blessedness of divine worship, heightened with singing and melody, whereby the heart is kept in a constant state of elevation towards God, under a full persuasion that he accepts such prayers and praises, on account of the divine bounty in imparting blessedness." Some of the company added further, that this glorification would be attended with magnificent illuminations, with most fragrant incense, and with stately processions, preceded by the chief priest with a grand trumpet, who would be followed by primates and officers of various orders, by men carrying palms, and by women with golden images in their hand.

4. The SEVENTH COMPANY, which, from its superior light, was invisible to the rest, came from the east of heaven, and consisted of angels of the same society as the angel that had sounded the trumpet. When these heard in their heaven, that not a single person throughout the Christian world was acquainted with the true nature of heavenly joy and eternal happiness, they said one to another, "Surely this cannot be true; it is impossible that such thick darkness and stupidity should

prevail amongst Christians: let us even go down and hear whether it be true; for if it be so, it is indeed wonderful." Then those angels said to the one that had the trumpet, "You know that every one that has desired heaven, and has formed any definite conception in his mind respecting its joys, is introduced after death into those particular joys which he had imagined; and after he experiences that such joys are only the offspring of the vain delusions of his own fancy, he is led out of his error, and instructed in the truth. This is the case with most of those in the world of spirits, who in their former life have thought about heaven, and from their notions of its joys have desired to possess them." On hearing this, the angel that had the trumpet said to the six companies of the assembled wise ones, "Follow me; and I will introduce you into your respective joys, and thereby into heaven."

5. When the angel had thus spoken, he went before them; and he was first attended by the company who were of opinion that the joys of heaven consisted solely in pleasant associations and entertaining conversation. These the angel introduced to an assembly of spirits in the northern quarter, who, during their abode in the former world, had entertained the same ideas of the joys of heaven. There was in the place a large and spacious house, wherein all these spirits were assembled. In the house there were more than fifty different apartments, allotted to different kinds and subjects of conversation: in some of these apartments they conversed about such matters as they had seen or heard in the public places of resort and the streets of the city; in others the conversation turned upon the various charms of the fair sex, with a mixture of wit and humor, producing cheerful smiles on the countenances of all present; in others they talked about the news relating to courts, to public ministers, and state policy, and to various matters which had transpired from privy councils, interspersing many conjectures and reasonings of their own respecting the issues of such councils; in others again they conversed about trade and merchandise; in others upon subjects of literature; in others upon points of civil prudence and morals; and in others about affairs relating to the Church, its sects, &c. Permission was granted me to enter and look about the house; and I saw people running from one apartment to another, seeking such company as was most suited to their own tempers and inclinations; and in the different parties I could distinguish three kinds of persons; some as it were panting to converse, some eager to ask questions, and others greedily devouring what was said. The house had four doors, one towards each quarter; and I observed several leaving their respective companies with a great desire to get out of the house. I followed some of them to the east door, where I saw several sitting with great marks of dejection

on their faces; and on my inquiring into the cause of their trouble, they replied, "The doors of this house are kept shut against all persons who wish to go out; and this is the third day since we entered, to be entertained according to our desire with company and conversation; and now we are grown so weary with continual discoursing, that we can scarcely bear to hear the sound of a human voice; wherefore, from mere irksomeness, we have betaken ourselves to this door; but on our knocking to have it opened, we were told, that the doors of this house are never opened to let any persons out, but only to let them in, and that we must stay here and enjoy the delights of heaven; from which information we conclude, that we are to remain here to eternity; and this is the cause of our sorrow and lowness of spirits; now too we begin to feel an oppression in the breast, and to be overwhelmed with anxiety." The angel then addressing them said: "These things in which you imagined the true joys of heaven to consist, prove, you find, the destruction of all happiness; since they do not of themselves constitute true heavenly joys, but only contribute thereto." "In what then," said they to the angel, "does heavenly joy consist?" The angel replied briefly, "In the delight of doing something that is useful to ourselves and others; which delight derives its essence from love and its existence from wisdom. The delight of being useful, originating in love, and operating by wisdom, is the very soul and life of all heavenly joys. In the heavens there are frequent occasions of cheerful intercourse and conversation, whereby the minds (*mentes*) of the angels are exhilarated, their minds (*animi*) entertained, their bosoms delighted, and their bodies refreshed; but such occasions do not occur, till they have fulfilled their appointed uses in the discharge of their respective business and duties. It is this fulfilling of uses that gives soul and life to all their delights and entertainments; and if this soul and life be taken away, the contributory joys gradually cease, first exciting indifference, then disgust, and lastly sorrow and anxiety." As the angel ended, the door was thrown open, and those who were sitting near it burst out in haste, and went home to their respective labors and employments, and so found relief and refreshment to their spirits.

6. After this the angel addressed those who fancied the joys of heaven and eternal happiness consisted of partaking of feasts with Abraham, Isaac, and Jacob, succeeded by sports and public exhibitions, and these by other feasts, and so on to eternity. He said, "Follow me; and I will introduce you into the possession of your enjoyments:" and immediately he led them through a grove into a plain floored with planks, on which were set tables, fifteen on one side and fifteen on the other. They then asked, "What is the meaning of so many tables?"

and the angel replied, "The first table is for Abraham, the second for Isaac, the third for Jacob, and the rest in order for the twelve apostles: on the other side are the same number of tables for their wives; the first three are for Sarah, Abraham's wife, for Rebecca, the wife of Isaac, and for Leah and Rachel, the wives of Jacob; and the other twelve are for the wives of the twelve apostles." They had not waited long before the tables were covered with dishes; between which, at stated distances, were ornaments of small pyramids holding sweetmeats. The guests stood around the tables waiting to see their respective presidents: these soon entered according to their order of precedency, beginning with Abraham, and ending with the last of the apostles; and then each president, taking his place at the head of his own table, reclined on a couch, and invited the bystanders to take their places, each on his couch: accordingly the men reclined with the patriarchs and apostles, and the women with their wives: and they ate and drank with much festivity, but with due decorum. When the repast was ended, the patriarchs and apostles retired; and then were introduced various sports and dances of virgins and young men; and these were succeeded by exhibitions. At the conclusion of these entertainments, they were again invited to feasting; but with this particular restriction, that on the first day they should eat with Abraham, on the second with Isaac, on the third with Jacob, on the fourth with Peter, on the fifth with James, on the sixth with John, on the seventh with Paul, and with the rest in order till the fifteenth day, when their festivity should be renewed again in like order, only changing their seats, and so on to eternity. After this the angel called together the company that had attended him, and said to them, "All those whom you have observed at the several tables, had entertained the same imaginary ideas as yourselves, respecting the joys of heaven and eternal happiness; and it is with the intent that they may see the vanity of such ideas, and be withdrawn from them, that those festive representations were appointed and permitted by the Lord. Those who with so much dignity presided at the tables, were merely old people and feigned characters, many of them husbandmen and peasants, who, wearing long beards, and from their wealth being exceedingly proud and arrogant, were easily induced to imagine that they were those patriarchs and apostles. But follow me to the ways that lead from this place of festivity." They accordingly followed, and observed groups of fifty or more, here and there, surfeited with the load of meat which lay on their stomachs, and wishing above all things to return to their domestic employments, their professions, trades, and handicraft works; but many of them were detained by the keepers of the grove, who questioned them concerning the days they had feasted, and whether they had as yet taken their turns with Peter and Paul; representing to them the shame and indecency of departing till they had paid equal respect to the apostles. But the general reply was, "We are surfeited with our entertainment; our food has become insipid to us, we have lost all relish for it, and the very sight of it is loathsome to us; we have spent many days and nights in such repasts of luxury, and can endure it no longer: we therefore earnestly request leave to depart." Then the keepers dismissed them, and they made all possible haste to their respective homes.

After this the angel called the company that attended him, and as they went along he gave them the following information respecting heaven:—"There are in heaven," says he, "as in the world, both meats and drinks, both feasts and repasts; and at the tables of the great there is a variety of the most exquisite food, and all kinds of rich dainties and delicacies, wherewith their minds are exhilarated and refreshed. There are likewise sports and exhibitions, concerts of music, vocal and instrumental, and all these things in the highest perfection. Such things are a source of joy to them, but not of happiness; for happiness ought to be within external joys, and to flow from them. This inward happiness abiding in external joys, is necessary to give them their proper relish, and make them joys; it enriches them, and prevents their becoming loathsome and disgusting; and this happiness is derived to every angel from the use he performs in his duty or employment. There is a certain vein latent in the affection of the will of every angel, which attracts his mind to the execution of some purpose or other, wherein his mind finds itself in tranquillity, and is satisfied. This tranquillity and satisfaction form a state of mind capable of receiving from the Lord the love of uses; and from the reception of this love springs heavenly happiness, which is the life of the above-mentioned joys. Heavenly food in its essence is nothing but love, wisdom, and use united together; that is, use effected by wisdom and derived from love; wherefore food for the body is given to every one in heaven according to the use which he performs; sumptuous food to those who perform eminent uses; moderate, but of an exquisite relish, to those who perform less eminent uses; and ordinary to such as live in the performance of ordinary uses; but none at all to the slothful.

7. After this the angel called to him the company of the so-called wise ones, who supposed heavenly joys, and the eternal happiness thence derived, to consist in exalted power and dominion, with the possession of abundant treasures, attended with more than princely splendor and magnificence, and who had been betrayed into this supposition by what is written in the Word,—that they should be kings and princes, and should reign for ever with Christ, and should be ministered unto by

angels; with many other similar expressions. "Follow me," said the angel to them, " and I will introduce you to your joys." So he led them into a portico constructed of pillars and pyramids: in the front there was a low porch, through which lay the entrance to the portico; through this porch he introduced them, and lo! there appeared to be about twenty people assembled. After waiting some time, they were accosted by a certain person, having the garb and appearance of an angel, and who said to them, "The way to heaven is through this portico; wait awhile and prepare yourselves; for the elder among you are to be kings, and the younger princes." As he said this, they saw near each pillar a throne, and on each throne a silken robe, and on each robe a sceptre and crown; and near each pyramid a seat raised three feet from the ground, and on each seat a massive gold chain, and the ensigns of an order of knighthood, fastened at each end with diamond clasps. After this they heard a voice, saying, "Go now and put on your robes; be seated, and wait awhile:" and instantly the elder ones ran to the thrones, and the younger to the seats; and they put on their robes and seated themselves. When lo! there arose a mist from below, which, communicating its influence to those on the thrones and the seats, caused them instantly to assume airs of authority, and to swell with their new greatness, and to be persuaded in good earnest that they were kings and princes. That mist was an *aura* of phantasy or imagination with which their minds were possessed. Then on a sudden, several young pages presented themselves, as if they came on wings from heaven; and two of them stood in waiting behind every throne, and one behind every seat. Afterwards at intervals a herald proclaimed:—" Ye kings and princes, wait a little longer; your palaces in heaven are making ready for you; your courtiers and guards will soon attend to introduce you." Then they waited and waited in anxious expectation, till their spirits were exhausted, and they grew weary with desire.

After about three hours, the heavens above them were seen to open, and the angels looked down in pity upon them, and said, "Why sit ye in this state of infatuation, assuming characters which do not belong to you? They have made a mockery of you, and have changed you from men into mere images, because of the imagination which has possessed you, that you should reign with Christ as kings and princes, and that angels should minister unto you. Have you forgotten the Lord's words, that whosoever would be the greatest in the kingdom of heaven must be the least of all, and the servant of all? Learn then what is meant by kings and princes, and by reigning with Christ; that it is to be wise and perform uses. The kingdom of Christ, which is heaven, is a kingdom of uses; for the Lord loves every one, and is desirous to do good to every one; and good is the same thing as use: and as the Lord promotes good or use by the mediation of angels in heaven, and of men on earth, therefore to such as faithfully perform uses, he communicates the love thereof, and its reward, which is internal blessedness; and this is true eternal happiness. There are in the heavens, as on earth, distinctions of dignity and eminence, with abundance of the richest treasures; for there are governments and forms of government, and consequently a variety of ranks and orders of power and authority. Those of the highest rank have courts and palaces to live in, which for splendor and magnificence exceed every thing that the kings and princes of the earth can boast of; and they derive honor and glory from the number and magnificence of their courtiers, ministers, and attendants; but then these persons of high rank are chosen from those whose heartfelt delight consists in promoting the public good, and who are only externally pleased with the distinctions of dignity for the sake of order and obedience; and as the public good requires that every individual, being a member of the common body, should be an instrument of use in the society to which he belongs, which use is from the Lord and is effected by angels and men as of themselves, it is plain that this is meant by reigning with the Lord." As soon as the angels had concluded, the kings and princes descended from their thrones and seats, and cast away their sceptres, crowns, and robes; and the mist which contained the *aura* of phantasy was dispersed, and a bright cloud, containing the *aura* of wisdom encompassed them, and thus they were presently restored to their sober senses.

8. After this the angel returned to the house of assembly, and called to him those who had conceived the joys of heaven and eternal happiness to consist in paradisiacal delights; to whom he said, "Follow me, and I will introduce you into your paradisiacal heaven, that you may enter upon the beatitudes of your eternal happiness." Immediately he introduced them through a lofty portal, formed of the boughs and shoots of the finest trees interwoven with each other. After their admission, he led them through a variety of winding paths in different directions. The place was a real paradise, on the confines of heaven, intended for the reception of such as, during their abode on earth, had fancied the whole heaven to be a single paradise, because it is so called, and had been led to conceive that after death there would be a perfect rest from all kinds of labor; which rest would consist in a continual feast of pleasures, such as walking among roses, being exhilarated with the most exquisite wines, and participating in continual mirth and festivity; and that this kind of life could only be enjoyed in a heavenly paradise. As they followed the angel, they saw a great number of old and young, of both sexes, sitting by threes and tens in a

company on banks of roses; some of whom were wreathing garlands to adorn the heads of the seniors, the arms of the young, and the bosoms of the children; others were pressing the juice out of grapes, cherries, and mulberries, which they collected in cups, and then drank with much festivity; some were delighting themselves with the fragrant smells that exhaled far and wide from the flowers, fruits, and odoriferous leaves of a variety of plants; others were singing most melodious songs, to the great entertainment of the hearers; some were sitting by the sides of fountains, and directing the bubbling streams into various forms and channels; others were walking, and amusing one another with cheerful and pleasant conversation; others were retiring into shady arbors to repose on couches; besides a variety of other paradisiacal entertainment. After observing these things, the angel led his companions through various winding paths, till he brought them at length to a most beautiful grove of roses, surrounded by olive, orange, and citron trees. Here they found many persons sitting in a disconsolate posture, with their heads reclined on their hands, and exhibiting all the signs of sorrow and discontent. The companions of the angel accosted them, and inquired into the cause of their grief. They replied, "This is the seventh day since we came into this paradise: on our first admission we seemed to ourselves to be elevated into heaven, and introduced into a participation of its inmost joys; but after three days our pleasures began to pall on the appetite, and our relish was lost, till at length we became insensible to their taste, and found that they had lost the power of pleasing. Our imaginary joys being thus annihilated we were afraid of losing with them all the satisfaction of life, and we began to doubt whether any such thing as eternal happiness exists. We then wandered through a variety of paths and passages, in search of the gate at which we were admitted; but our wandering was in vain: for on inquiring the way of some persons we met, they informed us, that it was impossible to find the gate, as this paradisiacal garden is a spacious labyrinth of such a nature, that whoever wishes to go out, enters further and further into it; 'wherefore,' said they, 'you must of necessity remain here to eternity; you are now in the middle of the garden, where all delights are centred.'" They further said to the angel's companions, "We have now been in this place for a day and a half, and as we despair of ever finding our way out, we have sat down to repose on this bank of roses, where we view around us olive-trees, vines, orange and citron-trees, in great abundance; but the longer we look at them, the more our eyes are wearied with seeing, our noses with smelling, and our palates with tasting: and this is the cause of the sadness, sorrow, and weeping, in which you now behold us." On hearing this relation, the attendant angel said to them, "This paradisiacal laby rinth is truly an entrance into heaven; I know the way that leads out of it; and if you will follow me, I will show it you." No sooner had he uttered those words than they arose from the ground, and, embracing the angel, attended him with his companions. The angel as they went along, instructed them in the true nature of heavenly joy and eternal happiness thence derived. "They do not," said he, "consist in external paradisiacal delights, unless they are also attended with internal. External paradisiacal delights reach only the senses of the body; but internal paradisiacal delights reach the affections of the soul; and the former without the latter are devoid of all heavenly life, because they are devoid of soul; and every delight without its corresponding soul, continually grows more and more languid and dull, and fatigues the mind more than labor. There are in every part of heaven paradisiacal gardens, in which the angels find much joy; and so far as it is attended with a delight of the soul, the joy is real and true." Hereupon they all asked, "What is the delight of the soul, and whence is it derived?" The angel replied, "The delight of the soul is derived from love and wisdom proceeding from the Lord; and as love is operative, and that by means of wisdom, therefore they are both fixed together in the effect of such operation; which effect is use. This delight enters into the soul by influx from the Lord, and descends through the superior and inferior regions of the mind into all the senses of the body, and in them is full and complete; becoming hereby a true joy, and partaking of an eternal nature from the eternal fountain whence it proceeds. You have just now seen a paradisiacal garden; and I can assure you that there is not a single thing therein, even the smallest leaf, which does not exist from the marriage of love and wisdom in use: wherefore if a man be in this marriage, he is in a celestial paradise, and therefore in heaven."

9. After this, the conducting angel returned to the house of assembly, and addressed those who had persuaded themselves that heavenly joy and eternal happiness consist in a perpetual glorification of God, and a continued festival of prayer and praise to eternity; in consequence of a belief they had entertained in the world that they should then see God, and because the life of heaven, originating in the worship of God, is called a perpetual sabbath. "Follow me," said the angel to them, "and I will introduce you to your joy." So he led them into a little city, in the middle of which was a temple, and where all the houses were said to be consecrated chapels. In that city they observed a great concourse of people flocking together from all parts of the neighboring country; and among them a number of priests, who received and saluted them on their arrival, and led them by the hand to the gates of the temple, and from thence into some of the chapels around it, where they initiated them into the per

petual worship of God; telling them that the city was one of the courts leading to heaven, and that the temple was an entrance to a most spacious and magnificent temple in heaven, where the angels glorify God by prayers and praises to eternity. "It is ordained," said they, "both here and in heaven, that you are first to enter into the temple, and remain there for three days and three nights· and after this initiation you are to enter the houses of the city, which are so many chapels consecrated by us to divine worship, and in every house join the congregation in a communion of prayers, praises, and repetitions of holy things; you are to take heed also that nothing but pious, holy, and religious subjects enter into your thoughts, or make a part of your conversation." After this the angel introduced his companions into the temple, which they found filled and crowded with many persons, who on earth had lived in exalted stations, and also with many of an inferior class: guards were stationed at the doors to prevent any one from departing until he had completed his stay of three days. Then said the angel, "This is the second day since the present congregation entered the temple: examine them, and you will see their manner of glorifying God." On their examining them, they observed that most of them were fast asleep, and that those who were awake were listless and yawning; many of them, in consequence of the continual elevation of their thoughts to God, without any attention to the inferior concerns of the body, seemed to themselves, and thence also to others, as if their faces were unconnected with their bodies; several again had a wild and raving look with their eyes, because of their long abstraction from visible objects; in short, every one, being quite tired out, seemed to feel an oppression at the chest, and great weariness of spirits, which showed itself in a violent aversion to what they heard from the pulpit, so that they cried out to the preacher to put an end to his discourse, for their ears were stunned, they could not understand a single word he said, and the very sound of his voice was become painful to them. They then all left their seats, and, crowding in a body to the doors, broke them open, and by mere violence made their way through the guards. The priests hereupon followed, and walked close beside them, teaching, praying, sighing, and encouraging them to celebrate the solemn festival, and to glorify God, and sanctify themselves; "and then," said they, "we will initiate you into the eternal glorification of God in that most magnificent and spacious temple which is in heaven, and so will introduce you to the enjoyment of eternal happiness." These words, however, made but little impression upon them, on account of the listlessness of their minds, arising from the long elevation of their thoughts above their ordinary labors and employments. But when they attempted to disengage themselves from them, the priests caught hold of their hands and garments, in order to force

them back again into the temple to a repetition of their prayers
and praises; but in vain: they insisted on being left to themselves to recruit their spirits; "we shall else die," they said,
"through mere faintness and weariness." At that instant, lo!
there appeared four men in white garments, with mitres on their
heads; one of them while on earth had been an archbishop, and
the other three bishops, all of whom had now become angels. As
they approached, they addressed themselves to the priests, and
said, "We have observed from heaven how you feed these sheep.
Your instruction tends to their infatuation. Do you not know
that to glorify God means to bring forth the fruits of love; that
is, to discharge all the duties of our callings with faithfulness,
sincerity, and diligence? for this is the nature of love towards
God and our neighbor; and this is the bond and blessing of
society. Hereby God is glorified, as well as by acts of worship
at stated times after these duties. Have you never read these
words of the Lord, *Herein is my Father glorified, that ye bring
forth much fruit; so shall ye be my disciples*, John xv. 8. Ye
priests indeed may glorify God by your attendance on his worship, since this is your office, and from the discharge of it you
derive honor, glory, and recompense; but it would be as impossible for you as for others thus to glorify God, unless honor,
glory, and recompense were annexed to your office." Having
said this, the bishops ordered the doorkeepers to give free ingress
and egress to all, there being so great a number of people, who,
from their ignorance of the state and nature of heaven, can form
no other idea of heavenly joy than that it consists in the perpetual worship of God.

10. After this the angel returned with his companions to the
place of assembly, where the several companions of the wise ones
were still waiting; and next he addressed those who fancied that
heavenly joy and eternal happiness depend only on admittance
into heaven, which is obtained merely by divine grace and favor;
and that in such case the persons introduced would enter into the
enjoyments of heaven, just as those introduced to a court-festival
or a marriage, enter into the enjoyment of such scenes. "Wait
here awhile," said the angel, "until I sound my trumpet, and
call together those who have been most distinguished for their
wisdom in regard to the spiritual things of the Church." After
some hours, there appeared nine men, each having a wreath of
laurel on his head as a mark of distinction: these the angel introduced into the house of assembly, where all the companies before
collected were still waiting; and then in their presence he addressed the nine strangers, and said, "I am informed, that in
compliance with your desire, you have been permitted to ascend
into heaven, according to you ideas thereof, and that you have
returned to this inferior or sub-celestial earth, perfectly well
informed as to the nature and state of heaven: tell us therefore

what you have seen, and how heaven appeared to you." Then they replied in order; and the FIRST thus began: "My idea of heaven from my earliest infancy to the end of my life on earth was, that it was a place abounding with all sorts of blessings, satisfactions, enjoyments, gratifications, and delights; and that if I were introduced there, I should be encompassed as by an atmosphere of such felicities, and should receive it with the highest relish, like a bridegroom at the celebration of his nuptials, and when he enters the chamber with his bride. Full of this idea, I ascended into heaven, and passed the first guard and also the second; but when I came to the third, the captain of the guard accosted me and said, " Who are you, friend ?" I replied, " Is not this heaven ? My longing desire to ascend into heaven has brought me hither; I pray you therefore permit me to enter." Then he permitted me; and I saw angels in white garments, who came about me and examined me, and whispered to each other, ' What new guest is this, who is not clothed in heavenly raiment ?' I heard what they said, and thought within myself, This is a similar case to that which the Lord describes, of the person who came to the wedding, and had not on a wedding garment: and I said, 'Give me such garments;' at which they smiled: and instantly one came from the judgment-hall with this command: 'Strip him naked, cast him out, and throw his clothes after him;' and so I was cast out." The SECOND in order then began as follows: " I also supposed that if I were but admitted into heaven, which was over my head, I should there be encompassed with joys, which I should partake of to eternity. I likewise wished to be there, and my wish was granted; but the angels on seeing me fled away, and said one to another, ' What prodigy is this! how came this bird of night here ?' On hearing which, I really felt as if I had undergone some change, and was no longer a man: this however was merely imaginary, and arose from my breathing the heavenly atmosphere. Presently, however, there came one running from the judgment-hall, with an order that two servants should lead me out, and conduct me back by the way I had ascended, till I had reached my own home; and when I arrived there, I again appeared to others and also to myself as a man." The THIRD said, " I always conceived heaven to be some place of blessedness independent of the state of the affections; wherefore as soon as I came into this world, I felt a most ardent desire to go to heaven. Accordingly I followed some whom I saw ascending thither, and was admitted along with them; but I did not proceed far; for when I was desirous to delight my mind (*animus*) according to my idea of heavenly blessedness, a sudden stupor, occasioned by the light of heaven, which is as white as snow, and whose essence is said to be wisdom, seized my mind (*mens*), and darkness my eyes, and I was reduced to a state of insanity: and presently, from the heat of heaven, which corresponds with the brightness of its light, and whose essence is said to be love, there arose in my heart a violent palpitation, a general uneasiness seized my whole frame, and I was inwardly excruciated to such a degree that I threw myself flat on the ground. While I was in this situation, one of the attendants came from the judgment-hall with an order to carry me gently to my own light and heat; and when I came there my spirit and my heart presently returned to me." The FOURTH said, that he also had conceived heaven to be some place of blessedness independent of the state of the affections. "As soon therefore," said he, "as I came into the spiritual world, I inquired of certain wise ones whether I might be permitted to ascend into heaven, and was informed that this liberty was granted to all, but that there was need of caution how they used it, lest they should be cast down again. I made light of this caution, and ascended in full confidence that all were alike qualified for the reception of heavenly bliss in all its fulness: but alas! I was no sooner within the confines of heaven, than my life seemed to be departing from me, and from the violent pains and anguish which seized my head and body, I threw myself prostrate on the ground, where I writhed about like a snake when it is brought near the fire. In this state I crawled to the brink of a precipice, from which I threw myself down, and being taken up by some people who were standing near the place where I fell, by proper care I was soon brought to myself again." The other FIVE then gave a wonderful relation of what befell them in their ascents into heaven, and compared the changes they experienced as to their states of life, with the state of fish when raised out of water into air, and with that of birds when raised out of air into ether; and they declared that, after having suffered so much pain, they had no longer any desire to ascend into heaven, and only wished to live a life agreeable to the state of their own affections, among their like in any place whatever. "We are well informed," they added, "that in the world of spirits, where we now are, all persons undergo a previous preparation, the good for heaven, and the wicked for hell; and that after such preparation they discover ways open for them to societies of their like, with whom they are to live eternally; and that they enter such ways with the utmost delight, because they are suitable to their love." When those of the first assembly had heard these relations, they all likewise acknowledged, that they had never entertained any other notion of heaven than as of a place where they should enter upon the fruition of never-ceasing delights. Then the angel who had the trumpet thus addressed them: "You see now that the joys of heaven and eternal happiness arise not from the place, but from the state of the man's life; and a state of heavenly life is derived from love and wisdom; and since it is use which contains love and wisdom, and in which they are fixed and subsist, therefore a state of heavenly life is derived from the conjunction of love and wisdom in use. It amounts to the same if we call them charity, faith, and good works; for charity is love, faith is truth whence wisdom is derived, and good works are uses. Moreover in our spiritual world there are places as in the natural world; otherwise there could be no habitations and distinct abodes; nevertheless place with us is not place, but an appearance of place according to the state of love and wisdom, or of charity and faith. Every one who becomes an angel, carries his own heaven within himself, because he carries in himself the love of his own heaven; for a man from creation is the smallest effigy, image, and type of the great heaven, and the human form is nothing else; wherefore every one after death comes into that society of heaven of whose general form he is an individual effigy; consequently, when he enters into that society he enters into a form corresponding to his own; thus he passes as it were from himself into that form as into another self, and again from that other self into the same form in himself, and enjoys his own life in that of the society, and that of the society in his own; for every society in heaven may be considered as one common body, and the constituent angels as the similar parts thereof, from which the common body exists. Hence it follows, that those who are in evils, and thence in falses, have formed in themselves an effigy of hell, which suffers torment in heaven from the influx and violent activity of one opposite upon another; for infernal 'ove is opposite to heavenly love, and consequently the delights of those two loves are in a state of discord and enmity, and whenever they meet they endeavor to destroy each other."

11. After this a voice was heard from heaven, saying to the angel that had the trumpet, "Select ten out of the whole assembly, and introduce them to us. We have heard from the Lord that He will prepare them so as to prevent the heat and light, or the love and wisdom, of our heaven, from doing them any injury during the space of three days." Ten were then selected and followed the angel. They ascended by a steep path up a certain hill, and from thence up a mountain, on the summit of which was situated the heaven of those angels, which had before appeared to them at a distance like an expanse in the clouds. The gates were opened for them; and after they had passed the third gate, the introducing angel hastened to the prince of the society, or of that heaven, and announced their arrival. The prince said, " Take some of my attendants, and carry them word that their arrival is agreeable to me, and introduce them into my reception-room, and provide for each a separate apartment with a chamber, and appoint some of my attendants and servants to wait upon them and attend to their wishes:" all which was done. On being introduced by the angel, they asked whether they might go and see the prince; and the angel replied, " It is now morning, and it is not allowable before noon; till that time every one is engaged in his particular duty and employment: but you are invited to dinner, and then you will sit at table with our

prince; in the meantime I will introduce you into his palace, and show you its splendid and magnificent contents."

12. When they were come to the palace, they first viewed it from without. It was large and spacious, built of porphyry, with a foundation of jasper; and before the gates were six lofty columns of lapis lazuli; the roof was of plates of gold, the lofty windows, of the most transparent crystal, had frames also of gold. After viewing the outside they were introduced within, and were conducted from one apartment to another; in each of which they saw ornaments of inexpressible elegance and beauty; and beneath the roof were sculptured decorations of inimitable workmanship. Near the walls were set silver tables overlaid with gold, on which were placed various implements made of precious stones, and of entire gems in heavenly forms, with several other things, such as no eye had ever seen on earth, and consequently such as could never be supposed to exist in heaven. While they were struck with astonishment at these magnificent sights, the angel said, " Be not surprised; the things which you now behold are not the production and workmanship of any angelic hand, but are framed by the Builder of the universe, and presented as a gift to our prince; wherefore the architectonic art is here in its essential perfection, and hence are derived all the rules of that art which are known and practised in the world." The angel further said, "You may possibly conceive that such objects charm our eyes, and infatuate us by their grandeur, so that we consider them as constituting the joys of our heaven: this however is not the case; for our affections not being set on such things, they are only contributory to the joys of our hearts; and therefore, so far as we contemplate them as such, and as the workmanship of God, so far we contemplate in them the divine omnipotence and mercy."

13. After this the angel said to them, "It is not yet noon: come with me into our prince's garden, which is near the palace." So they went with him; and as they were entering, he said, " Behold here the most magnificent of all the gardens in our heavenly society!" But they replied, "How! there is no garden here. We see only one tree, and on its branches and at its top as it were golden fruit and silver leaves, with their edges adorned with emeralds, and beneath the tree little children with their nurses." Hereupon the angel, with an inspired voice said, "This tree is in the midst of the garden; some of us call it the tree of our heaven, and some, the tree of life. But advance nearer, and your eyes will be opened, and you will see the garden." They did so, and their eyes were opened, and they saw numerous trees bearing an abundance of fine flavored fruit, entwined about with young vines, whose tops with their fruit inclined towards the tree of life in the midst. These trees were planted in a continuous series, which, proceeding from a point, and being continued into endless circles, or gyrations, as of a perpetual spiral, formed a perfect spiral of trees, wherein one species continually succeeded another, accord-

ing to the worth and excellence of their fruit. The circumgyration began at a considerable distance from the tree in the midst, and the intervening space was radiant with a beam of light, which caused the trees in the circle to shine with a graduated splendor that was continued from the first to the last. The first trees were the most excellent of all, abounding with the choicest fruits, and were called paradisiacal trees, being such as are never seen in any country of the natural world, because none such ever grew or could grow there. These were succeeded by olive-trees, the olives by vines, these by sweet-scented shrubs, and these again by timber trees, whose wood was useful for building. At stated intervals in this spiral or gyre of trees, were interspersed seats, formed of the young shoots of the trees behind, brought forward and entwined in each other, while the fruit of the trees hanging over at the same time enriched and adorned them. At this perpetually winding circle of trees, there were passages which opened into flower-gardens, and from them into shrubberies, laid out into areas and beds. At the sight of all these things the companions of the angels exclaimed, "Behold heaven in form! wherever we turn our eyes we feel an influx of somewhat celestially-paradisiacal, which is not to be expressed." At this the angel rejoicing said, "All the gardens of our heaven are representative forms or types of heavenly beatitudes in their origins; and because the influx of these beatitudes elevated your minds, therefore you exclaimed, 'Behold heaven in form!' but those who do not receive that influx, regard these paradisiacal gardens only as common woods or forests. All those who are under the influence of the love of use receive the influx; but those who are under the influence of the love of glory not originating in use, do not receive it." Afterwards he explained to them what every particular thing in the garden represented and signified.

14. While they were thus employed, there came a messenger from the prince, with an invitation to them to dine with him; and at the same time two attendants brought garments of fine linen, and said, "Put on these; for no one is admitted to the prince's table unless he be clothed in the garments of heaven." So they put them on, and accompanied their angel, and were shewn into a drawing-room belonging to the palace, where they waited for the prince; and there the angel introduced them to the company and conversation of the grandees and nobles, who were also waiting for the prince's appearing. And lo! in about an hour the doors were opened, and through one larger than the rest, on the western side, he was seen to enter in stately procession. His inferior counsellors went before him, after them his privy-counsellors, and next the chief officers belonging to the court; in the middle of these was the prince; after him followed courtiers of various ranks, and lastly the guards; in all they amounted to a hundred and twenty. Then the angel, advancing before the ten strangers, who by their dress now appeared like

inmates of the place, approached with them towards the prince, and reverently introduced them to his notice; and the prince, without stopping the procession, said to them, "Come and dine with me." So they followed him into the dining-hall, where they saw a table magnificently set out, having in the middle a tall golden pyramid with a hundred branches in three rows, each branch having a small dish, or basket, containing a variety of sweetmeats and preserves, with other delicacies made of bread and wine; and through the middle of the pyramid there issued as it were a bubbling fountain of nectareous wine, the stream of which, falling from the summit of the pyramid separated into different channels and filled the cups. At the sides of this pyramid were various heavenly golden forms, on which were dishes and plates covered with all kinds of food. The heavenly forms supporting the dishes and plates were forms of art, derived from wisdom, such as cannot be devised by any human art, or expressed by any human words: the dishes and plates were of silver, on which were engraved forms similar to those that supported them; the cups were transparent gems. Such was the splendid furniture of the table.

15. As regards the dress of the prince and his ministers, the prince wore a long purple robe, set with silver stars wrought in needle-work; under this robe he had a tunic of bright silk of a blue or hyacinthine color; this was open about the breast, where there appeared the forepart of a kind of zone or ribbon, with the ensign of his society; the badge was an eagle sitting on her young at the top of a tree; this was wrought in polished gold set with diamonds. The counsellors were dressed nearly after the same manner, but without the badge; instead of which they wore sapphires curiously cut, hanging from their necks by a golden chain. The courtiers wore brownish cloaks, wrought with flowers encompassing young eagles; their tunics were of an opal-colored silk, so were also their lower garments; thus were they dressed.

16. The privy-counsellors, with those of inferior order, and the grandees stood around the table, and by command of the prince folded their hands, and at the same time in a low voice said a prayer of thanksgiving to the Lord; and after this, at a sign from the prince, they reclined on couches at the table. The prince then said to the ten strangers, "Do ye also recline with me; behold, there are your couches:" so they reclined; and the attendants, who were before sent by the prince to wait upon them, stood behind them. Then said the prince to them, "Take each of you a plate from its supporting form, and afterwards a dish from the pyramid;" and they did so; and lo! instantly new plates and dishes appeared in the place of those that were taken away; and their cups were filled with wine that streamed from the fountain out of the tall pyramid: and they ate and drank. When dinner was about half ended, the prince addressed the

ten new guests, and said, "I have been informed that you were convened in the country which is immediately under this heaven, in order to declare your thoughts respecting the joys of heaven and eternal happiness thence derived, and that you professed different opinions each according to his peculiar ideas of delight originating in the bodily senses. But what are the delights of the bodily senses without those of the soul? The former are animated by the latter. The delights of the soul in themselves are imperceptible beatitudes; but, as they descend into the thoughts of the mind, and thence into the sensations of the body, they become more and more perceptible: in the thoughts of the mind they are perceived as satisfactions, in the sensations of the body as delights, and in the body itself as pleasures. Eternal happiness is derived from the latter and the former taken together; but from the latter alone there results a happiness not eternal but temporary, which quickly comes to an end and passes away, and in some cases becomes unhappiness. You have now seen that all your joys are also joys of heaven, and that these are far more excellent than you could have conceived; yet such joys do not inwardly affect our minds. There are three things which enter by influx from the Lord as a one into our souls; these three as a one, or this trine, are love, wisdom, and use. Love and wisdom of themselves exist only ideally, being confined to the affections and thoughts of the mind; but in use they exist really, because they are together in act and bodily employment; and where they exist really, there they also subsist. And as love and wisdom exist and subsist in use, it is by use we are affected; and use consists in a faithful, sincere, and diligent discharge of the duties of our calling. The love of use, and a consequent application to it, preserve the powers of the mind, and prevent their dispersion; so that the mind is guarded against wandering and dissipation, and the imbibing of false lusts, which with their enchanting delusions flow in from the body and the world through the senses, whereby the truths of religion and morality, with all that is good in either, become the sport of every wind; but the application of the mind to use binds and unites those truths, and disposes the mind to become a form receptible of the wisdom thence derived; and in this case it extirpates the idle sports and pastimes of falsity and vanity, banishing them from its centre towards the circumference. But you will hear more on this subject from the wise ones of our society, when I will send to you in the afternoon. So saying, the prince arose, and the new guests along with him, and bidding them farewell, he charged the conducting angel to lead them back to their private apartments, and there to show them every token of civility and respect, and also to invite some courteous and agreeable company to entertain them with conversation respecting the various joys of this society.

17. The angel executed the prince's charge; and when they

were turned to their private apartments, the company, invited from the city to inform them respecting the various joys of the society, arrived, and after the usual compliments entered into conversation with them as they walked along in a strain at once entertaining and elegant. But the conducting angel said, "These ten men were invited into this heaven to see its joys, and to receive thereby a new idea concerning eternal happiness. Acquaint us therefore with some of its joys which affect the bodily senses; and afterwards, some wise ones will arrive, who will acquaint us with what renders those joys satisfactory and happy." Then the company who were invited from the city related the following particulars:—"1. There are here days of festivity appointed by the prince, that the mind, by due relaxation, may recover from the weariness which an emulative desire may occasion in particular cases. On such days we have concerts of music and singing in the public places, and out of the city are exhibited games and shows: in the public places at such times are raised orchestras surrounded with balusters formed of vines wreathed together, from which hang bunches of ripe grapes; within these balusters in three rows, one above another, sit the musicians, with their wind and stringed instruments of various tones, both high and low, loud and soft; and near them are singers of both sexes who entertain the citizens with the sweetest music and singing, both in concert and solo, varied at times as to its particular kind: these concerts continue on those days of festivity from morning till noon, and afterwards till evening. 2. Moreover, every morning from the houses around the public places we hear the sweetest songs of virgins and young girls, which resound though the whole city. It is an affection of spiritual love, which is sung every morning; that is, it is rendered sonorous by modifications of the voice in singing, or by modulations. The affection in the song is perceived as the real affection, flowing into the minds of the hearers, and exciting them to a correspondence with it: such is the nature of heavenly singing. The virgin-singers say, that the sound of their song is as it were self-inspired and self-animated from within, and exalted with delight according to the reception it meets with from the hearers. When this is ended, the windows of the houses around the public places, and likewise of those in the streets, are shut, and so also are the doors; and then the whole city is silent, and no noise heard in any part of it, nor is any person seen loitering in the streets, but all are intent on their work and the duties of their calling. 3. At noon, however, the doors are opened, and in the afternoon also the windows in some houses, and boys and girls are seen playing in the streets, while their masters and mistresses sit in the porches of their houses, watching over them, and keeping them in order. 4. At the extreme parts of the city there are various sports of boys and young men, as running, hand-ball, tennis, &c.; there are besides trials of skill among the boys, in order to discover the readiness of their wit in speaking, acting, and perceiving; and such as excel receive some leaves of laurel as a reward; not to mention other things of a like nature, designed to call forth and exercise the latent talents of the young people. 5. Moreover out of the city are exhibited stage-entertainments, in which the actors represent the various graces and virtues of moral life, among whom are inferior characters for the sake of relatives." And one of the ten asked, "How for the sake of relatives?" And they replied, "No virtue with its graces and beauties, can be suitably represented except by means of relatives, in which are comprised and represented all its graces and beauties, from the greatest to the least; and the inferior characters represent the least, even till they become extinct; but it is provided by law, that nothing of the opposite, which is indecorous and dishonorable, should be exhibited, except figuratively, and as it were remotely. The reason of which provision is, because nothing that is honorable and good in any virtue can by successive progressions pass over to what is dishonorable and evil: it only proceeds to its least, when it perishes; and when that is the case, the opposite commences; wherefore heaven, where all things are honorable and good, has nothing in common with hell, where all things are dishonorable and evil."

18. During this conversation, a servant came in and brought word, that the eight wise ones, invited by the prince's order, were arrived, and wished to be admitted; whereupon the angel went out to receive and introduce them: and presently the wise ones, after the customary ceremonies of introduction, began to converse with them on the beginnings and increments of wisdom, with which they intermixed various remarks respecting its progression, shewing, that with the angels it never ceases or comes to a period, but advances and increases to eternity. Hereupon the attendant angel said to them, "Our prince at table while talking with these strangers respecting the seat or abode of wisdom, showed that it consists in use: if agreeable to you, be pleased to acquaint them further on the same subject." They therefore said, "Man, at his first creation, was endued with wisdom and its love, not for the sake of himself, but that he might communicate it to others from himself. Hence it is a maxim inscribed on the wisdom of the wise, that no one is wise for himself alone, or lives for himself, but for others at the same time: this is the origin of society, which otherwise could not exist. To live for others is to perform uses. Uses are the bonds of society, which are as many in number as there are good uses; and the number of uses is infinite. There are spiritual uses, such as regard love to God and love towards our neighbour; there are moral and civil uses, such as regard the love of the society and state to which a man belongs, and of his fellow-citizens among whom he lives; there are natural uses,

which regard the love of the world and its necessities; and there are corporeal uses, such as regard the love of self-preservation with a view to superior uses. All these uses are inscribed on man, and follow in order one after another; and when they are together, one is in the other. Those who are in the first uses, which are spiritual, are in all the succeeding ones, and such persons are wise; but those who are not in the first, and yet are in the second, and thereby in the succeeding ones, are not so highly principled in wisdom, but only appear to be so by virtue of an external morality and civility; those who are neither in the first nor second, but only in the third and fourth, have not the least pretensions to wisdom; for they are satans, loving only the world and themselves for the sake of the world; but those who are only in the fourth, are least wise of all; for they are devils, because they live to themselves alone, and only to others for the sake of themselves. Moreover, every love has its particular delight; for it is by delight that love is kept alive; and the delight of the love of uses is a heavenly delight, which enters into succeeding delights in their order, and according to the order of succession, exalts them and makes them eternal." After this they enumerated the heavenly delights proceeding from the love of uses, and said, that they are a thousand times ten thousand; and that all who enter heaven enter into those delights. With further wise conversation on the love of use, they passed the day with them until evening.

19. Towards evening there came a messenger clothed in linen to the ten strangers who attended the angel, and invited them to a marriage-ceremony which was to be celebrated the next day, and the strangers were much rejoiced to think that they were also to be present at a marriage-ceremony in heaven. After this they were conducted to the house of one of the counsellors, and supped with him; and after supper they returned to the palace, and each retired to his own chamber, where they slept till morning. When they awoke, they heard the singing of the virgins and young girls from the houses around the public places of resort, which we mentioned above. They sung that morning the affection of conjugial love; the sweetness of which so affected and moved the hearers, that they perceived sensibly a blessed serenity instilled into their joys, which at the some time exalted and renewed them. At the hour appointed the angel said, "Make yourselves ready, and put on the heavenly garments which our prince sent you;" and they did so, and lo! the garments were resplendent as with a flaming light; and on their asking the angel, "Whence is this?" he replied, "Because you are going to a marriage-ceremony; and when that is the case, our garments always assume a shining appearance, and become marriage-garments."

20. After this the angel conducted them to the house where

the nuptials were to be celebrated, and the porter opened the door; and presently being admitted within the house, they were received and welcomed by an angel sent from the bridegroom, and were introduced and shewn to the seats intended for them: and soon after they were invited into an ante-chamber, in the middle of which they saw a table, and on it a magnificent candlestick with seven branches and sconces of gold: against the walls there were hung silver lamps, which being lighted made the atmosphere appear of a golden hue: and they observed on each side of the candlestick two tables, on which were set loaves in three rows; there were tables also at the four corners of the room, on which were placed crystal cups. While they were viewing these things, lo! a door opened from a closet near the marriage-chamber, and six virgins came out, and after them the bridegroom and the bride, holding each other by the hand, and advancing towards a seat placed opposite to the candlestick, on which they seated themselves, the bridegroom on the left hand, and the bride on the right, while the six virgins stood by the seat near the bride. The bridegroom was dressed in a robe of bright purple, and a tunic of fine shining linen, with an ephod, on which was a golden plate set round with diamonds, and on the plate was engraved a young eagle, the marriage-ensign of that heavenly society; on his head he wore a mitre: the bride was dressed in a scarlet mantle, under which was a gown, ornamented with fine needle-work, that reached from her neck to her feet, and beneath her bosom she wore a golden girdle, and on her head a golden crown set with rubies. When they were thus seated, the bridegroom turning himself towards the bride, put a golden ring on her finger; he then took bracelets and a pearl necklace, and clasped the bracelets about her wrists, and the necklace about her neck, and said, "*Accept these pledges;*" and as she accepted them he kissed her, and said, "Now thou art mine;" and he called her his wife. On this all the company cried out, "May the divine blessing be upon you!" These words were first pronounced by each separately, and afterwards by all together. They were pronounced also in turn by a certain person sent from the prince as his representative; and at that instant the ante-chamber was filled with an aromatic smoke, which was a token of blessing from heaven. Then the servants in waiting took loaves from the two tables near the candlestick, and cups, now filled with wine, from the tables at the corners of the room, and gave to each of the guests his own loaf and his own cup, and they ate and drank. After this the husband and his wife arose, and the six virgins attended them with the silver lamps, now lighted, in their hands to the threshold; and the married pair entered their chamber; and the door was shut.

21. Afterwards the conducting angel talked with the guests about his ten companions, acquainting them how he was com-

missioned to introduce them, and shew them the magnificent things contained in the prince's palace, and other wonderful sights; and how they had dined at table with him, and afterwards had conversed with the wise ones of the society; and he said, "May I be permitted to introduce them also to you, in order that they may enjoy the pleasure of your conversation?" So he introduced them, and they entered into discourse together. Then a certain wise personage, one of the marriage-guests, said, "Do you understand the meaning of what you have seen?" They replied, "But little;" and then they asked him, "Why was the bridegroom, who is now a husband, dressed in that particular manner?" He answered, "Because the bridegroom, now a husband, represented the Lord, and the bride, who is now a wife, represented the church; for marriages in heaven represent the marriage of the Lord with the church. This is the reason why he wore a mitre on his head, and was dressed in a robe, a tunic, and an ephod, like Aaron; and why the bride had a crown on her head, and wore a mantle like a queen; but to-morrow they will be dressed differently, because this representation lasts no longer than to-day." They further asked, "Since he represented the Lord, and she the church, why did she sit at his right hand?" The wise one replied, "Because there are two things which constitute the marriage of the Lord with the church—love and wisdom; the Lord is love, and the church is wisdom; and wisdom is at the right hand of love; for every member of the church is wise as of himself, and in proportion as he is wise he receives love from the Lord. The right hand also signifies power; and love has power by means of wisdom; but, as we have just observed, after the marriage-ceremony the representation is changed; for then the husband represents wisdom, and the wife the love of his wisdom. This love however is not primary, but secondary love; being derived from the Lord to the wife through the wisdom of the husband: the love of the Lord, which is the primary love, is the husband's love of being wise; therefore after marriage, both together, the husband and his wife, represent the church." They asked again, "Why did not you men stand by the bridegroom, now the husband, as the six virgins stood by the bride, now the wife?" The wise one answered, "Because we to-day are numbered among the virgins; and the number six signifies all and what is complete." But they said, "Explain your meaning." He replied, "Virgins signify the church; and the church consists of both sexes: therefore also we, with respect to the church, are virgins. That this is the case, is evident from these words in the Revelation: '*These are those who were not defiled with women; for they are* VIRGINS: *and they follow the Lamb whithersoever he goeth,*' chap. xiv. 4. And as virgins signify the church, therefore the Lord likened it to ten virgins invited to a marriage, Mat. xxv.

And as Israel, Zion, and Jerusalem, signify the church, therefore mention is so often made in the Word, of the VIRGIN AND DAUGHTER OF ISRAEL, OF ZION, AND OF JERUSALEM. The Lord also describes his marriage with the church in these words: ' UPON THY RIGHT HAND DID STAND THE QUEEN *in gold of Ophir: her clothing is of wrought gold: she shall be brought unto the king in* RAIMENT OF NEEDLEWORK: THE VIRGINS *her companions* THAT FOLLOW HER *shall enter into the king's palace*,' Psalm xlv. 9—16." Lastly they asked, "Is it not expedient that a priest be present and minister at the marriage-ceremony?" The wise one answered, "This is expedient on the earth, but not in the heavens, by reason of the representation of the Lord himself and the church. On the earth they are not aware of this; but even with us a priest ministers in whatever relates to betrothings, or marriage-contracts, and hears, receives, confirms, and consecrates the consent of the parties. Consent is the essential of marriage; all succeeding ceremonies are its formalities."

22. After this the conducting angel went to the six virgins, and gave them an account of his companions, and requested that they would vouchsafe to join company with them. Accordingly they came; but when they drew near, they suddenly retired, and went into the ladies' apartment to the virgins their companions. On seeing this, the conducting angel followed them, and asked why they retired so suddenly without entering into conversation? They replied, "We cannot approach:" and he said, " Why not?" They answered, " We do not know; but we perceived something which repelled us and drove us back again. We hope they will excuse us." The angel then returned to his companions, and told them what the virgins had said, and added, " I conjecture that your love of the sex is not chaste. In heaven we love virgins for their beauty and the elegance of their manners; and we love them intensely, but chastely." Hereupon his companions smiled and said, "You conjecture right: who can behold such beauties near and not feel some excitement?"

23. After much entertaining conversation the marriage-guests departed, and also the ten strangers with their attendant angel; and the evening being far advanced, they retired to rest. In the morning they heard a proclamation, TO-DAY IS THE SABBATH. They then arose and asked the angel what it meant: he replied, "It is for the worship of God, which returns at stated periods, and is proclaimed by the priests. The worship is performed in our temples and lasts about two hours; wherefore if it please you, come along with me, and I will introduce you." So they made themselves ready, and attended the angel, and entered the temple. It was a large building capable of containing about three thousand persons, of a semicircular form, with benches or seats carried round in a continued sweep according to the figure

of the temple; the hinder ones being more elevated than those in front. The pulpit in front of the seats was drawn a little from the centre; the door was behind the pulpit on the left hand. The ten strangers entered with their conducting angel, who pointed out to them the places where they were to sit; telling them, " Every one that enters the temple knows his own place by a kind of innate perception ; nor can he sit in any place but his own : in case he takes another place, he neither hears nor perceives anything, and he also disturbs the order; the consequence of which is, that the priest is not inspired."

24. When the congregation had assembled, the priest ascended the pulpit, and preached a sermon full of the spirit of wisdom. The discourse was concerning the sanctity of the Holy Scriptures, and the conjunction of the Lord with both worlds, the spiritual and the natural, by means thereof. In the illustration in which he then was, he fully proved, that that holy book was dictated by Jehovah the Lord, and that consequently He is in it, so as to be the wisdom it contains; but that the wisdom which is Himself therein, lies concealed under the sense of the letter, and is opened only to those who are in the truths of doctrine, and at the same time in goodness of life, and thus who are in the Lord, and the Lord in them. To his discourse he added a votive prayer and descended. As the audience were going out, the angel requested the priest to speak a few words of peace with his ten companions; so he came to them, and they conversed together for about half an hour. He discoursed concerning the divine trinity—that it is in Jesus Christ, in whom all the fulness of the Godhead dwells bodily, according to the declaration of the apostle Paul; and afterwards concerning the union of charity and faith; but he said, " the union of charity and truth ;" because faith is truth.

25. After expressing their thanks they returned home ; and then the angel said to them, " This is the third day since you came into the society of this heaven, and you were prepared by the Lord to stay here three days ; it is time therefore that we separate; put off therefore the garments sent you by the prince, and put on your own." When they had done so, they were inspired with a desire to be gone ; so they departed and descended, the angel attending them to the place of assembly ; and there they gave thanks to the Lord for vouchsafing to bless them with knowledge, and thereby with intelligence, concerning heavenly joys and eternal happiness.

26. "I again solemnly declare, that these things were done and said as they are related; the former in the world of spirits, which is intermediate between heaven and hell, and the latter in the society of heaven to which the angel with the trumpet and the conductor belonged. Who in the Christian world would have known anything concerning heaven, and the joys and hap-

piness there experienced, the knowledge of which is the knowledge of salvation, unless it had pleased the Lord to open to some person the sight of his spirit, in order to shew and teach them? That similar things exist in the spiritual world is very manifest from what were seen and heard by the apostle John, as described in the Revelation; as that he saw the Son of Man in the midst of seven candlesticks; also a tabernacle, temple, ark, and altar in heaven; a book sealed with seven seals; the book opened, and horses going forth thence; four animals around the throne; twelve thousand chosen out of every tribe; locusts ascending out of the bottomless pit; a dragon, and his combat with Michael; a woman bringing forth a male child, and flying into a wilderness on account of the dragon; two beasts, one ascending out of the sea, the other out of the earth; a woman sitting upon a scarlet beast; the dragon cast out into a lake of fire and brimstone; a white horse and a great supper; a new heaven and a new earth, and the holy Jerusalem descending described as to its gates, wall, and foundation; also a river of the water of life, and trees of life bearing fruits every month; besides several other particulars; all which things were seen by John, while as to his spirit he was in the spiritual world and in heaven: not to mention the things seen by the apostles after the Lord's resurrection; and what were afterwards seen and heard by Peter, Acts xi.; also by Paul; moreover by the prophets; as by EZEKIEL, who saw four animals which were cherubs, chap i. and chap x.; a new temple and a new earth, and an angel measuring them, chap. xl.—xlviii.; and was led away to Jerusalem, and saw there abominations: and also into Chaldea into captivity, chap. viii. and chap. xi. The case was similar with ZECHARIAH, who saw a man riding among myrtles; also four horns, chap. i. 8, and following verses; and afterwards a man with a measuring-line in his hand, chap. ii. 1, and following verses; likewise a candlestick and two olive trees, chap. iv. 2, and following verses; also a flying roll and an ephah, chap. v. 1, 6; also four chariots going forth between two mountains, and horses, chap. vi. 1, and following verses. So likewise with DANIEL, who saw four beasts coming up out of the sea, chap. vii. 1, and following verses; also combats of a ram and he-goat, chap. viii. 1, and following verses; who also saw the angel Gabriel, and had much discourse with him, chap. ix.: the youth of Elisha saw chariots and horses of fire round about Elisha, and saw them when his eyes were opened, 2 Kings vi. 15, and following verses. From these and several other instances in the Word, it is evident, that the things which exist in the spiritual world, appeared to many both before and after the Lord's coming: is it any wonder then, that the same things should now also appear when the church is commencing, or when the New Jerusalem is coming down from the Lord out of heaven?"

ON MARRIAGES IN HEAVEN.

27. THAT there are marriages in heaven cannot be admitted as an article of faith by those who imagine that a man after death is a soul or spirit, and who conceive of a soul or spirit as of a rarefied ether or vapor; who imagine also, that a man will not live as a man till after the day of the last judgment; and in general who know nothing respecting the spiritual world, in which angels and spirits dwell, consequently in which there are heavens and hells: and as that world has been heretofore unknown, and mankind have been in total ignorance that the angels of heaven are men, in a perfect form, and in like manner infernal spirits, but in an imperfect form, therefore it was impossible for anything to be revealed concerning marriages in that world; for if it had it would have been objected, "How can a soul be joined with a soul, or a vapor with a vapor, as one married partner with another here on earth?" not to mention other similar objections, which, the instant they were made, would take away and dissipate all faith respecting marriages in another life. But now, since several particulars have been revealed concerning that world, and a description has also been given of its nature and quality, in the treatise on HEAVEN AND HELL, and also in the APOCALYPSE REVEALED, the assertion, that marriages take place in that world, may be so far confirmed as even to convince the reason by the following propositions: I. *A man* (homo) *lives a man after death.* II. *In this case a male is a male, and a female a female.* III. *Every one's peculiar love remains with him after death.* IV. *The love of the sex especially remains; and with those who go to heaven, which is the case with all who become spiritual here on earth, conjugial love remains.* V. *These things fully confirmed by ocular demonstration.* VI. *Consequently that there are marriages in the heavens.* VII. *Spiritual nuptials are to be understood by the Lord's words, where he says, that after the resurrection they are not given in marriage.* We will now give an explanation of these propositions in their order.

28. I. A MAN LIVES A MAN AFTER DEATH. That a man lives a man after death has been heretofore unknown in the world, for the reasons just now mentioned; and, what is surprising, it has been unknown even in the Christian world, where they have the Word, and illustration thence concerning eternal life, and where the Lord himself teaches, *That all the dead rise again; and that God is not the God of the dead but of the living*, Matt. xxii. 31, 32. Luke xx. 37, 38. Moreover, a man, as to the affections and thoughts of his mind, is in the midst of angels and spirits, and is so consociated with them that were he to be separated from them he would instantly die. It is still more surprising that this

is unknown, when yet every man that has departed this life since the beginning of creation, after his decease has come and does still come to his own, or, as it is said in the Word, has been gathered and is gathered to his own: besides every one has a common perception, which is the same thing as the influx of heaven into the interiors of his mind, by virtue of which he inwardly perceives truths, and as it were sees them, and especially this truth, that he lives a man after death; a happy man if he has lived well, and an unhappy one if he has lived ill. For who does not think thus, while he elevates his mind in any degree above the body, and above the thought which is nearest to the senses; as is the case when he is interiorly engaged in divine worship, and when he lies on his death-bed expecting his dissolution; also when he hears of those who are deceased, and their lot? I have related a thousand particulars respecting departed spirits, informing certain persons that are now alive concerning the state of their deceased brethren, their married partners, and their friends. I have written also concerning the state of the English, the Dutch, the Papists, the Jews, the Gentiles, and likewise concerning the state of Luther, Calvin, and Melancthon; and hitherto I never heard any one object, "How can such be their lot, when they are not yet risen from their tombs, the last judgement not being yet accomplished? Are they not in the meantime mere vaporous and unsubstantial souls residing, in some place of confinement (*in quodam pu seu ubi*)?" Such objections I have never yet heard from any quarter; whence I have been led to conclude, that every one perceives in himself that he lives a man after death. Who that has loved his married partner and his children when they are dying or are dead, will not say within himself (if his thought be elevated above the sensual principles of the body) that they are in the hand of God, and that he shall see them again after his own death, and again be joined with them in a life of love and joy?

29. Who, that is willing, cannot see from reason, that a man after death is not a mere vapor, of which no idea can be formed but as of a breath of wind, or of air and ether, and that such vapor constitutes or contains in it the human soul, which desires and expects conjunction with its body, in order that it may enjoy the bodily senses and their delights, as previously in the world? We cannot see, that if this were the case with a man after death, his state would be more deplorable than that of fishes, birds, and terrestrial animals, whose souls are not alive, and consequently are not in such anxiety of desire and expectation? Supposing a man after death to be such a vapor, and thus a breath of wind, he would either fly about in the universe, or according to certain traditions, would be reserved in a place of confinement, or in the *limbo* of the ancient fathers, until the last judgement. Who cannot hence from reason conclude, that those

who have lived since the beginning of creation, which is computed to be about six thousand years ago, must be still in a similar anxious state, and progressively more anxious, because all expectation arising from desire produces anxiety, and being continued from time to time increases it; consequently, that they must still be either floating about in the universe, or be kept shut up in confinement, and thereby in extreme misery; and that must be the case with Adam and his wife, with Abraham, Isaac, and Jacob, and with all who have lived since that time? All this being supposed true, it must needs follow, that nothing would be more deplorable than to be born a man. But the reverse of this is provided by the Lord, who is Jehovah from eternity and the Creator of the universe; for the state of the man that conjoins himself with him by a life according to his precepts, becomes more blessed and happy after death than before it in the world; and it is more blessed and happy from this circumstance, that the man then is spiritual, and a spiritual man is sensible of and perceives spiritual delight, which is a thousand times superior to natural delight.

30. That angels and spirits are men, may plainly appear from those seen by Abraham, Gideon, Daniel, and the prophets, and especially by John when he wrote the Revelation, and also by the women in the Lord's sepulchre, yea, from the Lord himself as seen by the disciples after his resurrection. The reason of their being seen was, because the eyes of the spirits of those who saw them were opened; and when the eyes of the spirit are opened, angels appear in their proper form, which is the human; but when the eyes of the spirit are closed, that is, when they are veiled by the vision of the bodily eyes, which derive all their impressions from the material world, then they do not appear.

31. It is however to be observed, that a man after death is not a natural, but a spiritual man; nevertheless he still appears in all respects like himself; and so much so, that he knows not but that he is still in the natural world: for he has a similar body, countenance, speech, and senses; for he has a similar affection and thought, or will and understanding. He is indeed actually not similar, because he is a spiritual, and consequently an interior man; but the difference does not appear to him, because he cannot compare his spiritual state with his former natural state, having put off the latter, and being in the former; therefore I have often heard such persons say, that they know not but that they are in the former world, with this difference, however, that they no longer see those whom they had left in that world; but that they see those who had departed out of it, or were deceased. The reason why they now see the latter and not the former, is, because they are no longer natural men, but spiritual or substantial; and a spiritual or substantial man sees a spiritual or substantial man, as a natural or material man sees a natural or

material man, but not *vice versa*, on account of the difference between what is substantial and what is material, which is like the difference between what is prior and what is posterior; and what is prior, being in itself purer, cannot appear to what is posterior, which in itself is grosser; nor can what is posterior, being grosser, appear to what is prior, which in itself is purer; consequently an angel cannot appear to a man of this world, nor a man of this world to an angel. The reason why a man after death is a spiritual or substantial man, is, because this spiritual or substantial man lay inwardly concealed in the natural or material man; which natural or material man was to it as a covering, or as a skin about to be cast off; and when the covering or skin is cast off, the spiritual or substantial man comes forth, a purer, interior, and more perfect man. That the spiritual man is still a perfect man, notwithstanding his being invisible to the natural man, is evident from the Lord's being seen by the apostles after his resurrection, when he appeared, and presently he did not appear; and yet he was a man like to himself both when seen and when not seen: it is also said, that when they saw him, their eyes were opened.

32. II. IN THIS CASE A MALE IS A MALE, AND A FEMALE A FEMALE. Since a man (*homo*) lives a man after death, and man is male and female, and there is such a distinction between the male principle and the female principle, that the one cannot be changed into the other, it follows, that after death the male lives a male, and the female a female, each being a spiritual man. It is said that the male principle cannot be changed into the female principle, nor the female into the male, and that therefore after death the male is a male, and the female a female; but as it is not known in what the masculine principle essentially consists, and in what the feminine, it may be expedient briefly to explain it. The essential distinction between the two is this: in the masculine principle, love is inmost, and its covering is wisdom; or, what is the same, the masculine principle is love covered (or veiled) by wisdom; whereas in the feminine principle, the wisdom of the male is inmost, and its covering is love thence derived; but this latter love is feminine, and is given by the Lord to the wife through the wisdom of the husband; whereas the former love is masculine, which is the love of growing wise, and is given by the Lord to the husband according to the reception of wisdom. It is from this circumstance, that the male is the wisdom of love, and the female is the love of that wisdom; therefore from creation there is implanted in each a love of conjunction so as to become a one; but on this subject more will be said in the following pages. That the female principle is derived from the male, or that the woman was taken out of the man, is evident from these words in Genesis: *Jehovah God took out one of the man's ribs, and closed up the flesh in the place thereof; and he*

builded the rib, which he had taken out of the man, into a woman; and he brought her to the man; and the man said, This is bone of my bones, and flesh of my flesh; hence she shall be called Eve, because she was taken out of man, chap. ii. 21—23: the signification of a rib and of flesh will be shown elsewhere.

33. From this primitive formation it follows, that by birth the character of the male is intellectual, and that the female character partakes more of the will principle; or, what amounts to the same, that the male is born into the affection of knowing, understanding, and growing wise, and the female into the love of conjoining herself with that affection in the male. And as the interiors form the exteriors to their own likeness, and the masculine form is the form of intellect, and the feminine is the form of the love of that intellect, therefore the male and the female differ as to the features of the face, the tone of the voice, and the form of the body; the male having harder features, a harsher tone of voice, a stronger body, and also a bearded chin, and in general a form less beautiful than that of the female; they differ also in their gestures and manners; in a word, they are not exactly similar in a single respect; but still, in every particular of each, there is a tendency to conjunction; yea, the male principle in the male, is male in every part of his body, even the most minute, and also in every idea of his thought, and every spark of his affection; the same is true of the female principle in the female; and since of consequence the one cannot be changed into the other, it follows, that after death a male is a male, and a female a female.

34. III. EVERY ONE'S PECULIAR LOVE REMAINS WITH HIM AFTER DEATH. Man knows that there is such a thing as love; but he does not know what love is. He knows that there is such a thing from common discourse; as when it is said, that such a one loves me, that a king loves his subjects, and subjects love their king; that a husband loves his wife, and a mother her children, and *vice versa;* also when it is said, that any one loves his country, his fellow citizens, and his neighbour; in like manner of things abstracted from persons; as when it is said that a man loves this or that. But although the term love is thus universally applied in conversation, still there is scarcely any one that knows what love is: even while meditating on the subject, as he is not then able to form any distinct idea concerning it, and thus not to fix it as present in the light of the understanding, because of its having relation not to light but to heat, he either denies its reality, or he calls it merely an influent effect arising from the sight, the hearing, and the conversation, and thus accounts for the motions to which it gives birth; not being at all aware, that love is his very life, not only the common life of his whole body and of all his thoughts, but also the life of all their particulars. A wise man may perceive this from the con

sideration, that if the affection of love be removed, he is incapable both of thinking and acting; for in proportion as that affection grows cold, do not thought, speech, and action grow cold also? and in proportion as that affection grows warm, do not they also grow warm in the same degree? Love therefore is the heat of the life of man (*hominis*), or his vital heat. The heat of the blood, and also its redness, are from this source alone. The fire of the angelic sun, which is pure love, produces this effect.

35. That every one has his own peculiar love, or a love distinct from that of another; that is, that no two men have exactly the same love, may appear from the infinite variety of human countenances, the countenance being a type of the love; for it is well known that the countenance is changed and varied according to the affection of love; a man's desires also, which are of love, and likewise his joys and sorrows, are manifested in the countenance. From this consideration it is evident, that every man is his own peculiar love; yea, that he is the form of his love. It is however to be observed, that the interior man, which is the same with his spirit which lives after death, is the form of his love, and not so the exterior man which lives in this world, because the latter has learnt from infancy to conceal the desires of his love; yea, to make a pretence and show of desires which are different from his own.

36. The reason why every one's peculiar love remains with him after death, is, because, as was said just above, n. 34, love is a man's (*hominis*) life; and hence it is the man himself. A man also is his own peculiar thought, thus his own peculiar intelligence and wisdom; but these make a one with his love; for a man thinks from this love and according to it; yea, if he be in freedom, he speaks and acts in like manner; from which it may appear, that love is the *esse* or essence of a man's life, and that thought is the *existere* or existence of his life thence derived; therefore speech and action, which are said to flow from the thought, do not flow from the thought, but from the love through the thought. From much experience I have learned that a man after death is not his own peculiar thought, but that he is his own peculiar affection and derivative thought; or that he is his own peculiar love and derivative intelligence; also that a man after death puts off everything which does not agree with his love; yea, that he successively puts on the countenance, the tone of voice, the speech, the gestures, and the manners of the love proper to his life: hence it is, that the whole heaven is arranged in order according to all the varieties of the affections of the love of good, and the whole hell according to all the affections of the love of evil.

37. IV. THE LOVE OF THE SEX ESPECIALLY REMAINS; AND WITH THOSE WHO GO TO HEAVEN, WHICH IS THE CASE WITH ALL WHO BECOME SPIRITUAL HERE ON EARTH, CONJUGIAL LOVE RE-

MAINS. The reason why the love of the sex remains with man (*homo*) after death, is, because after death a male is a male and a female a female; and the male principle in the male is male (or masculine) in the whole and in every part thereof; and so is the female principle in the female; and there is a tendency to conjunction in all their parts, even the most singular; and as this conjunctive tendency was implanted from creation, and thence perpetually influences, it follows, that the one desires and seeks conjunction with the other. Love, considered itself, is a desire and consequent tendency to conjunction; and conjugial love to conjunction into a one; for the male-man and the female-man were so created, that from two they may become as it were one man, or one flesh; and when they become a one, then, taken together they are a man (*homo*) in his fulness; but without such conjunction, they are two, and each is a divided or half-man. Now as the above conjunctive tendency lies concealed in the inmost of every part of the male, and of every part of the female, and the same is true of the faculty and desire to be conjoined together into a one, it follows, that the mutual and reciprocal love of the sex remains with men (*homines*) after death.

38. We speak distinctively of the love of the sex and of conjugial love, because the one differs from the other. The love of the sex exists with the natural man; conjugial love with the spiritual man. The natural man loves and desires only external conjunctions, and the bodily pleasures thence derived; whereas the spiritual man loves and desires internal conjunctions and the spiritual satisfactions thence derived; and these satisfactions he perceives are granted with one wife, with whom he can perpetually be more and more joined together into a one: and the more he enters into such conjunction the more he perceives his satisfactions ascending in a similar degree, and enduring to eternity; but respecting anything like this the natural man has no idea. This then is the reason why it is said, that after death conjugial love remains with those who go to heaven, which is the case with all those who become spiritual here on earth.

39. V. THESE THINGS FULLY CONFIRMED BY OCULAR DEMONSTRATION. That a man (*homo*) lives as a man after death, and that in this case a male is a male, and a female a female; and that every one's peculiar love remains with him after death, especially the love of the sex and conjugial love, are positions which I have wished hitherto to confirm by such arguments as respect the understanding, and are called rational; but since man (*homo*) from his infancy, in consequence of what has been taught him by his parents and masters, and afterwards by the learned and the clergy, has been induced to believe, that he shall not live a man after death until the day of the last judgement, which has now been expected for six thousand years; and several have regarded this article of faith as one which ought to be believed.

but not intellectually conceived, it was therefore necessary that the above positions should be confirmed also by ocular proofs; otherwise a man who belives only the evidence of his senses, in consequence of the faith previously implanted, would object thus: "If men lived men after death, I should certainly see and hear them: who has ever descended from heaven, or ascended from hell, and given such information?" In reply to such objections it is to be observed, that it never was possible, nor can it ever be, that any angel of heaven should descend, or any spirit of hell ascend, and speak with any man, except with those who have the interiors of the mind or spirit opened by the Lord; and this opening of the interiors cannot be fully effected except with those who have been prepared by the Lord to receive the things which are of spiritual wisdom: on which accounts it has pleased the Lord thus to prepare me, that the state of heaven and hell, and of the life of men after death, might not remain unknown, and be laid asleep in ignorance, and at length buried in denial. Nevertheless, ocular proofs on the subjects above mentioned, by reason of their copiousness, cannot here be adduced; but they have been already adduced in the treatise on HEAVEN and HELL, and in the CONTINUATION RESPECTING THE SPIRITUAL WORLD, and afterwards in the APOCALYPSE REVEALED; but especially, in regard to the present subject of marriages, in the MEMORABLE RELATIONS which are annexed to the several paragraphs or chapters of this work.

40. VI. CONSEQUENTLY THERE ARE MARRIAGES IN HEAVEN. This position having been confirmed by reason, and at the same time by experience, needs no further demonstration.

41. VII. SPIRITUAL NUPTIALS ARE TO BE UNDERSTOOD BY THE LORD'S WORDS, "AFTER THE RESURRECTION THEY ARE NOT GIVEN IN MARRIAGE." In the Evangelists are these words, *Certain of the Sadducees, who say that there is no resurrection, asked Jesus, saying, Master, Moses wrote, If a man die, having no children, his brother shall take his wife, and raise up seed unto his brother. Now there were with us seven brethren; and the first, when he had married a wife, deceased, and having no issue, left his wife unto his brother; likewise the second also, and the third unto the seventh; last of all the woman died also; therefore in the resurrection whose wife shall she be of the seven? But Jesus answering, said unto them, The sons of this generation marry, and are given in marriage; but those who shall be accounted worthy to attain to another generation, and the resurrection from the dead, shall neither marry nor be given in marriage, neither can they die any more; for they are like unto the angels, and are the sons of God, being sons of the resurrection. But that the dead rise again, even Moses shewed at the bush, when he called the Lord the God of Abraham, and the God of Isaac, and the God of Jacob; for he is not the God of the dead, but of the*

living; for all live unto him, Luke xx. 27—38, Matt. xxii. 29—32; Mark xii. 18—27. By these words the Lord taught two things; first, that a man (*homo*) rises again after death; and secondly, that in heaven they are not given in marriage. That a man rises again after death, he taught by these words, *God is not the God of the dead, but of the living,* and when he said that Abraham, Isaac, and Jacob, are alive: he taught the same also in the parable concerning the rich man in hell, and Lazarus in heaven, Luke xvi. 22—31. Secondly, that in heaven they are not given in marriage, he taught by these words, "*Those who shall be accounted worthy to attain to another generation, neither marry nor are given in marriage.*" That none other than spiritual nuptials are here meant, is very evident from the words which immediately follow—"*neither can they die any more; because they are like unto the angels, and are the sons of God, being sons of the resurrection.*" Spiritual nuptials mean conjunction with the Lord, which is effected on earth; and when it is effected on earth, it is also effected in the heavens; therefore in the heavens there is no repetition of nuptials, nor are they again given in marriage: this is also meant by these words, "*The sons of this generation marry and are given in marriage; but those who are accounted worthy to attain to another generation, neither marry nor are given in marriage.*" The latter are also called by the Lord "*sons of nuptials,*" Matt. ix. 15; Mark ii. 19; and in this place, *angels, sons of God, and sons of the resurrection.* That to celebrate nuptials, signifies to be joined with the Lord, and that to enter into nuptials is to be received into heaven by the Lord, is manifest from the following passages: *The kingdom of heaven is like unto a man, a king, who made a marriage* (nuptials) *for his son, and sent out servants and invited to the marriage,* Matt. xxii. 2—14. *The kingdom of heaven is like unto ten virgins, who went forth to meet the bridegroom: of whom five being prepared entered into the marriage* (nuptials), Matt. xxv. 1, and the following verses. That the Lord here meant himself, is evident from verse 13, where it is said, *Watch ye; because ye know not the day and hour in which the Son of Man will come:* also from the Revelation, *The time of the marriage of the Lamb is come, and his wife hath made herself ready: blessed are those who are called to the marriage supper of the Lamb,* xix. 7, 9. That there is a spiritual meaning in everything which the Lord spake, has been fully shewn in the DOCTRINE OF THE NEW JERUSALEM CONCERNING THE SACRED SCRIPTURE, published at Amsterdam in the year 1763.

* * * * *

42. To the above I shall add two MEMORABLE RELATIONS RESPECTING THE SPIRITUAL WORLD. The first is as follows: One morning I was looking upwards into heaven and saw over me **three** expanses one above another; I saw that the first expanse,

which was nearest, opened, and presently the second which was above it, and lastly the third which was highest; and by virtue of illustration thence, I perceived, that above the first expanse were the angels who compose the first or lowest heaven; above the second expanse were the angels who compose the second or middle heaven; and above the third expanse were the angels who compose the third or highest heaven. I wondered at first what all this meant: and presently I heard from heaven a voice as of a trumpet, saying, "We have perceived, and now see, that you are meditating on CONJUGIAL LOVE; and we are aware that no one on earth as yet knows what true conjugial love is in its origin and in its essence; and yet it is of importance that it should be known: therefore it has pleased the Lord to open the heavens to you in order that illustrating light and consequent perception may flow into the interiors of your mind. With us in the heavens, especially in the third heaven, our heavenly delights are principally derived from conjugial love; therefore, in consequence of leave granted us, we will send down to you a conjugial pair for your inspection and observation;" and lo! instantly there appeared a chariot descending from the highest or third heaven, in which I saw one angel; but as it approached I saw therein two. The chariot at a distance glittered before my eyes like a diamond, and to it were harnessed young horses white as snow; and those who sat in the chariot held in their hands two turtle-doves, and called to me, saying, "Do you wish us to come nearer to you? but in this case take heed, lest the radiance, which is from the heaven whence we have descended, and is of a flaming quality, penetrate too interiorly; by its influence the superior ideas of your understanding, which are in themselves heavenly, may indeed be illustrated; but these ideas are ineffable in the world in which you dwell: therefore what you are about to hear, receive rationally, that you may explain it so that it may be understood." I replied, "I will observe your caution; come nearer:" so they came nearer; and lo! it was a husband and his wife; who said, "We are a conjugial pair: we have lived happy in heaven from the earliest period, which you call the golden age, and have continued during that time in the same bloom of youth in which you now see us." I viewed each of them attentively, because I perceived they represented conjugial love in its life and in its decoration; in its life in their faces, and in its decoration in their raiment; for all the angels are affections of love in a human form. The ruling affection itself shines forth from their faces; and from the affection, and according to it, the kind and quality of their raiment is derived and determined: therefore it is said in heaven, that every one is clothed by his own affection. The husband appeared of a middle age, between manhood and youth: from his eyes darted forth sparkling light derived from the wisdom of love; by virtue of

which light his face was radiant from its inmost ground; and in
consequence of such radiance the surface of his skin had a kind
of refulgence, whereby his whole face was one resplendent comeliness. He was dressed in an upper robe which reached down to
his feet, and underneath it was a vesture of hyacinthine blue,
girded about with a golden band, upon which were three precious
stones, two sapphires on the sides, and a carbuncle in the
middle; his stockings were of bright shining linen, with threads
of silver interwoven, and his shoes were of velvet: such was the
representative form of conjugial love with the husband. With
the wife it was this; I saw her face, and I did not see it: I saw
it as essential beauty, and I did not see it because this beauty
was inexpressible; for in her face there was a splendor of
flaming light, such as the angels in the third heaven enjoy, and
this light made my sight dim; so that I was lost in astonishment: she observing this addressed me, saying, "What do you
see?" I replied, "I see nothing but conjugial love and the form
thereof; but I see, and I do not see." Hereupon she turned
herself sideways from her husband; and then I was enabled to
view her more attentively. Her eyes were bright and sparkling
from the light of her own heaven, which light, as was said, is of
a flaming quality, which it derives from the love of wisdom; for
in that heaven wives love their husbands from their wisdom and
in it, and husbands love their wives from that love of wisdom
and in it, as directed towards themselves; and thus they are
united. This was the origin of her beauty; which was such
that it would be impossible for any painter to imitate and exhibit
it in its form, for he has no colors bright and vivid enough to
express its lustre; nor is it in the power of his art to depict
such beauty: her hair was arranged in becoming order so as to
correspond with her beauty; and in it were inserted diadems of
flowers; she had a necklace of carbuncles, from which hung a
rosary of chrysolites; and she wore pearl bracelets: her upper
robe was scarlet, and underneath it she had a purple stomacher,
fastened in front with clasps of rubies; but what surprised me
was, that the colors varied according to her aspect in regard to
her husband, being sometimes more glittering, sometimes less;
if she were looking towards him, more, if sideways, less. When
I had made these observations, they again talked with me; and
when the husband was speaking, he spoke at the same time as
from his wife; and when the wife was speaking, she spoke at
the same time as from her husband; such was the union of
their minds from whence speech flows; and on this occasion I
also heard the tone of voice of conjugial love; inwardly it was
simultaneous, and it proceeded from the delights of a state of
peace and innocence. At length they said, "We are recalled;
we must depart:" and instantly they again appeared to be conveyed in a chariot as before. They went by a paved way through

flowering shrubberies, from the beds of which arose olive and orange-trees laden with fruit: and when they approached their own heaven, they were met by several virgins, who welcomed and introduced them.

43. After this I saw an angel from that heaven holding in his hand a roll of parchment, which he unfolded, saying, " I see that you are meditating on conjugial love; in this parchment are contained arcana of wisdom respecting that love, which have never yet been disclosed in the world. They are now to be disclosed, because it is of importance that they should be: those arcana abound more in our heaven than in the rest, because we are in the marriage of love and wisdom; but I prophesy that none will appropriate to themselves that love, but those who are received by the Lord into the New Church, which is the New Jerusalem." Having said this, the angel let down the unfolded parchment, which a certain angelic spirit received from him, and laid on a table in a certain closet, which he instantly locked, and holding out the key to me, said, " Write."

44. THE SECOND MEMORABLE RELATION. I once saw three spirits recently deceased, who were wandering about in the world of spirits, examining whatever came in their way, and inquiring concerning it. They were all amazement to find that men lived altogether as before, and that the objects they saw were similar to those they had seen before: for they knew that they were departed out of the former or natural world, and that in that world they believed that they should not live as men until after the day of the last judgement, when they should be again clothed with the flesh and bones that had been laid in the tomb; therefore, in order to remove all doubt of their being really and truly men, they by turns viewed and touched themselves and others, and felt the surrounding objects, and by a thousand proofs convinced themselves that they now were men as in the former world; besides which they saw each other in a brighter light, and the surrounding objects in superior splendor, and thus their vision was more perfect. At that instant two angelic spirits happening to meet them, accosted them, saying, " Whence are you?" They replied, " We have departed out of a world, and again we live in a world; thus we have removed from one world to another; and this surprises us." Hereupon the three novitiate spirits questioned the two angelic spirits concerning heaven; and as two of the three novitiates were youths, and there darted from their eyes as it were a sparkling fire of lust for the sex, the angelic spirit said, " Possibly you have seen some females;" and they replied in the affirmative; and as they made inquiry respecting heaven, the angelic spirits gave them the following information: " In heaven there is every variety of magnificent and splendid objects, and such things as the eye had never seen; there are also virgins and young men; virgins

of such beauty that they may be called personifications of beauty, and young men of such morality that they may be called personifications of morality; moreover the beauty of the virgins and the morality of the young men correspond to each other, as forms mutually suited to each other. Hereupon the two novitiates asked, " Are there in heaven human forms altogether similar to those in the natural world?" And it was replied, "They are altogether similar; nothing is wanting in the male, and nothing in the female; in a word, the male is a male, and the female a female, in all the perfection of form in which they were created: retire, if you please, and examine if you are deficient in anything, and whether you are not a complete man as before." Again, the novitiates said, " We have been told in the world we have left, that in heaven they are not given in marriage, because they are angels;—is there then the love of the sex there?" And the angelic spirits replied, "In heaven *your* love of the sex does not exist; but we have the angelic love of the sex, which is chaste, and devoid all libidinous allurement." Hereupon the novitiates observed, " If there be a love of the sex devoid of all allurement, what in such cases is the love of the sex?" And while they were thinking about this love they sighed, and said, " Oh, how dry and insipid is the joy of heaven! What young man, if this be the case, can possibly wish for heaven? Is not such love barren and devoid of life?" To this the angelic spirits replied, with a smile, " The angelic love of the sex, such as exists in heaven, is nevertheless full of the inmost delights: it is the most agreeable expansion of all the principles of the mind, and thence of all the parts of the breast, existing inwardly in the breast, and sporting therein as the heart sports with the lungs, giving birth thereby to respiration, tone of voice, and speech; so that the intercourse between the sexes, or between youths and virgins, is an intercourse of essential celestial sweets, which are pure. All novitiates, on ascending into heaven, are examined as to the quality of their chastity, being let into the company of virgins, the beauties of heaven, who from their tone of voice, their speech, their face, their eyes, their gesture, and their exhaling sphere, perceive what is their quality in regard to the love of the sex; and if their love be unchaste, they instantly quit them, and tell their fellow-angels that they have seen satyrs or priapuses. The new comers also undergo a change, and in the eyes of the angels appear rough and hairy, and with feet like calves' or leopards', and presently they are cast down again, lest by their lust they should defile the heavenly atmosphere." On receiving this information, the two novitiates again said, "According to this, there is no love of the sex in heaven; for what is a chaste love of the sex, but a love deprived of the essence of its life? And must not all the intercourse of youths and virgins, in such case, consist of dry insipid joys? We are not stocks and stones, but perceptions and affections of life." To this the angelic spirits indignantly replied, "You are altogether ignorant what a chaste love of the sex is; because as yet you are not chaste. This love is the very essential delight of the mind, and thence of the heart; and not at the same time of the flesh beneath the heart. Angelic chastity, which is common to each sex, prevents the passage of that love beyond the enclosure of the heart; but within that and above it, the morality of a youth is delighted with the beauty of a virgin in the delights of the chaste love of the sex: which delights are of too interior a nature, and too abundantly pleasant, to admit of any description in words. The angels have this love of the sex, because they have conjugial love only; which love cannot exist together with the unchaste love of the sex. Love truly conjugial is chaste, and has nothing in common with unchaste love, being confined to one of the sex, and separate from all others; for it is a love of the spirit and thence of the body, and not a love of the body and thence of the spirit; that is, it is not a love infesting the spirit." On hearing this, the two young novitiates rejoiced, and said, "There still exists in heaven a love of the sex; what else is conjugial love?" But the angelic spirits replied, "Think more profoundly, weigh the matter well in your minds, and you will perceive, that your love of the sex is a love extra-conjugial, and quite different from conjugial love; the latter being as distinct from the former, as wheat is from chaff, or rather as the human principle is from the bestial. If you should ask the females in heaven, 'What is love extra-conjugial?' I take upon me to say, their reply will be, 'What do you mean? What do you say? How can you utter a question which so wounds our ears? How can a love that is not created be implanted in any one?' If you should then ask them, 'What is love truly conjugial?' I know they will reply, 'It is not the love of the sex, but the love of one of the sex; and it has no other ground of existence than this, that when a youth sees a virgin provided by the Lord, and a virgin sees a youth, they are each made sensible of a conjugial principle kindling in their hearts, and perceive that each is the other's, he hers, and she his; for love meets love and causes them to know each other, and instantly conjoins their souls, and afterwards their minds, and thence enters their bosoms, and after the nuptials penetrates further, and thus becomes love in its fulness, which grows every day into conjunction, till they are no longer two, but as it were one.' I know also that they will be ready to affirm in the most solemn manner, that they are not acquainted with any other love of the sex; for they say, 'How can there be a love of the sex, unless it be tending mutually to meet, and reciprocal, so as to seek an eternal union, which consists in two becoming one flesh?'" To this the angelic spirits added, "In heaven they are in total ignorance what whoredom is; nor do they know that it exists, or that its existence is even possible. The angels feel a chill all over the body at the idea of unchaste or extra-conjugial love; and on the other hand, they feel a genial warmth throughout the body arising from chaste or conjugial love. With the males, all the nerves lose their proper tension at the sight of a harlot, and recover it again at the sight of a wife." The three novitiates, on hearing this, asked, "Does a similar love exist between married partners in the heavens as in the earths?" The two angelic spirits replied, that it was altogether similar; and as they perceived in the novitiates an inclination to know, whether in heaven there were similar ultimate delights, they said, that they were exactly similar, but much more blessed, because angelic perception and sensation is much more exquisite than human: "and what," added they, " is the life of that love unless derived from a flow of vigor? When this vigor fails, must not the love itself also fail and grow cold? Is not this vigor the very measure, degree, and basis of that love? It it not its beginning, its support, and its fulfilment? It is a universal law, that things primary exist, subsist, and persist from things ultimate: this is true also of that love; therefore unless there were ultimate delights, there would be no delights of conjugial love." The novitiates then asked, whether from the ultimate delights of that love in heaven any offspring were produced; and if not, to what use did those delights serve? The angelic spirit answered, that natural offspring were not produced, but spiritual offspring: and the novitiates said, "What are spiritual offspring?" They replied, "Two conjugial partners by ultimate delights are more and more united in the marriage of good and truth, which is the marriage of love and wisdom; and love and wisdom are the offspring produced therefrom: in heaven the husband is wisdom, and the wife is the love thereof, and both are spiritual; therefore, no other than spiritual offspring can be there conceived and born: hence it is that the angels, after such delights, do not experience sadness, as some do on earth, but are cheerful; and this in consequence of a continual influx of fresh powers succeeding the former, which serve for their renovation, and at the same time illustration: for all who come into heaven, return into their vernal youth, and into the vigor of that age, and thus continue to eternity." The three novitiates, on hearing this, said, "Is it not written in the Word, that in heaven they are not given in marriage, because they are angels?" To which the angelic spirits replied, " Look up into heaven and you will receive an answer:" and they asked, " Why are we to look up into heaven?" They said, " Because thence we receive all interpretations of the Word. The Word is altogether spiritual and the angels being spiritual, will teach the spiritual understanding of it. They did not wait long before heaven was opened over their heads, and two angels appeared in view, and said, "There are nuptials in the heavens, as on earth; but only with those in the heavens who are in the marriage of good and truth; nor are any other angels: therefore it is spiritual nuptials, which relate to the marriage of good and truth, that are there understood. These (viz. spiritual nuptials) take place on earth, but not after departure thence, thus not in the heavens; as it is said of the five foolish virgins, who were also invited to the nuptials, that they could not enter, because they were not in the marriage of good and truth; for they had no oil, but only lamps. Oil signifies good, and lamps truth; and to be given in marriage denotes to enter heaven, where the marriage of good and truth takes place." The three novitiates were made glad by this intelligence; and being filled with a desire of heaven, and with the hope of heavenly nuptials, they said, " We will apply ourselves with all diligence to the practice of morality and a becoming conduct of life, that we may enjoy our wishes."

ON THE STATE OF MARRIED PARTNERS AFTER DEATH.

45. THAT there are marriages in the heavens, has been shewn just above; it remains now to be considered, whether the marriage-covenant ratified in the world will remain and be in force after death, or not. As this is a question not of judgement but of experience, and as experience herein has been granted me by consociation with angels and spirits, I will here adduce it; but yet so that reason may assent thereto. To have this question determined, is also an object of the wishes and desires of all married persons; for husbands who have loved their wives, in case they die, are desirous to know whether it be well with them, and whether they shall ever meet again; and the same is true of wives in regard to their husbands. Many married pairs also wish to know beforehand whether they are to be separated after death, or to live together: those who have disagreed in their tempers, wish to know whether they are to be separated; and those who have agreed, whether they are to live together. Information on this subject then being much wished for, we will now proceed to give it in the following order: I. *The love of the sex remains with every man* (homo) *after death, according to its interior quality; that is, such as it had been in his interior will and thought in the world.* II. *The same is true of conjugial love.* III. *Married partners most commonly meet after death, know each other, again associate and for a time live together: this is the case in the first state, thus while they are in externals as in the world.* IV. *But successively, as they put off their externals, and enter into their internals, they perceive what had been the quality of their love and inclination for each other, and conse-*

quently whether they can live together or not. V. *If they can live together, they remain married partners; but if they cannot they separate; sometimes the husband from the wife, sometimes the wife from the husband, and sometimes each from the other.* VI. *In this case there is given to the man a suitable wife, and to the woman a suitable husband.* VII. *Married partners enjoy similar communications with each other as in the world, but more delightful and blessed, yet without prolification; in the place of which they experience spiritual prolification, which is that of love and wisdom.* VIII. *This is the case with those who go to heaven; but it is otherwise with those who go to hell.* We now proceed to an explanation of these propositions, by which they may be illustrated and confirmed.

46. I. THE LOVE OF THE SEX REMAINS WITH EVERY MAN AFTER DEATH, ACCORDING TO ITS INTERIOR QUALITY; THAT IS, SUCH AS IT HAD BEEN IN HIS INTERIOR WILL AND THOUGHT IN THE WORLD. Every love follows a man after death, because it is the *esse* of his life; and the ruling love, which is the head of the rest, remains with him to eternity, and together with it the subordinate loves. The reason why they remain, is, because love properly appertains to the spirit of man, and to the body by derivation from the spirit; and a man after death becomes a spirit and thereby carries his love along with him; as love is the *esse* of a man's life, it is evident, that such as a man's life has been in the world, such is his lot after death. The love of the sex is the most universal of all loves, being implanted from creation in the very soul of man, from which the essence of the whole man is derived, and this for the sake of the propagation of the human race. The reason why this love chiefly remains, is, because after death a male is a male, and a female a female, and because there is nothing in the soul, the mind, and the body, which is not male (or masculine) in the male, and female (or feminine) in the female; and these two (the male and female) are so created, that they have a continual tendency to conjunction, yea, to such a conjunction as to become a one. This tendency is the love of the sex, which precedes conjugial love. Now, since a conjunctive inclination is inscribed on every part and principle of the male and of the female, it follows, that this inclination cannot be destroyed and die with the body.

47. The reason why the love of the sex remains such as it was interiorly in the world, is, because every man has an internal and an external, which are also called the internal and external man; and hence there is an internal and an external will and thought. A man when he dies, quits his external, and retains his internal; for externals properly belong to his body, and internals to his spirit. Now since every man is his own love, and love resides in the spirit, it follows, that the love of the sex remains with him after death, such as it was interiorly with him;

as for example, if the love interiorly had been conjugial and chaste, it remains such after death; but if it had been interiorly adulterous (anti-conjugial), it remains such also after death. It is however to be observed that the love of the sex is not the same with one person as with another; its differences are infinite: nevertheless, such as it is in any one's spirit, such it remains.

48. II. CONJUGIAL LOVE IN LIKE MANNER REMAINS SUCH AS IT HAD BEEN INTERIORLY; THAT IS, SUCH AS IT HAD BEEN IN THE MAN'S INTERIOR WILL AND THOUGHT IN THE WORLD. As the love of the sex is one thing, and conjugial love another, therefore mention is made of each; and it is said, that the latter also remains after death such as it has been internally with a man, during his abode in the world: but as few know the distinction between the love of the sex and conjugial love, therefore, before we proceed further in the subject of this treatise, it may be expedient briefly to point it out. The love of the sex is directed to several, and contracted with several of the sex; but conjugial love is directed to only one, and contracted with one of the sex; moreover, love directed to and contracted with several is a natural love; for it is common to man with beasts and birds, which are natural: but conjugial love is a spiritual love, and peculiar and proper to men; because men were created, and are therefore born to become spiritual; therefore, so far as a man becomes spiritual, so far he puts off the love of the sex, and puts on conjugial love. In the beginning of marriage the love of the sex appears as if conjoined with conjugial love; but in the progress of marriage they are separated; and in this case, with such as are spiritual, the love of the sex is removed, and conjugial love is imparted; but with such as are natural, the contrary happens. From these observations it is evident, that the love of the sex, being directed to and contracted with several and being in itself natural, yea, animal, is impure and unchaste, and being vague and indeterminate in its object, is adulterous; but the case is altogether different with conjugial love. That conjugial love is spiritual, and truly human, will manifestly appear from what follows.

47.* III. MARRIED PARTNERS MOST COMMONLY MEET AFTER DEATH, KNOW EACH OTHER, AGAIN ASSOCIATE, AND FOR A TIME LIVE TOGETHER: THIS IS THE CASE IN THE FIRST STATE, THUS WHILE THEY ARE IN EXTERNALS AS IN THE WORLD. There are two states in which a man (*homo*) enters after death, an external and an internal state. He comes first into his external state, and afterwards into his internal; and during the external state, married partners meet each other, (supposing they are both deceased,) know each other, and if they have lived together in the world, associate again, and for some time live together; and while they are in this state they do not know the inclination of each to the other, this being concealed in the internals of each; but afterwards, when they come into their internal state, the inclination manifests itself; and if it be in mutual agreement and sympathy, they continue to live together a conjugial life; but if it be in disagreement and antipathy, their marriage is dissolved. In case a man had had several wives, he successively joins himself with them, while he is in his external state; but when he enters into his internal state, in which he perceives the inclinations of his love, and of what quality they are, he then either adopts one or leaves them all; for in the spiritual world, as well as in the natural, it is not allowable for any Christian to have more than one wife, as it infests and profanes religion. The case is the same with a woman that had had several husbands: nevertheless the women in this case do not join themselves to their husbands; they only present themselves, and the husbands join them to themselves. It is to be observed that husbands rarely know their wives, but that wives well know their husbands, women having an interior perception of love, and men only an exterior.

48.* IV. BUT SUCCESSIVELY, AS THEY PUT OFF THEIR EXTERNALS AND ENTER INTO THEIR INTERNALS, THEY PERCEIVE WHAT HAD BEEN THE QUALITY OF THEIR LOVE AND INCLINATION FOR EACH OTHER, AND CONSEQUENTLY WHETHER THEY CAN LIVE TOGETHER OR NOT. There is no occasion to explain this further, as it follows from what is shewn in the previous section; suffice it here to shew how a man (*homo*) after death puts off his externals and puts on his internals. Every one after death is first introduced into the world which is called the world of spirits, and which is intermediate between heaven and hell; and in that world he is prepared, for heaven if he is good, and for hell if he is evil. The end or design of this preparation is, that the internal and external may agree together and make a one, and not disagree and make two: in the natural world they frequently make two, and only make a one with those who are sincere in heart. That they make two is evident from the deceitful and the cunning; especially from hypocrites, flatterers, dissemblers, and liars: but in the spiritual world it is not allowable thus to have a divided mind; for whoever has been internally wicked must also be externally wicked; in like manner, whoever has been good, must be good in each principle: for every man after death becomes of such a quality as he had been interiorly, and not such as he had been exteriorly. For this end, after his decease, he is let alternately into his external and his internal; and every one, while he is in his external, is wise, that is, he wishes to appear wise, even though he be wicked; but a wicked person internally is insane. By those changes he is enabled to see his follies, and to repent of them: but if he had not repented in the world, he cannot afterwards; for he loves his follies, and wishes to remain in them: therefore he forces his external also to be equally insane; thus his internal and his external become a one; and when this is effected, he is prepared for hell. But it is otherwise with a good spirit: such a one, as in the world he had looked unto God and had repented, was more wise in his internal than in his external: in his external also, through the allurements and vanities of the world, he was sometimes led astray; therefore his external is likewise reduced to agreement with his internal, which, as was said, is wise; and when this is effected he is prepared for heaven. From these considerations it may plainly appear, how the case is in regard to putting off the external and putting on the internal after death.

49. V. IF THEY CAN LIVE TOGETHER, THEY REMAIN MARRIED PARTNERS; BUT IF THEY CANNOT, THEY SEPARATE; SOMETIMES THE HUSBAND FROM THE WIFE, SOMETIMES THE WIFE FROM THE HUSBAND, AND SOMETIMES EACH FROM THE OTHER. The reason why separations take place after death is, because the conjunctions which are made on earth are seldom made from any internal perception of love, but from an external perception, which hides the internal. The external perception of love originates in such things as regard the love of the world and of the body. Wealth and large possessions are peculiarly the objects of worldly love, while dignities and honors are those of the love of the body: besides these objects, there are also various enticing allurements, such as beauty and an external polish of manners, and sometimes even an unchasteness of character. Moreover, matrimonial engagements are frequently contracted within the particular district, city, or village, in which the parties were born, and where they live; in which case the choice is confined and limited to families that are known, and to such as are in similar circumstances in life: hence matrimonial connections made in the world are for the most part external, and not at the same time internal; when yet it is the internal conjunction, or the conjunction of souls, which constitutes a real marriage; and this conjunction is not perceivable until the man puts off the external and puts on the internal; as is the case after death. This then is the reason why separations take place, and afterwards new conjunctions are formed with such as are of a similar nature and disposition; unless these conjunctions have been provided on earth, as happens with those who from an early age have loved, have desired, and have asked of the Lord an honorable and lovely connection with one of the sex, shunning and abominating the impulses of a loose and wandering lust.

50. VI. IN THIS CASE THERE IS GIVEN TO THE MAN A SUITABLE WIFE, AND TO THE WOMAN A SUITABLE HUSBAND. The reason of this is, because no married partners can be received into heaven, so as to remain there, but such as have been interiorly

united, or as are capable of being so united; for in heaven two married partners are not called two, but one angel; this is understood by the Lord's words *" They are no longer two, but one flesh."* The reason why no other married partners are there received is, because in heaven no others can live together in one house, and in one chamber and bed; for all in the heavens are associated according to the affinities and relationships of love, and have their habitations accordingly. In the spiritual world there are not spaces, but the appearance of spaces; and these appearances are according to the states of life of the inhabitants, which are according to their states of love; therefore in that world no one can dwell but in his own house, which is provided for him and assigned to him according to the quality of his love: if he dwells in any other, he is straitened and pained in his breast and breathing; and it is impossible for two to dwell together in the same house unless they are likenesses; neither can married partners so dwell together, unless they are mutual inclinations; if they are external inclinations, and not at the same time internal, the very house or place itself separates, and rejects and expels them. This is the reason why for those who after preparation are introduced into heaven, there is provided a marriage with a consort whose soul inclines to mutual union with the soul of another, so that they no longer wish to be two lives, but one. This is the reason why after separation there is given to the man a suitable wife and to the woman in like manner a suitable husband.

51. VII. MARRIED PAIRS ENJOY SIMILAR COMMUNICATIONS WITH EACH OTHER AS IN THE WORLD, BUT MORE DELIGHTFUL AND BLESSED, YET WITHOUT PROLIFICATION; IN THE PLACE OF WHICH THEY EXPERIENCE SPIRITUAL PROLIFICATION, WHICH IS THAT OF LOVE AND WISDOM. The reason why married pairs enjoy similar communications as in the world, is, because after death a male is a male, and a female a female, and there is implanted in each at creation an inclination to conjunction; and this inclination with man is the inclination of his spirit and thence of his body; therefore after death, when a man becomes a spirit, the same mutual inclination remains, and this cannot exist without similar communications; for after death a man is a man as before; neither is there any thing wanting either in the male or in the female: as to form they are like themselves, and also as to affections and thoughts; and what must be the necessary consequence, but that they must enjoy like communications? And as conjugial love is chaste, pure, and holy, therefore their communications are ample and complete; but on this subject see what was said in the MEMORABLE RELATION, n. 44. The reason why such communications are more delightful and blessed than in the world, is, because conjugial love, as it is the love of the

spirit, becomes interior and purer, and thereby more perceivable; and every delight increases according to perception, and to such a degree that its blessedness is discernible in its delight.

52. The reason why marriages in the heavens are without prolification, and that in place thereof there is experienced spiritual prolification, which is that of love and wisdom, is, because with the inhabitants of the spiritual world, the third principle—the natural, is wanting; and it is this which contains the spiritual principles; and these without that which contains them have no consistence, like the productions of the natural world: moreover spiritual principles, considered in themselves, have relation to love and wisdom; therefore love and wisdom are the births produced from marriages in the heavens. These are called births, because conjugial love perfects an angel, uniting him with his consort, in consequence whereof he becomes more and more a man (*homo*); for, as was said above, two married partners in heaven are not two but one angel; wherefore by conjugial unition they fill themselves with the human principle, which consists in desiring to grow wise, and in loving whatever relates to wisdom.

53. VIII. THIS IS THE CASE WITH THOSE WHO GO TO HEAVEN; BUT IT IS OTHERWISE WITH THOSE WHO GO TO HELL. That after death a suitable wife is given to a husband, and a suitable husband to a wife, and that they enjoy delightful and blessed communications, but without prolification, except of a spiritual kind, is to be understood of those who are received into heaven and become angels; because such are spiritual, and marriages in themselves are spiritual and thence holy: but with respect to those who go to hell, they are all natural; and marriages merely natural are not marriages, but conjunctions which originate in unchaste lust. The nature and quality of such conjunctions will be shewn in the following pages, when we come to treat of the chaste and the unchaste principles, and further when we come to treat of adulterous love.

54. To what has been above related concerning the state of married partners after death, it may be expedient to add the following circumstances. I. That all those married partners who are merely natural, are separated after death; because with them the love of marriage grows cold, and the love of adultery grows warm: nevertheless after separation, they sometimes associate as married partners with others; but after a short time they withdraw from each other: and this in many cases is done repeatedly; till at length the man is made over to some harlot, and the woman to some adulterer; which is effected in an infernal prison: concerning which prison, see the APOCALYPSE REVEALED, n. 153, § x., where promiscuous whoredom is forbidden each party under certain pains and penalties. II. Married partners, of whom one is spiritual and the other natural, are also separated after death; and to the spiritual is given a suitable

married partner; whereas the natural one is sent to the resorts of the lascivious among his like. III. But those, who in the world have lived a single life, and have altogether alienated their minds from marriage, in case they be spiritual, remain single; but if natural, they become whoremongers. It is otherwise with those, who in their single state have desired marriage, and especially if they have solicited it without success; for such, if they are spiritual, blessed marriages are provided, but not until they come into heaven. IV. Those who in the world have been shut up in monasteries, both men and women, at the conclusion of the monastic life, which continues some time after death, are let loose and discharged, and enjoy the free indulgence of their desires, whether they are disposed to live in a married state or not: if they are disposed to live in a married state, this is granted them; but if otherwise, they are conveyed to those who live in celibacy on the side of heaven; such, however, as have indulged the fires of prohibited lust, are cast down. V. The reason why those who live in celibacy are on the side of heaven, is, because the sphere of perpetual celibacy infests the sphere of conjugial love, which is the very essential sphere of heaven; and the reason why the sphere of conjugial love is the very essential sphere of heaven, is, because it descends from the heavenly marriage of the Lord and the church.

* * * * *

55. To the above, I shall add two MEMORABLE RELATIONS: the FIRST is this. On a certain time I heard from heaven the sweetest melody, arising from a song that was sung by wives and virgins in heaven. The sweetness of their singing was like the affection of some kind of love flowing forth harmoniously. Heavenly songs are in reality sonorous affections, or affections expressed and modified by sounds; for as the thoughts are expressed by speech, so the affections are expressed by songs; and from the measure and flow of the modulation, the angels perceive the object of the affection. On this occasion there were many spirits about me; and some of them informed me that they heard this delightful melody, and that it was the melody of some lovely affection, the object of which they did not know: they therefore made various conjectures about it, but in vain. Some conjectured that the singing expressed the affection of a bridegroom and bride when they sign the marriage-articles; some that it expressed the affection of a bridegroom and a bride at the solemnizing of the nuptials; and some that it expressed the primitive love of a husband and a wife. But at that instant there appeared in the midst of them an angel from heaven, who said, that they were singing the chaste love of the sex. Hereupon some of the bystanders asked, "What is the chaste love of the sex?" And the angel answered, "It is the love which a man bears towards a beautiful and elegant virgin or wife, free from

every lascivious idea, and the same love experienced by a virgin or a wife towards a man." As he said this, he disappeared. The singing continued; and as the bystanders then knew the subject of the affection which it expressed, they heard it very variously, every one according to the state of his love. Those who looked upon women chastely, heard it as a song of symphony and sweetness; those who looked upon them unchastely, heard it as a discordant and mournful song; and those who looked upon them disdainfully, heard it as a song that was harsh and grating. At that instant the place on which they stood was suddenly changed into a theatre, and a voice was heard, saying, "INVESTIGATE THIS LOVE:" and immediately spirits from various societies presented themselves, and in the midst of them some angels in white. The latter then said, "We in this spiritual world have inquired into every species of love, not only into the love which a man has for a man, and a woman for a woman; and into the reciprocal love of a husband and a wife; but also into the love which a man has for woman, and which a woman has for men; and we have been permitted to pass through societies and examine them, and we have never yet found the common love of the sex chaste, except with those who from true conjugial love are in continual potency, and these are in the highest heavens. We have also been permitted to perceive the influx of this love into the affections of our hearts, and have been made sensible that it surpasses in sweetness every other love, except the love of two conjugial partners whose hearts are as one: but we have besought you to investigate this love, because it is new and unknown to you; and since it is essential pleasantness, we in heaven call it heavenly sweetness." They then began the investigation; and those spoke first who were unable to think chastely of marriages. They said, "What man when he beholds a beautiful and lovely virgin or wife, can so correct or purify the ideas of his thought from concupiscence, as to love the beauty and yet have no inclination to taste it, if it be allowable? Who can convert concupiscence, which is innate in every man, into such chastity, thus into somewhat not itself, and yet love? Can the love of the sex, when it enters by the eyes into the thoughts, stop at the face of a woman? Does it not descend instantly into the breast, and beyond it? The angels talk idly in saying that this love is chaste, and yet is the sweetest of all loves, and that it can only exist with husbands who are in true conjugial love, and thence in an extreme degree of potency with their wives. Do such husbands possess any peculiar power more than other men, when they see a beautiful woman, of keeping the ideas of their thought in a state of elevation, and as it were of suspending them, so that they cannot descend and proceed to what constitutes that love?" The argument was next taken up by those who were in cold and in heat; in cold towards their wives, and in heat towards the sex; and they said, "What is the chaste love of the sex? Is it not a contradiction in terms to talk of such a love? If chastity be predicated of the love of the sex, is not this destroying the very thing of which it is predicated? How can the chaste love of the sex be the sweetest of all loves, when chastity deprives it of its sweetness? You all know where the sweetness of that love resides; when therefore the idea connected therewith is banished from the mind, where and whence is the sweetness?" At that instant certain spirits interrupted them, and said, "We have been in company with the most beautiful females and have had no lust; therefore we know what the chaste love of the sex is." But their companions, who were acquainted with their lasciviousness, replied, "You were at those times in a state of loathing towards the sex, arising from impotence; and this is not the chaste love of the sex, but the ultimate of unchaste love." On hearing what had been said, the angels were indignant and requested those who stood on the right, or to the south, to deliver their sentiments. They said, "There is a love of one man to another, and also of one woman to another; and there is a love of a man to a woman, and of a woman to a man; and these three pairs of loves totally differ from each other. The love of one man to another is as the love of understanding and understanding; for the man was created and consequently born to become understanding: the love of one woman to another is as the love of affection and affection of the understanding of men; for the woman was created and born to become a love of the understanding of a man. These loves, viz., of one man to another, and of one woman to another, do not enter deeply into the bosom, but remain without, and only touch each other; thus they do not interiorly conjoin the two parties: wherefore also two men, by their mutual reasonings, sometimes engage in combat together like two wrestlers; and two women, by their mutual concupiscences, are at war with each other like two prize-fighters. But the love of a man and a woman is the love of the understanding and of its affection; and this love enters deeply and effects conjunction, which is that love; but the conjunction of minds, and not at the same time of bodies, or the endeavour towards that conjunction alone, is spiritual love, and consequently chaste love; and this love exists only with those who are in true conjugial love, and thence in an eminent degree of potency; because such, from their chastity, do not admit an influx of love from the body of any other woman than of their own wives; and as they are in an extreme degree of potency, they cannot do otherwise than love the sex, and at the same time hold in aversion whatever is unchaste. Hence they are principled in a chaste love of the sex, which, considered in itself, is interior spiritual friendship, deriving its sweetness from an eminent degree of potency, but still being chaste. This eminent degree of potency they possess in consequence of a total renunciation of whoredom; and as each loves his own wife alone, the potency is chaste. Now, since this love with such partakes not of the flesh, but only of the spirit, therefore it is chaste; and as the beauty of the woman, from innate inclination, enters at the same time into the mind, therefore the love is sweet." On hearing this, many of the bystanders put their hands to their ears, saying, "What has been said offends our ears; and what you have spoken is of no account with us." These spirits were unchaste. Then again was heard the singing from heaven, and sweeter now than before; but to the unchaste it was so grating and discordant that they hurried out of the theatre and fled, leaving behind them only the few who from wisdom loved conjugial chastity.

56. THE SECOND MEMORABLE RELATION. As I was conversing with angels some time ago in the spiritual world, I was inspired with a desire, attended with a pleasing satisfaction, to see the TEMPLE OF WISDOM, which I had seen once before; and accordingly I asked them the way to it. They said, "Follow the light and you will find it." I said, "What do you mean by following the light?" They replied, "Our light grows brighter and brighter as we approach that temple; wherefore, follow the light according to the increase of its brightness; for our light proceeds from the Lord as a sun, and thence considered in itself is wisdom." I immediately directed my course, in company with two angels, according to the increase of the brightness of the light, and ascending by a steep path to the summit of a hill in the southern quarter. There we found a magnificent gate, which the keeper, on seeing the angels with me, opened; and lo! we saw an avenue of palm-trees and laurels, according to which we directed our course. It was a winding avenue, and terminatad in a garden, in the middle of which was the TEMPLE OF WISDOM. On arriving there, and looking about me, I saw several small sacred buildings, resembling the temple, inhabited by the WISE. We went towards one of them, and coming to the door accosted the person who dwelt there, and told him the occasion and manner of our coming. He said, "You are welcome; enter and be seated, and we will improve our acquaintance by discourses respecting wisdom." I viewed the building within, and observed that it was divided into two, and still was but one; it was divided into two by a transparent wall; but it appeared as one from its translucence, which was like that of the purest crystal. I inquired the reason of this? He said, "I am not alone; my wife is with me, and we are two; yet still we are not two, but one flesh." But I replied, "I know that you are a wise one; and what has a wise one or a wisdom to do with a woman?" Hereupon our host, becoming

59

somewhat indignant, changed countenance, and beckoned with his hand, and lo! instantly other wise ones presented themselves from the neighboring buildings, to whom he said humorously, "Our stranger here asks, 'What has a wise one or a wisdom to do with a woman?'" At this they smiled and said, "What is a wise one or a wisdom without a woman, or without love, a wife being the love of a wise man's wisdom?" Our host then said, "Let us now endeavor to improve our acquaintance by some discourse respecting wisdom; and let it be concerning causes, and at present concerning the cause of beauty in the female sex." Then they spoke in order; and the first assigned as a cause, that women were created by the Lord's affections of the wisdom of men, and the affection of wisdom is essential beauty. A second said, that the woman was created by the Lord through the wisdom of the man, because from the man; and that hence she is a form of wisdom inspired with love-affection; and since love-affection is essential life, a female is the life of wisdom, whereas a male is wisdom; and the life of wisdom is essential beauty. A third said, that women have a perception of the delights of conjugial love; and as their whole body is an organ of that perception, it must needs be that the habitation of the delights of conjugial love, with its perception, be beauty. A fourth assigned this cause; that the Lord took away from the man beauty and elegance of life, and transferred it to the woman; and that hence the man, unless he be re-united with his beauty and elegance in the woman, is stern, austere, joyless, and unlovely; so one man is wise only for himself, and another is foolish: whereas, when a man is united with his beauty and elegance of life in a wife, he becomes engaging, pleasant, active, and lovely, and thereby wise. A fifth said, that women were created beauties, not for the sake of themselves, but for the sake of the men; that men, who of themselves are hard, might be made soft: that their minds, of themselves grave and severe, might become gentle and cheerful; and that their hearts, of themselves cold, might be made warm; which effects take place when they become one flesh with their wives. A sixth assigned as a cause, that the universe was created by the Lord a most perfect work; but that nothing was created in it more perfect than a beautiful and elegant woman, in order that man may give thanks to the Lord for his bounty herein, and may repay it by the reception of wisdom from him. These and many other similar observations having been made, the wife of our host appeared beyond the crystal wall, and said to her husband, "Speak if you please;" and then when he spoke, the life of wisdom from the wife was perceived in his discourse; for in the tone of his speech was her love: thus experience testified to the truth. After this we took a view of the temple of wisdom, and also of the paradisiacal scenes which encompassed it, and being thereby filled with joy, we departed, and passed through the avenue to the gate, and descended by the way we had ascended.

ON LOVE TRULY CONJUGIAL.

57. THERE are infinite varieties of conjugial love, it being in no two persons exactly similar. It appears indeed as if it were similar with many; but this appearance arises from corporeal judgement, which, being gross and dull, is little qualified to discern aright respecting it. By corporeal judgement we mean the judgement of the mind from the evidence of the external senses; but to those whose eyes are opened to see from the judgment of the spirit, the differences are manifest; and more distinctly to those who are enabled to elevate the sight arising from such judgement to a higher degree, which is effected by withdrawing it from the senses, and exalting it into a superior light; these can at length confirm themselves in their understanding, and thereby see that conjugial love is never exactly similar in any two persons. Nevertheless no one can see the infinite varieties of this love in any light of the understanding however elevated, unless he first know what is the nature and quality of that love in its very essence and integrity, thus what was its nature and quality when, together with life, it was implanted in man from God. Unless this its state, which was most perfect, be known, it is in vain to attempt the discovery of its differences by any investigation; for there is no other fixed point, from which as a first principle those differences may be deduced, and to which as the focus of their direction they may be referred, and thus may appear truly and without fallacy. This is the reason why we here undertake to describe that love in its essence; and as it was in this essence when, together with life from God, it was infused into man, we undertake to describe it such as it was in its primeval state; and as in this state it was truly conjugial, therefore we have entitled this section, ON LOVE TRULY CONJUGIAL. The description of it shall be given in the following order: I. *There exists a love truly conjugial, which at this day is so rare that it is not known what is its quality, and scarcely that it exists.* II. *This love originates in the marriage of good and truth.* III. *There is a correspondence of this love with the marriage of the Lord and the church.* IV. *This love from its origin and correspondence, is celestial, spiritual, holy, pure, and clean, above every other love imparted by the Lord to the angels of heaven and the men of the church.* V. *It is also the foundation love of all celestial and spiritual loves, and*

thence of all natural loves. **VI.** *Into this love are collected all joys and delights from first to last.* **VII.** *None however come into this love, and can be in it, but those who approach the Lord, and love the truths of the church and practise its goods.* **VIII.** *This love was the love of loves with the ancients, who lived in the golden, silver, and copper ages; but afterwards it successively departed.* We now proceed to the explanation of each article.

58. I. THERE EXISTS A LOVE TRULY CONJUGIAL, WHICH AT THIS DAY IS SO RARE THAT IS NOT KNOWN WHAT IS ITS QUALITY, AND SCARCELY THAT IT EXISTS. That there exists such conjugial love as is described in the following pages, may indeed be acknowledged from the first state of that love, when it insinuates itself, and enters into the hearts of a youth and a virgin; thus from its influence on those who begin to love one alone of the sex, and to desire to be joined therewith in marriage; and still more at the time of courtship and the interval which precedes the marriage-ceremony; and lastly during the marriage-ceremony and some days after it. At such times who does not acknowledge and consent to the following positions; that this love is the foundation of all loves, and also that into it are collected all joys and delights from first to last? And who does not know that, after this season of pleasure, the satisfactions thereof successively pass away and depart, till at length they are scarcely sensible? In the latter case, if it be said as before, that this love is the foundation of all loves, and that into it are collected all joys and delights, the positions are neither agreed to nor acknowledged, and possibly it is asserted that they are nonsense or incomprehensible mysteries. From these considerations it is evident, that primitive marriage love bears a resemblance to love truly conjugial, and presents it to view in a certain image. The reason of which is, because then the love of the sex, which is unchaste, is put away, and in its place the love of one of the sex, which is truly conjugial and chaste, remains implanted: in this case, who does not regard other women with indifference, and the one to whom he is united with love and affection?

59. The reason why love truly conjugial is notwithstanding so rare, that its quality is not known, and scarcely its existence, is, because the state of pleasurable gratifications before and at the time of marriage, is afterwards changed into a state of indifference arising from an insensibility to such gratifications. The causes of this change of state are too numerous to be here adduced; but they shall be adduced in a future part of this work, when we come to explain in their order the causes of coldnesses, separations, and divorces; from which it will be seen, that with the generality at this day this image of conjugial love is so far abolished, and with the image the knowledge thereof, that its quality and even its existence are scarcely known. It is well

known, that every man by birth is merely corporeal, and that from corporeal he becomes natural more and more interiorly, and thus rational, and at length spiritual. The reason why this is effected progressively is, because the corporeal principle is like ground, wherein things natural, rational, and spiritual are implanted in their order; thus a man becomes more and more a man. The case is nearly similar when he enters into marriage; on this occasion a man becomes a more complete man, because he is joined with a consort, with whom he acts as one man : but this, in the first state spoken of above, is effected only in a sort of image : in like manner he then commences from what is corporeal, and proceeds to what is natural as to conjugial life, and thereby to a conjunction into a one. Those who, in this case, love corporeal natural things, and rational things only as grounded therein, cannot be conjoined to a consort as into a one, except as to those externals : and when those externals fail, cold takes possession of the internals; in consequence whereof the delights of that love are dispersed and driven away, as from the mind so from the body, and afterwards as from the body so from the mind; and this until there is nothing left of the remembrance of the primeval state of their marriage, consequently no knowledge respecting it. Now since this is the case with the generality of persons at this day, it is evident that love truly conjugial is not known as to its quality, and scarcely as to its existence. It is otherwise with those who are spiritual. With them the first state is an initiation into lasting satisfactions, which advance in degree, in proportion as the spiritual rational principle of the mind, and thence the natural sensual principle of the body, in each party, conjoin and unite themselves with the same principles in the other party; but such instances are rare.

60. II. THIS LOVE ORIGINATES IN THE MARRIAGE OF GOOD AND TRUTH. That all things in the universe have relation to good and truth, is acknowledged by every intelligent man, because it is a universal truth ; that likewise in every thing in the universe good is conjoined with truth, and truth with good, cannot but be acknowledged, because this also is a universal truth, which agrees with the former. The reason why all things in the universe have relation to good and truth, and why good is conjoined with truth, and truth with good, is, because each proceeds from the Lord, and they proceed from him as a one. The two things which proceed from the Lord, are love and wisdom, because these are himself, thus from himself; and all things relating to love are called good, or goods, and all things relating to wisdom are called true, or truths; and as these two proceed from him as the creator, it follows that they are in the things created. This may be illustrated by heat and light which proceed from the sun : from them all things appertaining to the earth are derived, which germinate according to their presence and conjunction;

and natural heat corresponds to spiritual heat, which is love, as natural light corresponds to spiritual light, which is wisdom.

61. That conjugial love proceeds from the marriage of good and truth, will be shewn in the following section or paragraph: t is mentioned here only with a view of shewing that this love is celestial, spiritual, and holy, because it is from a celestial, spiritual, and holy origin. In order to see that the origin of conjugial love is from the marriage of good and truth, it may be expedient in this place briefly to premise somewhat on the subject. It was said just above, that in every created thing there exists a conjunction of good and truth; and there is no conjunction unless it be reciprocal; for conjunction on one part, and not on the other in its turn, is dissolved of itself. Now as there is a conjunction of good and truth, and this is reciprocal, it follows that there is a truth of good, or truth grounded in good, and that there is a good of truth, or good grounded in truth; that the truth of good, or truth grounded in good, is in the male, and that it is the very essential male (or masculine) principle, and that the good of truth, or good grounded in truth, is in the female, and that it is the very essential female (or feminine) principle; also that there is a conjugial union between those two, will be seen in the following section: it is here only mentioned in order to give some preliminary idea on the subject.

62. III. THERE IS A CORRESPONDENCE OF THIS LOVE WITH THE MARRIAGE OF THE LORD AND THE CHURCH; that is, that as the Lord loves the church, and is desirous that the church should love him, so a husband and a wife mutually love each other. That there is a correspondence herein, is well known in the Christian world: but the nature of that correspondence as yet is not known; therefore we will explain it presently in a particular paragraph. It is here mentioned in order to show that conjugial love is celestial, spiritual, and holy, because it corresponds to the celestial, spiritual, and holy marriage of the Lord and the church. This correspondence also follows as a consequence of conjugial love's originating in the marriage of good and truth, spoken of in the preceding article; because the marriage of good and truth constitutes the church with man: for the marriage of good and truth is the same as the marriage of charity and faith; since good relates to charity, and truth to faith. That this marriage constitutes the church must at once be acknowledged, because it is a universal truth; and every universal truth is acknowledged as soon as it is heard, in consequence of the Lord's influx and at the same time of the confirmation of heaven. Now since the church is the Lord's, because it is from him, and since conjugial love corresponds to the marriage of the Lord and the church, it follows that this love is from the Lord.

63. But in what manner the church from the Lord is formed with two married partners, and how conjugial love is formed

thereby, shall be illustrated in the paragraph spoken of above: we will at present only observe, that the church from the Lord is formed in the husband, and through the husband in the wife; and that when it is formed in each, it is a full church; for in this case is effected a full conjunction of good and truth; and the conjunction of good and truth constitutes the church. That the uniting inclination, which is conjugial love, is in a similar degree with the conjunction of good and truth, which is the church, will be proved by convincing arguments in what follows in the series.

64. IV. THIS LOVE, FROM ITS ORIGIN AND CORRESPONDENCE, IS CELESTIAL, SPIRITUAL, HOLY, PURE, AND CLEAN, ABOVE EVERY OTHER LOVE IMPARTED BY THE LORD TO THE ANGELS OF HEAVEN AND THE MEN OF THE CHURCH. That such is the nature and quality of conjugial love from its origin, which is the marriage of good and truth, was briefly shewn above; but the subject was then barely touched upon: in like manner that such is the nature and quality of that love, from its correspondence with the marriage of the Lord and the church. These two marriages, from which conjugial love, as a slip or shoot, descends, are essentially holy, therefore if it be received from its author, the Lord, holiness from him follows of consequence, which continually cleanses and purifies it: in this case, if there be in the man's will a desire and tendency to it, this love becomes daily and continually cleaner and purer. Conjugial love is called celestial and spiritual because it is with the angels of heaven; celestial, as with the angels of the highest heaven, these being called celestial angels; and spiritual, as with the angels beneath that heaven, these being called spiritual angels. Those angels are so called, because the celestial are loves, and thence wisdoms, and the spiritual are wisdoms and thence loves; similar thereto is their conjugial principle. Now as conjugial love is with the angels of both the superior and the inferior heavens, as was also shewn in the first paragraph concerning marriages in heaven, it is manifest that it is holy and pure. The reason why this love in its essence, considered in regard to its origin, is holy and pure above every other love with angels and men, is, because it is as it were the head of the other loves: concerning its excellence something shall be said in the following article.

65. V. IT IS ALSO THE FOUNDATION LOVE OF ALL CELESTIAL AND SPIRITUAL LOVES, AND THENCE OF ALL NATURAL LOVES. The reason why conjugial love considered in its essence is the foundation love of all the loves of heaven and the church, is, because it originates in the marriage of good and truth, and from this marriage proceed all the loves which constitute heaven and the church with man: the good of this marriage constitutes love, and its truth constitutes wisdom; and when love draws near to wisdom, or joins itself therewith, then love becomes love; and when

wisdom in its turn draws near to love, and joins itself therewith. then wisdom becomes wisdom. Love truly conjugial is the conjunction of love and wisdom. Two married partners, between or in whom this love subsists, are an image and form of it: all likewise in the heavens, where faces are the genuine types of the affections of every one's love, are likenesses of it; for, as was shewn above, it pervades them in the whole and in every part. Now as two married partners are an image and form of this love, it follows that every love which proceeds from the form of essential love itself, is a resemblance thereof; therefore if conjugial love be celestial and spiritual, the loves proceeding from it are also celestial and spiritual. Conjugial love therefore is as a parent, and all other loves are as the offspring. Hence it is, that from the marriages of the angels in the heavens are produced spiritual offspring, which are those of love and wisdom, or of good and truth; concerning which production, see above, n. 51, 52.

66. The same is evident from man's having been created for this love, and from his formation afterwards by means of it. The male was created to become wisdom grounded in the love of growing wise, and the female was created to become the love of the male grounded in his wisdom, and consequently was formed according thereto; from which consideration it is manifest, that two married partners are the very forms and images of the marriage of love and wisdom, or of good and truth. It is well to be observed, that there is not any good or truth which is not in a substance as in its subject: there are no abstract goods and truths; for, having no abode or habitation, they no where exist, neither can they appear as airy unfixed principles; therefore in such case they are mere entities, concerning which reason seems to itself to think abstractedly; but still it cannot conceive of them except as annexed to subjects: for every human idea, however elevated, is substantial, that is, affixed to substances. It is moreover to be observed, that there is no substance without a form; an unformed substance not being any thing, because nothing can be predicated of it; and a subject without predicates is also an entity which has no existence in reason. These philosophical considerations are adduced in order to shew still more clearly, that two married partners who are principled in love truly conjugial, are actually forms of the marriage of good and truth, or of love and wisdom.

67. Since natural loves flow from spiritual, and spiritual from celestial, therefore it is said that conjugial love is the foundation love of all celestial and spiritual loves, and thence of all natural loves. Natural loves relate to the loves of self and of the world; spiritual loves to love towards the neighbour; and celestial loves to love to the Lord; and such as are the relations of the

loves, it is evident in what order they follow and are present with man. When they are in this order, then the natural loves live from the spiritual, and the spiritual from the celestial, and all in this order from the Lord, in whom they originate.

68. VI. INTO THIS LOVE ARE COLLECTED ALL JOYS AND DELIGHTS FROM FIRST TO LAST. All delights whatever, of which a man (*homo*) has any perception, are delights of his love; the love manifesting itself, yea, existing and living thereby. It is well known that the delights are exalted in proportion as the love is exalted, and also in proportion as the incident affections touch the ruling love more nearly. Now as conjugial love is the foundation love of all good loves, and as it is inscribed on all the parts and principles of man, even the most particular, as was shewn above, it follows that its delights exceed the delights of all other loves, and also that it gives delight to the other loves, according to its presence and conjunction with them; for it expands the inmost principles of the mind, and at the same time the inmost principles of the body, as the delicious current of its fountain flows through and opens them. The reason why all delights from first to last are collected into this love, is on account of the superior excellence of its use, which is the propagation of the human race, and thence of the angelic heaven; and as this use was the chief end of creation, it follows that all the beatitudes, satisfactions, delights, pleasantnesses, and pleasures, which the Lord the Creator could possibly confer upon man, are collected into this his love. That delights follow use, and are also communicated to man according to the love thereof, is manifest from the delights of the five senses, seeing, hearing, smelling, taste, and touch: each of these has its delights with variations according to the specific uses of each; what then must be the delight annexed to the sense of conjugial love, the use of which comprehends all other uses?

69. I am aware that few will acknowledge that all joys and delights from first to last are collected into conjugial love; because love truly conjugial, into which they are collected, is at this day so rare that its quality is not known, and scarcely its existence, agreeably to what was explained and confirmed above, n. 58, 59; for such joys and delights exist only in genuine coningial love; and as this is so rare on earth, it is impossible to describe its super-eminent felicities any otherwise than from the mouth of angels, because they are principled in it. They have declared, that the inmost delights of this love, which are delights of the soul, into which the conjugial principle of love and wisdom, or of good and truth from the Lord, first flows, are imperceptible and thence ineffable, because they are the delights of peace and innocence conjointly; but that in their descent they become more and more perceptible; in the superior principles of the mind as beatitudes, in the inferior as satisfactions, in the

breast as delights thence derived; and that from the breast they diffuse themselves into every part of the body, and at length unite themselves in ultimates and become the delight of delights. Moreover the angels have related wonderful things respecting these delights; adding further, that their varieties in the souls of conjugial pairs, and from their souls in their minds, and from their minds in their breasts, are infinite and also eternal; that they are exalted according to the prevalence of wisdom with the husband; and this, because they live to eternity in the bloom of their age, and because they know no greater blessedness than to grow wiser and wiser. But a fuller account of these delights, as given by the angels, may be seen in the MEMORABLE RELATIONS, especially in those added to some of the following chapters.

70. VII. NONE HOWEVER COME INTO THIS LOVE, AND CAN REMAIN IN IT, BUT THOSE WHO APPROACH THE LORD, AND LOVE THE TRUTHS OF THE CHURCH AND PRACTISE ITS GOODS. The reason why none come into that love but those who approach the Lord, is, because monogamical marriages, which are of one husband with one wife, correspond to the marriage of the Lord and the church, and because such marriages originate in the marriage of good and truth; on which subject, see above, n. 60 and 62. That from this origin and correspondence it follows, that love truly conjugial is from the Lord, and exists only with those who come directly to him, cannot be fully confirmed unless these two arcana be specifically treated of, as shall be done in the chapters which immediately follow; one of which will treat on the origin of conjugial love as derived from the marriage of good and truth, and the other on the marriage of the Lord and the church, and on its correspondence. That it hence follows, that conjugial love with man (*homo*) is according to the state of the church with him, will also be seen in those chapters.

71. The reason why none can be principled in love truly conjugial but those who receive it from the Lord, that is, who come directly to him, and by derivation from him live the life of the church, is, because this love, considered in its origin and correspondence, is celestial, spiritual, holy, pure, and clean, above every love implanted in the angels of heaven and the men of the church; as was shewn above, n. 64; and these its distinguishing characters and qualities cannot possibly exist, except with those who are conjoined to the Lord, and by him are consociated with the angels of heaven; for these shun extra-conjugial loves, which are conjunctions with others than their own conjugial partner, as they would shun the loss of the soul and the lakes of hell; and in proportion as married partners shun such conjunctions, even as to the libidinous desires of the will and the intentions thence derived, so far love truly conjugial is purified with them, and becomes successively spiritual, first during their abode on earth,

and afterwards in heaven. It is not however possible that any love should become perfectly pure either with men or with angels; consequently neither can this love: nevertheless, since the intention of the will is what the Lord principally regards, therefore so far as any one is in this intention, and perseveres in it, so far he is initiated into its purity and sanctity, and successively advances therein. The reason why none can be principled in spiritual conjugial love, but those who are of the above description by virtue of conjunction with the Lord, is, because heaven is in this love; and the natural man, whose conjugial love derives its pleasure only from the flesh, cannot approach to heaven nor to any angel, no, nor to any man principled in this love, it being the foundation of all celestial and spiritual loves; which may be seen above, n. 65—67. That this is the case, has been confirmed to me by experience. I have seen genii in the spiritual world, who were in a state of preparation for hell, approaching to an angel while he was being entertained by his consort; and at a distance, as they approached, they became like furies, and sought out caverns and ditches as asylums, into which they cast themselves. That wicked spirits love what is similar to their affection, however unclean it is, and hold in aversion the spirits of heaven, as what is dissimilar, because it is pure, may be concluded from what was said in the PRELIMINARY MEMORABLE RELATION, n. 10.

72. The reason why those who love the truths of the church and practise its goods, come into this love and are capable of remaining in it, is, because no others are received by the Lord; for these are in conjunction with him, and thereby are capable of being kept in that love by influence from him. The two constituents of the church and heaven in man (*homo*) are the truth of faith and the good of life; the truth of faith constitutes the Lord's presence, and the good of life according to the truths of faith constitutes conjunction with him, and thereby the church and heaven. The reason why the truth of faith constitutes the Lord's presence, is, because it relates to light, spiritual light being nothing else; and the reason why the good of life constitutes conjunction, is, because it relates to heat; and spiritual heat is nothing but the good of life, for it is love; and the good of life originates in love; and it is well known, that all light, even that of winter, causes presence, and that heat united to light causes conjunction; for gardens and shrubberies appear in all degrees of light, but they do not bear flowers and fruits unless when heat joins itself to light. From these considerations the conclusion is obvious, that those are not gifted by the Lord with love truly conjugial, who merely know the truths of the church, but those who know them and practise their good.

73. VIII. THIS LOVE WAS THE LOVE OF LOVES WITH THE ANCIENTS, WHO LIVED IN THE GOLDEN, SILVER, AND COPPER AGES. That conjugial love was the love of loves with the most

ancient and the ancient people, who lived in the ages thus named, cannot be known from historical records, because their writings are not extant; and there is no account given of them except by writers in succeeding ages, who mention them, and describe the purity and integrity of their lives, and also the successive decrease of such purity and integrity, resembling the debasement of gold to iron: but an account of the last or iron age, which commenced from the time of those writers, may in some measure be gathered from the historical records of the lives of some of their kings, judges, and wise men, who were called *sophi*, in Greece and other countries. That this age however should not endure, as iron endures in itself, but that it should be like iron mixed with clay, which do not cohere, is foretold by Daniel, chap. ii. 43. Now as the golden, silver, and copper ages passed away before the time when writing came into use, and thus it is impossible on earth to acquire any knowledge concerning their marriages, it has pleased the Lord to unfold to me such knowledge by a spiritual way, by conducting me to the heavens inhabited by those most ancient people, that I might learn from their own mouths the nature and quality of their marriages during their abode here on earth in their several ages: for all, who from the beginning of creation have departed by death out of the natural world, are in the spiritual world, and as to their loves resemble what they were when alive in the natural world, and continue such to eternity. As the particulars of this knowledge are worthy to be known and related, and tend to confirm the sanctity of marriages, I am desirous to make them public as they were shown me in the spirit when awake, and were afterwards recalled to my remembrance by an angel, and thus described. And as they are from the spiritual world, like the other accounts annexed to each chapter, I am desirous to arrange them so as to form six MEMORABLE RELATIONS according to the progressions of the several periods of time.

* * * * * * *

74. THESE SIX MEMORABLE RELATIONS from the spiritual world, concerning conjugial love, discover the nature and quality of that love in the earliest times and afterwards, and also at the present day; whence it appears that that love has successively fallen away from its sanctity and purity, until it became adulterous; but that nevertheless there is a hope of its being brought back again to its primeval or ancient sanctity."

75. THE FIRST MEMORABLE RELATION. On a time, while I was meditating on conjugial love, my mind was seized with a desire of knowing what had been the nature and quality of that love among those who lived in the GOLDEN AGE, and afterwards among those who lived in the following ages, which have their names from silver, copper, and iron: and as I knew that all who lived well in those ages are in the heavens, I prayed to the Lord that

I might be allowed to converse with them and be informed: and lo! an angel presented himself and said, "I am sent by the Lord to be your guide and companion: I will first lead and attend you to those who lived in the first age or period of time, which is called golden:" and he said, "The way to them is difficult; it lies through a shady forest, which none can pass unless he receive a guide from the Lord." I was in the spirit, and prepared myself for the journey; and we turned our faces towards the east; and as we advanced I saw a mountain, whose height extended beyond the region of the clouds. We passed a great wilderness, and came to the forest planted with various kinds of trees and rendered shady by their thickness, of which the angel had advertised me. The forest was divided by several narrow paths; and the angel said, that according to the number of those paths are the windings and intricacies of error: and that unless his eyes were opened by the Lord, so as to see olives entwined with vine tendrils, and his steps were directed from olive to olive, the traveller would miss his way, and fall into the abodes of Tartarus, which are round about at the sides. This forest is of such a nature, to the end that the passage may be guarded; for none but a primeval nation dwells upon that mountain. After we had entered the forest, our eyes were opened, and we saw here and there olives entwined with vines, from which hung bunches of grapes of a blue or azure color, and the olives were ranged in continual wreaths; we therefore made various circuits as they presented themselves to our view; and at length we saw a grove of tall cedars and some eagles perched on their branches; on seeing which the angel said, "We are now on the mountain not far from its summit:" so we went forward, and lo! behind the grove was a circular plain, where there were feeding he and she-lambs, which were representative forms of the state of innocence and peace of the inhabitants of the mountain. We passed over this plain, and lo! we saw tabernacles, to the number of several thousands in front on each side in every direction as far as the eye could reach. And the angel said, "We are now in the camp, where are the armies of the Lord Jehovah; for so they call themselves and their habitations. These most ancient people, while they were in the world, dwelt in tabernacles; therefore now also they dwell in the same. But let us bend our way to the south, where the wiser of them live, that we may meet some one to converse with." In going along I saw at a distance three boys and three girls sitting at a door of a certain tent; but as we approached, the boys and girls appeared like men and women of a middle stature. The angel then said, "All the inhabitants of this mountain appear at a distance like infants, because they are in a state of innocence; and infancy is the appearance of innocence." The men on seeing us hastened towards us and said, "Whence are you; and how came you here your faces are not like those of our mountain." But the angel in reply told them how, by permission, we had had access through the forest, and what was the cause of our coming. On nearing this, one of the three men invited and introduced us into his tabernacle. The man was dressed in a blue robe and a tunic of white wool: and his wife had on a purple gown, with a stomacher under it of fine linen wrought in needle-work. And as my thought was influenced by a desire of knowing the state of marriages among the most ancient people, I looked by turns on the husband and the wife, and observed as it were a unity of their souls in their faces; and I said, "You are one:" and the man answered, "We are one; her life is in me, and mine in her; we are two bodies, but one soul: the union between us is like that of the two viscera in the breast, which are called the heart and the lungs; she is my heart and I am her lungs; but as by the heart we here mean love, and by the lungs wisdom, she is the love of my wisdom, and I am the wisdom of her love; therefore her love from without veils my wisdom, and my wisdom from within enters into her love: hence, as you said, there is an appearance of the unity of our souls in our faces." I then asked, "If such a union exists, is it possible for you to look at any other woman than your own?" He replied, "It is possible but as my wife is united to my soul, we both look together, and in this case nothing of lust can enter; for while I behold the wives of others, I behold them by my own wife, whom alone I love: and as my own wife has a perception of all my inclinations, she, as an intermediate, directs my thoughts and removes every thing discordant, and therewith impresses cold and horror at every thing unchaste; therefore it is as impossible for us to look unchastely at the wife of any other of our society, as it is to look from the shades of Tartarus to the light of our heaven therefore neither have we any idea of thought, and still less any expression of speech, to denote the allurements of libidinous love." He could not pronounce the word whoredom, because the chastity of their heaven forbade it. Hereupon my conducting angel said to me, "You hear now that the speech of the angels of this heaven is the speech of wisdom, because they speak from causes." After this, as I looked around, I saw their tabernacle as it were overlaid with gold; and I asked, "Whence is this?" He replied, "It is in consequence of a flaming light, which, like gold, glitters, irradiates, and glances on the curtains of our tabernacle while we are conversing about conjugial love; for the heat from our sun, which in its essence is love, on such occasions bares itself, and tinges the light, which in its essence is wisdom, with its golden color; and this happens because conjugial love in its origin is the sport of wisdom and love; for the man was born to be wisdom, and the woman to be the love of the man's wisdom: hence spring the delights of that sport, in and derived from conjugial love between us and our wives. We have seen clearly for thousands of years in our heaven, that those delights, as to quantity, degree, and intensity, are excellent and eminent according to our worship of the Lord Jehovah, from whom flows that heavenly union or marriage, which is the union and marriage of love and wisdom." As he said this, I saw a great light upon the hill in the middle of the tabernacles; and I inquired, "Whence is that light?" And he said, "It is from the sanctuary of the tabernacle of our worship." I asked whether I might approach it; to which he assented. I approached therefore, and saw the tabernacle without and within, answering exactly to the description of the tabernacle which was built for the sons of Israel in the wilderness; the form of which was showed to Moses on Mount Sinai, Exod. xxv. 40; chap. xxvi. 30. I then asked, "What is within in that sanctuary, from which so great a light proceeds?" He replied, "It is a tablet with this inscription, THE COVENANT BETWEEN JEHOVAH AND THE HEAVENS:" he said no more. And as by this time we were ready to depart, I asked, "Did any of you, during your abode in the natural world, live with more than one wife?" He replied, "I know not one; for we could not think of more. We have been told by those who had thought of more, that instantly the heavenly blessedness of their souls withdrew from their inmost principles to the extreme parts of their bodies, even to the nails, and together therewith the honorable badges of manhood; when this was perceived they were banished the land." On saying this, the man ran to his tabernacle, and returned with a pomegranate, in which there was abundance of seeds of gold: and he gave it me, and I brought it away with me, as a sign that we had been with those who had lived in the golden age. And then, after a salutation of peace, we took our leave, and returned home.

76. THE SECOND MEMORABLE RELATION. The next day the same angel came to me, and said, "Do you wish me to lead and attend you to the people who lived in the SILVER AGE OR PERIOD, that we may hear from them concerning the marriages of their time?" And he added, "Access to these also can only be obtained by the Lord's favor and protection." I was in the spirit as before, and accompanied my conductor. We first came to a hill on the confines between the east and the south; and while we were ascending it, he shewed me a great extent of country: we saw at a distance an eminence like a mountain, between which and the hill on which we stood was a valley, and behind the valley a plain, and from the plain a rising ground of easy ascent. We descended the hill intending to pass through the valley, and we saw here and there on each side pieces of wood and stone, carved into the figures of men, and of various beasts, birds, and fishes; and I asked the angel what they meant,

and whether they were idols? He replied, ' By no means: they are representative forms of various moral virtues and spiritual truths. The people of that age were acquainted with the science of correspondences; and as every man, beast, bird, and fish, corresponds to some quality, therefore each particular carved figure represents partially some virtue or truth, and several together represent virtue itself, or truth, in a common extended form. These are what in Egypt were called hieroglyphics. We proceeded through the valley, and as we entered the plain, lo! we saw horses and chariots; horses variously harnessed and caparisoned, and chariots of different forms; some carved in the shape of eagles, some like whales, and some like stags with horns, and like unicorns; and likewise beyond them some carts, and stables round about at the sides; and as we approached, both horses and chariots disappeared, and instead thereof we saw men (*homines*), in pairs, walking, talking, and reasoning. And the angel said to me, "The different species of horses, chariots, and stables, seen at a distance, are appearances of the rational intelligence of the men of that period; for a horse, by correspondence, signifies the understanding of truth, a chariot, its doctrine, and stables, instructions: you know that in this world all things appear according to correspondences." But we passed by these things, and ascended by a long acclivity, and at length saw a city, which we entered; and in walking through the streets and places of public resort, we viewed the houses: they were so many palaces built of marble, having steps of alabaster in front, and at the sides of the steps pillars of jasper: we saw also temples of precious stone of a sapphire and lazure color. And the angel said to me, "Their houses are of stone, because stones signify natural truths, and precious stones spiritual truths; and all those who lived in the silver age had intelligence grounded in spiritual truths, and thence in natural truths: silver also has a similar signification." In taking a view of the city, we saw here and there consorts in pairs: and as they were husbands and wives, we expected that some of them would invite us to their houses; and while we were in this expectation, as we were passing by, we were invited by two into their house, and we ascended the steps and entered; and the angel, taking upon him the part of speaker, explained to them the occasion of our coming to this heaven; informing them that it was for the sake of instruction concerning marriages among the ancients, "of whom," says he, " you in this heaven are a part." They said, " We were from a people in Asia; and the chief pursuit of our age was the truths whereby we had intelligence. This was the occupation of our souls and minds; but our bodily senses were engaged in representations of truths in form; and the science of correspondences conjoined the sensual things of our bodies with the perceptions of our minds, and procured us intelligence."

On hearing this, the angel asked them to give some account of their marriages: and the husband said, "There is a correspondence between spiritual marriage, which is that of truth with good, and natural marriage, which is that of a man with one wife; and as we have studied correspondences, we have seen that the church, with its truths and goods, cannot at all exist but with those who live in love truly conjugial with one wife: for the marriage of good and truth constitutes the church with man: therefore all we in this heaven say, that the husband is truth, and the wife the good thereof; and that good cannot love any truth but its own, neither can truth in return love any good but its own: if any other were loved, internal marriage, which constitutes the church, would perish, and there would remain only external marriage, to which idolatry, and not the church, corresponds; therefore marriage with one wife we call sacrimony; but if it should have place with more than one among us, we should call it sacrilege." As he said this, we were introduced into an ante-chamber, where there were several devices on the walls, and little images as it were of molten silver; and I inquired, "What are these?" They said, "They are pictures and forms representative of several qualities, characters, and delights, relating to conjugial love. These represent unity of souls, these conjunction of minds, these harmony of bosoms, these the delights thence arising." While we were viewing these things, we saw as it were a rainbow on the wall, consisting of three colors, purple (or red), blue and white; and we observed how the purple passed the blue, and tinged the white with an azure color, and that the latter color flowed back through the blue into the purple, and elevated the purple into a kind of flaming lustre: and the husband said to me, "Do you understand all this?" I replied, "Instruct me:" and he said, "The purple color, from its correspondence, signifies the conjugial love of the wife, the white the intelligence of the husband, the blue the beginning of conjugial love in the husband's perception from the wife, and the azure, with which the white was tinged, signifies conjugial love in this case in the husband; and this latter color flowing back through the blue into the purple, and elevating the purple into a kind of flaming lustre, signifies the conjugial love of the husband flowing back to the wife. Such things are represented on these walls, while from meditating on conjugial love, its mutual, successive, and simultaneous union, we view with eager attention the rainbows which are there painted." Hereupon I observed, "These things are more than mystical at this day; for they are appearances representative of the arcana of the conjugial love of one man with one wife." He replied, "They are so; yet to us in our heaven they are not arcana, and consequently neither are they mystical." As he said this, there appeared at a distance a chariot drawn by small white horses; on seeing which the angel said, "That chariot is a sign for us to take our leave;" and then, as we were descending the steps, our host gave us a bunch of white grapes hanging to the vine leaves: and lo! the leaves became silver; and we brought them down with us for a sign that we had conversed with the people of the silver age.

77. THE THIRD MEMORABLE RELATION. The next day, my conducting and attendant angel came to me and said, "Make ready, and let us go to the heavenly inhabitants in the west, who are from the men that lived in the third period, or in the copper age. Their dwellings are from the south by the west towards the north; but they do not reach into the north." Having made myself ready, I attended him, and we entered their heaven on the southern quarter. There was a magnificent grove of palm trees and laurels. We passed through this, and immediately on the confines of the west we saw giants, double the size of ordinary men. They asked us, "Who let you in through the grove?" The angel said, "The God of heaven." They replied, "We are guards to the ancient western heaven; but pass on." We passed on, and from a rising ground we saw a mountain rising to the clouds, and between us and the mountain a number of villages, with gardens, groves, and plains intermixed. We passed through the villages and came to the mountain, which we ascended; and lo! its summit was not a point but a plain, on which was a spacious and extensive city. All the houses of the city were built of the wood of the pine-tree, and their roofs consisted of joists or rafters; and I asked, "Why are the houses here built of wood?" The angel replied, "Because wood signifies natural good; and the men of the third age of the earth were principled in this good; and as copper also signifies natural good, therefore the age in which they lived the ancients named from copper. Here are also sacred buildings constructed of the wood of the olive, and in the middle of them is the sanctuary, where is deposited in an ark the Word that was given to the inhabitants of Asia before the Israelitish Word; the historical books of which are called the WARS OF JEHOVAH, and the prophetic books, ENUNCIATIONS; both mentioned by Moses, Numb. xxi. verses 14, 15, and 27—30. This Word at this day is lost in the kingdoms of Asia, and is only preserved in Great Tartary." Then the angel led me to one of the sacred buildings, which we looked into, and saw in the middle of it the sanctuary, the whole in the brightest light; and the angel said, "This light is from that ancient Asiatic Word: for all divine truth in the heavens gives forth light." As we were leaving the sacred building, we were informed that it had been reported in the city that two strangers had arrived there; and that they were to be examined as to whence they came, and what was their business; and immediately one of the public officers came running towards us, and took us for examination

before the judges: and on being asked whence we came, and what was our business, we replied, " We have passed the grove of palm-trees, and also the abodes of the giants, the guards of your heaven, and afterwards the region of villages; from which circumstances you may conclude, that we have not come here of ourselves, but by direction of the God of heaven. The business on which we are come is, to be instructed concerning your marriages, whether they are monogamical or polygamical." and they said, " What are polygamical marriages? Are not they adulterous?" And immediately the bench of judges deputed an intelligent person to instruct us in his own house on this point: and when we were come to his house, he set his wife by his side, and spoke as follows: " We are in possession of precepts concerning marriages, which have been handed down to us from the primeval or most ancient people, who were principled in love truly conjugial, and thereby excelled all others in the virtue and potency of that love while they were in the world, and who are now in a most blessed state in their heaven, which is in the east. We are their posterity, and they, as fathers, have given us, their sons, rules of life, among which is the following concerning marriages: 'Sons, if you are desirous to love God and your neighbour, and to become wise and happy to eternity, we counsel you to live married to one wife; if you depart from this precept, all heavenly love will depart from you, and therewith internal wisdom; and you will be banished.' This precept of our Fathers we have obeyed as sons, and have perceived its truth, which is, that so far as any one loves his conjugial partner alone, so far he becomes celestial and internal, and that so far as any one does not love his married partner alone, so far he becomes natural and external; and in this case he loves only himself and the images of his own mind, and is doating and foolish. From these considerations, all of us in this heaven live married to one wife; and this being the case, all the borders of our heaven are guarded against polygamists, adulterers, and whoremongers; if polygamists invade us, they are cast out into the darkness of the north; if adulterers, they are cast out into fires of the west; and if whoremongers, they are cast out into the delusive lights of the south." On hearing this, I asked, " What he meant by the darkness of the north, the fires of the west, and the delusive lights of the south?" He answered, "The darkness of the north is dulness of mind and ignorance of truths; the fires of the west are the loves of evil; and the delusive lights of the south are the falsifications of truth, which are spiritual whoredoms." After this, he said, " Follow me to our repository of curiosities:" so we followed him, and he shewed us the writings of the most ancient people, which were on the tables of wood and stone, and afterwards on smooth blocks of wood; the writings of the second age were on sheets of parchment; of these he brought me a sheet, on which were copied the rules of the people of the first age from their tables of stone, among which also was the precept concerning marriages. Having seen these and other ancient curiosities, the angel said, "It is now time for us to take our leave; and immediately our host went into the garden, and plucked some twigs off a tree, and bound them into a little bunch, and gave them to us, saying, "These twigs are from a tree, which is native of or peculiar to our heaven, and whose juice has a balsamic fragrance." We brought the bunch down with us, and descended by the eastern way, which was not guarded; and lo! the twigs were changed into shining brass, and the upper ends of them into gold, as a sign that we had been with the people of the third age, which is named from copper or brass.

78. THE FOURTH MEMORABLE RELATION. After two days the angel again addressed me, saying, "Let us complete the period of the ages; the last still remains, which is named from IRON. The people of this age dwell in the north on the side of the west, in the inner parts or breadth-ways: they are all from the old inhabitants of Asia, who were in possession of the ancient Word, and thence derived their worship; consequently they were before the time of our Lord's coming into the world. This is evident from the writings of the ancients, in which those times are so named. These same periods are meant by the statue seen by Nebuchadnezzar, whose head was of gold, the breast and arms of silver, the belly and thighs of brass, the legs of iron, and the feet of iron and of clay, Dan. ii. 32, 33." These particulars the angel related to me in the way, which was contracted and anticipated by changes of state induced in our minds according to the genius or disposition of the inhabitants whom we passed; for spaces and consequent distances in the spiritual world are appearances according to the state of their minds. When we raised our eyes, lo! we were in a forest consisting of beeches, chestnut-trees and oaks; and on looking around us, there appeared bears to the left, and leopards to the right: and when I wondered at this, the angel said, "They are neither bears nor leopards, but men, who guard these inhabitants of the north; by their nostrils they have a scent of the sphere of life of those who pass by, and they rush violently on all who are spiritual, because the inhabitants are natural. Those who only read the Word, and imbibe thence nothing of doctrine, appear at a distance like bears; and those who confirm false principles thence derived, appear like leopards." On seeing us, they turned away, and we proceeded. Beyond the forest there appeared thickets, and afterwards fields of grass divided into areas, bordered with box: this was succeeded by a declivity which led to a valley, wherein were several cities. We passed some of them, and entered into one of a considerable size: its streets were irregular, and so were the

houses, which were built of brick, with beams between, and plastered. In the places of public resort were consecrated buildings of hewn lime-stone; the under-structure of which was below the ground, and the super-structure above. We went down into one of them by three steps, and saw on the walls idols of various forms, and a crowd on their knees paying adoration to them: in the middle of the building was a company, above whom might be seen the head of the tutelary god of that city. As we went out, the angel said to me, "Those idols, with the ancients who lived in the silver age, as above described, were images representative of spiritual truths and moral virtues; and when the science of correspondence was forgotten and extinct, they first became objects of worship, and afterwards were adored as deities: hence came idolatry." When we were come out of the consecrated building, we made our observations on the men and their dress. Their faces were like steel, of a grayish color, and they were dressed like comedians, with napkins about their loins hanging from a tunic buttoned close at the breast; and on their heads they wore curled caps like sailors. But the angel said, "Enough of this; let us seek some instruction concerning the marriages of the people of this age." We then entered into the house of one of the grandees, who wore on his head a high cap. He received us kindly, and said, "Come in and let us converse together." We entered into the vestibule, and there seated ourselves; and I asked him about the marriages of his city and country. He said, "We do not here live with one wife, but some with two or three, and some with more, because we are delighted with variety, obedience, and honor, as marks of dignity; and these we receive from our wives according to their number. With one wife there would be no delight arising from variety; but disgust from sameness: neither would there be any flattering courteousness arising from obedience, but a troublesome disquietude from equality; neither would there be any satisfaction arising from dominion and the honor thence derived, but vexation from wrangling about superiority. And what is a woman? Is she not born subject to man's will; to serve, and not to domineer? Wherefore in this place every husband in his own house enjoys as it were royal dignity; and as this is suited to our love, it constitutes also the blessedness of our life." But I asked, "In such case, what becomes of conjugial love, which from two souls makes one, and joins minds together, and renders a man (*homo*) blessed? This love cannot be divided; for if it be it becomes a heat which effervesces and passes away." To this he replied, "I do not understand what you say; what else renders a man (*homo*) blessed, but the emulation of wives contending for the honor of the first place in the husband' favor?" As he said this, a man entered into the women's apartment and opened the two doors; whence there issued a libidinous effluvium, which had a stench like mire; this arose from polygamical love, which is connubial, and at the same time adulterous; so I rose and shut the doors. Afterwards I said, "How can you subsist upon this earth, when you are void of any love truly conjugial, and also when you worship idols?" He replied, "As to connubial love, we are so jealous of our wives, that we do not suffer any one to enter further within our houses than the vestibule; and where there is jealousy, there must also be love. In respect to idols, we do not worship them; but we are not able to think of the God of the universe, except by means of such forms presented to our eyes; for we cannot elevate our thoughts above the sensual things of the body, nor think of God above the objects of bodily vision." I then asked him again, "Are not your idols of different forms? How then can they excite the idea of one God?" He replied, "This is a mystery to us; somewhat of the worship of God lies concealed in each form." I then said, "You are merely sensual corporeal spirits; you have neither the love of God nor the love of a married partner grounded in any spiritual principle; and these loves together form a man (*homo*), and from sensual make him celestial." As I said this, there appeared through the gate as it were lightning: and on my asking what it meant, he said, "Such lightning is a sign to us that there will come the ancient one from the east, who teaches us concerning God, that He is one, the alone omnipotent, who is the first and the last; he also admonishes us not to worship idols, but only to look at them as images representative of the virtues proceeding from the one God, which also together form his worship. This ancient one is our angel, whom we revere and obey. He comes to us, and raises us, when we are falling into obscure worship of God from mere fancies respecting images." On hearing this, we left the house and went out of the city; and in the way, from what we had seen in the heavens, we drew some conclusions respecting the circuit and the progression of conjugial love; of the circuit that it had passed from the east to the south, from the south to the west, and from the west to the north; and of the progression, that it had decreased according to its circulation, namely, that in the east it was celestial, in the south spiritual, in the west natural, and in the north sensual; and also that it had decreased in a similar degree with the love and the worship of God: from which considerations we further concluded, that this love in the first age was like gold, in the second like silver, in the third like brass, and in the fourth like iron, and that at length it ceased. On this occasion the angel, my guide and companion, said, "Nevertheless I entertain a hope that this love will be revived by the God of heaven, who is the Lord, because it is capable of being so revived."

79. THE FIFTH MEMORABLE RELATION. The angel that had

been my guide and companion to the ancients who had lived in the four ages, the golden, the silver, the copper, and the iron, again presented himself to me, and said, "Are you desirous of seeing the age which succeeded those ancient ones, and to know what its quality formerly was, and still is? Follow me, and you shall see. They are those concerning whom Daniel thus prophesied: '*A kingdom shall arise after those four in which iron shall be mixed with miry clay: they shall mingle themselves together by the seed of man: but they shall not cohere one with the other, as iron is not mixed with clay*, Dan. ii. 41—43:'" and he said, "By the seed of man, whereby iron shall be mixed with clay, and still they shall not cohere, is meant the truth of the Word falsified." After he had said this, I followed him, and in the way, he related to me these particulars. "They dwell in the borders between the south and the west, but at a great distance beyond those who lived in the four former ages, and also at a greater depth." We then proceeded through the south to the region bordering on the west, and passed though a formidable forest; for in it there were lakes, out of which crocodiles raised their heads, and opened at us their wide jaws beset with teeth; and between the lakes were terrible dogs, some of which were three-headed like Cerberus, some two-headed, all looking at us as we passed with a horrible hungry snarl and fierce eyes. We entered the western tract of this region, and saw dragons and leopards, such as are described in the Revelation, chap. xii. 3; chap. xiii. 2. Then the angel said to me, "All these wild beasts which you have seen, are not wild beasts but correspondences, and thereby representative forms of the lusts of the inhabitants whom we shall visit. The lusts themselves are represented by those horrible dogs; their deceit and cunning by crocodiles; their falsities and depraved inclinations to the things which relate to worship, by dragons and leopards: nevertheless the inhabitants represented do not live close behind the forest, but behind a great wilderness which lies intermediate, that they may be fully withheld and separated from the inhabitants of the foregoing ages, being of an entirely different genius and quality from them: they have indeed heads above their breasts, and breasts above their loins, and loins above their feet, like the primeval men; but in their heads there is not any thing of gold, nor in their breasts any thing of silver, nor in their loins any thing of brass, no, nor in their feet any thing of pure iron; but in their heads is iron mixed with clay, in their breasts is each mixed with brass, in their loins is also each mixed with silver, and in their feet is each mixed with gold: by this inversion they are changed from men (*homines*) into graven images of men, in which inwardly nothing coheres; for what was highest, is made lowest, thus what was the head is become the heel, and *vice versa.* They appear to us from heaven like stage-players, who lie upon their elbows with the body inverted, and put themselves in a walking motion; or like beasts, which lie on their backs, and lift the feet upwards, and from the head, which they plunge in the earth, look towards heaven." We passed through the forest, and entered the wilderness, which was not less terrible: it consisted of heaps of stones, and ditches between them, out of which crept hydras and vipers, and there flew forth venomous flying serpents. This whole wilderness was on a continual declivity: we descended by a long steep descent, and at length came into the valley inhabited by the people of that region and age. There were here and there cottages, which appeared at length to meet, and to be joined together in the form of a city: this we entered, and lo! the houses were built of the scorched branches of trees, cemented together with mud, and covered with black slates. The streets were irregular; all of them at the entrance narrow, but wider as they extended, and at the end spacious, where there were places of public resort: hence there were as many places of public resort as there were streets. As we entered the city, it became dark, because the sky did not appear; we therefore looked up and light was given us, and we saw: and then I asked those we met, "Are you able to see, because the sky does not appear above you?" They replied, "What a question is this! we see clearly; we walk in full light." On hearing this, the angel said to me, "Darkness to them is light, and light darkness, as is the case with birds of night; for they look downwards and not upwards." We entered into some of the cottages, and saw in each a man with his woman, and we asked them, "Do all live here in their respective houses with one wife only?" And they replied with a hissing, "What do you mean by one wife only? Why do not you ask, whether we live with one harlot? What is a wife but a harlot? By our laws it is not allowable to commit fornication with more than one woman; but still we do not hold it dishonorable or unbecoming to do so with more; yet out of our own houses we glory in this one among another: thus we rejoice in the license we take, and the pleasure attending it, more than polygamists. Why is a plurality of wives denied us, when yet it has been granted, and at this day is granted in the whole world about us? What is life with one woman only, but captivity and imprisonment! We however in this place have broken the bolt of this prison, and have rescued ourselves from slavery, and made ourselves free; and who is angry with a prisoner for asserting his freedom when it is in his power?" to this we replied, "You speak, friend, as if without any sense of religion. What rational person does not know that adulteries are profane and infernal, and that marriages are holy and heavenly. Do not adulteries take place with devils in hell, and marriages with angels in heaven? Did you never read the sixth* commandment of the decalogue? and in Paul, that adulterers can by no means enter heaven?" Hereupon our host laughed heartily, and regarded me as a simpleton, and almost as out of my senses. But just then there came running a messenger from the chief of the city, and said, " Bring the two strangers into the town-hall; and if they refuse to come, drag them there: we have seen them in a shade of light; they have entered privately; they are spies." Hereupon the angel said to me, "The reason why we were seen in a shade, is, because the light of heaven in which we have been, is to them a shade, and the shade of hell is to them light; and this is because they regard nothing as sin, not even adultery: hence they see what is false altogether as what is true; and what is false is lucid in hell before satans, and what is true darkens their eyes like the shade of night." We said to the messenger, "We will not be pressed, still less will we be dragged into the town-hall; but we will go with you of our own accord." So we went: and lo! there was a great crowd assembled, out of which came some lawyers, and whispered to us, saying, "Take heed to yourselves how you speak any thing against religion, the form of our government, and good manners:" and we replied, "We will not speak against them, but for them and from them." Then we asked, "What are your religious notions respecting marriages?" At this the crowd murmured, and said, " What have you to do here with marriages? Marriages are marriages." Again we asked, "What are your religious notions respecting whoredoms?" At this also they murmured, saying, "What have you to do here with whoredoms? Whoredoms are whoredoms: let him that is guiltless cast the first stone." And we asked thirdly, " Does your religion teach that marriages are holy and heavenly, and that adulteries are profane and infernal?" Hereupon several in the crowd laughed aloud, jested, and bantered, saying, "Inquire of our priests, and not of us, as to what concerns religion. We acquiesce entirely in what they declare; because no point of religion is an object of decision in the understanding. Have you never heard that the understanding is without any sense or discernment in mysteries, which constitute the whole of religion? And what have actions to do with religion? Is not the soul made blessed by the muttering of words from a devout heart concerning expiation, satisfaction, and imputation, and not by works?" But at this instant there came some of the wise ones of the city, so called, and said, "Retire hence;' the crowd grows angry; a storm is gathering: let us talk in private on this subject; there is a retired walk behind the town-hall; come with us there." We followed them; and they asked

---

* According to the division of the commandments adopted by the Church of England, it is the *seventh* that is here referred to.

83

us whence we came, and what was our business there?" And we said, "to be instructed concerning marriages, whether they are holy with you, as they were with the ancients who lived in the golden, silver, and copper ages; or whether they are not holy." And they replied, "What do you mean by holiness? Are not marriages works of the flesh and of the night?" And we answered, "Are they not also works of the spirit? and what the flesh does from the spirit, is not that spiritual? and all that the spirit does, it does from the marriage of good and truth. Is not this marriage spiritual, which enters the natural marriage of husband and wife?" To this the wise ones, so called, made answer, "There is too much subtlety and sublimity in what you say on this subject; you ascend far above rational principles to spiritual: and who, beginning at such an elevation, can descend thence, and thus form any decision?" To this they added with a smile of ridicule, "Perhaps you have the wings of an eagle, and can fly in the highest region of heaven, and make these discoveries: this we cannot do." We then asked them to tell us, from the altitude or region in which the winged ideas of their minds fly, whether they knew, or were able to know, that the love of one man with one wife is conjugial love, into which are collected all the beatitudes, satisfactions, delights, pleasantnesses, and pleasures of heaven; and that this love is from the Lord according to the reception of good and truth from him; thus according to the state of the church?" On hearing this, they turned away, and said, "These men are out of their senses; they enter the ether with their judgement, and scatter about vain conjectures like nuts and almonds." After this they turned to us, saying, "We will give a direct answer to your windy conjectures and dreams;" and they said, "What has conjugial love in common with religion and inspiration from God? Is not this love with every one according to the state of his potency? Is it not the same with those who are out of the church as with those who are in it, with Gentiles as with Christians, yea, with the impious as with the pious? Has not every one the strength of this love either hereditarily, or from bodily health, or from temperance of life, or from warmth of climate? By medicines also it may be strengthened and stimulated. Is not the case similar with the brute creation, especially with birds which unite in pairs? Moreover, is not this love carnal? and what has a carnal principle in common with the spiritual state of the church? Does this love, as to its ultimate effect with a wife, differ at all from love as to its effect with a harlot? Is not the lust similar, and the delight similar? Wherefore it is injurious to deduce the origin of conjugial love from the holy things of the church." On hearing this, we said to them, "You reason from the stimulus of lasciviousness, and not from conjugial love; you are altogether ignorant what conjugial love is, because it is cold with you; from what you have said we are convinced that you are of the age which has its name from and consists of iron and clay, which do not cohere, according to the prophecy in Daniel, chap. ii. 43; for you make conjugial love and adulterous love the same thing; and do these two cohere any more than iron and clay? You are believed and called wise, and yet you have not the smallest pretensions to that character." On hearing this, they were inflamed with rage and made a loud cry, and called the crowd together to cast us out; but at that instant, by virtue of power given us by the Lord, we stretched out our hands, and lo! the flying serpents, vipers, and hydras, and also the dragons from the wilderness, presented themselves, and entered and filled the city; at which the inhabitants being terrified fled away. The angel then said to me, " Into this region new comers from the earth daily enter, and the former inhabitants are by turns separated and cast down into the gulphs of the west, which appear at a distance like lakes of fire and brimstone. All in those gulphs are spiritual and natural adulterers.

80. THE SIXTH MEMORABLE RELATION. As the angel said this, I looked to the western boundary, and lo! there appeared as it were lakes of fire and brimstone; and I asked him, why the hells in that quarter had such an appearance? He replied, "They appear as lakes in consequence of the falsifications of truth; because water in the spiritual sense signifies truth; and there is an appearance as it were of fire round about them, and in them, in consequence of the love of evil, and as it were of brimstone in consequence of the love of what is false. Those three things, the lake, the fire, and the brimstone, are appearances, because they are correspondences of the evil loves of the inhabitants. All in that quarter are shut up in eternal work-houses, where they labor for food, for clothing, and for a bed to lie on; and when they do evil, they are grievously and miserably punished." I further asked the angel, why he said that in that quarter are spiritual and natural adulterers, and why he had not rather said, that they were evil doers and impious? He replied, "Because all those who make light of adulteries, that is, who commit them from a confirmed persuasion that they are not sins, and thus are in the purpose of committing them from a belief of their being harmless, are in their hearts evil doers and impious; for the conjugial human principle ever goes hand in hand with religion; and every step and movement made under the influence of religion, and leading to it, is also a step and movement made under the influence of the conjugial principle, and leading to it, which is peculiar and proper to the Christian." On asking what that conjugial principle was, he said, "It is the desire of living with one wife; and every Christian has this desire according to his religion." I was afterwards grieved in spirit to think that marriages, which in the most ancient times had been most holy,

were so wretchedly changed into adulteries. The angel said, "The case is the same at this day with religion; for the Lord says, '*In the consummation of the age there will be the abomination of desolation foretold by Daniel. And there will be great affliction, such as there has not been from the beginning of the world,*' Matt. xxiv. 15, 21. The abomination of desolation signifies the falsification and deprivation of all truth; affliction signifies the state of the church infested by evils and falses; and the consummation of the age, concerning which those things are spoken, signifies the last time or end of the church. The end is now, because there does not remain a truth which is not falsified; and the falsification of truth is spiritual whoredom, which acts in unity with natural whoredom, because they cohere."

81. As we were conversing and lamenting together on this occasion, there suddenly appeared a beam of light, which, darting powerfully upon my eyes, caused me to look up: and lo! the whole heaven above us appeared luminous; and from the east to the west in an extended series we heard a GLORIFICATION: and the angel said to me, "That is a glorification of the Lord on account of his coming, and is made by the angels of the eastern and western heavens." From the northern and southern heavens nothing was heard but a soft and pleasing murmur. As the angel understood everything, he told me first, that glorifications and celebrations of the Lord are made from the Word, because then they are made from the Lord; for the Lord is the Word, that is, the essential divine truth therein; and he said, " Now in particular they glorify and celebrate the Lord by these words, which were spoken by Daniel the prophet, '*Thou sawest iron mixed with miry clay; they shall mingle themselves together by the seed of man; but they shall not cohere. Nevertheless in those days the God of the heavens shall cause a kingdom to arise, which shall not perish for ages. It shall bruise and consume those kingdoms; but itself shall stand for ages,*' Dan. ii. 43, 44." After this, I heard as it were the voice of singing, and further in the east I saw a glittering of light more resplendent than the former; and I asked the angel what was the subject of their glorification? He said, "These words in Daniel; '*I saw in the visions of the night, and lo! with the clouds of heaven there came as it were the* SON OF MAN: *and to him was given dominion and a kingdom; and all people and nations shall worship him. His dominion is the dominion of an age, which shall not pass away; and his kingdom that which shall not perish,*' Dan. vii. 13, 14. They are further celebrating the Lord from these words in the Revelation: '*To* JESUS CHRIST *be glory and strength: behold he cometh with clouds. He is alpha and omega, the beginning and the end, the first and the last; who is, who was, and who is to come, the almighty. I, John, heard this from the* SON OF MAN, *out of the midst of the seven*

candlesticks,' Rev. i. 5—7, 10—13; chap. xxii. 13; Matt. xxiv. 30, 31." I looked again into the eastern heaven: it was enlightened on the right side, and the light entered the southern expanse. I heard a sweet sound; and I asked the angel, what was the subject of their glorification in that quarter respecting the Lord? He said, "These words in the Revelation: '*I saw a new heaven and a new earth; and I saw the holy city, New Jerusalem, coming down from God out of heaven, prepared as a* BRIDE *for her* HUSBAND: *and the angel spake with me, and said, Come, I will shew thee the* BRIDE, THE LAMB'S WIFE: *and he carried me away in the spirit to a great and high mountain, and shewed me the holy city, Jerusalem,*' Rev. xxi. 1, 2, 9, 10: also these words, 'I JESUS *am the bright and morning star; and the spirit and the bride say,* COME; AND HE SAID, EVEN I COME QUICKLY; *Amen: even* COME, LORD JESUS," Rev. xxii. 16, 17, 20.' After these and several other subjects of glorification, there was heard a common glorification from the east to the west of heaven, and also from the south to the north; and I asked the angel, "What now is the subject?" He said, "These words from the prophets; '*Let all flesh know that* I, JEHOVAH, AM THY SAVIOUR AND THY REDEEMER,' Isaiah xlix. 26. '*Thus saith* JEHOVAH, *the King of Israel, and* HIS REDEEMER, JEHOVAH ZEBAOTH, *I am the first and the last,* and BESIDE ME THERE IS NO GOD,' Isaiah xliv. 6. '*It shall be said in that day,* Lo! THIS IS OUR GOD, *whom we have expected to deliver us;* THIS IS JEHOVAH WHOM WE HAVE EXPECTED.' Isaiah xxv. 9. '*The voice of him that crieth in the wilderness, Prepare a way for* JEHOVAH. *Behold* THE LORD JEHOVAH *cometh in strength. He shall feed his flock like a* SHEPHERD,' Isaiah xl. 3, 10, 11. ' *Unto us a child is born; unto us a son is given; whose name is Wonderful, Counsellor,* GOD, *Hero,* FATHER OF ETERNITY, *Prince of Peace,*' Isaiah ix. 6. '*Behold the days will come, and I will raise up to David a righteous branch, who shall reign a King: and this is his name,* JEHOVAH OUR RIGHTEOUSNESS,' Jeremiah xxiii. 5, 6; chap. xxxiii. 15, 16. 'JEHOVAH ZEBAOTH *is his name, and* THY REDEEMER *the holy one of Israel:* THE GOD OF THE WHOLE EARTH SHALL HE BE CALLED,' Isaiah liv. 5. 'IN THAT DAY THERE SHALL BE ONE JEHOVAH, AND HIS NAME ONE,' Zech. xiv. 9." On hearing and understanding these words, my heart exulted, and I went home with joy; and there I returned out of a state of the spirit into a state of the body; in which latter state I committed to writing what I had seen and heard: to which I now add the following particular. That conjugial love, such as it was with the ancients, will be revived again by the Lord after his coming; because this love is from the Lord alone, and is the portion of those who from him, by means of the Word, are made spiritual.

82. After this, a man from the northern quarter came run-

ning in great haste, and looked at me with a threatening countenance, and addressing me in a passionate tone of voice, said, "Are you the man that wishes to seduce the world, under the notion of re-establishing a new church, which you understand by the New Jerusalem coming down out of heaven from God; and teaching, that the Lord will endow with love truly conjugial those who embrace the doctrines of that church; the delights and felicity of which love you exalt to the very heaven? Is not this a mere fiction? and do you not hold it forth as a bait and enticement to accede to your new opinions? But tell me briefly, what are the doctrinals of the New Church, and I will see whether they agree or disagree." I replied, "The doctrines of the church, which is meant by the New Jerusalem, are as follow: I. That there is one God, in whom there is a divine trinity; and that he is the LORD JESUS CHRIST. II. That a saving faith is to believe on him. III. That evils are to be shunned, because they are of the devil and from the devil. IV. That goods are to be done, because they are of God and from God. V. That these are to be done by a man as from himself; but that it ought to be believed, that they are done from the Lord with him and by him." On hearing these doctrines, his fury for some moments abated; but after some deliberation he again looked at me sternly, and said, "Are these five precepts the doctrines of faith and charity of the New Church?" I replied, "They are." He then asked sharply, "How can you demonstrate the FIRST, 'that there is one God in whom there is a divine trinity; and that he is the Lord Jesus Christ?" I said, "I demonstrate it thus: Is not God one and individual? Is not there a trinity? If God be one and individual, is not he one person? If he be one person, is not the trinity in that person? That this God is the LORD JESUS CHRIST, is evident from these considerations, that he was conceived from God the Father, Luke i. 34, 35; and thus that as to his soul he is God; and hence, as he himself saith, that the Father and himself are one, John x. 30; that he is in the Father, and the Father in him, John xix. 10, 11; that he that seeth him and knoweth him, seeth and knoweth the Father, John xiv. 7, 9; that no one seeth and knoweth the Father, except he that is in the bosom of the Father, John i. 18; that all things of the Father are his, John iii. 35; chap. xvi. 15; that he is the Way, the Truth, and the Life; and that no one cometh to the Father but by him, John xiv. 6; thus of or from him, because the Father is in him; and, according to Paul, that all the fulness of the Godhead dwelleth bodily in him, Coloss. ii. 9; and moreover, that he hath power over all flesh, John xvii. 2; and that he hath all power in heaven and in earth, Matt. xxviii. 18: from which declarations it follows, that he is God of heaven and earth." He afterwards asked how I proved the SECOND, "that a saving faith is to believe on him?"

I said, "By these words of the Lord, 'This is the will of the Father, that every one that BELIEVETH ON THE SON should have eternal life, John vi. 40.' 'God so loved the world, that he gave his only-begotten Son, that every one that BELIEVETH ON HIM should not perish, but should have eternal life,' John iii. 15, 16. HE THAT BELIEVETH ON THE SON, hath eternal life; but he that believeth not the Son will not see life; but the wrath of God abideth on him,' John iii. 36." He afterwards said, "Demonstrate also the THIRD, and the next two doctrines:" I replied, "What need is there to demonstrate 'that evils ought to be shunned, because they are of the devil and from the devil; and that goods ought to be done, because they are of God and from God;' also 'that the latter are to be done by a man as from himself; but that he ought to believe that they are from the Lord with him and by him?" That these three doctrines are true, is confirmed by the whole Sacred Scripture from beginning to end; for what else is therein principally insisted on, but to shun evils and do goods, and believe on the Lord God? Moreover, without these three doctrines there can be no religion: for does not religion relate to life? and what is life but to shun evils and do goods? and how can a man do the latter and shun the former but as from himself? Therefore if you remove these doctrines from the church, you remove from it the Sacred Scripture, and also religion; and these being removed, the church is no longer a church." The man on hearing this retired, and mused on what he had heard; but still he departed in indignation.

ON THE ORIGIN OF CONJUGIAL LOVE AS GROUNDED IN THE MARRIAGE OF GOOD AND TRUTH.

83. THERE are both internal and external origins of conjugial love, and several of each; nevertheless there is but one inmost or universal origin of all. That this origin is the marriage of good and truth, shall be demonstrated in what now follows. The reason why no one heretofore has deduced the origin of that love from this ground, is, because it has never yet been discovered that there is any union between good and truth; and the reason why this discovery has not been made, is, because good does not appear in the light of the understanding, as truth does, and hence the knowledge of it conceals itself and evades every inquiry: and as from this circumstance good is as it were unknown, it was impossible for any one to conjecture that any marriage subsisted between it and truth: yea, before the rational natural sight, good appears so different from truth, that no conjunction between them can be supposed. That this is the case, may be seen from

common discourse whenever they are mentioned; as when it is said, "This is good," truth is not at all thought of; and when it is said, "This is true," neither is good at all thought of; therefore at this day it is believed by many, that truth is one thing and good another; and by many also, that a man is intelligent and wise, and thereby a man (*homo*), according to the truths which he thinks, speaks, writes, and believes, and not at the same time according to goods. That nevertheless there is no good without truth, nor any truth without good, consequently that there is an eternal marriage between them; also that this marriage is the origin of conjugial love, shall now be shewn and explained in the following order: I. *Good and truth are the universals of creation, and thence are in all created things; but they are in created subjects according to the form of each.* II. *There is neither solitary good nor solitary truth, but in all cases they are conjoined.* III. *There is the truth of good, and from this the good of truth; or truth grounded in good, and good grounded in that truth: and in those two principles is implanted from creation an inclination to join themselves together into a one.* IV. *In the subjects of the animal kingdom, the truth of good, or truth grounded in good, is male (or masculine); and the good of that truth, or good grounded in that truth, is female (or feminine).* V. *From the influx of the marriage of good and truth from the Lord, the love of the sex and conjugial love are derived.* VI. *The love of the sex belongs to the external or natural man, and hence it is common to every animal.* VII. *But conjugial love belongs to the internal or spiritual man; and hence this love is peculiar to man.* VIII. *With man conjugial love is in the love of the sex, as a gem in its matrix.* IX. *The love of the sex with man is not the origin of conjugial love, but its first rudiment; thus it is like an external natural principle, in which an internal spiritual principle is implanted.* X. *During the implantation of conjugial love, the love of the sex inverts itself and becomes the chaste love of the sex.* XI. *The male and the female were created to be the essential form of the marriage of good and truth.* XII. *They are that form in their inmost principles, and thence in what is derived from those principles, in proportion as the interiors of their minds are opened.* We will now proceed to the explanation.

84. I. GOOD AND TRUTH ARE THE UNIVERSALS OF CREATION, AND THENCE ARE IN ALL CREATED THINGS; BUT THEY ARE IN CREATED SUBJECTS ACCORDING TO THE FORM OF EACH. The reason why good and truth are the universals of creation, is, because these two are in the Lord God the Creator; yea, they are himself; for he is essential divine good and essential divine truth. But this enters more clearly into the perception of the understanding, and thereby into the ideas of thought, if instead of good we say love, and instead of truth we say wisdom; conse-

quently that in the Lord God the Creator there are divine love and divine wisdom, and that they are himself; that is, that he is essential love and essential wisdom ; for those two are the same as good and truth. The reason of this is, because good has relation to love, and truth to wisdom ; for love consists of goods, and wisdom truths. As the two latter and the two former are one and the same, in the following pages we shall sometimes speak of the latter and sometimes of the former, while by both the same is understood. This preliminary observation is here made, lest different meanings should be attached to the expressions when they occur in the following pages.

85. Since therefore the Lord God the Creator is essential love and essential wisdom, and from him was created the universe, which thence is as a work proceeding from him, it must needs be, that in all created things there is somewhat of good and of truth from him ; for whatever is done and proceeds from any one, derives from him a certain similarity to him. That this is the case, reason also may see from the order in which all things in the universe were created ; which order is, that one exists for the sake of another, and that thence one depends upon another, like the links of a chain : for all things are for the sake of the human race, that from it the angelic heaven may exist, through which creation returns to the Creator himself, in whom it originated : hence there is a conjunction of the created universe with its Creator, and by conjunction everlasting conservation. Hence it is that good and truth are called the universals of creation. That this is the case, is manifested to every one who takes a rational view of the subject : he sees in every created thing something which relates to good, and something which relates to truth.

86. The reason why good and truth in created subjects are according to the form of each, is, because every subject receives influx according to its form. The conservation of the whole consists in the perpetual influx of divine good and divine truth into forms created from those principles ; for thereby subsistence or conservation is perpetual existence or creation. That every subject receives influx according to its form, may be illustrated variously ; as by the influx of heat and light from the sun into vegetables of every kind ; each of which receives influx according to its form ; thus every tree and shrub according to its form, every herb and every blade of grass according to its form : the influx is alike into all ; but the reception, which is according to the form, causes every species to continue a peculiar species. The same thing may also be illustrated by the influx into animals of every kind according to the form of each. That the influx is according to the form of every particular thing, may also be seen by the most unlettered person, if he attends to the various instruments of sound, as pipes, flutes, trumpets, horns, and organs.

which give forth a sound from being blown alike, or from a like influx of air, according to their respective forms.

87. II. THERE IS NEITHER SOLITARY GOOD NOR SOLITARY TRUTH, BUT IN ALL CASES THEY ARE CONJOINED. Whoever is desirous from any of the senses to acquire an idea respecting good, cannot possibly find it without the addition of something which exhibits and manifests it: good without this is a nameless entity; and this something, by which it is exhibited and manifested, has relation to truth. Pronounce the term *good* only, and say nothing at the same time of this or that thing with which it is conjoined; or define it abstractedly, or without the addition of anything connected with it; and you will see that it is a mere nothing, and that it becomes something with its addition; and if you examine the subject with discernment, you will perceive that good, without some addition, is a term of no predication, and thence of no relation, of no affection, and of no state; in a word, of no quality. The case is similar in regard to truth, if it be pronounced and heard without what it is joined with: that what it is joined with relates to good, may be seen by refined reason. But since goods are innumerable, and each ascends to its greatest, and descends to its least, as by the steps of a ladder, and also, according to its progression and quality, varies its name, it is difficult for any but the wise to see the relation of good and truth to their objects, and their conjunction in them. That nevertheless there is not any good without truth, nor any truth without good, is manifest from common perception, provided it be first acknowledged that every thing in the universe has relation to good and truth; as was shewn in the foregoing article, n. 84, 85. That there is neither solitary good nor solitary truth, may be illustrated and at the same time confirmed by various considerations; as by the following: that there is no essence without a form, nor any form without an essence; for good is an essence or *esse;* and truth is that by which the essence is formed and the *esse* exists. Again in a man (*homo*) there are the will and the understanding. Good is of the will, and truth is of the understanding; and the will alone does nothing but by the understanding; nor does the understanding alone do anything but from the will. Again, in a man there are two fountains of bodily life, the heart and the lungs. The heart cannot produce any sensitive and moving life without the respiring lungs; neither can the lungs without the heart. The heart has relation to good, and the respiration of the lungs to truth: there is also a correspondence between them. The case is similar in all the things of the mind and of the body belonging to him; but we have not leisure to produce further confirmations in this place; therefore the reader is referred to the ANGELIC WISDOM CONCERNING THE DIVINE PROVIDENCE, n. 3–16, where this subject is more fully confirmed and explained in the following order: I. That the

universe with all its created subjects, is from the divine love by the divine wisdom; or, what is the same thing, from the divine good by the divine truth. II. That the divine good and the divine truth proceed as a one from the Lord. III. That this one, in a certain image, is in every created thing. V. That good is not good, only so far as it is united with truth; and that truth is not truth, only so far as it is united with good. VII. That the Lord does not suffer that anything should be divided; wherefore a man must either be in good and at the same time in truth, or in evil and at the same time in falsehood: not to mention several other considerations.

88. THERE IS THE TRUTH OF GOOD, AND FROM THIS THE GOOD OF TRUTH; OR TRUTH GROUNDED IN GOOD, AND GOOD GROUNDED IN THAT TRUTH; AND IN THOSE TWO PRINCIPLES IS IMPLANTED FROM CREATION AN INCLINATION TO JOIN THEMSELVES TOGETHER INTO A ONE. It is necessary that some distinct idea be acquired concerning these principles; because on such idea depends all knowledge respecting the essential origin of conjugial love: for, as will be seen presently, the truth of good, or truth grounded on good, is male (or masculine), and the good of truth, or good grounded in that truth, is female (or feminine): but this may be comprehended more distinctly, if instead of good we speak of love, and instead of truth we speak of wisdom; which are one and the same, as may be seen above, n. 84. Wisdom cannot exist with a man but by means of the love of growing wise; if this love be taken away, it is altogether impossible for him to become wise. Wisdom derived from this love is meant by the truth of good, or by truth grounded in good: but when a man has procured to himself wisdom from that love, and loves it in himself, or himself for its sake, he then forms a love which is the love of wisdom, and is meant by the good of truth, or by good grounded in that truth. There are therefore two loves belonging to a man, whereof one, which is prior, is the love of growing wise; and the other, which is posterior, is the love of wisdom: but this latter love if it remains with man, is an evil love, and is called self-conceit, or the love of his own intelligence. That it was provided from creation, that this love should be taken out of the man, lest it should destroy him, and should be transferred to the woman, for the effecting of conjugial love, which restores man to integrity, will be confirmed in the following pages. Something respecting those two loves, and the transfer of the latter to the woman, may be seen above, n. 32, 33, and in the preliminary MEMORABLE RELATION, n. 20. If therefore instead of love is understood good, and instead of wisdom truth, it is evident, from what has been already said, that there exists the truth of good, or truth grounded in good, and from this the good of truth, or good grounded in that truth.

89. The reason why in these two principles there is implanted from creation an inclination to join themselves together into a one, is because the one was formed from the other; wisdom being formed from the love of growing wise, or truth being formed from good; and the love of wisdom being formed from that wisdom, or the good of truth from that truth; from which formation it may be seen, that there is a mutual inclination to re-unite themselves, and to join themselves together into a one. This effect takes place with men who are in genuine wisdom, and with women who are in the love of that wisdom in the husband; thus with those who are in love truly conjugial. But concerning the wisdom which ought to exist with the man, and which should be loved by the wife, more will be said in what follows.

90. IV. IN THE SUBJECT OF THE ANIMAL KINGDOM THE TRUTH OF GOOD, OR TRUTH GROUNDED IN GOOD, IS MALE (OR MASCULINE); AND THE GOOD OF THAT TRUTH, OR GOOD GROUNDED IN THAT TRUTH, IS FEMALE (OR FEMININE). That from the Lord, the Creator and Supporter of the universe, there flows a perpetual union of love and wisdom, or a marriage of good and truth, and that created subjects receive the influx, each according to its form, was shewn above, n. 84—86: but that the male from this marriage, or from that union, receives the truth of wisdom, and that the good of love from the Lord is conjoined thereto according to reception, and that this reception takes place in the intellect, and that hence the male is born to become intellectual, reason, by its own light, may discover from various particulars respecting him, especially from his affection, application, manners, and form. It is discoverable from his AFFECTION, which is the affection of knowing, of understanding, and of growing wise; the affection of knowing takes place in childhood, the affection of understanding in youth and in the entrance upon manhood, and the affection of growing wise takes place from the entrance upon manhood even to old age; from which it is evident, that his nature or peculiar temper is inclinable to form the intellect; consequently that he is born to become intellectual: but as this cannot be effected except by means of love, therefore the Lord adjoins love to him according to his reception; that is, according to his intention in desiring to grow wise. The same is discoverable from his APPLICATION, which is to such things as respect the intellect, or in which the intellect is predominant; several of which relate to public offices and regard the public good. The same is discoverable too from his MANNERS, which are all grounded in the intellect as a ruling principle; in consequence whereof the actions of his life, which are meant by manners, are rational; and if not, still he is desirous they should appear so; masculine rationality is also discernible in every one of his virtues. Lastly, the same is discoverable from his FORM, which is different and totally distinct from the female form;

on which subject see also what was said above, n. 33. Add to this, that the principle of prolification is in him, which is derived from the intellect alone; for it is from truth grounded in good in the intellect: that the principle of prolification is from this source may be seen in the following pages.

91. But that the female is born to be a subject of the will (*ut sit voluntaria*), yet a subject of the will as grounded in the intellectual principle of the man, or what is the same, to be the love of the man's wisdom, because she was formed through his wisdom, (on which subject see above, n. 88, 89,) may also appear from the female's affection, application, manners, and form. From her AFFECTION, which is the affection of loving knowledge, intelligence, and wisdom; nevertheless not in herself but in the man; and thus of loving the man: for the man (*vir*) cannot be loved merely on account of his form, in that he appears as a man (*homo*), but on account of the talent with which he is gifted, which causes him to be a man. From her APPLICATION; in that it is to such manual works as knitting, needlework, and the like, serving for ornament, both to decorate herself and to exalt her beauty: and moreover from her application to various domestic duties, which connect themselves with the duties of men, which, as was said, relate to public offices. They are led to these duties from an inclination to marriage, that they may become wives, and thereby one with their husbands. That the same is also discoverable from their MANNERS and FORM, needs no explanation.

92. V. FROM THE INFLUX OF THE MARRIAGE OF GOOD AND TRUTH FROM THE LORD, THE LOVE OF THE SEX AND CONJUGIAL LOVE ARE DERIVED. That good and truth are the universals of creation, and thence are in all created subjects; and that they are in created subjects according to the form of each; and that good and truth proceed from the Lord not as two but as one, was shewn above, n. 84—87: from these considerations it follows, that the UNIVERSAL CONJUGIAL SPHERE proceeds from the Lord, and pervades the universe from its primaries to its ultimates; thus from angels even to worms. The reason why such a sphere of the marriage of good and truth proceeds from the Lord, is, because it is also the sphere of propagation, that is, of prolification and fructification; and this sphere is the same with the divine providence relating to the preservation of the universe by successive generations. Now since this universal sphere, which is that of the marriage of good and truth, flows into its subjects according to the form of each, see n. 86, it follows that the male receives it according to his form, thus in the intellect, because he is in an intellectual form; and that the female receives it according to her form, thus in the will, because she is a form of the will grounded in the intellect of the man; and since tha

sphere is also the sphere of prolification, it follows that hence is the love of the sex.

93. The reason why conjugial love also is from this same source, is, because that sphere flows into the form of wisdom with men, and also with angels; for a man may increase in wisdom to the end of his life in the world, and afterwards to eternity in heaven; and in proportion as he increases in wisdom, his form is perfected; and this form receives not the love of the sex, but the love of one of the sex; for with one of the sex it may be united to the inmost principles in which heaven with its felicities consists, and this union is conjugial love.

94. VI. THE LOVE OF THE SEX BELONGS TO THE EXTERNAL OR NATURAL MAN, AND HENCE IT IS COMMON TO EVERY ANIMAL. Every man is born corporeal, and becomes more and more interiorly natural, and in proportion as he loves intelligence he becomes rational, and afterwards, if he loves wisdom, he becomes spiritual. What the wisdom is by which a man becomes spiritual, will be shewn in the following pages, n. 130. Now as a man advances from knowledge into intelligence, and from intelligence into wisdom, so also his mind changes its form; for it is opened more and more, and conjoins itself more nearly with heaven, and by heaven with the Lord; hence it becomes more enamored of truth, and more desirous of the good of life. If therefore he halts at the threshold in the progression to wisdom, the form of his natural mind remains; and this receives the influx of the universal sphere, which is that of the marriage of good and truth, in the same manner as it is received by the inferior subjects of the animal kingdom—beasts and birds; and as these are merely natural, the man in such case becomes like them, and thereby loves the sex just as they do. This is what is meant by the assertion,—the love of the sex belongs to the external or natural man, and hence it is common to every animal.

95. VII. BUT CONJUGIAL LOVE BELONGS TO THE INTERNAL OR SPIRITUAL MAN; AND HENCE THIS LOVE IS PECULIAR TO MAN. The reason why conjugial love belongs to the internal or spiritual man is, because in proportion as a man becomes more intelligent and wise, in the same proportion he becomes more internal and spiritual, and in the same proportion the form of his mind is more perfected; and this form receives conjugial love: for therein it perceives and is sensible of a spiritual delight, which is inwardly blessed, and a natural delight thence arising, which derives its soul, life, and essence from the spiritual delight.

96. The reason why conjugial love is peculiar to man, is because he only can become spiritual, he being capable of elevating his intellect above his natural loves, and from that state of elevation of seeing them beneath him, and of judging of their quality, and also of amending, correcting, and removing them

No other animal can do this; for the loves of other animals are altogether united with their inborn knowledge; on which account this knowledge cannot be elevated into intelligence, and still less into wisdom; in consequence of which every other animal is led by the love implanted in his knowledge, as a blind person is led through the streets by a dog. This is the reason why conjugial love is peculiar to man; it may also be called native and near akin to him; because man has the faculty of growing wise, with which faculty this love is united.

97. VIII. WITH MAN CONJUGIAL LOVE IS IN THE LOVE OF THE SEX AS A GEM IN ITS MATRIX. As this however is merely a comparison, we will explain it in the article which immediately follows: this comparison also illustrates what was shewn just above, n. 94, 95,—that the love of the sex belongs to the external or natural man, and conjugial love to the internal or spiritual man.

98. IX. THE LOVE OF THE SEX WITH MAN IS NOT THE ORIGIN OF CONJUGIAL LOVE, BUT ITS FIRST RUDIMENT; THUS IT IS LIKE AN EXTERNAL NATURAL PRINCIPLE, IN WHICH AN INTERNAL SPIRITUAL PRINCIPLE IS IMPLANTED. The subject here treated of is love truly conjugial, and not ordinary love, which also is called conjugial, and which with some is merely the limited love of the sex. Love truly conjugial exists only with those who desire wisdom, and who consequently advance more and more into wisdom. These the Lord foresees, and provides for them conjugial love; which love indeed commences with them from the love of the sex, or rather by it; but still it does not originate in it; for it originates in proportion to the advancement in wisdom and the dawning of the light thereof in man; for wisdom and that love are inseparable companions. The reason why conjugial love commences by the love of the sex is, because before a suitable consort is found, the sex in general is loved and regarded with a fond eye, and is treated with civility from a moral ground: for a young man has to make his choice; and while this is determining, from an innate inclination to marriage with one, which lies concealed in the interiors of his mind, his external receives a gentle warmth. A further reason is, because determinations to marriage are delayed from various causes even to riper years, and in the mean time the beginning of that love is as lust; which with some actually goes astray into the love of the sex; yet with them it is indulged no further than may be conducive to health. This, however, is to be understood as spoken of the male sex, because it has enticements which actually inflame it; but not of the female sex. From these considerations it is evident that the love of the sex is not the origin of love truly conjugial; but that it is its first rudiment in respect to time, yet not in respect to end; for what is first in respect to end, is first in the mind and its intention, because it is regarded as primary;

but to this first there is no approaching unless successively through mediums, and these are not first in themselves, but only conducive to what is first in itself.

99. X. DURING THE IMPLANTATION OF CONJUGIAL LOVE, THE LOVE OF THE SEX INVERTS ITSELF AND BECOMES THE CHASTE LOVE OF THE SEX. It is said that in this case the love of the sex inverts itself; because while conjugial love is coming to its origin, which is in the interiors of the mind, it sees the love of the sex not before itself but behind, or not above itself but beneath, and thus as somewhat which it passes by and leaves. The case herein is similar to that of a person climbing from one office to another through a great variety, till he reaches one which exceeds the rest in dignity; when he looks back upon the offices through which he had passed, as behind or beneath him; or as when a person intends a journey to the palace of some king, after his arrival at his journey's end, he inverts his view in regard to the objects which he had seen in the way. That in this case the love of the sex remains and becomes chaste, and yet, to those who are principled in love truly conjugial, is sweeter than it was before, may be seen from the description given of it by those in the spiritual world, in the two MEMORABLE RELATIONS, n. 44, and 55.

100. XI. THE MALE AND THE FEMALE WERE CREATED TO BE THE ESSENTIAL FORM OF THE MARRIAGE OF GOOD AND TRUTH. The reason of this is, because the male was created to be the understanding of truth, thus truth in form; and the female was created to be the will of good, thus good in form; and there is implanted in each, from their inmost principles, an inclination to conjunction into a one, as may be seen above, n. 88; thus the two make one form, which emulates the conjugial form of good and truth. It is said to emulate it, because it is not the same, but is like it; for the good which joins itself with the truth belonging to the man, is from the Lord immediately; whereas the good of the wife, which joins itself with the truth belonging to the man, is from the Lord mediately through the wife; therefore there are two goods, the one internal, the other external, which join themselves with the truth belonging to the husband, and cause him to be constantly in the understanding of truth, and thence in wisdom, by love truly conjugial: but on this subject more will be said in the following pages.

101. XII. MARRIED PARTNERS ARE THAT FORM IN THEIR INMOST PRINCIPLES, AND THENCE IN WHAT IS DERIVED FROM THOSE PRINCIPLES, IN PROPORTION AS THE INTERIORS OF THEIR MINDS ARE OPENED. There are three things of which every man consists, and which follow in an orderly connection,—the soul, the mind, and the body: his inmost is the soul, his middle is the mind, and his ultimate is the body. Every thing which flows from the Lord into a man, flows into his inmost principle,

which is the soul, and descends thence into his middle principle, which is the mind, and through this into his ultimate principle, which is the body. Such is the nature of the influx of the marriage of good and truth from the Lord with man: it flows immediately into his soul, and thence proceeds to the principles next succeeding, and through these to the extreme or outermost: and thus conjointly all the principles constitute conjugial love. From an idea of this influx it is manifest, that two married partners are the form of conjugial love in their inmost principles, and thence in those derived from the inmost.

102. But the reason why married partners become that form in proportion as the interiors of their minds are opened, is, because the mind is successively opened from infancy even to extreme old age: for a man is born corporeal: and in proportion as the mind is opened proximately above the body, he becomes rational; and in proportion as his rational principle is purified, and as it were drained of the fallacies which flow in from the bodily senses, and of the concupiscences which flow in from the allurements of the flesh, in the same proportion it is opened; and this is affected solely by wisdom: and when the interiors of the rational mind are open, the man becomes a form of wisdom; and this form is the receptacle of love truly conjugial. "The wisdom which constitutes this form, and receives this love, is rational, and at the same time moral, wisdom: rational wisdom regards the truths and goods which appear inwardly in man, not as its own, but as flowing in from the Lord; and moral wisdom shuns evils and falses as leprosies, especially the evils of lasciviousness, which contaminate its conjugial love."

* * * * *

103. To the above I shall add two MEMORABLE RELATIONS: the FIRST is this. One morning before sun-rise I was looking towards the east in the spiritual world, and I saw four horsemen as it were issuing from a cloud refulgent with the flame of the dawing day. On their heads they had crested helmets, on their arms as it were wings, and around their bodies light orange-colored tunics; thus clad as for expedition, they rose in their seats, and gave their horses the reins, which thus ran as if they had had wings to their feet. I kept my eye fixed on their course or flight, desiring to know where they were going; and lo! three of the horsemen took their direction towards three different quarters, the south, the west, and the north; and the fourth in a short space of time halted in the east. Wondering at all this, I looked up into heaven, and inquired where those horsemen were going? I received for answer, "To the wise men in the kingdoms of Europe, who with clear reasoning and acute discernment discuss the subjects of their investigation, and are distinguished above the rest for their genius, that they may assemble together and explain the secret RESPECTING THE ORIGIN

OF CONJUGIAL LOVE, AND RESPECTING ITS VIRTUE OR POTENCY." It was then said from heaven, "Wait awhile, and you will see twenty-seven chariots; three, in which are Spaniards; three, in which are Frenchmen; three, in which are Italians; three, in which are Germans; three, in which are Dutchmen or Hollanders; three, in which are Englishmen; three, in which are Swedes; three, in which are Danes; and three, in which are Poles." In about two hours I saw the chariots, drawn by horses of a pale-red color, with remarkable trappings: they passed rapidly along towards a spacious house in the confines of the east and south, around which all alighted from their several chariots, and entered in with much confidence. Then it was said to me, "Go, and do you also enter, and you will hear." I went and entered: and on examining the house within, I saw that it was square, the sides looking to the four quarters: in each side there were three high windows of crystalline glass, the frames of which were of olive-wood; on each side of the frames were projections from the walls, like chambers vaulted above, in which there were tables. The walls of these chambers were of cedar, the roof of the noble almug wood, and the floor of poplar boards. Near the eastern wall, where no windows were seen, there was set a table overlaid with gold, on which was placed a TURBAN set with precious stones, which was to be given as a prize or reward to him who should by investigation discover the secret about to be proposed. While my attention was directed to the chamber projections like closets near the windows, I saw five men in each from every kingdom of Europe, who were prepared and waiting to know the object for the exercise of their judgements. An angel then presented himself in the middle of the palace, and said, "The object for the exercise of your judgements shall be RESPECTING THE ORIGIN OF CONJUGIAL LOVE, AND RESPECTING ITS VIRTUE OR POTENCY. Investigate this and decide upon it; and write your decision on a piece of paper, and put it into the silver urn which you see placed near the golden table, and subscribe the initial letter of the kingdom from which you come; as F for French, B for Batavians or Hollanders, I for Italians, E for English, P for Poles, G for German, H for Spaniards (*Hispani*), D for Danes, S for Swedes." As he said this, the angel departed, saying, "I will return." Then the five men, natives of the same country, in each closet near the windows, took into consideration the proposed subject, examined it attentively, and came to a decision according to their respective talents and powers of judgement, which they wrote on a piece of paper, and placed it in the silver urn, having first subscribed the initial letter of their kingdom. This business being accomplished in about three hours, the angel returned and drew the papers in order from the urn, and read them before the assembly.

104. From the FIRST PAPER which he happened to lay hold

of, he read as follows; "We five, natives of the same country, in our closet have decreed that the origin of conjugial love is from the most ancient people in the golden age, and that it was derived to them from the creation of Adam and his wife: hence is the origin of marriages, and with marriages the origin of conjugial love. The virtue or potency of conjugial love we derive from no other source than climate or situation in regard to the sun, and the consequent heat of the country; and we are confirmed in this sentiment, not by vain conjectures of reason, but by evident proofs of experience, as by the case of the people who live under the line, or the equinoctial, where the heat of the day is intense, and by the case of those who live nearer to the line, or more distant from it; and also from the co-operation of the sun's heat with the vital heat in the living creatures of the earth and the fowls of heaven, in the time of spring during prolification. Moreover, what is conjugial love but heat, which becomes virtue or potency, if the heat supplied from the sun be added to it?" To this decision was subscribed the letter H, the initial of the kingdom from which they were.

105. After this he put his hand into the urn a SECOND TIME, and took out a paper from which he read as follows: "We, natives of the same country, in our lodge have agreed that the origin of conjugial love is the same with the origin of marriages, which were sanctioned by laws in order to restrain man's innate concupiscences prompting him to adultery, which ruins the soul, defiles the reason, pollutes the morals, and infects the body with disease: for adultery is not human but bestial, not rational but brutish, and thus not in any respect Christian but barbarous: with a view to the condemnation of such adultery, marriages originated, and at the same time conjugial love. The case is the same with the virtue or potency of this love; for it depends on chastity, which consists in abstaining from the rovings of whoredom: the reason is, because virtue or potency, with him who loves his married partner alone, is confined to one, and is thus collected and as it were concentrated; and then it becomes refined like a quintessence from which all defilement is separated, which would otherwise be dispersed and cast away in every direction. One of us five, who is a priest, has also added predestination as a cause of that virtue or potency, saying, 'Are not marriages predestinated? and this being the case, are not the progeny thence issuing and the means conducive thereto, predestinated also?' He insisted on adding this cause because he had sworn to it." To this decision was subscribed the letter B. On hearing it, a certain spirit observed with a smile, "How fair an apology is predestination for weakness or impotence!"

106. Presently he drew from the urn a THIRD PAPER, from which he read as follows: "We, natives of the same country,

in our department have deliberated concerning the causes of the origin of conjugial love, and have seen this to be the principal, that it is the same with the origin of marriage, because conjugial love had no existence before marriage; and the ground of its existence is, that when any one is desperately in love with a virgin, he desires in heart and soul to possess her as being lovely above all things; and as soon as she betroths herself to him he regards her as another self. That this is the origin of conjugial love, is clearly manifest from the fury of every man against his rivals, and from the jealousy which takes place in case of violation. We afterwards considered the origin of the virtue or potency of this love; and the sentiments of three prevailed against the other two, viz., that virtue or potency with a married partner arises from some degree of licentiousness with the sex. They affirmed that they knew from experience that the potency of the love of the sex is greater than the potency of conjugial love." To this decision was subscribed the letter I. On hearing it, there was a cry from the table, "Remove this paper and take another out of the urn."

107. And instantly he drew out a FOURTH, from which he read as follows: "We, natives of the same country, under our window have come to this conclusion, that the origin of conjugial love and of the love of the sex is the same, the former being derived from the latter; only that the love of the sex is unlimited, indeterminate, loose, promiscuous, and roving; whereas conjugial love is limited, determinate, fixed, regular, and constant; and that this love therefore has been sanctioned and established by the prudence of human wisdom as necessary to the existence of every empire, kingdom, commonwealth, and even society; for without it men would wander like droves of cattle in fields and forests, with harlots and ravished females, and would fly from one habitation to another to avoid the bloody murders, violations, and depredations, whereby the whole human race would be in danger of being extirpated. This is our opinion concerning the origin of conjugial love. But the virtue or potency of conjugial love we deduce from an uninterrupted state of bodily health continuing from infancy to old age; for the man who always retains a sound constitution and enjoys a continual freedom from sickness, feels his vigor unabated, while his fibres, nerves, muscles, and sinews, are neither torpid, relaxed, nor feeble, but retain the full strength of their powers: farewell." To this decision was subscribed the letter E.

108. FIFTHLY, he drew a paper out of the urn, from which he read as follows: "We, natives of the same country, at our table, from the rationality of our minds, have examined into the origin of conjugial love and of its virtue or potency; and from all the considerations which have presented themselves, we have seen and concluded upon no other origin of conjugial love than

this; that every man, from incentives and consequent incitements which are concealed in the interiors of his mind and body, after indulging in various desires of his eyes, at length fixes his mind and inclination on one of the female sex, until his passion is determined entirely to her: from this moment his warmth is enkindled more and more, until at length it becomes a flame; in this state the inordinate love of the sex is banished, and conjugial love takes its place. A youthful bridegroom under the influence of this flame, knows no other than that the virtue or potency of this love will never cease; for he wants experience and therefore knowledge respecting a state of the failure of his powers, and of the coldness of love which then succeeds to delights: conjugial love therefore has its origin in this first ardor before the nuptial ceremony, and from the same source it derives its virtue or potency; but this virtue or potency changes its aspect after the nuptial ceremony, and decreases and increases; yet still it continues with regular changes, or with decrease and increase, even to old age, by means of prudent moderation, and by restraining the libidinous desires which burst forth from the lurking places of the mind not yet thoroughly purified: for libidinous desire precedes wisdom. This is our judgement concerning the origin and continuance of conjugial virtue or potency." To this decision was subscribed the letter P.

109. SIXTHLY, he drew out a paper, from which he read as follows: "We, natives of the same country, from the fellowship subsisting among us, have attentively considered the causes of the origin of conjugial love, and have agreed in assigning two; one of which is the right education of children, and the other the distinct possession of inheritances. We have assigned these two, because they aim at and regard the same end, which is the public good: and this end is obtained, because infants conceived and born from conjugial love become proper and true children; and these in consequence of the natural love of the parents, exalted by the consideration of their offspring being legitimate, are educated to be heirs of all their parents' possessions both spiritual and natural. That the public good is founded on a right education of children and on a distinct possession of inheritances, is obvious to reason. Of the love of the sex and conjugial love, the latter appears as if it were one with the former, but it is distinctly different; neither is the one love near to the other, but within it; and what is within is more excellent than what is without: and we have seen that conjugial love from creation is within, and lies hid in the love of the sex, just as an almond does in its shell; therefore when conjugial love comes out of its shell, which is the love of the sex, it glitters before the angels like a gem, a beryl, and astroites. The reason of this is, because on conjugial love is inscribed the safety of the whole human race, which we conceive to be understood by the

public good. This is our judgement respecting the origin of this love. With respect to the origin of its virtue or potency, from a consideration of its causes, we have concluded it to be the development and separation of conjugial love from the love of the sex, which is effected by wisdom on the man's part, and by the love of the man's wisdom on the part of the wife: for the love of the sex is common to man and beast; whereas conjugial love is peculiar to men: therefore so far as conjugial love is developed and separated from the love of the sex, so far a man is a man and not a beast; and a man acquires virtue or potency from his love, as a beast does from his." To this decision was subscribed the letter G.

110. SEVENTHLY, he drew out a paper from which he read as follows: "We, natives of the same country, in the chamber under the light of our window, have found our thoughts and thence our judgements exhilarated by meditating on conjugial love; for who is not exhilarated by this love, which, while, it prevails in the mind, prevails also through the whole body? We judge of the origin of this love from its delights; for who in any case knows or has known the trace of any love except from its delight and pleasurableness? The delights of conjugial love in their origins are felt as beatitudes, satisfactions, and happinesses, in their derivations as pleasantnesses and pleasures, and in their ultimates as superlative delights. The love of the sex therefore originates when the interiors of the mind, and thence the interiors of the body, are opened for the influx of those delights; but conjugial love originated at the time when, from entering into marriage engagements, the primitive sphere of that love ideally promoted those delights. The virtue or potency of this love arises from its passing, with its inmost principles, from the mind into the body; for the mind, by derivation from the head, is in the body, while it feels and acts, especially when it is delighted from this love: hence we judge of the degrees of its potency and the regularity of its alterations. Moreover we also deduce the virtue of potency from the stock whence a man is descended: if this be noble on the father's side, it becomes also by transmission noble with his offspring. That such nobility is generated, inherited and descends by transmission, is agreeable to the dictates of reason supported by experience." To this decision was subscribed the letter F.

111. From the paper which came forth the EIGHTH in order, he read as follows: "We, natives of the same country, in our place of assembly have not discovered the real origin of conjugial love, because it lies deeply concealed in the sacred repositories of the mind. The most consummate vision cannot, by any intellectual effort, reach that love in its origin. We have made many conjectures; but after the vain exertion of subtle inquiry, we have been in doubt whether our conjectures might not be called

rather trifling than judicious; therefore whoever is desirous to extract the origin of that love from the sacred repositories of his mind, and to exhibit it clearly before his eyes, let him go to *Delphos*. We have contemplated that love beneath its origin, and have seen that in the mind it is spiritual, and as a fountain from which a sweet stream flows, whence it descends into the breast, where it becomes delightful, and is called bosom love, which in itself is full of friendship and confidence, from a full inclination to reciprocality; and that when it has passed the breast, it becomes genial love. These and similar considerations, which a young man revolves in his mind while he is determining his choice to one of the sex, kindle in his heart the fire of conjugial love; which fire, as it is the primitive of that love is its origin. In respect to the origin of its virtue or potency, we acknowledge no other than that love itself, they being inseparable companions, yet still they are such that sometimes the one precedes and sometimes the other. When the love precedes and the virtue or potency follows it, each is noble because in this case potency is the virtue of conjugial love; but if the potency precedes and the love follows, each is then ignoble; because in this case the love is subordinate to carnal potency: we therefore judge of the quality of each from the order in which the love descends or ascends, and thus proceeds from its origin to its proposed end." To this decision was subscribed the letter D.

112. Lastly, or NINTHLY, he took up a paper, from which he read as follows: "We, natives of the same country, in our council-chamber have exercised our judgement on the two points proposed, viz., the origin of conjugial love, and the origin of its virtue or potency. In the subtleties of inquiry respecting the origin of conjugial love, in order to avoid obscurity in our reasonings, we have distinguished between the love of the sex as being spiritual, natural, and carnal; and by the spiritual love of the sex we have understood love truly conjugial, because this is spiritual; and by the natural love of the sex we have understood polygamical love, because this is natural; and by the merely carnal love of the sex we have understood adulterous love because this is merely carnal. In exercising our judgements to examine into love truly conjugial, we have clearly seen that this love exists only between one male and one female, and that from creation it is celestial and inmost, the soul and father of all good loves, being inspired into the first parents, and capable of being inspired into Christians; it is also of such a conjunctive nature that by it two minds may become one mind, and two men (*homines*) as it were one man (*homo*); which is meant by becoming one flesh. Tha this love was inspired at creation, is plain from these words in the book of creation, "*And a man shall leave father and mother, and shall cleave to his wife; and they shall be one flesh,*' Gen. ii. 24. That it can be inspired into Christians,

is evident from these words, '*Jesus said, Have ye not read, that he who made them from the beginning, made them male and female, and said, For this cause shall a man leave father and mother, and shall cleave to his wife; and they two shall be one flesh? Wherefore they are no longer two but one flesh,*' *Matt.* xix. 4—6. So far in regard to the origin of conjugial love: but as to the origin of the virtue or potency of love truly conjugial, we conceive it to proceed from a similitude of minds and unanimity; for when two minds are conjugially united, their thoughts spiritually kiss each other, and these inspire into the body their virtue or potency." To this decision was subscribed the letter S.

113. There were standing behind an oblong stage in the palace, erected before the doors, some strangers from Africa, who cried out to the natives of Europe, "Permit one of us to deliver his sentiments respecting the origin of conjugial love, and respecting its virtue or potency." And immediately all the tables gave signs of assent with their hands. Then one of them entered and stood at the table on which the turban was placed, and said, "You Christians deduce the origin of conjugial love from love itself; but we Africans deduce it from the God of heaven and earth. Is not conjugial love a chaste, pure, and holy love? Are not the angels of heaven principled therein? Is not the whole human race, and thence the whole angelic heaven, the seed of that love? And can such super-eminent principle derive its existence from any other source than from God himself, the Creator and Preserver of the universe? You Christians deduce conjugial virtue or potency from various causes rational and natural; but we Africans deduce it from the state of man's conjunction with the God of the universe. This state we call a state of religion; but you call it a state of the church: for when the love is derived from that state, and is fixed and permanent, it must needs produce its own virtue, which resembles it, and thus also is fixed and permanent. Love truly conjugial is known only to those few who live near to God; consequently the potency of that love is known to none else. This potency is described by the angels in the heavens as the delight of a perpetual spring."

114. As he said these word, the whole assembly arose, and lo! behind the golden table on which lay the turban, there appeared a window that had not before been seen; and through it was heard a voice, saying, "THE AFRICAN IS TO HAVE THE TURBAN." The angel then gave it into his hand, but did not place it upon his head; and he went home with it. The inhabitants of the kingdoms of Europe then left the assembly and entered their chariots, in which they returned to their respective societies.

115. THE SECOND MEMORABLE RELATION. Awaking from sleep at midnight, I saw at some elevation towards the east at

angel holding in his right hand a paper, which appeared extremely bright, being illuminated by the light flowing from the sun. In the middle of the paper there was written in golden letters, THE MARRIAGE OF GOOD AND TRUTH. From the writing there darted forth a splendor which formed a wide circle about the paper. This circle or encompassing splendor appeared like the early dawn in spring. After this I saw the angel descending with the paper in his hand; and as he descended the paper became less and less lucid, and the writing, which was THE MARRIAGE OF GOOD AND TRUTH, changed from a golden into a silver color, afterwards into a copper color, next into an iron color, and at length into the color of iron and copper rust: finally, I saw the angel enter an obscure mist, and through the mist descend upon the ground; and here I did not see the paper, although he still held it in his hand. This happened in the world of spirits, in which all men first assemble after their decease. The angel then said to me, "Ask those who come hither whether they see me, or anything in my hand." There came a great number; one company from the east, another from the south, another from the west, and another from the north; and I asked those who came from the east and from the south, who in the world had applied themselves to literary pursuits, "Do you see any one here with me, and anything in his hand?" They all said, "No." I then put the same question to those who came from the west and from the north, who in the world had believed in the words of the learned; and these gave the same answer: nevertheless the last of them, who in the world had been principled in simple faith grounded in charity, or in some degree of truth grounded in good, when the rest were gone away, said, that they saw a man with a paper, the man in a graceful dress, and the paper with letters written upon it: and when they applied their eyes nearer to it, they said that they could read these words, *The marriage of good and truth;* and they addressed the angel, intreating him to explain to them the meaning of the writing. He said, "All things in the whole heaven and in the whole world, are a marriage of good and truth; for all things whatever, both those which live and communicate life and those which do not live and do not communicate life, were created from and into the marriage of good and truth. There does not exist anything which was created into truth alone, or any thing which was created into good alone: solitary good or solitary truth is not any thing; but by marriage they exist and become something which derives its nature and quality from that of the marriage. In the Lord the Creator are divine good and divine truth in their very substance: the *esse* of his substance is divine good, and its *existere* is divine truth: in him also they are in their very essential union; for in him they infinitely make a one: and since these two in the Creator himself are a one, therefore also they are a one in all things created from him; hereby also the Creator is conjoined in an eternal covenant as of marriage with all things created from himself." The angel further said, that the Sacred Scripture, which proceeded immediately from the Lord, is in general and in particular a marriage of good and truth; and since the church, which is formed by the truth of doctrine, and religion, which is formed by the good of life agreeable to the truth of doctrine, are with Christians derived solely from the Sacred Scripture, therefore it may manifestly appear, that the church in general and in particular is a marriage of good and truth; (that this is the case, may be seen in the APOCALYPSE REVEALED, n. 373, 483.) What has just been said concerning the marriage of good and truth, is applicable also to the MARRIAGE OF CHARITY AND FAITH; for good relates to charity, and truth to faith. Some of the spirits above-mentioned who did not see the angel and the writing, being still near, and hearing these things, said in an under tone, " *Yes, we also comprehend what has been spoken;*" but the angel then said to them, "Turn aside a little from me and speak in like manner." They turned aside, and then said alond, " *It is not so.*" After this the angel spoke concerning the MARRIAGE OF GOOD AND TRUTH with married pairs, saying, that if their minds were in that marriage, the husband being truth, and the wife the good thereof, they would both be in the delights of the blessedness and innocence, and thence in the happiness which the angels of heaven enjoy; and in this state the prolific principle of the husband would be in a continual spring, and thereby in the endeavour and vigor of propagating its truth, and the wife would be in a continual reception thereof from a principle of love. The wisdom which husbands derive from the Lord, is sensible of no greater delight than to propagate its truths; and the love of wisdom which wives have from the Lord is sensible of no higher gratification than to receive those truths as it were in the womb, and thus to conceive them, to carry them in the womb, and to bring them forth. Spiritual prolifications with the angels of heaven are of this sort; and if you are disposed to believe it, natural prolifications are also from the same origin. The angel, after a salutation of peace, raised himself from the ground, and passing through the mist ascended into heaven; and then the paper shone as before according to the degrees of ascent; and behold! the circle, which before appeared as the dawn of day, descended and dispelled the mist which caused darkness on the ground, and a bright sunshine succeeded.

ON THE MARRIAGE OF THE LORD AND THE CHURCH, AND ITS CORRESPONDENCE.

116. THE reason why the marriage of the Lord and the church, together with its correspondence, is here also treated of, is, because without knowledge and intelligence on this subject, scarcely any one can know, that conjugial love in its origin is holy, spiritual, and celestial, and that it is from the Lord. It is said indeed by some in the church, that marriages have relation to the marriage of the Lord with the church; but the nature and quality of this relationship is unknown, in order therefore that this relationship may be exhibited to the understanding so as to be seen in some degree of light, it is necessary to treat particularly of that holy marriage which has place with and in those who are the Lord's church. These also, and no others, are principled in love truly conjugial. But for the better elucidation of this arcanum, it may be expedient to consider the subject distinctly, as arranged under the following articles: I. *The Lord in the Word is called the Bridegroom and Husband, and the church the bride and wife; and the conjunction of the Lord with the church, and the reciprocal conjunction of the church with the Lord, is called a marriage.* II. *The Lord is also called a Father, and the church, a mother.* III. *The offspring derived from the Lord as a husband and father, and from the church as a wife and mother, are all spiritual; and in the spiritual sense of the Word are understood by sons and daughters, brothers and sisters, sons-in-law and daughters-in-law, and by other names of relations.* IV. *The spiritual offspring, which are born from the Lord's marriage with the church are truths and goods; truths, from which are derived understanding, perception, and all thought; and goods, from which are derived love, charity, and all affection.* V. *From the marriage of good and truth, which proceeds from the Lord in the way of influx, man* (homo) *receives truth, and the Lord conjoins good thereto; and thus the church is formed by the Lord with man.* VI. *The husband does not represent the Lord and the wife the church; because both together, the husband and the wife, constitute the church.* VII. *Therefore there is not a correspondence of the husband with the Lord and of the wife with the church, in the marriages of the angels in the heavens and of men on earth.* VIII. *But there is a correspondence with conjugial love, semination, prolification, the love of infants, and similar things which exist in marriages, and are derived from them.* IX. *The Word is the medium of conjunction, because it is from the Lord, and therefore is the Lord.* X. *The church is from the Lord, and exists with those who come to him, and live according to his precepts.* XI. *Conjugial love is according to the state of the church, because* *it is according to the state of wisdom with man* (homo). XII. *And as the church is from the Lord, conjugial love is also from him.* We proceed to the explanation of each article.

117. I. THE LORD IN THE WORD IS CALLED THE BRIDEGROOM AND HUSBAND, AND THE CHURCH THE BRIDE AND WIFE; AND THE CONJUNCTION OF THE LORD WITH THE CHURCH, AND THE RECIPROCAL CONJUNCTION OF THE CHURCH WITH THE LORD, IS CALLED A MARRIAGE. That the Lord in the Word is called the Bridegroom and Husband, and the church the bride and wife, may appear from the following passages: "*He that hath the* BRIDE *is the* BRIDEGROOM; *but the friend of the* BRIDEGROOM, *who standeth and heareth him, rejoiceth with joy because of the* BRIDEGROOM's *voice*," John iii. 29: this was spoken by John the Baptist concerning the Lord. "*Jesus said, So long as the* BRIDEGROOM *is with them, the* SONGS OF THE NUPTIALS *cannot fast: the days will come when the* BRIDEGROOM *will be taken away from them, and then will they fast*," Matt. ix. 15; Mark ii. 19, 20; Luke v. 34, 35. "*I saw the holy city, New Jerusalem, prepared as a* BRIDE *adorned for* HER HUSBAND," Rev. xxi. 2. The New Jerusalem signifies the New Church of the Lord, as may be seen in the APOCALYPSE REVEALED, n. 880, 881. "*The angel said to John, Come, and I will shew thee the* BRIDE, THE LAMB'S WIFE: *and he shewed him the holy city, New Jerusalem*," Rev. xxi. 9, 10. "*The time of the* MARRIAGE OF THE LAMB *is come, and his* WIFE *hath made herself ready. Blessed are those who are called to the supper of the* MARRIAGE OF THE LAMB," Rev. xix. 7, 9. The BRIDEGROOM, whom the five prepared virgins went forth to meet, and with WHOM they entered in to the MARRIAGE, Matt. xxv. 1—10, denotes the Lord; as is evident from verse 13, where it is said, "Watch, therefore; because ye know neither the day nor the hour in which the SON OF MAN will come:" not to mention many passages in the prophets.

118. II. THE LORD IS ALSO CALLED A FATHER, AND THE CHURCH, A MOTHER. The Lord is called a Father, as appears from the following passages: "*Unto us a child is born; unto us a son is given; and his name shall be called, Wonderful, Counsellor,* GOD, THE FATHER OF ETERNITY, *the Prince of Peace,*" Isaiah ix. 6. "*Thou,* JEHOVAH, *art* OUR FATHER, *our* REDEEMER; *thy name is from an age,*" Isaiah lxiii. 16. Again, "*Jesus said, He that seeth* ME, *seeth the* FATHER *that sent* ME," John xii. 45. "*If ye have known* ME, *ye have known my* FATHER *also; and henceforth ye have known him, and have seen him.*" John xiv. 7. "*Philip said, Shew us the* FATHER: *Jesus said unto him, He that seeth me, seeth the* FATHER; *how sayest thou then, Shew us the* FATHER?" John xiv. 8, 9. "*Jesus said, The* FATHER *and I are one,*" John x. 30. "*All things that the* FATHER *hath are* MINE," John xvi. 15; chap. xvii. 10. "*The* FATHER *is in* ME, *and I* IN THE FATHER," John x. 38; chap. xiv

10, 11, 20. That the Lord and his Father are one, as the soul and the body are one, and that God the Father descended from heaven, and assumed the human (nature or principle), to redeem and save men, and that his human nature is what is called the Son, and is said to be sent into the world, has been fully shewn in the APOCALYPSE REVEALED.

119. The church is called a mother, as appears from the following passages : " *Jehovah said, Contend with* YOUR MOTHER : *she is not* MY WIFE, *and I am not her* HUSBAND," Hosea ii. 2, 5. " *Thou art thy* MOTHER'S *daughter, that loatheth her* HUSBAND," Ezek. xvi. 45. " *Where is the bill of thy* MOTHER'S *divorcement, whom I have put away ?*" Isaiah l. 1. " *Thy* MOTHER *was like a vine planted by the waters, bearing fruit,*" Ezek. xix. 10 ; speaking of the Jewish church. " *Jesus stretching out his hand to the disciples, said,* MY MOTHER *and my brethren are those who hear the Word of God, and do it,*" Luke viii. 21 ; Matt. xii. 49, 50 ; Mark iii. 33—35 : the Lord's disciples means the church. " *There was standing at the cross of Jesus his mother : and Jesus seeing his mother and the disciple whom he loved, standing by, he saith unto his mother, Woman, behold thy son ; and he saith to the disciple, Behold thy mother : wherefore from that hour the disciple took her unto his own,*" John xix. 25—27. This implies, that the Lord did not acknowledge Mary as a mother, but the church ; therefore he calls her Woman, and the disciple's mother. The reason why the Lord called her the mother of this disciple, or of John, was, because John represented the church as to the goods of charity, which are the church in real effect; therefore it is said, He took her unto his own. Peter represented truth and faith, James charity, and John the works of charity, as may be seen in the APOCALYPSE REVEALED, n. 5, 6, 790, 798, 879 ; and the twelve disciples together represented the church as to all its constituent principles, as may be seen, n. 233, 790, 903, 915.

120. III. THE OFFSPRING DERIVED FROM THE LORD AS A HUSBAND AND FATHER, AND FROM THE CHURCH AS A WIFE AND MOTHER, ARE ALL SPIRITUAL; AND IN THE SPIRITUAL SENSE OF THE WORD ARE UNDERSTOOD BY SONS AND DAUGHTERS, BROTHERS AND SISTERS, SONS-IN-LAW, AND DAUGHTERS-IN-LAW, AND BY OTHER NAMES OF RELATIONS. That no other than spiritual offspring are born of the Lord by the church, is a proposition which wants no demonstration, because reason sees it to be self-evident; for it is the Lord from whom every good and truth proceeds, and it is the church which receives them and brings them into effect; and all the spiritual things of heaven and the church relate to good and truth. Hence it is that sons and daughters in the Word, in its spiritual sense, signify truths and goods ; sons, truths conceived in the spiritual man, and born in the natural ; and daughters, goods in like manner: therefore those who are regenerated by the Lord, are called in the Word

sons of God, sons of the kingdom, born of him; and the Lord called the disciples sons: the male child, that the woman brought forth, and that was caught up to God, Rev. xii. 5, has a similar signification; see APOCALYPSE REVEALED, n. 543. Since daughters signify goods of the church, therefore in the Word mention is so frequently made of the daughter of Zion, the daughter of Jerusalem, the daughter of Israel, and the daughter of Judah; by whom is signified not any daughter, but the affection of good, which is an affection of the church; see also APOCALYPSE REVEALED, n. 612. The Lord also calls those who are of his church, brethren and sisters; see Matt. xii. 49, 50; chap. xxv. 40; chap. xxviii. 10; Mark iii. 35; Luke viii. 21.

121. IV. THE SPIRITUAL OFFSPRING, WHICH ARE BORN FROM THE LORD'S MARRIAGE WITH THE CHURCH, ARE TRUTHS AND GOODS; TRUTHS, FROM WHICH ARE DERIVED UNDERSTANDING, PERCEPTION, AND ALL THOUGHT; AND GOODS, FROM WHICH ARE DERIVED LOVE, CHARITY, AND ALL AFFECTION. The reason why truths and goods are the spiritual offspring, which are born of the Lord by the church, is, because the Lord is essential good and essential truth, and these in him are not two but one; also, because nothing can proceed from the Lord but what is in him, and what he is. That the marriage of truth and good proceeds from the Lord, and flows in with men, and is received according to the state of the mind and life of those who are of the church, was shewn in the foregoing section on the MARRIAGE OF GOOD AND TRUTH. The reason why by means of truths a man has understanding, perception, and all thought, and by means of goods has love, charity, and all affection, is, because all things of man relate to truth and good; and there are two constituents of man—the will and the understanding; the will being the receptacle of good, and the understanding of truth. That love, charity and affection, belong to the will, and that perception and thought belong to the understanding, may appear without the aid of light arising from demonstration; for there is a light derived from the understanding itself by which these propositions are seen to be self-evident.

122. V. FROM THE MARRIAGE OF GOOD AND TRUTH, WHICH PROCEEDS FROM THE LORD IN THE WAY OF INFLUX, MAN (*homo*) RECEIVES TRUTH, AND THE LORD CONJOINS GOOD THERETO; AND THUS THE CHURCH IS FORMED BY THE LORD WITH MAN. The reason why a man receives truth by virtue of the good and truth which proceed as a one from the Lord, is, because he receives this as his own, and appropriates it to himself as his own; for he thinks what is true as from himself, and in like manner speaks from what is true; and this takes place because truth is in the light of the understanding, and hence he sees it: and whatever he sees in himself, or in his mind, he knows not whence it is; for he does not see the influx, as he sees those

objects which strike upon the bodily vision; hence he supposes that it is himself. That it should appear thus, is granted by the Lord to him, in order that he may be a man (*homo*), and that he may have a reciprocal principle of conjunction: add to this, that every man is born a faculty of knowing, understanding, and growing wise; and this faculty receives truths, whereby it has knowledges, intelligence, and wisdom. And since the female was created through the truth of the male, and is formed into the love thereof more and more after marriage, it follows, that she also receives the husband's truth in herself, and conjoins it with her own good.

123. The Lord adjoins and conjoins good to the truths which a man receives, because he cannot take good as of himself, it being no object of his sight, as it does not relate to light, but to heat, which is felt and not seen; therefore when a man sees truth in his thought, he seldom reflects upon the good which flows into it from the love of the will, and which gives it life: neither does a wife reflect upon the good belonging to her, but upon the husband's inclination towards her, which is according to the assent of his understanding to wisdom: the good which belongs to her from the Lord, she applies, without the husband's knowing any thing respecting such application. From these considerations then it plainly appears, that a man receives truth from the Lord, and that the Lord adjoins good to that truth, according to the application of truth to use; consequently as the man is desirous to think, and thence to live, wisely.

124. The church is thus formed with a man by the Lord, because in such case he is in conjunction with the Lord, in good from Him, and in truth as from himself; thus he is in the Lord, and the Lord in him, according to the Lord's words in John xv. 4, 5. The case is the same, if instead of good we say charity, and instead of truth faith; because good is of charity, and truth is of faith.

125. VI. THE HUSBAND DOES NOT REPRESENT THE LORD, AND THE WIFE THE CHURCH; BECAUSE BOTH TOGETHER, THE HUSBAND AND THE WIFE, CONSTITUTE THE CHURCH. It is a common saying in the church, that as the Lord is the Head of the church, so the husband is the head of the wife; whence it should follow, that the husband represents the Lord, and the wife the church: but the Lord is the Head of the church; and man (*homo*), the man (*vir*) and the woman, are the church; and still more the husband and wife together. With these the church is first implanted in the man, and through him in the wife; because the man with his understanding receives the truth of the church, and the wife from the man; but if it be *vice versa*, it is not according to order: sometimes, however, this is the case; but then it is with men, who either are not lovers of wisdom, and consequently are not of the church, or who are in a servile dependence on the

will of their wives. Something on this subject may be seen in the preliminary RELATIONS, n. 21.

126. VII. THEREFORE THERE IS NOT A CORRESPONDENCE OF THE HUSBAND WITH THE LORD AND OF THE WIFE WITH THE CHURCH, IN THE MARRIAGES OF THE ANGELS IN THE HEAVENS AND OF MEN ON EARTH. This follows as a consequence from what has just been said; to which, nevertheless, it may be expedient to add, that it appears as if truth was the primary constituent of the church, because it is first in respect to time: from this appearance, the prelates of the church have exalted faith, which is of truth, above charity, whch is of good; in like manner the learned have exalted thought, which is of the understanding, above affection, which is of the will; therefore the knowledge of what the good of charity and the affection of the will are, lies deeply buried as in a tomb, while some even cast earth upon them, as upon the dead, to prevent their rising again. That the good of charity, notwithstanding, is the primary constituent of the church, may be plainly seen by those who have not closed the way from heaven to their understandings, by confirmations in favor of faith, as the sole constituent of the church, and in favor of thought, as the sole constituent of man. Now as the good of charity is from the Lord, and the truth of faith is with a man as from himself, and these two principles cause conjunction of the Lord with man, and of man with the Lord, such as is understood by the Lord's words, that He is in them, and they in Him, John xv. 4, 5, it is evident that this conjunction constitutes the church.

127. VIII. BUT THERE IS A CORRESPONDENCE WITH CONJUGIAL LOVE, SEMINATION, PROLIFICATION, THE LOVE OF INFANTS, AND SIMILAR THINGS WHICH EXIST IN MARRIAGES AND ARE DERIVED FROM THEM. These, however, are arcana of too deep a nature to enter the understanding with any degree of light, unless preceded by knowledge concerning correspondence; nor is it possible, if this knowledge be wanting, so to explain them as to make them comprehensible. But what correspondence is, and that it exists between natural things and spiritual, is abundantly shown in the APOCALYPSE REVEALED, also in the ARCANA CŒLESTIA, and specifically in the DOCTRINE OF THE NEW JERUSALEM CONCERNING THE SACRED SCRIPTURE, and particularly in a MEMORABLE RELATION respecting it in the following pages. Before some knowledge on this subject is acquired, we will only present to the intellectual view, as in a shade, these few particulars: conjugial love corresponds to the affection of genuine truth, its chastity, purity, and sanctity; semination corresponds to the potency of truth; prolification corresponds to the propagation of truth; and the love of infants corresponds to the defence of truth and good. Now as truth with a man (*homo*) appears as his own, and good is adjoined thereto from the Lord, it is evident that these corre-

spondences are those of the natural or external man with the spiritual or internal man : but some degree of light will be reflected on this subject from the MEMORABLE RELATIONS which follow

128. IX. THE WORD IS THE MEDIUM OF CONJUNCTION, BECAUSE IT IS FROM THE LORD, AND THEREFORE IS THE LORD. The Word is the medium of conjunction of the Lord with man (*homo*), and of man with the Lord, because in its essence it is divine truth united to divine good, and divine good united to divine truth : that this union exists in every part of the Word in its celestial and spiritual sense, may be seen in the APOCALYPSE REVEALED, n. 373, 483, 689, 881; whence it follows, that the Word is the perfect marriage of good and truth ; and as it is from the Lord, and what is from him is also himself, it follows, that while a man reads the Word, and collects truths out of it, the Lord adjoins good. For a man does not see the goods which affect him in reading ; because he reads the Word from the understanding, and the understanding acquires thence only such things as are of its own nature, that is, truths. That good is adjoined thereto from the Lord, is made sensible to the understanding from the delight which flows in during a state of illustration ; but this takes place interiorly with those only who read the Word to the end that they may become wise; and such persons are desirous of learning the genuine truths contained in the Word, and thereby of forming the church in themselves ; whereas those who read the Word only with a view to gain the reputation of learning, and those also who read it from an opinion that the mere reading or hearing it inspires faith and conduces to salvation, do not receive any good from the Lord; for the end proposed by the latter is to save themselves by the mere expressions contained in the Word, in which there is nothing of truth ; and the end proposed by the former is to be distinguished for their learning; which end has no conjunction with any spiritual good, but only with the natural delight arising from worldly glory. As the Word is the medium of conjunction, it is therefore called the old and the new Covenant: a covenant signifies conjunction.

129. X. THE CHURCH IS FROM THE LORD, AND EXISTS WITH THOSE WHO COME TO HIM AND LIVE ACCORDING TO HIS PRECEPTS. It is not denied at this day that the church is the Lord's, and consequently that it is from the Lord. The reason why it exists with those who come to him, is, because his church in that part of the globe which is called Christian, is derived from the Word; and the Word is from him, and in such a manner from him, that it is himself, the divine truth being therein united to the divine good, and this also is the Lord. This is meant by the Word, "*which was with God, and which was God, from which men have life and light, and which was made flesh,*" John i. 1—14. Moreover, the reason why the church exists with

those who come to him, is, because it exists with those who believe in him; and to believe that he is God the Saviour and Redeemer, that he is Jehovah our justice, that he is the door by which we are to enter into the sheepfold, that is, into the church, that he is the way, the truth, and the life, and that no one comes to the Father but by him, that the Father and he are one, besides many other particulars which he himself teaches; to believe these things, I say, is impossible for any one, except by influence from him; and the reason why this is impossible unless he be approached, is, because he is the God of heaven and earth, as he also teaches. Who else is to be approached, and who else can be? The reason why the church exists with those who live according to his precepts, is, because there is conjunction with none else; for he says, "*He that hath my precepts, and doeth them, he it is that loveth me; and I will love him, and will make my abode with him: but he that doth not love me, doth not keep my precepts,*" John xiv. 21—24. Love is conjunction; and conjunction with the Lord is the church.

130. XI. CONJUGIAL LOVE IS ACCORDING TO THE STATE OF THE CHURCH, BECAUSE IT IS ACCORDING TO THE STATE OF WISDOM WITH MAN (*homo*). That conjugial love is according to the state of wisdom with man, has been often said above, and will be often repeated in the following pages: at present therefore we will shew what wisdom is, and that it makes one with the church. "There are belonging to man knowledge, intelligence, and wisdom. Knowledge relates to information; intelligence, to reason; and wisdom to life. Wisdom considered in its fulness relates at the same time to information, to reason, and to life: information precedes, reason is formed by it, and wisdom by both; as is the case when a man lives rationally according to the truths which he knows. Wisdom therefore relates to both reason and life at once; and it becomes (or is making) wisdom while it is a principle of reason and thence of life; but it is wisdom when it is made a principle of life and thence of reason. The most ancient people in this world acknowledged no other wisdom than the wisdom of life; which was the wisdom of those who were formerly called SOPHI: but the ancient people, who succeeded the most ancient, acknowledged the wisdom of reason as wisdom; and these were called PHILOSOPHERS. At this day, however, many call even knowledge, wisdom; for the learned, the erudite, and the mere sciolists, are called wise; thus wisdom has declined from its mountain-top to its valley. But it may be expedient briefly to shew what wisdom is in its rise, in its progress, and thence in its full state. The things relating to the church, which are called spiritual, reside in the inmost principles with man; those relating to the public weal, which are called things of a civil nature, hold a place below these; and those relating to science, to experience, and to art, which are called natural things, constitute their seat

or basis. The reason why the things relating to the church, which are called spiritual, reside in the inmost principles with man, is, because they conjoin themselves with heaven, and by heaven with the Lord; for no other things enter from the Lord through heaven with man. The reason why the things relating to the public weal, which are called things of a civil nature, hold a place beneath spiritual things, is, because they have relation to the world, and conjoin themselves with it; for statutes, laws, and rules, are what bind men, so that a civil society and state may be composed of them in a well-connected order. The reason why the things relating to science, to experience, and to art, which are called natural, constitute their seat or basis, is, because they conjoin themselves closely with the five bodily senses; and these senses are the ultimates on which the interior principles of the mind and the inmost principles of the soul, as it were sit or rest. Now as the things relating to the church, which are called spiritual, reside in the inmost principles, and as the things residing in the inmost principles constitute the head, and the succeeding things beneath them, which are called things of a civil nature, constitute the body, and the ultimate things, which are called natural, constitute the feet; it is evident, that while these three kinds of things follow in their order, a man is a perfect man; for in such case there is an influx like that of the things of the head into those of the body, and through the body into the feet; thus spiritual things flow into things of a civil nature, and through them into natural things. Now as spiritual things are in the light of heaven, it is evident that by their light they illustrate the things which succeed in order, and by their heat, which is love, animate them; and when this is the case the man has wisdom. As wisdom is a principle of life, and thence of reason, as was said above, it may be asked, What is wisdom as a principle of life? In a summary view, it is to shun evils, because they are hurtful to the soul, to the public weal, and to the body; and it is to do goods, because they are profitable to the soul, to the public weal, and to the body. This is the wisdom which is meant by the wisdom to which conjugial love binds itself; for it binds itself thereto by shunning the evil of adultery as the pest of the soul, of the public weal, and of the body: and as this wisdom originates in spiritual things relating to the church, it follows, that conjugial love is according to the state of the church; because it is according to the state of wisdom with men. Hereby also is understood what has been frequently said above, that so far as a man becomes spiritual, so far he is principled in love truly conjugial; for a man becomes spiritual by means of the spiritual things of the church." More observations respecting the wisdom with which conjugial love conjoins itself, may be seen below, n. 163—165.

131. XII. AND AS THE CHURCH IS FROM THE LORD, CON-

jugial love is also from him. As this follows as a consequence from what has been said above, it is needless to dwell upon the confirmation of it. Moreover, that love truly conjugial is from the Lord, all the angels of heaven testify; and also that this love is according to their state of wisdom, and that their state of wisdom is according to the state of the church with them. That the angels of heaven thus testify, is evident from the MEMORABLE RELATIONS annexed to the chapters, containing an account of what was seen and heard in the spiritual world.

* * * * * * * *

132. To the above I shall add TWO MEMORABLE RELATIONS. FIRST. I was conversing on a time with two angels, one from the eastern heaven and the other from the southern; who perceiving me engaged in meditation on the arcana of wisdom relating to conjugial love, said, "Are you at all acquainted with the SCHOOLS OF WISDOM in our world?" I replied, "Not as yet." And they said, "There are several; and those who love truths from spiritual affection, or because they are truths, and because they are the means of attaining wisdom, meet together on a given signal, and investigate and decide upon such questions as require deeper consideration than common." They then took me by the hand, saying, "Follow us; and you shall see and hear: to-day the signal for meeting is given." I was led across a plain to a hill; and lo! at the foot of the hill was an avenue of palms continued even to its summit, which we entered and ascended: on the summit or top of the hill was a grove, the trees of which, on an elevated plot of ground, formed as it were a theatre, within which was a court paved with various colored stones: around it in a square form were placed seats, on which the lovers of wisdom were seated; and in the middle of the theatre was a table, on which was laid a sealed paper. Those who sat on the seats invited us to sit down where there was room: and I replied, "I was led here by two angels to see and hear, and not to sit down." Then those two angels went into the middle of the court to the table, and broke the seal of the paper, and read in the presence of those who were seated the arcana of wisdom written on the paper, which were now to be investigated and explained. They were written by angels of the third heaven, and let down upon the table. There were three arcana, FIRST, What is the image of God, and what the likeness of God, into which man (*homo*) was created? SECOND, Why is not a man born into the knowledge of any love, when yet beasts and birds, from the highest to the lowest, are born into the knowledge of all their loves? THIRD, What is signified by the tree of life, and what by the tree of the knowledge of good and evil, and what by eating thereof? Underneath was written, Collect your opinions on these three questions into one decision, and write it on a new piece of paper, and lay it on this table, and we shall see it: if the decision, on

examination, appear just and reasonable, each of you shall receive a prize of wisdom. Having read the contents of the paper, the two angels withdrew, and were carried up into their respective heavens.

Then those who sat on the seats began to investigate and explain the arcana proposed to them, and delivered their sentiments in order; first those who sat on the north, next those on the west, afterwards those on the south, and lastly those on the east. They began with the first subject of inquiry, WHAT IS THE IMAGE OF GOD, AND WHAT THE LIKENESS OF GOD, INTO WHICH MAN WAS CREATED? But before they proceeded, these words were read in the presence of them all out of the book of creation, " *God said, Let us make man into* OUR IMAGE, *according to* OUR LIKENESS : *and God created man into* HIS IMAGE; *into the* IMAGE OF GOD *created he him*," Gen. i. 26, 27. " *In the day that God created man, into the* LIKENESS OF GOD *made he him*," Gen. v. 1. Those who sat on the north spoke first, saying, "The image of God and the likeness of God are the two lives breathed into man by God, which are the life of the understanding; for it is written, ' *Jehovah God breathed into Adam's nostril the soul of* LIVES ; *and man became a living soul*,' Gen. ii. 7 ; into the nostrils denotes into the perception, that the will of good and the understanding of truth, and thereby the soul of lives, was in him; and since life from God was breathed into him, the image and likeness of God signify integrity derived from wisdom and love, and from justice and judgment in him." These sentiments were favored by those who sat to the west ; only they added, that the state of integrity then breathed in from God is continually breathed into every man since ; but that it is a man as in a receptacle ; and a man, as he is a receptacle, is an image and likeness of God. After this, the third in order, who were those who were seated on the south, delivered their sentiments as follows : " An image of God and a likeness of God are two distinct things ; but in man they are united from creation ; and we see, as from an interior light, that the image of God may be destroyed by man, but not the likeness of God. This appears as clear as the day from this consideration, that Adam retained the likeness of God after that he had lost the image of God ; for it is written after the curse, ' *Behold the man is as one of us, knowing good and evil*,' Gen. iii. 22 ; and afterwards he is called a likeness of God, and not an image of God, Gen. v. 1. But we will leave to our associates who sit on the east, and are thence in superior light, to say what is properly meant by an image of God, and what by a likeness of God." And then, after silence was obtained, those who sat on the east arose from their seats, and looked up to the Lord, and afterwards sat down again, and thus began : " An image of God is a receptacle of God ; and since God is love itself and wisdom itself, an image of God is a receptacle of love and wisdom from God in it; but a likeness of God is a perfect likeness and full appearance, as if love and wisdom are in a man, and thence altogether as his; for a man has no other sensation than that he loves and is wise from himself, or that he wills good and understands truth from himself; when nevertheless nothing of all this is from himself, but from God. God alone loves from himself and is wise from himself; because God is love itself and wisdom itself. The likeness or appearance that love and wisdom, or good and truth, are in a man as his, causes a man to be a man, and makes him capable of being conjoined to God, and thereby of living to eternity: from which consideration it follows, that a man is a man from this circumstance, that he can will good and understand truth altogether as from himself, and yet know and believe that it is from God; for as he knows and believes this, God places his image in him, which could not be if he believed it was from himself and not from God." As they said this, being overpowered with zeal derived from the love of truth, they thus continued: "How can a man receive any thing of love and wisdom, and retain it, and reproduce it, unless he feel it as his own? And how can there be conjunction with God by love and wisdom, unless a man have some reciprocity of conjunction? For without such a reciprocity conjunction is impossible; and the reciprocity of conjunction is, that a man should love God, and enjoy the things which are of God, as from himself, and yet believe that it is from God. Also, how can a man live eternally, unless he be conjoined to an eternal God? Consequently how can a man be a man without such a likeness of God in him?" These words met with the approbation of the whole assembly; and they said, Let this conclusive decision be made from them, " A man is a recipient of God, and a recipient of God is an image of God; and since God is love itself and wisdom itself, a man is a recipient of those principles; and a recipient becomes an image of God in proportion to reception; and a man is a likeness of God from this circumstance, that he feels in himself that the things which are of God are in him as his own; but still from that likeness he is only so far an image of God, as he acknowledges that love and wisdom, or good and truth, are not his own in him, and consequently are not from him, but are only in God, and consequently from God."

133. After this, they entered upon the next subject of discussion, WHY IS NOT A MAN BORN INTO THE KNOWLEDGE OF ANY LOVE, WHEN YET BEASTS AND BIRDS, FROM THE HIGHEST TO THE LOWEST, ARE BORN INTO THE KNOWLEDGE OF ALL THEIR LOVES? They first confirmed the truth of the proposition by various considerations; as in regard to a man, that he is born into no knowledge, not even into the knowledge of conjugial love; and they inquired, and were informed by attentive ex-

aminers, that an infant from connate knowledge cannot even move itself to the mother's breast, but must be moved thereto by the mother or nurse; and that it knows only how to suck, and this in consequence of habit acquired by continual suction in the womb; and that afterwards it does not know how to walk, or to articulate any human expression; no, nor even to express by its tone of voice the affection of its love, as the beasts do : and further, that it does not know what is salutary for it in the way of food, as all the beasts do, but catches at whatever falls in its way, whether it be clean or unclean, and puts it into its mouth. The examiners further declared, that a man without instruction is an utter stranger to every thing relating to the sexes and their connection; and that neither virgins nor young men have any knowledge thereof without instruction from others, notwithstanding their being educated in various sciences : in a word, a man is born corporeal as a worm; and he remains such, unless he learns to know, to understand, and to be wise, from others. After this, they gave abundant proofs that beasts, from the highest to the lowest, as the animals of the earth, the fowls of the air, reptiles, fishes, the small creatures called insects, are born into all the knowledges of the loves of their life, as into the knowledge of all things relating to nourishment, to habitation, to the love of the sex and prolification, and to the rearing of their young. This they confirmed by many wonderful things which they recollected to have seen, heard, and read, in the natural world, (so they called our world, in which they had formerly lived), in which not representative but real beasts exist. When the truth of the proposition was thus fully proved they applied all the powers of their minds to search out and discover the ends and causes which might serve to unfold and explain this arcanum; and they all said, that the divine wisdom must needs have ordained these things, to the end that a man may be a man, and a beast a beast; and thus, that the imperfection of a man at his birth becomes his perfection, and the perfection of a beast at his birth is his imperfection.

134. Those on the NORTH then began to declare their sentiments, and said, "A man is born without knowledges, to the end that he may receive them all; whereas supposing him to be born into knowledges, he could not receive any but those into which he was born, and in this case neither could he appropriate any to himself; which they illustrated by this comparison : a man at his first birth is like ground in which no seeds are implanted, but which nevertheless is capable of receiving all seeds, and of bringing them forth and fructifying them; whereas a beast is like ground already sown, and filled with grasses and herbs, which receives no other seeds than what are sown in it, or if it received any it would choke them. Hence it is, that a man requires many years to bring him to maturity of growth; during

which time he is capable of being cultivated like ground, and of bringing forth as it were grain, flowers, and trees of every kind; whereas a beast arrives at maturity in a few years, during which no cultivation can produce any thing in him but what is born with him." Afterwards, those on the WEST delivered their sentiments, and said, "A man is not born knowledge, as a beast is; but he is born faculty and inclination; faculty to know, and inclination to love; and he is born faculty not only to know but also to understand and be wise; he is likewise born the most perfect inclination to love not only the things relating to self and the world, but also those relating to God and heaven; consequently a man, by birth from his parents, is an organ which lives merely by the external senses, and at first by no internal senses, to the end that he may successively become a man, first natural, afterwards rational, and lastly spiritual; which could not be the case if he was born into knowledges and loves, as the beasts are: for connate knowledges and affections set bounds to that progression; whereas connate faculty and inclination set no such bounds: therefore a man is capable of being perfected in knowledge, intelligence, and wisdom to eternity." Those on the SOUTH next took up the debate, and expressed their sentiments as follows: "It is impossible for a man to take any knowledge from himself, since he has no connate knowledge; but he may take it from others; and as he cannot take any knowledge from himself, so neither can he take any love; for where there is no knowledge there is no love; knowledge and love being undivided companions, and no more capable of separation than will and understanding, or affection and thought; yea, no more than essence and form: therefore in proportion as a man takes knowledge from others, so love joins itself thereto as its companion. The universal love which joins itself is the love of knowing, of understanding, and of growing wise; this love is peculiar to man alone, and not to any beast, and flows in from God. We agree with our companions from the west, that a man is not born into any love, and consequently not into any knowledge; but that he is only born into an inclination to love, and thence into a faculty to receive knowledges, not from himself but from others, that is, by others: we say, by others, because neither have these received any thing of knowledge from themselves, but from God. We agree also with our companions to the north, that a man is first born as ground, in which no seeds are sown, but which is capable of receiving all seeds, both useful and hurtful. To these considerations we add, that beasts are born into natural loves, and thereby into knowledges corresponding to them; and that still they do not know, think, understand, and enjoy any knowledges, but are led through them by their loves, almost as blind persons are led through the streets by dogs, for as to understanding they are blind; or rather like people walking in their sleep, who act from the impulse of blind knowledge, the understanding being asleep." Lastly, those on the EAST declared their sentiments, and said, "We agree with our brethren in the opinions they have delivered, that a man knows nothing from himself, but from and by others, to the end that he may know and acknowledge that all knowledge, understanding, and wisdom, is from God; and that a man cannot otherwise be conceived, born, and generated of the Lord, and become an image and likeness of him; for he becomes an image of the Lord by acknowledging and believing, that he has received and does receive from the Lord all the good of love and charity, and all the truth of wisdom and faith, and not the least portion thereof from himself; and he becomes a likeness of the Lord by his being sensible of those principles in himself, as if they were from himself. This he is sensible of, because he is not born into knowledges, but receives them; and what he receives, appears to him as if it was from himself. This sensation is given him by the Lord, to the end that he may be a man and not a beast; since by willing, thinking, loving, knowing, understanding, and growing wise, as from himself, he receives knowledges, and exalts them into intelligence, and by the use thereof into wisdom; thus the Lord conjoins man to himself, and man conjoins himself to the Lord. This could not have been the case, unless it had been provided by the Lord, that man should be born in total ignorance." When they had finished speaking, it was the desire of all present, that a conclusion should be formed from the sentiments which had been expressed; and they agreed upon the following: "That a man is born into no knowledge, to the end that he may come into all knowledge, and may advance into intelligence, and thereby into wisdom, and that he is born into no love, to the intent that he may come into all love, by application of the knowledges from intelligence, and into love to the Lord by love towards his neighbour, and may thereby be conjoined to the Lord, and by such conjunction be made a man, and live for ever."

135. After this they took the paper, and read the third subject of investigation, which was, WHAT IS SIGNIFIED BY THE TREE OF LIFE, WHAT BY THE TREE OF THE KNOWLEDGE OF GOOD AND EVIL, AND WHAT BY EATING THEREOF? and all the others :ntreated as a favor, that those who were from the east would unfold this arcanum, because it required a more than ordinary depth of understanding, and because those who were from the east are in flaming light, that is, in the wisdom of love, this wisdom being understood by the garden of Eden, in which those two trees were placed. They said, "We will declare our sentiments; but as man does not take any thing from himself, but from the Lord, therefore we will speak from him; but yet from ourselves as of ourselves:" and then they continued, "A tree signifies a man, and the fruit thereof the good of life; hence

the tree of life signifies a man living from God, or God living in man; and since love and wisdom, and charity and faith, or good and truth, constitute the life of God in man, therefore these are signified by the tree of life, and hence man has eternal life: the like is signified by the tree of life, of which it will be given to eat, Rev. ii. 7; chap xxii. 2, 14. The tree of the knowledge of good and evil signifies a man believing that he lives from himself and not from God; thus that in man love and wisdom, charity and faith, that is, good and truth, are his and not God's; believing this, because he thinks and wills, and speaks and acts to all appearance, as from himself: and as a man from this faith persuades himself, that God has implanted himself, or infused his divine into him, therefore the serpent said, "*God doth know, in the day that ye eat of the fruit of that tree, your eyes will be opened, and ye will be as God, knowing good and evil,*" Gen. iii. 5. Eating of those trees signifies reception and appropriation; eating of the tree of life, the reception of life eternal, and eating of the tree of the knowledge of good and evil, the reception of damnation; therefore also both Adam and his wife, together with the serpent, were cursed: the serpent means the devil as to self-love and the conceit of his own intelligence. This love is the possessor of that tree; and the men who are in conceit, grounded in that love, are those trees. Those persons, therefore, are grievously mistaken who believe that Adam was wise and did good from himself, and that this was his state of integrity; when yet Adam himself was cursed by reason of that belief; for this is signified by eating of the tree of the knowledge of good and evil; therefore he then fell from the state of integrity in which he had been, in consequence of believing that he was wise and did good from God and not at all from himself; for this is meant by eating of the tree of life. The Lord alone, when he was in the world, was wise and did good from himself; because the essential divine from birth was in him and was his; therefore also from his own ability he was made the Redeemer and Saviour." From all these considerations they came to this conclusion, "That by the tree of life, and the tree of the knowledge of good and evil, and eating thereof, is signified that life for man is God in him, and that in this case he has heaven and eternal life; but that death for man is the persuasion and belief, that life for him is not God but self; whence he has hell and eternal death, which is condemnation."

136. After this they looked into the paper left by the angels upon the table, and saw written underneath, COLLECT YOUR OPINIONS ON THESE THREE QUESTIONS INTO ONE DECISION. Then they collected them, and saw that they cohered in one series, and that the series or decision was this, "That man is created to receive love and wisdom from God, and yet to all appearance as from himself; and this for the sake of reception

and conjunction : and that therefore a man is not born into any love, or into any knowledge, and also not into any ability of loving and growing wise from himself; therefore if he ascribes all the good of love and truth of wisdom to God, he becomes a living man; but if he ascribes them to himself, he becomes a dead man." These words they wrote on a new piece of paper, and placed it on the table: and lo! on a sudden the angels appeared in bright light, and carried the paper away into heaven; and after it was read there, those who sat on the seats heard these words from thence, "Well, well;" and instantly there appeared a single angel as it were flying from heaven, with two wings about his feet, and two about his temples, having in his hand prizes, consisting of robes, caps, and wreaths of laurel; and he alighted on the ground, and gave those who sat on the north robes of an opaline color; those who sat on the west robes of scarlet color; those who sat on the south caps whose borders were ornamented with bindings of gold and pearls, and which on the left side upwards were set with diamonds cut in the form of flowers; but to those who sat to the east he gave wreaths of laurel, intermixed with rubies and sapphires. Then all of them, adorned with their respective prizes, went home from the school of wisdom; and when they shewed themselves to their wives, their wives came to meet them, being distinguished also with ornaments presented to them from heaven; at which the husbands wondered.

137. THE SECOND MEMORABLE RELATION. On a time when I was meditating on conjugial love, lo! there appeared at a distance two naked infants with baskets in their hands, and turtle-doves flying around them; and on a nearer view, they seemed as if they were naked, handsomely ornamented with garlands; chaplets of flowers decorated their heads, and wreaths of liles and roses of a hyacinthine blue, hanging obliquely from the shoulders to the loins, adorned their bosoms; and round about both of them there was as it were a common band woven of small leaves interspersed with olives. But when they came nearer, they did not appear as infants, or naked, but as two persons in the prime of their age, wearing cloaks and tunics of shining silk, embroidered with the most beautiful flowers: and when they were near me, there breathed forth from heaven through them a vernal warmth, attended with an odoriferous fragrance, like what arises from gardens and fields in the time of spring. They were two married partners from heaven, and they accosted me; and because I was musing on what I had just seen, they inquired, "What did you see?" And when I told them that at first they appeared to me as naked infants, afterwards as infants decorated with garlands, and lastly as grown up persons in embroidered garments, and that instantly I experienced a vernal warmth with its delights, they smiled pleasantly, and said, "In

the way we did not seem to ourselves as infants, or naked, or adorned with garlands, but constantly in the same appearance which we now have: thus at a distance was represented our conjugial love; its state of innocence by our seeming like naked infants, its delights by garlands, and the same delights now by our cloaks and tunics being embroidered with flowers; and as you said that, as we approached, a vernal warmth breathed on you, attended with its pleasant fragrance as from a garden, we will explain to you the reason of all this." They said, "We have now been married partners for ages, and constantly in the prime of our age in which you now see us: our first state was like the first state of a virgin and a youth, when they enter into consociation by marriage; and we then believed, that this state was the very essential blessedness of our life; but we were informed by others in our heaven, and have since perceived ourselves, that this was a state of heat not tempered by light; and that it is successively tempered, in proportion as the husband is perfected in wisdom, and the wife loves that wisdom in the husband; and that this is effected by and according to the uses which each, by mutual aid, affords to society; also that delights succeed according to the temperature of heat and light; or of wisdom and its love. The reason why on our approach there breathed on you as it were a vernal warmth, is, because conjugial love and that warmth in our heaven act in unity; for warmth with us is love; and the light, wherewith warmth is united, is wisdom; and use is as it were the atmosphere which contains each in its bosom. What are heat and light without that which contains them? In like manner, what are love and wisdom without their use? In such case there is nothing conjugial in them, because the subject is wanting in which they should exist to produce it. In heaven where there is vernal warmth, there is love truly conjugial; because the vernal principle exists only where warmth is equally united to light, or where warmth and light are in equal proportions; and it is our opinion, that as warmth is delighted with light, and *vice versa,* so love is delighted with wisdom, and wisdom in its turn with love." He further added, "With us in heaven there is perpetual light, and on no occasion do the shades of evening prevail, still less is there darkness; because our sun does not set and rise like yours, but remains constantly in a middle altitude between the zenith and the horizon, which, as you express it, is at an elevation of 45 degrees. Hence, the heat and light proceeding from our sun cause perpetual spring, and a perpetual vernal warmth inspires those with whom love is united with wisdom in just proportion; and our Lord, by the eternal union of heat and light, breathes nothing but uses: hence also come the germinations of your earth, and the connubial associations of your birds and animals in the spring; for the vernal warmth opens their interiors even to the inmost, which are called their souls, and affects them, and communicates to them its conjugial principle, and causes their principle of prolification to come into its delights, in consequence of a continual tendency to produce fruits of use, which use is the propagation of their kind. But with men (*homines*) there is a perpetual influx of vernal warmth from the Lord; wherefore they are capable of enjoying marriage delights at all times, even in the midst of winter; for the males of the human race were created to be recipients of light, that is, of wisdom from the Lord, and the females to be recipients of heat, that is, of the love of the wisdom of the male from the Lord. Hence then it is, that, as we approached, there breathed on you a vernal warmth attended with an odoriferous fragrance, like what arises from gardens and fields in the spring." As he said this, he gave me his right hand, and conducted me to houses inhabited by married partners in a like prime of their age with himself and his partner; and said, "These wives, who now seem like young virgins, were in the world infirm old women; and their husbands, who now seem in the spring of youth, were in the world decrepit old men; and all of them were restored by the Lord to this prime of their age, because they mutually loved each other, and from religious motives shunned adulteries as enormous sins:" and he added, "No one knows the blessed delights of conjugial love, unless he rejects the horrid delights of adultery; and no one can reject these delights, unless he is under the influence of wisdom from the Lord; and no one is under the influence of wisdom from the Lord, unless he performs uses from the love of uses." I also saw on this occasion their house utensils, which were all in celestial forms, and glittered with gold, which had a flaming appearance from the rubies with which it was studded.

ON THE CHASTE PRINCIPLE AND THE NON-CHASTE.

138. As we are yet only at the entrance of our subject respecting conjugial love specifically considered, and as conjugial love cannot be known specifically, except in a very indistinct and obscure manner, unless its opposite, which is the unchaste principle, also in some measure appear; and as this unchaste principle appears in some measure, or in a shade, when the chaste principle is described together with the non-chaste, non-chastity being only a removal of what is unchaste from what is chaste; therefore we will now proceed to treat of the chaste principle and the non-chaste. But the unchaste principle, which is altogether opposite to the chaste, is treated of in the latter part of this

work, entitled ADULTEROUS LOVE AND ITS SINFUL PLEASURES, where it is fully described with all its varieties. But what the unchaste principle is, and what the non-chaste, and with what persons each of them prevails, shall be illustrated in the following order: I. *The chaste principle and the non-chaste are predicated only of marriages and of such things as relate to marriages.* II. *The chaste principle is predicated only of monogamical marriages, or of the marriage of one man with one wife.* III. *The Christian conjugial principle alone is chaste.* IV. *Love truly conjugial is essential chastity.* V. *All the delights of love truly conjugial, even the ultimate, are chaste.* VI. *With those who are made spiritual by the Lord, conjugial love is more and more purified and rendered chaste.* VII. *The chastity of marriage exists by a total renunciation of whoredoms from a principle of religion.* VIII. *Chastity cannot be predicated of infants, or of boys and girls, or of young men and virgins before they feel in themselves the love of the sex.* IX. *Chastity cannot be predicated of eunuchs so born, or of eunuchs so made.* X. *Chastity cannot be predicated of those who do not believe adulteries to be evils in regard to religion; and still less of those who do not believe them to be hurtful to society.* XI. *Chastity cannot be predicated of those who abstain from adulteries only for various external reasons.* XII. *Chastity cannot be predicated of those who believe marriages to be unchaste.* XIII. *Chastity cannot be predicated of those who have renounced marriage by vows of perpetual celibacy, unless there be and remain in them the love of a life truly conjugial.* XIV. *A state of marriage is to be preferred to a state of celibacy.* We will now proceed to an explanation of each article.

139. I. THE CHASTE PRINCIPLE AND THE NON-CHASTE ARE PREDICATED ONLY OF MARRIAGES AND OF SUCH THINGS AS RELATE TO MARRIAGES. The reason of this is, because, as will be shewn presently, love truly conjugial is essential chastity; and the love opposite to it, which is called adulterous, is essential unchastity; so far therefore as any one is purified from the latter love, so far he is chaste; for so far the opposite, which is destructive of chastity, is taken away; whence it is evident that the purity of conjugial love is what is called chastity. Nevertheless there is a conjugial love which is not chaste, and yet it is not unchastity; as is the case with married partners, who, for various external reasons, abstain from the effects of lasciviousness so as not to think about them; howbeit, if that love is not purified in their spirits, it is still not chaste; its form is chaste, but it has not in it a chaste essence.

140. The reason why the chaste principle and the non-chaste are predicated of such things as relate to marriages, is, because the conjugial principle is inscribed on both sexes from inmost principles to ultimates; and a man's quality as to his thoughts and affections, and consequently as to his bodily actions and

behaviour, is according thereto. That this is the case, appears more evidently from such as are unchaste. The unchaste principle abiding in their minds is heard from the tone of their voice in conversation, and from their applying whatever is said, even though it be chaste, to wanton and loose ends; (the tone of the voice in conversation is grounded in the will-affection, and the conversation itself is grounded in the thought of the understanding;) which is a proof that the will and the understanding, with everything belonging to them, consequently the whole mind, and thence everything belonging to the body, from inmost principles to ultimates, abound with what is unchaste. I have been informed by the angels, that, with the greatest hypocrites, the unchaste principle is perceivable from hearing their conversation, however chastely they may talk, and also is made sensible from the sphere that issues from them; which is a further proof that unchastity resides in the inmost principles of their minds, and thence in the inmost principles of their bodies, and that the latter principles are exteriorly covered like a shell painted with figures of various colors. That a sphere of lasciviousness issues forth from the unchaste, is manifest from the statutes prescribed to the sons of Israel, ordaining that everything should be unclean that was touched even by the hand of those who were defiled by such unchaste persons. From these considerations it may be concluded that the case is similar in regard to the chaste, viz., that with them everything is chaste from inmost principles to ultimates, and that this is an effect of the chastity of conjugial love. Hence it is, that in the world it is said, "To the pure all things are pure, and to the defiled all things are defiled."

141. THE CHASTE PRINCIPLE IS PREDICATED ONLY OF MONOGAMICAL MARRIAGES, OR OF THE MARRIAGE OF ONE MAN WITH ONE WIFE. The reason of this is, because with them conjugial love does not reside in the natural man, but enters into the spiritual man, and successively opens to itself a way to the essential spiritual marriage, or the marriage of good and truth, which is its origin, and conjoins itself therewith; for that love enters according to the increase of wisdom, which is according to the implantation of the church from the Lord, as has been abundantly shewn above. This cannot be effected with polygamists; for they divide conjugial love; and this love when divided, is not unlike the love of the sex, which in itself is natural; but on this subject something worthy of attention may be seen in the section on POLYGAMY.

142. III. THE CHRISTIAN CONJUGIAL PRINCIPLE ALONE IS CHASTE. This is, because love truly conjugial keeps pace with the state of the church in man (*homo*), and because the state of the church is from the Lord, as has been shewn in the foregoing section, n. 130, 131, and elsewhere; also because the church in its genuine truths is in the Word, and the Lord is there present

in those truths. From these considerations it follows, that the chaste conjugial principle exists nowhere but in the Christian world, and still that there is a possibility of its existing elsewhere. By the Christian conjugial principle we mean the marriage of one man with one wife. That this conjugial principle is capable of being ingrafted into Christians, and of being transplanted hereditarily into the offspring from parents who are principled in love truly conjugial, and that hence both the faculty and the inclination to grow wise in the things of the church and of heaven may become connate, will be seen in its proper place. Christians, if they marry more wives than one, commit not only natural but also spiritual adultery: this will be shewn in the section on POLYGAMY.

143. IV. LOVE TRULY CONJUGIAL IS ESSENTIAL CHASTITY. The reasons for this are, 1. Because it is from the Lord, and corresponds to the marriage of the Lord and the church. 2. Because it descends from the marriage of good and truth. 3. Because it is spiritual, in proportion as the church exists with man (*homo*). 4. Because it is the foundation and head of all celestial and spiritual loves. 5. Because it is the orderly seminary of the human race, and thereby of the angelic heaven. 6. Because on this account it also exists with the angels of heaven, and gives birth with them to spiritual offspring, which are love and wisdom. 7. And because its uses are thus more excellent than the other uses of creation. From these considerations it follows, that love truly conjugial, viewed from its origin and in its essence, is pure and holy, so that it may be called purity and holiness, consequently essential chastity: but that nevertheless it is not altogether pure, either with men or angels, may be seen below in article VI., n. 146.

144. V. ALL THE DELIGHTS OF LOVE TRULY CONJUGIAL, EVEN THE ULTIMATE, ARE CHASTE. This follows from what has been above explained, that love truly conjugial is essential chastity, and from the considerations that delights constitute its life. That the delights of this love ascend and enter heaven, and in the way pass through the delights of the heavenly loves, in which the angels of heaven are principled; also, that they conjoin themselves with the delights of the conjugial love of the angels, has been mentioned above. Moreover, I have heard it declared by the angels, that they perceive those delights with themselves to be exalted and filled, while they ascend from chaste marriages on the earths: and when some by-standers, who were unchaste, inquired concerning the ultimate delights whether they were chaste, they assented and said, "How should it be otherwise? Are not these the delights of true conjugial love in their fulness?" The origin, nature, and quality of the delights of this love, may be seen above, n. 69: and also in the MEMORABLE RELATIONS, especially those which follow.

145 VI. WITH THOSE WHO ARE MADE SPIRITUAL BY THE LORD, CONJUGIAL LOVE IS MORE AND MORE PURIFIED AND RENDERED CHASTE. The reasons for this are, 1. Because the first love, by which is meant the love previous to the nuptials and immediately after them, partakes somewhat of the love of the sex, and thus of the ardor belonging to the body not as yet moderated by the love of the spirit. 2. Because a man (*homo*) from natural is successively made spiritual; for he becomes spiritual in proportion as his rational principle, which is the medium between heaven and the world, begins to drive a soul from influx out of heaven, which is the case so far as it is affected and delighted with wisdom; concerning which wisdom see above, n. 130; and in proportion as this is effected, in the same proportion his mind is elevated into a superior *aura*, which is the continent of celestial light and heat, or, what is the same, of the wisdom and love in which the angels are principled; for heavenly light acts in unity with wisdom, and heavenly heat with love; and in proportion as wisdom and the love thereof increase with married pairs, in the same proportion conjugial love is purified with them; and as this is effected successively, it follows that conjugial love is rendered more and more chaste. This spiritual purification may be compared with the purification of natural spirits, which is effected by the chemists, and is called defecation, rectification, castigation, acution, decantation, and sublimation; and wisdom purified may be compared with alcohol, which is a highly rectified spirit. 3. Now as spiritual wisdom in itself is of such a nature that it becomes more and more warmed with the love of growing wise, and by virtue of this love increases to eternity; and as this is effected in proportion as it is perfected by a kind of defecation, castigation, rectification, acution, decantation, and sublimation, and this by elevating and abstracting the intellect from the fallacies of the senses, and the will from the allurements of the body; it is evident that conjugial love, whose parent is wisdom, is in like manner rendered successively more and more pure, and thereby chaste. That the first state of love between married partners is a state of heat not yet tempered by light; but that it is successively tempered in proportion as the husband is perfected in wisdom, and the wife loves it in her husband, may be seen in the MEMORABLE RELATION, n. 137.

146. It is however to be observed, that there is no conjugial love altogether chaste or pure either with men (*homines*) or with angels; there is still somewhat not chaste or not pure which adjoins or subjoins itself thereto; but this has a different origin from that which gives birth to what is unchaste: for with the angels the chaste principle is above and the non-chaste beneath, and there is as it were a door with a hinge interposed by the Lord, which is opened by determination, and is carefully pre-

vented from standing open, lest the one principle should pass into the other, and they should mix together: for the natural principle of man from his birth is defiled and fraught with evils; whereas his spiritual principle is not so, because its birth is from the Lord, for it is regeneration; and regeneration is a successive separation from the evils to which a man is naturally inclined. That no love with either men or angels is altogether pure, or can be pure; but that the end, purpose, or intention of the will, is principally regarded by the Lord: and that therefore so far as a man is principled in a good end, purpose, or intention, and perseveres therein, so far he is initiated into purity, and so far he advances and approaches towards purity, may be seen above, n. 71.

147. VII. THE CHASTITY OF MARRIAGE EXISTS BY A TOTAL RENUNCIATION OF WHOREDOMS FROM A PRINCIPLE OF RELIGION. The reason of this is, because chastity is the removal of unchastity; it being a universal law, that so far as any one removes evil, so far a capacity is given for good to succeed in its place; and further, so far as evil is hated, so far good is loved; and also *vice versa;* consequently, so far as whoredom is renounced, so far the chastity of marriage enters. That conjugial love is purified and rectified according to the renunciation of whoredoms, every one sees from common perception as soon as it is mentioned and heard; thus before confirmation; but as all have not common perception, it is of importance that the subject should also be illustrated in the way of proof by such considerations as may tend to confirm it. These considerations are, that conjugial love grows cold as soon as it is divided, and this coldness causes it to perish; for the heat of unchaste love extinguishes it, as two opposite heats cannot exist together, but one must needs reject the other and deprive it of its potency. Whenever therefore the heat of conjugial love begins to acquire a pleasant warmth, and from a sensation of its delights to bud and flourish, like an orchard and garden in spring; the latter from the vernal temperament of light and heat from the sun of the natural world, but the former from the vernal temperament of light and heat from the sun of the spiritual world.

148. There is implanted in every man (*homo*) from creation, and consequently from his birth, an internal and an external conjugial principle; the internal is spiritual, and the external natural: a man comes first into the latter, and as he becomes spiritual, he comes into the former. If therefore he remains in the external or natural conjugial principle, the internal or spiritual conjugial principle is veiled or covered, until he knows nothing respecting it; yea, until he calls it an ideal shadow without a substance: but if a man becomes spiritual, he then begins to know something respecting it, and afterwards to per-

ceive something of its quality, and successively to be made sensible of its pleasantness, agreeableness, and delights; and in proportion as this is the case, the veil or covering between the external and internal, spoken of above, begins to be attenuated, and afterwards as it were to melt, and lastly to be dissolved and dissipated. When this effect takes place, the external conjugial principle remains indeed; but it is continually purged and purified from its dregs by the internal; and this until the external becomes as it were the face of the internal, and derives its delight from the blessedness which is in the internal, and at the same time its life, and the delights of its potency. Such is the renunciation of whoredoms, by which the chastity of marriage exists. It may be imagined, that the external conjugial principle, which remains after the internal has separated itself from it, or it from itself, resembles the external principle not separated: but I have heard from the angels that they are altogether unlike; for that the external principle in conjunction with the internal, which they called the external of the internal, was void of all lasciviousness, because the internal cannot be lascivious, but only be delighted chastely; and that it imparts the same disposition to its external, wherein it is made sensible of its own delights: the case is altogether otherwise with the external separated from the internal; this they said, was lascivious in the whole and in every part. They compared the external conjugial principle derived from the internal to excellent fruit, whose pleasant taste and flavor insinuate themselves into its outward rind, and form this into correspondence with themselves; they compared it also to a granary, whose store is never diminished, but is continually recruited according to its consumption; whereas they compared the external principle, separate from the internal, to wheat in a winnowing machine, when it is put in motion about its axis; in which case the chaff only remains, which is dispersed by the wind; so it is with the conjugial principle, unless the adulterous principle be renounced.

149. The reason why the chastity of marriage does not exist by the renunciation of whoredoms, unless it be made from a principle of religion, is, because a man (*homo*) without religion is not spiritual, but remains natural; and if the natural man renounces whoredoms, still his spirit does not renounce them; and thus, although it seems to himself that he is chaste by such renunciation, yet nevertheless unchastity lies inwardly concealed like corrupt matter in a wound only outwardly healed. That conjugial love is according to the state of the church with man, may be seen above n. 130. More on this subject may be seen in the exposition of article XI.

150. VIII. CHASTITY CANNOT BE PREDICATED OF INFANTS, OR OF BOYS AND GIRLS, OR OF YOUNG MEN AND VIR-

GINS BEFORE THEY FEEL IN THEMSELVES THE LOVE OF THE SEX. This is because the chaste principle and the unchaste are predicated only of marriages, and of such things as relate to marriages, as may be seen above, n. 139; and of those who know nothing of the things relating to marriage, chastity is not predicable; for it is as it were nothing relating to them; and nothing cannot be an object either of affection or thought: but after this nothing there arises something, when the first motion towards marriage is felt, which is the love of the sex. That virgins and young men, before they feel in themselves the love of the sex, are commonly called chaste, is owing to ignorance of what chastity is.

151. XI. CHASTITY CANNOT BE PREDICATED OF EUNUCHS SO BORN, OR OF EUNUCHS SO MADE. Eunuchs so born are those more especially with whom the ultimate of love is wanting from birth; and as in such case the first and middle principles are without a foundation on which to stand, they have therefore no existence; and if they exist, the persons in whom they exist have no concern to distinguish between the chaste principle and the unchaste, each being indifferent to them; but of these persons there are several distinctions. The case is nearly the same with eunuchs so made as with some eunuchs so born; but eunuchs so made, as they are both men and women, cannot possibly regard conjugial love any otherwise than as a phantasy, and the delights thereof as idle stories. If they have any inclination, it is rendered mute, which is neither chaste nor unchaste: and what is neither chaste nor unchaste, derives no quality from either the one or the other.

152. X. CHASTITY CANNOT BE PREDICATED OF THOSE WHO DO NOT BELIEVE ADULTERIES TO BE EVILS IN REGARD TO RELIGION; AND STILL LESS OF THOSE WHO DO NOT BELIEVE THEM TO BE HURTFUL TO SOCIETY. The reason why chastity cannot be predicated of such is, because they neither know what chastity is nor even that it exists; for chastity relates to marriage, as was shown in the first article of this section. Those who do not believe adulteries be evil in regard to religion, regard even marriages as unchaste; whereas religion with married pairs constitutes their chastity; thus such persons have nothing chaste in them, and therefore it is in vain to talk to them of chastity; these are confirmed adulterers: but those who do not believe adulteries to be hurtful to society, know still less than the others, either what chastity is or even that it exists; for they are adulterers from a determined purpose: if they say that marriages are less unchaste than adulteries, they say so merely with the mouth, but not with the heart, because marriages with them are cold, and those who speak from such cold concerning chaste heat, cannot have an idea of chaste heat in regard to conjugial love. The nature and quality of such persons, and of the ideas of their thought, and hence of the interior principles of their conversation,

will be seen in the second part of this work,—ADULTEROUS LOVE AND ITS SINFUL PLEASURES.

153. XI. CHASTITY CANNOT BE PREDICATED OF THOSE WHO ABSTAIN FROM ADULTERIES ONLY FOR VARIOUS EXTERNAL REASONS. Many believe that the mere abstaining from adulteries in the body is chastity; yet this is not chastity, unless at the same time there is an abstaining in spirit. The spirit of man (*homo*), by which is here meant his mind as to affections and thoughts, constitutes the chaste principle and the unchaste, for hence it flows into the body, the body being in all cases such as the mind or spirit is. Hence it follows, that those who abstain from adulteries in the body, without being influenced from the spirit are not chaste; neither are those chaste who abstain from them in spirit as influenced from the body. There are many assignable causes which make a man desist from adulteries in the body, and also in the spirit as influenced from the body; but still, he that does not desist from them in the body as influenced from the spirit, is unchaste; for the Lord says, "*That whosoever looketh upon another's woman, so as to lust after her, hath already committed adultery with her in his heart,*" Matt. v. 28. It is impossible to enumerate all the causes of abstinence from adulteries in the body only, they being various according to states of marriage, and also according to states of the body; for there are some persons who abstain from them from fear of the civil law and its penalties; some from fear of the loss of reputation and thereby of honor; some from fear of diseases which may be thereby contracted; some from fear of domestic quarrels on the part of the wife, whereby the quiet of their lives may be disturbed; some from fear of revenge on the part of the husband or relations; some from fear of chastisement from the servants of the family; some also abstain from motives of poverty, avarice, or imbecility, arising either from disease, from abuse, from age, or from impotence. Of these there are some also, who, because they cannot or dare not commit adultery in the body, condemn adulteries in the spirit; and thus they speak morally against adulteries, and in favor of marriages; but such person, unless in spirit they call adulteries accursed, and this from a religious principle in the spirit, are still adulterers; for although they do not commit them in the body, yet they do in the spirit; wherefore after death, when they become spirits, they speak openly in favor of them. From these considerations it is manifest, that even a wicked person may shun adulteries as hurtful; but that none but a Christian can shun them as sins. Hence then the truth of the proposition is evident, that chastity cannot be predicated of those who abstain from adulteries merely for various external reasons.

154. XII. CHASTITY CANNOT BE PREDICATED OF THOSE WHO BELIEVE MARRIAGES TO BE UNCHASTE. These, like the persons

spoken of just above, n. 152, do not know either what chastity is, or even that it exists; and in this respect they are like those who make chastity to consist merely in celibacy, of whom we shall speak presently.

155. XIII. CHASTITY CANNOT BE PREDICATED OF THOSE WHO HAVE RENOUNCED MARRIAGE BY VOWS OF PERPETUAL CELIBACY, UNLESS THERE BE AND REMAIN IN THEM THE LOVE OF A LIFE TRULY CONJUGIAL. The reason why chastity cannot be predicated of these, is, because after a vow of perpetual celibacy, conjugial love is renounced; and yet it is of this love alone that chastity can be predicated: nevertheless there still remains an inclination to the sex implanted from creation, and consequently innate by birth; and when this inclination is restrained and subdued, it must needs pass away into heat, and in some cases into a violent burning, which, in rising from the body into the spirit, infests it, and with some persons defiles it; and there may be instances where the spirit thus defiled may defile also the principles of religion, casting them down from their internal abode, where they are in holiness, into things external, where they become mere matters of talk and gesture; therefore it was provided by the Lord, that celibacy should have place only with those who are in external worship, as is the case with all who do not address themselves to the Lord, or read the Word. With such, eternal life is not so much endangered by vows of celibacy attended with engagements to chastity, as it is with those who are principled in internal worship: moreover, in many instances that state of life is not entered upon from any freedom of the will, many being engaged therein before they attain to freedom grounded in reason, and some in consequence of alluring worldly motives. Of those who adopt that state with a view to have their minds disengaged from the world, that they may be more at leisure to apply themselves to divine things, those only are chaste with whom the love of a life truly conjugial either preceded that state or followed it, and with whom it remains; for the love of a life truly conjugial is that alone of which chastity is predicated. Wherefore also, after death, all who have lived in monasteries are at length freed from their vows and set at liberty, that, according to the interior vows and desires of their love, they may be led to choose a life either conjugial or extra-conjugial: if in such case they enter into conjugial life, those who have loved also the spiritual things of divine worship are given in marriage in heaven; but those who enter into extra-conjugial life are sent to their like, who dwell on the confines of heaven. I have inquired of the angels, whether those who have devoted themselves to works of piety, and given themselves up entirely to divine worship, and who thus have withdrawn themselves from the snares of the world and the concupiscences of the flesh, and with this view have vowed per-

petual virginity, are received into heaven, and there admitted among the blessed to enjoy an especial portion of happiness according to their faith. To this the angels replied, that such are indeed received into heaven; but when they are made sensible of the sphere of conjugial love there, they become sad and fretful, and then, some of their own accord, some by asking leave, and some from being commanded, depart and are dismissed, and when they are out of that heaven, a way is opened for them to their consociates, who had been in a similar state of life in the world; and then from being fretful they become cheerful, and rejoice together.

156. XIV. A STATE OF MARRIAGE IS TO BE PREFERRED TO A STATE OF CELIBACY. This is evident from what has been said above respecting marriage and celibacy. A state of marriage is to be preferred because it is a state ordained from creation; because it originates in the marriage of good and truth; because it corresponds with the marriage of the Lord and the church; because the church and conjugial love are constant companions; because its use is more excellent than all the other uses of the things of creation, for thence according to order is derived the increase of the human race, and also of the angelic heaven, which is formed from the human race: moreover, marriage constitutes the completeness of a man (*homo*); for by it he becomes a complete man, as will be shewn in the following chapter. All these things are wanting in celibacy. But if the proposition be taken for granted, that a state of celibacy is preferable to a state of marriage, and if this proposition be left to the mind's examination, to be assented to and established by confirming proofs, then the conclusion must be, that marriages are not holy, neither can they be chaste; yea, that chastity in the female sex belongs only to those, who abstain from marriage and vow perpetual virginity: and moreover, that those who have vowed perpetual celibacy are understood by the eunuchs *who make themselves eunuchs for the kingdom of heaven's sake*, Matt. xix. 12; not to mention other conclusions of a like nature; which, being grounded in a proposition that is not true, are also not true. The eunuchs who make themselves eunuchs for the kingdom of heaven's sake, are spiritual eunuchs, who are such as in marriages abstain from the evils of whoredoms: that Italian eunuchs are not meant, is evident.

* * * * * *

151.* To the above I shall add TWO MEMORABLE RELATIONS. FIRST. As I was going home from the school of wisdom (concerning which, see above, n. 132), I saw in the way an angel dressed in blue. He joined me and walked by my side, and said, "I see that you are come from the school of wisdom, and are made glad by what you heard there; and as I perceive that you are not a full inhabitant of this world, because you are at the same time in the natural world, and therefore know nothing of our olympic gymnasia, where the ancient *sophi* meet together, and by the information they collect from every new comer, learn what changes and successions wisdom has undergone and is still undergoing in your world; if you are willing I will conduct you to the place where several of those ancient *sophi* and their sons, that is, their disciples, dwell." So he led me to the confines between the north and east; and while I was looking that way from a rising ground, lo! I saw a city, and on one side of it two small hills; that which was nearer to the city being lower than the other. "That city," said he, is called Athens, the lower hill Parnassus, and the higher Helicon. They are so called, because in the city and around it dwell the wise men who formerly lived in Greece, as Pythagoras, Socrates, Aristippus, Xenophon, with their disciples and scholars." On my asking him concerning Plato and Aristotle, he said, "They and their followers dwell in another region, because they taught principles of rationality which relate to the understanding; whereas the former taught morality which relates to the life." He further informed me, that it was customary at times to depute from the city of Athens some of the students to learn from the literati of the Christians, what sentiments they entertain at this day respecting God, the creation of the universe, the immortality of the soul, the relative state of men and beasts, and other subjects of interior wisdom: and he added, that a herald had that day announced an assembly, which was a token that the emissaries had met with some strangers newly arrived from the earth, who had communicated some curious information. We then saw several persons going from the city and its suburbs, some having their heads decked with wreaths of laurel, some holding palms in their hands, some with books under their arms, and some with pens under the hair of the left temple. We mixed with the company, and ascended the hill with them; and lo! on the top was an octagonal palace, which they called the Palladium, into which we entered: within there were eight hexangular recesses, in each of which was a book-case and a table: at these recesses were seated the laureled *sophi*, and in the Palladium itself there were seats cut out of the rock, on which the rest were seated. A door on the left was then opened, through which the two strangers newly arrived from the earth were introduced; and after the compliments of salutation were paid, one of the laureled *sophi* asked them, "WHAT NEWS FROM THE EARTH?" They replied, "This is news, that in forests there have been found men like beasts, or beasts like men: from their face and body they were known to have been born men, and to have been lost or left in the forests when they were two or three years old; they were not able to give utterance to any thought, nor could they learn to articulate the voice into any distinct expression; neither did they know the food suitable for them as the beasts do, but put greedily into their mouths whatever they found in the forest, whether it was clean or unclean; besides many other particulars of a like nature: from which some of the learned among us have formed several conjectures and conclusions concerning the relative state of men and beasts." On hearing this account, some of the ancient *sophi* asked, "What were the conjectures and conclusions formed from the circumstances you have related?" The two strangers replied, "There were several: but they may all be comprised under the following: 1. That a man by nature, and also by birth, is more stupid and consequently viler than any beast; and that he remains so, unless he is instructed. 2. That he is capable of being instructed, because he has learnt to frame articulate sounds, and thence to speak, and thereby has begun to express his thoughts, and this successively more and more perfectly until he has been able to express the laws of civil society; several of which are nevertheless impressed on beasts from their birth. 3. That beasts have rationality like men. 4. Therefore, that if beasts could speak, they would reason on any subject as acutely as men; a proof of which is, that they think from reason and prudence just as men do. 5. That the understanding is only a modification of light from the sun; the heat co-operating by means of ether, so that it is only an activity of interior nature; and that this activity may be so exalted as to appear like wisdom. 6. That therefore it is ridiculous to believe that a man lives after death any more than a beast; unless perchance, for some days after his decease, in consequence of an exhalation of the life of the body, he may appear as a mist under the form of a spectre, before he is dissipated into nature; just as a shrub raised up from its ashes, appears in the likeness of its own form. 7. Consequently that religion, which teaches a life after death, is a mere device, in order to keep the simple inwardly in bonds by its laws, as they are kept outwardly in bonds by the laws of the state." To this they added, that "people of mere ingenuity reason in this manner, but not so the intelligent:" and they were asked, "How do the intelligent reason?" They said they had not been informed; but they supposed that they must reason differently.

152.* On hearing this relation, all those who were sitting at the tables exclaimed, "Alas! what times are come on the earth! What changes has wisdom undergone? How is she transformed into a false and infatuated ingenuity! The sun is set, and in his station beneath the earth is in direct opposition to his meridian altitude. From the case here adduced respecting such as have been left and found in forests, who cannot see that an uninstructed man is such as here represented? For is not the nature of his life determined by the nature of the instruction he receives? Is he not born in a state of greater ignorance than the beasts?

Must he not learn to walk and to speak? Supposing he never learnt to walk, would he ever stand upright? And if he never learnt to speak, would he ever be able to express his thoughts? Is not every man such as instruction makes him,—insane from false principles, or wise from truths? and is not he that is insane from false principles, entirely possessed with an imagination that he is wiser than he that is wise from truths? Are there not instances of men who are so wild and foolish, that they are no more like men than those who have been found in forests? Is not this the case with such as have been deprived of memory? From all these considerations we conclude, that a man without instruction is neither a man nor a beast; but that he is a form, which is capable of receiving in itself that which constitutes a man; and thus that he is not born a man, but that he is made a man; and that a man is born such a form as to be an organ receptive of life from God, to the end that he may be a subject into which God may introduce all good, and, by union with himself, may make him eternally blessed. We have perceived from your conversation, that wisdom at this day is so far extinguished or infatuated, that nothing at all is known concerning the relative state of the life of men and of beasts; and hence it is that the state of the life of man after death is not known: but those who are capable of knowing this, and yet are not willing, and in consequence deny it, as many Christians do, may fitly be compared to such as are found in forests: not that they are rendered so stupid from a want of instruction, but that they have rendered themselves so by the fallacies of the senses, which are the darkness of truths."

153.* At that instant a certain person standing in the middle of the Palladium, and holding in his hand a palm, said, "Explain, I pray, this arcanum, How a man, created a form of God, could be changed into a form of the devil. I know that the angels of heaven are forms of God and that the angels of hell are forms of the devil, and that the two forms are opposite to each other, the latter being insanities, the former wisdoms. Tell me, therefore, how a man, created a form of God, could pass from day into such night, as to be capable of denying God and life eternal." To this the several teachers replied in order; first the Pythagoreans, next the Socratics, and afterwards the rest: but among them there was a certain Platonist, who spoke last; and his opinion prevailed, which was to this effect; That the men of the saturnine or golden age knew and acknowledged that they were forms receptive of life from God; and that on this account wisdom was inscribed on their souls and hearts, and hence they saw truth from the light of truth, and by truths perceived good from the delight of the love thereof: but as mankind in the following ages receded from the acknowledgement that all the truth of wisdom and the consequent good of love belonging to them, continually flowed in from God, they ceased to be habitations of God; and then also discourse with God, and consociation with angels ceased: for the interiors of their minds were bent from their direction, which had been elevated upwards to God from God, into a direction more and more oblique, outwardly into the world, and thereby to God from God through the world, and at length inverted into an opposite direction, which is downwards to self; and as God cannot be looked at by a man interiorly inverted, and thereby averted, men separated themselves from God, and were made forms of hell or devils. From these considerations it follows, that in the first ages they acknowledged in heart and soul, that all the good of love and the consequent true wisdom, were derived to them from God, and also that they were God's in them: and thus that they were mere recipients of life from God, and hence were called images of God, sons of God, and born of God: but that in succeeding ages they did not acknowledge this in heart and soul, but by a certain persuasive faith, next by an historical faith, and lastly only with the mouth; and this last kind of acknowledgement is no acknowledgement at all; yea, it is in fact a denial at heart. From these considerations it may be seen what is the quality of the wisdom which prevails at this day on the earth among Christians, while they do not know the distinction between a man and a beast, notwithstanding their being in possession of a written revelation, whereby they may be inspired by God: and hence many believe, that in case a man lives after death, a beast must live also; or because a beast is not to live after death, neither will a man. Is not our spiritual light, which enlightens the sight of the mind, become thick darkness with them? and is not their natural light, which only enlightens the bodily sight, become brightness to them?

154.* After this they all turned towards the two strangers, and thanked them for their visit, and for the relation they had given, and entreated them to go and communicate to their brethren what they had heard. The strangers replied that they would endeavor to confirm their brethren in this truth, that so far as they ascribe all the good of charity and the truth of faith to the Lord, and not to themselves, so far they are men, and so far they become angels of heaven.

155.* THE SECOND MEMORABLE RELATION. One morning I was awoke by some delightful singing which I heard at a height above me, and in consequence, during the first watch, which is internal, pacific, and sweet, more than the succeeding part of the day, I was in a capacity of being kept for some time in the spirit as it were out of the body, and of attending carefully to the affection which was sung. The singing of heaven is an affection of the mind, sent forth through the mouth as a tune: for the tone of the voice in speaking, separate from the discourse of the speaking, and grounded in the affection of love, is what gives life to the speech. In that state I perceived that it was the affection of the delights of conjugial love, which was made musical by wives in heaven: that this was the case, I observed from the sound of the song, in which those delights were varied in a wonderful manner. After this I arose, and looked into the spiritual world; and lo! in the east, beneath the sun, there appeared as it were a GOLDEN SHOWER. It was the morning dew descending in great abundance, which, catching the sun's rays, exhibited to my eyes the appearance of a golden shower. In consequence of this I became fully awake, and went forth in the spirit, and asked an angel who then happened to meet me, whether he saw a golden shower descending from the sun? He replied, that he saw one whenever he was meditating on conjugial love; and at the same time turning his eyes towards the sun, he added, "That shower falls over a hall, in which are three husbands with their wives, who dwell in the midst of an eastern paradise. Such a shower is seen falling from the sun over that hall, because with those husbands and wives there resides wisdom respecting conjugial love and its delights; with the husbands respecting conjugial love, and with the wives respecting its delights. But I perceive that you are engaged in meditating on the delights of conjugial love: I will therefore conduct you there, and introduce you to them." He led me through paradisiacal scenery to houses built of olive wood, having two cedar columns before the gate, and introduced me to the husbands, and asked their permission for me to converse with them in the presence of the wives. They consented, and called their wives. These looked into my eyes most shrewdly; upon which I asked them, " Why do you do so?" They said, "We can thereby discover exquisitely what is your inclination and consequent affection, and your thought grounded in affection, respecting the love of the sex; and we see that you are meditating intensely, but still chastely, concerning it." And they added, "What do you wish us to tell you on the subject?" I replied, "Tell me, I pray, something respecting the delights of conjugial love." The husbands assented, saying, " If you are so disposed, give them some information in regard to those delights: their ears are chaste." They asked me, " Who taught you to question us respecting the delights of that love? Why did you not question our husbands?" I replied, " This angel, who accompanies me, informed me, that wives are the recipients and sensories of those delights, because they are born loves; and all delights are of love." To this they replied with a smile, " Be prudent, and declare nothing of this sort except ambiguously; because it is a wisdom deeply seated in the hearts of our sex, and is not discovered to any husband, unless he be principled in love truly conjugial. There are several reasons for this, which we keep entirely to ourselves." Then the husbands said, " Our wives know all the states of our minds, none of which are hid from them: they see, perceive, and are sensible of whatever proceeds from our will. We, on the other hand, know nothing of what passes with our wives. This faculty is given to wives, because they are most tender loves, and as it were burning zeals for the preservation of friendship and conjugial confidence, and thereby of all the happiness of life, which they carefully attend to, both in regard to their husbands and themselves, by virtue of a wisdom implanted in their love, which is so full of prudence, that they are unwilling to say, and consequently cannot say, that they love, but that they are loved." I asked the wives, "Why are you unwilling, and consequently cannot say so?" They replied, "If the least hint of the kind were to escape from the mouth of a wife, the husband would be seized with coolness, which would entirely separate him from all communication with his wife, so that he could not even bear to look upon her; but this is the case only with those husbands who do not hold marriages to be holy, and therefore do not love their wives from spiritual love: it is otherwise with those who do. In the minds of the latter this love is spiritual, and by derivation thence in the body is natural. We in this hall are principled in the latter love by derivation from the former; therefore we trust our husbands with our secrets respecting our delights of conjugial love." Then I courteously asked them to disclose to me some of those secrets: they then looked towards a window on the southern quarter, and lo! there appeared a white dove, whose wings shone as if they were of silver, and its head was crested with a crown as of gold: it stood upon a bough, from which there went forth an olive; and while it was in the attempt to spread out its wings, the wives said, "We will communicate something: the appearing of that dove is a token that we may. "Every man (*vir*)," they continued, "has five senses, seeing, hearing, smelling, taste, and touch; but we have likewise a sixth, which is the sense of all the delights of the conjugial love of the husband; and this sense we have in the palms of our hands, while we touch the breasts, arms, hands, or cheeks, of our husbands, especially their breasts; and also while we are touched by them. All the gladness and pleasantness of the thoughts of their minds (*mentium*), all the joys and delights of their minds (*animorum*), and all the festive and cheerful principles of their bosoms, pass from them to us, and become perceptible, sensible, and tangible: we discern them as exquisitely and distinctly as the ear does the tune of a song, and the tongue the taste of dainties; in a word, the spiritual delights of our husbands put on with us a kind of natural embodiment; therefore they call us the sensory organs of chaste conjugial love, and thence its de-.ights. But this sixth sense of ours exists, subsists, persists, and is exalted in the degree in which our husbands love us from wisdom and judgement, and in which we in our turn love them from the same principles in them. This sense in our sex is called in the heavens the sport of wisdom with its love, and of love with its wisdom." From this information I became desirous of asking further questions concerning the variety of their delights. They said, "It is infinite; but we are unwilling and therefore unable to say more; for the dove at our window, with the olive branch under his feet, is flown away." I waited for its return, but in vain. In the meantime I asked the husbands, "Have you a like sense of conjugial love?" They replied, "We have a like sense in general, but not in particular. We enjoy a general blessedness, delight, and pleasantness, arising from the particulars of our wives; and this general principle, which we derive from them, is serenely peaceful." As they said this, lo! through the window there appeared a swan standing on a branch of a fig-tree, which spread out his wings and flew away. On seeing this, the husbands said, "This is a sign for us to be silent respecting conjugial love: come again some other time, and perhaps you may hear more." They then withdrew, and we took our leave.

ON THE CONJUNCTION OF SOULS AND MINDS BY MARRIAGE, WHICH IS MEANT BY THE LORD'S WORDS,—THEY ARE NO LONGER TWO, BUT ONE FLESH.

156.* THAT at creation there was implanted in the man and the woman an inclination and also a faculty of conjunction as into a one, and that this inclination and this faculty are still in man and woman, is evident from the book of creation, and at the same time from the Lord's words. In the book of creation, called GENESIS, it is written, "*Jehovah God builded the rib, which he had taken from the man, into a woman, and brought her to the man. And the man said, This now is bone of my bones, and flesh of my flesh. She shall be called Woman, because she was taken out of man; for this cause shall a man leave his father and his mother, and shall cleave to his wife: and they shall be one flesh,*" chap. ii. 22—24. The Lord also says in Matthew, "*Have ye not read, that he that made them from the beginning, made them a male and a female, and said, For this cause shall a man leave father and mother, and shall cleave to his wife; and they* TWO SHALL BECOME ONE FLESH? WHEREFORE THEY ARE NO LONGER TWO, BUT ONE FLESH," chap. xix. 4—6. From this it is evident, that the woman was created out of the man (*vir*), and that each has an inclination and faculty to reunite themselves into a one. That such reunion means into one man (*homo*), is also evident from the book of creation, where both together are called man (*homo*); for it is written, "*In the day that God created man* (homo), *he created them a male and a female, and called their name Man* (homo)," chap. v. 2. It is there written, he called their name Adam; but Adam and man are one expression in the Hebrew tongue: moreover, both together are called man in the same book, chap. i. 27; chap. iii. 22—24. One flesh also signifies one man; as is evident from the passages in the Word where mention is made of all flesh, which signifies every man, as Gen. chap. vi. 12, 13, 17, 19; Isaiah xl. 5, 6; chap. xlix. 26; chap. lxvi. 16, 23, 24; Jer. xxv. 31; chap. xxxii. 27; chap. xlv. 5; Ezek. xx. 48; chap. xxi. 4, 5; and other passages. But what is meant by the man's rib, which was builded into a woman; what by the flesh, which was closed up in the place thereof, and thus what by bone of my bones, and flesh of my flesh; and what by a father and a mother, whom a man (*vir*) shall leave after marriage; and what by cleaving to a wife, has been shewn in the ARCANA CŒLESTIA; in which work the two books, Genesis and Exodus, are explained as to the spiritual sense. It is there proved that a rib does not mean a rib,—nor flesh, flesh,—nor a bone, a bone,—nor cleaving to, cleaving to; but that they signify spiritual things, which correspond thereto, and consequently are signified thereby. That spiritual things are understood, which from two make one man (*homo*), is evident from this consideration, that conjugial love conjoins them, and this love is spiritual. That the love of the man's wisdom is transferred into the wife, has been occasionally observed above, and will be more fully proved in the following sections: at this time it is not allowable to digress from the subject proposed, which is concerning the conjunction of two married partners into one flesh by a union of souls and minds. This union we will elucidate by treating of it in the following order. I. *From creation there is implanted in each sex a faculty and inclination, whereby they are able and willing to be conjoined together as it were into a one.* II. *Conjugial love conjoins two souls, and thence two minds into a one.* III. *The will of the wife conjoins itself with the understanding of the man, and thence the understanding of the man conjoins itself with the will of the wife.* IV. *The inclination to unite the man to herself is constant and perpetual with the wife; but is inconstant and alternate with the man.* V. *Conjunction is inspired into the man from the wife according to her love, and is received by the man according to his wisdom.* VI. *This conjunction is effected successively from the first days of marriage; and with those who are principled in love truly conjugial, is effected more and more thoroughly to eternity.* VII. *The conjunction of the wife with the rational wisdom of the husband is effected from within, but with this moral wisdom from without.* VIII. *For the sake of this conjunction as an end, the wife has a perception of the affections of the husband, and also the utmost prudence in moderating them.* IX. *Wives conceal this perception with themselves, and hide it from their husbands, for reasons of necessity, in order that conjugial love, friendship, and confidence, and thereby the blessedness of dwelling together, and the happiness of life may be secured.* X. *This perception is the wisdom of the wife, and is not communicable to the man; neither is the rational wisdom of the man communicable to the wife.* XI. *The wife, from a principle of love, is continually thinking about the man's inclination to her, with the purpose of joining him to herself: it is otherwise with the man.* XII. *The wife conjoins herself to the man, by applications to the desires of his will.* XIII. *The wife is conjoined to her husband by the sphere of her life flowing from the love of him.* XIV. *The wife is conjoined to the husband by the appropriation of the powers of his virtue; which however is effected according to their mutual spiritual love.* XV. *Thus the wife receives in herself the image of her husband, and thence perceives, sees, and is sensible of, his affections.* XVI. *There are duties proper to the husband, and others proper to the wife; and the wife cannot enter into the duties proper to the husband, nor the husband into the duties proper to the wife, so as to perform them aright.* XVII. *These duties, also, according to mutual aid, conjoin the two into a one, and at the same time constitute one house.* XVIII. *Married partners, according to these conjunctions, become one man* (homo) *more and more.* XIX. *Those who are principled in love truly conjugial, are sensible of their being a united man, and as it were one flesh.* XX. *Love truly conjugial, considered in itself, is a union of souls, a conjunction of minds, and an endeavor towards conjunction in the bosoms and thence in the body.* XXI. *The states of this love are innocence, peace, tranquillity, inmost friendship, full confidence, and a mutual desire of mind and heart to do every good to each other; and the states derived from these are blessedness, satisfaction, delight, and pleasure; and from the eternal enjoyment of these is derived heavenly felicity.* XXII. *These things can only exist in the marriage of one man with one wife.* We proceed now to the explanation of these articles.

157. I. FROM CREATION THERE IS IMPLANTED IN EACH SEX A FACULTY AND INCLINATION, WHEREBY THEY ARE ABLE AND WILLING TO BE JOINED TOGETHER, AS IT WERE INTO A ONE. That the woman was taken out of the man, was shewn just above from the book of creation; hence it follows, that there is in each sex a faculty and inclination to join themselves together into a one; for that which is taken out of anything, derives and retains its constituent principle, from the principle proper to the thing whence it was taken; and as this derived principle is of a similar nature with that from which it was derived, it seeks after a reunion; and when it is reunited, it is as in itself when it

is in that from whence it came, and *vice versa*. That there is a faculty of conjunction of the one sex with the other, or that they are capable of being united, is universally allowed; and also that there is an inclination to join themselves the one with the other; for experience supplies sufficient confirmation in both cases.

158. II. CONJUGIAL LOVE CONJOINS TWO SOULS, AND THENCE TWO MINDS, INTO A ONE. Every man consists of a soul, a mind, and a body. The soul is his inmost, the mind his middle, and the body his ultimate constituent. As the soul is a man's inmost principle, it is, from its origin, celestial; as the mind is his middle principle, it is, from its origin, spiritual; and as the body is his ultimate principle, it is, from its origin, natural. Those things, which, from their origin, are celestial and spiritual, are not in space, but in the appearance of space. This also is well known in the word; therefore it is said, that neither extension nor place can be predicated of spiritual things. Since therefore spaces are appearances, distances also and presences are appearances. That the appearances of distances and presences in the spiritual world are according to proximities, relationships, and affinities of love, has been frequently pointed out and confirmed in small treatises respecting that world. These observations are made, in order that it may be known that the souls and minds of men are not in space like their bodies; because the former, as was said above, from their origin, are celestial and spiritual; and as they are not in space, they may be joined together as into a one, although their bodies at the same time are not so joined. This is the case especially with married partners, who love each other intimately: but as the woman is from the man, and this conjunction is a species of reunion, it may be seen from reason, that it is not a conjunction into a one, but an adjunction, close and near according to the love, and approaching to contact with those who are principled in love truly conjugial. This adjunction may be called spiritual dwelling together; which takes place, with married partners who love each other tenderly, however distant their bodies may be from each other. Many experimental proofs exist, even in the natural world, in confirmation of these observations. Hence it is evident, that conjugial love conjoins two souls and minds into a one.

159. III. THE WILL OF THE WIFE CONJOINS ITSELF WITH THE UNDERSTANDING OF THE MAN, AND THENCE THE UNDERSTANDING OF THE MAN WITH THE WILL OF THE WIFE. The reason of this is, because the male is born to become understanding, and the female to become will, loving the understanding of the male; from which consideration it follows, tha conjugial conjunction is that of the will of the wife with the understanding of the man, and the reciprocal conjunction of the understanding of the man with the will of the wife. Every one sees that the conjunction of the understanding and the will is

of the most intimate kind; and that it is such, that the one faculty can enter into the other, and be delighted from and in the conjunction.

160. IV. THE INCLINATION TO UNITE THE MAN TO HERSELF IS CONSTANT AND PERPETUAL WITH THE WIFE, BUT INCONSTANT AND ALTERNATE WITH THE MAN. The reason of this is, because love cannot do otherwise than love and unite itself, in order that it may be loved in return, this being its very essence and life; and women are born loves; whereas men, with whom they unite themselves in order that they may be loved in return, are receptions. Moreover love is continually efficient; being like heat, flame, and fire, which perish if their efficiency is checked. Hence the inclination to unite the man to herself is constant and perpetual with the wife: but a similar inclination does not operate with the man towards the wife, because the man is not love, but only a recipient of love; and as a state of reception is absent or present according to intruding cares, and to the varying presence or absence of heat in the mind, as derived from various causes, and also according to the increase and decrease of the bodily powers, which do not return regularly and at stated periods, it follows, that the inclination to conjunction is inconstant and alternate with men.

161. V. CONJUNCTION IS INSPIRED INTO THE MAN FROM THE WIFE ACCORDING TO HER LOVE, AND IS RECEIVED BY THE MAN ACCORDING TO HIS WISDOM. That love and consequent conjunction is inspired into the man by the wife, is at this day concealed from the men; yea, it is universally denied by them; because wives insinuate that the men alone love, and that they themselves receive; or that the men are loves, and themselves obediences: they rejoice also in heart when the men believe it to be so. There are several reasons why they endeavour to persuade the men of this, which are all grounded in their prudence and circumspection; respecting which, something shall be said in a future part of this work, particularly in the chapter ON THE CAUSES OF COLDNESS, SEPARATIONS, AND DIVORCES BETWEEN MARRIED PARTNERS. The reason why men receive from their wives the inspiration or insinuation of love, is, because nothing of conjugial love, or even of the love of the sex, is with the men, but only with wives and females. That this is the case, has been clearly shewn me in the spiritual world. I was once engaged in conversation there on this subject; and the men, in consequence of a persuasion infused from their wives, insisted that they loved and not the wives; but that the wives received love from them. In order to settle the dispute respecting this arcanum, all the females, married and unmarried, were withdrawn from the men, and at the same time the sphere of the love of the sex was removed with them. On the removal of this sphere, the men were reduced to a very unusual state, such as they had never

before perceived, at which they greatly complained. Then, while they were in this state, the females were brought to them, and the wives to the husbands; and both the wives and the other females addressed them in the tenderest and most engaging manner; but they were cold to their tenderness, and turned away, and said one to another, "What is all this? what is a female?" And when some of the women said that they were their wives, they replied, "What is a wife? we do not know you." But when the wives began to be grieved at this absolutely cold indifference of the men, and some of them to shed tears, the sphere of the love of the female sex, and the conjugial sphere, which had for a time been withdrawn from the men, was restored; and then the men instantly returned into their former state, the lovers of marriage into their state, and the lovers of the sex into theirs. Thus the men were convinced, that nothing of conjugial love, or even of the love of the sex, resides with them, but only with the wives and females. Nevertheless, the wives afterwards from their prudence induced the men to believe, that love resides with the men, and that some small spark of it may pass from them into the wives. This experimental evidence is here adduced, in order that it may be known, that wives are loves and men recipients. That men are recipients according to their wisdom, especially according to this wisdom grounded in religion, that the wife only is to be loved, is evident from this consideration, that so long as the wife only is loved, the love is concentrated; and because it is also ennobled, it remains in its strength, and is fixed and permanent; and that in any other case it would be as when wheat from the granary is cast to the dogs, whereby there is scarcity at home.

162. VI. THIS CONJUNCTION IS EFFECTED SUCCESSIVELY FROM THE FIRST DAYS OF MARRIAGE; AND WITH THOSE WHO ARE PRINCIPLED IN LOVE TRULY CONJUGIAL, IT IS EFFECTED MORE AND MORE THOROUGHLY TO ETERNITY. The first heat of marriage does not conjoin; for it partakes of the love of the sex, which is the love of the body and thence of the spirit; and what is in the spirit, as derived from the body, does not long continue; but the love which is in the body, and is derived from the spirit, does continue. The love of the spirit, and of the body from the spirit, is insinuated into the souls and minds of married partners, together with friendship and confidence. When these two [friendship and confidence] conjoin themselves with the first love of marriage, there is effected conjugial love, which opens the bosoms, and inspires the sweets of that love; and this more and more thoroughly, in proportion as those two principles adjoin themselves to the primitive love, and that love enters into them, and *vice versa*.

163. VII. THE CONJUNCTION OF THE WIFE WITH THE RATIONAL WISDOM OF THE HUSBAND IS EFFECTED FROM WITHIN,

BUT WITH HIS MORAL WISDOM FROM WITHOUT. That wisdom with men is two-fold, rational and moral, and that their rational wisdom is of the understanding alone, and their moral wisdom is of the understanding and the life together, may be concluded and seen from mere intuition and examination. But in order that it may be known what we mean by the rational wisdom of men, and what by their moral wisdom, we will enumerate some of the specific distinctions. The principles constituent of their rational wisdom are called by various names; in general they are called knowledge, intelligence, and wisdom; but in particular they are called rationality, judgement, capacity, erudition, and sagacity; but as every one has knowledge peculiar to his office, therefore they are multifarious; for the clergy, magistrates, public officers, judges, physicians and chemists, soldiers and sailors, artificers and laborers, husbandmen, &c., have each their peculiar knowledge. To rational wisdom also appertain all the knowledge into which young men are initiated in the schools, and by which they are afterwards initiated into intelligence, which also are called by various names, as philosophy, physics, geometry, mechanics, chemistry, astronomy, jurisprudence, politics, ethics, history, and several others, by which, as by doors, an entrance is made into things rational, which are the ground of rational wisdom.

164. But the constituents of moral wisdom with men are all the moral virtues, which have respect to life, and enter into it, and also all the spiritual virtues, which flow from love to God and love towards our neighbour, and centre in those loves. The virtues which appertain to the moral wisdom of men are also of various kinds, and are called temperance, sobriety, probity, benevolence, friendship, modesty, sincerity, courtesy, civility, also carefulness, industry, quickness of wit, alacrity, munificence, liberality, generosity, activity, intrepidity, prudence and many others. Spiritual virtues with men are the love of religion, charity, truth, conscience, innocence, and many more. The latter virtues and also the former, may in general be referred to love and zeal for religion, for the public good, for a man's country, for his fellow-citizens, for his parents, for his married partner, and for his children. In all these, justice and judgement have dominion; justice having relation to moral, and judgement to rational wisdom.

165. The reason why the conjunction of the wife with the man's rational wisdom is from within, is, because this wisdom belongs to the man's understanding, and ascends into the light in which women are not, and this is the reason why women do not speak from that wisdom; but, when the conversation of the men turns on subjects proper thereto, they remain silent and listen. That nevertheless such subjects have place with the wives from within, is evident from their listening thereto, and from their inwardly recollecting what had been said, and favoring

those things which they had heard from their husbands. But the reason why the conjunction of the wife with the moral wisdom of the man is from without, is, because the virtues of that wisdom for the most part are akin to similar virtues with the women, and partake of the man's intellectual will, with which the will of the wife unites and constitutes a marriage; and since the wife knows those virtues appertaining to the man more than the man himself does, it is said that the conjunction of the wife with those virtues is from without.

166. VIII. FOR THE SAKE OF THIS CONJUNCTION AS AN END, THE WIFE HAS A PERCEPTION OF THE AFFECTIONS OF THE HUSBAND, AND ALSO THE UTMOST PRUDENCE IN MODERATING THEM. That wives know the affections of their husbands, and prudently moderate them, is among the arcana of conjugial love which lie concealed with wives. They know those affections by three senses, the sight, the hearing, and the touch, and moderate them while their husbands are not at all aware of it. Now as the reasons of this are among the arcana of wives, it does not become me to disclose them circumstantially; but as it is becoming for the wives themselves to do so, therefore four MEMORABLE RELATIONS are added to this chapter, in which those reasons are disclosed by the wives: two of the RELATIONS are taken from the three wives that dwelt in the hall, over which was seen falling as it were a golden shower; and two from the seven wives that were sitting in the garden of roses. A perusal of these RELATIONS will unfold this arcanum.

167. IX. WIVES CONCEAL THIS PERCEPTION WITH THEMSELVES AND HIDE IT FROM THEIR HUSBANDS, FOR REASONS OF NECESSITY, IN ORDER THAT CONJUGIAL LOVE, FRIENDSHIP, AND CONFIDENCE, AND THEREBY THE BLESSEDNESS OF DWELLING TOGETHER AND THE HAPPINESS OF LIFE MAY BE SECURED. The concealing and hiding of the perception of the affections of the husband by the wives, are said to be of necessity; because if they should reveal them, they would cause a complete alienation of their husbands, both in mind and body. The reason of this is, because there resides deep in the minds of many men a conjugial coldness, originating in several causes, which will be enumerated in the chapter ON THE CAUSES OF COLDNESSES, SEPARATION, AND DIVORCES BETWEEN MARRIED PARTNERS. This coldness, in case the wives should discover the affections and inclinations of their husbands, would burst forth from its hiding places, and communicate its cold, first to the interiors of the mind, afterwards to the breast, and thence to the ultimates of love which are appropriated to generation; and these being affected with cold, conjugial love would be banished to such a degree, that there would not remain any hope of friendship, of confidence, of the blessedness of dwelling together, and thence of the happiness of life; when nevertheless wives are continually

feeding on this hope. To make this open declaration, that they know their husbands' affections and inclinations of love, carries with it a declaration and publication of their own love: and it is well known, that so far as wives make such a declaration, so far the men grow cold and desire a separation. From these considerations the truth of this proposition is manifest, that the reasons why wives conceal their perception with themselves, and hide it from their husbands, are reasons of necessity.

168. X. THIS PERCEPTION IS THE WISDOM OF THE WIFE, AND IS NOT COMMUNICABLE TO THE MAN; NEITHER IS THE RATIONAL WISDOM OF THE MAN COMMUNICABLE TO THE WIFE. This follows from the distinction subsisting between the male principle and the female. The male principle consists in perceiving from the understanding, and the female in perceiving from love: and the understanding perceives also those things which are above the body and are out of the world; for the rational and spiritual sight reaches to such objects; whereas love reaches no further than to what it feels; when it reaches further, it is in consequence of conjunction with the understanding of the man established from creation: for the understanding has relation to light, and love to heat; and those things which have relation to light, are seen, and those which have relation to heat, are felt. From these considerations it is evident, that from the universal distinction subsisting between the male principle and the female, the wisdom of the wife is not communicable to the man, neither is the wisdom of the man communicable to the wife: nor, further, is the moral wisdom of the man communicable to women, so far as it partakes of his rational wisdom.

169. XI. THE WIFE FROM A PRINCIPLE OF LOVE IN CONTINUALLY THINKING ABOUT THE MAN'S INCLINATION TO HER, WITH THE PURPOSE OF JOINING HIM TO HERSELF: IT IS OTHERWISE WITH THE MAN. This agrees with what was explained above; namely, that the inclination to unite the man to herself is constant and perpetual with the wife, but inconstant and alternate with the man; see n. 160: hence it follows, that the wife's thoughts are continually employed about her husband's inclination to her, with the purpose of joining him to herself. Her thoughts concerning her husband are interrupted indeed by domestic concerns; but still they remain in the affection of her love; and this affection does not separate itself from the thoughts with women, as it does with men: these things, however, I relate from hearsay; see the two MEMORABLE RELATIONS from the seven wives sitting in the rose-garden, which are annexed to some of the following chapters.

170. XII. THE WIFE CONJOINS HERSELF TO THE MAN BY APPLICATIONS TO THE DESIRES OF HIS WILL. This being generally known and admitted, it is needless to explain it.

171. XIII. THE WIFE IS CONJOINED TO HER HUSBAND BY

THE SPHERE OF HER LIFE FLOWING FROM THE LOVE OF HIM. There flows, yea there overflows, from every man (*homo*) a spiritual sphere, derived from the affections of his love, which encompasses him, and infuses itself into the natural sphere derived from the body, so that the two spheres are conjoined. That a natural sphere is continually flowing, not only from men, but also from beasts, yea from trees, fruits, flowers, and also from metals, is generally known. The case is the same in the spiritual world; but the spheres flowing from subjects in that world are spiritual, and those which emanate from spirits and angels are altogether spiritual; because there appertain thereto affections of love, and thence interior perceptions and thoughts. This is the origin of all sympathy and antipathy, and likewise of all conjunction and disjunction, and, according thereto, of presence and absence in the spiritual world: for what is of a similar nature or concordant causes conjunction and presence, and what is of a dissimilar nature and discordant causes disjunction and absence; therefore those spheres cause distances in that world. What effects those spiritual spheres produce in the natural world, is also known to some. The inclinations of married partners towards each other are from no other origin. They are united by unanimous and concordant spheres, and disunited by adverse and discordant spheres; for concordant spheres are delightful and grateful, whereas discordant spheres are undelightful and ungrateful. I have been informed by the angels, who are in a clear perception of those spheres, that every part of a man, both interior and exterior, renews itself; which is effected by solutions and reparations; and that hence arises the sphere which continually issues forth. I have also been informed that this sphere encompasses a man on the back and on the breast, lightly on the back, but more densely on the breast, and that the sphere issuing from the breast conjoins itself with the respiration; and that this is the reason why two married partners, who are of different minds and discordant affections, lie in bed back to back, and, on the other hand, why those who agree in minds and affections, mutually turn towards each other. I have been further informed by the angels, that these spheres, because they flow from every part of a man (*homo*), and are abundantly continued around him, conjoin and disjoin two married partners not only externally, but also internally; and that hence come all the differences and varieties of conjugial love. Lastly, I have been informed, that the sphere of love, flowing from a wife who is tenderly loved, is perceived in heaven as sweetly fragrant, by far more pleasant than it is perceived in the world by a newly married man during the first days after marriage. From these considerations is manifested the truth of the assertion, that a wife is conjoined to a man by the sphere of her life flowing from the love of him.

172. XIV. THE WIFE IS CONJOINED TO THE HUSBAND BY THE APPROPRIATION OF THE POWERS OF HIS VIRTUE; WHICH HOWEVER IS EFFECTED ACCORDING TO THEIR MUTUAL SPIRITUAL LOVE. That this is the case, I have also gathered from the mouth of angels. They have declared that the prolific principles imparted from the husbands are received universally by the wives and add themselves to their life; and that thus the wives lead a life unanimous, and successively more unanimous with their husbands; and that hence is effectively produced a union of souls and a conjunction of minds. They declared the reason of this was, because in the prolific principle of the husband is his soul, and also his mind as to its interiors, which are conjoined to the soul. They added, that this was provided from creation, in order that the wisdom of the man, which constitutes his soul, may be appropriated to the wife, and that thus they may become, according to the Lord's words, one flesh: and further, that this was provided, lest the husband (*homo vir*) from some caprice should leave the wife after conception. But they added further, that applications and appropriations of the life of the husband with the wife are effected according to conjugial love, because love which is spiritual union, conjoins; and that this also is provided for several reasons.

173. XV. THUS THE WIFE RECEIVES IN HERSELF THE IMAGE OF HER HUSBAND, AND THENCE PERCEIVES, SEES, AND IS SENSIBLE OF, HIS AFFECTIONS. From the reasons above adduced it follows as an established fact, that wives receive in themselves those things which appertain to the wisdom of their husbands, thus which are proper to the souls and minds of their husbands, and thereby from virgins make themselves wives. The reasons from which this follows, are, 1. That the woman was created out of the man. 2. That hence she has an inclination to unite, and as it were to reunite herself with the man. 3. That by virtue of this union with her partner, and for the sake of it, the woman is born the love of the man, and becomes more and more the love of him by marriage; because in this case the love is continually employing its thoughts to conjoin the man to itself. 4. That the woman is conjoined to her only one (*unico suo*) by application to the desires of his life. 5. That they are conjoined by the spheres which encompass them, and which unite themselves universally and particularly according to the quality of the conjugial love with the wives, and at the same time according to the quality of the wisdom recipient thereof with the husbands. 6. That they are also conjoined by appropriations of the powers of the husbands by the wives. 7. From which reasons it is evident, that there is continually somewhat of the husband being transferred to the wife, and inscribed on her as her own. From all these considerations it follows, that the image of the husband is formed in the wife; by virtue of which image the wife perceives, sees, and is sensible of, the things which are in her hus

band, in herself, and thence as it were herself in him. She perceives from communication, she sees from aspect, and she is made sensible from the touch. That she is made sensible of the reception of her love by the husband from the touch in the palms of the hands, on the cheeks, the shoulders, the hands, and the breasts, I learnt from the three wives in the hall, and the seven wives in the rose garden, spoken of in the MEMORABLE RELATIONS which follow.

174. XVI. THERE ARE DUTIES PROPER TO THE HUSBAND AND OTHERS PROPER TO THE WIFE; AND THE WIFE CANNOT ENTER INTO THE DUTIES PROPER TO THE HUSBAND, NOR THE HUSBAND INTO THE DUTIES PROPER TO THE WIFE, SO AS TO PERFORM THEM ARIGHT. That there are duties proper to the husband, and others proper to the wife, needs not to be illustrated by an enumeration of them; for they are many and various: and every one that chooses to do so can arrange them numerically according to their genera and species. The duties by which wives principally conjoin themselves with their husbands, are those which relate to the education of the children of each sex, and of the girls till they are marriageable.

175. The wife cannot enter into the duties proper to the husband, nor on the other hand the husband into the duties proper to the wife, because they differ like wisdom and the love thereof, or like thought and the affection thereof, or like understanding and the will thereof. In the duties proper to husbands, the primary agent is understanding, thought, and wisdom; whereas in the duties proper to wives, the primary agent is will, affection, and love; and the wife from the latter performs her duties, and the husband from the former performs his; wherefore their duties are naturally different, but still conjunctive in a successive series. Many believe that women can perform the duties of men, if they are initiated therein at an early age, as boys are. They may indeed be initiated into the practice of such duties, but not into the judgement on which the propriety of duties interiorly depends; wherefore such women as have been initiated into the duties of men, are bound in matters of judgement to consult men, and then, if they are left to their own disposal, they select from the counsels of men that which suits their own inclination. Some also suppose that women are equally capable with men of elevating their intellectual vision, and into the same sphere of light, and of viewing things with the same depth; and they have been led into this opinion by the writings of certain learned authoresses: but these writings, when examined in the spiritual world in the presence of the authoresses, were found to be the productions, not of judgement and wisdom, but of ingenuity and wit; and what proceeds from these on account of the elegance and neatness of the style in which it is written, has the appearance of sublimity and erudition; yet only in the eyes

of those who dignify all ingenuity by the name of wisdom. In like manner men cannot enter into the duties proper to women, and perform them aright, because they are not in the affections of women, which are altogether distinct from the affections of men. As the affections and perceptions of the male [and of the female] sex are thus distinct by creation and consequently by nature, therefore among the statutes given to the sons of Israel this also was ordained, " *A woman shall not put on the garment of a man, neither shall a man put on the garment of a woman; because this is an abomination.* Deut. xxii. 5. This was, because, all in the spiritual world are clothed according to their affections; and the two affections, of the woman and of the man, cannot be united except [as subsisting] between two, and in no case [as subsisting] in one.

176. XVII. THESE DUTIES ALSO, ACCORDING TO MUTUAL AID, CONJOIN THE TWO INTO A ONE, AND AT THE SAME TIME CONSTITUTE ONE HOUSE. It is well known in the world that the duties of the husband in some way conjoin themselves with the duties of the wife, and that the duties of the wife adjoin themselves to the duties of the husband, and that these conjunctions and adjunctions are a mutual aid, and according thereto: but the primary duties, which confederate, consociate, and gather into one the souls and lives of two married partners, relate to the common care of educating their children; in relation to which care, the duties of the husband and of the wife are distinct, and yet join themselves together. They are distinct; for the care of suckling and nursing the infants of each sex, and also the care of instructing the girls till they become marriageable, is properly the duty of the wife; whereas the care of instructing the boys, from childhood to youth, and from youth till they become capable of governing themselves, is properly the duty of the husband: nevertheless the duties, of both the husband and the wife, are blended by means of counsel and support, and several other mutual aids. That these duties, both conjoined and distinct, or both common and peculiar, combine the minds of conjugial partners into one; and that this is effected by the love called *storge*, is well known. It is also well known, that these duties, regarded in their distinction and conjunction, constitute one house.

177. XVIII. MARRIED PARTNERS, ACCORDING TO THESE CONJUNCTIONS, BECOME ONE MAN (*homo*) MORE AND MORE. This coincides with what is contained in article VI.; where it was observed, that conjunction is effected successively from the first days of marriage and that with those who are principled in love truly conjugial, it is effected more and more thoroughly to eternity; see above. They become one man in proportion as conjugial love increases; and as this love in the heavens is genuine by virtue of the celestial and spiritual life of the angels, therefore two married partners are there called two, when they

are regarded as husband and wife, but one, when they are regarded as angels.

178. XIX. THOSE WHO ARE PRINCIPLED IN LOVE TRULY CONJUGIAL, ARE SENSIBLE OF THEIR BEING A UNITED MAN, AND AS IT WERE ONE FLESH. That this is the case, must be confirmed not from the testimony of any inhabitant of the earth, but from the testimony of the inhabitants of heaven; for there is no love truly conjugial at this day with men on earth; and moreover, men on earth are encompassed with a gross body, which deadens and absorbs the sensation that two married partners are a united man, and as it were one flesh; and besides, those in the world who love their married partners only exteriorly, and not interiorly, do not wish to hear of such a thing: they think also on the subject lasciviously under the influence of the flesh. It is otherwise with the angels of heaven, who are principled in spiritual and celestial conjugial love, and are not encompassed with so gross a body as men on earth. From those among them who have lived for ages with their conjugial partners in heaven, I have heard it testified, that they are sensible of their being so united, the husband with the wife, and the wife with the husband, and each in the other mutually and interchangeably, as also in the flesh, although they are separate. The reason why this phenomenon is so rare on earth, they have declared to be this; because the union of the souls and minds of married partners on earth is made sensible in their flesh; for the soul constitutes the inmost principles not only of the head, but also of the body: in like manner the mind, which is intermediate between the soul and the body, and which, although it appears to be in the head, is yet also actually in the whole body: and they have declared, that this is the reason why the acts, which the soul and mind intend, flow forth instantly from the body; and that hence also it is, that they themselves, after the rejection of the body in the former world, are perfect men. Now, since the soul and the mind join themselves closely to the flesh of the body, in order that they may operate and produce their effects, it follows that the union of soul and mind with a married partner is made sensible also in the body as one flesh. As the angels made these declarations, I heard it asserted by the spirits who were present, that such subjects belong to angelic wisdom, being above ordinary apprehension; but these spirits were rational-natural, and not rational-spiritual.

179. XX. LOVE TRULY CONJUGIAL, CONSIDERED IN ITSELF, IS A UNION OF SOULS, A CONJUNCTION OF MINDS, AND AN ENDEAVOUR TOWARDS CONJUNCTION IN THE BOSOMS AND THENCE IN THE BODY. That it is a union of souls and a conjunction of minds, may be seen above, n. 158. The reason why it is an endeavour towards conjunction in the bosoms is, because the bosom (or breast) is as it were a place of public assembly, and a

royal council-chamber, while the body is as a populous city around it. The reason why the bosom is as it were a place of public assembly, is, because all things, which by derivation from the soul and mind have their determination in the body, first flow into the bosom; and the reason why it is as it were a royal council-chamber, is, because in the bosom there is dominion over all things of the body; for in the bosom are contained the heart and lungs; and the heart rules by the blood, and the lungs by the respiration, in every part. That the body is as a populous city around it, is evident. When therefore the souls and minds of married partners are united, and love truly conjugial unites them, it follows that this lovely union flows into their bosoms, and through their bosoms into their bodies, and causes an endeavour towards conjunction; and so much the more, because conjugial love determines the endeavour to its ultimates, in order to complete its satisfactions; and as the bosom is intermediate between the body and the mind, it is evident on what account conjugial love has fixed therein the seat of its delicate sensation.

180. XXI. THE STATES OF THIS LOVE ARE INNOCENCE, PEACE, TRANQUILLITY, INMOST FRIENDSHIP, FULL CONFIDENCE, AND A MUTUAL DESIRE OF MIND AND HEART TO DO EVERY GOOD TO EACH OTHER; AND THE STATES DERIVED FROM THESE ARE BLESSEDNESS, SATISFACTION, DELIGHT AND PLEASURE; AND FROM THE ETERNAL ENJOYMENT OF THESE IS DERIVED HEAVENLY FELICITY. All these things are in conjugial love, and thence are derived from it, because its origin is from the marriage of good and truth, and this marriage is from the Lord; and because love is of such a nature, that it desires to communicate with another, whom it loves from the heart, yea, confer joys upon him, and thence to derive its own joys. This therefore is the case in an infinitely high degree with the divine love, which is in the Lord, in regard to man, whom he created a receptacle of both love and wisdom proceeding from himself; and as he created man (*homo*) for the reception of those principles, the man (*vir*) for the reception of wisdom, and the woman for the reception of the love of the man's wisdom, therefore from inmost principles he infused into men (*homines*) conjugial love into which love he might insinuate all things blessed, satisfactory, delightful, and pleasant, which proceed solely from his divine love through his divine wisdom, together with life, and flow into their recipients; consequently, which flow into those who are principled in love truly conjugial; for these alone are recipients. Mention is made of innocence, peace, tranquillity, inmost friendship, full confidence, and the mutual desire of doing every good to each other; for innocence and peace relate to the soul, tranquillity to the mind, inmost friendship to the breast, full confidence to the heart, and the mutual desire of doing every good to each other, to the body as derived from the former principles.

181. XXII. These things can only exist in the marriage of one man with one wife. This is a conclusion from all that has been said above, and also from all that remains to be said; therefore there is no need of any particular comment for its confirmation.

* * * * * * * *

182. To the above I will add two memorable relations. First. After some weeks, I heard a voice from heaven, saying, "Lo! there is again an assembly on Parnassus: come hither, and we will shew you the way." I accordingly came; and as I drew near, I saw a certain person on Helicon with a trumpet, with which he announced and proclaimed the assembly. And I saw the inhabitants of Athens and its suburbs ascending as before; and in the midst of them three novitiates from the world. They were of a Christian community; one a priest, another a politician, and the third a philosopher. These they entertained on the way with conversation on various subjects, especially concerning the wise ancients, whom they named. They inquired whether they should see them, and were answered in the affirmative, and were told, that if they were desirous, they might pay their respects to them, as they were courteous and affable. The novitiates then inquired after Demosthenes, Diogenes, and Epicurus; and were answered, "Demosthenes is not here, but with Plato; Diogenes, with his scholars, resides under Helicon, because of his little attention to worldly things, and his being engaged in heavenly contemplations; Epicurus dwells in a border to the west, and has no intercourse with us; because we distinguish between good and evil affections, and say, that good affections are one with wisdom, and evil affections are contrary to it." When they had ascended the hill Parnassus, some guards there brought water in crystal cups from a fountain in the mount, and said, "This is water from the fountain which, according to ancient fable, was broken open by the hoof of the horse Pegasus, and was afterwards consecrated to nine virgins: but by the winged horse Pegasus they meant the understanding of truth, by which comes wisdom; by the hoofs of his feet they understood experiences whereby comes natural intelligence; and by the nine virgins they understood knowledges and sciences of every kind. These things are now called fables; but they were correspondences, agreeable to the primeval method of speaking." Then those who attended the three strangers said, "Be not surprised; the guards are told thus to speak; but we know that to drink water from the fountain, means to be instructed concerning truths, and by truths concerning goods, and thereby to grow wise." After this, they entered the Palladium, and with them the three novitiates, the priest, the politician, and the philosopher; and immediately the laurelled phi who were seated at the tables, asked, "What news from the earth?" They replied, "This is news; that a certain person

declares that he converses with angels, and has his sight opened into the spiritual world, equally as into the natural world; and he brings thence much new information, and, among other particulars, asserts, that a man lives a man after death, as he lived before in the world; that he sees, hears, speaks, as before in the world; that he is clothed and decked with ornaments, as before in the world; that he hungers and thirsts, eats and drinks, as before in the world; that he enjoys conjugial delights, as before in the world; that he sleeps and wakes, as before in the world; that in the spiritual world there are land and water, mountains and hills, plains and valleys, fountains and rivers, paradises and groves; also that there are palaces and houses, cities and villages, as in the natural world; and further, that there are writings and books, employments and trades; also precious stones, gold and silver; in a word, that there are all such things there as there are on earth, and that those things in the heavens are infinitely more perfect; with this difference only, that all things in the spiritual world are from a spiritual origin, and therefore are spiritual, because they are from the sun of that world, which is pure love; whereas all things in the natural world are from a natural origin, and therefore are natural and material, because they are from the sun of that world, which is pure fire; in short, that a man after death is perfectly a man, yea more perfectly than before in the world; for before in the world he was in a material body, but in the spiritual world he is in a spiritual body." Hereupon the ancient sages asked, "What do the people on the earth think of such information?" The three strangers replied, "We know that it is true, because we are here, and have viewed and examined everything; wherefore we will tell you what has been said and reasoned about it on earth." Then the PRIEST said, "Those of our order, when they first heard such relations, called them visions, then fictions; afterwards they insisted that the man had seen spectres, and lastly they hesitated, and said, 'Believe them who will; we have hitherto taught that a man will not be in a body after death until the day of the last judgement.'" Then the sages asked, "Are there no intelligent persons among those of your order, who can prove and evince the truth, that a man lives a man after death?" The priest said, "There are indeed some who prove it, but not to the conviction of others. Those who prove it say, that it is contrary to sound reason to believe, that a man does not live a man till the day of the last judgement, and that in the mean while he is a soul without a body. What is the soul, or where is it in the interim? Is it a vapor, or some wind floating in the atmosphere, or some thing hidden in the bowels of the earth? Have the souls of Adam and Eve, and of all their posterity, now for six thousand years, or sixty ages, been flying about in the universe, or been shut up in the bowels of the earth, waiting for the last judgement? What can be more anxious and miserable than such an expectation? May not their lot in such a case be compared with that of prisoners bound hand and foot, and lying in a dungeon? If such be a man's lot after death, would it not be better to be born an ass than a man? Is it not also contrary to reason to believe, that the soul can be re-clothed with its body? Is not the body eaten up by worms, mice, and fish? And can a bony skeleton that has been parched in the sun, or mouldered into dust, be introduced into a new body? And how could the cadaverous and putrid materials be collected, and reunited to the souls? When such questions as these are urged, those of our order do not offer any answers grounded in reason, but adhere to their creed, saying, 'We keep reason under obedience to faith.' With respect to collecting all the parts of the human body from the grave at the last day, they say, 'This is a work of omnipotence;' and when they name omnipotence and faith, reason is banished; and I am free to assert, that in such case sound reason is not appreciated, and by some is regarded as a spectre; yea, they can say to sound reason, 'Thou art unsound.'" On hearing these things, the Grecian sages said, "Surely such paradoxes vanish and disperse of themselves, as being full of contradiction; and yet in the world at this day they cannot be dispersed by sound reason. What can be believed more paradoxical than what is told respecting the last judgement; that the universe will then be destroyed, and that the stars of heaven will then fall down upon the earth, which is less than the stars; and that then the bodies of men, whether they be mouldering carcases, or mummies eaten by men, or reduced to mere dust, will meet and be united again with their souls? We, during our abode in the world, from the inductions of reason, believed the immortality of the souls of men; and we also assigned regions for the blessed, which we call the elysian fields; and we believed that the soul was a human image or appearance, but of a fine and delicate nature, because spiritual." After this, the assembly turned to the other stranger, who in the world had been a POLITICIAN. He confessed that he did not believe in a life after death, and that respecting the new information which he had heard about it, he thought it all fable and fiction. "In my meditations on the subject," said he, "I used to say to myself, 'How can souls be bodies?—does not the whole man lie dead in the grave?—is not the eye there; how can he see?—is not the ear there, how can he hear?—whence must he have a mouth wherewith to speak? Supposing anything of a man to live after death, must it not resemble a spectre? and how can a spectre eat and drink, or how can it enjoy conjugial delights? whence can it have clothes, houses, meats, &c.? Besides, spectres, which are mere aërial images, appear as if they really existed; and yet they do not. These and similar sentiments I used to entertain in the world concerning the life of men after death; but now, since I have seen all things, and touched them with my hands, I am convinced by my very senses that I am a man as I was in the world; so that I know no other than that I live now as I lived formerly; with only this difference, that my reason now is sounder. At times I have been ashamed of my former thoughts." The PHILOSOPHER gave much the same account of himself as the politician had done; only differing in this respect, that he considered the new relations which he had heard concerning a life after death, as having reference to opinions and hypotheses which he had collected from the ancients and moderns. When the three strangers had done speaking, the sophi were all in amazement; and those who were of the Socratic school, said, that from the news they had heard from the earth, it was quite evident, that the interiors of human minds had been successively closed; and that in the world at this time a belief in what is false shines as truth, and an infatuated ingenuity as wisdom; and that the light of wisdom, since their times, has descended from the interiors of the brain into the mouth beneath the nose, where it appears to the eyes as a shining of the lip, while the speech of the mouth thence proceeding appears as wisdom. Hereupon one of the young scholars said, "How stupid are the minds of the inhabitants of the earth at this day! I wish we had here the disciples of Heraclitus, who weep at every thing, and of Democritus, who laugh at every thing; for then we should hear much lamentation and much laughter." When the assembly broke up, they gave the three novitiates the insignia of their authority, which were copper plates, on which were engraved some hieroglyphic characters; with which they took their leave and departed.

183. THE SECOND MEMORABLE RELATION. I saw in the eastern quarter a grove of palm-trees and laurels, set in winding rows, which I approached and entered; and walking in the winding paths I saw at the end a garden, which formed the centre of the grove. There was a little bridge dividing the grove from the garden, and at the bridge two gates, one on the side next the grove, and the other on the side next the garden. And as I drew near, the keeper opened the gates, and I asked him the name of the garden. He said, "ADRAMANDONI; which is the delight of conjugial love." I entered, and lo! there were olive-trees; and among them ran pendulous vines, and underneath and among them were shrubs in flower. In the midst of the garden was a grassy circus, on which were seated husbands and wives, and youths and maidens, in pairs; and in the midst of the circus, on an elevated piece of ground, there was a little fountain, which, from the strength of its spring, threw its water to a considerable height. On approaching the circus I saw two angels clad in purple and scarlet, in conversation with those who were seated on

the grass. They were conversing respecting the origin of conjugial love, and respecting its delights; and this being the subject of their discourse, the attention was eager, and the reception full; and hence there was an exaltation in the speech of the angels as from the fire of love. I collected the following summary of what was said. They began with the difficulty of investigating and perceiving the origin of conjugial love; because its origin is divinely celestial, it being divine love, divine wisdom, and divine use, which three proceed as a one from the Lord, and thence flow as a one into the souls of men, and through their souls into their minds, and there into the interior affections and thoughts, and through these into the desires next to the body, and from these through the breast into the genital region, where all principles derived from their first origin exist together, and, in union with successive principles, constitute conjugial love. After this the angels said, "Let us communicate together by questions and answers; since the perception of a thing, imbibed by hearing only, flows in indeed, but does not remain unless the hearer also thinks of it from himself, and asks questions concerning it." Then some of that conjugial assembly said to the angels, "We have heard that the origin of conjugial love is divinely celestial; because it is by virtue of influx from the Lord into the souls of men; and, as it is from the Lord, that it is love, wisdom, and use, which are three essentials, together constituting one divine essence, and that nothing but what is of the divine essence can proceed from him, and flow into the inmost principle of man (*homo*), which is called his soul; and that these three essentials are changed into analogous and corresponding principles in their descent into the body. We ask therefore now in the first place, What is meant by the third proceeding divine essential, which is called use?" The angels replied, "Love and wisdom, without use, are only abstract ideas of thought; which also after some continuance in the mind pass away like the winds; but in use they are collected together, and therein become one principle, which is called real. Love cannot rest unless it is as work; for love is the essential active principle of life; neither can wisdom exist and subsist unless when it is at work from and with love; and to work is use; therefore we define use to be the doing good from love by wisdom; use being essential good. As these three essentials, love, wisdom, and use, flow into the souls of men, it may appear from what ground it is said, that all good is from God; for every thing done from love by wisdom, is called good; and use also is something done. What is love without wisdom but a mere infatuation? and what is love with wisdom without use, but a puff of the mind? Whereas love and wisdom with use not only constitute man (*homo*), but also are man; yea, what possibly you will be surprised at, they propagate man; for in the seed of a man (*vir*) is his soul in a perfect human form, covered with substances from the purest principles of nature; whereof a body is formed in the womb of the mother. This is the supreme and ultimate use of the divine love by the divine wisdom." Finally the angels said, "We will hence come to this conclusion, that all fructification, propagation, and prolification, is originally derived from the influx of love, wisdom, and use from the Lord, from an immediate influx into the souls of men, from a mediate influx into the souls of animals, and from an influx still more mediate into the inmost principles of vegetables; and all these effects are wrought in ultimates from first principles. That fructifications, propagations, and prolifications, are continuations of creation, is evident; for creation cannot be from any other source, than from divine love by divine wisdom in divine use; wherefore all things in the universe are procreated and formed from use, in use, and for use." Afterwards those who were seated on the grassy couches, asked the angels, "Whence are the innumerable and ineffable delights of conjugial love?" The angels replied, "They are from the uses of love and wisdom, as may be plain from this consideration, that so far as any one loves to grow wise, for the sake of genuine use, so far he is in the vein and potency of conjugial love; and so far as he is in these two, so far he is in the delights thereof. Use effects this; because love and wisdom are delighted with each other, and as it were sport together like little children; and as they grow up, they enter into genial conjunction, which is effected by a kind of betrothing, nuptial solemnity, marriage, and propagation, and this with continual variety to eternity. These operations take place between love and wisdom inwardly in use. Those delights in their first principles are imperceptible; but they become more and more perceptible as they descend thence by degrees and enter the body. They enter by degrees from the soul into the interiors of a man's mind, from these into its exteriors, from these into the bosom, and from the bosom into the genital region. Those celestial nuptial sports in the soul are not at all perceived by man; but they thence insinuate themselves into the interiors of the mind under a species of peace and innocence, and into the exteriors of the mind under a species of blessedness, satisfaction, and delight; in the bosom under a species of the delights of inmost friendship; and in the genital region, from continual influx even from the soul with the essential sense of conjugial love, as the delight of delights. These nuptial sports of love and wisdom in use in the soul, in proceeding towards the bosom, become permanent, and present themselves sensible therein under an infinite variety of delights; and from the wonderful communication of the bosom with the genital region, the delights therein become the delights of conjugial love, which are superior to all other delights in heaven and in the world; because the use of conjugial love is the most excellent of a.l uses, the procreation of the human race being thence derived, and from the human race the angelic heaven." To this the angels added, that those who are not principled in the love of wisdom for the sake of use from the Lord, do not know anything concerning the variety of the innumerable delights of love truly conjugial; for with those who do not love to grow wise from genuine truths, but love to be insane from false principles, and by this insanity perform evil uses from some particular love, the way to the soul is closed: hence the heavenly nuptial sports of love and wisdom in the soul, being more and more intercepted, cease, and together with them conjugial love ceases with its vein, its potency, and its delights." On hearing these statements the audience said, "We now perceive that conjugial love is according to the love of growing wise for the sake of uses from the Lord." The angels replied that it was so. And instantly upon the heads of some of the audience there appeared wreaths of flowers; and on their asking, "Why is this?" the angels said, "Because they have understood more profoundly:" and immediately they departed from the garden, and the latter in the midst of them.

ON THE CHANGE OF THE STATE OF LIFE WHICH TAKES PLACE WITH MEN AND WOMEN BY MARRIAGE.

184. WHAT is meant by states of life, and their changes, is very well known to the learned and the wise, but unknown to the unlearned and the simple; wherefore it may be expedient to premise somewhat on the subject. The state of a man's life is its quality; and as there are in every man two faculties which constitute his life, and which are called the understanding and the will, the state of a man's life is its quality as to the understanding and the will. Hence it is evident, that changes of the state of life mean changes of quality as to the things appertaining to the understanding and the will. That every man is continually changing as to those two principles, but with a distinction of variations before marriage and after it, is the point proposed to be proved in this section; which shall be done in the following propositions:—I. *The state of a man's* (homo) *life from infancy even to the end of his life, and afterwards to eternity, is continually changing.* II. *In like manner a man's internal form which is that of his spirit, is continually changing.* III. *These changes differ in the case of men and of women; since men from creation are forms of knowledge, intelligence, and wisdom, and women are forms of the love of those principles as existing with men.* IV. *With men there is an elevation of the mind into superior light, and with women an elevation of the mind into*

superior heat: and that the woman is made sensible of the delights of her heat in the man's light. V. *With both men and women, the states of life before marriage are different from what they are afterwards.* VI. *With married partners the states of life after marriage are changed and succeed each other according to the conjunctions of their minds by conjugial love.* VII. *Marriage also induces other forms in the souls and minds of married partners.* VIII. *The woman is actually formed into a wife according to the description in the book of creation.* IX. *This formation is effected on the part of the wife by secret means; and this is meant by the woman's being created while the man slept.* X. *This formation on the part of the wife is affected by the conjunction of her own will with the internal will of the man.* XI. *The end herein is, that the will of both become one, and that thus both may become one man* (homo). XII. *This formation on the part of the wife is effected by an appropriation of the affections of the husband.* XIII. *This formation on the part of the wife is effected by a reception of the propagations of the soul of the husband, with the delight arising from her desire to be the love of her husband's wisdom.* XIV. *Thus a maiden is formed into a wife, and a youth into a husband.* XV. *In the marriage of one man with one wife, between whom there exists love truly conjugial, the wife becomes more and more a wife, and the husband more and more a husband.* XVI. *Thus also their forms are successively perfected and ennobled from within.* XVII. *Children born of parents who are principled in love truly conjugial, derive from them the conjugial principle of good and truth; whence they have an inclination and faculty, if sons, to perceive the things relating to wisdom, and if daughters, to love those things which wisdom teaches.* XVIII. *The reason of this is because the soul of the offspring is from the father and its clothing from the mother.* We proceed to the explanation of each article.

185. I. THE STATE OF A MAN'S (*homo*) LIFE, FROM INFANCY EVEN TO THE END OF HIS LIFE, AND AFTERWARDS TO ETERNITY, IS CONTINUALLY CHANGING. The common states of a man's life are called infancy, childhood, youth, manhood, and old age. That every man, whose life is continued in the world, successively passes from one state into another, thus from the first to the last, is well known. The transitions into those ages only become evident by the intervening spaces of time: that nevertheless they are progressive from one moment to another, thus continual, is obvious to reason; for the case is similar with a man as with a tree, which grows and increases every instant of time, even the most minute, from the casting of the seed into the earth. These momentaneous progressions are also changes of state; for the subsequent adds something to the antecedent, which perfects the state. The changes which take place in a man's internals, are

more perfectly continuous than those which take place in his externals; because a man's internals, by which we mean the things appertaining to his mind or spirit, are elevated into a superior degree above his externals; and in those priciples which are in a superior degree, a thousand effects take place in the same instant in which one effect is wrought in externals. The changes which take place in internals, are changes of the state of the will as to affections, and of the state of the understanding as to thoughts. The successive changes of state of the latter and of the former are specifically meant in the proposition. The changes of these two lives or faculties are perpetual with every man from infancy even to the end of his life, and afterwards to eternity; because there is no end to knowledge, still less to intelligence, and least of all to wisdom; for there is infinity and eternity in the extent of these principles, by virtue of the Infinite and Eternal One, from whom they are derived. Hence comes the philosophical tenet of the ancients, that everything is divisible *in infinitum;* to which may be added, that it is multiplicable in like manner. The angels assert, that by wisdom from the Lord they are being perfected to eternity; which also means to infinity; because eternity is the infinity of time.

186. II. IN LIKE MANNER A MAN'S (*homo*), INTERNAL FORM WHICH IS THAT OF HIS SPIRIT, IS CONTINUALLY CHANGING. The reason why this form is continually changing as the state of the man's life is changed, is, because there is nothing that exists but in a form, and state induces that form; wherefore it is the same whether we say that the state of a man's life is changed, or that its form is changed. All a man's affections and thoughts are in forms, and thence from forms; for forms are their subjects. If affections and thoughts were not in subjects, which are formed, they might exist also in skulls without a brain; which would be the same thing as to suppose sight without an eye, hearing without an ear, and taste without a tongue. It is well known that there are subjects of these senses, and that these subjects are forms. The state of life, and thence the form, with a man, is continually changing; because it is a truth which the wise have taught and still teach, that there does not exist a sameness, or absolute identity of two things, still less of several; as there are not two human faces the same, and still less several: the case is similar in things successive, in that no subsequent state of life is the same as a preceding one; whence it follows, that there is a perpetual change of the state of life with every man, consequently also a perpetual change of form, especially of his internals. But as these considerations do not teach anything respecting marriages, but only prepare the way for knowledges concerning them, and since also they are mere philosophical inquiries of the understanding, which, with some persons, are difficult of apprehension, we will pass them without further discussion.

187. III. THESE CHANGES DIFFER IN THE CASE OF MEN AND OF WOMEN; SINCE MEN FROM CREATION ARE FORMS OF KNOWLEDGE, INTELLIGENCE, AND WISDOM; AND WOMEN ARE FORMS OF THE LOVE OF THOSE PRINCIPLES AS EXISTING WITH MEN. That men were created forms of the understanding, and that women were created forms of the love of the understanding of men, may be explained above, n. 90. That the changes of state, which succeed both with men and women from infancy to mature age, are for the perfecting of forms, the intellectual form with men, and the voluntary with women, follows as a consequence: hence it is clear, that the changes with men differ from those with women; nevertheless with both, the external form which is of the body is perfected according to the perfecting of the internal form which is of the mind; for the mind acts upon the body, and not *vice versa*. This is the reason why infants in heaven become men of stature and comeliness according as they increase in intelligence; it is otherwise with infants on earth, because they are encompassed with a material body like the animals; nevertheless they agree in this, that they first grow in inclination to such things as allure their bodily senses, and afterwards by little and little to such things as affect the internal thinking sense, and by degrees to such things as tincture the will with affection; and when they arrive at an age which is midway between mature and immature, the conjugial inclination begins, which is that of a maiden to a youth, and of a youth to a maiden; and as maidens in the heavens, like those on earth from an innate prudence conceal their inclination to marriage, the youths there know no other than that they affect the maidens with love; and this also appears to them in consequence of their masculine eagerness; which they also derive from an influx of love from the fair sex; concerning which influx we shall speak particularly elsewhere. From these considerations the truth of the proposition is evident, that the changes of state with men differ from those with women; since men from creation are forms of knowledge, intelligence and wisdom, and women are forms of the love of those principles as existing with men.

188. IV. WITH MEN THERE IS AN ELEVATION OF THE MIND INTO SUPERIOR LIGHT, AND WITH WOMEN AN ELEVATION OF THE MIND INTO SUPERIOR HEAT; AND THE WOMAN IS MADE SENSIBLE OF THE DELIGHTS OF HER HEAT IN THE MAN'S LIGHT. By the light into which men are elevated, we mean intelligence and wisdom; because spiritual light, which proceeds from the sun of the spiritual world, which sun in its essence is love, acts in equality or unity with those two principles; and by the heat into which women are elevated, we mean conjugial love; because spiritual heat, which proceeds from the sun of that world, in its essence is love, and with women it is love conjoining itself with intelligence and wisdom in men; which love in its complex

is called conjugial love, and by determination becomes that love. It is called elevation into superior light and heat, because it is elevation into the light and heat which the angels of the superior heavens enjoy: it is also an actual elevation, as from a thick mist into pure air, and from an inferior region of the air into a superior, and from thence into ether; therefore elevation into superior light with men is elevation into superior intelligence, and thence into wisdom; in which also there are ascending degrees of elevation; but elevation into superior heat with women is an elevation into chaster and purer conjugial love, and continually towards the conjugial principle, which from creation lies concealed in their inmost principles. These elevations, considered in themselves, are openings of the mind; for the human mind is distinguished into regions, as the world is distinguished into regions as to the atmosphere; the lowest of which is the watery, the next above is the aerial, and still higher is the ethereal, above which there is also the highest: into similar regions the mind of man is elevated as it is opened, with men by wisdom, and with women by love truly conjugial.

189. We have said, that the woman is made sensible of the delights of her heat in the man's light; by which we mean that the woman is made sensible of the delights of her love in the man's wisdom, because wisdom is the receptacle; and wherever love finds such a receptacle corresponding to itself, it is in the enjoyment of its delights: but we do not mean, that heat with its light is delighted out of forms, but within them; and spiritual heat is delighted with spiritual light in their forms to a greater degree, because those forms by virtue of wisdom and love are vital, and thereby susceptible. This may be illustrated by what are called the sports of heat with light in the vegetable kingdom: out of the vegetable there is only a simple conjunction of heat and light, but within it there is a kind of sport of the one with the other; because there they are in forms or receptacles; for they pass through astonishing meandering ducts, and in the inmost principles therein they tend to use in bearing fruit, and also breathe forth their satisfactions far and wide into the atmosphere, which they fill with fragrance. The delight of spiritual heat with spiritual light is more vividly perceivable in human forms, in which spiritual heat is conjugial love, and spiritual light is wisdom.

190. V. WITH BOTH MEN AND WOMEN, THE STATES OF LIFE BEFORE MARRIAGE ARE DIFFERENT FROM WHAT THEY ARE AFTERWARDS. Before marriage, each sex passes through two states, one previous and the other subsequent to the inclination for marriage. The changes of both these states, and the consequent formations of minds, proceed in successive order according to their continual increase; but we have not leisure now to describe these changes, which are various and different in their

several subjects. The inclination to marriage, previous to marriage, are only imaginary in the mind, and become more and more sensible in the body; but the states thereof after marriage are states of conjunction and also of prolification, which, it is evident, differ from the forgoing states as effects differ from intentions.

191. VI. WITH MARRIED PARTNERS THE STATES OF LIFE AFTER MARRIAGE ARE CHANGED AND SUCCEED EACH OTHER ACCORDING TO THE CONJUNCTIONS OF THEIR MINDS BY CONJUGIAL LOVE. The reason why changes of the state and the successions thereof after marriage, with both the man and the wife, are according to conjugial love with each, and thus are either conjunctive or disjunctive of their minds, is, because conjugial love is not only various but also different with conjugial pairs: various, with those who love each other interiorly; for with such it has its intermissions, notwithstanding its being inwardly in its heat regular and permanent; but it is different with those who love each other only exteriorly; for with such its intermissions do not proceed from similar causes, but from alternate cold and heat. The true ground of these differences is, that with the latter the body is the principal agent, the ardour of which spreads itself around, and forcibly draws into communion with it the inferior principles of the mind; whereas, with the former, who love each other interiorly, the mind is the principal agent, and brings the body into communion with it. It appears as if love ascended from the body into the soul; because as soon as the body catches the allurement, it enters through the eyes, as through doors, into the mind, and thus through the sight, as through an outer court, into the thoughts, and instantly into the love: nevertheless it descends from the mind, and acts upon the inferior principles according to their orderly arrangement; therefore the lascivious mind acts lasciviously, and the chaste mind chastely; and the latter arranges the body, whereas the former is arranged by the body.

192. VII. MARRIAGE ALSO INDUCES OTHER FORMS IN THE SOULS AND MINDS OF MARRIED PARTNERS. That marriage has this effect cannot be observed in the natural world; because in this world souls and minds are encompassed with a material body, through which the mind rarely shines: the men (*homines*) also of modern times, more than the ancients, are taught from their infancy to assume feigned countenances, whereby they deeply conceal the affections of their minds; and this is the reason why the forms of minds are not known and distinguished according to their different quality, as existing before marriage and after it: nevertheless that the forms of souls and minds differ after marriage from what they were before, is very manifest from their appearance in the spiritual world; for they are then spirits and angels, who are minds and souls in a human form,

stripped of their outward coverings, which had been composed of watery and earthy elements, and of aerial vapors thence arising; and when these are cast off, the forms of the minds are plainly seen, such as they had been inwardly in their bodies; and then it is clearly perceived, that there is a difference in regard to those forms with those who live in marriage, and with those who do not. In general, married partners have an interior beauty of countenance, the man deriving from the wife the ruddy bloom of her love, and the wife from the man the fair splendor of his wisdom; for two married partners in the spiritual world are united as to their souls; and moreover there appears in each a human fulness. This is the case in heaven, because there are no marriages (*conjugia*) in any other place; beneath heaven there are only nuptial connections (*connubia*), which are alternately tied and loosed.

193. VIII. THE WOMAN IS ACTUALLY FORMED INTO A WIFE, ACCORDING TO THE DESCRIPTION IN THE BOOK OF CREATION. In this book it is said, that the woman was created out of the man's rib, and that the man said, when she was brought to him, "This is bone of my bones, and flesh of my flesh; and she shall be called Eve (*Ischah*), because she was taken out of man (*Isch*):" Gen. chap. ii. 21—23. A rib of the breast, in the Word, signifies, in the spiritual sense, natural truth. This is signified by the ribs which the bear carried between his teeth, Dan. vii. 5; for bears signify those who read the Word in the natural sense, and see truths therein without understanding: the man's breast signifies that essential and peculiar principle, which is distinguished from the breast of the woman: that this is wisdom, may be seen above, n. 187; for truth supports wisdom as the ribs do the breast. These things are signified, because the breast is that part of a man in which all his principles are as in their centre. From these considerations, it is evident, that the woman was created out of the man by a transfer of his peculiar wisdom, which is the same thing as to be created out of natural truth; and that the love thereof was transferred from the man into the woman, to the end that conjugial love might exist; and that this was done in order that the love of the wife and not self-love might be in the man: for the wife, in consequence of her innate disposition, cannot do otherwise than convert self-love, as existing with the man, into his love to herself; and I have been informed, that this is effected by virtue of the wife's love itself, neither the man nor the wife being conscious of it: hence, no man can possibly love his wife with true conjugial love, who from a principle of self-love is vain and conceited of his own intelligence. When this arcanum relating to the creation of the woman from the man, is understood, it may then be seen, that the woman in like manner is as it were created or formed from the man in marriage; and that this is effected by the wife, or rather through her by the Lord, who

imparts inclinations to women whereby they produce such an effect: for the wife receives into herself the image of a man, and thereby appropriates to herself his affections, as may be seen above, n. 183; and conjoins the man's internal will with her own, of which we shall treat presently; and also claims to herself the propagated forms (*propagines*) of his soul, of which also we shall speak elsewhere. From these considerations it is evident, that, according to the description in the book of Genesis, interiorly understood, a woman is formed into a wife by such things as she takes out of the husband and his breast, and implants in herself.

194. IX. THIS FORMATION IS EFFECTED ON THE PART OF THE WIFE BY SECRET MEANS; AND THIS IS MEANT BY THE WOMAN'S BEING CREATED WHILE THE MAN SLEPT. It is written in the book of Genesis, that Jehovah God caused a deep sleep to fall upon Adam, so that he slept; and that then he took one of his ribs, and builded it into a woman: chap. ii. 21, 22. That by the man's sleep and sleeping is signified his entire ignorance that the wife is formed and as it were created from him, appears from what was shewn in the preceding chapter, and also from the innate prudence and circumspection of wives, not to divulge anything concerning their love, or their assumption of the affections of the man's life, and thereby of the transfer of his wisdom into themselves. That this is effected on the part of the wife without the husband's knowledge, and while he is as it were sleeping, thus by secret means, is evident from what was explained above, n. 166—168; where also it is clearly shewn, that the prudence with which women are influenced herein, was implanted in them from creation, and consequently from their birth, for reasons of necessity, so that conjugial love, friendship, and confidence, and thereby the blessedness of dwelling together and a happy life, may be secured: wherefore for the right accomplishing of this, the man is enjoined to *leave his father and mother and to cleave to his wife*, Gen. ii. 24; Matt. xix. 4, 5. The father and mother, whom the man is to leave, in a spiritual sense signify his *proprium* of will and *proprium* of understanding; and the *proprium* of a man's (*homo*) will is to love himself, and the *proprium* of his understanding is to love his own wisdom; and to cleave to his wife signifies to devote himself to the love of his wife. Those two *propriums* are deadly evils to man, if they remain with him, and the love of those two *propriums* is changed into conjugial love, so far as a man cleaves to his wife, that is, so far as he receives her love; see above, n. 193, and elsewhere. To sleep signifies to be in ignorance and unconcern; a father and a mother signify the two *propriums* of a man (*homo*), the one of the will and the other of the understanding; and to cleave to, signifies to devote one's self to the love of any one, as might be abundantly confirmed from passages in other parts of the Word; but this would be foreign to our present subject.

195. X. THIS FORMATION ON THE PART OF THE WIFE IS EFFECTED BY THE CONJUNCTION OF HER OWN WILL WITH THE INTERNAL WILL OF THE MAN. That the man possesses rational and moral wisdom, and that the wife conjoins herself with those things which relate to his moral wisdom, may be seen above, n. 163—165. The things which relate to rational wisdom constitute the man's understanding, and those which relate to moral wisdom constitute his will. The wife conjoins herself with those things which constitute the man's will. It is the same, whether we say that the wife conjoins herself, or that she conjoins her will to the man's will; because she is born under the influence of the will, and consequently in all her actions acts from the will. The reason why it is said *with the man's internal will,* is, because the man's will resides in his understanding, and the man's intellectual principle is the inmost principle of the woman, according to what was observed above concerning the formation of the woman from the man, n. 32, and in other places. The man has also an external will; but this frequently takes its tincture from simulation and dissimulation. This will the wife notices; but she does not conjoin herself with it, except pretendedly or in the way of sport.

196. XI. THE END HEREIN IS, THAT THE WILL OF BOTH MAY BECOME ONE, AND THAT THUS BOTH MAY BECOME ONE MAN (*homo*): for whoever conjoins to himself the will of another, also conjoins to himself his understanding; for the understanding regarded in itself is merely the minister and servant of the will. That this is the case, appears evidently from the affection of love, which moves the understanding to think as it directs. Every affection of love belongs to the will; for what a man loves that he also wills. From these considerations it follows, that whoever conjoins to himself the will of a man conjoins to himself the whole man: hence it is implanted as a principle in the wife's love to unite the will of her husband to her own will; for hereby the wife becomes the husband's, and the husband the wife's; thus both become one man (*homo*).

197. XII. THIS FORMATION [ON THE PART OF THE WIFE] IS EFFECTED BY AN APPROPRIATION OF THE AFFECTIONS OF THE HUSBAND. This article agrees with the two preceding, because affections are of the will; for affections which are merely derivations of the love, form the will, and make and compose it; but these affections with men are in the understanding, whereas with women they are in the will.

198. XIII. THIS FORMATION [ON THE PART OF THE WIFE] IS EFFECTED BY A RECEPTION OF THE PROPAGATIONS OF THE SOUL OF THE HUSBAND, WITH THE DELIGHT ARISING FROM HER DESIRE TO BE THE LOVE OF HER HUSBAND'S WISDOM. This coincides with what was explained above, n. 172, 173, therefore any further explanation is needless. Conjugial delights

with wives arise solely from their desire to be one with their husbands, as good is one with truth in the spiritual marriage. That conjugial love descends from this spiritual marriage, has been proved above in the chapter which treats particularly on that subject; hence it may be seen, as in an image, that the wife conjoins the man to herself, as good conjoins truth to itself; and that the man reciprocally conjoins himself to the wife, according to the reception of her love in himself, as truth reciprocally conjoins itself to good, according to the reception of good in itself; and that thus the love of the wife forms itself by the wisdom of the husband, as good forms itself by truth; for truth is the form of good. From these considerations it is also evident, that conjugial delights with the wife originate principally in her desiring to be one with the husband, consequently to be the love of her husband's wisdom; for in such case she is made sensible of the delights of her own heat in the man's light, according to what was explained in Article IV., n. 188.

199. XIV. THUS A MAIDEN IS FORMED INTO A WIFE, AND A YOUTH INTO A HUSBAND. This flows as a consequence, from what has been said above in this and the foregoing chapter respecting the conjunction of married partners into one flesh. A maiden becomes or is made a wife, because in a wife there are principles taken out of the husband, and therefore supplemental, which were not previously in her as a maiden: a youth also becomes or is made a husband, because in a husband there are principles taken out of the wife, which exalt his receptibility of love and wisdom, and which were not previously in him as a youth: this is the case with those who are principled in love truly conjugial. That it is these who feel themselves a united man (*homo*), and as it were one flesh, may be seen in the preceding chapter, n. 178. From these considerations it is evident, that with females the maiden principle is changed into that of a wife, and with men the youthful principle is changed into that of a husband. That this is the case, was experimentally confirmed to me in the spiritual world, as follows: Some men asserted, that conjunction with a female before marriage is like conjunction with a wife after marriage.—On hearing this, the wives were very indignant, and said: "There is no likeness at all in the two cases. The difference between them is like that between what is fancied and what is real." Hereupon the men rejoined, "Are you not females as before?" To this the wives replied more sharply, "We are not females, but wives; you are in fancied and not in real love; you therefore talk fancifully." Then the men said, "If you are not females (*feminae*) still you are women (*mulieres*):" and they replied, "In the first states of marriage we were women (*mulieres*); but now we are wives."

200. XV. IN THE MARRIAGE OF ONE MAN WITH ONE

WIFE, BETWEEN WHOM THERE EXISTS LOVE TRULY CONJUGIAL, THE WIFE BECOMES MORE AND MORE A WIFE, AND THE HUSBAND MORE AND MORE A HUSBAND. That love truly conjugial more and more conjoins two into one man (*homo*), may be seen above n. 178, 179; and as a wife becomes a wife from and according to conjunction with the husband, and in like manner the husband with the wife; and as love truly conjugial endures to eternity, it follows, that the wife becomes more and more a wife, and the husband more and more a husband. The true reason of this is, because in the marriage of love truly conjugial, each married partner becomes continually a more interior man; for that love opens the interiors of their minds; and as these are opened, a man becomes more and more a man (*homo*): and to become more a man (*homo*) in the case of the wife is to become more a wife, and in the case of the husband to become more a husband. I have heard from the angels, that the wife becomes more and more a wife as the husband becomes more and more a husband, but not *vice versa ;* because it rarely, if ever, happens, that a chaste wife is wanting in love to her husband, but that the husband is wanting in a return of love to his wife ; and that this return of love is wanting because he has no elevation of wisdom, which alone receives the love of the wife: respecting this wisdom see above n. 130, 163—165. These things however they said in regard to marriages on earth.

201. XVI. THUS ALSO THEIR FORMS ARE SUCCESSIVELY PERFECTED AND ENNOBLED FROM WITHIN. The most perfect and noble human form results from the conjunction of two forms by marriage so as to become one form; thus from two fleshes becoming one flesh, according to creation. That in such case the man's mind is elevated into superior light, and the wife's into superior heat, and that then they germinate, and bear flowers and fruits, like trees in the spring, may be seen above, n. 188, 189. That from the nobleness of this form are produced noble fruits, which in the heavens are spiritual, and on earth natural, will be seen in the following article.

202. XVII. CHILDREN BORN OF PARENTS WHO ARE PRINCIPLED IN LOVE TRULY CONJUGIAL, DERIVE FROM THEM THE CONJUGIAL PRINCIPLE OF GOOD AND TRUTH, WHENCE THEY HAVE AN INCLINATION AND FACULTY, IF SONS, TO PERCEIVE THE THINGS RELATING TO WISDOM, AND IF DAUGHTERS, TO LOVE THOSE THINGS WHICH WISDOM TEACHES. That children derive from their parents inclination to such things as had been objects of the love and life of the parents, is a truth most perfectly agreeable to the testimony of history in general, and of experience in particular ; but that they do not derive or inherit from their parents the affections themselves, and thence the lives of those affections, but only inclinations and faculties thereto, has been shewn me by the wise in the spiritual world ; con-

cerning whom, see the two MEMORABLE RELATIONS above adduced. That children to the latest posterity, from innate inclinations, if they are not modified, are led into affections, thoughts, speech, and life, similar to those of their parents, is clearly manifest from the Jews, who at this day are like their fathers in Egypt, in the wilderness, in the land of Canaan, and in the Lord's time; and this likeness is not confined to their minds only, but extends to their countenances; for who does not know a Jew by his look? The case is the same with the descendants of others: from which considerations it may infallibly be concluded, that children are born with inclinations to such things as their parents were inclined to. But it is of the divine providence, lest thought and act should follow inclination, that perverse inclinations may be corrected; and also that a faculty has been implanted for this purpose, by virtue whereof parents and masters have the power of amending the morals of children, and children may afterwards, when they come to years of discretion, amend their own morals.

203. We have said that children derive from their parents the conjugial principle of good and truth, because this is implanted from creation in the soul of every one; for it is that which flows into every man from the Lord, and constitutes his human life. But this conjugial principle passes into derivatives from the soul even to the ultimates of the body. In its passage through these ultimates and those derivatives, it is changed by the man himself in various ways, and sometimes into the opposite, which is called the conjugial or connubial principle of what is evil and false. When this is the case, the mind is closed from beneath, and is sometimes twisted as a spire into the contrary; but with some that principle is not closed, but remains half-open above, and with some open. The latter and the former conjugial principle is the source of those inclinations which children inherit from their parents, a son after one manner, and a daughter after another. The reason why such inclinations are derived from the conjugial principle, is, because, as was proved above, n. 65, conjugial love is the foundation of all loves.

204. The reason why children born of parents who are principled in love truly conjugial, derive inclinations and faculties, if a son, to perceive the things relating to wisdom, and if a daughter, to love the things which wisdom teaches, is, because the conjugial principle of good and truth is implanted from creation in every soul, and also in the principles derived from the soul; for it was shewn above, that this conjugial principle fills the universe from first principles to last, and from a man even to a worm; and also that the faculty to open the inferior principles of the mind even to conjunction with its superior principles, which are in the light and heat of heaven, is also implanted in every man from creation: hence it is evident, that a superior suitableness and facility to conjoin good to truth, and truth to

good, and thus to grow wise, is inherited by those who are born from such a marriage; consequently they have a superior suitableness and facility also to embrace the things relating to the church and heaven; for that conjugial love is conjoined with these things, has been frequently shewn above. From these considerations, reason may clearly discover the end for which the Lord the Creator has provided, and still provides, marriages of love truly conjugial.

205. I have been informed by the angels, that those who lived in the most ancient times, live at this day in the heavens, in separate houses, families, and nations, as they had lived on earth, and that scarce any one of a house is wanting; and this because they were principled in love truly conjugial; and that hence their children inherited inclinations to the conjugial principle of good and truth, and were easily initiated into it more and more interiorly by education received from their parents, and afterwards as from themselves, when they become capable of judging for themselves, were introduced into it by the Lord.

206. XVIII. THE REASON OF THIS IS BECAUSE THE SOUL OF THE OFFSPRING IS FROM THE FATHER AND ITS CLOTHING FROM THE MOTHER. No wise man entertains a doubt that the soul is from the father; it is also manifestly conspicuous from minds, and likewise from faces which are the types of minds, in descendants from fathers of families in a regular series; for the father returns as in an image, if not in his sons, yet in his grandsons and great grandsons; and this because the soul constitutes a man's (*homo*) inmost principle, which may be covered and concealed by the offspring nearest in descent, but nevertheless it comes forth and manifests itself in the more remote issue. That the soul is from the father, and its clothing from the mother, may be illustrated by analogies in the vegetable kingdom. In this kingdom the earth or ground is the common mother, which in itself, as in a womb, receives and clothes seeds; yea, as it were conceives, bears, brings forth, and educates them, as a mother her offspring from the father.

* * * * * * * *

207. To the above I will add TWO MEMORABLE RELATIONS. FIRST. After some time I was looking towards the city Athens, of which mention was made in a former memorable relation, and I heard thence an unusual clamor. There was in it something of laughter, and in the laughter something of indignation, and in the indignation something of sadness: still however the clamor was not thereby dissonant, but consonant: because one tone was not together with the other, but one was within another. In the spiritual world a variety and commixture of affections is distinctly perceived in sound. I inquired from afar what was the matter. They said, " A messenger is arrived from the place where the new comers from the Christian world first appear,

bringing information of what he has heard there from three persons, that in the world whence they came they had believed with the generality, that the blessed and happy after death enjoy absolute rest from labor; and since administrations, offices, and employments, are labor, they enjoy rest from these: and as those three persons are now conducted hither by our emissary, and are at the gate waiting for admission, a clamor was made, and it was deliberately resolved they should not be introduced into the Palladium on Parnassus, as the former were, but into the great auditory, to communicate the news they brought from the Christian world: accordingly some deputies have been sent to introduce them in form." Being at that time myself in the spirit, and distances with spirits being according to the states of their affections, and having at that time a desire to see and hear them, I seemed to myself to be present there, and saw them introduced, and heard what they said. The seniors or wiser part of the audience sat at the sides of the auditory, and the rest in the midst; and before these was an elevated piece of ground. Hither the three strangers, with the messenger, were formally conducted by attendants, through the middle of the auditory. When silence was obtained, they were addressed by a kind of president of the assembly, and asked, "WHAT NEWS FROM THE EARTH?" They replied, "There is a variety of news: but pray tell us what information you want." The president answered, "WHAT NEWS IS THERE FROM THE EARTH CONCERNING OUR WORLD AND HEAVEN?" They replied, "When we first came into this world, we were informed, that here and in heaven there are administrations, offices, employments, trades, studies, relating to all sciences and professions, together with wonderful mechanical arts; and yet we believed that after our removal or translation from the natural world into the spiritual, we should enter upon an eternal rest from labor; and what are employments but labor?" To this the president replied, "By eternal rest from labor did you understand eternal inactivity, in which you should be continually sitting and laying down, with your bosoms and mouths open, attracting and inhaling delights and joys?" "We conceived something of this sort," said the three strangers smiling courteously. Then they were asked, "What connection have joys and delights and the happiness thence resulting, with a state of inactivity?" By inactivity the mind is enfeebled and contracted, instead of being strengthened and expanded; or in other words, the man is reduced to a state of death, instead of being quickened into life. Suppose a person to sit still in the most complete inactivity, with his hands hanging down, his eyes fixed on the ground, and withdrawn from all other objects, and suppose him at the same time to be encompassed by an atmosphere of gladness, would not a lethargy seize both his head and body, and the vital expansion of his countenance would be contracted, and at length with relaxed fibres he would nod and totter, till he fell to the earth? What is it that keeps the whole bodily system in its due expansion and tension, but the tension of the mind? and whence comes the tension of the mind but from administrations and employments, while the discharge of them is attended with delight? I will therefore tell you some news from heaven: in that world there are administrations, offices, judicial proceedings both in greater and lesser cases, also mechanical arts and employments." The strangers on hearing of judicial proceedings in heaven, said, "To what purpose are such proceedings? are not all in heaven inspired and led by God, and in consequence thereof taught what is just and right? what need then is there of judges?" The president replied, "In this world we are instructed and learn what is good and true, also what is just and equitable, as in the natural world; and these things we learn, not immediately from God, but mediately through others; and every angel, like every man, thinks what is true, and does what is good, as from himself; and this, according to the state of the angel, is mixed and not pure: and moreover, there are among the angels some of a simple and some of a wise character; and it is the part of the wise to judge, when the simple, from their simplicity and ignorance, are doubtful about what is just, or through mistake wander from it. But as you are as yet strangers in this world, if it be agreeable to you to accompany me into our city, we will shew you all that is contained therein." Then they quitted the auditory, and some of the elders also accompanied them. They were introduced into a large library, which was divided into classes arranged according to the sciences. The three strangers, on seeing so many books, were astonished, and said, "There are books also in this world! whence do you procure parchment and paper, pens and ink?" The elders replied, "We perceive that in the former world you believed that this world is empty and void, because it is spiritual; and you believed so because you had conceived an idea of what is spiritual abstracted from what is material; and that which is so abstracted appeared to you as nothingness, thus as empty and void; when nevertheless in this world there is a fulness of all things. Here all things are SUBSTANTIAL and not material: and material things derive their origin from things substantial. We who live here are spiritual men, because we are substantial and not material; hence in this world we have all things that are in the natural world, in their perfection, even books and writings, and many other things which are not in the natural world." The three strangers, when they heard talk of things SUBSTANTIAL, conceived that it must be so, as well because they saw written books, as because they heard it asserted that material things originate in substantial. For their further confirmation in these particulars, they were conducted to the houses of the scribes, who were copying the writings of the wise ones of the city; and they inspected the writings, and wondered to see them so beautiful and elegant. After this they were conducted to the museums, schools, and colleges, and to the places where they had their literary sports. Some of these were called the sports of the Heliconides, some of the Parnassides, some of the Athænides, and some the sports of the maidens of the fountain. They were told that the latter were so called, because maidens signify affections of the sciences, and every one has intelligence according to his affection for the sciences: the sports so called were spiritual exercises and trials of skill. Afterwards they were led about the city to see the rulers, administrators, and their officers, by whom they were conducted to see several wonderful works executed in a spiritual manner by the artificers. When they had taken a view of all these things, the president again conversed with them about the eternal rest from labor, into which the blessed and happy enter after death, and said, "Eternal rest is not inactivity; for inactivity occasions a thorough languor, dulness, stupor, and drowsiness of the mind and thence of the body; and these things are death and not life, still less eternal life which the angels of heaven enjoy; therefore eternal rest is that which dispels such mischiefs, and causes a man to live; and it is this which elevates the mind; consequently it is by some employment and work that the mind is excited, vivified, and delighted; which is affected according to the use, from which, in which, and to which the mind is actuated. Hence the universal heaven is regarded by the Lord as containing uses; and every angel is an angel according to use; the delight of use carries him along, as a prosperous gale a ship, and causes him to be in eternal peace, and the rest of peace. This is the meaning of eternal rest from labor. That an angel is alive according as his mind is directed to use, is evident from the consideration, that every one has conjugial love with its energy, ability and delights, according as he devotes himself to the genuine use in which he is." When the three strangers were convinced that eternal rest is not inactivity, but the delight of some useful employment, there came some maidens with pieces of embroidery and net-work, wrought with their own hands, which they presented to them. When the novitiate spirits were gone, the maidens sang an ode, wherein they expressed with angelic melody the affection of useful works with the pleasures attending it.

208. THE SECOND MEMORABLE RELATION. While I was meditating on the arcana of conjugial love stored up with wives, there again appeared the GOLDEN SHOWER described above; and I recollected that it fell over a hall in the east where there lived three conjugial loves, that is, three married pairs, who loved each other tenderly. On seeing it, and as if invited by the sweetness of meditating on that love, I hastened towards it, and as I approached, the shower from golden became purple, afterwards

scarlet, and when I came near, it was sparkling like dew. I knocked at the door, and when it was opened, I said to the attendant, "Tell the husbands that the person who before came with an angel, is come again, and begs the favor of being admitted into their company." Presently the attendant returned with a message of assent from the husbands, and I entered. The three husbands with their wives were together in an open gallery, and as I paid my respects to them, they returned the compliment. I then asked the wives, Whether the white dove in the window afterwards appeared? They said, "Yes; and to-day also; and it likewise expanded its wings; from which we concluded that you were near at hand, and were desirous of information respecting one other arcanum concerning conjugial love." I inquired, "Why do you say *one* arcanum; when I came here to learn several?" They replied, "They are arcana, and some of them transcend your wisdom to such a degree, that the understanding of your thought cannot comprehend them. You glory over us on account of your wisdom; but we do not glory over you on account of ours; and yet ours is eminently distinguished above yours, because it enters your inclinations and affections, and sees, perceives, and is sensible of them. You know nothing at all of the inclinations and affections of your own love; and yet these are the principles from and according to which your understanding thinks, consequently from and according to which you are wise; and yet wives are so well acquainted with those principles in their husbands, that they see them in their faces, and hear them from the tone of their voices in conversation, yea, they feel them on their breasts, arms, and cheeks: but we, from the zeal of our love for your happiness, and at the same time for our own, pretend not to know them; and yet we govern them so prudently, that wherever the fancy, good pleasure, and will of our husbands lead, we follow by permitting and suffering it; only bending its direction when it is possible, but in no case forcing it." I asked, "Whence have you this wisdom?" They replied, "It is implanted in us from creation and consequently from birth. Our husbands compare it to instinct; but we say that it is of the divine providence, in order that the men may be rendered happy by their wives. We have heard from our husbands, that the Lord wills that the husband (*homo masculus*) should act freely according to reason; and that on this account the Lord himself from within governs his freedom, so far as respects the inclinations and affections, and governs it from without by means of his wife; and that thus he forms a man with his wife into an angel of heaven; and moreover love changes its essence, and does not become conjugial love, if it be compelled. But we will be more explicit on this subject: we are moved thereto, that is, to prudence in governing the inclinations and affections of our husbands, so that they may seem to themselves to act freely according-ing to their reason, from this motive, because we a⁙ ⁙ ⁙ght. ⁙ with their love; and we love nothing more than that t⁙⁙/ should be delighted with our delights, which, in case of their being lightly esteemed by our husbands, become insipid also to us." Having said this, one of the wives entered her chamber, and on her return said, "My dove still flutters its wings, which is a sign that we may make further disclosures." They then said, "We have observed various changes of the inclinations and affections of the men; as that they grow cold towards their wives, while the husbands entertain vain thoughts against the Lord and the church; that they grow cold while they are conceited of their own intelligence; that they grow cold while they regard with desire the wives of others; that they grow cold while their love is adverted to by their wives; not to mention other occasions; and that there are various degrees of their coldness: this we discover from a withdrawal of the sense from their eyes, ears, and bodies, on the presence of our senses. From these few observations you may see, that we know better than the men whether it be well or ill with them; if they are cold towards their wives, it is ill with them, but if they are warm towards them, it is well; therefore wives are continually devising means whereby the men may become warm and not cold towards them; and these means they devise with a sagacity inscrutable to the men." As they said this, the dove was heard to make a sort of moaning; and immediately the wives said, "This is a token to us that we have a wish to communicate greater arcana, but that it is not allowable: probably you will reveal to the men what you have heard." I replied, "I intend to do so: what harm can come from it?" Hereupon the wives talked together on the subject, and then said, "Reveal it, if you like. We are well aware of the power of persuasion which wives possess. They will say to their husbands, 'The man is not in earnest; he tells idle tales: he is but joking from appearances, and from strange fancies usual with men. Do not believe him, but believe us: we know that you are loves, and we obediences.' Therefore you may reveal it if you like; but still the husbands will place no dependence on what comes from your lips, but on that which comes from the lips of their wives which they kiss."

UNIVERSALS RESPECTING MARRIAGES.

209. THERE are so many things relating to marriages that, if particularly treated of, they would swell this little work into a large volume: for we might treat particularly of the similitude

and dissimilitude subsisting among married partners; of the elevation of natural conjugial love into spiritual, and of their conjunction; of the increase of the one and the decrease of the other; of the varieties and diversities of each; of the intelligence of wives; of the universal conjugial sphere proceeding from heaven, and of its opposite from hell, and of their influx and reception; with many other particulars, which, if individually enlarged upon, would render this work so bulky as to tire the reader. For this reason, and to avoid useless prolixity, we will condense these particulars into UNIVERSALS RESPECTING MARRIAGES. But these, like the foregoing subjects, must be considered distinctly as arranged under the following articles: I. *The sense proper to conjugial love is the sense of touch.* II. *With those who are in love truly conjugial, the faculty of growing wise gradually increases; but with those who are not it decreases.* III. *With those who are in love truly conjugial, the happiness of dwelling together increases; but with those who are not it decreases.* IV. *With those who are in love truly conjugial, conjunction of minds increases, and therewith friendship; but with those who are not they both decrease.* V. *Those who are in love truly conjugial, continually desire to be one man* (homo); *but those who are not desire to be two.* VI. *Those who are in love truly conjugial, in marriage have respect to what is eternal; but with those who are not the case is reversed.* VII. *Conjugial love resides with chaste wives; but still their love depends on the husbands.* VIII. *Wives love the bonds of marriage if the men do.* IX. *The intelligence of women is in itself modest, elegant, pacific, yielding, soft, tender; but the intelligence of men is in itself grave, harsh, hard, daring, fond of licentiousness.* X. *Wives are in no excitation as men are; but they have a state of preparation for reception.* XI. *Men have abundant store according to the love of propagating the truths of their wisdom, and to the love of doing uses.* XII. *Determination is in the good pleasure of the husband.* XIII. *The conjugial sphere flows from the Lord through heaven into everything in the universe, even to its ultimates.* XIV. *This sphere is received by the female sex, and through that is transferred into the male sex; and not vice versa.* XV. *Where there is love truly conjugial, this sphere is received by the wife, and only through her by the husband.* XVI. *Where there is love not conjugial, this sphere is received indeed by the wife, but not by the husband through her.* XVII. *Love truly conjugial may exist with one of the married partners, and not at the same time with the other.* XVIII. *There are various similitudes and dissimilitudes, both internal and external, with married partners.* XIX. *Various similitudes can be conjoined, but not with dissimilitudes.* XX. *The Lord provides similitudes for those who desire love truly conjugial; and if not on earth, he yet provides them in heaven.* XXI. *A man* (homo) *according to the deficiency and loss of conjugial love, approaches to the nature of a beast.* We proceed to the explanation of each article.

210. I. THE SENSE PROPER TO CONJUGIAL LOVE IS THE SENSE OF TOUCH. Every love has its own proper sense. The love of seeing, grounded in the love of understanding, has the sense of seeing; and the gratifications proper to it are the various kinds of symmetry and beauty. The love of hearing grounded in the love of hearkening to and obeying, has the sense of hearing; and the gratifications proper to it are the various kinds of harmony. The love of knowing these things which float about in the air, grounded in the love of perceiving, is the sense of smelling; and the gratifications proper to it are the various kinds of fragrance. The love of self-nourishment, grounded in the love of imbibing goods, is the sense of tasting; and the delights proper to it are the various kinds of delicate foods. The love of knowing objects, grounded in the love of circumspection and self-preservation, is the sense of touching, and the gratifications proper to it are the various kinds of titillation. The reason why the love of conjunction with a partner, grounded in the love of uniting good and truth, has the sense of touch proper to it, is, because this sense is common to all the senses, and hence borrows from them somewhat of support and nourishment. That this love brings all the above-mentioned senses into communion with it, and appropriates their gratification, is well known. That the sense of touch is devoted to conjugial love, and is proper to it, is evident from all its sports, and from the exaltation of its subtleties to the highest degree of what is exquisite. But the further consideration of this subject we leave to lovers.

211. II. WITH THOSE WHO ARE IN LOVE TRULY CONJUGIAL, THE FACULTY OF GROWING WISE INCREASES; BUT WITH THOSE WHO ARE NOT IT DECREASES. The faculty of growing wise increases with those who are in love truly conjugial, because this love appertains to married partners on account of wisdom, and according to it, as has been fully proved in the preceding sections; also, because the sense of that love is the touch, which is common to all the senses, and also is full of delights; in consequence of which it opens the interiors of the mind, as it opens the interiors of the senses, and therewith the organical principles of the whole body. Hence it follows, that those who are principled in that love, prefer nothing to growing wise; for a man grows wise in proportion as the interiors of his mind are opened; because by such opening, the thoughts of the understanding are elevated into superior light, and the affections of the will into superior heat; and superior light is wisdom, and superior heat is the love thereof. Spiritual delights conjoined to natural delights, which are the portion of those who are in love truly conjugial, constitute loveliness, and thence the faculty of

growing wise. Hence it is that the angels have conjugial love according to wisdom; and the increase of that love and at the same time of its delights is according to the increase of wisdom; and spiritual offspring, which are produced from their marriages, are such things as are of wisdom from the father, and of love from the mother, which they love from a spiritual *storge;* which love unites with their conjugial love, and continually elevates it, and joins them together.

212. The contrary happens with those who are not in any conjugial love, from not having any love of wisdom. These enter the marriage state with no other end in view than lasciviousness, in which is also the love of growing insane; for every end considered in itself is a love, and lasciviousness in its spiritual origin is insanity. By insanity we mean a delirium in the mind occasioned by false principles; and an eminent degree of delirium is occasioned by truths which are falsified until they are believed to be wisdom. That such persons are opposed to conjugial love, is confirmed or evinced by manifest proof in the spiritual world; where, on perceiving the first scent of conjugial love, they fly into caverns, and shut the doors; and if these are opened, they rave like madmen in the world.

213. III. WITH THOSE WHO ARE IN LOVE TRULY CONJUGIAL, THE HAPPINESS OF DWELLING TOGETHER INCREASES; BUT WITH THOSE WHO ARE NOT IT DECREASES. The happiness of dwelling together increases with those who are in love truly conjugial, because they mutually love each other with every sense. The wife sees nothing more lovely than the husband, and the husband nothing more lovely than the wife; neither do they hear, smell, or touch any thing more lovely; hence the happiness they enjoy of living together in the same house, chamber, and bed. That this is the case, you that are husbands can assure yourselves from the first delights of marriage, which are in their fulness; because at that time the wife is the only one of the sex that is loved. That the reverse is the case with those who are not in conjugial love, is well known.

214. IV. WITH THOSE WHO ARE IN LOVE TRULY CONJUGIAL CONJUNCTION OF MINDS INCREASES, AND THEREWITH FRIENDSHIP; BUT WITH THOSE WHO ARE NOT, THEY BOTH DECREASE. That conjunction of minds increases with those who are in love truly conjugial, was proved in the chapter ON THE CONJUNCTION OF SOULS AND MINDS BY MARRIAGE, WHICH IS MEANT BY THE LORD'S WORDS, THAT THEY ARE NO LONGER TWO BUT ONE FLESH, see n. 156*—191. But that conjunction increases as friendship unites with love; because friendship is as it were the face and also the raiment of that love; for it not only joins itself to love as raiment, but also conjoins itself thereto as a face. Love preceding friendship is like the love of the sex, which, after the marriage vow, takes its leave and departs; whereas love conjoined to

friendship after the marriage vow, remains and is strengthened it likewise enters more interiorly into the breast, friendship introducing it, and making it truly conjugial. In this case the love makes its friendship also conjugial, which differs greatly from the friendship of every other love; for it is full. That the case is reversed with those who are not principled in conjugial love, is well known. With these, the first friendship, which was insinuated during the time of courtship, and afterwards during the period immediately succeeding marriage, recedes more and more from the interiors of the mind, and thence successively at length retires to the cuticles; and with those who think of separation, it entirely departs; but with those who do not think of separation, love remains in the externals, yet it is cold in the internals.

215. V. THOSE WHO ARE IN LOVE TRULY CONJUGIAL, CONTINUALLY DESIRE TO BE ONE MAN, BUT THOSE WHO ARE NOT IN CONJUGIAL LOVE, DESIRE TO BE TWO. Conjugial love essentially consists in the desire of two to become one; that is, in their desire that two lives may become one life. This desire is the perpetual *conatus* of that love, from which flow all its effects. That *conatus* is the very essence of motion, and that desire is the living *conatus* appertaining to man, is confirmed by the researches of philosophers, and is also evident to such as take a view of the subject from refined reason. Hence it follows, that those who are in love truly conjugial, continually endeavour, that is, desire to be one man. That the contrary is the case with those who are not in conjugial love, they themselves very well know; for as they continually think themselves two from the disunion of their souls and minds, so they do not comprehend what is meant by the Lord's words, "*They are no longer two, but one flesh:*" Matt. xix. 6.

216. VI. THOSE WHO ARE IN LOVE TRULY CONJUGIAL, IN MARRIAGE HAVE RESPECT TO WHAT IS ETERNAL; BUT WITH THOSE WHO ARE NOT THE CASE IS REVERSED. Those who are in love truly conjugial have respect to what is eternal, because in that love there is eternity; and its eternity is grounded in this, that love with the wife, and wisdom with the husband, increases to eternity; and in the increase or progression the married partners enter more and more interiorly into the blessedness of heaven, which their wisdom and its love have stored up together in themselves: if therefore the idea of what is eternal were to be plucked away, or by any casualty to escape from their minds, it would be as if they were cast down from heaven. What is the state of conjugial partners in heaven, when the idea of what is eternal falls out of their minds, and the idea of what is temporal takes its place, was made evident to me from the following case. On a certain time, permission having been granted for the purpose, two married partners were present with me from heaven: and at that instant the idea of what is eternal respecting marriage

was taken away from them by an idle disorderly spirit who was talking with craft and subtlety. Hereupon they began to bewail themselves, saying, that they could not live any longer, and that they felt such misery as they had never felt before. When this was perceived by their co-angels in heaven, the disorderly spirit was removed and cast down; whereupon the idea of what is eternal instantly returned to them, and they were gladdened in heart, and most tenderly embraced each other. Besides this, I have heard two married partners, who at one instant entertained an idea of what is eternal respecting their marriage, and the next an idea of what is temporal. This arose from their being internally dissimilar. When they were in the idea of what is eternal, they were mutually glad; but when in the idea of what is temporal, they said, "There is no longer any marriage between us;" and the wife, "I am no longer a wife, but a concubine;" and the husband, "I am no longer a husband, but an adulterer;" wherefore while their internal dissimilitude was open to them, the man left the woman, and the woman the man: afterwards, however, as each had an idea of what is eternal respecting marriage, they were consociated with suitable partners. From these instances it may be clearly seen, that those who are in love truly conjugial have respect to what is eternal; and if this idea escapes from their inmost thoughts, they are disunited as to conjugial love, though not at the same time as to friendship; for friendship dwells in externals, but conjugial love in internals. The case is similar with marriages on earth, where married partners who tenderly love each other, think of what is eternal respecting the marriage-covenant, and not at all of its termination by death; and if this should enter their thoughts, they are grieved; nevertheless they are cherished again by hope from the thought of its continuance after their decease.

216.* VII. CONJUGIAL LOVE RESIDES WITH CHASTE WIVES; BUT STILL THEIR LOVE DEPENDS ON THE HUSBANDS. The reason of this is, because wives are born loves; and hence it is innate to them to desire to be one with their husbands and from this thought of their will they continually feed their love; wherefore to recede from the *conatus* of uniting themselves to their husbands, would be to recede from themselves: it is otherwise with the husbands, who are not born loves, but recipients of that love from their wives; and on this account, so far as they receive it, so far the wives enter with their love; but so far as they do not receive it, so far the wives stand aloof with their love, and wait in expectation. This is the case with chaste wives; but it is otherwise with the unchaste. From these considerations it is evident, that conjugial love resides with the wives, but that their love depends on the husbands.

217. VIII. WIVES LOVE THE BONDS OF MARRIAGE IF THE MEN DO. This follows from what was said in the foregoing

article: moreover, wives naturally desire to be, and to be called wives; this being to them a name of respect and honor; they therefore love the bonds of marriage. And as chaste wives desire, not in name only, but in reality, to be wives, and this is effected by a closer and closer binding with their husbands, therefore they love the bonds of marriage as establishing the marriage-covenant, and this so much the more as they are loved again by their husbands, or what is tantamount, as the men love those bonds.

218. IX. THE INTELLIGENCE OF WOMEN IS IN ITSELF MODEST, ELEGANT, PACIFIC, YIELDING, SOFT, TENDER; BUT THE INTELLIGENCE OF MEN IN ITSELF IS GRAVE, HARSH, HARD, DARING, FOND OF LICENTIOUSNESS. That such is the characteristic distinction of the woman and the man, is very evident from the body, the face, the tone of voice, the conversation, the gesture, and the manners of each: from the BODY, in that there is more hardness in the skin and flesh of men, and more softness in that of women; from the FACE, in that it is harder, more fixed, harsher, of darker complexion, also bearded, thus less beautiful in men; whereas in women it is softer, more yielding, more tender, of fairer complexion, and thence more beautiful; from the TONE OF VOICE, in that it is deeper with men, and sweeter with women; from the CONVERSATION in that with men it is given to licentiousness and daring, but with women it is modest and pacific; from the GESTURE, in that with men it is stronger and firmer, whereas with women it is more weak and feeble; from the MANNERS, in that with men they are more unrestrained, but with women more elegant. How far from the very cradle the genius of men differs from that of women, was discovered to me clearly from seeing a number of boys and girls met together. I saw them at times through a window in the street of a great city, where more than twenty assembled every day. The boys, agreeably to the disposition born with them, in their pastimes were tumultuous, vociferous, apt to fight, to strike, and to throw stones at each other; whereas the girls sat peaceably at the doors of the houses, some playing with little children, some dressing dolls or working on bits of linen, some kissing each other; and to my surprise, they still looked with satisfaction at the boys whose pastimes were so different from their own. Hence I could see plainly, that a man by birth is understanding, and a woman, love; and also the quality of understanding and of love in their principles; and thereby what would be the quality of a man's understanding without conjuction with female love, and afterwards with conjugial love.

219. X. WIVES ARE IN NO EXCITATION AS MEN ARE; BUT THEY HAVE A STATE OF PREPARATION FOR RECEPTION. That men have semination and consequent excitation, and that women have not the latter because they have not the former, is evident; but that women have a state of preparation for reception, and

thus for conception, I relate from what has been told me; but what the nature and quality of this state with the women is, I am not allowed to describe; besides, it is known to them alone: but whether their love, while they are in that state, is in the enjoyment of its delight, or in what is undelightful, as some say, they have not made known. This only is generally known, that it is not allowed the husband to say to the wife, that he is able and not willing: for thereby the state of reception is greatly hurt, which is prepared according to the state of the husband's ability.

220. XI. MEN HAVE ABUNDANT STORE ACCORDING TO THE LOVE OF PROPAGATING THE TRUTHS OF WISDOM, AND TO THE LOVE OF DOING USES. This position is one of the arcana which were known to the ancients, and which are now lost. The ancients knew that everything which was done in the body is from a spiritual origin: as that from the will, which in itself is spiritual, actions flow; that from the thought, which also is spiritual, speech flows; also that natural sight is grounded in spiritual sight, which is that of the understanding; natural hearing in spiritual hearing, which is attention of the understanding and at the same time accommodation of the will; and natural smelling in spiritual smelling, which is perception; and so forth: in like manner they saw that semination with men is from a spiritual origin. That it is from the truths of which the understanding consists, they concluded from several deductions both of reason and of experience; and they asserted, that nothing is received by males from the spiritual marriage, which is that of good and truth, and which flows into everything in the universe, but truth, and whatever has relation to truth; and that this in its progress into the body is formed into seed; and that hence it is, that seeds spiritually understoood are truths. As to formation, they asserted, that the masculine soul, as being intellectual, is thus truth; for the intellectual principle is nothing else; wherefore while the soul descends, truth also descends: that this is effected by this circumstance, that the soul, which is the inmost principle of every man (*homo*) and every animal, and which in its essence is spiritual, from an implanted tendency to self-propagation, follows in the descent, and is desirous to procreate itself; and that when this is the case, the entire soul forms itself, and clothes itself, and becomes seed: and that this may be done thousands of times, because the soul is a spiritual substance, which is not a subject of extension but of impletion, and from which no part can be taken away, but the whole may be produced, without any loss thereof: hence it is, that it is as fully present in the smallest receptacles, which are seeds, as in its greatest receptacle, the body. Since therefore the principle of truth in the soul is the origin of seed, it follows, that men have abundant store according to their love of propagating the truths of their wisdom: it is also according to their love of doing uses;

because uses are the goods which truths produce. In the world also it is well known to some, that the industrious have abundant store, but not the idle. I inquired, "How is a feminine principle produced from a male soul?" and I received for answer, that it was from intellectual good; because this in its essence is truth: for the intellect can think that this is good, thus that it is true that it is good. It is otherwise with the will: this does not think what is good and true, but loves and does it. Therefore in the Word sons signify truths, and daughters goods, as may be seen above, n. 120; and seed signifies truth, as may be seen in the APOCALYPSE REVEALED, n. 565.

221. XII. DETERMINATION IS IN THE GOOD PLEASURE OF THE HUSBAND. This is, because with men there is the abundant store above mentioned; and this varies with them according to the states of their minds and bodies: for the understanding is not so constant in its thoughts as the will is in its affections; since it is sometimes carried upwards, sometimes downwards; at one time it is in a serene and clear state in another in a turbulent and obscure one; sometimes it is employed on agreeable objects, sometimes on disagreeable; and as the mind, while it acts, is also in the body, it follows, that the body has similar states: hence the husband at times recedes from conjugial love, and at times accedes to it, and the abundant store is removed in the one state, and restored in the other. These are the reasons why determination at all times is to be left to the good pleasure of the husband: hence also it is that wives, from a wisdom implanted in them, never offer any admonition on such subjects.

222. XIII. THE CONJUGIAL SPHERE FLOWS FROM THE LORD THROUGH HEAVEN INTO EVERYTHING IN THE UNIVERSE, EVEN TO ITS ULTIMATES. That love and wisdom, or, what is the same, good and truth, proceed from the Lord, was shewn above in a chapter on the subject. Those two principles in a marriage proceed continually from the Lord, because they are himself, and from him are all things; and the things which proceed from him fill the universe, for unless this were the case, nothing which exists would subsist. There are several spheres which proceed from him; the sphere of the conservation of the created universe; the sphere of the defence of good and truth against evil and false, the sphere of reformation and regeneration, the sphere of innocence and peace, the sphere of mercy and grace, with several others; but the universal of all is the conjugial sphere, because this also is the sphere of propagation, and thus the supereminent sphere of the conservation of the created universe by successive generations. That this conjugial sphere fills the universe, and pervades all things from first to last, is evident from what has been shewn above, that there are marriages in the heavens, and the most perfect in the third or supreme heaven: and that besides taking place with men it takes place also with

all the subjects of the animal kingdom in the earth, even down to worms; and moreover with all the subjects of the vegetable kingdom, from olives and palms even to the smallest grasses. That this sphere is more universal than the sphere of heat and light, which proceeds from the sun of our world, may appear reasonable from this consideration, that it operates also in the absence of the sun's heat, as in winter, and in the absence of its light, as in the night, especially with men (*homines*). The reason why it so operates is, because it was from the sun of the angelic heaven, and thence there is a constant equation of heat and light, that is, a conjunction of good and truth; for it is in a continual spring. The changes of good and truth, or of its heat and light, are not variations thereof, like the variations on earth arising from changes of the heat and light proceeding from the natural sun; but they arise from the recipient subjects.

223. XIV. THIS SPHERE IS RECEIVED BY THE FEMALE SEX, AND THROUGH THAT IS TRANSFERRED TO THE MALE SEX. There is not any conjugial love appertaining to the male sex, but it appertains solely to the female sex, and from this sex is transferred to the male: this I have seen evidenced by experience; concerning which see above, n. 161. A further proof of it is supplied from this consideration, that the male form is the intellectual form, and the female the voluntary; and the intellectual form cannot grow warm with conjugial heat from itself, but from the conjunctive heat of some one, in whom it was implanted from creation; consequently it cannot receive that love except by the voluntary form of the woman adjoined to itself; because this also is a form of love. This same position might be further confirmed by the marriage of good and truth; and, to the natural man, by the marriage of the heart and lungs; for the heart corresponds to love, and the lungs to understanding; but as the generality of mankind are deficient in the knowledge of these subjects, confirmation thereby would tend rather to obscure than to illustrate. It is in consequence of the transferrence of this sphere from the female sex into the male, that the mind is also inflamed solely from thinking about the sex; that hence also comes propagative formation and thereby excitation, follows of course; for unless heat is united to light on earth, nothing flourishes and is excited to cause fructification there.

224. XV. WHERE THERE IS LOVE TRULY CONJUGIAL, THIS SPHERE IS RECEIVED BY THE WIFE, AND ONLY THROUGH HER BY THE HUSBAND. That this sphere, with those who are in love truly conjugial, is received by the husband only through the wife, is at this day an arcanum; and yet in itself it is not an arcanum, because the bridegroom and new-married husband may know this; is he not affected conjugially by whatever proceeds from the bride and new-married wife, but not at that time by what proceeds from others of the sex? The case is the same with

those who live together in love truly conjugial. And since everyone, both man and woman, is encompassed by his own sphere of life, densely on the breast, and less densely on the back, it is manifest whence it is that husbands who are very fond of their wives, turn themselves to them, and in the day-time regard them with complacency; and on the other hand, why those who do not love their wives, turn themselves away from them, and in the day-time regard them with aversion. By the reception of the conjugial sphere by the husband only through the wife, love truly conjugial is known and distinguished from that which is spurious, false, and cold.

225. XVI. WHERE THERE IS LOVE NOT CONJUGIAL, THIS SPHERE IS RECEIVED INDEED BY THE WIFE, BUT NOT BY THE HUSBAND THROUGH HER. This conjugial sphere flowing into the universe is in its origin divine; in its progress in heaven with the angels it is celestial and spiritual; with men it is natural, with beasts and birds animal, with worms merely corporeal, with vegetables it is void of life; and moreover in all its subjects it is varied according to their forms. Now as this sphere is received immediately by the female sex, and mediately by the male, and as it is received according to forms, it follows, that this sphere, which in its origin is holy, may in the subjects be turned into what is not holy, yea may be even inverted into what is opposite. The sphere opposite to it is called meretricious with such women, and adulterous with such men; and as such men and women are in hell, this sphere is from thence: but of this sphere there is also much variety, and hence there are several species of it; and such a species is attracted and appropriated by a man (*vir*) as is agreeable to him, and as is conformable and correspondent with his peculiar temper and disposition. From these considerations it may appear, that the man who does not love his wife, receives that sphere from some other source than from his wife; nevertheless it is a fact, that it is also inspired by the wife, but without the husband's knowing it, and while he grows warm.

226. XVII. LOVE TRULY CONJUGIAL MAY EXIST WITH ONE OF THE MARRIED PARTNERS, AND NOT AT THE SAME TIME WITH THE OTHER. For one may from the heart devote himself to chaste marriage, while the other knows not what chaste marriage is; one may love the things which are of the church, but the other those which are of the world alone: as to their minds, one may be in heaven, the other in hell; hence there may be conjugial love with the one, and not with the other. The minds of such, since they are turned in a contrary direction, are inwardly in collision with each other; and if not outwardly, still, he that is not in conjugial love, regards his lawful consort as a tiresome old woman; and so in other cases.

227. XVIII. THERE ARE VARIOUS SIMILITUDES AND DISSIMILITUDES, BOTH INTERNAL AND EXTERNAL, WITH MARRIED

PARTNERS. It is well known, that between married partners there are similitudes and dissimilitudes, and that the external appear, but not the internal, except after some time of living together, to the married partners themselves, and by indications to others; but it would be useless to mention each so that they might be known, since several pages might be filled with an account and description of their varieties. Similitudes may in part be deduced and concluded from the dissimilitudes on account of which conjugial love is changed into cold; of which we shall speak in the following chapter. Similitudes and dissimilitudes in general originate from connate inclinations, varied by education, connections, and persuasions that have been imbibed.

228. XIX. VARIOUS SIMILITUDES CAN BE CONJOINED, BUT NOT WITH DISSIMILITUDES. The varieties of similitudes are very numerous, and differ more or less from each other; but still those which differ may in time be conjoined by various things, especially by accommodations to desires, by mutual offices and civilities, by abstaining from what is unchaste, by the common love of infants and the care of children, but particularly by conformity in things relating to the church; for things relating to the church effect a conjunction of similitudes differing interiorly, other things only exteriorly. But with dissimilitudes no conjunction can be effected, because they are antipathetical.

229. XX. THE LORD PROVIDES SIMILITUDES FOR THOSE WHO DESIRE LOVE TRULY CONJUGIAL, AND IF NOT ON EARTH, HE YET PROVIDES THEM IN HEAVEN. The reason of this is, because all marriages of love truly conjugial are provided by the Lord. That they are from him, may be seen above, n. 130, 131; but in what manner they are provided in heaven, I have heard thus described by the angels: The divine providence of the Lord extends to everything, even to the minutest particulars, concerning marriages and in marriages, because all the delights of heaven spring from the delights of conjugial love, as sweet waters from the fountain-head; and on this account it is provided that conjugial pairs be born; and that they be continually educated to their several marriages under the Lord's auspices, neither the boy nor the girl knowing anything of the matter; and after a stated time, when they both become marriageable, they meet in some place as by chance, and see each other, and in this case they instantly know, as by a kind of instinct, that they are a pair, and by a kind of inward dictate think within themselves, the youth, that she is mine, and the maiden, that he is mine; and when this thought has existed some time in the mind of each, they accost each other from a deliberate purpose, and betroth themselves. It is said, as by chance, by instinct, and by dictate; and the meaning is, by divine providence; since, while the divine providence is, unknown, it has such an appearance; for the Lord opens internal similitudes, so that they may see themselves.

230. XXI. A MAN (*homo*), ACCORDING TO THE DEFICIENCY AND LOSS OF CONJUGIAL LOVE, APPROACHES TO THE NATURE OF A BEAST. The reason of this is, because so far as a man (*homo*) is in conjugial love, so far he is spiritual, and so far as he is spiritual, so far he is a man (*homo*); for a man is born to a life after death, and attains the possession thereof in consequence of having in him a spiritual soul, and is capable of being elevated thereto by the faculty of his understanding; if in this case his will, from the faculty also granted to it, is elevated at the same time, he lives after death the life of heaven. The contrary comes to pass, if he is in a love opposite to conjugial love; for so far as he is in this opposite love, so far he is natural; and a merely natural man is like a beast as to lusts and appetites, and to their delights; with this difference only, that he has the faculty of elevating his understanding into the light of wisdom, and also of elevating his will into the heat of celestial love. These faculties are never taken away from any man (*homo*); therefore the merely natural man, although as to concupiscences and appetites and their delights, he is like a beast, still lives after death, but in a state corresponding to his past life. From these considerations it may appear that a man, according to the deficiency of conjugial love, approaches to the nature of a beast. This position may seem to be contradicted by the consideration, that there are a deficiency and loss of conjugial love with some who yet are men (*homines*); but the position is meant to be confined to those who make light of conjugial love from a principle of adulterous love, and who therefore are in such deficiency and loss.

* * * * * * * *

231. To the above I shall add THREE MEMORABLE RELATIONS. FIRST. I once heard loud exclamations, which issued from the hells, with a noise as if they bubbled up through water: one to the left hand, in these words, "O HOW JUST!" another to the right, "O HOW LEARNED!" and a third from behind, "O HOW WISE!" and as I was in doubt whether there are also in hell persons of justice, learning, and wisdom, I was impressed with a strong desire of seeing what was the real case; and a voice from heaven said to me, "You shall see and hear." I therefore in spirit went out of the house, and saw before me an opening, which I approached; and looked down; and lo! there was a ladder, by which I descended: and when I was down, I observed a level country set thick with shrubs, intermixed with thorns and nettles; and on my asking, whether this was hell, I was told it was the lower earth next above hell. I then continued my course in a direction according to the exclamations in order; first to those who exclaimed, "O HOW JUST!" where I saw a company consisting of such as in the world had been judges influenced by friendship and gifts; then to the second exclamation, O HOW LEARNED!" where I saw a company of such as in the world had

been reasoners; and lastly to the third exclamation, "O now WISE!" where I saw a company such as in the world had been confirmators. From these I returned to the first, where there were judges influenced by friendship and gifts, and who were proclaimed "Just." On one side I saw as it were an amphitheatre built of brick, and covered with black slates; and I was told that they called it a tribunal. There were three entrances to it on the north, and three on the west, but none on the south and east; a proof that their decisions were not those of justice, but were arbitrary determinations. In the middle of the amphitheatre there was a fire, into which the servants who attended threw torches of sulphur and pitch; the light whereof, by its vibrations on the plastered walls, presented pictured images of birds of the evening and night; but both the fire and the vibrations of light thence issuing, together with the forms of the images thereby produced, were representations that in their decisions they could adorn the matter of any debate with colored dyes, and give it a form according to their own interest. In about half an hour I saw some old men and youths in robes and cloaks, enter the amphitheatre, who, laying aside their caps, took their seats at the tables, in order to sit in judgement. I heard and perceived with what cunning and ingenuity, under the impulse of prejudice in favor of their friends, they warped and inverted judgement so as to give it an appearance of justice, and this to such a degree, that they themselves saw what was unjust as just, and on the other hand what was just as unjust. Such persuasions respecting the points to be decided upon, appeared from their countenances, and were heard from their manner of speaking. I then received illustration from heaven, from which I perceived how far each point was grounded in right or not; and I saw how industriously they concealed what was unjust, and gave it a semblance of what was just; and how they selected some particular statute which favored their own side of the question, and by cunning reasonings warped the rest to the same side. After judgement was given, the decrees were conveyed to their clients, friends and favorers, who, to recompense them for their services, continued to shout, "O HOW JUST, O HOW JUST!" After this I conversed respecting them with the angels of heaven, and related to them some of the things I had seen and heard. The angels said to me, "Such judges appear to others to be endowed with a most extraordinary acuteness of intellect; when yet they do not at all see what is just and equitable. If you remove the prejudices of friendship in favor of particular persons, they sit mute in judgement like so many statues, and only say, 'I acquiesce, and am entirely of your opinion on this point.' This happens because all their judgements are prejudices; and prejudice with partiality influences the case in question from beginning to end. Hence they see nothing but what is connected with their friend's interest; and whatever is contrary thereto, they set aside; or if they pay any attention to it, they involve it in intricate reasonings, as a spider wraps up its prey in a web, and make an end of it; hence, unless they follow the web of their prejudice, they see nothing of what is right. They were examined whether they were able to see it, and it was discovered that they were not. That this is the case, will seem wonderful to the inhabitants of your world; but tell them it is a truth that has been investigated by the angels of heaven. As they see nothing of what is just, we in heaven regard them not as men but as monsters, whose heads are constituted of things relating to friendship, their breasts of those relating to injustice, their feet of those which relate to confirmation, and the soles of the feet of those things which relate to justice, which they supplant and trample under foot, in case they are unfavorable to the interests of their friend. But of what quality they appear to us from heaven, you shall presently see; for their end is at hand." And lo! at that instant the ground was cleft asunder, and the tables fell one upon another, and they were swallowed up, together with the whole amphitheatre, and were cast into caverns, and imprisoned. It was then said to me, "Do you wish to see them where they now are?" And lo! their faces appeared as of polished steel, their bodies from the neck to the loins as graven images of stone clothed with leopards' skins, and their feet like snakes: the law books too, which they had arranged in order on the tables, were changed into packs of cards: and now, instead of sitting in judgement, the office appointed to them is to prepare vermilion and mix it up into a paint, to bedaub the faces of harlots and thereby turn them into beauties.

After seeing these things, I was desirous to visit the two other assemblies, one of which consisted of mere reasoners, and the other of mere confirmators; and it was said to me, "Stop awhile, and you shall have attendant angels from the society next above them; by these you will receive light from the Lord and will see what will surprise you."

232. THE SECOND MEMORABLE RELATION. After some time I heard again from the lower earth voices exclaiming as before, " O HOW LEARNED! O HOW WISE!" I looked round to see what angels were present; and lo! they were from the heaven immediately above those who cried out, " O HOW LEARNED!" and I conversed with them respecting the cry, and they said, "Those learned ones are such as only reason *whether a thing be so or not*, and seldom think *that it is so;* therefore, they are like winds which blow and pass away, like the bark about trees which are without sap, or like shells about almonds without a kernel, or like the outward rind about fruit without pulp; for their minds are void of interior judgement, and are united only with the bodily senses; therefore unless the senses themselves decide,

they can conclude nothing; in a word, they are merely sensual, and we call them REASONERS. We give them this name, because they never conclude anything, and make whatever they hear a matter of argument, and dispute whether it be so, with perpetual contradiction. They love nothing better than to attack essential truths, and so to pull them in pieces as to make them a subject of dispute. These are those who believe themselves learned above the rest of the world." On hearing this account, I entreated the angels to conduct me to them: so they led me to a cave, from which there was a flight of steps leading to the earth below. We descended and followed the shout, "O now LEARNED!" and lo! there were some hundreds standing in one place, beating the ground with their feet. Being at first surprised at this sight, I inquired the reason of their standing in that manner and beating the ground with the soles of their feet, and said, "They may thus by their feet make holes in the floor." At this the angel smiled and said, "They appear to stand in this manner, because they never think on any subject that it is so, but only whether it is so, and dispute about it; and when the thinking principle proceeds no further than this, they appear only to tread and trample on a single clod, and not to advance." Upon this I approached the assembly, and lo! they appeared to me to be good-looking men and well dressed; but the angels said, "This is their appearance when viewed in their own light; but if light from heaven flows in, their faces are changed, and so is their dress; and so it came to pass: they then appeared with dark faces, and dressed in black sackcloth; but when this light was withdrawn, they appeared as before. I presently entered into conversation with some of them, and said, "I heard the shout of a crowd about you, '*O how learned!*' may I be allowed therefore to have a little conversation with you on subjects of the highest learning?" they replied, "Mention any subject, and we will give you satisfaction." I then asked, "What must be the nature of that religion by which a man is saved?" They said, "We will divide this subject into several parts; and we cannot answer it until we have concluded on its subdivisions. The first inquiry shall be, Whether religion be anything? the second, Whether there be such a thing as salvation or not? the third, Whether one religion be more efficacious than another? the fourth, Whether there be a heaven and a hell? the fifth, Whether there be eternal life after death? besides many more inquiries. Then I desired to know their opinion concerning the first article of inquiry, Whether religion be anything? They began to discuss the subject with abundance of arguments, whether there be any such thing as religion, and whether what is called religion be anything? I requested them to refer it to the assembly, and they did so; and the general answer was, that the proposition required so much investigation that it could not be

197

finished within the evening. I then asked, "Can you finish it within the year?" and one of them said, "Not within a hundred years:" so I observed, "In the mean while you are without religion;" and he replied, "Shall it not be first demonstrated whether there be such a thing as religion, and whether what is called religion be anything? if there be such a thing, it must be also for the wise; if there be no such thing, it must be only for the vulgar. It is well known that religion is called a bond; but it is asked, for whom? if it be only for the vulgar, it is not anything in itself; if it be likewise for the wise, it is something." On hearing these arguments, I said to them, "There is no character you deserve less than that of being learned; because all your thoughts are confined to the single inquiry, whether a thing be, and to canvass each side of the question. Who can become learned, unless he know something for certain, and progressively advance into it, as a man in walking progressively advances from step to step, and thereby successively arrives at wisdom! If you follow any other rule, you make no approach to truths, but remove them more and more out of sight. To reason only whether a thing be, is it not like reasoning about a cap or a shoe, whether they fit or not, before they are put on? and what must be the consequence of such reasoning, but that you will not know whether anything exist, yea, whether there be any such thing as salvation, or eternal life after death; whether one religion be more efficacious than another, and whether there be a heaven and a hell? On these subjects you cannot possibly think at all, so long as you halt at the first step, and beat the sand at setting out, instead of setting one foot before another and going forward. Take heed to yourselves, lest your minds, standing thus without in a state of indetermination, should inwardly harden and become statues of salt, and yourselves friends of Lot's wife." With these words I took my leave, and they being indignant threw stones after me; and then they appeared to me like graven images of stone, without any human reason in them. On my asking the angels concerning their lot, they said, "Their lot is, that they are cast down into the deep, into a wilderness, where they are forced to carry burdens; and in this case, as they are no longer capable of rational conversation, they give themselves up to idle prattle and talk, and appear at a distance like asses that are heavily laden."

233. THE THIRD MEMORABLE RELATION. After this one of the angels said, "Follow me to the place where they exclaim, 'O HOW WISE!' and you shall see prodigies of men; you shall see faces and bodies, which are the faces and bodies of a man, and yet they are not men." I said, "Are they beasts then?" he replied, "They are not beasts, but beast-men; for they are such as cannot at all see whether truth be truth or not, and yet they can make whatever they will to be truth. Such persons

with us are called CONFIRMATORS." We followed the vociferation, and came to the place; and lo! there was a company of men, and around them a crowd, and in the crowd some of noble blood, who, on hearing that they confirmed whatever they said, and favored themselves with such manifest consent, turned, and said, "O how WISE!" But the angel said to me, "Let us not go to them, but call one out of the company." We called him and went aside with him, and conversed on various subjects; and he confirmed every one of them, so that they appeared altogether as true; and we asked him, whether he could also confirm the contrary? he said, "As well as the former." Then he spoke openly and from the heart, and said, "What is truth? Is there anything true in the nature of things, but what a man makes true? Advance any proposition you please, and I will make it to be true." Hereupon I said, "Make this true; That faith is the all of the church." This he did so dexterously and cunningly, that the learned who were standing by admired and applauded him. I afterwards requested him to make it true, That charity is the all of the church; and he did so: and afterwards, That charity is nothing of the church: and he dressed up each side of the question, and adorned it so with appearances, that the bystanders looked at each other, and said, "Is not this a wise man?" But I said, "Do not you know that to live well is charity, and that to believe well is faith? does not he that lives well also believe well? and consequently, is not faith of charity, and charity of faith? do you not see that this is true?" He replied, "I will make it true, and will then see." He did so, and said, "Now I see it;" but presently he made the contrary to be true, and then said, "I also see that this is true." At this we smiled and said, "Are they not contraries? how can two contraries appear true?" To this he replied with indignation, "You are mistaken; each is true; since truth is nothing but what a man makes true." There was a certain person standing near, who in the world had been a legate of the first rank. He was surprised at this assertion, and said, "I acknowledge that in the world something like this method of reasoning prevails; but still you are out of your senses. Try if you can make it to be true, that light is darkness, and darkness light." He replied, "I will easily do this. What are light and darkness but a state of the eye? Is not light changed into shade when the eye comes out of sunshine, and also when it is kept intensely fixed on the sun? Who does not know, that the state of the eye in such a case is changed, and that in consequence light appears as shade; and on the other hand, when the state or the eye is restored, that shade appears as light? Does not an owl see the darkness of night as the light of day, and the light of day as the darkness of night, and also the sun itself as an opaque and dusky globe? If any man had the eyes of an owl, which would he call light and which darkness? What then is light but the state of the eye? and if it be a state of the eye, is not light darkness, and darkness light? therefore each of the propositions is true." Afterwards the legate asked him to make this true, That a raven is white and not black; and he replied, "I will do this also with ease; and he said, "Take a needle or razor, and lay open the feathers or quills of a raven; are they not white within? Also remove the feathers and quills, and look at its skin; is it not white? What is the blackness then which envelops it but a shade, which ought not to determine the raven's color? That blackness is merely a shade, I appeal to the skilful in the science of optics, who will tell you, that if you pound a black stone or glass into fine powder, you will see that the powder is white." But the legate replied, "Does not the raven appear black to the sight?" The confirmator answered, "Will you, who are a man, think in any case from appearance? you may indeed say from appearance, that a crow is black, but you cannot think so; as for example, you may speak from the appearance and say that the sun rises, advances to its meridian altitude, and sets; but, as you are a man, you cannot think so; because the sun stands unmoved and the earth only changes its position. The case is the same with the raven; appearance is appearance; and say what you will, a raven is altogether and entirely white; it grows white also as it grows old; and this I have seen." We next requested him to tell us from his heart, whether he was in joke, or whether he really believed that nothing is true but what a man makes true? and he replied, "I swear that I believe it." Afterwards the legate asked him, whether he could make it true that he was out of his senses; and he said, "I can; but I do not choose: who is not out of his senses?" When the conversation was thus ended, this universal confirmator was sent to the angels, to be examined as to his true quality; and the report they afterwards made was, that he did not possess even a single grain of understanding; because all that is above the rational principle was closed in him, and that alone which is below was open. Above the rational principle is heavenly light, and below it is natural light; and this light is such that it can confirm whatever it pleases; but if heavenly light does not flow into natural light, a man does not see whether any thing true is true, and consequently neither does he see that any thing false is false. To see in either case is by virtue of heavenly light in natural light; and heavenly light is from the God of heaven, who is the Lord; therefore this universal confirmator is not a man or a beast, but a beast-man. I questioned the angel concerning the lot of such persons, and whether they can be together with those who are alive, since every one has life from heavenly light, and from this light has understanding. He said, that such persons when they are alone, can neither think nor express their thoughts, but stand mute like machines, and as in a deep sleep; but that they awake as soon as any sound strikes their ears: and he added, that those become such, who are inmostly wicked; into these no heavenly light can flow from above, but only somewhat spiritual through the world, whence they derive the faculty of confirming. As he said this, I heard a voice from the angels who had examined the confirmation, saying to me, "From what you have now heard form a general conclusion." I accordingly formed the following: "That intelligence does not consist in being able to confirm whatever a man pleases, but in being able to see that what is true is true, and what is false is false." After this I looked towards the company where the confirmators stood, and where the crowd about them shouted, "*O how wise!*" and lo! a dusky cloud covered them, and in the cloud were owls and bats on the wing; and it was said to me, "The owls and bats flying in the dusky cloud, are correspondences and consequent appearances of their thoughts; because confirmations of falsities so as to make them appear like truths, are represented in this world under the forms of birds of night, whose eyes are inwardly illuminated by a false light, from which they see objects in the dark as if in the light. By such a false spiritual light are those influenced who confirm falses until they seem as truths, and afterwards are said and believed to be truths: all such see backwards, and not forwards.

ON THE CAUSES OF COLDNESS, SEPARATION, AND DIVORCE IN MARRIAGES.

234. IN treating here on the causes of coldness in marriages, we shall treat also at the same time on the causes of separation, and likewise of divorce, because they are connected; for separations come from no other source than from coldnesses, which are successively inborn after marriage, or from causes discovered after marriage, from which also coldness springs; but divorces come from adulteries; for these are altogether opposite to marriages; and opposites induce coldness, if not in both parties, at least in one. This is the reason why the causes of coldness, separations, and divorces, are brought together into one chapter. But the coherence of the causes will be more clearly discerned from viewing them in the following series:—
I. *There are spiritual heat and spiritual cold; and spiritual heat is love, and spiritual cold the privation thereof.* II. *Spiritual cold in marriages is a disunion of souls and a disjunction of minds, whence come indifference, discord, contempt, disdain, and aversion; from which, in several cases, at length comes separation as to bed, chamber, and house.* III. *There are several successive causes of cold, some internal, some external, and some*

accidental. IV. *Internal causes of cold are from religion.* V. *The first of these causes is the rejection of religion by each of the parties.* VI. *The second is, that one has religion and not the other.* VII. *The third is, that one is of one religion and the other of another.* VIII. *The fourth is the falsity of the religion imbibed.* IX. *With many, these are causes of internal cold, but not at the same time of external.* X. *There are also several external causes of cold; the first of which is dissimilitude of minds and manners.* XI. *The second is, that conjugial love is believed to be the same. as adulterous love, only that the latter is not allowed by law, but the former is.* XII. *The third is, a striving for pre-eminence between married partners.* XIII. *The fourth is, a want of determination to any employment or business, whence comes wandering passion.* XIV. *The fifth is, inequality of external rank and condition.* XV. *There are also causes of separation.* XVI. *The first of them is a vitiated state of mind.* XVII. *The second is a vitiated state of body.* XVIII. *The third is impotence before marriage.* XIX. *Adultery is the cause of divorce.* XX. *There are also several accidental causes of cold; the first of which is, that enjoyment is common (or cheap), because continually allowed.* XXI. *The second is, that living with a married partner, from a covenant and compact, seems to be forced and not free.* XXII. *The third is, affirmation on the part of the wife, and her talking incessantly about love.* XXIII. *The fourth is, the man's continually thinking that his wife is willing; and on the other hand, the wife's thinking that the man is not willing.* XXIV. *As cold is in the mind it is also in the body; and according to the increase of that cold, the externals also of the body are closed.* We proceed to an explanation of each article.

235. THERE ARE SPIRITUAL HEAT AND SPIRITUAL COLD; AND SPIRITUAL HEAT IS LOVE, AND SPIRITUAL COLD IS THE PRIVATION THEREOF. Spiritual heat is from no other source than the sun of the spiritual world; for there is in that world a sun proceeding from the Lord, who is in the midst of it; and as it is from the Lord, it is in its essence pure love. This sun appears fiery before the angels, just as the sun of our world appears before men. The reason of its appearing fiery is, because love is spiritual fire. From that sun proceed both heat and light; but as that sun is pure love, the heat thence derived in its essence is love, and the light thence derived in its essence is wisdom; hence it is manifest what is the source of spiritual heat, and that spiritual heat is love. But we will also briefly explain the source of spiritual cold. It is from the sun of the natural world, and its heat and light. The sun of the natural world was created that its heat and light might receive in them spiritual heat and light, and by means of the atmospheres might convey spiritual heat and light even to ultimates in the earth, in order to produce effects

of ends, which are of the Lord in his sun, and also to clothe spiritual principles with suitable garments, that is, with materials, to operate ultimate ends in nature. These effects are produced when spiritual heat is joined to natural heat; but the contrary comes to pass when natural heat is separated from spiritual heat, as is the case with those who love natural things, and reject spiritual: with such, spiritual heat becomes cold. The reason why these two loves, which from creation are in agreement, become thus opposite, is, because in such case the dominant heat becomes the servant, and *vice versa;* and to prevent this effect, spiritual heat, which from its lineage is lord, then recedes; and in those subjects, spiritual heat grows cold, because it becomes opposite. From these considerations it is manifest that spiritual cold is the privation of spiritual heat. In what is here said, by heat is meant love; because that heat living in subjects is felt as love. I have heard in the spiritual world, that spirits merely natural grow intensely cold while they apply themselves to the side of some angel who is in a state of love; and that the case is similar in regard to the infernal spirits, while heat flows into them out of heaven; and that nevertheless among themselves, when the heat of heaven is removed from them, they are inflamed with great heat.

236. II. SPIRITUAL COLD IN MARRIAGES IS A DISUNION OF SOULS AND A DISJUNCTION OF MINDS, WHENCE COME INDIFFERENCE, DISCORD, CONTEMPT, DISDAIN, AND AVERSION; FROM WHICH, IN SEVERAL CASES, AT LENGTH COMES SEPARATION AS TO BED, CHAMBER, AND HOUSE. That these effects take place with married partners, while their primitive love is on the decline, and becomes cold, is too well known to need any comment. The reason is; because conjugial cold above all others resides in human minds; for the essential conjugial principle is inscribed on the soul, to the end that a soul may be propagated from a soul, and the soul of the father into the offspring. Hence it is that this cold originates there, and successively goes downward into the principles thence derived, and infects them; and thus changes the joys and delights of the primitive love into what is sad and undelightful.

237. III. THERE ARE SEVERAL SUCCESSIVE CAUSES OF COLD, SOME INTERNAL, SOME EXTERNAL, AND SOME ACCIDENTAL. That there are several causes of cold in marriages, is known in the world; also that they arise from many external causes; but it is not known that the origins of the causes lie concealed in the inmost principles, and that from these they descend into the principles thence derived, until they appear in externals; in order therefore that it may be known that external causes are not causes in themselves, but derived from causes in themselves, which, as was said, are in inmost principles, we will first distri-

bute the causes generally into internal and external, and afterwards will particularly examine them.

238. IV. INTERNAL CAUSES OF COLD ARE FROM RELIGION. That the very origin of conjugial love resides in the inmost principles of man, that is, in his soul, is demonstrable to every one from the following considerations alone; that the soul of the offspring is from the father, which is known from the similitude of inclinations and affections, and also from the general character of the countenance derived from the father and remaining with very remote posterity; also from the propagative faculty implanted in souls from creation; and moreover by what is analogous thereto in the subjects of the vegetable kingdom, in that there lies hid in the inmost principles of germination the propagation of the seed itself, and thence of the whole, whether it be a tree, a shrub, or a plant. This propagative or plastic force in seeds in the latter kingdom, and in souls in the other, is from no other source than the conjugial sphere, which is that of good and truth, and which perpetually emanates and flows in from the Lord the Creator and Supporter of the universe; concerning which sphere, see above, n. 222—225; and from the endeavour of those two principles, good and truth, therein, to unite into a one. This conjugial endeavour remains implanted in souls, and conjugial love exists by derivation from it as its origin. That this same marriage, from which the above universal sphere is derived, constitutes the church with man, has been abundantly shewn above in the chapter ON THE MARRIAGE OF GOOD AND TRUTH, and frequently elsewhere. Hence there is all the evidence of rational demonstration, that the origin of the church and of conjugial love are in one place of abode, and in a continual embrace; but on this subject see further particulars above, n. 130, where it was proved, that conjugial love is according to the state of the church with man; thus that it is grounded in religion, because religion constitutes this state. Man also was created with a capacity of becoming more and more interior, and thereby of being introduced or elevated nearer and nearer to that marriage, and thus into love truly conjugial, and this even so far as to perceive a state of its blessedness. That religion is the only means of introduction and elevation, appears clearly from what was said above, namely, that the origin of the church and of conjugial love are in the same place of abode, and in mutual embrace there, and that hence they must needs be conjoined.

239. From what has been said above it follows, that where there is no religion, there is no conjugial love; and that where there is no conjugial love, there is cold. That conjugial cold is the privation of that love, may be seen above, n. 235; consequently that conjugial cold is also a privation of a state of the

church, or of religion. Sufficient evidence of the truth of this may be deduced from the general ignorance that now prevails concerning love truly conjugial. In these times, who knows, and who is willing to acknowledge, and who will not be surprised to hear, that the origin of conjugial love is deduced hence? But the only cause and source of this ignorance is, that, notwithstanding there is religion, still there are not the truths of religion; and what is religion without truths? That there is a want of the truths of religion, is fully shown in the APOCALYPSE REVEALED; see also the MEMORABLE RELATION, n. 566 of that work.

240. V. OF INTERNAL CAUSES OF COLD THE FIRST IS THE REJECTION OF RELIGION BY EACH OF THE PARTIES. Those who reject the holy things of the church from the face to the hinder part of the head, or from the breast to the back, have not any good love; if any proceeds apparently from the body, still there is not any in the spirit. With such persons goods place themselves on the outside of evils, and cover them, as raiment glittering with gold covers a putrid body. The evils which reside within, and are covered, are in general hatreds, and thence intestine combats against everything spiritual; for all things of the church which they reject, are in themselves spiritual; and as love truly conjugial is the fundamental love of all spiritual loves, as was shewn above, it is evident that interior hatred is contrary to it, and that the interior or real love with such is in favor of the opposite, which is the love of adultery; therefore such persons, more than others, will be disposed to ridicule this truth, that every one has conjugial love according to the state of the church; yea, they will possibly laugh at the very mention of love truly conjugial; but be it so; nevertheless they are to be pardoned, because it is as impossible for them to distinguish in thought between the marriage embrace and the adulterous, as it is for a camel to go through the eye of a needle. Such persons, as to conjugial love, are starved with cold more than others. If they keep to their married partners, it is only on account of some of the external causes mentioned above, n. 153, which withhold and bind them. Their interiors of the soul and thence of the mind are more and more closed, and in the body are stopped up; and in this case even the love of the sex is thought little of, or becomes insanely lascivious in the interiors of the body, and thence in the lowest principles of their thought. It is these who are meant in the MEMORABLE RELATION, n. 79, which they may read if they please.

241. VI. OF INTERNAL CAUSES OF COLD THE SECOND IS, THAT ONE OF THE PARTIES HAS RELIGION AND NOT THE OTHER. The reason of this is, because the souls must of course disagree; for the soul of one is open to the reception of conjugial love, while the soul of the other is closed to it. It is closed with the

party that has not religion, and it is open with the one that has; hence such persons cannot live together harmoniously; and when once conjugial love is banished, there ensues cold; but this is with the party that has no religion. This cold cannot be dissipated except by the reception of a religion agreeing with that of the other party, if it be true; otherwise, with the party that has no religion, there ensues cold, which descends from the soul into the body, even to the cuticles; in consequence of which he can no longer look his married partner directly in the face, or accost her in a communion of respirations, or speak to her except in a subdued tone of voice, or touch her with the hand, and scarcely with the back; not to mention the insanities which, proceeding from that cold, make their way into the thoughts, which they do not make known; and this is the reason why such marriages dissolve of themselves. Moreover, it is well known, that an impious man thinks meanly of a married partner; and all who are without religion are impious.

242. VII. OF INTERNAL CAUSES OF COLD THE THIRD IS, THAT ONE OF THE PARTIES IS OF ONE RELIGION AND THE OTHER OF ANOTHER. The reason of this is, because with such persons good cannot be conjoined with its corresponding truth; for as was shewn above, the wife is the good of the husband's truth, and he is the truth of the wife's good. Hence of two souls there cannot be made one soul; and hence the stream of that love is closed: and consequently a conjugial principle is entered upon, which has a lower place of abode, and which is that of good with another truth, or of truth with another good than its own, between which there cannot be any harmonious love: hence with the married partner that is in a false religion, there commences a cold, which grows more intense in proportion as he differs from the other party. On a certain time, as I was wandering through the streets of a great city inquiring for a lodging, I entered a house inhabited by married partners of a different religion; being ignorant of this circumstance, the angels instantly accosted me, and said, "We cannot remain with you in that house; for the married partners who dwell there differ in religion." This they perceived from the internal disunion of their souls.

243. VIII. OF INTERNAL CAUSES OF COLD THE FOURTH IS, THE FALSITY OF THE RELIGION. This is, because falsity in spiritual things either takes away religion or defiles it. It takes it from those with whom genuine truths are falsified; it defiles it, where there are indeed falsities, but not genuine truths, which therefore could not be falsified. In the latter case there may be imputed goods with which those falses may be conjoined by applications from the Lord; for these falses are like various discordant tones, which by artful arrangements and combinations are brought into harmony, and communicate to harmony its

agreeableness: in this case some conjugial love is communicable; but with those who have falsified with themselves the genuine truths of the church, it is not communciable. The prevailing ignorance concerning love truly conjugial, or a negative doubting respecting the possibility of the existence of such love, is from persons of the latter description; and from the same source also comes the wild imagination, in the minds of the generality, that adulteries are not evils in a religious point of view.

244. IX. WITH MANY, THE ABOVE-MENTIONED ARE CAUSES OF INTERNAL COLD, BUT NOT AT THE SAME TIME OF EXTERNAL. If the causes above pointed out and confirmed, which are the causes of internal cold, produced similar external cold, as many separations would ensue as there are cases of internal cold, which are as many as there are marriages of those who are in a false or a different religion, or in no religion; respecting whom we have already treated; and yet it is well-known, that many such live together as if they mutually loved and were friendly to each other: but whence this originates, with those who are in internal cold, will be shewn in the following chapter CONCERNING THE CAUSES OF APPARENT LOVE, FRIENDSHIP, AND FAVOR IN MARRIAGES. There are several causes which conjoin minds (*animos*), but still do not conjoin souls; among these are some of those mentioned above, n. 183; but still cold lies interiorly concealed, and makes itself continually observed and felt. With such married partners the affections depart from each other; but the thoughts, while they come forth into speech and behaviour, for the sake of apparent friendship and favor, are present; therefore such persons know nothing of the pleasantness and delight, and still less of the satisfaction and blessedness of love truly conjugial, accounting them to be little else than fables. These are of the number of those who deduce the origin of conjugial love from the same causes with the nine companies of wise ones assembled from the several kingdoms of Europe; concerning whom see the MEMORABLE RELATION above, n. 103—114.

245. It may be urged as an objection to what has been proved above, that still the soul is propagated from the father although it is not conjoined to the soul of the mother, yea, although cold residing therein causes separation; but the reason why souls or offspring are nevertheless propagated is, because the understanding of the man is not closed, but is capable of being elevated into the light into which the soul is; but the love of his will is not elevated into the heat corresponding to the light there, except by the life, which makes him from natural become spiritual; hence it is, that the soul is still procreated, but, in the descent, while it becomes seed, it is veiled over by such things as belong to his natural love; from this springs hereditary evil. To these considerations I will add an arcanum from heaven, namely, that between the disjoined souls of two persons,

especially of married partners, there is effected conjunction in a middle love; otherwise there would be no conception with men (*homines*). Besides what is here said of conjugial cold, and its place of abode in the supreme region of the mind, see the LAST MEMORABLE RELATION of this chapter, n. 270.

246. X. THERE ARE ALSO SEVERAL EXTERNAL CAUSES OF COLD, THE FIRST OF WHICH IS DISSIMILITUDE OF MINDS AND MANNERS. There are both internal and external similitudes and dissimilitudes. The internal arise from no other source than religion; for religion is implanted in souls, and by them is transmitted from parents to their offspring as the supreme inclination; for the soul of every man derives life from the marriage of good and truth, and from this marriage is the church; and as the church is various and different in the several parts of the world, therefore also the souls of all men are various and different; wherefore internal similitudes and dissimilitudes are from this source, and according to them the conjugial conjunctions of which we have been treating; but external similitudes and dissimilitudes are not of the souls but of minds; by minds (*animos*) we mean the affections and thence the external inclinations, which are principally insinuated after birth by education, social intercourse, and consequent habits of life; for it is usual to say, I have a mind to do this or that; which indicates an affection and inclination to it. Persuasions conceived respecting this or that kind of life also form those minds; hence come inclinations to enter into marriage even with such as are unsuitable, and likewise to refuse consent to marriage with such as are suitable; but still these marriages, after a certain time of living together, vary according to the similitudes and dissimilitudes contracted hereditarily and also by education; and dissimilitudes induce cold. So likewise dissimilitudes of manners; as for example, an ill-mannered man or woman, joined with a well-bred one; a neat man or woman, joined with a slovenly one; a litigious man or woman, joined with one that is peaceably disposed; in a word, an immoral man or woman, joined with a moral one. Marriages of such dissimilitudes are not unlike the conjunctions of different species of animals with each other, as of sheep and goats, of stags and mules, of turkeys and geese, of sparrows and the nobler kind of birds, yea, as of dogs and cats, which from their dissimilitudes do not consociate with each other, but in the human kind these dissimilitudes are indicated not by faces, but by habits of life; wherefore external colds are from this source.

247. XI. OF EXTERNAL CAUSES OF COLD THE SECOND IS, THAT CONJUGIAL LOVE IS BELIEVED TO BE THE SAME AS ADULTEROUS LOVE, ONLY THAT THE LATTER IS NOT ALLOWED BY LAW, BUT THE FORMER IS. That this is a source of cold, is obvious to reason, while it is considered that adulterous love is diametrically

opposite to conjugial love; wherefore when it is believed that conjugial love is the same as adulterous, they both become alike in idea; and in such case a wife is regarded as a harlot, and marriage as uncleanness; the man himself also is an adulterer, if not in body, still in spirit. That hence ensue contempt, disdain, and aversion, between the man and his woman, and thereby intense cold, is an unavoidable consequence; for nothing stores up in itself conjugial cold more than adulterous love; and as adulterous love also passes into such cold, it may not undeservedly be called essential conjugial cold.

248. XII. OF EXTERNAL CAUSES OF COLD THE THIRD IS, A STRIVING FOR PRE-EMINENCE BETWEEN MARRIED PARTNERS. This is, because conjugial love principally respects the union of wills, and the freedom of decision thence arising; both which are ejected from the married state by a striving for pre-eminence or superiority; for this divides and tears wills into pieces, and changes the freedom of decision into servitude. During the influence of such striving, the spirit of one of the parties meditates violence against the other; if in such case their minds were laid open and viewed by spiritual sight, they would appear like two boxers engaged in combat, and regarding each other with hatred and favor alternately; with hatred while in the vehemence of striving, and with favor while in the hope of dominion, and while under the influence of lust. After one has obtained the victory over the other, this contention is withdrawn from the externals, and betakes itself into the internals of the mind, and there abides with its restlessness stored up and concealed. Hence cold ensues both to the subdued party or servant, and to the victor or dominant party. The reason why the latter also suffers cold is, because conjugial love no longer exists with them, and the privation of this love is cold; see n. 235. In the place of conjugial love succeeds heat derived from pre-eminence; but this heat is utterly discordant with conjugial heat, yet it can exteriorly resemble it by means of lust. After a tacit agreement between the parties, it appears as if conjugial love was made friendship; but the difference between conjugial and servile friendship in marriages, is like that between light and shade, between a living fire and an *ignis fatuus*, yea, like that between a well-conditioned man and one consisting only of bone and skin.

249. XIII. OF EXTERNAL CAUSES OF COLD THE FOURTH IS, A WANT OF DETERMINATION TO ANY EMPLOYMENT OR BUSINESS, WHENCE COMES WANDERING PASSION. Man (*homo*) was created for use, because use is the continent of good and truth, from the marriage of which proceeds creation, and also conjugial love, as was shewn above. By employment and business we mean every application to uses; while therefore a man is in any employment and business, or in any use, in such case his mind is limited and circumscribed as in a circle, within which it is successively ar-

ranged into a form truly human, from which as from a house he sees various concupiscences out of himself, and by sound reason within exterminates them; consequently also he exterminates the wild insanities of adulterous lust.; hence it is that conjugial heat remains better and longer with such than with others. The reverse happens with those who give themselves up to sloth and ease; in such case the mind is unlimited and undetermined, and hence the man (*homo*) admits into the whole of it everything vain and ludicrous which flows in from the world and the body, and leads to the love thereof; that in this case conjugial love also is driven into banishment, is evident; for in consequence of sloth and ease the mind grows stupid and the body torpid, and the whole man becomes insensible to every vital love, especially to conjugial love, from which as from a fountain issue the activities and alacrities of life. Conjugial cold with such is different from what it is with others; it is indeed the privation of conjugial love, but arising from defect.

250. XIV. OF EXTERNAL CAUSES OF COLD THE FIFTH IS, INEQUALITY OF EXTERNAL RANK AND CONDITION. There are several inequalities of rank and condition, which while parties are living together put an end to the conjugial love which commenced before marriage; but they may all be referred to inequalities as to age, station, and wealth. That unequal ages induce cold in marriage, as in the case of a lad with an old woman, and of a young girl with a decrepit old man, needs no proof. That inequality of station has a similar effect, as in the marriage of a prince with a servant maid, or of an illustrious matron with a servant man, is also acknowledged without further proof. That the case is the same in regard to wealth, unless a similitude of minds and manners, and an application of one party to the inclinations and native desires of the other, consociate them, is evident. But in all such cases, the compliance of one party on account of the pre-eminence of station and condition of the other, effects only a servile and frigid conjunction; for the conjugial principle is not of the spirit and heart, but only nominal and of the countenance; in consequence of which the inferior party is given to boasting, and the superior blushes with shame. But in the heavens there is no inequality of age, station, or wealth; in regard to age, all there are in the flower of their youth, and continue so into eternity; in regard to station, they all respect others according to the uses which they perform. The more eminent in condition respect inferiors as brethren, neither do they prefer station to the excellence of use, but the excellence of use to station; also when maidens are given in marriage, they do not know from what ancestors they are descended; for no one in heaven knows his earthly father, but the Lord is the Father of all. The case is the same in regard to wealth, which in heaven is the faculty of growing wise, according to which a suf-

ficiency of wealth is given. How marriages are there entered into, may be seen above, n. 229.

251. XV. THERE ARE ALSO CAUSES OF SEPARATION. There are separations from the bed and also from the house. There are several causes of such separations; but we are here treating of legitimate causes. As the causes of separation coincide with the causes of concubinage, which are treated of in the latter part of this work in their own chapter, the reader is referred thereto that he may see the causes in their order. The legitimate causes of separation are the following.

252. XVI. THE FIRST CAUSE OF LEGITIMATE SEPARATION IS A VITIATED STATE OF MIND. The reason of this is, because conjugial love is a conjunction of minds ; if therefore the mind of one of the parties takes a direction different from that of the other, such conjunction is dissolved, and with the conjunction the love vanishes. The states of vitiation of the mind which cause separation, may appear from an enumeration of them; they are for the most part, the following: madness, frenzy, furious wildness, actual foolishness and idiocy, loss of memory, violent hysterics, extreme silliness so as to admit of no perception of good and truth, excessive stubbornness in refusing to obey what is just and equitable; excessive pleasure in talkativeness and conversing only on insignificant and trifling subjects ; an unbridled desire to publish family secrets, also to quarrel, to strike, to take revenge, to do evil, to steal, to tell lies, to deceive, to blaspheme ; carelessness about the children, intemperance, luxury, excessive prodigality, drunkenness, uncleanness, immodesty, application to magic and witchcraft, impiety, with several other causes. By legitimate causes we do not here mean judicial causes, but such as are legitimate in regard to the other married partner; separation from the house also is seldom ordained in a court of justice.

253. XVII. THE SECOND CAUSE OF LEGITIMATE SEPARATION IS A VITIATED STATE OF BODY. By vitiated states of body we do not mean accidental diseases, which happen to either of the married partners during their marriage, and from which they recover ; but we mean inherent diseases, which are permanent. The science of pathology teaches what these are. They are manifold, such as diseases whereby the whole body is so far infected that the contagion may prove fatal; of this nature are malignant and pestilential fevers, leprosies, the venereal disease, gangrenes, cancers, and the like ; also diseases whereby the whole body is so far weighed down, as to admit of no consociability, and from which exhale dangerous effluvia and noxious vapors, whether from the surface of the body, or from its inward parts, in particular from the stomach and lungs ; from the surface of the body proceed malignant pocks, warts, pustules, scorbutic phthisic, virulent scab, especially if the face be defiled thereby: from the stomach proceed foul, stinking, rank and

crude eructations: from the lungs, filthy and putrid exhalations, arising from imposthumes, ulcers, abcesses, or from vitiated blood or lymph therein. Besides these there are also various other diseases, as lipothamia, which is a total faintness of body and defect of strength; paralysis, which is a loosing and relaxation of the membranes and ligaments which serve for motion; certain chronic diseases, arising from a loss of the sensibility and elasticity of the nerves, or from too great a thickness; tenacity, and acrimony of the humors; epilepsy; fixed weakness arising from apoplexy; certain phthisical complaints, whereby the body is wasted; the cholic, cœliac affection, rupture, and other like diseases.

254. XVIII. THE THIRD CAUSE OF LEGITIMATE SEPARATION IS IMPOTENCE BEFORE MARRIAGE. The reason why this is a cause of separation is, because the end of marriage is the procreation of children, which cannot take place where this cause of separation operates; and as this is foreknown by the parties, they are deliberately deprived of the hope of it, which hope nevertheless nourishes and strengthens their conjugial love.

255. XIX. ADULTERY IS THE CAUSE OF DIVORCE. There are several reasons for this, which are discernible in rational light, and yet at this day they are concealed. From rational light it may be seen that marriages are holy and adulteries profane; and thus that marriages and adulteries are diametrically opposite to each other; and that when opposites act upon each other, one destroys the other even to the last spark of its life. This is the case with conjugial love, when a married person commits adultery from a confirmed principle, and thus from a deliberate purpose. With those who know anything of heaven and hell, these things are more clearly discernible by the light of reason: for they know that marriages are in and from heaven, and that adulteries are in and from hell, and that these two cannot be conjoined, as heaven cannot be conjoined with hell, and that instantly, if they are conjoined with man (*homo*), heaven recedes, and hell enters. Hence then it is, that adultery is the cause of divorce; wherefore the Lord saith, that "*whosoever shall put away his wife, except for whoredom, and shall marry another, committeth adultery,*" Matt. xix. 9. He saith, if, except for whoredom, he shall put away his wife, and marry another, he committeth adultery; because putting away for this cause is a plenary separation of minds, which is called divorce; whereas other kinds of putting away, grounded in their particular causes are separations, of which we have just treated; after these, if another wife is married, adultery is committed; but not so after a divorce.

256. XX. THERE ARE ALSO SEVERAL ACCIDENTAL CAUSES OF COLD; THE FIRST OF WHICH IS, THAT ENJOYMENT IS COMMON (OR CHEAP), BECAUSE CONTINUALLY ALLOWED. The reason

why this consideration is an accidental cause of cold is, because it exists with those who think lasciviously respecting marriage and a wife, but not with those who think holily respecting marriage, and securely respecting a wife. That from being common (or cheap) in consequence of being continually allowed, even joys become indifferent, and also tiresome, is evident from the case of pastimes and public shows, musical entertainments, dancing, feasting, and the like, which in themselves are agreeable, because vivifying. The case is the same with the intimacy and connection between married partners, especially between those who have not removed the unchaste love of the sex from the love which they bear to each other; and when they think of enjoyment's being common (or cheap) in consequence of being continually allowed, they think vainly in the absence of the faculty of enjoyment. That this consideration is to such persons a cause of cold is self-evident. It is called accidental, because it joins inward cold as a cause, and ranks on its side as a reason. To remove the cold arising from this circumstance, it is usual with wives, from the prudence implanted in them, to offer resistance to what is allowable. But the case is altogether otherwise with those who think chastely respecting wives; wherefore with the angels the consideration of enjoyment's being common in consequence of being continually allowed, is the very delight of their souls, and contains their conjugial love; for they are continually in the delight of that love, and in its ultimates according to the presence of their minds uninterrupted by cares, thus from the decisions of the judgement of the husbands.

257. XXI. OF ACCIDENTAL CAUSES OF COLD THE SECOND IS, THAT LIVING WITH A MARRIED PARTNER, FROM A COVENANT AND CONTRACT, SEEMS FORCED AND NOT FREE. This cause operates only with those with whom conjugial love in the inmost principles is cold; and since it unites with internal cold, it becomes an additional or accidental cause. With such persons, extra-conjugial love, arising from consent and the favor thereof, is interiorly in heat; for the cold of the one is the heat of the other; which, if it is not sensibly felt, is still within, yea, in the midst of cold; and unless it was thus also within, there would be no reparation. This heat is what constitutes the force or compulsion, which is increased in proportion as, by one of the parties, the covenant grounded in agreement and the contract grounded in what is just, are regarded as bonds not to be violated; it is otherwise if those bonds are loosed by each of the parties. The case is reversed with those who have rejected extra-conjugial love as detestable, and think of conjugial love as of what is heavenly and heaven; and the more so if they perceive it to be so: with such that covenant with its articles of agreement, and that contract with its sanctions, are inscribed on their hearts, and are continually being inscribed thereon more and more. In

this case the bond of that love is neither secured by a covenant agreed upon, nor by a law enacted; but both covenant and law are from creation implanted in the love itself, which influences the parties; from the latter [namely, the covenant and the law implanted from creation in the love itself] are derived the former [namely, the covenant and law] in the world, but not *vice versa*. Hence, whatever relates to that love is felt as free; neither is there any freedom but what is of love: and I have heard from the angels, that love truly conjugial is most free, because it is the love of loves.

258. XXII. OF ACCIDENTAL CAUSES OF COLD THE THIRD IS, AFFIRMATION ON THE PART OF THE WIFE, AND HER TALKING INCESSANTLY ABOUT LOVE. With the angels in heaven there is no refusal and repugnance on the part of the wives, as there is with some wives on earth: with the angels in heaven also the wives converse about love, and are not silent as some wives on earth; but the causes of these differences I am not allowed to declare, because it would be unbecoming; nevertheless they are declared in four MEMORABLE RELATIONS at the close of the chapters, by the angels' wives, who freely speak of them to their husbands, by the three in the hall over which there was a golden shower, and by the seven who were sitting in a rosary. These memorable relations are adduced, to the end that every thing may be explained that relates to conjugial love, which is the subject here treated of both in general and in particular.

259. XXIII. OF ACCIDENTAL CAUSES OF COLD THE FOURTH IS, THE MAN'S CONTINUALLY THINKING THAT HIS WIFE IS WILLING; AND ON THE OTHER HAND THE WIFE'S THINKING THAT THE MAN IS NOT WILLING. That the latter circumstance is a cause of love's ceasing with wives, and the former a cause of cold with men, is too obvious to need any comment. For that the man who thinks that his wife, when in his sight by day, and when lying at his side by night, is desirous or willing, should grow cold to the extremities, and on the other hand that the wife, who thinks that the man is able and not willing, should lose her love, are circumstances among many others well known to husbands who have considered the arcana relating to conjugial love. These circumstances are adduced also, to the end that this work may be perfected, and THE CONJUGIAL LOVE AND ITS CHASTE DELIGHTS may be completed.

260. XXIV. As COLD IS IN THE MIND IT IS ALSO IN THE BODY; AND ACCORDING TO THE INCREASE OF THAT COLD, THE EXTERNALS ALSO OF THE BODY ARE CLOSED. It is believed at the present day that the mind of man (*homo*) is in the head, and nothing of it in the body, when yet the soul and the mind are both in the head and in the body; for the soul and the mind are the man (*homo*), since both constitute the spirit which lives after death; and that this spirit is in a perfect human form, has

been fully shown in the treatises we have published. Hence, as soon as a man thinks anything, he can in an instant utter it by means of his bodily mouth, and at the same time represent it by gesture; and as soon as he wills anything, he can in an instant bring it into act and effect by his bodily members: which could not be the case unless the soul and the mind were together in the body, and constituted his spiritual man. From these considerations it may be seen, that while conjugial love is in the mind, it is similar to itself in the body; and since love is heat, that it opens the externals of the body from the interiors; but on the other hand, that the privation thereof, which is cold, closes the externals of the body from the interiors: hence it is manifest what is the cause of the faculty [of conjugial love] with the angels enduring for ever, and what is the cause of its failing with men who are cold.

* * * * *

261. To the above I shall add THREE MEMORABLE RELATIONS. FIRST. In the superior northern quarter near the east in the spiritual world, there are places of instruction for boys, for youths, for men, and also for old men: into these places all who die infants are sent and are educated in heaven; so also all who arrive fresh from the world, and desire information about heaven and hell, are sent to the same places. This tract is near the east, that all may be instructed by influx from the Lord; for the Lord is the east, because he is in the sun there, which from him is pure love; hence the heat from that sun in its essence is love, and the light from it in its essence is wisdom. These are inspired into them from the Lord out of that sun; and they are inspired according to reception, and reception is according to the love of growing wise. After periods of instruction, those who are made intelligent are sent forth thence, and are called disciples of the Lord. They are sent forth first into the west, and those who do not remain there, into the south, and some through the south into the east, and are introduced into the societies where they are to reside. On a time, while I was meditating respecting heaven and hell, I began to desire a universal knowledge of the state of each, being aware, that whoever knows universals, may afterwards comprehend particulars, because the latter are contained in the former, as parts in a whole. In this desire I looked to the above tract in the northern quarter near the east, where were the places of instruction, and went there by a way then open to me. I entered one of the colleges, where there were some young men, and addressed the chief teachers there who gave instruction, and asked them whether they were acquainted with the universals respecting heaven and hell. They replied, that they knew some little; "but if we look," said they, "towards the east to the Lord, we shall receive illustration and knowledge." They did so, and said, "There are three universals

of hell, which are diametrically opposite to the universals of heaven. The universals of hell are these three loves; the love of dominion grounded in self-love, the love of possessing the goods of others grounded in the love of the world, and adulterous love. The universals of heaven opposite to these are the three following loves; the love of dominion grounded in the love of use, the love of possessing worldly goods grounded in the love of performing uses therewith, and love truly conjugial." Hereupon, after expressing my good wishes towards them, I took my leave, and returned home. When I was come home, it was said to me from heaven, "Examine those three universals above and beneath, and afterwards we shall see them in your hand." It was said *in the hand*, because whatever a man examines intellectually, appears to the angels as if inscribed on his hands.

262. After this I examined the first universal love of hell, which is the love of dominion grounded in self-love, and afterwards the universal love of heaven corresponding to it, which is the love of dominion grounded in the love of uses; for I was not allowed to examine one love without the other, because, being opposites, the understanding does not perceive the one without the other; wherefore that each may be perceived, they must be set in opposition to each other; for a beautiful and handsome face is rendered conspicuous by contrasting it with an ugly and deformed one. While 1 was considering the love of dominion grounded in self-love, I perceived that this love was in the highest degree infernal, and consequently prevailed with those who are in the deepest hell; and that the love of dominion grounded in the love of uses was in the highest degree heavenly, and consequently prevailed with those who are in the highest heaven. The love of dominion grounded in self-love is in the highest degree infernal, because to exercise dominion from self-love, is to exercise it from *proprium*, and a man's *proprium* from his birth is essential evil, which is diametrically opposite to the Lord; wherefore the more persons who are under the influence of such evil, advance therein, the more they deny God and the holy things of the church, and worship themselves and nature. Let such persons, I entreat them, examine that evil in themselves, and they will see this to be the case. This love also is of such a nature, that in proportion as it is left unrestrained, which is the case so long as it is not checked by impossibilities, in the same proportion it rushes impetuously from step to step, even to the highest, and there also finds no bounds, but is sad and sorrowful because there is no higher step for it to ascend. This love with statesmen is so intense that they wish to be kings and emperors, and if it were possible, to have dominion over all things of the world, and to be called kings of kings and emperors of emperors; while the same love with the clergy is so intense that they wish to be gods and, as far as is possible, to have dominion over all

things of heaven, and to be called gods of gods. That neither of these acknowledge any God, will be seen in what follows. On the other hand, those who desire to exercise dominion from the love of uses, do not desire it from themselves, but from the Lord; since the love of uses is from the Lord, and is the Lord himself: these regard dignities only as means to the performance of uses, setting uses far above dignities; whereas the former set dignities far above uses.

263. While I was meditating on these things, an angel from the Lord said to me, "You shall presently see, and be convinced by ocular demonstration, what is the nature and quality of that infernal love." Then suddenly the earth opened on the left, and I saw a devil ascending from hell, with a square cap on his head let down over his forehead even to his eyes: his face was full of pimples as of a burning fever, his eyes fierce and firy, his breast swelling immensely; from his mouth he belched smoke like a furnace, his loins seemed all in a blaze, instead of feet he had bony ankles without flesh, and from his body exhaled a stinking and filthy heat. On seeing him I was alarmed, and cried out, "Approach no nearer; tell me, whence are you?" He replied in a hoarse tone of voice, "I am from below, where I am with two hundred in the most supereminent of all societies. We are all emperors of emperors, king of kings, dukes of dukes, and princes of princes; no one in our society is barely an emperor, a king, a duke, or a prince. We sit there on thrones of thrones, and despatch thence mandates through the whole world and beyond it." I then said to him, "Do you not see that you are insane from the phantasy of super-eminence?" and he replied, "How can you say so, when we absolutely seem to ourselves, and are also acknowledged by each other, to have such distinction?" On hearing this, I was unwilling to repeat my charge of insanity, as he was insane from phantasy; and I was informed that this devil, during his abode in the world, had been only a house-steward, and at that time he was so lifted up in spirit, that he despised all mankind in comparison with himself, and indulged in the phantasy that he was more worthy than a king, and even than an emperor; in consequence of which proud conceit, he had denied God, and had regarded all the holy things of the church as of no concern to himself, but of some to the stupid multitude. At length I asked him, "How long do you two hundred thus glory among yourselves?" He replied to eternity; but such of us as torture others for denying our super-eminence, sink under ground; for we are allowed to glory, but not to do mischief to any one." I asked him again, "Do you know what befalls those who sink under ground?" He said, "They sink down into a certain prison, where they are called viler than the vile, or the vilest, and are set to work." I

then said to him. "Take heed therefore, lest you also should sink down."

264. After this the earth again opened, but now on the right; and I saw another devil rising thence, who had on his head a kind of turban, wrapped about with spires as of a snake, the head of which stood out from the crown; his face was leprous from the forehead to the chin, and so were his hands; his loins were naked and as black as soot, through which was discernible in dusky transparence the fire as of a furnace; and the ankles of his feet were like two vipers. The former devil, on seeing him, fell on his knees, and adored him. On my asking why he did so, he said, "He is the God of heaven and earth, and is omnipotent." I then asked the other, "What do you say to this?" he replied, "What shall I say? I have all power over heaven and hell; the lot of all souls is in my hand." Again I enquired, "How can he, who is emperor of emperors, so submit himself, and how can you receive adoration?" he answered, "He is still my servant; what is an emperor before God? the thunder of excommunication is in my right hand." I then said to him, "How can you be so insane? In the world you were only a canon; and because you were infected with the phantasy that you also had the keys of heaven, and thence the power of binding and loosing, you have inflamed your spirit to such a degree of madness, that you now believe yourself to be very God." Upon this he swore with indignation that it was so, and said, "The Lord has not any power in heaven, because he has transferred it all to us. We have only to give the word of command, and heaven and hell reverently obey us. If we send any one to hell, the devils immediately receive him; and so do the angels receive those whom we send to heaven." I asked further, "How many are there in your society?" he said, "Three hundred; and we are all gods there; but I am god of gods." After this the earth opened beneath the feet of each, and they sank down into their respective hells; and I saw that beneath their hells were workhouses, into which those who injure others would fall; for every one in hell is left to his phantasy, and is also permitted to glory in it; but he is not allowed to injure another. The reason why such are there, is, because a man is then in his spirit; and the spirit, after it is separated from the body, comes into the full liberty of acting according to its affections and consequent thoughts. I was afterwards permitted to look into their hells: that which contained the emperors of emperors and kings of kings, was full of all uncleanness; and the inhabitants appeared like various kinds of wild beasts, with fierce eyes; and so it was in the other, which contained the gods and the god of gods: in it there appeared the direful birds of night, which are called *ochim* and *ijim*, flying about them. The images of their

phantasies were presented to me under this appearance. From these circumstances it was manifest, what is the nature and quality of political and ecclesiastical self-love; that the latter would make its votaries desirous of being gods, while the former would make them desirous of being emperors; and that under the influence of such loves men wish and strive to attain the objects of their desires, so far as they are left without restraint.

265. Afterwards a hell was opened, where I saw two men, one sitting on a bench, holding his feet in a basket full of serpents which seemed to be creeping upwards by his breast even to his neck; and the other sitting on a blazing ass, at whose sides red serpents were creeping, raising their heads and necks, and pursuing the rider. I was told that they had been popes who had compelled emperors to resign their dominions, and had ill-treated them both in word and deed at Rome, whither they went to supplicate and adore them; and that the basket in which were the serpents, and the blazing ass with snakes at his sides, were representations of their love of dominion grounded on self-love, and that such appearances are seen only by those who look at them from a distance. There were some canons present, whom I asked whether those had really been popes? They said, that they were acquainted with them, and knew that they had been such.

266. After beholding these sad and hideous spectacles, I looked around, and saw two angels in conversation standing near me. One wore a woollen robe that shone bright with flaming purple, and under it a vest of fine bright linen; the other had on similar garments of scarlet, together with a turban studded on the right side with carbuncles. I approached them, and, greeting them with a salutation of peace, respectfully asked them, "For what purpose are you here below?" They replied, "We have let ourselves down from heaven by the Lord's command, to speak with you respecting the blessed lot of those who are desirous to have dominion from the love of uses. We are worshipers of the Lord. I am prince of a society; my companion is chief priest of the same." The prince moreover said, "I am the servant of my society, because I serve it by doing uses:" the other said, "I am minister of the church there, because in serving them I minister holy things to the uses of their souls. We both are in perpetual joys grounded in the eternal happiness which is in them from the Lord. All things in our society are splendid and magnificent; they are splendid from gold and precious stones, and magnificent from palaces and paradises. The reason of this is, because our love of dominion is not grounded in self-love, but in the love of uses: and as the love of uses is from the Lord, therefore all good uses in the heavens are splendid and refulgent; and as all in our society are in this love, therefore the atmosphere appears golden from the light which partakes of the

sun's flame-principle, and the sun's flame-principle corresponds to that love." As they said this, they appeared to me to be encompassed with such a sphere, from which an aromatic odor issued that was perceivable by the senses. I mentioned this circumstance to them, and intreated them to continue their discourse respecting the love of uses; and they proceeded thus: "The dignities which we enjoy, we indeed sought after and solicited for no other end than that we might be enabled more fully to perform uses, and to extend them more widely. We are also encompassed with honor, and we accept it, not for ourselves, but for the good of the society; for the brethren and consociates, who form the commonalty of the society, scarcely know but that the honors of our dignities are in ourselves, and consequently that the uses which we perform are from ourselves; but we feel otherwise, being sensible that the honors of the dignities are out of ourselves, and that they are as the garments with which we are clothed; but that the uses which we perform, from the love of them, are within us from the Lord: and this love receives its blessedness from communication by uses with others; and we know from experience, that so far as we do uses from the love thereof, so far that love increases, and with it wisdom, whereby communication is effected; but so far as we retain uses in ourselves, and do not communicate them, so far blessedness perishes; and in such case use becomes like food stored up in the stomach, which, not being dispersed, affords no nourishment to the body and its parts, but remains undigested, and thereby causes loathing: in a word, the whole heaven is nothing but a continent of use, from first principles to last. What is use but the actual love of our neighbor? and what holds the heavens together with this love?" On hearing this I asked, "How can any one know whether he performs uses from self-love, or from the love of uses? every man, both good and bad, performs uses, and that from some love. Suppose that in the world there be a society composed of mere devils, and another composed of mere angels; I am of opinion that the devils in their society, from the fire of self-love, and the splendor of their own glory, would do as many uses as the angels in their society; who then can know from what love, and from what origin uses flow?" To this the two angels replied, "Devils do uses for the sake of themselves and of reputation, that they may be raised to honors or may gain wealth; but angels do not do uses from such motives, but for the sake of uses from the love thereof. A man cannot discern the true quality of those uses; but the Lord discerns it. Every one who believes in the Lord, and shuns evils as sins, performs uses from the Lord; but every one who neither believes in the Lord, nor shuns evils as sins, does uses from self and for the sake of self. This is the difference between the uses done by devils and those done by angels." Having said this, the two angels departed; and I saw them from afar carried in a firy chariot like Elias, and conveyed into their respective heavens.

267. THE SECOND MEMORABLE RELATION. Not long after this interview with the angels, I entered a certain grove, and while I was walking there, I meditated on those who are in the concupiscence and consequent phantasy of possessing the things of the world; and then at some distance from me I saw two angels in conversation, and by turns looking at me; I therefore went nearer to them, and as I approached they thus accosted me: "We have perceived in ourselves that you are meditating on what we are conversing about, or that we are conversing on what you are meditating about, which is a consequence of the reciprocal communication of affections." I asked therefore what they were conversing about? they replied, "About phantasy, concupiscence, and intelligence; and just now about those who lelight themselves in the vision and imagination of possessing whatever the world contains." I then entreated them to favor me with their sentiments on those three subjects,—concupiscence, phantasy, and intelligence. They began by saying, "Every one is by birth interiorly in concupiscence, but by education exteriorly in intelligence; and no one is in intelligence, still less in wisdom, interiorly, thus as to his spirit, but from the Lord: for every one is withheld from the concupiscence of evil, and held in intelligence, according as he looks to the Lord, and is at the same time in conjunction with him; without this, a man is mere concupiscence; yet still in externals, or as to the body, he is in intelligence arising from education; for a man lusts after honors and wealth, or eminence and opulence, and in order to attain them, it is necessary that he appear moral and spiritual, thus intelligent and wise; and he learns so to appear from infancy. This the reason why, as soon as he comes among men, or into company, he inverts his spirit, and removes it from concupiscence, and speaks and acts from the fair and honorable maxims which he has learnt from infancy, and retains in the bodily memory: and he is particularly cautious, lest anything of the wild concupiscence prevalent in his spirit should discover itself. Hence every man who is not interiorly led by the Lord, is a pretender, a sycophant, a hypocrite, and thereby an apparent man, and yet not a man; of whom it may be said, that his shell or body is wise, and his kernel or spirit insane; also that his external is human, and his internal bestial. Such persons, with the hinder part of the head look upwards, and with the fore part downwards; thus they walk as if oppressed with heaviness, with the head hanging down and the countenance prone to the earth; and when they put off the body, and become spirits, and are thereby set at liberty from external restraints, they become the madnesses of their respective concupiscences. Those who are in self-love desire to domineer over the universe, yea, to extend its

limits in order to enlarge their dominion, of which they see no end: those who are in the love of the world desire to possess whatever the world contains, and are full of grief and envy in case any of its treasures are hid and concealed from them by others: therefore to prevent such persons from becoming mere concupiscences, and thereby no longer men, they are permitted in the spiritual world to think from a fear of the loss of reputation, and thereby of honor and gain, and also from a fear of the law and its penalties, and also to give their mind to some study or work whereby they are kept in externals and thus in a state of intelligence, however wild and insane they may be interiorly." After this I asked them, whether all who are in any concupiscence, are also in the phantasy thereof; they replied, that those are in the phantasy of their respective concupiscences, who think interiorly in themselves, and too much indulge their imagination by talking with themselves; for these almost separate their spirit from connection with the body, and by vision overflow the understanding, and take a foolish delight as if they were possessed of the universe and all that it contains: into this delirium every man comes after death, who has abstracted his spirit from the body, and has not wished to recede from the delight of the delirium by thinking at all religiously respecting evils and falses, and least of all respecting the inordinate love of self as being destructive of love to the Lord, and respecting the inordinate love of the world, as being destructive of neighborly love.

268. After this the two angels and also myself were seized with a desire of seeing those who from worldly love are in the visionary concupiscence or phantasy of possessing all wealth; and we perceived that we were inspired with this desire to the end that such visionaries might be known. Their dwellings were under the earth of our feet, but above hell: we therefore looked at each other and said, "Let us go." There was an opening, and in it a ladder by which we descended; and we were told that we must approach them from the east, lest we should enter into the mist of their phantasy, whereby our understanding and at the same time our sight would be obscured; and lo! there appeared a house built of reeds, and consequently full of chinks, standing in a mist, which continually issued like smoke through the chinks of three of the walls. We entered, and saw perhaps fifty here and fifty there sitting on benches, with their faces turned from the east and south, and looking towards the west and north. Before each person there was a table, on which were large purses, and by the purses a great quantity of gold coin: so we asked them, "Is that the wealth of all the persons in the world?" they replied, "Not of all in the world, but of all in the kingdom." The sound of their voice was hissing; and they had round faces, which glistened like the shell of a snail, and the pupils of their eyes in a green plane as it were shot forth light-

ning, which was an effect of the light of phantasy. We stood in the midst of them, and said, "You believe that you possess all the wealth of the kingdom;" they replied, "We do possess it." We then asked, "Which of you?" they said, "Every one;" and we asked, "How every one? there are many of you:" they said, "Every one of us knows that all which another has is his own. No one is allowed to think, and still less to say, 'Mine are not thine; but every one may think and say, 'Thine are mine.'" The coin on the tables appeared, even to us, to be pure gold; but when we let in light from the east, we saw that they were little grains of gold, which they had magnified to such a degree by a union of their common phantasy. They said, that every one that enters ought to bring with him some gold, which they cut into small pieces, and these again into little grains, and by the unanimous force of their phantasy they increase them into larger coin. We then said, "Were you not born men of reason; whence then have you this visionary infatuation?" they said, "We know that it is an imaginary vanity; but as it delights the interiors of our minds, we enter here and are delighted as with the possession of all things: we continue in this place, however, only a few hours, at the end of which we depart; and as often as we do so we again become of sound mind; yet still our visionary delight alternately succeeds and occasions our alternate entrance into and departure from these habitations: thus we are alternately wise and foolish; we also know that a hard lot awaits those who by cunning rob others of their goods." We inquired, "What lot?" they said, "They are swallowed up and are thrust naked into some infernal prison, where they are kept to hard labor for clothes and food, and afterwards for some pieces of coin of trifling value, which they collect, and in which they place the joy of their hearts; but if they do any harm to their companions, they are fined a part of their coin."

269. Afterwards we ascended from these hells to the south, where we had been before, and the angels related there several interesting particulars respecting concupiscence not visionary or phantastic, in which all men are born; namely, that while they are in it, they are like persons infatuated, and yet seem to themselves to be most eminently wise; and that from this infatuation they are alternately let into the rational principle which is in their externals; in which state they see, acknowledge, and confess their insanity; but still they are very desirous to quit their rational and enter their insane state; and also do let themselves into it, as into a free and delightful state succeeding a forced and undelightful one; thus it is concupiscence and not intelligence that interiorly pleases them. There are three universal loves which form the constituent principles of every man by creation; neighbourly love, which also is the love of doing uses; the love of the world, which also is the love of possessing wealth; and

the love of self, which also is the love of bearing rule over others. Neighbourly love, or the love of doing uses, is a spiritual love; but the love of the world, or the love of possessing wealth, is a material love; whereas the love of self, or the love of bearing rule over others, is a corporeal love. A man is a man while neighbourly love, or the love of doing uses, constitutes the head, the love of the world the body, and the love of self the feet; whereas if the love of the world constitutes the head, the man is as it were hunched-backed; but when the love of self constitutes the head, he is like a man standing not on his feet, but on the palms of his hands with his head downwards and his haunches upwards. When neighbourly love constitutes the head, and the two other loves in order constitute the body and feet, the man appears from heaven of an angelic countenance, with a beautiful rainbow about his head; whereas if the love of the world constitutes the head, he appears from heaven of a pale countenance like a corpse, with a yellow circle about his head; but if the love of self constitutes the head, he appears from heaven of a dusky countenance, with a white circle about his head." Hereupon I asked, "What do the circles about the head represent?" they replied, "They represent intelligence; the white circle about the head of the dusky countenance represents, that his intelligence is in externals, or about him, but insanity is in his internals, or in him. A man also who is of such a quality and character, is wise while in the body, but insane while in the spirit; and no man is wise in spirit but from the Lord, as is the case when he is regenerated and created again or anew by him." As they said this, the earth opened to the left, and through the opening I saw a devil rising with a white lucid circle around his head, and I asked him, Who he was? He said, "I am Lucifer, the son of the morning: and because I made myself like the Most High, I was cast down." Nevertheless he was not Lucifer, but believed himself to be so. I then said, 'Since you were cast down, how can you rise again out of hell?" he replied, "There I am a devil, but here I am an angel of light: do you not see that my head is surrounded by a lucid sphere? you shall also see, if you wish, that I am super-moral among the moral, super-rational among the rational, yea, super-spiritual among the spiritual: I can also preach; yea, I have preached." I asked him, "What have you preached?" he said, "Against fraudulent dealers and adulterers, and against all infernal loves; on this occasion too I, Lucifer, called myself a devil, and denounced vengeance against myself as a devil; and therefore I was extolled to the skies with praises. Hence it is that I am called the son of the morning; and, what I myself was surprised at, while I was in the pulpit, I thought no other than that I was speaking rightly and properly; but I discovered that this arose from my being in externals, which at that time were separated from my internals; but although I discovered this, still I could not change myself, because through my haughtiness I did not look to God." I next asked him, "How could you so speak, when you are yourself a fraudulent dealer, an adulterer, and a devil?" He answered, "I am one character when I am in externals or in the body, and another when in internals or in the spirit; in the body I am an angel, but in the spirit a devil; for in the body I am in the understanding, but in the spirit I am in the will; and the understanding carries me upwards, whereas the will carries me downwards. When I am in the understanding my head is surrounded by a white belt, but when the understanding submits itself entirely to the will, and becomes subservient to it, which is our last lot, the belt grows black and disappears; and when this is the case, we cannot again ascend into this light." Afterwards he spoke of his twofold state, the external and the internal, more rationally than any other person; but on a sudden when he saw the angels attendant on me, his face and voice were inflamed, and he became black, even as to the belt round his head, and he sunk down into hell through the opening from which he arose. The bystanders, from what they had seen, came to this conclusion, that a man is such as his love, and not such as his understanding is; since the love easily draws over the understanding to its side, and enslaves it. I then asked the angels, "Whence have devils such rationality?" They said, "It is from the glory of self-love; for self-love is surrounded by glory, and glory elevates the understanding even into the light of heaven; for with every man the understanding is capable of being elevated according to knowledges, but the will only by a life according to the truths of the church and of reason: hence even atheists, who are in the glory of reputation arising from self-love, and thence in a high conceit of their own intelligence, enjoy a more sublime rationality than many others; this, however, is only when they are in the thought of the understanding, and not when they are in the affection of the will. The affection of the will possesses a man's internal, whereas the thought of the understanding possesses his external." The angel further declared the reason why every man is constituted of the three loves above mentioned; namely, the love of use, the love of the world, and the love of self; which is, that he may think from God, although as from himself. He also said, that the supreme principles in a man are turned upwards to God, the middle outwards to the world, and the lowest downwards to self; and since the latter are turned downwards, a man thinks as from himself, when yet it is from God.

270. THE THIRD MEMORABLE RELATION. One morning on awaking from sleep my thoughts were deeply engaged on some arcana of conjugial love, and at length on this, "*In what region of the human mind does love truly conjugial reside, and thence in what region does conjugial cold reside?*" I knew that there are

three regions of the human mind, one above the other, and that in the lowest region dwells natural love; in the superior, spiritual love; and in the supreme, celestial love; and that in each region there is a marriage of good and truth; and good is of love, and truth is of wisdom; that in each region there is a marriage of love and wisdom; and that this marriage is the same as the marriage of the will and the understanding, since the will is the receptacle of love, and the understanding the receptacle of wisdom. While I was thus deeply engaged in thought, lo! I saw two swans flying towards the north, and presently two birds of paradise flying towards the south, and also two turtle doves flying in the east: as I was watching their flight, I saw that the two swans bent their course from the north to the east, and the two birds of paradise from the south, also that they united with the two doves in the east, and flew together to a certain lofty palace there, about which there were olives, palms, and beeches. The palace had three rows of windows, one above the other; and while I was making my observations, I saw the swans fly into the palace through open windows in the lowest row, the birds of paradise through others in the middle row, and the doves through others in the highest. When I had observed this, an angel presented himself, and said, "Do you understand what you have seen?" I replied, "In a small degree." He said, "That palace represents the habitations of conjugial love, such as are in human minds. Its highest part, into which the doves flew, represents the highest region of the mind, where conjugial love dwells in the love of good with its wisdom; the middle part, into which the birds of paradise flew, represents the middle region, where conjugial love dwells in the love of truth with its intelligence: and the lowest part, into which the swans flew, represents the lowest region of the mind, where conjugial love dwells in the love of what is just and right with its knowledge. The three pairs of birds also signify these things; the pair of turtle doves signifies conjugial love of the highest region, the pair of birds of paradise conjugial love of the middle region, and the pair of swans conjugial love of the lowest region. Similar things are signified by the three kinds of trees about the palace, the olives, palms, and beeches. We in heaven call the highest region of the mind celestial, the middle spiritual, and the lowest natural; and we perceive them as stories in a house, one above another, and an ascent from one to the other by steps as by stairs; and in each part as it were two apartments, one for love, the other for wisdom, and in front as it were a chamber, where love with its wisdom, or good with its truth, or, what is the same, the will with its understanding, consociate in bed. In that palace are presented as in an image all the arcana of conjugial love." On hearing this, being inflamed with a desire of seeing it, I asked whether anyone was permitted to enter and see it, as it was a representative palace? He replied, "None but those who are in the third heaven, because to them every representative of love and wisdom becomes real: from them I have heard what I have related to you, and also this particular, that love truly conjugial dwells in the highest region in the midst of mutual love, in the marriage-chamber or apartment of the will, and also in the midst of the perceptions of wisdom in the marriage-chamber or apartment of the understanding, and that they consociate in bed in the chamber which is in front, in the east." I also asked, "Why are there two marriage-chambers?" He said, "The husband is in the marriage-chamber of the understanding, and the wife in that of the will." I then asked, "Since conjugial love dwells there, where then does conjugial cold dwell?" He replied, "It dwells also in the supreme region, but only in the marriage-chamber of the understanding, that of the will being closed there: for the understanding with its truths, as often as it pleases, can ascend by a winding staircase into the highest region into its marriage-chamber; but if the will with the good of its love does not ascend at the same time into the consociate marriage-chamber, the latter is closed, and cold ensues in the other: this is *conjugial cold*. The understanding, while such cold prevails towards the wife, looks downwards to the lowest region, and also, if not prevented by fear, descends to warm itself there at an illicit fire." Having thus spoken, he was about to recount further particulars respecting conjugial love from its images in that palace; but he said, "Enough at this time; inquire first whether what has been already said is above the level of ordinary understandings; if it is, what need of saying any more? but if not, more will be discovered."

ON THE CAUSES OF APPARENT LOVE, FRIENDSHIP, AND FAVOR IN MARRIAGES.

271. HAVING treated of the causes of cold and separation, it follows from order that the causes of apparent love, friendship, and favor in marriages, should also be treated of; for it is well known, that although cold separates the minds (*animos*) of married partners at the present day, still they live together, and have children; which would not be the case, unless there were also apparent loves, alternately similar to or emulous of the warmth of genuine love. That these appearances are necessary and useful, and that without them there would be no houses, and consequently no societies, will be seen in what follows. Moreover, some conscientious persons may be distressed with the idea, that the disagreement of mind subsisting between them and their married partners, and the internal alienation thence arising, may

be their own fault, and may be imputed to them as such, and on this account they are grieved at the heart; but as it is out of their power to prevent internal disagreements, it is enough for them, by apparent love and favor, from conscientious motives to subdue the inconveniences which might arise: hence also friendship may possibly return, in which conjugial love lies concealed on the part of such, although not on the part of the other. But this subject, like the foregoing, from the great variety of its matter, shall be treated of in the following distinct articles: I. *In the natural world almost all are capable of being joined together as to external, but not as to internal affections, if these disagree and are apparent.* II. *In the spiritual world all are joined together according to internal, but not according to external affections, unless these act in unity with the internal.* III. *It is the external affections, according to which matrimony is generally contracted in the world.* IV. *But in case they are not influenced by internal affections, which conjoin minds, the bonds of matrimony are loosed in the house.* V. *Nevertheless those bonds must continue in the world till the decease of one of the parties.* VI. *In cases of matrimony, in which the internal affections do not conjoin, there are external affections, which assume a semblance of the internal and tend to consociate.* VII. *Hence come apparent love, friendship, and favor between married partners.* VIII. *These appearances are assumed conjugial semblances, and they are commendable, because useful and necessary.* IX. *These assumed conjugial semblances, in the case of a spiritual man* (homo) *conjoined to a natural, are founded in justice and judgement.* X. *For various reasons these assumed conjugial semblances with natural men are founded in prudence.* XI. *They are for the sake of amendment and accommodation.* XII. *They are for the sake of preserving order in domestic affairs, and for the sake of mutual aid.* XIII. *They are for the sake of unanimity in the care of infants and the education of children.* XIV. *They are for the sake of peace in the house.* XV. *They are for the sake of reputation out of the house.* XVI. *They are for the sake of various favors expected from the married partner, or from his or her relations; and thus from the fear of losing such favors.* XVII. *They are for the sake of having blemishes excused, and thereby of avoiding disgrace.* XVIII. *They are for the sake of reconciliation.* XIX. *In case favor does not cease with the wife, when faculty ceases with the man, there may exist a friendship resembling conjugial friendship, when the parties grow old.* XX. *There are various kinds of apparent love and friendship between married partners, one of whom is brought under the yoke, and therefore is subject to the other.* XXI. *In the world there are infernal marriages between persons who interiorly are the most inveterate enemies, and exteriorly are as the closest friends.* We proceed to an explanation of each article.

272. I. IN THE NATURAL WORLD ALMOST ALL ARE CAPABLE OF BEING JOINED TOGETHER AS TO EXTERNAL, BUT NOT AS TO INTERNAL AFFECTIONS, IF THESE DISAGREE AND ARE APPARENT. The reason of this is, because in the world every one is clothed with a material body, and this is overcharged with lusts, which are in it as dregs that fall to the bottom, when the must of the wine is clarified. Such are the constituent substances of which the bodies of men in the world are composed. Hence it is that the internal affections, which are of the mind, do not appear; and in many cases, scarce a grain of them transpires; for the body either absorbs them, and involves them in its dregs, or by simulation which has been learned from infancy conceals them deeply from the sight of others; and by these means the man puts himself into the state of every affection which he observes in another, and allures his affection to himself, and thus they unite. The reason why they unite is, because every affection has its delight, and delights tie minds together. But it would be otherwise if the internal affections, like the external, appeared visibly in the face and gesture, and were made manifest to the hearing by the tone of the speech; or if their delights were sensible to the nostrils or smell, as they are in the spiritual world: in such case, if they disagreed so as to be discordant, they would separate minds from each other, and according to the perception of antipathy, the minds would remove to a distance. From these considerations it is evident, that in the natural world almost all are capable of being joined together as to external, but not as to internal affections, if these disagree and are apparent.

273. II. IN THE SPIRITUAL WORLD ALL ARE CONJOINED ACCORDING TO INTERNAL, BUT NOT ACCORDING TO EXTERNAL AFFECTIONS, UNLESS THESE ACT IN UNITY WITH THE INTERNAL. This is, because in the spiritual world the material body is rejected, which could receive and bring forth the forms of all affections, as we have said just above; and a man (*homo*) when stripped of that body is in his internal affections, which his body had before concealed: hence it is, that in the spiritual world similarities and dissimilarities, or sympathies and antipathies, are not only felt, but also appear in the face, the speech, and the gesture; wherefore in that world similitudes are conjoined, and dissimilitudes separated. This is the reason why the universal heaven is arranged by the Lord according to all the varieties of the affections of the love of good and truth, and, on the contrary, hell according to all the varieties of the love of what is evil and false. As angels and spirits, like men in the world, have internal and external affections, and as, in the spiritual world, the internal affections cannot be concealed by the external, they therefore transpire and manifest themselves: hence with angels and spirits both the internal and external affections are reduced to similitude and correspondence; after which their internal affections are, by

the external, imaged in their faces, and perceived in the tone of their speech; they also appear in their behaviour and manners. Angels and spirits have internal and external affections, because they have minds and bodies; and affections with the thoughts thence derived belong to the mind, and sensations with the pleasures thence derived to the body. It frequently happens in the world of spirits, that friends meet after death, and recollect their friendships in the former world, and on such occasions believe that they shall live on terms of friendship as formerly; but when their consociation, which is only of the external affections, is perceived in heaven, a separation ensues according to their internal; and in this case some are removed from the place of their meeting into the north, some into the west, and each to such a distance from the other, that they can no longer see or know each other; for in the places appointed for them to remain at, their faces are changed so as to become the image of their internal affections. From these considerations it is manifest, that in the spiritual world all are conjoined according to internal affections, and not according to external, unless these act in unity with the internal.

274. III. IT IS THE EXTERNAL AFFECTIONS ACCORDING TO WHICH MATRIMONY IS GENERALLY CONTRACTED IN THE WORLD. The reason of this is, because the internal affections are seldom consulted; and even if they are, still their similitude is not seen in the woman; for she, by a peculiar property with which she is gifted from her birth, withdraws the internal affections into the inner recesses of her mind. There are various external affections which induce men to engage in matrimony. The first affection of this age is an increase of property by wealth, as well with a view to becoming rich as for a plentiful supply of the comforts of life; the second is a thirst after honors, with a view either of being held in high estimation or of an increase of fortune: besides these, there are various allurements and concupiscences which do not afford an opportunity of ascertaining the agreement of the internal affections. From these few considerations it is manifest, that matrimony is generally contracted in the world according to external affections.

275. IV. BUT IN CASE THEY ARE NOT INFLUENCED BY INTERNAL AFFECTIONS, WHICH CONJOIN MINDS, THE BONDS OF MATRIMONY ARE LOOSED IN THE HOUSE. It is said *in the house*, because it is done privately between the parties; as is the case when the first warmth, excited during courtship and breaking out into a flame as the nuptials approach, successively abates from the discordance of the internal affections, and at length passes off into cold. It is well known that in this case the external affections, which had induced and allured the parties to matrimony, disappear, so that they no longer effect conjunction. That cold arises from various causes, internal, external, and accidental.

all which originate in a dissimilitude of internal inclinations, was proved in the foregoing chapter. From these considerations the truth of what was asserted is manifest, that unless the external affections are influenced by internal, which conjoin minds, the bonds of matrimony are loosed in the house.

276. V. NEVERTHELESS THOSE BONDS MUST CONTINUE IN THE WORLD TILL THE DECEASE OF ONE OF THE PARTIES. This proposition is adduced to the intent that to the eye of reason it may more evidently appear how necessary, useful, and true it is, that where there is not genuine conjugial love, it ought still to be assumed, that it may appear as if there were. The case would be otherwise if the marriage contract was not to continue to the end of life, but might be dissolved at pleasure; as was the case with the Israelitish nation, who claimed to themselves the liberty of putting away their wives for every cause This is evident from the following passage in Matthew: "*The pharisees came, and said unto Jesus, Is it lawful for a man to put away his wife for every cause? And when Jesus answered, that it is not lawful to put away a wife and to marry another; except on account of whoredom, they replied that nevertheless Moses commanded to give a bill of divorce and to put her away; and the disciples said, If the case of a man with his wife be so, it is not expedient to marry,*" xix. 3—10. Since therefore the covenant of marriage is for life, it follows that the appearances of love and friendship between married partners are necessary. That matrimony, when contracted, must continue till the decease of one of the parties, is grounded in the divine law, consequently also in rational law, and thence in civil law: in the divine law, because, as said above, it is not lawful to put away a wife and marry another, except for whoredom; in rational law, because it is founded upon spiritual, for divine law and rational are one law; from both these together, or by the latter from the former, it may be abundantly seen what enormities and destructions of societies would result from the dissolving of marriage, or the putting away of wives, at the good pleasure of the husbands, before death. Those enormities and destructions of societies may in some measure be seen in the MEMORABLE RELATION respecting the origin of conjugial love, discussed by the spirits assembled from the nine kingdoms, n. 103—115; to which there is no need of adding further reasons. But these causes do not operate to prevent the permission of separations grounded in their proper causes, respecting which see above, n. 252—254; and also of concubinage, respecting which see the second part of this work.

277. VI. IN CASE OF MATRIMONY IN WHICH THE INTERNAL AFFECTIONS DO NOT CONJOIN, THERE ARE EXTERNAL AFFECTIONS WHICH ASSUME A SEMBLANCE OF THE INTERNAL AND TEND TO CONSOCIATE. By internal affections we mean the mutual incli-

nations which influence the mind of each of the parties from heaven; whereas by external affections we mean the inclinations which influence the mind of each of the parties from the world. The latter affections or inclinations indeed equally belong to the mind, but they occupy its inferior regions, whereas the former occupy the superior: but since both have their allotted seat in the mind, it may possibly be believed that they are alike and agree; yet although they are not alike, still they can appear so: in some cases they exist as agreements, and in some as insinuating semblances. There is a certain communion implanted in each of the parties from the earliest time of the marriage-covenant, which, notwithstanding their disagreement in minds (*animis*) still remains implanted; as a communion of possessions, and in many cases a communion of uses, and of the various necessities of the house, and thence also a communion of thoughts and of certain secrets; there is also a communion of bed, and of the love of children: not to mention several others, which, as they are inscribed on the conjugial covenant, are also inscribed on their minds. Hence originate especially those external affections which resemble the internal; whereas those which only counterfeit them are partly from the same origin and partly from another; but on the subject of each more will be said in what follows.

278. VII. HENCE COME APPARENT LOVE, FRIENDSHIP, AND FAVOR BETWEEN MARRIED PARTNERS. Apparent loves, friendships, and favors between married partners, are a consequence of the conjugial covenant being ratified for the term of life, and of the conjugial communion thence inscribed on those who ratify it; whence spring external affections resembling the internal, as was just now indicated: they are moreover a consequence of their causes, which are usefulness and necessity: from which in part exist conjunctive external affections, or their counterfeit, whereby external love and friendship appear as internal.

279. VIII. THESE APPEARANCES ARE ASSUMED CONJUGIAL SEMBLANCES; AND THEY ARE COMMENDABLE, BECAUSE USEFUL AND NECESSARY. They are called assumed semblances, because they exist with those who disagree in mind, and who from such disagreement are interiorly in cold: in this case, when they still appear to live united, as duty and decency require, their kind offices to each other may be called assumed conjugial semblances; which, as being commendable for the sake of uses, are altogether to be distinguished from hypocritical semblances; for hereby all those good things are provided for, which are commemorated in order below, from article XI—XX. They are commendable for the sake of necessity, because otherwise those good things would be unattained; and yet the parties are enjoined by a covenant and compact to live together, and hence it behoves each of them to consider it a duty to do so.

280. IX. These assumed conjugial semblances, in the case of a spiritual man (*homo*) conjoined to a natural, are founded in justice and judgement. The reason of this is, because the spiritual man, in all he does, acts from justice and judgement; wherefore he does not regard these assumed semblances as alienated from their internal affections, but as connected with them; for he is in earnest, and respects amendment as an end; and if he does not obtain this, he respects accommodation for the sake of domestic order, mutual aid, the care of children, and peace and tranquillity. To these things he is led from a principle of justice; and from a principle of judgement he gives them effect. The reason why a spiritual man so lives with a natural one is, because a spiritual man acts spiritually, even with a natural man.

281. X. For various reasons, these assumed conjugial semblances with natural men are founded in prudence. In the case of two married partners of whom one is spiritual and the other natural, (by the spiritual we mean the one that loves spiritual things, and thereby is wise from the Lord, and by the natural, the one that loves only natural things, and thereby is wise from himself,) when they are united in marriage, conjugial love with the spiritual partner is heat, and with the natural is cold. It is evident that heat and cold cannot remain together, also that heat cannot inflame him that is in cold, unless the cold be first dispersed, and that cold cannot flow into him that is in heat, unless the heat be first removed: hence it is that inward love cannot exist between married partners, one of whom is spiritual and the other natural; but that a love resembling inward love may exist on the part of the spiritual partner, as was said in the foregoing article; whereas between two natural married partners no inward love can exist, since each is cold; and if they have any heat, it is from something unchaste; nevertheless such persons may live together in the same house, with separate minds (*animis*), and also assume looks of love and friendship towards each other, notwithstanding the disagreement of their minds (*mentes*): in such case, the external affections, which for the most part relate to wealth and possessions, or to honor and dignities, may as it were be kindled into a flame; and as such enkindling induces fear for their loss, therefore assumed conjugial semblances are in such cases necessities, which are principally those adduced below in articles XV.—XVII. The rest of the causes adduced with these may have somewhat in common with those relating to the spiritual man; concerning which see above, n. 280; but only in case the prudence with the natural man is founded in intelligence.

282. XI. They are for the sake of amendment and accommodation. The reason why assumed conjugial semblances, which are appearances of love and friendship subsisting between

married partners who disagree in mind, are for the sake of amendment, is because a spiritual man (*homo*), connected with a natural one by the matrimonial covenant, intends nothing else but amendment of life; which he effects by judicious and elegant conversation, and by favors which soothe and flatter the temper of the other; but in case these things prove ineffectual, he intends accommodation, for the preservation of order in domestic affairs, for mutual aid, and for the sake of the infants and children, and other similar things; for, as was shown above, n. 280, whatever is said and done by a spiritual man (*homo*) is founded in justice and judgement. But with married partners, neither of whom is spiritual, but both natural, similar conduct may exist, but for other ends; if for the sake of amendment and accommodation, the end is, either that the other party may be reduced to a similitude of manners, and be made subordinate to his desires, or that some service may be made subservient to his own, or for the sake of peace within the house, of reputation out of it, or of favors hoped for by the married partner or his relations; not to mention other ends: but with some these ends are grounded in the prudence of their reason, with some in natural civility, with some in the delights of certain cupidities which have been familiar from the cradle, the loss of which is dreaded; besides several ends, which render the assumed kindnesses as of conjugial love more or less counterfeit. There may also be kindnesses as of conjugial love out of the house, and none within; those however respect as an end the reputation of both parties; and if they do not respect this, they are merely deceptive.

283. XII. THEY ARE FOR THE SAKE OF PRESERVING ORDER IN DOMESTIC AFFAIRS, AND FOR THE SAKE OF MUTUAL AID. Every house in which there are children, their instructors, and other domestics, is a small society resembling a large one. The latter also consists of the former, as a whole consists of its parts, and thereby it exists; and further, as the security of a large society depends on order, so does the security of this small society; wherefore as it behoves public magistrates to see and provide that order may exist and be preserved in a compound society, so it concerns married partners in their single society. But there cannot be this order if the husband and wife disagree in their minds (*animis*); for thereby mutual counsels and aids are drawn different ways, and are divided like their minds, and thus the form of the small society is rent asunder; wherefore to preserve order, and thereby to take care of themselves and at the same time of the house, or of the house and at the same time of themselves, lest they should come to hurt and fall to ruin, necessity requires that the master and mistress agree, and act in unity; and if, from the difference of their minds (*mentium*), this cannot be done so wel as it might, both duty and propriety

require that it be done by representative conjugial friendship. That hereby concord is established in houses for the sake of necessity and consequent utility, is well known.

284. XIII. THEY ARE FOR THE SAKE OF UNANIMITY IN THE CARE OF INFANTS AND THE EDUCATION OF CHILDREN. It is very well known that assumed conjugial semblances, which are appearances of love and friendship resembling such as are truly conjugial, exist with married partners for the sake of infants and children. The common love of the latter causes each married partner to regard the other with kindness and favor. The love of infants and children with the mother and the father unite as the heart and lungs in the breast. The love of them with the mother is as the heart, and the love towards them with the father is as the lungs. The reason of this comparison is, because the heart corresponds to love, and the lungs to the understanding; and love grounded in the will belongs to the mother, and love grounded in the understanding to the father. With spiritual men (*homines*) there is conjugial conjunction by means of that love grounded in justice and judgement; in justice, because the mother had carried them in her womb, had brought them forth with pain, and afterwards with unwearied care suckles, nourishes, washes, dresses, and educates them, [and in judgement, because the father provides for their instruction in knowledge, intelligence, and wisdom.]*

285. XIV. THEY ARE FOR THE SAKE OF PEACE IN THE HOUSE. Assumed conjugial semblances, or external friendships for the sake of domestic peace and tranquillity, relate principally to the men, who, from their natural characteristic, act from the understanding in whatever they do; and the understanding, being exercised in thought, is engaged in a variety of objects which disquiet, disturb, and distract the mind; wherefore if there were not tranquillity at home, it would come to pass that the vital spirits of the parties would grow faint, and their interior life would as it were expire, and thereby the health of both mind and body would be destroyed. The dreadful apprehension of these and several other dangers would possess the minds of the men, unless they had an asylum with their wives at home for appeasing the disturbances arising in their understandings. Moreover peace and tranquillity give serenity to their minds, and dispose them to receive agreeably the kind attentions of their wives, who spare no pains to disperse the mental clouds which they are very quick-sighted to observe in their husbands: moreover, the same peace and tranquillity make the presence of their wives agreeable. Hence it is evident, that an assumed semblance of love, as if it was truly conjugial, for the sake of peace and

---

* This passage within the brackets is inserted to supply what evidently appears to be an omission in the original.

tranquillity at home, is both necessary and useful. It is further to be observed, that with the wives such semblances are not assumed as with the men; but if they appear to resemble them, they are the effect of real love, because wives are born loves of the understanding of the men; wherefore they accept kindly the favors of their husbands, and if they do not confess it with their lips, still they acknowledge it in heart.

286. XV. THEY ARE FOR THE SAKE OF REPUTATION OUT OF THE HOUSE. The fortunes of men in general depend on their reputation for justice, sincerity, and uprightness; and this reputation also depends on the wife, who is acquainted with the most familiar circumstances of her husband's life; therefore if the disagreements of their minds should break out into open enmity, quarrels, and threats of hatred, and these should be noised abroad by the wife and her friends, and by the domestics, they would easily be turned into tales of scandal, which would bring disgrace and infamy upon the husband's name. To avoid such mischiefs, he has no other alternative than either to counterfeit affection for his wife, or that they be separated as to house.

287. XVI. THEY ARE FOR THE SAKE OF VARIOUS FAVORS EXPECTED FROM THE MARRIED PARTNER, OR FROM HIS OR HER RELATIONS, AND THUS FROM THE FEAR OF LOSING SUCH FAVORS. This is the case more especially in marriages where the rank and condition of the parties are dissimilar, concerning which, see above, n. 250; as when a man marries a wealthy wife who stores up her money in purses, or her treasures in coffers; and the more so if she boldly insists that the husband is bound to support the house out of his own estate and income: that hence come forced likenesses of conjugial love, is generally known. The case is similar where a man marries a wife, whose parents, relations, and friends, are in offices of dignity, in lucrative business, and in employments with large salaries, who have it in their power to better her condition: that this also is a ground of counterfeit love, as if it were conjugial, is generally known. It is evident that in both cases it is the fear of the loss of the above favors that is operative.

288. XVII. THEY ARE FOR THE SAKE OF HAVING BLEMISHES EXCUSED, AND THEREBY OF AVOIDING DISGRACE. There are several blemishes for which conjugial partners fear disgrace, some criminal, some not. There are blemishes of the mind and of the body slighter than those mentioned in the foregoing chapter n. 252 and 253, which are causes of separation; wherefore those blemishes are here meant, which, to avoid disgrace, are buried in silence by the other married partner. Besides these, in some cases there are contingent crimes, which, if made public, are subject to heavy penalties; not to mention a deficiency of that ability which the men usually boast of. That excuses of such blemishes, in order to avoid disgrace, are the causes of counter-

feit love and friendship with a married partner, is too evident to need further confirmation.

289. XVIII. THEY ARE FOR THE SAKE OF RECONCILIATION. That between married partners who have mental disagreements from various causes, there subsist alternate distrust and confidence, alienation and conjunction, yea, dispute and compromise, thus reconciliation; and also that apparent friendships promote reconciliation, is well known in the world. There are also reconciliations which take place after partings, which are not so alternate and transitory.

290. XIX. IN CASE FAVOR DOES NOT CEASE WITH THE WIFE, WHEN FACULTY CEASES WITH THE MAN, THERE MAY EXIST A FRIENDSHIP RESEMBLING CONJUGIAL FRIENDSHIP WHEN THE PARTIES GROW OLD. The primary cause of the separation of minds (*animorum*) between married partners is a falling off of favor on the wife's part in consequence of the cessation of ability on the husband's part, and thence a falling off of love; for just as heats communicate with each other, so also do colds. That from a falling off of love on the part of each, there ensues a cessation of friendship, and also of favor, if not prevented by the fear of domestic ruin, is evident both from reason and experience. In case therefore the man tacitly imputes the causes to himself, and still the wife perseveres in chaste favor towards him, there may thence result a friendship, which, since it subsists between married partners, appears to resemble conjugial love. That a friendship resembling the friendship of that love, may subsist between married partners, when old, experience testifies from the tranquillity, security, loveliness, and abundant courtesy with which they live, communicate, and associate together.

291. XX. THERE ARE VARIOUS KINDS OF APPARENT LOVE AND FRIENDSHIP BETWEEN MARRIED PARTNERS, ONE OF WHOM IS BROUGHT UNDER THE YOKE, AND THEREFORE IS SUBJECT TO THE OTHER. It is no secret in the world at this day, that as the first fervor of marriage begins to abate, there arises a rivalship between the parties respecting right and power; respecting right, in that according to the statutes of the covenant entered into, these is an equality, and each has dignity in the offices of his or her function; and respecting power, in that it is insisted on by the men, that in all things relating to the house, superiority belongs to them, because they are men, and inferiority to the women because they are women. Such rivalships, at this day familiar, arise from no other source than a want of conscience respecting love truly conjugial, and of sensible perception respecting the blessedness of that love; in consequence of which want, lust takes the place of that love, and counterfeits it; and, on the removal of genuine love, there flows from this lust a grasping for power, in which some are influenced by the delight of the love of domineering, which in some is implanted

by artful women before marriage, and which to some is unknown. Where such grasping prevails with the men, and the various turns of rivalship terminate in the establishment of their sway, they reduce their wives either to become their rightful property, or to comply with their arbitrary will, or into a state of slavery, every one according to the degree and qualified state of that grasping implanted and concealed in himself; but where such grasping prevails with the wives, and the various turns of rivalship terminate in establishing their sway, they reduce their husbands either into a state of equality of right with themselves, or of compliance with their arbitrary will, or into a state of slavery: but as when the wives have obtained the sceptre of sway, there remains with them a desire which is a counterfeit of conjugial love, and is restrained both by law and by the fear of legitimate separation, in case they extend their power beyond the rule of right into what is contrary thereto, therefore they lead a life in consociation with their husbands. But what is the nature and quality of the love and friendship between a ruling wife and a serving husband, and also between a ruling husband and a serving wife, cannot be briefly described; indeed, if their differences were to be specifically pointed out and enumerated, it would occupy several pages; for they are various and diverse—various according to the nature of the grasping for power prevalent with the men, and in like manner with the wives; and diverse in regard to the differences subsisting in the men and the women; for such men have no friendship of love but what is infatuated, and such wives are in the friendship of spurious love grounded in lust. But by what arts wives procure to themselves power over the men, will be shown in the following article.

292. XXI. IN THE WORLD THERE ARE INFERNAL MARRIAGES BETWEEN PERSONS WHO INTERIORLY ARE THE MOST INVETERATE ENEMIES, AND EXTERIORLY ARE AS THE CLOSEST FRIENDS. I am indeed forbidden by the wives of this sort, in the spiritual world, to present such marriages to public view; for they are afraid lest their art of obtaining power over the men should at the same time be divulged, which yet they are exceedingly desirous to have concealed: but as I am urged by the men in that world to expose the causes of the intestine hatred and as it were fury excited in their hearts against their wives, in consequence of their clandestine arts, I shall be content with adducing the following particulars. The men said, that unwittingly they contracted a terrible dread of their wives, in consequence of which they were constrained to obey their decisions in the most abject manner, and be at their beck more than the vilest servants, so that they lost all life and spirit; and that this was the case not only with those who were in inferior stations of life, but also with those who were advanced in high dignities, yea with brave and famous generals: they also said, that after they had

contracted this dread, they could not help on every occasion expressing themselves to their wives in a friendly manner, and doing what was agreeable to their humors, although they cherished in their hearts a deadly hatred against them; and further, that their wives still behaved courteously to them both in word and deed, and complaisantly attended to some of their requests. Now as the men themselves greatly wondered, whence such an antipathy could arise in their internals, and such an apparent sympathy in their externals, they examined into the causes thereof from some women who were acquainted with the above secret art. From this source of information they learned, that women (*mulieres*) are skilled in a knowledge which they conceal deeply in their own minds, whereby, if they be so disposed, they can subject the men to the yoke of their authority; and that this is effected in the case of ignorant wives, sometimes by alternate quarrel and kindness, sometimes by harsh and unpleasant looks, and sometimes by other means; but in the case of polite wives, by urgent and persevering petitions, and by obstinate resistance to their husbands in case they suffer hardships from them, insisting on their right of equality by law, in consequence of which they are firm and resolute in their purpose; yea, insisting that if they should be turned out of the house, they would return at their pleasure, and would be urgent as before; for they know that the men by their nature cannot resist the positive tempers of their wives but that after compliance they submit themselves to their disposal; and that in this case the wives make a show of all kinds of civility and tenderness to their husbands subjected to their sway. The genuine cause of the dominion which the wives obtain by this cunning is, that the man acts from the understanding and the woman from the will, and that the will can persist, but not so the understanding. I have been told, that the worst of this sort of women, who are altogether a prey to the desire of dominion, can remain firm in their positive humors even to the last struggle for life. I have also heard the excuses pleaded by such women (*mulieres*) for entering upon the exercise of this art; in which they urged that they would not have done so unless they had foreseen supreme contempt and future rejection, and consequent ruin on their part, if they should be subdued by their husbands: and that thus they had taken up these their arms from necessity. To this excuse they add this admonition for the men; to leave their wives their own rights, and while they are in alternations of cold, not to consider them as beneath their maid-servants: they said also that several of their sex, from their natural timidity, are not in a state of exercising the above art; but I added, from their natural modesty. From the above considerations it may now be known what is meant by infernal marriages in the world between persons who interiorly are the most inveterate enemies, and exteriorly are like the most attached friends.

* * * * * *

293. To the above I will add TWO MEMORABLE RELATIONS. FIRST. Some time ago as I was looking through a window to the east, I saw seven women sitting in a garden of roses at a certain fountain, and drinking the water. I strained my eye-sight greatly to see what they were doing, and this effort of mine affected them; wherefore one of them beckoned me, and I immediately quitted the house and came to them. When I joined them, I courteously inquired whence they were. They said, " We are wives, and are here conversing respecting the delights of conjugial love, and from much consideration we conclude, that they are also the delights of wisdom." This answer so delighted my mind (*animum*), that I seemed to be in the spirit, and thence in perception more interior and more enlightened than on any former occasion; wherefore I said to them, " Give me leave to propose a few questions respecting those satisfactions." On their consenting, I asked, " How do you wives know that the delights of conjugial love are the same as the delights of wisdom?" They replied, " We know it from the correspondence of our husbands' wisdom with our own delights of conjugial love; for the delights of this love with ourselves are exalted and diminished and altogether qualified, according to the wisdom of our husbands." On hearing this, I said, "I know that you are affected by the agreeable conversation of your husbands and their cheerfulness of mind, and that you derive thence a bosom delight; but I am surprised to hear you say, that their wisdom produces this effect; but tell me what is wisdom, and what wisdom [produces this effect]?" To this the wives indignantly replied, " Do you suppose that we do not know what wisdom is, and what wisdom [produces that effect], when yet we are continually reflecting upon it as in our husbands, and learn it daily from their mouths? For we wives think of the state of our husbands from morning to evening; there is scarcely an hour in the day, in which our intuitive thought is altogether withdrawn from them, or is absent; on the other hand, our husbands think very little in the day respecting our state; hence we know what wisdom of theirs it is that gives us delight. Our husbands call that wisdom spiritual rational, and spiritual moral. Spiritual rational wisdom, they say, is of the understanding and knowledges, and spiritual moral wisdom of the will and life; but these they join together and make a one, and insist that the satisfactions of this wisdom are transferred from their minds into the delights in our bosoms, and from our bosoms into theirs, and thus return to wisdom their origin." I then asked, " Do you know anything more respecting the wisdom of your husbands which gives you delight?"

They said, "We do, There is spiritual wisdom, and thence rational and moral wisdom. Spiritual wisdom is to acknowledge the Lord the Saviour as the God of heaven and earth, and from Him to procure the truths of the church, which is effected by means of the Word and of preachings derived therefrom, whence comes spiritual rationality; and from Him to live according to those truths, whence comes spiritual morality. These two our husbands call the wisdom which in general operates to produce love truly conjugial. We have heard from them also that the reason of this is, because, by means of that wisdom, the interiors of their minds and thence of their bodies are opened, whence there exists a free passage from first principles even to last for the stream of love; on the flow, sufficiency, and virtue of which conjugial love depends and lives. The spiritual rational and moral wisdom of our husbands, specifically in regard to marriage, has for its end and object to love the wife alone, and to put away all concupiscence for other women; and so far as this is effected, so far that love is exalted as to degree, and perfected as to quality; and also so far we feel more distinctly and exquisitely the delights in ourselves corresponding to the delights of the affections and the satisfactions of the thoughts of our husbands." I inquired afterwards, whether they knew how communication is effected. They said, "In all conjunction by love there must be action, reception, and reaction. The delicious state of our love is acting or action, the state of the wisdom of our husbands is recipient or reception, and also is reacting or reaction according to perception; and this reaction we perceive with delights in the breast according to the state continually expanded and prepared to receive those things which in any manner agree with the virtue belonging to our husbands, thus also with the extreme state of love belonging to ourselves, and which thence proceed." They said further, "Take heed lest by the delights which we have mentioned, you understand the ultimated delights of that love: of these we never speak, but of our bosom delights, which always correspond with the state of the wisdom of our husbands." After this there appeared at a distance as it were a dove flying with the leaf of a tree in its mouth: but as it approached, instead of a dove I saw it was a little boy with a paper in his hand: on coming to us he held it out to me, and said, "Read it before these Maidens of the fountain." I then read as follows. "Tell the inhabitants of your earth, that there is a love truly conjugial having myriads of delights, scarce any of which are as yet known to the world; but they will be known, when the church betroths herself to her Lord, and is married." I then asked, "Why did the little boy call you Maidens of the fountain?" They replied, "We are called maidens when we sit at this fountain; because we are affections of the truths of the wisdom of our husbands, and the affection of truth is called a maiden; a fountain also signifies the true of wisdom, and the bed of roses, on which we sit, the delights thereof." Then one of the seven wove a garland of roses, and sprinkled it with water of the fountain, and placed it on the boy's cap round his little head, and said, "Receive the delights of intelligence; know that a cap signifies intelligence; and a garland from this rose-bed delights." The boy thus decorated then departed, and again appeared a distance like a flying dove, but now with a coronet on his head.

294. THE SECOND MEMORABLE RELATION. After some days I again saw the seven wives in a garden of roses, but not in the same as before. Its magnificence was such as I had never before seen: it was round, and the roses in it formed as it were a rainbow. The roses or flowers of a purple color formed its outermost circle, others of a yellow golden color formed the next interior circle, within this were others of a bright blue, and the inmost of a shining green; and within this rainbow rose-bed was a small lake of limpid water. These seven wives, who were called the Maidens of the fountain, as they were sitting there seeing me again at the window, called me to them; and when I was come they said, "Did you ever see anything more beautiful upon the earth?" I replied, "Never." They then said, "Such scenery is created instantaneously by the Lord, and represents something new on the earth; for every thing created by the Lord is representative: but what is this? tell, if you can: we say it is the delights of conjugial love." On hearing this, I said, "What! the delights of conjugial love, respecting which you before conversed with so much wisdom and eloquence! After I had left you, I related your conversation to some wives in our country, and said, 'I now know from instruction that you have bosom delights arising from your conjugial love, which you can communicate to your husbands according to their wisdom, and that on this account you look at your husbands with the eyes of your spirit from morning to evening, and study to bend and draw their minds (*animos*) to become wise, to the end that you may secure those delights.' I mentioned also that by wisdom you understand spiritual rational and moral wisdom, and in regard to marriage, the wisdom to love the wife alone, and to put away all concupiscence for other women: but to these things the wives of our country answered with laughter, saying, "What is all this but mere idle talk? We do not know what conjugial love is. If our husbands possess any portion of it, still we do not: whence then come its delights to us? yea, in regard to what you call ultimate delights, we at times refuse them with violence, for they are unpleasant to us, almost like violations: and you will see, if you attend to it, no sign of such love in our faces: wherefore you are trifling or jesting, if you also assert, with those seven wives, that we think of our husbands from

morning to evening, and continually attend to their will and pleasure in order to catch from them such delights.' I have retained thus much of what they said, that I might relate it to you; since it is repugnant, and also in manifest contradiction, to what I heard from you near the fountain, and which I so greedily imbibed and believed." To this the wives sitting in the rose garden replied, "Friend, you know not the wisdom and prudence of wives; for they totally hide it from the men, and for no other end than that they may be loved: for every man who is not spiritually but only naturally rational and moral, is cold towards his wife; and the cold lies concealed in his inmost principles. This is exquisitely and acutely observed by a wise and prudent wife; who so far conceals her conjugial love, and withdraws it into her bosom, and there hides it so deeply that it does not at all appear in her face, in the tone of her voice, or in her be-behaviour. The reason of this is, because so far as it appears, so far the conjugial cold of the man diffuses itself from the inmost principles of his mind, where it resides, into its ultimates, and occasions in the body a total coldness, and a consequent endeavour to separate from bed and chamber." I then asked, "Whence arises that which you call conjugial cold?" They replied, "From the insanity of the men in regard to spiritual things; and every one who is insane in regard to spiritual things, in his inmost principles is cold towards his wife, and warm towards harlots; and since conjugial love and adulterous love are opposite to each other; it follows that conjugial love becomes cold when illicit love is warm; and when cold prevails with the man, he cannot endure any sense of love, and thus not any allusion thereto, from his wife; therefore the wife so wisely and prudently conceals that love; and so far as she conceals it by denying and refusing it, so far the man is cherished and recruited by the influent meretricious sphere. Hence it is, that the wife of such a man has no bosom delights such as we have, but only pleasures, which, on the part of the man, ought to be called the pleasures of insanity, because they are the pleasures of illicit love. Every chaste wife loves her husband, even if he be unchaste; but since wisdom is alone recipient of that love, therefore she exerts all her endeavours to turn his insanity into wisdom, that is, to prevent his lusting after other women besides herself. This she does by a thousand methods, being particularly cautious lest any of them should be discovered by the man; for she is well aware that love cannot be forced, but that it is insinuated in freedom; wherefore it is given to women to know from the sight, the hearing, and the touch, every state of the mind of their husbands; but on the other hand it is not given to the men to know any state of the mind of their wives. A chaste wife can look at her husband with an austere countenance, accost him with a harsh voice, and also be angry and quarrel, and yet in her heart cherish a soft and tender love towards him; but such anger and dissimulation have for their end wisdom, and thereby the reception of love with the husband: as is manifest from the consideration, that she can be reconciled in an instant. Besides, wives use such means of concealing the love implanted in their inmost heart, with a view to prevent conjugial cold bursting forth with the man, and extinguishing the fire of his adulterous heat, and, thus converting him from green wood into a dry stick." When the seven wives had expressed these and many more similar sentiments, their husbands came with clusters of grapes in their hands, some of which were of a delicate, and some of a disagreeable flavor; upon which the wives said, "Why have you also brought bad or wild grapes?" The husbands replied, "Because we perceived in our souls, with which yours are united, that you were conversing with that man respecting love truly conjugial, that its delights are the delights of wisdom, and also respecting adulterous love, that its delights are the pleasures of insanity. The latter are the disagreable or wild grapes; the former are those of delicate flavor." They confirmed what their wives had said, and added that, "in externals, the pleasures of insanity appear like the delights of wisdom, but not so in internals; just like the good and bad grapes which we have brought; for both the chaste and the unchaste have similar wisdom in externals, but altogether dissimilar in internals." After this the little boy came again with a piece of paper in his hand, and held it out to me, saying, "Read this;" and I read as follows: "Know that the delights of conjugial love ascend to the highest heaven, and both in the way thither and also there, unite with the delights of all heavenly loves, and thereby enter into their happiness, which endures for ever; because the delights of that love are also the delights of wisdom: and know also, that the pleasures of illicit love descend even to the lowest hell, and, both in the way thither and also there, unite with the pleasures of all infernal loves, and thereby enter into their unhappiness, which consists in the wretchedness of all heart-delights; because the pleasures of that love are the pleasures of insanity." After this the husbands departed with their wives, and accompanied the little boy as far as to the way of his ascent into heaven; and they knew that the society from which he was sent was a society of the new heaven, with which the new church in the world will be conjoined.

ON BETROTHINGS AND NUPTIALS.

295. THE subject of betrothings and nuptials, and also of the rites and ceremonies attending them, is here treated of principally from the reason of the understanding; for the object of

this book is that the reader may see truths rationally, and thereby give his consent, for thus his spirit is convinced; and those things in which the spirit is convinced, obtain a place above those which, without consulting reason, enter from authority and the faith of authority; for the latter enter the head no further than into the memory, and there mix themselves with fallacies and falses; thus they are beneath the rational things of the understanding. From these any one may seem to converse rationally, but he will converse preposterously; for in such case he thinks as a crab walks, the sight following the tail: it is otherwise if he thinks from the understanding; for then the rational sight selects from the memory whatever is suitable, whereby it confirms truth viewed in itself. This is the reason why in this chapter several particulars are adduced which are established customs, as that the right of choice belongs to the men, that parents ought to be consulted, that pledges are to be given, that the conjugial covenant is to be settled previous to the nuptials, that it ought to be performed by a priest, also that the nuptials ought to be celebrated; besides several other particulars, which are here mentioned in order that every one may rationally see that such things are assigned to conjugial love, as requisite to promote and complete it. The articles into which this section is divided are the following; I. *The right of choice belongs to the man, and not to the woman.* II. *The man ought to court and intreat the woman respecting marriage with him, and not the woman the man.* III. *The woman ought to consult her parents, or those who are in the place of parents, and then deliberate with herself, before she consents.* IV. *After a declaration of consent, pledges are to be given.* V. *Consent is to be secure and established by solemn betrothing.* VI. *By betrothing, each party is prepared for conjugial love.* VII. *By betrothing, the mind of the one is united to the mind of the other, so as to effect a marriage of the spirit previous to a marriage of the body.* VIII. *This is the case with those who think chastely of marriages; but it is otherwise with those who think unchastely of them.* IX. *Within the time of betrothing, it is not allowable to be connected corporeally.* X. *When the time of betrothing is completed, the nuptials ought to take place.* XI. *Previous to the celebration of the nuptials, the conjugial covenant is to be ratified in the presence of witnesses.* XII. *The marriage is to be consecrated by a priest.* XIII. *The nuptials are to be celebrated with festivity.* XIV. *After the nuptials, the marriage of the spirit is made also the marriage of the body, and thereby a full marriage.* XV. *Such is the order of conjugial love with its modes from its first heat to its first torch.* XVI. *Conjugial love precipitated without order and the modes thereof, burns up the marrows and is consumed.* XVII. *The states of the minds of each of the parties proceeding in successive order, flow into the state of marriage; nevertheless in one manner with the spiritual and in another with the natural.* XVIII *There are successive and simultaneous orders, and the latter is from the former and according to it.* We proceed to an explanation of each article.

296. THE RIGHT OF CHOICE BELONGS TO THE MAN, AND NOT TO THE WOMAN. This is because the man is born to be understanding, but the woman to be love; also because with the men there generally prevails a love of the sex, but with the women a love of one of the sex; and likewise because it is not unbecoming for men to speak openly about love, as it is for women; nevertheless women have the right of selecting one of their suitors. In regard to the first reason, that the right of choice belongs to the men, because they are born to understanding, it is grounded in the consideration that the understanding can examine agreements and disagreements, and distinguish them, and from judgement choose that which is suitable: it is otherwise with the women, because they are born to love, and therefore have no such discrimination; and consequently their determinations to marriage would proceed only from the inclinations of their love; if they have the skill of distinguishing between men and men, still their love is influenced by appearances. In regard to the other reason, that the right of choice belongs to the men, and not to the women, because with men there generally prevails a love of the sex, and with women a love of one of the sex, it is grounded in the consideration, that those in whom a love of the sex prevails, can freely look around and also determine: it is otherwise with women, in whom is implanted a love for one of the sex. If you wish for a proof of this, ask, if you please, the men you meet, what their sentiments are respecting monogamical and polygamical unions; and you will seldom meet one who will not reply in favor of the polygamical; and this also is a love of the sex: but ask the women their sentiments on the subject, and almost all, except the vilest of the sex, will reject polygamical unions; from which consideration it follows, that with the women there prevails a love of one of the sex, thus conjugial love. In regard to the third reason, that it is not unbecoming for men to speak openly about love, whereas it is for women, it is self-evident; hence also it follows, that declaration belongs to the men, and therefore so does choice. That women have the right of selecting in regard to their suitors, is well known; but this species of selection is confined and limited, whereas that of the men is extended and unlimited.

297. II. THE MAN OUGHT TO COURT AND INTREAT THE WOMAN RESPECTING MARRIAGE WITH HIM, AND NOT THE WOMAN THE MAN. This naturally follows the right of choice; and besides, to court and intreat women respecting marriage is in itself honorable and becoming for men, but not for women. If women were to court and entreat the men, they would not only

be blamed, but, after intreaty, they would be reputed as vile, or after marriage as libidinous, with whom there would be no association but what was cold and fastidious; wherefore marriages would thereby be converted into tragic scenes. Wives also take it as a compliment to have it said of them, that being conquered as it were, they yielded to the pressing intreaties of the men. Who does not foresee, that if the women courted the men, they would seldom be accepted? They would either be indignantly rejected, or be enticed to lasciviousness, and also would dishonor their modesty. Moreover, as was shewn above, the men have not any innate love of the sex; and without love there is no interior pleasantness of life: wherefore to exalt their life by that love, it is incumbent on the men to compliment the women; courting and intreating them with civility, courtesy, and humility, respecting this sweet addition to their life. The superior comeliness of the female countenance, person, and manners, above that of the men, adds itself as a proper object of desire.

298. III. THE WOMAN OUGHT TO CONSULT HER PARENTS, OR THOSE WHO ARE IN THE PLACE OF PARENTS, AND THEN DELIBERATE WITH HERSELF, BEFORE SHE CONSENTS. The reason why parents are to be consulted is, because they deliberate from judgement, knowledge, and love; from *judgement*, because they are in an advanced age, which excels in judgement, and discerns what is suitable and unsuitable: from *knowledge*, in respect to both the suitor and their daughter; in respect to the suitor they procure information, and in respect to their daughter they already know; wherefore they conclude respecting both with united discernment: from *love*, because to consult the good of their daughter, and to provide for her establishment, is also to consult and provide for their own and for themselves.

299. The case would be altogether different, if the daughter consents of herself to her urgent suitor, without consulting her parents, or those who are in their place; for she cannot from judgement, knowledge, and love, make a right estimate of the matter which so deeply concerns her future welfare: she cannot from *judgement*, because she is as yet in ignorance as to conjugial life, and not in a state of comparing reasons, and discovering the morals of men from their particular tempers; nor from *knowledge*, because she knows few things beyond the domestic concerns of her parents and of some of her companions; and is unqualified to examine into such things as relate to the family and property of her suitor: nor from *love*, because with daughters in their first marriageable age, and also afterwards, this is led by the concupiscences originating in the senses, and not as yet by the desires originating in a refined mind. The daughter ought nevertheless to deliberate on the matter with herself, before she consents, lest she should be led against her will to form a con-

nection with a man whom she does not love; for by so doing, consent on her part would be wanting; and yet it is consent that constitutes marriage, and initiates the spirit into conjugial love; and consent against the will, or extorted, does not initiate the spirit, although it may the body; and thus it converts chastity, which resides in the spirit, into lust; whereby conjugial love in its first warmth is vitiated.

300. IV. AFTER A DECLARATION OF CONSENT, PLEDGES ARE TO BE GIVEN. By pledges we mean presents, which, after consent, are confirmations, testifications, first favors, and gladnesses. Those presents are *confirmations*, because they are certificates of consent on each side; wherefore, when two parties consent to anything, it is customary to say, "Give me a token;" and of two, who have entered into a marriage-engagement, and have secured it by presents, that they are pledged, thus confirmed. They are *testifications*, because those pledges are continual visible witnesses of mutual love; hence also they are memorials thereof; especially if they be rings, perfume-bottles or boxes, and ribbons, which are worn in sight. In such things there is a sort of representative image of the minds (*animorum*) of the bridegroom and the bride. Those pledges are *first favors*, because conjugial love engages for itself everlasting favor; whereof those gifts are the first fruits. That they are the *gladnesses* of love, is well known, for the mind is exhilarated at the sight of them; and because love is in them, those favors are dearer and more precious than any other gifts, it being as if their hearts were in them. As those pledges are securities of conjugial love, therefore presents after consent were in use with the ancients; and after accepting such presents the parties were declared to be bridegroom and bride. But it is to be observed that it is at the pleasure of the parties to bestow those presents either before or after the act of betrothing; if before, they are confirmations and testifications of consent to betrothing; if after it, they are also confirmations and testifications of consent to the nuptial tie.

301. V. CONSENT IS TO BE SECURED AND ESTABLISHED BY SOLEMN BETROTHING. The reasons for betrothings are these: 1. That after betrothing the souls of the two parties may mutually incline towards each other. 2. That the universal love for the sex may be determined to one of the sex. 3. That the interior affections may be mutually known, and by applications in the internal cheerfulness of love, may be conjoined. 4. That the spirits of both parties may enter into marriage, and be more and more consociated. 4. That thereby conjugial love may advance regularly from its first warmth even to the nuptial flame. Consequently. 6. That conjugial love may advance and grow up in just order from its spiritual origin. The state of betrothing may be compared to the state of spring before summer; and the internal pleasantness of that state to the flowering of trees before

fructification. As the beginning and progressions of conjugial love proceed in order for the sake of their influx into the effective love, which commences at the nuptials, therefore, there are also betrothings in the heavens.

302. VI. BY BETROTHING EACH PARTY IS PREPARED FOR CONJUGIAL LOVE. That the mind or spirit of one of the parties is by betrothing prepared for union with the mind or spirit of the other, or what is the same, that the love of the one is prepared for union with the love of the other, appears from the arguments just adduced. Besides which it is to be noted, that on love truly conjugial is inscribed this order, that it ascends and descends; it ascends from its first heat progressively upwards towards the souls of the parties, with an endeavour to effect their conjunction, and this by continual interior openings of their minds; and there is no love which strives more intensely to effect such openings, or which is more powerful and expert in opening the interiors of minds, than conjugial love; for the soul of each of the parties intends this: but at the same moments in which that love ascends towards the soul, it descends also towards the body, and thereby clothes itself. It is however to be observed, that conjugial love is such in its descent as it is in the height to which it ascends: if it ascends high, it descends chaste; but if not, it descends unchaste: the reason of this is, because the lower principles of the mind are unchaste, but its higher are chaste; for the lower principles of the mind adhere to the body, but the higher separate themselves from them: but on this subject see further particulars below, n. 305. From these few considerations it may appear, that, by betrothing, the mind of each of the parties is prepared for conjugial love, although in a different manner according to the affections.

303. VII. BY BETROTHING THE MIND OF ONE IS UNITED TO THE MIND OF THE OTHER, SO AS TO EFFECT A MARRIAGE OF THE SPIRIT, PREVIOUS TO A MARRIAGE OF THE BODY. As this follows of consequence from what was said above, n. 301, 302, we shall pass it by, without adducing any further confirmations from reason.

304. VIII. THIS IS THE CASE WITH THOSE WHO THINK CHASTELY OF MARRIAGES; BUT IT IS OTHERWISE WITH THOSE WHO THINK UNCHASTELY OF THEM. With the chaste, that is, with those who think religiously of marriages, the marriage of the spirit precedes, and that of the body is subsequent; and these are those with whom love ascends towards the soul, and from its height thence descends; concerning whom see above, n. 302. The souls of such separate themselves from the unlimited love for the sex, and devote themselves to one, with whom they look for an everlasting and eternal union and its increasing blessednesses, as the cherishers of the hope which continually recreates their mind; but it is quite otherwise with the unchaste, that is, with

those who do not think religiously of marriages and their holiness. With these there is a marriage of the body, but not of the spirit: if, during the state of betrothment, there be any appearance of a marriage of the spirit, still, if it ascends by an elevation of the thoughts concerning it, it nevertheless falls back again to the concupiscences which arise from the flesh in the will; and thus from the unchaste principles therein it precipitates itself into the body, and defiles the ultimates of its love with an alluring ardor; and as, in consequence of this ardor, it was in the beginning all on fire, so its fire suddenly goes out, and passes off into the cold of winter; whence the failing [of power] is accelerated. The state of betrothing with such scarcely answers any other purpose, than that they may fill their concupiscences with lasciviousness, and thereby contaminate the conjugial principle of love.

305. IX. WITHIN THE TIME OF BETROTHING IT IS NOT ALLOWABLE TO BE CONNECTED CORPOREALLY; for thus the order which is inscribed on conjugial love, perishes. For in human minds there are three regions, of which the highest is called the celestial, the middle the spiritual, and the lowest the natural. In this lowest man is born; but he ascends into the next above it,—the spiritual, by a life according to the truths of religion, and into the highest by the marriage of love and wisdom. In the lowest or natural region, reside all the concupiscences of evil and lasciviousness; but in the superior or spiritual region, there are no concupiscences of evil and lasciviousness; for man is introduced into this region by the Lord, when he is re-born; but in the supreme or celestial region, there is conjugial chastity in its love: into this region a man is elevated by the love of uses; and as the most excellent uses are from marriages, he is elevated into it by love truly conjugial. From these few considerations, it may be seen that conjugial love, from the first beginnings of its warmth, is to be elevated out of the lowest region into a superior region, that it may become chaste, and that thereby from a chaste principle it may be let down through the middle and lowest regions into the body; and when this is the case, this lowest region is purified from all that is unchaste by this descending chaste principle: hence the ultimate of that love becomes also chaste. Now if the successive order of this love is precipitated by connections of the body before their time, it follows, that the man acts from the lowest region, which is by birth unchaste; and it is well known, that hence commences and arises cold in regard to marriage, and disdainful neglect in regard to a married partner. Nevertheless events of various kinds take place in consequence of hasty connections; also in consequence of too long a delay, and too quick a hastening, of the time of betrothing; but these, from their number and variety, can hardly be adduced.

306. X. When the time of betrothing is completed, the nuptials ought to take place. There are some customary rites which are merely formal, and others which at the same time are also essential: among the latter are nuptials; and that they are to be reckoned among essentials, which are to be manifested in the customary way, and to be formally celebrated, is confirmed by the following reasons: 1. That nuptials constitute the end of the foregoing state, into which the parties were introduced by betrothing, which principally was a state of the spirit, and the beginning of the following state, into which they are to be introduced by marriage, which is a state of the spirit and body together; for the spirit then enters into the body, and there becomes active: wherefore on that day the parties put off the state and also the name of bridegroom and bride, and put on the state and name of married partners and consorts. 2. That nuptials are an introduction and entrance into a new state, which is that a maiden becomes a wife, and a young man a husband, and both one flesh; and this is effected while love by ultimates unites them. That marriage actually changes a maiden into a wife, and a young man into a husband, was proved in the former part of this work; also that marriage unites two into one human form, so that they are no longer two but one flesh. 3. That nuptials are the commencement of an entire separation of the love of the sex from conjugial love, which is effected while, by a full liberty of connection, the knot is tied by which the love of the one is devoted to the love of the other. 4. It appears as if nuptials were merely an interval between those two states, and thus that they are mere formalities which may be omitted; but still there is also in them this essential, that the new state above-mentioned is then to be entered upon from covenant, and that the consent of the parties is to be declared in the presence of witnesses, and also to be consecrated by a priest; besides other particulars which establish it. As nuptials contain in them essentials, and as marriage is not legitimate till after their celebration, therefore also nuptials are celebrated in the heavens; see above, n. 21, and also, n. 27—41.

307. XI. Previous to the celebration of the nuptials, the conjugial covenant is to be ratified in the presence of witnesses. It is expedient that the conjugial covenant be ratified before the nuptials are celebrated, in order that the statutes and laws of love truly conjugial may be known, and that they may be remembered after the nuptials; also that the minds of the parties may be bound to just marriage: for after some introductory circumstances of marriage, the state which preceded betrothing returns at times, in which state remembrance fails and forgetfulness of the ratified covenant ensues; yea, it may be altogether effaced by the allurements of the unchaste to criminality; and if it is then recalled into the

memory, it is reviled: but to prevent these transgressions, society has taken upon itself the protection of that covenant, and has denounced penalties on the breakers of it. In a word, the ante-nuptial covenant manifests and establishes the sacred decrees of love truly conjugial, and binds libertines to the observance of them. Moreover, by this covenant, the right of propagating children, and also the right of the children to inherit the goods of their parents, become legitimate.

308. XII. MARRIAGE IS TO BE CONSECRATED BY A PRIEST. The reason of this is, because marriages, considered in themselves, are spiritual, and thence holy; for they descend from the heavenly marriage of good and truth, and things conjugial correspond to the divine marriage of the Lord and the church; and hence they are from the Lord himself, and according to the state of the church with the contracting parties. Now, as the ecclesiastical order on the earth administer the things which relate to the Lord's priestly character, that is, to his love, and thus also those which relate to blessing, it is expedient that marriages be consecrated by his ministers; and as they are then the chief witnesses, it is expedient that the consent of the parties to the covenant be also heard, accepted, confirmed, and thereby established by them.

309. XIII. THE NUPTIALS ARE TO BE CELEBRATED WITH FESTIVITY. The reasons are, because ante-nuptial love, which was that of the bridegroom and the bride, on this occasion descends into their hearts, and spreading itself thence in every direction into all parts of the body, the delights of marriage are made sensible, whereby the minds of the parties are led to festive thoughts and also let loose to festivities so far as is allowable and becoming; to favor which, it is expedient that the festivities of their minds be indulged in company, and they themselves be thereby introduced into the joys of conjugial love.

310. XIV. AFTER THE NUPTIALS, THE MARRIAGE OF THE SPIRIT IS MADE ALSO THE MARRIAGE OF THE BODY, AND THEREBY A FULL MARRIAGE. All things which a man does in the body, flow in from his spirit; for it is well known that the mouth does not speak of itself, but that it is the thinking principle of the mind which speaks by it; also that the hands do not act and the feet walk of themselves, but that it is the will of the mind which performs those operations by them; consequently, that the mind speaks and acts by its organs in the body: hence it is evident, that such as the mind is, such are the speech of the mouth and the actions of the body. From these premises it follows as a conclusion that the mind, by a continual influx, arranges the body so that it may act similarly and simultaneously with itself; wherefore the bodies of men viewed interiorly are merely forms of their minds exteriorly organized to effect the purposes of the soul. These things are premised, in order that

it may be perceived why the minds or spirits are first to be united as by marriage, before they are also further united in the body; namely, that while the marriages become of the body, they may also be marriages of the spirit; consequently, that married partners may mutually love each other from the spirit, and thence from the body. From this ground let us now take a view of marriage. When conjugial love unites the minds of two persons, and forms them into a marriage, in such case it also unites and forms their bodies into a marriage; for, as we have said, the form of the mind is also interiorly the form of the body; only with this difference, that the latter form is outwardly organized to effect that to which the interior form of the body is determined by the mind. But the mind formed from conjugial love is not only interiorly in the whole body, round about in every part, but moreover is interiorly in the organs appropriated to generation, which in their region are situated beneath the other regions of the body, and in which are terminated the forms of the mind with those who are united in conjugial love: consequently the affections and thoughts of their minds are determined thither; and the activities of such minds differ in this respect from the activities of minds arising from other loves, that the latter loves do not reach thither. The conclusion resulting from these considerations is, that such as conjugial love is in the minds or spirits of two persons, such is it interiorly in those its organs. But it is self-evident that a marriage of the spirit after the nuptials becomes also a marriage of the body, thus a full marriage, consequently, if a marriage in the spirit is chaste, and partakes of the sanctity of marriage, it is chaste also, and partakes of its sanctity, when it is in its fulness in the body; and the case is reversed if a marriage in the spirit is unchaste.

311. XV. SUCH IS THE ORDER OF CONJUGIAL LOVE WITH ITS MODES FROM ITS FIRST HEAT TO ITS FIRST TORCH. It is said from its first heat to its first torch, because vital heat is love, and conjugial heat or love successively increases, and at length as it were into a flame or torch. We have said " to its first torch," because we mean the first state after the nuptials, when that love burns; but what its quality becomes after this torch, in the marriage itself, has been described in the preceding chapters; but in this part we are explaining its order from the beginning of its career to this its first goal. That all order proceeds from first principles to last, and that the last become the first of some following order, also that all things of the middle order are the last of a prior and the first of a following order, and that thus ends proceed continually through causes into effects, may be sufficiently confirmed and illustrated to the eye of reason from what is known and visible in the world; but as at present we are treating only of the order in which love proceeds from its first starting-place to its goal, we shall pass by such confirmation and

illustration, and only observe on this subject, that such as the order of this love is from its first heat to its first torch, such it is in general, and such is its influence in its progression afterwards; for in this progression it unfolds itself, according to the quality of its first heat: if this heat was chaste, its chasteness is strengthened as it proceeds; but if it was unchaste, its unchasteness increases as it advances, until it is deprived of all that chasteness which, from the time of betrothing, belonged to it from without, but not from within.

312. XVI. CONJUGIAL LOVE PRECIPITATED WITHOUT ORDER AND THE MODES THEREOF, BURNS UP THE MARROWS AND IS CONSUMED. So it is said by some in the heavens; and by the marrows they mean the interiors of the mind and body. The reason why these are burnt up, that is, consumed, by precipitated conjugial love is, because that love in such case begins from a flame which eats up and corrupts those interiors, in which as in its principles conjugial love should reside, and from which it should commence. This comes to pass if the man and woman without regard to order precipitate marriage, and do not look to the Lord, and consult their reason, but reject betrothing and comply merely with the flesh: from the ardor of which, if that love commences, it becomes external and not internal, thus not conjugial; and such love may be said to partake of the shell, not of the kernel; or may be called fleshly, lean, and dry, because emptied of its genuine essence. See more on this subject above n. 305.

313. XVII. THE STATES OF THE MINDS OF EACH OF THE PARTIES PROCEEDING IN SUCCESSIVE ORDER, FLOW INTO THE STATE OF MARRIAGE; NEVERTHELESS IN ONE MANNER WITH THE SPIRITUAL AND IN ANOTHER WITH THE NATURAL. That the last state is such as that of the successive order from which it is formed and exists, is a rule, which from its truth must be acknowledged by the learned; for thereby we discover what influx is, and what it effects. By influx we mean all that which precedes, and constitutes what follows, and by things following in order constitutes what is last; as all that which precedes with a man, and constitutes his wisdom; or all that which precedes with a statesman, and constitutes his political skill; or all that which precedes with a theologian, and constitutes his erudition; in like manner all that which proceeds from infancy, and constitutes a man; also what proceeds in order from a seed and a twig, and makes a tree, and afterwards what proceeds from a blossom, and makes its fruit; in like manner all that which precedes and proceeds with a bridegroom and bride, and constitutes their marriage: this is the meaning of influx. That all those things which precede in minds form series, which collect together, one next to another, and one after another, and that these together compose a last or ultimate, is as yet unknown in the world; but as it is a truth from heaven, it is here adduced:

for it explains what influx effects, and what is the quality of the last or ultimate, in which the above-mentioned series successively formed co-exist. From these considerations it may be seen that the states of the minds of each of the parties proceeding in successive order flow into the state of marriage. But married partners after marriage are altogether ignorant of the successive things which are insinuated into, and exist in their minds (*animis*) from things antecedent; nevertheless it is those things which give form to conjugial love, and constitute the state of their minds; from which state they act the one with the other. The reason why one state is formed from one order with such as are spiritual, and from another with such as are natural, is, because the spiritual proceed in a just order, and the natural in an unjust order; for the spiritual look to the Lord, and the Lord provides and leads the order; whereas the natural look to themselves, and thence proceed in an inverted order; wherefore with the latter the state of marriage is inwardly full of unchasteness; and as that unchasteness abounds, so does cold; and as cold abounds so do the obstructions of the inmost life, whereby its vein is closed and its fountain dried.

314. XVIII. THERE ARE SUCCESSIVE AND SIMULTANEOUS ORDER, AND THE LATTER IS FROM THE FORMER AND ACCORDING TO IT. This is adduced as a reason tending to confirm what goes before. It is well known that there exist what is successive and what is simultaneous; but it is unknown that simultaneous order is grounded in successive, and is according to it; yet how things successive enter into things simultaneous, and what order they form therein, it is very difficult to present to the perception, since the learned are not in possession of any ideas that can elucidate the subject; and as the first idea respecting this arcanum cannot be suggested in few words, and to treat this subject at large would withdraw the mind from a more comprehensive view of the subject of conjugial love, it may suffice for illustration to quote what we have adduced in a compendium respecting those two orders, the successive and the simultaneous, and respecting the influx of the former into the latter, in THE DOCTRINE OF THE NEW JERUSALEM RESPECTING THE SACRED SCRIPTURE, where are these words: "There are in heaven and in the world successive order and simultaneous order. In successive order one thing follows after another from the highest to the lowest; but in simultaneous order one thing is next to another from the inmost to the outermost. Successive order is like a column with steps from the highest to the lowest; but simultaneous order is like a work cohering from the centre to the surface. Successive order becomes in the ultimate simultaneous in this manner; the highest things of successive order become the inmost of simultaneous, and the lowest things of successive order become the outermost of simultaneous; comparatively as

when a column of steps subsides, it becomes a body cohering in a plane. Thus what is simultaneous is formed from what is successive; and this in all things both of the spiritual and of the natural world." See n. 38, 65, of that work; and several further observations on this subject in the ANGELIC WISDOM RESPECTING THE DIVINE LOVE AND DIVINE WISDOM, n. 205—229. The case is similar with successive order leading to marriage, and with simultaneous order in marriage; namely, that the latter is from the former, and according to it. He that is acquainted with the influx of successive order into simultaneous, may comprehend the reason why the angels can see in a man's hand all the thoughts and intentions of his mind, and also why wives, from their husbands' hands on their bosoms, are made sensible of their affections; which circumstance has been occasionally mentioned in the MEMORABLE RELATIONS. The reason of this is, because the hands are the ultimates of man, wherein the deliberations and conclusions of his mind terminate, and there constitute what is simultaneous: therefore also in the Word, mention is made of a thing's being inscribed on the hands.

*   *   *   *   *   *

315. To the above I shall add TWO MEMORABLE RELATIONS. FIRST. On a certain time I saw not far from me a meteor—a cloud divided into smaller clouds, some of which were of an azure color, some opaque, and as it were in collision together. They were streaked with translucent irradiations of light, which at one time appeared sharp like the points of swords, at another, blunt like broken swords. The streaks sometimes darted out forwards, at others they drew themselves in again, exactly like combatants; thus those different colored lesser clouds appeared to be at war together; but it was only their manner of sporting with each other. And as this meteor appeared at no great distance from me, I raised my eyes, and looking attentively, I saw boys, youths, and old men, entering a house which was built of marble, on a foundation of porphyry; and it was over this house that the phenomenon appeared. Then addressing myself to one that was entering, I asked, "What house is this?" He answered, "It is a gymnasium, where young persons are initiated into various things relating to wisdom." On hearing this, I went in with them, being then in the spirit, that is, in a similar state with men of the spiritual world, who are called spirits and angels; and lo! in the gymnasium there were in front a desk, in the middle, benches, at the sides round about, chairs, and over the entrance, an orchestra. The desk was for the young men that were to give answers to the problem at that time to be proposed, the benches were for the audience, the chairs at the sides were for those who on former occasions had given wise answers, and the orchestra was for the seniors, who were arbitrators and judges: in the middle of the orchestra was a pulpit, where there sat a wise man,

whom they called the head master, who proposed the problems to which the young men gave their answers from the desk. When all were assembled, this man arose from the pulpit and said, "Give an answer now to this problem, and solve it if you can, WHAT IS THE SOUL, AND WHAT IS ITS QUALITY?" On hearing this problem all were amazed, and made a muttering noise; and some of the company on the benches exclaimed, "What mortal man, from the age of Saturn to the present time, has been able by any rational thought to see and ascertain what the soul is, still less what is its quality? Is not this subject above the sphere of all human understanding?" But it was replied from the orchestra, "It is not above the understanding, but within it and in its view; only let the problem be answered." Then the young men, who were chosen on that day to ascend the desk, and give an answer to the problem, arose. They were five in number, who had been examined by the seniors, and found to excel in sagacity, and were then sitting on couches at the sides of the desk. They afterwards ascended in the order in which they were seated; and every one, when he ascended, put on a silken tunic of an opaline color, and over it a robe of soft wool interwoven with flowers, and on his head a cap, on the crown of which was a bunch of roses encircled with small sapphires. The first youth thus clad ascended the desk, and thus began: "What the soul is, and what is its quality, has never been revealed to any one since the day of creation, being an arcanum in the treasuries of God alone; but this has been discovered, that the soul resides in a man as a queen; yet where her palace is, has been a matter of conjecture among the learned. Some have supposed it to be in a small tubercle between the cerebrum and the cerebellum, which is called the pineal gland: in this they have fixed the soul's habitation, because the whole man is ruled from those two brains, and they are regulated by that tubercle; therefore whatever regulates the brains, regulates also the whole man from the head to the heel." He also added, "Hence this conjecture appeared as true or probable to many in the world; but in the succeeding age it was rejected as groundless." When he had thus spoken, he put off the robe, the tunic, and the cap, which the second of the selected speakers put on, and ascended the desk. His sentiments concerning the soul are as follows: "In the whole heaven and the whole world it is unknown what the soul is, and what is its quality; it is however known that there is a soul, and that it is in man; but in what part of him is a matter of conjecture. This is certain, that it is in the head, since the head is the seat where the understanding thinks, and the will intends; and in front in the face of the head are man's five sensories, receiving life from the soul alone which resides in the head; but in what particular part of the head the soul has its more immediate residence, I dare not take upon me to say; yet I agree with those who fix its abode in the three ventricles of the brain, sometimes inclining to the opinion of those who fix it in the *corpora striata* therein, sometimes to theirs who fix it in the medullary substance of each brain, sometimes to theirs who fix it in the cortical substance, and sometimes to theirs who fix it in the *dura mater;* for arguments, and those too of weight, have not been wanting in the support of each of these opinions. The arguments in favor of the three ventricles of the brain have been, that those ventricles are the recipients of the animal spirits and of all the lymphs of the brain: the arguments in favor of the *corpora striata* have been, that these bodies constitute the marrow, through which the nerves are emitted, and by which each brain is continued into the spine; and from the spine and the marrow there is an emanation of fibres serving for the contexture of the whole body: the arguments in favor of the medullary substance of each brain have been, that this substance is a collection and congeries of all the fibres, which are the rudiments or beginnings of the whole man: the arguments in favor of the cortical substance have been, that in that substance are contained the prime and ultimate ends, and consequently the principles of all the fibres, and thereby of all the senses and motions: the arguments in favor of the *dura mater* have been, that it is the common covering of each brain, and hence by some kind of continuous principle extends itself over the heart and the viscera of the body. As to myself, I am undetermined which of these opinions is the most probable, and therefore I leave the matter to your determination and decision." Having thus concluded he descended from the desk, and delivered the tunic, the robe, and the cap, to the third, who mounting into the desk began as follows: "How little qualified is a youth like myself for the investigation of so sublime a theorem! I appeal to the learned who are here seated at the sides of the gymnasium; I appeal to you wise ones in the orchestra; yea, I appeal to the angels of the highest heaven, whether any person, from his own rational light, is able to form any idea concerning the soul; nevertheless I, like others, can guess about the place of its abode in man; and my conjecture is, that it is in the heart and thence in the blood; and I ground my conjecture on this circumstance, that the heart by its blood rules both the body and the head; for it sends forth a large vessel called the *aorta* into the whole body, and vessels called the carotids into the whole head; hence it is universally agreed, that the soul from the heart by means of the blood supports, nourishes, and vivifies the universal organical system both of the body and the head. As a further proof of this position it may be urged, that in the Sacred Scripture frequent mention is made of the soul and the heart; as where it is said, Thou shalt love God from the whole soul and the whole heart; and that God creates in man a new soul and a new heart, Deut. vi. 5 ; chap. x. 12 ; chap. xi. 13 ; chap. xxvi. 16 ; Jerem. xxxii. 41 ; Matt. xxii. 37 ; Mark xii. 30, 33 ; Luke x. 27 ; and in other places : it is also expressly said, that the blood is the soul of the flesh, Levit. xvii. 11, 14." At these words, the cry of " Learned ! learned !" was heard in the assembly, and was found to proceed from some of the canons. After this a fourth, clad in the garments of the former speaker, ascended the desk, and thus began : " I also am inclined to suspect that not a single person can be found of so subtle and refined a genius as to be able to discover what the soul is, and what is its quality ; therefore I am of opinion, that in attempting to make the discovery, subtlety will be spent in fruitless labor; nevertheless from my childhood I have continued firm in the opinion of the ancients, that the soul of man is in the whole of him, and in every part of the whole, and thus that it is in the head and in all its parts, as well as in the body and in all its parts ; and that it is an idle conceit of the moderns to fix its habitation in any particular part, and not in the body throughout; besides, the soul is a spiritual substance, of which there cannot be predicated either extension or place, but habitation and impletion ; moreover, when mention is made of the soul, who does not conceive life to be meant ? and is not life in the whole and in every part ?" These sentiments were favorably received by a great part of the audience. After him the fifth rose, and, being adorned with the same insignia, thus delivered himself from the desk : " I will not waste your time and my own in determining the place of the soul's residence, whether it be in some particular part of the body, or in the whole ; but from my mind's storehouse I will communicate to you my sentiments on the subject, What is the soul, and what is its quality ? No one conceives of the soul but as of a pure somewhat, which may be likened to ether, or air, or wind, containing a vital principle, from the rationality which man enjoys above the beasts. This opinion I conceive to be founded on the circumstance, that when a man expires, he is said to breathe forth or emit his soul or spirit ; hence also the soul which lives after death is believed to be such a breath or vapor animated by some principle of thinking life, which is called the soul ; and what else can the soul be ? But as I heard it declared from the orchestra, that this problem concerning the soul, its nature and quality, is not above the understanding, but is within it and in its view, I intreat and beseech you, who have made this declaration, to unfold this eternal arcanum yourselves." Then the elders in the orchestra turned their eyes towards the head master, who had proposed the problem, and who understood by their signs that they wished him to descend and teach the audience : so he instantly quitted the pulpit, passed through the auditory, and entered the desk, and there, stretching out his hand, he thus began: "Let me bespeak your attention: who does not believe the soul to be the inmost and most subtle essence of man? and what is an essence without a form, but an imaginary entity? wherefore the soul is a form, and a form whose qualities and properties I will now describe. It is a form of all things relating to love, and of all things relating to wisdom. All things relating to love are called affections, and those relating to wisdom are called perceptions. The latter derived from the former and thereby united with them constitute one form, in which are contained innumerable things in such an order, series, and coherence, that they may be called a one; and they may be called a one also for this reason, because nothing can be taken away from it, or added to it, but the quality of the form is changed. What is the human soul but such a form? are not all things relating to love and all things relating to wisdom essentials of that form? and are not these things appertaining to a man in his soul, and by derivation from the soul in his head and body? You are called spirits and angels; and in the world you believed that spirits and angels are like mere wind or ether, and thus mere mind and animation; and now you see clearly that you are truly, really, and actually men, who, during your abode in the world, lived and thought in a material body, and knew that a material body does not live and think, but a spiritual substance in that body; and this substance you called the soul, whose form you then were ignorant of, but now have seen and continue to see. You all are souls, of whose immortality you have heard, thought, said, and written so much; and because you are forms of love and wisdom from God, you can never die. The soul therefore is a human form, from which the smallest thing cannot be taken away, and to which the smallest thing cannot be added; and it is the inmost of all the forms of the whole body: and since the forms which are without receive from the inmost both essence and form, therefore you are souls, as you appear to yourselves and to us: in a word, the soul is the very man himself, because it is the inmost man; therefore its form is fully and perfectly the human form: nevertheless it is not life, but the proximate receptacle of life from God, and thereby the habitation of God." When he had thus spoken, many expressed their approbation; but some said, "We will weigh the matter." I immediately went home, and lo! over the gymnasium, instead of the foregoing meteor, there appeared a bright cloud, without streaks or rays that seemed to combat with each other, and which, penetrating through the roof, entered, and illuminated the walls; and I was informed, that they saw some pieces of writing, and among others this, "*Jehovah God breathed into the man's nostrils the* SOUL OF LIVES, *and the man became a* LIVING SOUL," Gen. ii. 7.

316. THE SECOND MEMORABLE RELATION. Some time ago,

as I was walking with my mind (*animus*) at rest, and in a state of delightful mental peace, I saw at a distance a grove, in the midst of which was an avenue leading to a small palace, into which maidens and youths, husbands and wives were entering. I also went thither in spirit, and asked the keeper who was standing at the entrance, whether I also might enter? He looked at me; upon which I said, "Why do you look at me?" He replied, "I look at you that I may see whether the delight of peace, which appears in your face, partakes at all of the delight of conjugial love. Beyond this avenue there is a little garden, and in the midst of it a house, where there are two novitiate conjugial partners, who to-day are visited by their friends of both sexes, coming to pay their congratulations. I do not know those whom I admit; but I was told that I should know them by their faces: those in whom I saw the delights of conjugial love, I was to admit, and none else?" All the angels can see from the faces of others the delights of their hearts; and he saw the delight of that love in my face, because I was then meditating on conjugial love. This meditation beamed forth from my eyes, and thence entered into the interiors of my face: he therefore told me that I might enter. The avenue through which I entered was formed of fruit trees connected together by their branches, which made on each side a continued espalier. Through the avenue I entered the little garden, which breathed a pleasant fragrance from its shrubs and flowers. The shrubs and flowers were in pairs; and I was informed that such little gardens appear about the houses where there are and have been nuptials, and hence they are challed nuptial gardens. I afterwards entered the house, where I saw the two conjugial partners holding each other by the hands, and conversing together from love truly conjugial; and as I looked, it was given me to see from their faces the image of conjugial love, and from their conversation the vital principle thereof. After I, with the rest of the company, had paid them my respects, and wished them all happiness, I went into the nuptial garden, and saw on the right side of it a company of youths, to whom all who came out of the house resorted. The reason of their resorting to them was, because they were conversing respecting conjugial love, and conversation on this subject attracts to it the minds (*animos*) of all by a certain occult power. I then listened to a wise one who was speaking on the subject; and the sum of what I heard is as follows: That the divine providence of the Lord is most particular and thence most universal in respect to marriages in the heavens: because all the felicities of heaven issue from the delights of conjugial love, like sweet waters from the sweet source of a fountain; and that on this account it is provided by the Lord that conjugial pairs be born, and that these pairs be continually educated for marriage, neither the maiden nor the youth knowing anything of the matter; and after a stated time, when they both become marriageable, they meet as by chance, and see each other; and that in this case they instantly know, as by a kind of instinct, that they are pairs, and by a kind of inward dictate think within themselves, the youth, that she is mine, and the maiden, that he is mine; and when this thought has existed for some time in the mind of each, they deliberately accost each other, and betroth themselves. It is said, "as by chance," and "as by instinct," and the meaning is, by the divine providence; since, while the divine providence is unknown, it has such an appearance. That conjugial pairs are born and educated to marriage, while each party is ignorant of it, he proved by the conjugial likeness visible in the faces of each; also by the intimate and eternal union of minds (*animorum*) and minds (*mentium*), which could not possibly exist, as it does in heaven, without being foreseen and provided by the Lord. When the wise one had proceeded thus far with his discourse, and had received the applauses of the company, he further added, that in the minutest things with man, both male and female, there is a conjugial principle; but still the conjugial principle with the male is different from what it is with the female; also that in the male conjugial principle there is what is conjunctive with the female conjugial principle, and *vice versa*, even in the minutest things. This he confirmed by the marriage of the will and the understanding in every individual, which two principles act together upon the minutest things of the mind and of the body; from which considerations it may be seen, that in every substance, even the smallest, there is a conjugial principle; and that this is evident from the compound substances which are made up of simple substances; as that there are two eyes, two ears, two nostrils, two cheeks, two lips, two arms with hands, two loins, two feet, and within in man two hemispheres of the brain, two ventricles of the heart, two lobes of the lungs, two kidneys, two testicles; and where there are not two, still they are divided into two. The reason why there are two is, because the one is of the will and the other of the understanding, which act wonderfully in each other to present a one; wherefore the two eyes make one sight, the two ears one hearing, the two nostrils one smell, the two lips one speech, the two hands one labor, the two feet one pace, the two hemispheres of the brain one habitation of the mind, the two chambers of the heart one life of the body by the blood, the two lobes of the lungs one respiration, and so forth; but the male and female principles, united by love truly conjugial, constitute one life fully human. While he was saying these things, there appeared red lightning on the right, and white lightning on the left; each was mild, and they entered through the eyes into the mind, and also enlightened it. After the lightning it also thundered; which was a gentle murmur from the angelic heaven flowing down and increasing. On hearing and seeing these things, the wise one said, "These are to remind me to add the following observations: that of the above pairs, the right one signifies their good, and the left their truth; and that this is from the marriage of good and truth, which is inscribed on man in general and in every one of his principles; and good has reference to the will, and truth to the understanding, and both together to a one. Hence, in heaven the right eye is the good of vision, and the left the truth thereof; also the right ear is the good of hearing, and the left the truth thereof; and likewise the right hand is the good of a man's ability, and the left the truth thereof; and in like manner in the rest of the above pairs; and since the right and left have such significations, therefore the Lord said, 'If thy right eye scandalize thee, pluck it out; and if thy right hand scandalize thee, cut it off'; whereby he meant, if good becomes evil, the evil must be cast out. This is the reason also why he said to his disciples that they should cast the net on the right side of the ship; and that when they did so, they took a great multitude of fishes; whereby he meant that they should teach the good of charity, and that thus they would collect men." When he had said these things, the two lightnings again appeared, but milder than before; and then it was seen, that the lightning on the left derived its whiteness from the red-shining fire of the lightning on the right; on seeing which he said, "This is a sign from heaven tending to confirm what I have said; because what is fiery in heaven is good, and what is white in heaven is truth; and its being seen that the lightning on the left derived its whiteness from the red-shining fire of the lightning on the right, is a demonstrative sign that the whiteness of light, or light, is merely the splendor of fire." On hearing this all went home, inflamed with the good and truth of gladness, in consequence of the above lightnings, and of the conversation respecting them.

ON REPEATED MARRIAGES.

317. It may come to be a matter of question, whether conjugial love, which is that of one man with one wife, after the death of one of the parties, can be separated, or transferred, or superinduced; also whether repeated marriages have any thing in common with polygamy, and thereby whether they may be called successive polygamies; with several other inquiries which often add scruples to scruples with men of a reasoning spirit. In order therefore that those who are curious in such researches, and who only grope in the shade respecting these marriages,

may see some light, I have conceived it would be worth while to present for their consideration the following articles on the subject: I. *After the death of a married partner, again to contract wedlock, depends on the preceding conjugial love.* II. *It depends also on the state of marriage, in which the parties had lived.* III. *With those who have not been in love truly conjugial there is no obstacle or hindrance to their again contracting wedlock.* IV. *Those who had lived together in love truly conjugial are unwilling to marry again, except for reasons separate from conjugial love.* V. *The state of the marriage of a youth with a maiden differs from that of a youth with a widow.* VI. *The state of the marriage of a widower with a maiden differs also from that of a widower with a widow.* VII. *The varieties and diversities of these marriages as to love and its attributes are innumerable.* VIII. *The state of a widow is more grievous than that of a widower.* We proceed to the explanation of each article.

318. I. AFTER THE DEATH OF A MARRIED PARTNER, AGAIN TO CONTRACT WEDLOCK, DEPENDS ON THE PRECEDING CONJUGIAL LOVE. Love truly conjugial is like a balance, in which the inclinations for repeated marriages are weighed : so far as the preceding conjugial love had been genuine, so far the inclination for another marriage is weak ; but so far as the preceding love had not been genuine, so far the inclination to another marriage is usually strong. The reason of this is obvious ; because conjugial love is in a similar degree a conjunction of minds, which remains in the life of the body of the one party after the decease of the other ; and this holds the inclination as a scale in a balance, and causes a preponderance according to the appropriation of true love. But since the approach to this love is seldom made at this day except for a few paces, therefore the scale of the preponderance of the inclination generally rises to a state of equilibrium, and from thence inclines and tends to the other side, that is, to marriage. The contrary is the case with those, whose preceding love in the former marriage has not been truly conjugial, because in proportion as that love is not genuine, there is in a like degree a disjunction of minds, which also remains in the life of the body of the one party after the decease of the other; and this enters the will disjoined from that of the other, and causes an inclination for a new connection ; in favor of which the thought arising from the inclination of the will induces the hope of a more united, and thereby a more delightful connection. That inclinations to repeated marriages arise from the state of the preceding love, is well known, and is also obvious to reason : for love truly conjugial is influenced by a fear of loss, and loss is followed by grief; and this grief and fear reside in the very inmost principles of the mind. Hence, so far as that love prevails, so far the soul inclines both in will and in thought, that is, in intention, to be in the subject with and in which it was : from

these considerations it follows, that the mind is kept balancing towards another marriage according to the degree of love in which it was in the former marriage. Hence it is that after death the same parties are re-united, and mutually love each other as they did in the world: but as we said above, such love at this day is rare, and there are few who make the slightest approach to it; and those who do not approach it, and still more those who keep at a distance from it, as they were desirous of separation in the matrimonial life heretofore passed, so after death they are desirous of being united to another. But respecting both these sorts of persons more will be said in what follows.

319. II. AFTER THE DEATH OF A MARRIED PARTNER, AGAIN TO CONTRACT WEDLOCK, DEPENDS ALSO ON THE STATE OF MARRIAGE IN WHICH THE PARTIES HAD LIVED. By the state of marriage here we do not mean the state of love treated of in the foregoing article, because the latter causes an internal inclination to marriage or from it; but we mean the state of marriage which causes an external inclination to it or from it; and this state with its inclinations is manifold: as, 1. If there are children in the house, and a new mother is to be provided for them. 2. If there is a wish for a further increase of children. 3. If the house is large and full of servants of both sexes. 4. If the calls of business abroad divert the mind from domestic concerns, and without a new mistress there is reason to fear misery and misfortune. 5. If mutual aids and offices require that married partners be engaged in various occupations and employments. 6. Moreover it depends on the temper and disposition of the separated partner, whether after the first marriage the other partner can or cannot live alone, or without a consort. 7. The preceding marriage also disposes the mind either to be afraid of married life, or in favor of it. 8. I have been informed that polygamical love and the love of the sex, also the lust of deflowering and the lust of variety, have induced the minds (*animos*) of some to desire repeated marriages; and that the minds of some have also been induced thereto by a fear of the law and of the loss of reputation, in case they commit whoredom: besides several other circumstances which promote external inclinations to matrimony.

320. III. WITH THOSE WHO HAVE NOT BEEN IN LOVE TRULY CONJUGIAL, THERE IS NO OBSTACLE OR HINDRANCE TO THEIR AGAIN CONTRACTING WEDLOCK. With those who have not been principled in conjugial love, there is no spiritual or internal, but only a natural or external bond; and if an internal bond does not keep the external in its order and tenor, the latter is but like a bundle when the bandage is removed, which flows every way according as it is tossed or driven by the wind. The reason of this is, because what is natural derives its origin from what is spiritual, and in its existence is merely a mass collected from

spiritual principles; wherefore if the natural be separated from the spiritual, which produced and as it were begot it, it is no longer kept together interiorly, but only exteriorly by the spiritual, which encompasses and binds it in general, and does not tie it and keep it tied together in particular. Hence it is, that the natural principle separated from the spiritual, in the case of two married partners, does not cause any conjunction of minds, and consequently of wills, but only a conjunction of some external affections, which are connected with the bodily senses. The reason why nothing opposes and hinders such persons from again contracting wedlock, is, because they have not been the essentials of marriage; and hence those essentials do not at all influence them after separation by death: therefore they are then absolutely at their own disposal, whether they be widowers or widows, to bind their sensual affections with whomsoever they please, provided there be no legal impediment. Neither do they themselves think of marriages in any other than a natural view, and from a regard to convenience in supplying various necessities and external advantages, which after the death of one of the parties may again be supplied by another; and possibly, if their interior thoughts were viewed, as in the spiritual world, there would not be found in them any distinction between conjugial unions and extra-conjugial connections. The reason why it is allowable for these to contract repeated marriages, is, as above-mentioned, because merely natural connections are after death of themselves dissolved and fall asunder; for by death the external affections follow the body, and are entombed with it; those only remaining which are connected with internal principles. But it is to be observed, that marriages interiorly conjunctive can scarcely be entered into in the world, because elections of internal likenesses cannot there be provided by the Lord as in the heavens; for they are limited in many ways, as to equals in rank and condition, within the country, city, and village where they live; and in the world for the most part married partners are held together merely by externals, and thus not by internals, which internals do not shew themselves till some time after marriage, and are only known when they influence the externals.

321. IV. THOSE WHO HAD LIVED TOGETHER IN LOVE TRULY CONJUGIAL ARE UNWILLING TO MARRY AGAIN, EXCEPT FOR REASONS SEPARATE FROM CONJUGIAL LOVE. The reasons why those who had lived in love truly conjugial, after the death of their married partners are unwilling to marry again, are as follow, 1. Because they were united as to their souls, and thence as to their minds; and this union, being spiritual, is an actual junction of the soul and mind of one of the parties to those of the other, which cannot possibly be dissolved; that such is the nature of spiritual conjunction, has been constantly shewn above. 2. Because they were also united as to their bodies by

the receptions of the propagation of the soul of the husband by the wife, and thus by the insertion of his life into hers, whereby a maiden becomes a wife; and on the other hand by the reception of the conjugial love of the wife by the husband, which disposes the interiors of his mind, and at the same time the interiors and exteriors of his body, into a state receptible of love and perceptible of wisdom, which makes him from a youth become a husband; see above, n. 198. 3. Because a sphere of love from the wife, and a sphere of understanding from the man, is continually flowing forth, and because it perfects conjunctions, and encompasses them with its pleasant influence, and unites them; see also above, n. 223. 4. Because married partners thus united think of, and desire what is eternal, and because on this idea their eternal happiness is founded; see n. 216. 5. From these several considerations it is, that they are no longer two, but one man, that is, one flesh. 6. That such a union cannot be destroyed by the death of one of the parties, is manifest to the sight of a spirit. 7. To the above considerations shall be added this new information, that two such conjugial partners, after the death of one, are still not separated; since the spirit of the deceased dwells continually with that of the survivor, and this even to the death of the latter, when they again meet and are reunited, and love each other more tenderly than before, because they are then in the spiritual world. Hence flows this undeniable consequence, that those who had lived in love truly conjugial, are unwilling to marry again. But if they afterwards contract something like marriage, it is for reasons separate from conjugial love, which are all external; as in case there are young children in the house, and the care of them requires attention; if the house is large and full of servants of both sexes; if the calls of business abroad divert the mind from domestic concerns; if mutual aids and offices are necessary; with other cases of a like nature.

322. V. THE STATE OF THE MARRIAGE OF A YOUTH WITH A MAIDEN DIFFERS FROM THAT OF A YOUTH WITH A WIDOW. By states of marriage we mean the states of the life of each party, the husband and the wife, after the nuptials, thus in the marriage, as to the quality of the intercourse at that time, whether it be internal, that is of souls and minds, which is intercourse in the principle idea, or whether it be only external, that is of minds (*animorum*), of the senses, and of the body. The state of marriage of a youth with a maiden is essentially itself initiatory to genuine marriage; for between these conjugial love can proceed in its just order, which is from its first heat to its first torch, and afterwards from its first seed with the youth-husband, and from its first flower with the maiden-wife, and thus generate, grow, and fructify, and introduce itself into those successive states with both parties mutually; but if otherwise, the youth or

the maiden was not really such, but only in external form. But between a youth and a widow there is not such an initiation to marriage from first principles, nor a like progression in marriage, since a widow is more at her own disposal, and under her own jurisdiction, than a maiden; wherefore a youth addresses himself differently to his wife if she were a widow, from what he does if she were a maiden. But herein there is much variety and diversity; therefore the subject is here mentioned only in a general way.

323. VI. THE STATE OF THE MARRIAGE OF A WIDOWER WITH A MAIDEN DIFFERS ALSO FROM THAT OF A WIDOWER WITH A WIDOW. For a widower has already been initiated into married life which a maiden has to be; and yet conjugial love perceives and is sensible of its pleasantness and delight in mutual initiation; a youth-husband and a maiden-wife perceive and are sensible of things ever new in whatever occurs, whereby they are in a kind of continual initiation and consequent amiable progression. The case is otherwise in the state of the marriage of a widower with a maiden: the maiden-wife has an internal inclination, whereas with the man that inclination has passed away; but herein there is much variety and diversity: the case is similar in a marriage between a widower and a widow; however, except this general notion, it is not allowable to add anything specifically.

324. VII. THE VARIETIES AND DIVERSITIES OF THESE MARRIAGES AS TO LOVE AND ITS ATTRIBUTES ARE INNUMERABLE. There is an infinite variety of all things, and also an infinite diversity. By varieties we here mean the varieties between those things which are of one genus or species, also between the genera and species; but by diversities we here mean the diversities between those things which are opposite. Our idea of the distinction of varieties and diversities may be illustrated as follows: The angelic heaven, which is connected as a one, in an infinite variety, no one there being absolutely like another, either as to souls and minds, or as to affections, perceptions, and consequent thoughts, or as to inclinations and consequent intentions, or as to tone of voice, face, body, gesture, and gait, and several other particulars, and yet, notwithstanding there are myriads of myriads, they have been and are arranged by the Lord into one form, in which there is full unanimity and concord; and this could not possibly be, unless they were all, with their innumerable varieties, universally and individually under the guidance of one: these are what we here mean by varieties. But by diversities we mean the opposites of those varieties, which exist in hell; for the inhabitants there are diametrically opposite to those in heaven; and hell, which consists of such, is kept together as a one by varieties in themselves altogether contrary to the varieties in heaven, thus by perpetual diversities. From these considerations it is evident what is perceived by infinite

variety and infinite diversity. The case is the same in marriages, namely, that there are infinite varieties with those who are in conjugial love, and infinite varieties with those who are in adulterous love; and hence, that there are infinite diversities between the latter and the former. From these premises it follows, that the varieties and diversities in marriages of every genus and species, whether of a youth with a maiden, or of a youth with a widow, or of a widower with a maiden, or of a widower with a widow exceed all number: who can divide infinity into numbers?

325. VIII. THE STATE OF A WIDOW IS MORE GRIEVOUS THAN THAT OF A WIDOWER. The reasons for this are both external and internal; the external are such as all can comprehend; as, 1. That a widow cannot provide for herself and her family the necessaries of life, nor dispose of them when acquired, as a man can, and as she previously did by and with her husband. 2. That neither can she defend herself and her family as is expedient; for, while she was a wife, her husband was her defence, and as it were her arm; and while she herself was her ow.1 [defence and arm], she still trusted to her husband. 3. That of herself she is deficient of counsel in such things as relate to interior wisdom and the prudence thence derived. 4. That a widow is without the reception of love, in which as a woman she is principled; thus she is in a state contrary to that which was innate and induced by marriage. These external reasons, which are natural, have their origin from internal reasons also, which are spiritual, like all other things in the world and in the body; respecting which see above, n. 220. Those external natural reasons are perceived from the internal spiritual reasons which proceed from the marriage of good and truth, and principally from the following: that good cannot provide or arrange anything but by truth; that neither can good defend itself but by truth; consequently that truth is the defence and as it were the arm of good; that good without truth is deficient of counsel, because it has counsel, wisdom, and prudence by means of truth. Now since by creation the husband is truth, and the wife the good thereof; or, what is the same thing, since by creation the husband is understanding, and the wife the love thereof, it is evident that the external or natural reasons, which aggravate the widowhood of a woman, have their origin from internal or spiritual reasons. These spiritual reasons, together with natural, are meant by what is said of widows in several passages in the Word; as may be seen in the APOCALYPSE REVEALED, n. 764.

* * * * * * *

326. To the above I shall add TWO MEMORABLE RELATIONS. FIRST. After the problem concerning the soul had been discussed and solved in the gymnasium, I saw them coming out in order: first came the chief teacher, then the elders, in the midst of whom were the five youths who had given the answers, and after

these the rest. When they were come out they went apart to the environs of the house, where there were piazzas surrounded by shrubs; and being assembled, they divided themselves into small companies, which were so many groups of youths conversing together on subjects of wisdom, in each of which was one of the wise persons from the orchestra. As I saw these from my apartment, I became in the spirit, and in that state I went out to them, and approached the chief teacher, who had lately proposed the problem concerning the soul. On seeing me, he said, "Who are you? I was surprised as I saw you approaching in the way, that at one instant you came into my sight, and the next instant went out of it; or that at one time I saw you, and suddenly I did not see you: assuredly you are not in the same state of life that we are." To this I replied, smiling, "I am neither a player nor a *vertumnus;* but I am alternate, at one time in your light, and at another in your shade; thus both a foreigner and a native." Hereupon the chief teacher looked at me, and said, "You speak things strange and wonderful: tell me who you are." I said, "I am in the world in which you have been, and from which you have departed, and which is called the natural world; and I am also in the world into which you have come, and in which you are, which is called the spiritual world. Hence I am in a natural state, and at the same time in a spiritual state; in a natural state with men of the earth and in a spiritual state with you; and when I am in the natural state, you do not see me, but when I am in the spiritual state, you do; that such should be my condition, has been granted me by the Lord. It is known to you, illustrious sir, that a man of the natural world does not see a man of the spiritual world, nor *vice versa;* therefore when I let my spirit into the body, you did not see me; but when I let it out of the body, you did see me. You have been teaching in the gymnasium, that you are souls, and that souls see souls, because they are human forms; and you know, that when you were in the natural world, you did not see yourself or your souls in your bodies; and this is a consequence of the difference between what is spiritual and what is natural." When he heard of the difference between what is spiritual and what is natural, he said, "What do you mean by that difference? is it not like the difference between what is more or less pure? for what is spiritual but that which is natural in a higher state of purity?" I replied, "The difference is of another kind; it is like that between prior and posterior, which bear no determinate proportion to each other: for the prior is in the posterior as the cause is in the effect; and the posterior is derived from the prior as the effect from its cause: hence, the one does not appear to the other." To this the chief teacher replied, "I have meditated and ruminated upon this difference, but heretofore in vain; I wish I could perceive it." I said, "You shall not only perceive the difference between what is spiritual and what is natural, but shall also see it." I then proceeded as follows: " You yourself are in a spiritual state with your associate spirits, but in a natural state with me; for you converse with your associates in the spiritual language, which is common to every spirit and angel, but with me in my mother-tongue; for every spirit and angel, when conversing with a man, speaks his peculiar language; thus French with a Frenchman, English with an Englishman, Greek with a Greek, Arabic with an Arabian, and so forth. That you may know therefore the difference between what is spiritual and what is natural in respect to languages, make this experiment; withdraw to your associates, and say something there: then retain the expressions, and return with them in your memory, and utter them before me." He did so, and returned to me with those expressions in his mouth, and uttered them; and they were altogether strange and foreign, such as do not occur in any language of the natural world. By this experiment several times repeated, it was made very evident that all the spiritual world have the spiritual language, which has in it nothing that is common to any natural language, and that every man comes of himself into the use of that language after his decease. At the same time also he experienced, that the sound of the spiritual language differs so far from the sound of natural language, that a spiritual sound, though loud, could not at all be heard by a natural man, nor a natural sound by a spirit. Afterwards I requested the chief teacher and the bystanders to withdraw to their associates, and write some sentence or other on a piece of paper, and then return with it to me, and read it. They did so, and returned with the paper in their hand; but when they read it, they could not understand any part of it, as the writing consisted only of some letters of the alphabet, with turns over them, each of which was significative of some particular sense and meaning: because each letter of the alphabet is thus significative, it is evident why the Lord is called Alpha and Omega. On their repeatedly withdrawing, and writing in the same manner, and returning to me, they found that their writing involved and comprehended innumerable things which no natural writing could possibly express; and they were given to understand, that this was in consequence of the spiritual man's thoughts being incomprehensible and ineffable to the natural man, and such as cannot flow and be brought into any other writing or language. Then as some present were unwilling to comprehend that spiritual thought so far exceeds natural thought, as to be respectively ineffable, I said to them, "Make the experiment; withdraw into your spiritual society, and think on some subject, and retain your thoughts, and return, and express them before me." They did so; but when they wanted to express the subject thought of, they were unable; for they did not find any idea of natural thought adequate to any idea of spiritual thought, consequently no words expressive of it; for ideas of thought are constituent of the words of language. This experiment they repeated again and again; whereby they were convinced that spiritual ideas are supernatural, inexpressible, ineffable, and incomprehensible to the natural man; and on account of this their super-eminence, they said, that spiritual ideas, or thoughts, as compared with natural, were ideas of ideas, and thoughts of thoughts; and that therefore they were expressive of qualities of qualities, and affections of affections; consequently that spiritual thoughts were the beginnings and origins of natural thoughts: hence also it was made evident that spiritual wisdom was the wisdom of wisdom, consequently that it was imperceptible to any wise man in the natural world. It was then told them from the third heaven, that there is a wisdom still interior and superior, which is called celestial, bearing a proportion to spiritual wisdom like that which spiritual wisdom bears to natural, and that these descend by an orderly influx according to the heavens from the divine wisdom of the Lord, which is infinite.

327. After this I said to the by-standers, "You have seen from these three experimental proofs what is the difference between spiritual and natural, and also the reason why the natural man does not appear to the spiritual, nor the spiritual to the natural, although they are consociated as to affections and thoughts, and thence as to presence. Hence it is that, as I approached, at one time you, Sir, (addressing the chief teacher), saw me, and at another you did not." After this, a voice was heard from the superior heaven to the chief teacher, saying, "Come up hither;" and he went up: and on his return, he said, that the angels, as well as himself, did not before know the differences between spiritual and natural, because there had never before been an opportunity of comparing them together, by any person's existing at the same time in both worlds; and without such comparison and reference those differences were not ascertainable.

328. After this we retired, and conversing again on this subject, I said, "Those differences originate solely in this circumstance of your existence in the spiritual world, that you are in substantials and not in materials: and substantials are the beginning of materials. You are in principles and thereby in singulars; but we are in principiates and composites; you are in particulars, but we are in generals; and as generals cannot enter into particulars, so neither can natural things, which are material, enter into spiritual things which are substantial, any more than a ship's cable can enter into, or be drawn though, the eye of a fine needle; or than a nerve can enter or be let into one of the fibres of which it is composed, or a fibre into one of the fibrils of which it is composed: this also is known in the world: there-

fore herein the learned are agreed, that there is no such thing as an influx of what is natural into what is spiritual, but of what is spiritual into what is natural. This now is the reason why the natural man cannot conceive that which the spiritual man conceives, nor consequently express such conceptions; wherefore Paul calls what he heard from the third heaven ineffable. Moreover, to think spiritually is to think abstractedly from space and time, and to think naturally is to think in conjunction with space and time; for in every idea of natural thought there is something derived from space and time, which is not the case with any spiritual idea; because the spiritual world is not in space and time, like the natural world, but in the appearances of space and time. In this respect also spiritual thoughts and perceptions differ from natural; therefore you can think of the essence and omnipresence of God from eternity, that is, of God before the creation of the world, since you think of the essence of God from eternity abstracted from time, and of his omnipresence abstracted from space, and thus comprehend such things as transcend the ideas of the natural man." I then related to them, how I once thought of the essence and omnipresence of God from eternity, that is of God before the creation of the world; and that because I could not yet remove spaces and times from the ideas of my thought, I was brought into anxiety; for the idea of nature entered instead of God: but it was said to me, " Remove the ideas of space and time, and you will see." I did so and then I saw; and from that time I was enabled to think of God from eternity, and not of nature from eternity; because God is in all time without time, and in all space without space, whereas nature in all time is in time, and in all space in space; and nature with her time and space, must of necessity have a beginning and a birth, but not God who is without time, and space; therefore nature is from God, not from eternity, but in time, that is, together with her time and space.

329. After the chief teacher and the rest of the assembly had left me, some boys who were also engaged in the gymnasian exercise, followed me home, and stood near me for a little while as I was writing: and lo! at that instant they saw a moth running upon my paper, and asked in surprise what was the name of that nimble little creature? I said, "It is called a moth; and I will tell you some wonderful things respecting it. This little animal contains in itself as many members and viscera as there are in a camel, such as brains, hearts, pulmonary pipes, organs of sense, motion, and generation, a stomach, intestines, and several others; and each of these organs consists of fibres, nerves, blood-vessels, muscles, tendons, membranes; and each of these of still purer parts, which escape the observation of the keenest eye." They then said that this little animal appeared to them just like a simple substance; upon which I said, "There

are nevertheless innumerable things within it I mention these things that you may know, that the case is similar in regard to every object which appears before you as one, simple and least, as well in your actions as in your affections and thoughts. I can assure you that every grain of thought, that every drop of your affection, is divisible *ad infinitum:* and that in proportion as your ideas are divisible, so you are wise. Know then, that every thing divided is more and more multiple, and not more and more simple; because what is continually divided approaches nearer and nearer to the infinite, in which all things are infinitely. What I am now observing to you is new and heretofore unheard of." When I concluded, the boys took their leave of me, and went to the chief teacher, and intreated him to take an opportunity to propose in the gymnasium somewhat new and unheard of as a problem. He inquired, "What?" they said, "That every thing divided is more and more multiple, and not more and more simple; because it approaches nearer and nearer to the infinite, in which all things are infinitely:" and he pledged himself to propose it, and said, "I see this, because I have perceived that one natural idea contains innumerable spiritual ideas; yea, that one spiritual idea contains innumerable celestial ideas. Herein is grounded the difference between the celestial wisdom of the angels of the third heaven, and the spiritual wisdom of the angels of the second heaven, and also the natural wisdom of the angels of the last heaven and likewise of men."

330. THE SECOND MEMORABLE RELATION. I once heard a pleasant discussion between some men respecting the female sex, whether it be possible for a woman to love her husband, who constantly loves her own beauty, that is, who loves herself from her form. They agreed among themselves first, that women have two-fold beauty; one natural, which is that of the face and body, and the other spiritual which is that of the love and manners; they agreed also, that these two kinds of beauty are often divided in the natural world, and are always united in the spiritual world; for in the latter world beauty is the form of the love and manners; therefore after death it frequently happens that deformed women become beauties, and beautiful women become deformities. While the men were discussing this point, there came some wives, and said, "Admit of our presence; because what you are discussing, you have learned by science, but we are taught it by experience; and you likewise know so little of the love of wives, that it scarcely amounts to any knowledge. Do you know that the prudence of the wives' wisdom consists in hiding their love from their husbands in the inmost recess of their bosoms, or in the midst of their hearts?" The discussion then proceeded; and the FIRST CONCLUSION made by the men was, That every woman is willing to appear beautiful as to face and manners, because she is born an affection of

love, and the form of this affection is beauty; therefore a woman that is not desirous to be beautiful, is not desirous to love and to be loved, and consequently is not truly a woman. Hereupon the wives observed, "The beauty of a woman resides in soft tenderness, and consequently in exquisite sensibility; hence comes the woman's love for the man, and the man's for the woman. This possibly you do not understand." The SECOND CONCLUSION of the men was, That a woman before marriage is desirous to be beautiful for the men, but after marriage, if she be chaste, for one man only, and not for the men. Hereupon the wives observed, "When the husband has sipped the natural beauty of the wife, he sees it no longer, but sees her spiritual beauty; and from this he re-loves, and recalls the natural beauty, but under another aspect." The THIRD CONCLUSION of their discussion was, That if a woman after marriage is desirous to appear beautiful in like manner as before marriage, she loves the men, and not a man: because a woman loving herself from her beauty is continually desirous that her beauty should be sipped; and as this no longer appears to her husband, as you observed, she is desirous that it may be sipped by the men to whom it appears. It is evident that such a one has a love of the sex, and not a love of one of the sex. Hereupon the wives were silent; yet they murmured, "What woman is so void of vanity, as not to desire to seem beautiful to the men also, at the same time that she seems beautiful to one man only?" These things were heard by some wives from heaven, who were beautiful, because they were heavenly affections. They confirmed the conclusions of the men; but they added, "Let them only love their beauty and its ornaments for the sake of their husbands, and from them."

331. Those three wives being indignant that the three conclusions of the men were confirmed by the wives from heaven, said to the men, "You have inquired whether a woman that loves herself from her beauty, loves her husband; we in our turn will therefore inquire whether a man who loves himself from his intelligence, can love his wife. Be present and hear." This was their FIRST CONCLUSION; No wife loves her husband on account of his face, but on account of his intelligence in his business and manners: know therefore, that a wife unites herself with a man's intelligence and thereby with the man: therefore if a man loves himself on account of his intelligence, he withdraws it from the wife into himself, whence comes disunion and not union: moreover to love his own intelligence is to be wise from himself, and this is to be insane; therefore it is to love his own insanity. Hereupon the men observed, "Possibly the wife unites herself with the man's strength or ability." At this the wives smiled, saying, "There is no deficiency of ability while the man loves the wife from intelligence; but there is if

he loves her from insanity. Intelligence consists in loving the wife only: and in this love there is no deficiency of ability; but insanity consists in not loving the wife but the sex, and in this love there is a deficiency of ability. You comprehend this." The SECOND CONCLUSION was; We women are born into the love of the men's intelligence; therefore if the men love their own intelligence, it cannot be united with its genuine love, which belongs to the wife; and if the man's intelligence is not united with its genuine love, which belongs to the wife, it becomes insanity grounded in haughtiness, and conjugial love becomes cold. What woman in such case can unite her love to what is cold; and what man can unite the insanity of his haughtiness to the love of intelligence? But the men said, "Whence has a man honor from his wife but by her magnifying his intelligence?" The wives replied, "From love, because love honors; and honor cannot be separated from love, but love may be from honor. Afterwards they came to this THIRD CONCLUSION; You seemed as if you loved your wives; and you do not see that you are loved by them, and thus that you re-love; and that your intelligence is a receptacle: if therefore you love your intelligence in yourselves, it becomes the receptacle of your love; and the love of *proprium* (or self-hood), since it cannot endure an equal, never becomes conjugial love; but so long as it prevails, so long it remains adulterous. Hereupon the men were silent; nevertheless they murmured, "What is conjugial love?" Some husbands in heaven heard what passed, and confirmed thence the three conclusions of the wives.

ON POLYGAMY.

332. THE reason why polygamical marriages are absolutely condemned by the Christian world cannot be clearly seen by any one, whatever powers of acute and ingenious investigation he may possess, unless he be previously instructed, THAT THERE EXISTS A LOVE TRULY CONJUGIAL; THAT THIS LOVE CAN ONLY EXIST BETWEEN TWO; NOR BETWEEN TWO, EXCEPT FROM THE LORD ALONE; AND THAT INTO THIS LOVE IS INSERTED HEAVEN WITH ALL ITS FELICITIES. Unless these knowledges precede, and as it were lay the first stone, it is in vain for the mind to desire to draw from the understanding any reasons for the condemnation of polygamy by the Christian world, which should be satisfactory, and on which it may firmly stand, as a house upon its stone or foundation. It is well known, that the institution of monogamical marriage is founded on the Word of the Lord,

"*That whosoever putteth away his wife, except on account of whoredom, and marrieth another, committeth adultery; and that from the beginning, or from the first establishment of marriages, it was [ordained], that two should become one flesh; and that man should not separate what God hath joined together,*" Matt. xix. 3—12. But although the Lord spake these words from the divine law inscribed on marriages, still if the understanding cannot support that law by some reason of its own, it may so warp it by the turnings and windings to which it is accustomed, and by sinister interpretations, as to render its principle obscure and ambiguous, and at length affirmative negative;— affirmative, because it is also grounded in the civil law; and negative, because it is not grounded in a rational view of those words. Into this principle the human mind will fall, unless it be previously instructed respecting the above-mentioned knowledges, which may be serviceable to the understanding as introductory to its reasons: these knowledges are, that there exists a love truly conjugial; that this love can only possibly exist between two; nor between two, except from the Lord alone; and that into this love is inserted heaven with all its felicities. But these, and several other particulars respecting the condemnation of polygamy by the Christian world, we will demonstrate in the following order: I. *Love truly conjugial can only exist with one wife, consequently neither can friendship, confidence, ability truly conjugial, and such conjunction of minds that two may be one flesh.* II. *Thus celestial blessednesses, spiritual satisfactions, and natural delights, which from the beginning were provided for those who are in love truly conjugial, can only exist with one wife.* III. *All those things can only exist from the Lord alone; and they do not exist with any but those who come to him alone, and at the same time live according to his commandments.* IV. *Consequently, love truly conjugial, with its felicities, can only exist with those who are of the Christian church.* V. *Therefore a Christian is not allowed to marry more than one wife.* VI. *If a Christian marries several wives, he commits not only natural but also spiritual adultery.* VII. *The Israelitish nation was permitted to marry several wives, because they had not the Christian church, and consequently love truly conjugial could not exist with them.* VIII. *At this day the Mahometans are permitted to marry several wives, because they do not acknowledge the Lord Jesus Christ to be one with Jehovah the Father, and thereby to be the God of heaven and earth; and hence they cannot receive love truly conjugial.* IX. *The Mahometan heaven is out of the Christian heaven and is divided into two heavens, the inferior and the superior; and only those are elevated into their superior heaven who renounce concubines and live with one wife, and acknowledge our Lord as equal to God the Father, to whom is given dominion over heaven and earth.* X. *Polygamy is lasciviousness.*

XI. *Conjugial chastity, purity, and sanctity, cannot exist with polygamists.* XII. *Polygamists, so long as they remain such, cannot become spiritual.* XIII. *Polygamy is not sin with those who live in it from a religious notion.* XIV. *That polygamy is not sin with those who are in ignorance respecting the Lord.* XV. *That of these, although polygamists, such are saved as acknowledge God, and from a religious notion live according to the civil laws of justice.* XVI. *But none either of the latter or of the former can be associated with the angels in the Christian heavens.* We proceed to an explanation of each article.

333. I. LOVE TRULY CONJUGIAL CAN ONLY EXIST WITH ONE WIFE, CONSEQUENTLY NEITHER CAN FRIENDSHIP, CONFIDENCE, ABILITY TRULY CONJUGIAL, AND SUCH A CONJUNCTION OF MINDS THAT TWO MAY BE ONE FLESH. That love truly conjugial is at this day so rare as to be generally unknown, is a subject which has been occasionally inquired into above; that nevertheless such love actually exists, was demonstrated in its proper chapter, and occasionally in following chapters. But apart from such demonstration, who does not know that there is such a love, which, for excellency and satisfaction, is paramount to all other loves, so that all other loves in respect to it are of little account? That it exceeds self-love, the love of the world, and even the love of life, experience testifies in a variety of cases. Have there not been, and are there not still, instances of men, who for a woman, the dear and desired object of their wishes, prostrate themselves on their knees, adore her as a goddess, and submit themselves as the vilest slaves to her will and pleasure? a plain proof that this love exceeds the love of self. Have there not been, and are there not still instances of men, who for such a woman, make light of wealth, yea of treasures presented in prospect, and are also prodigal of those which they possess? a plain proof that this love exceeds the love of the world. Have there not been, and are there not still, instances of men who for such a woman, account life itself as worthless, and desire to die rather than be disappointed in their wishes, as is evidenced by the many fatal combats between rival lovers on such occasions? a plain proof that this love exceeds the love of life. Lastly, have there not been, and are there not still, instances of men, who for such a woman, have gone raving mad in consequence of being denied a place in her favor? From such a commencement of this love in several cases, who cannot rationally conclude, that, from its essence, it holds supreme dominion over every other love; and that the man's soul in such case is in it, and promises itself eternal blessedness with the dear and desired object of its wishes? And who can discover, let him make what inquiry he pleases, any other cause of this than that he has devoted his soul and heart to one woman? for if the lover, while he is in that state, had the offer made him of choosing out of the whole sex the wor

thiest, the richest, and the most beautiful, would he not despise the offer, and adhere to her whom he had already chosen, his heart being riveted to her alone ?" These observations are made in order that you may acknowledge, that conjugial love of such super-eminence exists, while one of the sex alone is loved. What understanding which with quick discernment attends to a chain of connected reasonings, cannot hence conclude, that if a lover from his inmost soul constantly persisted in love to that one, he would attain those eternal blessednesses which he promised himself before consent, and promises in consent? That he also does attain them if he comes to the Lord, and from him lives a life of true religion, was shewn above. Who but the Lord enters the life of man from a superior principle, and implants therein internal celestial joys, and transfers them to the derivative principles which follow in order; and the more so, while at the same time he also bestows an enduring strength or ability? It is no proof that such love does not exist, or cannot exist, to urge that it is not experienced in one's self, and in this or that person.

334. Since love truly conjugial unites the souls and hearts of two persons, therefore also it is united with friendship, and by friendship with confidence, and makes each conjugial, and so exalts them above other friendships and confidences, that as that love is the chief love, so also that friendship and that confidence are the chief: that this is the case also with ability, is plain from several reasons, some of which are discovered in the SECOND MEMORABLE RELATION that follows this chapter; and from this ability follows the endurance of that love. That by love truly conjugial two consorts become one flesh, was shewn in a separate chapter, from n. 156—183.

335. II. THUS CELESTIAL BLESSEDNESS, SPIRITUAL SATISFACTIONS, AND NATURAL DELIGHTS, WHICH FROM THE BEGINNING WERE PROVIDED FOR THOSE WHO ARE IN LOVE TRULY CONJUGIAL, CAN ONLY EXIST WITH ONE WIFE. They are called celestial blessednesses, spiritual satisfactions, and natural delights, because the human mind is distinguished into three regions, of which the highest is called celestial, the second spiritual, and the third natural; and those three regions, with such as are principled in love truly conjugial, are open, and influx follows in order according to the openings. And as the pleasantnesses of that love are most eminent in the highest regions, they are perceived as blessednesses, and as in the middle region they are less eminent, they are perceived as satisfactions, and lastly, in the lowest region, as delights: that there are such blessednesses, satisfactions, and delights, and that they are perceived and felt, appears from the MEMORABLE RELATIONS in which they are described. The reason why all those happinesses were from the beginning provided for those who are principled in love truly

conjugial, is, because there is an infinity of all blessednesses in the Lord, and he is divine love; and it is the essence of love to desire to communicate all its goods to another whom it loves; therefore together with man he created that love, and inserted in it the faculty of receiving and perceiving those blessednesses. Who is of so dull and doting an apprehension as not to be able to see, that there is some particular love into which the Lord has collected all possible blessings, satisfactions, and delights?

336. III. ALL THOSE THINGS CAN ONLY EXIST FROM THE LORD ALONE; AND THEY DO NOT EXIST WITH ANY BUT THOSE WHO COME TO HIM ALONE, AND LIVE ACCORDING TO HIS COMMANDMENTS. This has been proved above in many places; to which proofs it may be expedient to add, that all those blessings, satisfactions, and delights can only be given by the Lord, and therefore no other is to be approached. What other can be approached, when by him all things were made which are made, John i. 3; when he is the God of heaven and earth, Matt. xxviii. 18: when no appearance of God the father was ever seen, or his voice heard, except through him, John i. 18; chap. v. 37; chap. xiv. 6—11? From these and very many other passages in the Word, it is evident that the marriage of love and wisdom, or of good and truth, from which alone all marriages derive their origin, proceeds from him alone. Hence it follows, that the above love with its felicities exists with none but those who come to him; and the reason why it exists with those who live according to his commandments, is, because he is conjoined with them by love, John xiv. 21—24.

337. IV. CONSEQUENTLY, LOVE TRULY CONJUGIAL WITH ITS FELICITIES CAN ONLY EXIST WITH THOSE WHO ARE OF THE CHRISTIAN CHURCH. The reason why conjugial love, such as was described in its proper chapter, n. 57—73, and in the following chapters, thus such as as it is in its essence, exists only with those who are of the Christian church, is, because that love is from the Lord alone, and the Lord is not so known elsewhere as that he can be approached as God; also because that love is according to the state of the church with every one, n. 130, and the genuine state of the church is from no other source than from the Lord, and thus is with none but those who receive it from him. That these two principles are the beginnings, introductions, and establishments of that love, has been already confirmed by such abundance of evident and conclusive reasons, that it is altogether needless to say any thing more on the subject. The reason why conjugial love is nevertheless rare in the Christian world, n. 58—59, is, because few in that world approach the Lord, and among those there are some who indeed believe the church, but do not live accordingly; besides other circumstances which are unfolded in the APOCALYPSE REVEALED, where the present state of the Christian church is fully described. But

nevertheless it is an established truth, that love truly conjugial can only exist with those who are of the Christian church; therefore also from this ground polygamy is in that church altogether rejected and condemned: that this also is of the divine providence of the Lord, appears very manifest to those who think justly concerning providence.

338. V. THEREFORE A CHRISTIAN IS NOT ALLOWED TO MARRY MORE THAN ONE WIFE. This follows as a conclusion from the confirmation of the preceding articles; to which this is to be added, that the genuine conjugial principle is more deeply inserted into the minds of Christians, than of the Gentiles who have embraced polygamy; and that hence the minds of Christians are more susceptible of that love than the minds of polygamists; for that conjugial principle is inserted in the interiors of the minds of Christians, because they acknowledge the Lord and his divine principle, and in the exteriors of their minds by civil laws.

339. VI. IF A CHRISTIAN MARRIES SEVERAL WIVES, HE COMMITS NOT ONLY NATURAL BUT ALSO SPIRITUAL ADULTERY. That a Christian who marries several wives, commits natural adultery, is agreeable to the Lord's words, "*That it is not lawful to put away a wife, because from the beginning they were created to be one flesh; and that he who putteth away a wife without just cause, and marrieth another, committeth adultery.*" Matt. xix. 3—12; thus still more does he commit adultery who does not put away his wife, but, while retaining her, connects himself with another. This law enacted by the Lord respecting marriages, has its internal ground in spiritual marriage; for whatever the Lord spoke was in itself spiritual; which is meant by this declaration, "*The words that I speak unto you are spirit and are life,*" John vi. 63. The spiritual [sense] contained therein is this, that by polygamical marriage in the Christian world, the marriage of the Lord and the Church is profaned; in like manner the marriage of good and truth; and still more the Word, and with the Word the church; and the profanation of those things is spiritual adultery. That the profanation of the good and truth of the church derived from the Word corresponds to adultery, and hence is spiritual adultery; and that the falsification of good and truth has a like correspondence, but in a less degree, may be seen confirmed in the APOCALYPSE REVEALED, n. 134. The reason why by polygamical marriages among Christians the marriage of the Lord and the church is profaned, is, because there is a correspondence between that divine marriage and the marriages of Christians; concerning which, see above, n. 83—102; which correspondence entirely perishes, if one wife is joined to another; and when it perishes, the married man is no longer a Christian The reason why by polygamical marriages among Christians the marriage of good and truth is profaned, is,

because from this spiritual marriage are derived marriages in the world; and the marriages of Christians differ from those of other nations in this respect, that as good loves truth, and truth good, and are a one, so it is with a wife and a husband; therefore if a Christian should join one wife to another, he would rend asunder in himself that spiritual marriage; consequently he would profane the origin of his marriage, and would thereby commit spiritual adultery. That marriages in the world are derived from the marriage of good and truth, may be seen above, n. 116—131. The reason why a Christian by polygamical marriage would profane the Word and the church, is, because the Word considered in itself is the marriage of good and truth, and the church in like manner, so far as this is derived from the Word; see above, n. 128—131. Now since a Christian is acquainted with the Lord, possesses the Word, and has also the church from the Lord by the Word, it is evident that he, much more than one who is not a Christian, has the faculty of being capable of being regenerated, and thereby of becoming spiritual, and also of attaining to love truly conjugial; for these things are connected together. Since those Christians who marry several wives, commit not only natural but also at the same time spiritual adultery, it follows that the condemnation of Christian polygamists after death is more grievous than that of those who commit only natural adultery. Upon inquiring into their state after death, I received for answer, that heaven is altogether closed in respect to them; that they appear in hell as lying in warm water in the recess of a bath, and that they thus appear at a distance, although they are standing on their feet, and walking, which is in consequence of their intestine frenzy; and that some of them are thrown into whirlpools in the borders of the worlds.

340. VII. THE ISRAELITISH NATION WAS PERMITTED TO MARRY SEVERAL WIVES, BECAUSE THEY HAD NOT THE CHRISTIAN CHURCH, AND CONSEQUENTLY LOVE TRULY CONJUGIAL COULD NOT EXIST WITH THEM. There are some at this day who are in doubt respecting the institution relative to monogamical marriages, or those of one man with one wife, and who are distracted by opposite reasonings on the subject; being led to suppose that because polygamical marriages were openly permitted in the case of the Israelitish nation and its kings, and in the case of David and Solomon, they are also in themselves permissible to Christians; but such persons have no distinct knowledge respecting the Israelitish nation and the Christian, or respecting the externals and internals of the church, or respecting the change of the church from external to internal by the Lord; consequently they know nothing from interior judgment respecting marriages. In general it is to be observed, that a man is born natural in order that he may be made spiritual; and that so long as he remains natural, he is

in the night, and as it were asleep as to spiritual things; and that in this case he does not even know the difference between the external natural man and the internal spiritual. That the Christian church was not with the Israelitish nation, is known from the Word; for they expected the Messiah, as they still expect him, who was to exalt them above all other nations and people in the world: if therefore they had been told, and were still to be told, that the Messiah's kingdom is over the heavens, and thence over all nations, they would have accounted it an idle tale; hence they not only did not acknowledge Christ or the Messiah, our Lord, when he came into the world, but also barbarously took him away out of the world. From these considerations it is evident, that the Christian church was not with that nation, as neither is it at this day; and those with whom the Christian church is not, are natural men both externally and internally: to such persons polygamy is not hurtful, since it is inherent in the natural man; for, in regard to love in marriages, the natural man perceives nothing but what has relation to lust. This is meant by these words of the Lord, "*That Moses, because of the* HARDNESS OF THEIR HEARTS, *suffered them to put away their wives: but that from the beginning it was not so,*" Matt. xix. 8. He says that Moses permitted it, in order that it may be known that it was not the Lord [who permitted it]. But that the Lord taught the internal spiritual man, is known from his precepts, and from the abrogation of the rituals which served only for the use of the natural man; from his precepts respecting washing, as denoting the purification of the internal man, Matt. xv. 1, 17—20; chap. xxiii. 25, 26; Mark vii. 14—23; respecting adultery, as denoting cupidity of the will, Matt. v. 28; respecting the putting away of wives, as being unlawful, and respecting polygamy, as not being agreeable to the divine law, Matt. xix. 3—9. These and several other things relating to the internal principle and the spiritual man, the Lord taught, because he alone opens the internals of human minds, and makes them spiritual, and implants these spiritual principles in the natural, that these also may partake of a spiritual essence: and this effect takes place if he is approached, and the life is formed according to his commandments, which in a summary are, to believe on him, and to shun evils because they are of and from the devil; also to do good works, because they are of the Lord and from the Lord; and in each case for the man to act as from himself, and at the same time to believe that all is done by the Lord through him. The essential reason why the Lord opens the internal spiritual man, and implants this in the external natural man, is, because every man thinks and acts naturally, and therefore could not perceive any thing spiritual, and receives it in his natural principle, unless the Lord had assumed the human natural, and had made this also divine. From these considerations now it appears a truth that the Israelitish nation was permitted to marry several wives, because the Christian church was not with them.

341. VIII. AT THIS DAY THE MAHOMETANS ARE PERMITTED TO MARRY SEVERAL WIVES, BECAUSE THEY DO NOT ACKNOWLEDGE THE LORD JESUS CHRIST TO BE ONE WITH JEHOVAH THE FATHER, AND THEREBY TO BE THE GOD OF HEAVEN AND EARTH, AND HENCE CANNOT RECEIVE LOVE TRULY CONJUGIAL. The Mahometans, in conformity to the religion which Mahomet gave them, acknowledge Jesus Christ to be the Son of God and a grand prophet, and that he was sent into the world by God the Father to teach mankind; but not that God the Father and he are one, and that his divine and human [principle] are one person, united as soul and body, agreeably to the faith of all Christians as grounded in the Athanasian Creed; therefore the followers of Mahomet could not acknowledge our Lord to be any God from eternity, but only to be a perfect natural man; and this being the opinion entertained by Mahomet, and thence by his disciples, and they knowing that God is one, and that that God is he who created the universe, therefore they could do no other than pass by our Lord in their worship; and the more so, because they declare Mahomet also to be a grand prophet; neither do they know what the Lord taught. It is owing to this cause, that the interiors of their minds, which in themselves are spiritual, could not be opened: that the interiors of the mind are opened by the Lord alone, may be seen just above, n. 340. The genuine cause why they are opened by the Lord, when he is acknowledged to be the God of heaven and earth, and is approached, and with those who live according to his commandments, is, because otherwise there is no conjunction, and without conjunction there is no reception. Man is receptible of the Lord's presence and of conjunction with him. To come to him causes presence, and to live according to his commandments causes conjunction; his presence alone is without reception, but presence and conjunction together are with reception. On this subject I will impart the following new information from the spiritual world. Every one in that world, when he is thought of, is brought into view as present; but no one is conjoined to another except from the affection of love; and this is insinuated by doing what he requires, and what is pleasing to him. This circumstance, which is common in the spiritual world, derives its origin from the Lord, who, in this same manner, is present and is conjoined. The above observations are made in order to show, that the Mahometans are permitted to marry several wives, because love truly conjugial, which subsists only between one man and one wife, was not communicable to them; since from their religious

tenets they did not acknowledge the Lord to be equal to God the Father, and so to be the God of heaven and earth. That conjugial love with every one is according to the state of the church, may be seen above, at n. 130, and in several other places.

342. IX. THE MAHOMETAN HEAVEN IS OUT OF THE CHRISTIAN HEAVEN AND IS DIVIDED INTO TWO HEAVENS, THE INFERIOR AND THE SUPERIOR; AND ONLY THOSE ARE ELEVATED INTO THEIR SUPERIOR HEAVEN WHO RENOUNCE CONCUBINES AND LIVE WITH ONE WIFE, AND ACKNOWLEDGE OUR LORD AS EQUAL TO GOD THE FATHER, TO WHOM IS GIVEN DOMINION OVER HEAVEN AND EARTH. Before we speak particularly to each of these points, it may be expedient to premise somewhat concerning the divine providence of the Lord in regard to the rise of Mahometanism. That this religion is received by more kingdoms than the Christian religion, may possibly be a stumbling-block to those who, while thinking of the divine providence, at the same time believe that no one can be saved that is not born a Christian; whereas the Mahometan religion is no stumbling-block to those who believe that all things are of the divine providence. These inquire in what respect the divine providence is manifested in the Mahometan religion; and they so discover in it this, that the Mahometan religion acknowledges our Lord to be the Son of God, the wisest of men, and a grand prophet, who came into the world to instruct mankind; but since the Mahometans have made the Koran the book of their religion, and consequently think much of Mahomet who wrote it, and pay him a degree of worship, therefore they think little respecting our Lord. In order to shew more fully that the Mahometan religion was raised up by the Lord's divine providence to destroy the idolatries of several nations, we will give a detail of the subject, beginning with the origin of idolatries. Previous to the Mahometan religion idolatrous worship prevailed throughout the whole world; because the churches before the Lord's coming were all representative; such also was the Israelitish church, in which the tabernacle, the garments of Aaron, the sacrifices, all things belonging to the temple at Jerusalem, and also the statutes, were representative. The ancients likewise had the science of correspondences, which is also the science of representations, the very essential science of the wise, which was principally cultivated by the Egyptians, whence their hieroglyphics were derived. From that science they knew what was signified by animals and trees of every kind, likewise by mountains, hills, rivers, fountains, and also by the sun, the moon, and the stars: by means of this science also they had a knowledge of spiritual things; since things represented, which were such as relate to the spiritual wisdom of the angels, were the origins [of those which represent]. Now since all their worship was representative, consisting of mere correspondences,

therefore they celebrated it on mountains and hills, and also in groves and gardens; and on this account they sanctified fountains, and in their adorations turned their faces to the rising sun: moreover they made graven horses, oxen, calves, and lambs; yea, birds, fishes, and serpents; and these they set in their houses and other places, in order, according to the spiritual things of the church to which they corresponded, or which they represented. They also set similar images in their temples, as a means of recalling to their remembrance the holy things of worship which they signified. In process of time, when the science of correspondences was forgotten, their posterity began to worship the very graven images as holy in themselves, not knowing that the ancients, their fathers, did not see anything holy in them, but only that according to correspondences they represented and thence signified holy things. Hence arose the idolatries which overspread the whole globe, as well Asia with its islands, as Africa and Europe. To the intent that all those idolatries might be eradicated, it came to pass of the Lord's divine providence, that a new religion, accommodated to the genius of the orientals, took its rise; in which something from each testament of the Word was retained, and which taught that the Lord had come into the world, and that he was a grand prophet, the wisest of all, and the Son of God. This was effected by means of Mahomet, from whom that religion took its name. From these considerations it is manifest, that this religion was raised up of the Lord's divine providence, and accommodated, as we have observed, to the genius of the orientals, to the end that it might destroy the idolatries of so many nations, and might give its professors some knowledge of the Lord, before they came into the spiritual world, as is the case with every one after death. This religion would not have been received by so many nations, neither could it have eradicated their idolatries, unless it had been made agreeable to their ideas; especially unless polygamy had been permitted; since without such permission, the orientals would have burned with the fire of filthy adultery more than the Europeans, and would have perished.

343. The Mahometans also have their heaven; for all in the universe, who acknowledge a God, and from a religious notion shuns evils as sins against him, are saved. That the Mahometan heaven is distinguished into two, the inferior and the superior, I have heard from themselves: and that in the inferior heaven they live with several wives and concubines as in the world; but that those who renounce concubines and live with one wife, are elevated into the superior heaven. I have heard also that it is impossible for them to think of our Lord as one with the Father; but that it is possible for them to think of him as his equal, and that he has dominion over heaven and earth, because he is his

Son; therefore such of them as are elevated by the Lord into their superior heaven, hold this belief.

344. On a certain time I was led to perceive the quality of the heat of conjugial love with polygamists. I was conversing with one who personated Mahomet. Mahomet himself is never present, but some one is substituted in his place, to the end that those who are lately deceased may as it were see him. This substitute, after I had been talking with him at a distance, sent me an ebony spoon and other things, which were proofs that they came from him; at the same time a communication was opened for the heat of their conjugial love in that place, which seemed to me like the warm stench of a bath; whereupon I turned myself away, and the communication was closed.

345. X. POLYGAMY IS LASCIVIOUSNESS. The reason of this is, because its love is divided among several, and is the love of the sex, and the love of the external or natural man, and thus is not conjugial love, which alone is chaste. It is well known that polygamical love is divided among several, and divided love is not conjugial love, which cannot be divided from one of the sex; hence the former love is lascivious, and polygamy is lasciviousness. Polygamical love is the love of the sex, differing from it only in this respect, that it is limited to a number, which the polygamist may determine, and that it is bound to the observance of certain laws enacted for the public good; also that it is allowed to take concubines at the same time as wives; and thus, as it is the love of the sex, it is the love of lasciviousness. The reason why polygamical love is the love of the external or natural man is, because it is inherent in that man; and whatever the natural man does from himself is evil, from which he cannot be released except by elevation into the internal spiritual man, which is effected solely by the Lord; and evil respecting the sex, by which the natural man is influenced, is whoredom; but since whoredom is destructive of society, instead thereof was induced its likeness, which is called polygamy. Every evil into which a man is born from his parents, is implanted in his natural man, but not any in his spiritual man; because into this he is born from the Lord. From what has now been adduced, and also from several other reasons, it may evidently be seen, that polygamy is lasciviousness.

346. XI. CONJUGIAL CHASTITY, PURITY, AND SANCTITY CANNOT EXIST WITH POLYGAMISTS. This follows from what has been just now proved, and evidently from what was demonstrated in the chapter ON THE CHASTE PRINCIPLE AND THE NON-CHASTE; especially from these articles of that chapter, namely, that a chaste, pure, and holy principle is predicated only of monogamica marriages, or of the marriage of one man with one wife, n. 141 also, that love truly conjugial is essential chastity, and that hence all the delights of that love, even the ultimate, are chaste, n.

143, 144; and moreover from what was adduced in the chapter ON LOVE TRULY CONJUGIAL, namely, that love truly conjugial, which is that of one man with one wife, from its origin and correspondence, is celestial, spiritual, holy, and clean above every other love, n. 64. Now since chastity, purity, and sanctity exist only in love truly conjugial, it follows, that it neither does nor can exist in polygamical love.

347. XII. A POLYGAMIST, SO LONG AS HE REMAINS SUCH, CANNOT BECOME SPIRITUAL. To become spiritual is to be elevated out of the natural, that is, out of the light and heat of the world, into the light and heat of heaven. Respecting this elevation no one knows anything but he that is elevated; nevertheless the natural man, although not elevated, perceives no other than that he is; because he can elevate his understanding into the light of heaven, and think and talk spiritually, like the spiritual man; but if the will does not at the same time follow the understanding to its altitude, he is still not elevated; for he does not remain in that elevation, but in a short time lets himself down to his will, and there fixes his station. It is said the will, but it is the love that is meant at the same time; because the will is the receptacle of the love; for what a man loves, that he wills. From these few considerations it may appear, that a polygamist, so long as he remains such, or what is the same, a natural man, so long as he remains such, cannot be made spiritual.

348. XIII. POLYGAMY IS NOT SIN WITH THOSE WHO LIVE IN IT FROM A RELIGIOUS NOTION. All that which is contrary to religion is believed to be sin, because it is contrary to God; and on the other hand, all that which agrees with religion, is believed not to be sin, because it agrees with God; and as polygamy existed with the sons of Israel from a principle of religion, and exists at this day with the Mahometans, it could not, and cannot, be imputed to them as sin. Moreover, to prevent its being sin to them, they remain natural, and do not become spiritual; and the natural man cannot see that there is any sin in such things as belong to the received religion: this is seen only by the spiritual man. It is on this account, that although the Mahometans are taught by the Koran to acknowledge our Lord as the Son of God, still they do not come to him, but to Mahomet; and so long they remain natural, and consequently do not know that there is in polygamy any evil, or indeed any lasciviousness. The Lord also saith, "*If ye were blind ye would not have sin; but now ye say, We see, therefore your sin remaineth,*" John ix. 41. Since polygamy cannot convict them of sin, therefore after death they have their heavens, n. 342, 343; and their joys there according to life.

349. XIV. POLYGAMY IS NOT SIN WITH THOSE WHO ARE IN IGNORANCE RESPECTING THE LORD. This is, because love

truly conjugial is from the Lord alone, and cannot be imparted by the Lord to any but those who know him, acknowledge him, believe on him, and live the life which is from him; and those to whom that love cannot be imparted know no other than that the love of the sex and conjugial love are the same thing; consequently also polygamy. Moreover, polygamists, who know nothing of the Lord, remain natural: for a man (*homo*) is made spiritual only from the Lord; and that is not imputed to the natural man as sin, which is according to the laws of religion and at the same time of society: he also acts according to his reason; and the reason of the natural man is in mere darkness respecting love truly conjugial; and this love in excellence is spiritual. Nevertheless the reason of polygamists is taught from experience, that both public and private peace require that promiscuous lust in general should be restrained, and be left to every one within his own house: hence comes polygamy.

350. It is well known, that a man (*homo*) by birth is viler than the beasts. All the beasts are born into the knowledges corresponding to the love of their life; for as soon as they are born, or are hatched from the egg, they see, hear, walk, know their food, their dam, their friends and foes; and soon after this they show attention to the sex, and to the affairs of love, and also to the rearing of their offspring. Man alone, at his birth, knows nothing of this sort; for no knowledge is connate to him; he has only the faculty and inclination of receiving those things which relate to knowledge and love; and if he does not receive these from others, he remains viler than a beast. That man is born in this condition, to the end that he may attribute nothing to himself, but to others, and at length every thing of wisdom and of the love thereof to God alone, and may hence become an image of God, see the MEMORABLE RELATION, n. 132—136. From these considerations it follows, that a man who does not learn from others that the Lord has come into the world, and that he is God, and has only acquired some knowledge respecting religion and the laws of his country, is not in fault if he thinks no more of conjugial love than of the love of the sex, and if he believes polygamical love to be the only conjugial love. The Lord leads such persons in their ignorance; and by his divine auspices providently withdraws from the imputation of guilt those who, from a religious notion, shun evils as sins, to the end that they may be saved; for every man is born for heaven, and no one for hell; and every one comes into heaven [by influence] from the Lord, and into hell [by influence] from himself.

351. XV. OF THESE, ALTHOUGH POLYGAMISTS, SUCH ARE SAVED AS ACKNOWLEDGE A GOD, AND FROM A RELIGIOUS NOTION LIVE ACCORDING TO THE CIVIL LAWS OF JUSTICE. All throughout the world who acknowledge a God and live according to the civil laws of justice from a religious notion, are saved. By the

civil laws of justice we mean such precepts as are contained in the Decalogue, which forbid murder, theft, adultery, and false witness. These precepts are the civil laws of justice in all the kingdoms of the earth; for without them no kingdom could subsist. But some are influenced in the practice of them by fear of the penalties of the law, some by civil obedience, and some also by religion; these last are saved, because in such case God is in them; and every one, in whom God is, is saved. Who does not see, that among the laws given to the sons of Israel, after they had left Egypt, were those which forbid murder, adultery, theft, and false witness, since without those laws their communion or society could not subsist? and yet these laws were promulgated by Jehovah God upon Mount Sinai with a stupendous miracle: but the cause of their being so promulgated was, that they might be also laws of religion, and thus that the people might practise them not only for the sake of the good of society, but also for the sake of God, and that when they practised them from a religious notion for the sake of God, they might be saved. From these considerations it may appear, that the pagans, who acknowledge a God, and live according to the civil laws of justice, are saved; since it is not their fault that they know nothing of the Lord, consequently nothing of the chastity of the marriage with one wife. For it is contrary to the divine justice to condemn those who acknowledge a God, and from their religion practise the laws of justice, which consist in shunning evils because they are contrary to God, and in doing what is good because it is agreeable to God.

352. XVI. BUT NONE EITHER OF THE LATTER OR OF THE FORMER CAN BE ASSOCIATED WITH THE ANGELS IN THE CHRISTIAN HEAVENS. The reason of this is, because in the Christian heavens there are celestial light, which is divine truth, and celestial heat, which is divine love; and these two discover the quality of goods and truths, and also of evils and falses; hence, there is no communication between the Christian and the Mahometan heavens, and in like manner between the heavens of the Gentiles. If there were a communication, none could have been saved but those who were in celestial light and at the same time in celestial heat from the Lord; yea neither would these be saved if there was a conjunction of the heavens: for in consequence of conjunction all the heavens would so far fall to decay that the angels would not be able to subsist; for an unchaste and lascivious principle would flow from the Mahometans into the Christian heaven, which in that heaven could not be endured; and a chaste and pure principle would flow from the Christians into the Mahometan heaven, which again could not be there endured. In such case, in consequence of communication and thence of conjunction, the Christian angels would become natural and thereby adulterers; or if they remained spiritual, they would

be continually sensible of a lascivious principle about them, which would intercept all the blessedness of their life. The case would be somewhat similar with the Mahometan heaven: for the spiritual principles of the Christian heaven would continually encompass and torment them, and would take away all the delight of their life, and would moreover insinuate that polygamy is sin, whereby they would be continually chided. This is the reason why all the heavens are altogether distinct from each other, so that there is no connection between them, except by an influx of light and heat from the Lord out of the sun, in the midst of which he is: and this influx enlightens and vivifies every one according to his reception; and reception is according to religion. This communication is granted, but not a communication of the heavens with each other.

* * * * * * * *

353. To the above I shall add TWO MEMORABLE RELATIONS. FIRST. I was once in the midst of the angels and heard their conversation. It was respecting intelligence and wisdom; that a man perceives no other than that each is in himself, and thus that whatever he thinks from his understanding and intends from his will, is from himself; when nevertheless not the least portion thereof is from the man, but only the faculty of receiving the things of the understanding and the will from God: and as every man (*homo*) is by birth inclined to love himself, it was provided from creation, to prevent man's perishing by self-love and the conceit of his own intelligence, that that love of the man (*vir*) should be transferred into the wife, and that in her should be implanted from her birth a love for the intelligence and wisdom of her husband, and thereby a love for him; therefore the wife continually attracts to herself her husband's conceit of his own intelligence, and extinguishes it in him, and vivifies it in herself, and thus changes it into conjugial love, and fills it with unbounded pleasantnesses. This is provided by the Lord, lest the conceit of his own intelligence should so far infatuate the man, as to lead him to believe that he has understanding and wisdom from himself and not from the Lord, and thereby make him willing to eat of the tree of the knowledge of good and evil, and thence to believe himself like unto God, and also a god, as the serpent, which was the love of his own intelligence, said and persuaded him: wherefore the man (*homo*) after eating was cast out of paradise, and the way to the tree of life was guarded by a cherub. Paradise, spiritually understood, denotes intelligence; to eat of the tree of life, in a spiritual sense, is to be intelligent and wise from the Lord; and to eat of the tree of the knowledge of good and evil, in a spiritual sense, is to be intelligent and wise from self.

354. The angels having finished this conversation departed; and there came two priests, together with a man who in the

world had been an ambassador of a kingdom, and to then. I related what I had heard from the angels. On hearing this they began to dispute with each other about intelligence and wisdom, and the prudence thence derived, whether they are from God or from man. The dispute grew warm. All three in heart believed that they are from man because they are in man, and that the perception and sensation of its being so confirm it; but the priests, who on this occasion were influenced by theological zeal, said, that there is nothing of intelligence and wisdom, and thus nothing of prudence from man; and when the ambassador retorted, that in such case there is nothing of thought from man, they assented to it. But as it was perceived in heaven, that all the three were in a similar belief, it was said to the ambassador, "Put on the garments of a priest, and believe that you are one, and then speak." He did so; and instantly he declared aloud that nothing of intelligence and wisdom, and consequently nothing of prudence, can possibly exist but from God; and he proved it with his usual eloquence full of rational arguments. It is a peculiar circumstance in the spiritual world, that a spirit thinks himself to be such as is denoted by the garment he wears; because in that world the understanding clothes every one. Afterwards, a voice from heaven said to the two priests, "Put off your own garments, and put on those of political ministers, and believe yourselves to be such." They did so; and in this case they at the same time thought from their interior self, and spoke from arguments which they had inwardly cherished in favor of man's own intelligence. At that instant there appeared a tree near the path; and it was said to them, "It is the tree of the knowledge of good and evil; take heed to yourselves lest ye eat of it." Nevertheless all the three, infatuated by their own intelligence, burned with a desire to eat of it, and said to each other, "Why should not we? Is not the fruit good?" And they went to it and eat of it. Immediately all the three, as they were in a like faith, became bosom friends; and they entered together into the way of self-intelligence, which led into hell: nevertheless I saw them return thence, because they were not yet prepared.

355. THE SECOND MEMORABLE RELATION. On a time as I was looking into the spiritual world, I saw in a certain green field some men, whose garments were like those worn by men of this world; from which circumstance I knew that they were lately deceased. I approached them and stood near them, that I might hear what they were conversing about. Their conversation was about heaven; and one of them who knew something respecting it, said, "In heaven there are wonderful things, such as no one can believe unless he has seen them: there are paradisiacal gardens, magnificent palaces constructed according to the rules of architecture, because the work of the art itself, resplen-

dent with gold; in the front of which are columns of silver; and on the columns heavenly forms made of precious stones; also houses of jasper and sapphire, in the front of which are stately porticos, through which the angels enter; and within the houses handsome furniture, which no art or words can describe. The angels themselves are of both sexes: there are youths and husbands, also maidens and wives: maids so beautiful, that nothing in the world bears any resemblance to their beauty; and wives still more beautiful, who are genuine images of celestial love, and their husbands images of celestial wisdom; and all these are ever approaching the full bloom of youth; and what is more, they know no other love of the sex than conjugial love; and, what you will be surprised to hear, the husbands there have a perpetual faculty of enjoyment." When the novitiate spirits heard that no other love of the sex prevailed in heaven than conjugial love, and that they had a perpetual faculty of enjoyment, they smiled at each other, and said, " What you tell us is incredible; there cannot be such a faculty: possibly you are amusing us with idle tales." But at that instant a certain angel from heaven unexpectedly stood in the midst of them, and said, " Hear me, I beseech you; I am an angel of heaven, and have lived now a thousand years with my wife, and during that time have been in the same flower of my age in which you here see me. This is in consequence of the conjugial love in which I have lived with my wife; and I can affirm, that the above faculty has been and is perpetual with me; and because I perceive that you believe this to be impossible, I will talk with you on the subject from a ground of rational argument according to the light of your understanding. You do not know anything of the primeval state of man, which you call a state of integrity. In that state all the interiors of the mind were open even to the Lord; and hence they were in the marriage of love and wisdom, or of good and truth; and as the good of love and the truth of wisdom perpetually love each other, they also perpetually desire to be united; and when the interiors of the mind are open, the conjugial spiritual love flows down freely with its perpetual endeavour, and presents the above faculty. The very soul of a man (*homo*), being in the marriage of good and truth, is not only in the perpetual endeavour of that union, but also in the perpetual endeavour of the fructification and production of its own likeness; and since the interiors of a man even from the soul are open by virtue of that marriage, and the interiors continually regard as an end the effect in ultimates that they may exist, therefore that perpetual endeavor for fructifying and producing its like, which is the property of the soul, becomes also of the body: and since the ultimate of the operation of the soul in the body with two conjugial partners is into the ultimates of love therein, and these depend on the state of the soul, it is evident whence they derive this perpetuality. Fructification also is perpetual, because the universal sphere of generating and propagating the celestial things which are of love, and the spiritual things which are of wisdom, and thence the natural things which are of offspring, proceeds from the Lord, and fills all heaven and all the world; and that celestial sphere fills the souls of all men, and descends through their minds into the body even to its ultimates, and gives the power of generating. But this cannot be the case with any but those with whom a passage is open from the soul through the superior and inferior principles of the mind into the body to its ultimates, as is the case with those who suffer themselves to be led back by the Lord into the primeval state of creation. I can confirm that now for a thousand years I have never wanted faculty, strength, or vigor, and that I am altogether a stranger to any diminution of powers, which are continually renewed by the influx of the above-mentioned sphere, and in such case also cheer the mind (*animum*), and do not make it sad, as is the case with those who suffer the loss of those powers. Moreover love truly conjugial is just like the vernal heat, from the influx of which all things tend to germination and fructification; nor is there any other heat in our heaven: wherefore with conjugial partners in that heaven there is spring in its perpetual *conatus*, and it is this perpetual *conatus* from which the above virtue is derived. But fructifications with us in heaven are different from those with men on earth. With us fructifications are spiritual, which are the fructifications of love and wisdom, or of good and truth: the wife from the husband's wisdom receives into herself the love thereof; and the husband from the love thereof in the wife receives into himself wisdom; yea the wife is actually formed into the love of the husband's wisdom, which is effected by her receiving the propagations of his soul with the delight arising therefrom, in that she desires to be the love of her husband's wisdom: thus from a maiden she becomes a wife and a likeness. Hence also love with its inmost friendship with the wife, and wisdom with its happiness with the husband, are continually increasing, and this to eternity. This is the state of the angels of heaven." When the angel had thus spoken, he looked at those who had lately come from the world, and said to them, 'You know that, while you were in the vigor of love, you loved our married partners; but when your appetite was gratified, you regarded them with aversion; but you do not know that we in heaven do not love our married partners in consequence of that vigor, but that we have vigor in consequence of love and derived from it; and that as we perpetually love our married partners, we have perpetual vigor: if therefore you can invert the state, you may be able to comprehend this. Does not he who perpetually loves a married partner, love her with the whole mind and with the whole body? for love turns every thing of the mind and of the body to that which it loves; and as this is done reciprocally, it conjoins the objects so that they become a one." He further said, "I will not speak to you of the conjugial love implanted from the creation in males and females, and of their inclination to legitimate conjunction, or of the faculty of prolification in the males, which makes one with the faculty of multiplying wisdom from the love of truth; and that so far as a man loves wisdom from the love thereof, or truth from good, so far he is in love truly conjugial and in its attendant vigor."

356. When he had spoken these words, the angel was silent; and from the spirit of his discourse the novitiates comprehended that a perpetual faculty of enjoyment is communicable; and as this consideration rejoiced their minds, they exclaimed, "O how happy is the state of angels! We perceive that you in the heavens remain for ever in a state of youth, and thence in the vigor of that age; but tell us how we also may enjoy that vigor." The angel replied, "Shun adulteries as infernal, and approach the Lord, and you will possess it." They said, "We will do so." But the angel replied, "You cannot shun adulteries as infernal evils, unless you in like manner shun all other evils, because adulteries are the complex of all; and unless you shun them, you cannot approach the Lord; for the Lord receives no others." After this the angel took his leave, and the novitiate spirits departed sorrowful.

ON JEALOUSY.

357. THE subject of jealousy is here treated of, because it also has relation to conjugial love. There is a just jealousy and an unjust;—a just jealousy with married partners who mutually love each other, with whom it is a just and prudent zeal lest their conjugial love should be violated, and thence a just grief if it is violated; and an unjust jealousy with those who are naturally suspicious, and whose minds are sickly in consequence of viscous and bilious blood. Moreover, all jealousy is by some accounted a vice; which is particularly the case with whoremongers, who censure even a just jealousy. The term JEALOUSY (*zelotypia*) is derived from ZELI TYPUS (the type of zeal), and there is a type or image of just and also of unjust zeal; but we will explain these distinctions in the following series of articles: I. *Zeal, considered in itself, is like the ardent fire of love.* II. *The burning or flame of that love, which is zeal, is a spiritual burning or flame, arising from an infestation and assault of the love.* III. *The quality of a man's* (homo) *zeal is according to the quality of his*

love; thus it differs according as the love is good or evil. IV. The zeal of a good love and the zeal of an evil love are alike in externals, but altogether unlike in internals. V. The zeal of a good love in its internals contains a hidden store of love and friendship; but the zeal of an evil love in its internals contains a hidden store of hatred and revenge. VI. The zeal of conjugial love is called jealousy. VII. Jealousy is like an ardent fire against those who infest love exercised towards a married partner, and like a terrible fear for the loss of that love. VIII. There is spiritual jealousy with monogamists, and natural with polygamists. IX. Jealousy with those married partners who tenderly love each other, is a just grief grounded in sound reason lest conjugial love should be divided, and should thereby perish. X. Jealousy with married partners who do not love each other, is grounded in several causes: arising in some instances from various mental weaknesses. XI. In some instances there is not any jealousy; and this also from various causes. XII. There is a jealousy also in regard to concubines, but not such as in regard to wives. XIII. Jealousy likewise exists among beasts and birds. XIV. The jealousy of men and husbands is different from that of women and wives. We proceed to an explanation of the above articles.

358. I. ZEAL, CONSIDERED IN ITSELF, IS LIKE THE ARDENT FIRE OF LOVE. What jealousy is cannot be known, unless it be known what zeal is; for jealousy is the zeal of conjugial love. The reason why zeal is like the ardent fire of love is, because zeal is of love, which is spiritual heat, and this in its origin is like fire. In regard to the first position, it is well known that zeal is of love: nothing else is meant by being zealous, and acting from zeal, than acting from the force of love: but since when it exists, it appears not as love, but as unfriendly and hostile, offended at and fighting against him who hurts the love, therefore it may also be called the defender and protector of love; for all love is of such a nature that it bursts into indignation and anger, yea into fury, whenever it is disturbed in its delights: therefore if a love, especially the ruling love, be touched, there ensues an emotion of the mind; and if it be hurt, there ensues wrath. From these considerations it may be seen, that zeal is not the highest degree of the love, but that it is ardent love. The love of one, and the correspondent love of another, are like two confederates; but when the love of one rises up against the love of another, they become like enemies; because love is the *esse* of a man's life; therefore he that assaults the love, assaults the life itself; and in such case there ensues a state of wrath against the assailant, like the state of every man whose life is attempted by another. Such wrath is attendant on every love, even that which is most pacific, as is very manifest in the case of hens, geese, and birds of every kind; which, without any fear,

rise against and fly at those who injure their young, or rob them of their meat. That some beasts are seized with anger, and wild beasts with fury, if their young are attacked, or their prey taken from them, is well known. The reason why love is said to burn like fire is, because love is spiritual heat, originating in the fire of the angelic sun, which is pure love. That love is heat as it were from fire, evidently appears from the heat of living bodies, which is from no other source than from their love; also from the circumstance that men grow warm and are inflamed according to the exaltation of their love. From these considerations it is manifest, that zeal is like the ardent fire of love.

359. II. THE BURNING OR FLAME OF THAT LOVE, WHICH IS ZEAL, IS A SPIRITUAL BURNING OR FLAME, ARISING FROM AN INFESTATION AND ASSAULT OF THE LOVE. That zeal is a spiritual burning or flame, is evident from what has been said above. As love in the spiritual world is heat arising from the sun of that world, therefore also love at a distance appears there as flame: it is thus that celestial love appears with the angels of heaven; and thus also infernal love appears with the spirits of hell: but it is to be observed, that that flame does not burn like the flame of the natural world. The reason why zeal arises from an assault of the love is, because love is the heat of every one's life; wherefore when the life's love is assaulted, the life's heat kindles itself, resists, and bursts forth against the assailant, and acts as an enemy by virtue of its own strength and ability, which is like flame bursting from a fire upon him who stirs it: that it is like fire, appears from the sparkling of the eyes from the face being inflamed, also from the tone of the voice and the gestures. This is the effect of love, as being the heat of life, to prevent its extinction, and with it the extinction of all cheerfulness, vivacity, and perceptibility of delight, grounded in its own love.

360. It may be expedient here to show how the love by being assaulted is inflamed and kindled into zeal, like fire into flame. Love resides in a man's will; nevertheless it is not inflamed in the will itself, but in the understanding; for in the will it is like fire, and in the understanding like flame. Love in the will knows nothing about itself, because there it is not sensible of anything relating to itself, neither does it there act from itself; but this is done in the understanding and its thought: when therefore the will is assaulted, it provokes itself to anger in the understanding, which is effected by various reasonings. These reasonings are like pieces of wood, which the fire inflames, and which thence burn: they are therefore like so much fuel, or so many combustible matters which give occasion to that spiritual flame, which is very variable.

361. We will here unfold the true reason why a man becomes inflamed in consequence of an assault of his love. The human form in its inmost principles is from creation a form of love and

wisdom. In man there are all the affections of love, and thence all the perceptions of wisdom, compounded in the most perfect order, so as to make together what is unanimous, and thereby a one. Those affections and perceptions are rendered substantial; for substances are their subjects. Since therefore the human form is compounded of these, it is evident that, if the love is assaulted, this universal form also, with everything therein, is assaulted at the same instant, or together with it. And as the desire to continue in its form is implanted from creation in all living things, therefore this principle operates in every general compound by derivation from the singulars of which it is compounded, and in the singulars by derivation from the general compound: hence when the love is assaulted, it defends itself by its understanding, and the understanding [defends itself] by rational and imaginative principles, whereby it represents to itself the event; especially by such as act in unity with the love which is assaulted: and unless this was the case the above form would wholly fall to pieces, in consequence of the privation of that love. Hence then it is that love, in order to resist assaults, hardens the substance of its form, and sets them erect, as it were in crests, like so many sharp prickles, that is, crisps itself; such is the provoking of love which is called zeal: wherefore if there is no opportunity of resistance, there arise anxiety and grief, because it foresees the extinction of interior life with its delights. But on the other hand, if the love is favored and cherished, the above form unbends, softens, and dilates itself; and the substances of the form become gentle, mild, meek, and alluring.

362. III. THE QUALITY OF A MAN'S ZEAL IS ACCORDING TO THE QUALITY OF HIS LOVE; THUS IT DIFFERS ACCORDING AS THE LOVE IS GOOD OR EVIL. Since zeal is of love, it follows that its quality is such as the quality of the love is; and as there are in general two loves, the love of what is good and thence of what is true, and the love of what is evil and thence of what is false, hence in general there is a zeal in favor of what is good and thence of what is true, and in favor of what is evil and thence of what is false. But it is to be noted, that of each love there is an infinite variety. This is very manifest from the angels of heaven and the spirits of hell; both of whom in the spiritual world are the forms of their respective love; and yet there is not one angel of heaven absolutely like another as to face, speech, gait, gesture, and manner; nor any spirit of hell; yea neither can there be to eternity, howsoever they be multiplied into myriads of myriads. Hence it is evident, that there is an infinite variety of loves, because there is of their forms. The case is the same with zeal, as being of the love; the zeal of one cannot be absolutely like or the same with the zeal of another. In general there are the zeal of a good and the zeal of an evil love.

363. IV. THE ZEAL OF A GOOD LOVE AND THE ZEAL OF AN EVIL LOVE ARE ALIKE IN EXTERNALS, BUT ALTOGETHER DIFFERENT IN INTERNALS. Zeal in externals, with every one, appears like anger and wrath; for it is love enkindled and inflamed to defend itself against a violator, and to remove him. The reason why the zeal of a good love and the zeal of an evil love appear alike in externals is, because in both cases love while it is in zeal, burns; but with a good man only in externals, whereas with an evil man it burns in both externals and internals; and when internals are not regarded, the zeals appear alike in externals; but that they are altogether different in internals will be seen in the next article. That zeal appears in externals like anger and wrath, may be seen and heard from all those who speak and act from zeal; as for example, from a priest while he is preaching from zeal, the tone of whose voice is high, vehement, sharp, and harsh; his face is heated and perspires; he exerts himself, beats the pulpit, and calls forth fire from hell against those who do evil: and so in many other cases.

364. In order that a distinct idea may be formed of zeal as influencing the good, and of zeal as influencing the wicked, and of their dissimilitude, it is necessary that some idea be previously formed of men's internals and externals. For this purpose, let us take a common idea on the subject, as being adapted to general apprehension, and let it be exhibited by the case of a nut or an almond, and their kernels. With the good, the internals are like the kernels within as to their soundness and goodness, encompassed with their usual and natural husk; with the wicked, the case is altogether different, their internals are like kernels which are either not eatable from their bitterness, or rotten, or worm-eaten; whereas their externals are like the shells or husks of those kernels, either like the natural shells or husks, or shining bright like shell-fish, or speckled like the stones called irises. Such is the appearance of their externals, within which the above-mentioned internals lie concealed. The case is the same with their zeal.

365. V. THE ZEAL OF A GOOD LOVE IN ITS INTERNALS CONTAINS A HIDDEN STORE OF LOVE AND FRIENDSHIP; BUT THE ZEAL OF AN EVIL LOVE IN ITS INTERNALS CONTAINS A HIDDEN STORE OF HATRED AND REVENGE. It was said just above, that zeal in externals appears like anger and wrath, as well with those who are in a good love, as with those who are in an evil love: but whereas the internals are different, the anger and wrath in each case differs from that of the other, and the difference is as follows: 1. The zeal of a good love is like a heavenly flame, which in one case bursts out upon another, but only defends itself, and that against a wicked person, as when he rushes into the fire and is burnt: but the zeal of an evil love is like an infernal flame, which of itself bursts forth and rushes on, and is desirous

to consume another. 2. The zeal of a good love instantly burns away and is allayed when the assailant ceases to assault; but the zeal of an evil love continues and is not extinguished. 3. This is because the internal of him who is in the love of good is it in itself mild, soft, friendly, and benevolent; wherefore when his external, with a view of defending itself, is fierce, harsh, and haughty, and thereby acts with rigor, still it is tempered by the good in which he is internally: it is otherwise with the wicked; with such the internal is unfriendly, without pity, harsh, breathing hatred and revenge, and feeding itself with their delights; and although it is reconciled, still those evils lie concealed as fires in wood underneath the embers; and these fires burst forth after death, if not in this world.

366. Since zeal in externals appears alike both in the good and the wicked, and since the ultimate sense of the Word consists of correspondence and appearances, therefore in the Word, it is very often said of Jehovah that he is angry and wrathful, that he revenges, punishes, casts into hell, with many other things which are appearances of zeal in externals; hence also it is that he is called zealous: whereas there is not the least of anger, wrath, and revenge in him; for he is essential mercy, grace and clemency, thus essential good, in whom it is impossible such evil passions can exist. But on this subject see more particulars in the treatise on HEAVEN AND HELL, n. 545—550; and in the APOCALYPSE REVEALED, n. 494, 498, 525, 714, 806.

367. VI. THE ZEAL OF CONJUGIAL LOVE IS CALLED JEALOUSY. Zeal in favor of truly conjugial love is the chief of zeals; because that love is the chief of loves, and its delights, in favor of which also zeal operates, are the chief delights; for, as was shewn above, that love is the head of all loves. The reason of this is, because that love induces in a wife the form of love, and in a husband the form of wisdom; and from these forms united into one, nothing can proceed but what savors of wisdom and at the same time of love. As the zeal of conjugial love is the chief of zeals, therefore it is called by a new name, JEALOUSY, which is the very type of zeal.

368. VII. JEALOUSY IS LIKE AN ARDENT FIRE AGAINST THOSE WHO INFEST LOVE EXERCISED TOWARDS A MARRIED PARTNER, AND LIKE A TERRIBLE FEAR FOR THE LOSS OF THAT LOVE. The subject here treated of is Jealousy of those who are in spiritual love with a married partner; in the following article we shall treat of the jealousy of those who are in natural love; and afterwards of the jealousy of those who are in love truly conjugial. With those who are in spiritual love the jealousy is various, because their love is various; for one love, whether spiritual or natural, is never altogether alike with two persons, still less with several. The reason why spiritual jealousy, or jealousy with the spiritual, is like an ardent fire raging against

those who infest their conjugial love, is, because with them the first principle of love is in the internals of each party, and their love from its first principle follows its principiates, even to its ultimates, by virtue of which ultimates and at the same time of first principles, the intermediates which are of the mind and body, are kept in lovely connection. These, being spiritual, in their marriage regard union as an end, and in union spiritual rest and the pleasantness thereof: now, as they have rejected disunion from their minds, therefore their jealousy is like a fire stirred up and darting forth against those who infest them. The reason why it is also like a terrible fear is, because their spiritual love intends that they be one; if therefore there exists a chance, or happens an appearance of separation, a fear ensues as terrible as when two united parts are torn asunder. This description of jealousy was given me from heaven by those who are in spiritual conjugial love; for there are a natural, a spiritual, and a celestial conjugial love; concerning the natural and the celestial conjugial love, and their jealousy, we shall take occasion to speak in the two following articles.

369. VIII. THERE IS SPIRITUAL JEALOUSY WITH MONOGAMISTS, AND NATURAL WITH POLYGAMISTS. The reason why spiritual jealousy exists with monogamists is, because they alone can receive spiritual conjugial love, as has been abundantly shown above. It is said that it exists; but the meaning is that it is capable of existing. That it exists only with a very few in the Christian world, where there are monogamical marriages, but that still it is capable of existing there, has also been confirmed above. That with polygamists conjugial love is natural, may be seen in the chapter on Polygamy, n. 345, 347; in like manner jealousy is natural in the same case, because this follows love. What the quality of jealousy is among polygamists, we are taught from the relations of those who have been eye-witnesses of its effects among the orientals: these effects are, that wives and concubines are guarded as prisoners in work-houses, and are withheld from and prohibited all communication with men; that into the women's apartments, or the closets of their confinement, no man is allowed to enter unless attended by a eunuch; and that the strictest watch it set to observe whether any of the women look with a lascivious eye or countenance at a man as he passes; and that if this be observed, the woman is sentenced to the whip; and in case she indulges her lasciviousness with any man, whether introduced secretly into her apartment, or from home, she is punished with death.

370. From these considerations it is plainly seen what is the quality of the fire of jealousy into which polygamical conjugial love enkindles itself,—that it is into anger and revenge; into anger with the meek, and into revenge with the fierce. The reason of this effect is, because their love is natural, and does

not partake of anything spiritual. This is a consequence of what is demonstrated in the chapter on Polygamy,—that polygamy is lasciviousness, n. 345; and that a polygamist, so long as he remains such, is natural, and cannot become spiritual, n. 347. But the fire of jealousy is different with natural monogamists, whose love is inflamed not so much against the women as against those who do violence, becoming anger against the latter, and cold against the former: it is otherwise with polygamists, whose fire of jealousy burns also with the rage of revenge: this likewise is one of the reasons why, after the death of polygamists, their concubines and wives are for the most part set free, and are sent to seraglios not guarded, to employ themselves in the various elegant arts proper to women.

371. IX. JEALOUSY WITH THOSE MARRIED PARTNERS WHO TENDERLY LOVE EACH OTHER, IS A JUST GRIEF GROUNDED IN SOUND REASON LEST CONJUGIAL LOVE SHOULD BE DIVIDED, AND SHOULD THEREBY PERISH. All love is attended with fear and grief; fear lest it should perish, and grief in case it perishes: it is the same with conjugial love; but the fear and grief attending this love is called zeal or jealousy. The reason why this zeal, with married partners who tenderly love each other, is just and grounded in sound reason, is, because it is at the same time a fear for the loss of eternal happiness, not only of its own but also of its married partner's, and because also it is a defence against adultery. In respect to the first consideration, —that it is a just fear for the loss of its own eternal happiness and of that of its married partner, it follows from every thing which has been heretofore adduced concerning love truly conjugial; and also from this consideration, that married partners derive from that love the blessedness of their souls, the satisfaction of their minds, the delight of their bosoms, and the pleasure of their bodies; and since these remain with them to eternity, each party has a fear for eternal happiness. That the above zeal is a just defence against adulteries, is evident: hence it is like a fire raging against violation, and defending itself against it. From these considerations it is evident, that whoever loves a married partner tenderly, is also jealous, but is just and discreet according to the man's wisdom.

372. It was said, that in conjugial love there is implanted a fear lest it should be divided, and a grief lest it should perish, and that its zeal is like a fire raging against violation. Some time ago, when meditating on this subject, I asked the zealous angels concerning the seat of jealousy? They said, that it is in the understanding of the man who receives the love of a married partner and returns it; and that its quality there is according to his wisdom: they said further, that jealousy has in it somewhat in common with honor, which also resides in conjugial love; for he that loves his wife, also honors her. In regard to zeal's

residing with a man in his understanding, they assigned this reason; because conjugial love defends itself by the understanding, as good does by truth; so the wife defends those things which are common with the man, by her husband; and that on this account zeal is implanted in the men, and by them, and for their sake, in the women. To the question as to the region of the mind in which jealousy resides with the men, they replied, in their souls, because it is also a defence against adulteries; and because adulteries principally destroy conjugial love, that when there is danger of the violation of that love, the man's understanding grows hard, and becomes like a horn, with which he strikes the adulterer.

373. X. JEALOUSY WITH MARRIED PARTNERS WHO DO NOT LOVE EACH OTHER, IS GROUNDED IN SEVERAL CAUSES; ARISING IN SOME INSTANCES FROM VARIOUS MENTAL WEAKNESSES. The causes why married partners who do not mutually love each other, are yet jealous, are principally the honor resulting from power, the fear of defamation with respect both to the man himself and also to his wife, and the dread lest domestic affairs should fall into confusion. It is well known that the men have honor resulting from power, that is, that they are desirous of being respected in consequence thereof; for so long as they have this honor, they are as it were of an elevated mind, and not dejected when in the company of men and women: to this honor also is attached the name of bravery; wherefore military officers have it more than others. That the fear of defamation, with respect both to the man himself and also to his wife, is a cause of jealousy that agrees with the foregoing: to which may be added, that living with a harlot, and debauched practices in a house, are accounted infamous. The reason why some are jealous through a dread lest their domestic affairs should fall into confusion, is because, so far as this is the case, the husband is made light of, and mutual services and aids are withdrawn; but with some in process of time this jealousy ceases and is annihilated, and with some it is changed into the mere semblance of love.

374. That jealousy in certain cases arises from various mental weaknesses, is not unknown in the world; for there are jealous persons, who are continually thinking that their wives are unfaithful, and believe them to be harlots, merely because they hear or see them talk in a friendly manner with or about men. There are several vitiated affections of the mind which induce this weakness; the principal of which is a suspicious fancy, which if it be long cherished, introduces the mind into societies of similar spirits, from whence it cannot without difficulty be rescued; it also confirms itself in the body, by rendering the serum, and consequently the blood, viscous, tenacious, thick, slow, and acrid, a defect of strength also increases it; for the consequence of such defect is, that the mind cannot be elevated from its suspicious

fancies; for the presence of strength elevates, and its absence depresses, the latter causing the mind to sink, give way, and become feeble; in which case it immerses itself more and more in the above fancy, till it grows delirious, and thence takes delight in quarrelling, and, so far as is allowable, in abuse.

375. There are also several countries, which more than others labor under this weakness of jealousy : in these the wives are imprisoned, are tyrannically shut out from conversation with men, are prevented from even looking at them through the windows, by blinds drawn down, and are terrified by threats of death if the cherished suspicion shall appear well grounded; not to mention other hardships which the wives in those countries suffer from their jealous husbands. There are two causes of this jealousy; one is, an imprisonment and suffocation of the thoughts in the spiritual things of the church; the other is, an inward desire of revenge. As to the first cause,—the imprisonment and suffocation of the thoughts in the spiritual things of the church, its operation and effect may be concluded from what has been proved above,—that every one has conjugial love according to the state of the church with him, and as the church is from the Lord, that that love is solely from the Lord, n. 130, 131 ; when therefore, instead of the Lord, living and deceased men are approached and invoked, it follows, that the state of the church is such that conjugial love cannot act in unity with it; and the less so while the mind is terrified into that worship by the threats of a dreadful prison : hence it comes to pass, that the thoughts, together with the expressions of them in conversation, are violently seized and suffocated; and when they are suffocated, there is an influx of such things as are either contrary to the church, or imaginary in favor of it; the consequence of which is, heat in favor of harlots and cold towards a married partner; from which two principles prevailing together in one subject, such an unconquerable fire of jealousy flows forth. As to the second cause,—the inward desire of revenge, this altogether checks the influx of conjugial love, and swallows it up, and changes the delight thereof, which is celestial, into the delight of revenge, which is infernal ; and the proximate determination of this latter is to the wife. There is also an appearance, that the unhealthiness of the atmosphere, which in those regions is impregnated with the poisonous exhalations of the surrounding country, is an additional cause.

376. XI. IN SOME INSTANCES THERE IS NOT ANY JEALOUSY; AND THIS ALSO FROM VARIOUS CAUSES. There are several causes of there being no jealousy, and of its ceasing. The absence of jealousy is principally with those who make no more account of conjugial than of adulterous love, and at the same time are so void of honorable feeling as to slight the reputation of a name: they are not unlike married pimps. There is no jealousy likewise with

those who have rejected it from a confirmed persuasion that it infests the mind, and thus it is useless to watch a wife, and that to do so serves only to incite her, and that therefore it is better to shut the eyes, and not even to look through the key-hole, lest any thing should be discovered. Some have rejected jealousy on account of the reproach attached to the name, and under the idea that any one who is a real man, is afraid of nothing: some have been driven to reject it lest their domestic affairs should suffer, and also lest they should incur public censure in case the wife was convicted of the disorderly passion of wich she is accused. Moreover jealousy passes off into no jealousy with those who grant license to their wives, either from a want of ability, or with a view to the procreation of children for the sake of inheritance, also in some cases with a view to gain, and so forth. There are also disorderly marriages, in which, by mutual consent, the licence of unlimited amour is allowed to each party, and yet they are civil and complaisant to each other when they meet.

377. XII. THERE IS A JEALOUSY ALSO IN REGARD TO CONCUBINES, BUT NOT SUCH AS IN REGARD TO WIVES. Jealousy in regard to wives originates in a man's inmost principles; but jealousy in regard to concubines originates in external principles; they therefore differ in kind. The reason why jealousy in regard to wives originates in inmost principles is, because conjugial love resides in them : the reason why it resides there is, because marriage from the eternity of its compact established by covenant, and also from an equality of right, the right of each party being transferred to the other, unites souls, and lays a superior obligation on minds: this obligation and that union, once impressed, remain inseparable, whatever be the quality of the love afterwards, whether it be warm or cold. Hence it is that an invitation to love coming from a wife chills the whole man from the inmost principles to the outermost; whereas an invitation to love coming from a concubine has not the same effect upon the object of her love. To jealousy in regard to a wife is added the earnest desire of reputation with a view to honor; and there is no such addition to jealousy in regard to a concubine. Nevertheless both kinds of jealousy vary according to the seat of the love received by the wife and by the concubine; and at the same time according to the state of the judgment of the man receiving it.

378. XIII. JEALOUSY LIKEWISE EXISTS AMONG BEASTS AND BIRDS. That it exists among wild beasts, as lions, tigers, bears, and several others, while they have whelps, is well known; and also among bulls, although they have not calves: it is most conspicuous among dung-hill cocks, who in favor of their hens fight with their rivals even to death : the reason why the latter have such jealousy is, because they are vain-glorious lovers, and the glory of that love cannot endure an equal; that they are

vain-glorious overs, above every genus and species of birds, is manifest from their gestures, nods, gait, and tone of voice. That the glory of honor with men, whether lovers or not, excites, increases, and sharpens jealousy, has been confirmed above.

379. XIV. THE JEALOUSY OF MEN AND HUSBANDS IS DIFFERENT FROM THAT OF WOMEN AND WIVES. The differences cannot however be distinctly pointed out, since the jealousy of married partners who love each other spiritually, differs from that of married parners who love each other merely naturally, and differs again with those who disagree in minds, and also with those who have subjected their consorts to the yoke of obedience. The jealousies of men and of women considered in themselves are different, because from different origins: the origin of the jealousies of men is in the understanding, whereas of women it is in the will applied to the understanding of the husband: the jealousy of a man therefore, is like a flame of wrath and anger; whereas that of a woman is like a fire variously restrained, by fear, by regard to the husband, by respect to her own love, and by her prudence in not revealing this love to her husband by jealousy: they differ also because wives are loves, and men recipients thereof; and wives are unwilling to squander their love upon the men, but the case is not so with the recipients towards the wives. With the spiritual, however, it is otherwise; with these the jealousy of the man is transferred into the wife, as the love of the wife is transferred into the husband; therefore with each party it appears like itself against the attempts of a violator; but the jealousy of the wife is inspired into the husband against the attempts of the violating harlot, which is like grief weeping, and moving the conscience.

* * * * * *

380. To the above I shall add two MEMORABLE RELATIONS. I was once in much amazement at the great multitude of men who ascribe creation, and consequently whatever is under the sun and above it, to nature; expressing the real sentiments of their hearts as to the visible things of the world, by this question, "What are these but the works of nature?" And when they are asked why they ascribe them to nature and not to God, when nevertheless they occasionally join in the general confession, that God has created nature, and therefore they might as well ascribe creation to God as to nature, they return for answer, with an internal tone of voice, which is scarcely audible, "What is God but nature?" From this persuasion concerning nature as the creator of the universe, and from this folly which has to them the semblance of wisdom, all such persons appear so full of their own importance, that they regard all those who acknowledge the creation of the universe to be from God, as so many ants which creep along the ground and tread in a beaten path, and in some cases as butterflies which fly in the air; ridiculing their opinions

as dreams, because they see what they do not see, and deciding all by the question, "Who has seen God, and who has not seen nature?" While I was thus amazed at the great multitude of such persons, there stood near me an angel, who asked me, "What is the subject of your meditation?" I replied, "It is concerning the great multitude of such as believe that nature created the universe." The angel then said to me, "All hell consists of such persons, who are there called satans and devils; satans, if they have confirmed themselves in favor of nature to the denial of God, and devils, if they have lived wickedly, and thereby rejected all acknowledgement of God from their hearts; but I will lead you to the *gymnasia*, which are in the south-west, where such persons dwell, having not yet departed to their infernal abodes." He took me by the hand and led me there. I saw some small houses, in which were apartments for the studious, and in the midst of them one which served as a principal hall to the rest. It was constructed of a pitchy kind of stone, covered with a sort of glazed plates, that seemed to sparkle with gold and silver, like the stones called *Glacies Mariæ;* and here and there were interspersed shells which glittered in like manner. We approached and knocked at the door, which was presently opened by one who bade us welcome. He then went to the table, and fetched four books, and said, "These books are the wisdom which is at this day the admiration of many kingdoms: this book or wisdom is the admiration of many in France, this of many in Germany, this of some in Holland, and this of some in England:" He further said, "If you wish to see it, I will cause these four books to shine brightly before your eyes: he then poured forth and spread around them the glory of his own reputation, and the books presently shone as with light; but this light instantly vanished from our sight. We then asked him what he was now writing? He replied, that he was now about to bring forth from his treasures, and publish to the world, things of inmost wisdom, which would be comprised under these general heads: I. Whether nature be derived from life, or life from nature. II. Whether the centre be derived from the expanse, or the expanse from the centre. III. On the centre and the expanse of nature and of life. Having said this, he reclined on a couch at the table; but we walked about in his spacious study. He had a candle on the table, because the light of the sun never shone in that room, but only the nocturnal light of the moon; and what surprised me, the candle seemed to be carried all round the room, and to illuminate it; but, for want of being snuffed, it gave but little light. While he was writing, we saw images in various forms flying from the table towards the walls, which in that nocturnal moon-light appeared like beautiful Indian birds; but on opening the door, lo! in the light of the sun they appeared like birds of the evening, with wings like network;

for they were semblances of truth made fallacies by being confirmed, which he had ingeniously connected together into series. After attending some time to this sight, we approached the table, and asked him what he was then writing? He replied, "On the first general head, WHETHER NATURE BE DERIVED FROM LIFE, OR LIFE FROM NATURE;" and on this question he said, that he could confirm either side, and cause it to be true; but as something lay concealed within which excited his fears, therefore he durst only confirm this side, that nature is of life, that is, from life, but not that life is of nature, that is, from it. We then civilly requested him to tell us, what lay concealed within, which excited his fears? He replied, he was afraid lest he should be called a naturalist, and so an atheist, by the clergy, and a man of unsound reason by the laity; as they both either believe from a blind credulity, or see from the sight of those who confirm that credulity. But just then, being impelled by a kind of indignant zeal for the truth, we addressed him saying, "Friend, you are much deceived; your wisdom, which is only an ingenious talent for writing, has seduced you, and the glory of reputation has led you to confirm what you do not believe. Do you know that the human mind is capable of being elevated above sensual things, which are derived into the thoughts from the bodily senses, and that when it is so elevated, it sees the things that are of life above, and those that are of nature beneath? What is life but love and wisdom? and what is nature but their recipient, whereby they may produce their effects or uses? Can these possibly be one in any other sense than as principal and instrumental are one? Can light be one with the eye, or sound with the ear? Whence are the senses of these organs but from life, and their forms but from nature? What is the human body but an organ of life? Are not all things therein organically formed to produce the things which the love wills and the understanding thinks? Are not the organs of the body from nature, and love and thought from life? And are not those things entirely distinct from each other? Raise the penetration of your ingenuity a little, and you will see that it is the property of life to be affected and to think, and that to be affected is from love, and to think is from wisdom, and each is from life; for, as we have said, love and wisdom are life: if you elevate your faculty of understanding a little higher, you will see that no love and wisdom exists, unless its origin be somewhere or other, and that its origin is wisdom itself, and thence life itself, and these, are God from whom is nature."

Afterwards we conversed with him about his second question, WHETHER THE CENTRE BE OF THE EXPANSE, OR THE EXPANSE OF THE CENTRE; and asked him why he discussed this question? He replied, "With a view to conclude concerning the centre and the expanse of nature and of life, thus concerning the origin of each." And when we asked him what were his sentiments on the subject, he answered, as in the former case, that he could confirm either side, but for fear of suffering in his reputation, he would confirm that the expanse is of the centre, that is, from the centre; although I know, said he, that something existed before the sun, and this in the universe throughout, and that these things flowed together of themselves into order, thus into centres. But here again we addressed him from the overflowing of an indignant zeal, and said, "Friend, you are insane." On hearing these words, he drew his couch aside from the table, and looked timidly at us, and then listened to our conversation, but with a smile upon his countenance, while we thus proceeded: "What is a surer proof of insanity, than to say that the centre is from the expanse? By your centre we understand the sun, and by your expanse the universe; and thus, according to you, the universe existed without the sun: but does not the sun make nature, and all its properties, which depend solely on the heat and light proceeding from the sun by the atmospheres? Where were those things previous to the sun's existence? But whence they originated we will shew presently. Are not the atmospheres and all things which exist on the earth, as surfaces, and the sun their centre? What are they all without the sun; or how could they subsist a single moment in the sun's absence? Consequently what were they all before the sun, or how could they subsist? Is not subsistence perpetual existence? Since therefore all the parts of nature derive their subsistence from the sun, they must of consequence derive also their existence from the same origin: every one sees and is convinced of this truth by the testimony of his own eyes. Does not that which is posterior subsist from what is prior, as it exists from what is prior? Supposing the surface to be the prior and the centre the posterior, would not the prior in such case subsist from the posterior, which yet is contrary to the laws of order? How can posterior things produce prior, or exterior things produce interior, or grosser things produce purer? consequently, how can surfaces, which constitute the expanse, produce centres? Who does not see that this is contrary to the laws of nature? We have adduced these arguments from a rational analysis, to prove that the expanse exists from the centre, and not the centre from the expanse; nevertheless every one who sees aright, sees it to be so without the help of such arguments. You have asserted, that the expanse flowed together of itself into a centre; did it thus flow by chance into so wonderful and stupendous an order, where one thing exists for the sake of another, and everything for the sake of man, and with a view to his eternal life? Is it possible that nature from any principle of love, by any principle of wisdom, should provide such things? And can nature make angels of men, and heaven of angels? Ponder and consider these things: and your idea of nature existing from nature will fall to the ground." Afterwards we questioned him as to his former and present sentiments concerning his third inquiry, relating to the CENTRE AND EXPANSE OF NATURE AND OF LIFE; whether he was of opinion that the centre and expanse of life are the same with the centre and expanse of nature? He replied, that he was in doubt about it, and that he formerly thought that the interior activity of nature is life; and that love and wisdom, which essentially constitute the life of man, are thence derived; and that the sun's fire, by the instrumentality of heat and light, through the mediums of the atmospheres, produce those principles; but that now, from what he had heard concerning the eternal life of men, he began to waver in his sentiments, and that in consequence of such wavering, his mind was sometimes carried upwards, sometimes downwards; and that when it was carried upwards, he acknowledged a centre of which he had before no idea; but when downwards, he saw a centre which he believed to be the only one that existed; and that life is from the centre which before was unknown to him; and nature is from the centre which he before believed to be the only one existing; and that each centre has an expanse around it. To this we said, Well, if he would only respect the centre and expanse of nature from the centre and expanse of life, and not contrariwise; and we informed him, that above the angelic heaven there is a sun which is pure love, in appearance firy like the sun of the world; and that from the heat which proceeds from that sun, angels and men derive will and love, and from its light they derive understanding and wisdom; and that the things which are of life, are called spiritual and that those which proceed from the sun of the world, are what contain life, and are called natural; also that the expanse of the centre of life is called the SPIRITUAL WORLD, which subsists from its sun, and that the expanse of nature is called the NATURAL WORLD, which subsists from its sun. Now, since of love and wisdom there cannot be predicated spaces and times, but instead thereof states, it follows, that the expanse around the sun of the angelic heaven is not extended, but still is in the extense of the natural sun, and present with all living subjects therein according to their receptions, which are according to forms. But he then asked, "Whence comes the fire of the sun of the world, or of nature?" We replied, that it is derived from the sun of the angelic heaven, which is not fire, but divine love proximately proceeding from God, who is love itself. As he was surprised at this, we thus proved it: "Love in its essence is spiritual fire; hence fire in the Word, in its spiritual sense, signifies love: it is on this account that priests, when officiating in the temple, pray that heavenly fire may fill their hearts, by which they mean heavenly love: the fire of the altar and of the candlestick in the tabernacle amongst the Israelites, represented divine love: the heat of the blood, or the vital heat of men and animals in general is from no other source than love, which constitutes their life; hence it is that a man is enkindled, grows warm, and becomes on fire, while his love is exalted into zeal, anger, and wrath; wherefore from the circumstance, that spiritual heat, which is love, produces natural heat with men, even to the kindling and inflaming of their faces and limbs, it may appear, that the fire of the natural sun has existed from no other source than the fire of the spiritual sun, which is divine love. Now, since the expanse originates from the centre, and not the centre from the expanse, as we said above, and the centre of life, which is the sun of the angelic heaven, is divine love proximately proceeding from God, who is in the midst of that sun; and since the expanse of that centre, which is called the spiritual world, is hence derived; and since from that sun existed the sun of the world, and from the latter its expanse, which is called the natural world; it is evident, that the universe was created by one God." With these words we took our leave, and he attended us out of the court of his study, and conversed with us respecting heaven and hell, and the divine government, from a new acuteness of genius.

381. THE SECOND MEMORABLE RELATION. On a time as I was looking around into the world of spirits, I saw at a distance a palace surrounded and as it were besieged by a crowd; I also saw many running towards it. Wondering what this could mean, I speedily left the house, and asked one of those who were running, what was the matter at the palace? He replied, that three new comers from the world had been taken up into heaven, and had there seen magnificent things, also maidens and wives of astonishing beauty; and that being let down from heaven they had entered into that palace, and were relating what they had seen; especially that they had beheld such beauties as their eyes had never before seen, or can see, unless illustrated by the light of heavenly *aura*. Respecting themselves they said, that in the world they had been orators, from the kingdom of France, and had applied themselves to the study of eloquence, and that now they were seized with a desire of making an oration on the origin of beauty. When this was made known in the neighbourhood, the multitude flocked together to hear them. Upon receiving this information, I hastened also myself, and entered the palace, and saw the three men standing in the midst, dressed in long robes of a sapphire color, which, having threads of gold in their texture at every change of posture shone as if they had been golden. They stood ready to speak behind a kind of stage; and presently one of them rose on a step behind the stage, and delivered his sentiments concerning the origin of the beauty of the female sex, in the following words.

382. "What is the origin of beauty but love, which, when it flows into the eyes of youths, and sets them on fire, becomes beauty? therefore love and beauty are the same thing;

for love, from an inmost principle, tinges the face of a marriageable maiden with a kind of flame, from the transparence of which is derived the dawn and bloom of her life. Who does not know that the flame emits rays into her eyes, and spreads from these as centres into the countenance, and also descends into the breast, and sets the heart on fire, and thereby affects [a youth], just as a fire with its heat and light affects a person standing near it? That heat is love, and that light is the beauty of love. The whole world is agreed, and firm in the opinion, that every one is lovely and beautiful according to his love: nevertheless the love of the male sex differs from that of the female. Male love is the love of growing wise, and female love is that of loving the love of growing wise in the male; so far therefore as a youth is the love of growing wise, so far he is lovely and beautiful to a maiden; and so far as a maiden is the love of a youth's wisdom, so far she is lovely and beautiful to a youth; wherefore as love meets and kisses the love of another, so also do beauties. I conclude therefore, that love forms beauty into a resemblance of itself."

383. After him arose a second, with a view of discovering, in a neat and elegant speech, the origin of beauty. He expressed himself thus: "I have heard that love is the origin of beauty; but I cannot agree with this opinion. What human being knows what love is? Who has ever contemplated it with any idea of thought? Who has ever seen it with the eye? Let such a one tell me where it is to be found. But I assert that wisdom is the origin of beauty; in women a wisdom which lies concealed and stored up in the inmost principles of the mind, in men a wisdom which manifests itself, and is apparent. Whence is a man (*homo*) a man but from wisdom? Were it not so, a man would be a statue or a picture. What does a maiden attend to in a youth, but the quality of his wisdom; and what does a youth attend to in a maiden, but the quality of her affection of his wisdom? By wisdom I mean genuine morality; because this is the wisdom of life. Hence it is, that when wisdom which lies concealed, approaches and embraces wisdom which is manifest, as is the case interiorly in the spirit of each, they mutually kiss and unite, and this is called love; and in such case each of the parties appears beautiful to the other. In a word, wisdom is like the light or brightness of fire, which impresses itself on the eyes, and thereby forms beauty."

384. After him the third arose, and spoke to this effect: "It is neither love alone nor wisdom alone, which is the origin of beauty; but it is the union of love and wisdom; the union of love with wisdom in a youth, and the union of wisdom with its love in a maiden: for a maiden does not love wisdom in herself but in a youth, and hence sees him as beauty, and when a youth sees this in a maiden, he then sees her as beauty; therefore love by wisdom forms beauty, and wisdom grounded in love receives

it. That this is the case, appears manifestly in Heaven. I have there seen maidens and wives, and have attentively considered their beauties, and have observed, that beauty in maidens differs from beauty in wives; in maidens being only the brightness, but in wives the splendor of beauty. The difference appeared like that of a diamond sparkling from light, and of a ruby shining from fire together with light. What is beauty but the delight of the sight? and in what does this delight originate but in the sport of love and wisdom? This sport gives brilliancy to the sight, and this brilliancy vibrates from eye to eye, and presents an exhibition of beauty. What constitutes beauty of countenance, but red and white, and the lovely mixture thereof with each other? and is not the red derived from love, and the white from wisdom? love being red from its fire, and wisdom, white from its light. Both these I have clearly seen in the faces of two married partners in heaven; the redness of white in the wife, and the whiteness of red in the husband; and I observed that they shone in consequence of mutually looking at each other." When the third had thus concluded, the assembly applauded and cried out, "He has gained the victory." Then on a sudden, a flaming light, which is the light of conjugial love, filled the house with its splendor, and the hearts of the company with satisfaction.

ON THE CONJUNCTION OF CONJUGIAL LOVE WITH THE LOVE OF INFANTS.

385. THERE are evident signs that conjugial love and the love of infants, which is called *storge*, are connected; and there are also signs which may induce a belief that they are not connected; for there is the love of infants with married partners who tenderly love each other, and also with married partners who disagree entirely, and likewise with those who are separated from each other, and in some cases it is more tender and stronger with the latter than the former; but that still the love of infants is always connected with conjugial love, may appear from the origin from which it flows in; for although this origin varies with the recipients, still those loves remain inseparable, just as the first end in the last, which is the effect. The first end of conjugial love is the procreation of offspring, and the last, or the effect, is the offspring procreated. That the first end enters into the effect, and is therein as in its origin, and does not withdraw from it, may be seen from a rational view of the orderly progression of ends and causes to effects. But as the reasonings of the generality commence merely from effects, and from them proceed to some consequences thence resulting, and do not com-

mence from causes, and from them proceed analytically to effects, and so forth; therefore the rational principles of light must needs become the obscure principles of cloud; whence come derivations from truth, arising from appearances and fallacies. But that it may be seen that conjugial love and the love of infants are interiorly connected, although exteriorly disjointed, we will proceed to demonstrate it in the following order. I. *Two universal spheres proceed from the Lord to preserve the universe in its created State; of which the one is the sphere of procreating, and the other the sphere of protecting the things procreated.* II. *These two universal spheres make a one with the sphere of conjugial love and the sphere of the love of infants.* III. *These two spheres universally and singularly flow into all things of heaven, and all things of the world from first to last.* IV. *The sphere of the love of infants is a sphere of protection and support of those who cannot protect and support themselves.* V. *This sphere affects both the evil and the good, and disposes every one to love, protect, and support his offspring from his own love.* VI. *This sphere principally affects the female sex, thus mothers, and the male sex, or fathers, by derivation from them.* VII. *This sphere is also a sphere of innocence and peace from the Lord.* VIII. *The sphere of innocence flows into infants, and through them into the parents, and affects them.* IX. *It also flows into the souls of the parents, and unites with the same sphere [as operative] with the infants; and it is principally insinuated by means of the touch.* X. *In the degree in which innocence retires from infants, affection and conjunction also abate, and this successively even to separation.* XI. *A state of rational innocence and peace with parents towards infants is grounded on the circumstance, that they know nothing and can do nothing from themselves, but from others, especially from the father and mother; and that this state also successively retires, in proportion as they know and have ability from themselves, and not from others.* XII. *The above sphere advances in order from the end through causes into effects and makes periods; whereby creation is preserved in the state foreseen and provided for.* XIII. *The love of infants descends and does not ascend.* XIV. *Wives have one state of love before conception and another after, even to the birth.* XV. *With parents conjugial love is conjoined with the love of infants by spiritual causes, and thence by natural.* XVI. *The love of infants and children is different with spiritual married partners from what it is with natural.* XVII. *With spiritual married partners that love is from what is interior or prior, but with natural from what is exterior or posterior.* XVIII. *In consequence hereof that love prevails with married partners who mutually love each other, and also with those who do not at all love each other.* XIX *The love of infants remains after death, especially with women.* XX. *Infants are educated under the*

Lord's auspices by such women, and grow in stature and intelligence as in the world. XXI. *It is there provided by the Lord, that with those infants the innocence of infancy becomes the innocence of wisdom, and thus the infants become angels.* We now proceed to an explanation of each article.

386. I. TWO UNIVERSAL SPHERES PROCEED FROM THE LORD TO PRESERVE THE UNIVERSE IN ITS CREATED STATE; OF WHICH THE ONE IS THE SPHERE OF PROCREATING AND THE OTHER THE SPHERE OF PROTECTING THE THINGS PROCREATED. The divine which proceeds from the Lord is called a sphere, because it goes forth from him, surrounds him, fills both the spiritual and the natural world, and produces the effects of the ends which the Lord predestinated in creation, and provides since creation. All that which flows from a subject, and surrounds and environs it, is named a sphere; as in the case of the sphere of light from the sun around it, of the sphere of life from man around him, of the sphere of odor from a plant around it, of the sphere of attraction from the magnet around it, and so forth: but the universal spheres of which we are here treating, are from the Lord around him; and they proceed from the sun of the spiritual world, in the midst of which he is. From the Lord by means of that sun, proceeds a sphere of heat and light, or what is the same, a sphere of love and wisdom, to produce ends, which are uses; but that sphere according to uses, is distinguished by various names: the divine sphere which looks to the preservation of the universe in its created state by successive generations, is called the sphere of procreating; and the divine sphere which looks to the preservation of generations in their beginnings, and afterwards in their progressions, is called the sphere of protecting the things procreated: besides these two, there are several other divine spheres which are named according to their uses, consequently variously, as may be seen above, n. 222. The operations of uses by these spheres are the divine providence.

387. II. THESE TWO UNIVERSAL SPHERES MAKE A ONE WITH THE SPHERE OF CONJUGIAL LOVE AND THE SPHERE OF THE LOVE OF INFANTS. That the sphere of conjugial love makes a one with the sphere of procreating, is evident; for procreation is the end, and conjugial love the mediate cause by which [the end is promoted], and the end and the cause in what is to be effected and in effects, act in unity, because they act together. That the sphere of the love of infants makes a one with the sphere of protecting the things procreated, is also evident, because it is the end proceeding from the foregoing end, which was procreation, and the love of infants is its mediate cause by which it is promoted: for ends advance in a series, one after another, and in their progress the last end becomes the first, and thereby advances further, even to the boundary, in which

they subsist or cease. But on this subject more will be seen in the explanation of article XII.

388. III. THESE TWO SPHERES UNIVERSALLY AND SINGULARLY FLOW INTO ALL THINGS OF HEAVEN AND ALL THINGS OF THE WORLD, FROM FIRST TO LAST. It is said universally and singularly, because when mention is made of a universal, the singulars of which it is composed are meant at the same time; for a universal exists from and consists of singulars; thus it takes its name from them, as a whole exists from, consists of, and takes its name from its parts; therefore, if you take away singulars, a universal is only a name, and is like a mere surface which contains nothing: consequently to attribute to God universal government, and to take away singulars, is vain talk and empty preaching: nor is it to the purpose, in this case, to urge a comparison with the universal government of the kings of the earth. From this ground then it is said, that those two spheres flow in universally and singularly.

389. The reason why the spheres of procreating and of protecting the things procreated, or the spheres of conjugial love and the love of infants, flow into all thing of heaven and all things of the world, from first [principles] to last, is because all things which proceed from the Lord, or from the sun which is from him and in which he is, pervade the created universe even to the last of all its principles: the reason of this is, because divine things, which in progression are called celestial and spiritual, have no relation to space and time. That extension cannot be predicated of things spiritual, in consequence of their not having any relation to space and time, is well known: hence whatever proceeds from the Lord, is in an instant from first [principles] in last. That the sphere of conjugial love is thus universal may be seen above, n. 222—225. That in like manner the sphere of the love of infants is universal, is evident from that love's prevailing in heaven, where there are infants from the earths; and from that love's prevailing in the world with men, beasts and birds, serpents and insects. Something resembling this love prevails also in the vegetable and mineral kingdoms; in the vegetable, in that seeds are guarded by shells or husks as by swaddling clothes, and moreover are in the fruit as in a house, and are nourished with juice as with milk; that there is something similar in minerals, is plain from the matrixes and external covering, in which noble gems and metals are concealed and guarded.

390. The reason why the sphere of procreating, and the sphere of protecting the things procreated, make a one in a continual series, is, because the love of procreating is continued into the love of what is procreated. The quality of the love of procreating is known from its delight, which is supereminent and transcendent. This love influences the state of procreating

with men, and in a remarkable manner the state of reception with women; and this very exalted delight with its love continues even to the birth, and there attains its fulness.

301. IV. THE SPHERE OF THE LOVE OF INFANTS IS A SPHERE OF PROTECTION AND SUPPORT OF THOSE WHO CANNOT PROTECT AND SUPPORT THEMSELVES. That the operations of uses from the Lord by spheres proceeding from him, are the divine providence, was said above, n. 386 ; this divine providence therefore is meant by the sphere of protection and support of those who cannot protect and support themselves : for it is a law of creation that the things created are to be preserved, guarded, protected, and supported ; otherwise the universe would fall to decay : but as this cannot be done immediately from the Lord with living creatures, who are left to their own choice, it is done mediately by his love implanted in fathers, mothers, and nurses. That their love is from the Lord influencing them, is not known to themselves, because they do not perceive the influx, and still less the Lord's omnipresence : but who does not see, that this principle is not of nature, but of the divine providence operating in and by nature ; and that such a universal principle cannot exist except from God, by a certain spiritual sun, which is in the centre of the universe, and whose operation, being without space and time, is instant and present from first principles in last ? But in what manner that divine operation, which is the Lord's divine providence, is received by animate subjects, will be shewn in what follows. That mothers and fathers protect and support infants, because they cannot protect and support themselves, is not the cause of that love, but is a rational cause derived from that love's falling into the understanding ; for a man, from this cause alone, without love inspired and inspiring it, or without law and punishment compelling him, would no more than a statue provide for infants.

302. V. THIS SPHERE AFFECTS BOTH THE EVIL AND THE GOOD, AND DISPOSES EVERY ONE TO LOVE, PROTECT, AND SUPPORT HIS OFFSPRING FROM HIS OWN LOVE. Experience testifies that the love of infants prevails equally with the evil and the good, and in like manner with tame and wild beasts ; yea, that in some cases it is stronger and more ardent in its influence on evil men, and also on wild beasts. The reason of this is, because all love proceeding from the Lord and flowing into subjects, is changed in the subject into the love of its life ; for every animate subject has no other sensation than that its love originates in itself, as it does not perceive the influx ; and while also it actually loves itself, it makes the love of infants proper to itself ; for it sees as it were itself in them, and them in itself, and itself thus united with them. Hence also this love is fiercer with wild beasts, as with lions and lionesses, he and she bears, leopards and leopardesses, he and she wolves, and others of a like nature, than with horses,

deer, goats, and sheep; because those wild beasts have dominion over the tame, and hence self-love is predominant, and this loves itself in its offspring; therefore as we said, the influent love is turned into self-love. Such an inversion of the influent love into self-love, and the consequent protection and support of the young offspring by evil parents, is of the Lord's divine providence; for otherwise there would remain but few of the human race, and none of the savage beasts, which, nevertheless, are of use. From these considerations it is evident, that every one is disposed to love, protect, and support his offspring, from his own love.

393. VI. THIS SPHERE PRINCIPALLY AFFECTS THE FEMALE SEX, THUS MOTHERS AND THE MALE SEX, OR FATHERS, BY DERIVATION FROM THEM. This follows from what was said above, in regard to the origin of conjugial love,—that the sphere of conjugial love is received by the women, and through them is transferred to the men: because women are born loves of the understanding of the men, and the understanding is a recipient. The case is the same with the love of infants, because this originates in conjugial love. It is well known that mothers are influenced by a most tender love of infants, and fathers by a love less tender. That the love of infants is inherent in conjugial love, into which women are born, is evident from the amiable and endearing love of girls towards infants, and towards their dolls, which they carry, dress, kiss, and press to their bosoms: boys are not influenced by any such affection. It appears as if mothers derived the love of infants from nourishing them in the womb out of their own blood, and from the consequent appropriation of their life, and thus from sympathetic union: but still this is not the origin of that love; for if another infant, without the mother's knowledge, were to be put after the birth in the place of the genuine infant, the mother would love it with equal tenderness as if it were her own: moreover infants are sometimes loved by their nurses more than by their mothers. From these considerations it follows, that this love is from no other source than from the conjugial love implanted in every woman, to which is joined the love of conceiving; from the delight of which the wife is prepared for reception. This is the first of the above love, which with its delight after the birth passes fully to the offspring.

394. VII. THIS SPHERE IS ALSO A SPHERE OF INNOCENCE AND PEACE [FROM THE LORD]. Innocence and peace are the two inmost principles of heaven; they are called inmost principles, because they proceed immediately from the Lord: for the Lord is innocence itself and peace itself. From innocence the Lord is called a Lamb, and from peace he saith, "*Peace I leave you; my peace I give you.*" John xiv. 27; and he is also meant by the peace with which the disciples were to salute a city or house which they entered; and of which it is said, that if it was worthy, peace would come upon it, and if not worthy, peace

would return, Matt. x. 11—15. Hence also the Lord is called the Prince of peace, Isaiah ix. 5, 6. A further reason why innocence and peace are the inmost principles of heaven, is, because innocence is the *esse* of every good, and peace is the blessed principle of every delight which is of good. See the work on HEAVEN AND HELL, as to the state of innocence of the angels of heaven, n. 276—283; and as to peace in heaven, n. 284—290.

395. VIII. THE SPHERE OF INNOCENCE FLOWS INTO INFANTS, AND THROUGH THEM INTO THE PARENTS, AND AFFECTS THEM. It is well known that infants are innocences; but it is not known that their innocence flows in from the Lord. It flows in from the Lord, because, as was said just above, he is innocence itself; neither can any thing flow in, since it cannot exist except from its first principle, which is IT itself. But we will briefly describe the nature and quality of the innocence of infants, which affects parents: it shines forth from their face, from some of their gestures, and from their first speech, and affects them. They have innocence, because they do not think from any interior principle; for they do not as yet know what is good and evil, and what is true and false, as the ground of their thoughts; in consequence of which they have not a prudence originating in selfhood, nor any deliberate purpose; of course they do not regard any evil as an end. They are free from selfhood acquired from self-love and the love of the world; they do not attribute any thing to themselves; they refer to their parents whatever they receive; content with the trifles which are given them as presents, they have no care about food and raiment, or about the future; they do not look to the world, and immerse themselves thereby in the desire of many things; they love their parents, their nurses, and their infant companions, with whom they play in innocence; they suffer themselves to be guided, they harken and obey. This is the innocence of infancy, which is the cause of the love called *storge*.

396. IX. IT ALSO FLOWS IN TO THE SOULS OF THE PARENTS, AND UNITES WITH THE SAME SPHERE [AS OPERATIVE] WITH THE INFANTS, AND IT IS PRINCIPALLY INSINUATED BY MEANS OF THE TOUCH. The Lord's innocence flows into the angels of the third heaven, where all are in the innocence of wisdom, and passes through the inferior heavens, but only through the innocences of the angels therein, and thus immediately and mediately flows into infants. These differ but little from graven forms; but still they are receptible of life from the Lord through the heavens. Yet, unless the parents also received that influx in their souls, and in the inmost principles of their minds, they would in vain be affected by the innocence of the infants. There must be something adequate and similar in another, whereby communication may be effected, and which may cause reception, affection, and thence conjunction; otherwise it would be like soft seed

falling upon a stone, or a lamb exposed to a wolf. From this ground then it is, that innocence flowing into the souls of the parents, unites with the innocence of the infants. Experience may shew that, with the parents, this conjunction is effected by the mediation of the bodily senses, but especially by the touch: as that the sight is intimately delighted by seeing them, the hearing by their speech, the smelling by their odor. That the communication and therefore the conjunction of innocence is principally effected by the touch, is evident from the satisfaction of carrying them in the arms, from fondling and kissing them, especially in the case of mothers, who are delighted in laying their mouth and face upon their bosoms, and at the same time in touching the same with the palms of their hands, in general, in giving them milk by suckling them at the breasts, moreover, in stroking their naked body, and the unwearied pains they take in washing and dressing them on their laps. That the communications of love and its delights between married partners are effected by the sense of the touch has been occasionally proved above. The reason why communications of the mind are also effected by the same sense is, because the hands are a man's ultimates, and his first principles are together in the ultimates, whereby also all things of the body and of the mind are kept together in an inseparable connection. Hence it is, that Jesus touched infants, Matt. xviii. 2—6; Mark x. 13—16; and that he healed the sick by the touch: and that those who touched him were healed: hence also it is, that inaugurations into the priesthood are at this day effected by the laying on of hands. From these considerations it is evident, that the innocence of parents and the innocence of infants meet each other by the touch, especially of the hands, and thereby join themselves together as by kisses.

397. That innocence produces similar effects with beasts and birds as with men, and that by contact, is well known: the reason of this is, because all that proceeds from the Lord, in an instant pervades the universe, as may be seen above, n. 388—390; and as it proceeds by degrees, and by continual mediations, therefore it passes not only to animals, but also to vegetables and minerals; see n. 389; it also passes into the earth itself, which is the mother of all vegetables and minerals; for the earth, in the spring, is in a prepared state for the reception of seeds, as it were in the womb; and when it receives them, it, as it were, conceives, cherishes them, bears, excludes, suckles, nourishes, clothes, educates, guards, and, as it were, loves the offspring derived from them, and so forth. Since the sphere of procreation proceeds thus far, how much more must it proceed to animals of every kind, even to worms! That as the earth is the common mother of vegetables, so there is also a common mother of bees in every hive, is a well known fact, confirmed by observation.

398. X. IN THE DEGREE IN WHICH INNOCENCE RETIRES FROM INFANTS, AFFECTION AND CONJUNCTION ALSO ABATE, AND THIS SUCCESSIVELY EVEN TO SEPARATION. It is well known that the love of infants, or *storge*, retires from parents according as innocence retires from them; and that, in the case of men, it retires even to the separation of children from home, and in the case of beasts and birds, to a rejection from their presence, and a total forgetfulness of relationship. From this circumstance, as an established fact, it may further appear, that innocence flowing in on each side produces the love called *storge*.

399. XI. A STATE OF RATIONAL INNOCENCE AND PEACE WITH PARENTS TOWARDS INFANTS, IS GROUNDED IN THE CIRCUMSTANCE, THAT THEY KNOW NOTHING AND CAN DO NOTHING FROM THEMSELVES, BUT FROM OTHERS, ESPECIALLY FROM THE FATHER AND MOTHER; AND THIS STATE SUCCESSIVELY RETIRES, IN PROPORTION AS THEY KNOW AND HAVE ABILITY FROM THEMSELVES, AND NOT FROM OTHERS. That the sphere of the love of infants is a sphere of protection and support of those who cannot protect and support themselves, was shewn above in its proper article, n. 391: that this is only a rational cause with men, but not the very essential cause of that love prevailing with them, was also mentioned in the same article. The real original cause of that love is innocence from the Lord, which flows in while the man is ignorant of it, and produces the above rational cause; therefore as the first cause produces a retiring from that love, so also does the second cause at the same time; or what is the same, as the communication of innocence retires, so also the persuading reason accompanies it; but this is the case only with man to the intent that he may do what he does from freedom according to reason, and from this, as from a rational and at the same time a moral law, may support his adult offspring according to the requirements of necessity and usefulness. This second cause does not influence animals who are without reason, they being affected only by the prior cause, which to them is instinct.

400. XII. THE SPHERE OF THE LOVE OF PROCREATING ADVANCES IN ORDER FROM THE END THROUGH CAUSES INTO EFFECTS, AND MAKES PERIODS; WHEREBY CREATION IS PRESERVED IN THE STATE FORESEEN AND PROVIDED FOR. All operations in the universe have a progression from ends through causes into effects. These three are in themselves indivisible, although in idea they appear divided; but still the end, unless the intended effect is seen together with it, is not any thing; nor does either become any thing, unless the cause supports, contrives, and conjoins it. Such a progression is inherent in every man in general, and in every particular, altogether as will, understanding, and action: every end in regard to man relates to the will, every cause to the understanding, and every effect to

the action; in like manner, every end relates to love, every efficient cause to wisdom, and every effect thence derived to use. The reason of this is, because the receptacle of love is the will, the receptacle of wisdom is the understanding, and the receptacle of use is action: since therefore operations in general and in particular with man advance from the will through the understanding into act, so also do they advance from love through wisdom into use. By wisdom here we mean all that which belongs to judgement and thought. That these three are a one in the effect, is evident. That they also make a one in ideas before the effect, is perceived from the consideration, that determination only intervenes; for in the mind an end goes forth from the will and produces for itself a cause in the understanding, and presents to itself an intention; and intention is as an act before determination; hence it is, that by a wise man, and also by the Lord, intention is accepted as an act. What rational person cannot see, or, when he hears, acknowledge, that those three principles flow from some first cause, and that that cause is, that from the Lord, the Creator and Conservator of the universe, there continually proceed love, wisdom, and use, and these three are one? Tell, if you can, in what other source they originate.

401. A similar progression from end through cause into effect belongs also to the sphere of procreating and of protecting the things procreated. The end in this case is the will or love of procreating; the middle cause, by which the end is effected and into which it infuses itself, is conjugial love; the progressive series of efficient causes is the loving, conception, gestation of the embryo or offspring to be procreated; and the effect is the offspring itself procreated. But although end, cause, and effect successively advance as three things, still in the love of procreating, and inwardly in all the causes, and in the effect itself, they make a one. They are the efficient causes only, which advance through times, because in nature; while the end or will, or love, remains continually the same: for ends advance in nature through times without time; but they cannot come forth and manifest themselves, until the effect or use exists and becomes a subject; before this, the love could love only the advance, but could not secure and fix itself. That there are periods of such progressions, and that creation is thereby preserved in the state foreseen and provided for, is well known. But the series of the love of infants from its greatest to its least, thus to the boundary in which it subsists or ceases, is retrograde; since it is according to the decrease of innocence in the subject, and also on account of the periods.

402. XIII. THE LOVE OF INFANTS DESCENDS, AND DOES NOT ASCEND. That it descends from generation to generation, or from sons and daughters to grandsons and granddaughters, and

does not ascend from these to fathers and mothers of families, is well known. The cause of its increase in descent is the love of fructifying, or of producing uses, and in respect to the human race, it is the love of multiplying it; but this derives its origin solely from the Lord, who, in the multiplication of the human race, regards the conservation of creation, and as the ultimate end thereof, the angelic heaven, which is solely from the human race; and since the angelic heaven is the end of ends, and thence the love of loves with the Lord, therefore there is implanted in the souls of men, not only the love of procreating, but also of loving the things procreated in successions: hence also this love exists only with man and not with any beast or bird. That this love with man descends increasing, is in consequence of the glory of honor, which in like manner increases with him according to amplifications. That the love of honor and glory receives into itself the love of infants flowing from the Lord, and makes it as it were its own, will be seen in article xvi.

403. XIV. WIVES HAVE ONE STATE OF LOVE BEFORE CONCEPTION AND ANOTHER AFTER, EVEN TO THE BIRTH. This is adduced to the end that it may be known, that the love of procreating, and the consequent love of what is procreated, is implanted in conjugial love with women, and that with them those two loves are divided, while the end, which is the love of procreating, begins its progression. That the love called *storge* is then transferred from the wife to the husband; and also that the love of procreating, which, as we said, with a woman makes one with her conjugial love, is then not alike, is evident from several indications.

404. XV. WITH PARENTS CONJUGIAL LOVE IS CONJOINED WITH THE LOVE OF INFANTS BY SPIRITUAL CAUSES, AND THENCE BY NATURAL. The spiritual causes are, that the human race may be multiplied, and from this the angelic heaven enlarged, and that thereby such may be born as will become angels, serving the Lord to promote uses in heaven, and by consociation with men also in the earths: for every man has angels associated with him from the Lord; and such is his conjunction with them, that if they were taken away, he would instantly die. The natural causes of the conjunction of those two loves are, to effect the birth of those who may promote uses in human societies, and may be incorporated therein as members. That the latter are the natural and the former the spiritual causes of the love of infants and of conjugial love, even married partners themselves think and sometimes declare, saying they have enriched heaven with as many angels as they have had descendants, and have furnished society with as many servants as they have had children.

405. XVI. THE LOVE OF CHILDREN AND INFANTS IS DIFFERENT WITH SPIRITUAL MARRIED PARTNERS FROM WHAT IT IS WITH NATURAL. With spiritual married partners the love of

infants as to appearance, is like the love of infants with natural married partners; but it is more inward, and thence more tender, because that love exists from innocence, and from a nearer reception of innocence, and thereby a more present preception of it in man's self; for the spiritual are such so far as they partake of innocence. But spiritual fathers and mothers, after they have sipped the sweet of innocence with their infants, love their children very differently from what natural fathers and mothers do. The spiritual love their children from their spiritual intelligence and moral life; thus they love them from the fear of God and actual piety, or the piety of life, and at the same time from affection and application to uses serviceable to society, consequently from the virtues and good morals which they possessed. From the love of these things they are principally led to provide for, and minister to, the necessities of their children; therefore if they do not observe such things in them, they alienate their minds from them and do nothing for them but so far as they think themselves bound in duty. With natural fathers and mothers the love of infants is indeed grounded also in innocence; but when the innocence is received by them, it is entwined around their own love, and consequently the love of their infants from the latter, and at the same time from the former, kissing, embracing, and dangling them, hugging them to their bosoms, and fawning upon and flattering them beyond all bounds, regarding them as one heart and soul with themselves; and afterwards, when they have passed the state of infancy even to boyhood and beyond it, in which state innocence is no longer operative, they love them not from any fear of God and actual piety, or the piety of life, nor from any rational and moral intelligence they may have; neither do they regard, or only very slightly, if at all, their internal affections, and thence their virtues and good morals, but only their externals, which they favor and indulge. To these externals their love is directed and determined: hence also they close their eyes to their vices, excusing, and favoring them. The reason of this is, because with such parents the love of their offspring is also the love of themselves; and this love adheres to the subject outwardly, without entering into it, as self does not enter into itself.

406. The quality of the love of infants and of the love of children with the spiritual and with the natural, is evidently discerned from them after death; for most fathers, when they come into another life, recollect their children who have died before them; they are also presented to and mutually acknowledge each other. Spiritual fathers only look at them, and inquire as to their present state, and rejoice if it is well with them, and grieve if it is ill; and after some conversation, instruction, and admonition respecting moral celestial life, they separate from them, telling them, that they are no longer to be remembered

as fathers because the Lord is the only Father to all in heaven, according to his words, Matt. xxiii. 9: and that they do not at all remember them as children. But natural fathers, when they first become conscious that they are living after death, and recall to mind their children who have died before them, and also when, agreeably to their wishes, they are presented to each other, they instantly embrace, and become united like bundles of rods; and in this case the father is continually delighted with beholding and conversing with them. If the father is told that some of his children are satans, and that they have done injuries to the good, he nevertheless keeps them in a group around him, if he himself sees that they are the occasion of hurt and do mischief, he still pays no attention to it, nor does he separate any of them from association with himself; in order, therefore, to prevent the continuance of such a mischievous company, they are of necessity committed forthwith to hell; and there the father, before the children, is shut up in confinement, and the children are separated, and each is removed to the place of his life.

407. To the above I will add this wonderful relation:—in the spiritual world I have seen fathers who, from hatred, and as it were rage, had looked at infants presented before their eyes, with a mind so savage, that, if they could, they would have murdered them; but on its being hinted to them, though without truth, that they were their own infants, their rage and savageness instantly subsided, and they loved them to excess. This love and hatred prevail together with those who in the world had been inwardly deceitful, and had set their minds in enmity against the Lord.

408. XVII. WITH THE SPIRITUAL THAT LOVE IS FROM WHAT IS INTERIOR OR PRIOR, BUT WITH THE NATURAL FROM WHAT IS EXTERIOR OR POSTERIOR. To think and conclude from what is interior or prior, is to think and conclude from ends and causes to effects; but to think and conclude from what is exterior or posterior, is to think and conclude from effects to causes and ends. The latter progression is contrary to order, but the former according to it; for to think and conclude from ends and causes, is to think and conclude from goods and truths, viewed in a superior region of the mind, to effects in an inferior region. Real human rationality from creation is of this quality. But to think and conclude from effects, is to think and conclude from an inferior region of the mind, where the sensual things of the body reside with their appearances and fallacies, to guess at causes and effects, which in itself is merely to confirm falsities and concupiscences, and afterwards to see and believe them to be truths of wisdom and goodnesses of the love of wisdom. The case is similar in regard to the love of infants and children with the spiritual and the natural; the spiritual love them from what is prior, thus according to order: but the natural love them from what is posterior, thus contrary to order. These observations

are adduced only for the confirmation of the preceding article.

409. XVIII. IN CONSEQUENCE HEREOF THAT LOVE PREVAILS WITH MARRIED PARTNERS WHO MUTUALLY LOVE EACH OTHER, AND ALSO WITH THOSE WHO DO NOT AT ALL LOVE EACH OTHER; consequently it prevails with the natural as well as with the spiritual; but the latter are influenced by conjugial love, whereas the former are influenced by no such love but what is apparent and pretended. The reason why the love of infants and conjugial love still act in unity, is, because, as we have said, conjugial love is implanted in every woman from creation, and together with it the love of procreating, which is determined to and flows into the procreated offspring, and from the women is communicated to the men. Hence in houses, in which there is no conjugial love between the man and his wife, it nevertheless is with the wife, and thereby some external conjunction is effected with the man. From this same ground it is, that even harlots love their offspring; for that which from creation is implanted in souls, and respects propagation, is indelible, and cannot be extirpated.

410. XIX. THE LOVE OF INFANTS REMAINS AFTER DEATH, ESPECIALLY WITH WOMEN. Infants, as soon as they are raised up, which happens immediately after their decease, are elevated into heaven, and delivered to angels of the female sex, who in the life of the body in the world loved infants, and at the same time feared God. These, having loved all infants with maternal tenderness, receive them as their own; and the infants in this case, as from an innate feeling, love them as their mothers: as many infants are consigned to them, as they desire from a spiritual *storge*. The heaven in which infants are appears in front in the region of the forehead, in the line in which the angels look directly at the Lord. That heaven is so situated, because all infants are educated under the immediate auspices of the Lord. There is an influx also into this heaven from the heaven of innocence, which is the third heaven. When they have passed through this first period, they are transferred to another heaven, where they are instructed.

411. XX. INFANTS ARE EDUCATED UNDER THE LORD'S AUSPICES BY SUCH WOMEN, AND GROW IN STATURE AND INTELLIGENCE AS IN THE WORLD. Infants in heaven are educated in the following manner; they learn to speak from the female angel who has the charge of their education; their first speech is merely the sound of affection, in which however there is some beginning of thought, whereby what is human in the sound is distinguished from the sound of an animal; this speech gradually becomes more distinct, as ideas derived from affection enter the thought: all their affections, which also increase, proceed from innocence. At first, such things are insinuated into them as appear before their eyes, and are delightful; and as these are from a spiritual origin, heavenly things flow into them at the same time, whereby

the interiors of their minds are opened. Afterwards, as the infants are perfected in intelligence, so they grow in stature, and viewed in this respect, they appear also more adult, because intelligence and wisdom are essential spiritual nourishment; therefore those things which nourish their minds, also nourish their bodies. Infants in heaven, however, do not grow up beyond their first age, where they stop, and remain in it to eternity. And when they are in that age, they are given in marriage, which is provided by the Lord, and is celebrated in the heaven of the youth, who presently follows the wife into her heaven, or into her house, if they are of the same society. That I might know of a certainty, that infants grow in stature, and arrive at maturity as they grow in intelligence, I was permitted to speak with some while they were infants, and afterwards when they were grown up; and they appeared as full-grown youths, in a stature, like that of young men full grown in the world.

412. Infants are instructed especially by representatives adequate and suitable to their genius; the great beauty and interior wisdom of which can scarcely be credited in the world. I am permitted to adduce here two representations, from which a judgement may be formed in regard to the rest. On a certain time they represented the Lord ascending from the sepulchre, and at the same time the unition of his human with the divine. At first they presented the idea of a sepulchre, but not at the same time the idea of the Lord, except so remotely, that it was scarcely, and as it were at a distance, perceived that it was the Lord; because in the idea of a sepulchre there is somewhat funereal, which they hereby removed. Afterwards they cautiously admitted into the sepulchre a sort of atmosphere, appearing nevertheless as a thin vapor, by which they signified, and this with a suitable degree of remoteness, spiritual life in baptism. They afterwards represented the Lord's descent to those who were bound, and his ascent with them into heaven; and in order to accommodate the representation to their infant minds, they let down small cords that were scarcely discernible, exceedingly soft and yielding, to aid the Lord in the ascent, being always influenced by a holy fear lest any thing in the representation should affect something that was not under heavenly influence: not to mention other representations, whereby infants are introduced into the knowledges of truth and the affections of good, as by games adapted to their capacities. To these and similar things infants are led by the Lord by means of innocence passing through the third heaven; and thus spiritual things are insinuated into their affections, and thence into their tender thoughts, so that they know no other than that they do and think such things from themselves, by which their understanding commences.

413. XXI. It is there provided by the Lord, that with those infants the innocence of infancy becomes the inno-

CENCE OF WISDOM [AND THUS THEY BECOME ANGELS]. Many may conjecture that infants remain infants, and become angels immediately after death: but it is intelligence and wisdom that make an angel: therefore so long as infants are without intelligence and wisdom, they are indeed associated with angels, yet are not angels: but they then first become so when they are made intelligent and wise. Infants therefore are led from the innocence of infancy to the innocence of wisdom, that is, from external innocence to internal: the latter innocence is the end of all their instruction and progression: therefore when they attain to the innocence of wisdom, the innocence of infancy is adjoined to them, which in the mean time had served them as a plane. I saw a representation of the quality of the innocence of infancy; it was of wood almost without life, and was vivified in proportion as the knowledges of truth and the affections of good were imbibed: and afterwards there was represented the quality of the innocence of wisdom, by a living infant. The angels of the third heaven, who are in a state of innocence from the Lord above other angels, appear like naked infants before the eyes of spirits who are beneath the heavens; and as they are wiser than all others, so are they also more truly alive: the reason of this is, because innocence corresponds to infancy, and also to nakedness; therefore it is said of Adam and his wife, when they were in a state of innocence, that they were naked and were not ashamed, but that when they had lost their state of innocence, they were ashamed of their nakedness, and hid themselves, Gen. ii. 25; chap. iii. 7, 10, 11. In a word, the wiser the angels are the more innocent they are. The quality of the innocence of wisdom may in some measure be seen from the innocence of infancy above described, n. 395, if only instead of parents, the Lord be assumed as the Father by whom they are led, and to whom they ascribe what they have received.

414. On the subject of innocence I have often conversed with the angels who have told me that innocence is the *esse* of every good, and that good is only so far good as it has innocence in it: and, since wisdom is of life and thence of good, that wisdom is only so far wisdom as it partakes of innocence: the like is true of love, charity, and faith; and hence it is that no one can enter heaven unless he has innocence; which is meant by these words of the Lord, " *Suffer infants to come to me, and forbid them not; for of such is the kingdom of the heavens; verily I say unto you, Whosoever shall not receive the kingdom of the heavens as an infant, he will not enter therein,*" Mark x. 14, 15; Luke xviii. 16, 17. In this passage, as well as in other parts of the Word, infants denote those who are in innocence. The reason why good is good, so far as it has innocence in it, is, because all good is from the Lord, and innocence consists in being led by the Lord.

* * * * * * *

415. To the above I shall add this MEMORABLE RELATION. One morning, as I awoke out of sleep, the light beginning to dawn and it being very serene, while I was meditating and not yet quite awake, I saw through the window as it were a flash of lightning, and presently I heard as it were a clap of thunder; and while I was wondering whence this could be, I heard from heaven words to this effect, "There are some not far from you, who are reasoning sharply about God and nature. The vibration of light like lightning, and the clapping of the air like thunder, are correspondences and consequent appearances of the conflict and collision of arguments, on one side in favor of God, and on the other in favor of nature." The cause of this spiritual combat was as follows: there were some satans in hell who expressed a wish to be allowed to converse with the angels of heaven; "for," said they, "we will clearly and fully demonstrate, that what they call God, the Creator of all things, is nothing but nature; and thus that God is a mere unmeaning expression, unless nature be meant by it." And as those satans believed this with all their heart and soul, and also were desirous to converse with the angels of heaven, they were permitted to ascend out of the mire and darkness of hell, and to converse with two angels at that time descending from heaven. They were in the world of spirits, which is intermediate between heaven and hell. The satans on seeing the angels there, hastily ran to them, and cried out with a furious voice, "Are you the angels of heaven with whom we are allowed to engage in debate, respecting God and nature? You are called wise because you acknowledge a God; but, alas! how simple you are! Who sees God? who understands what God is? who conceives that God governs, and can govern the universe, with everything belonging thereto? and who but the vulgar and common herd of mankind acknowledges what he does not see and understand? What is more obvious than that nature is all in all? Is it not nature alone that we see with our eyes, hear with our ears, smell with our nostrils, taste with our tongues, and touch and feel with our hands and bodies? And are not our bodily senses the only evidences of truth? Who would not swear from them that it is so? Are not your heads in nature, and is there any influx into the thoughts of your heads but from nature? Take away nature, and can you think at all? Not to mention several other considerations of a like kind." On hearing these words the angels replied, "You speak in this manner because you are merely sensual. All in the hells have the ideas of their thoughts immersed in the bodily senses, neither are they able to elevate their minds above them; therefore we excuse you. The life of evil and the consequent belief of wha is false have closed the interiors of your minds, so that you ar incapable of any elevation above the things of sense, except in a state removed from evils of life, and from false principles of

faith: for a satan, as well as an angel, can understand truth when he hears it; but he does not retain it, because evil obliterates truth and induces what is false: but we perceive that you are now in a state of removal from evil, and thus that you can understand the truth which we speak; attend therefore to what we shall say:" and they proceeded thus: "You have been in the natural world, and have departed thence, and are now in the spiritual world. Have you known anything till now concerning a life after death? Have you not till now denied such a life, and degraded yourselves to the beasts? Have you known any thing heretofore about heaven and hell, or the light and heat of this world? or of this circumstance, that you are no longer within the sphere of nature, but above it; since this world and all things belonging to it are spiritual, and spiritual things are above natural, so that not the least of nature can flow into this world? But, in consequence of believing nature to be a God or a goddess, you believe also the light and heat of this world to be the light and heat of the natural world, when yet it is not at all so; for natural light here is darkness, and natural heat is cold. Have you known anything about the sun of this world from which our light and heat proceed? Have you known that this sun is pure love, and the sun of the natural world pure fire; and the sun of the world, which is pure fire, is that from which nature exists and subsists; and that the sun of heaven, which is pure love, is that from which life itself, which is love with wisdom exists and subsists; and thus that nature, which you make a god or a goddess, is absolutely dead? You can, under the care of a proper guard, ascend with us into heaven; and we also, under similar protection, can descend with you into hell; and in heaven you will see magnificent and splendid objects, but in hell such as are filthy and unclean. The ground of the difference is, because all in the heavens worship God, and all in the hells worship nature; and the magnificent and splendid objects in the heavens are correspondences of the affections of good and truth, and the filthy and unclean objects in the hells are correspondences of the lusts of what is evil and false. Judge now, from these circumstances, whether God or nature be all in all." To this the satans replied, "In the state wherein we now are, we can conclude, from what we have heard, that there is a God; but when the delight of evil seizes our minds, we see nothing but nature." These two angels and two satans were standing to the right, at no great distance from me; therefore I saw and heard them; and lo! I saw near them many spirits who had been celebrated in the natural world for their erudition; and I was surprised to observe that those great scholars at one time stood near the angels and at another near the satans, and that they favored the sentiments of those near whom they stood; and I was led to understand that the changes of their situation were changes of the state of their minds, which sometimes favored one side and sometimes the other; for they were *vertumni*. Moreover, the angels said, "We will tell you a mystery; on our looking down upon the earth, and examining those who were celebrated for erudition, and who have thought about God and nature from their own judgement, we have found six hundred out of a thousand favorers of nature, and the rest favorers of God; and that these were in favor of God, in consequence of having frequently maintained in their conversation, not from any convictions of their understandings, but only from hear-say, that nature is from God; for frequent conversation from the memory and recollection, and not at the same time from thought and intelligence, induces a species of faith." After this, the satans were entrusted to a guard and ascended with the two angels into heaven, and saw the magnificent and splendid objects contained therein; and being then an illustration from the light of heaven, they acknowledged the being of a God, and that nature was created to be subservient to the life which is in God and from God; and that nature in itself is dead, and consequently does nothing of itself, but is acted upon by life. Having seen and perceived these things, they descended: and as they descended the love of evil returned and closed their understanding above and opened it beneath; and then there appeared above it as it were a veil sending forth lightning from infernal fire; and as soon as they touched the earth with their feet, the ground cleaved asunder beneath them, and they returned to their associates.

416. After these things those two angels seeing me near, said to the by-standers respecting me, "We know that this man has written about God and nature; let us hear what he has written." They therefore came to me, and intreated that what I had written about God and nature might be read to them: I therefore read as follows. "Those who believe in a Divine operation in everything of nature, may confirm themselves in favor of the Divine, from many things which they see in nature, equally, yea more than those who confirm themselves in favor of nature: for those who confirm themselves in favor of the Divine, attend to the wonderful things, which are conspicuous in the productions of both vegetables and animals:—in the PRODUCTION OF VEGETABLES, that from a small seed sown in the earth there is sent forth a root, by means of the root a stem, and successively buds, leaves, flowers, fruits, even to new seeds; altogether as if the seed was acquainted with the order of succession, or the process by which it was to renew itself. What rational person can conceive, that the sun which is pure fire, is acquainted with this, or that it can endue its heat and light with a power to effect such things; and further, that it can form wonderful things therein, and intend use? When a man of elevated reason sees and considers such things, he cannot

think otherwise than that they are from him who has infinite wisdom, consequently from God. Those who acknowledge the Divine, also see and think so; but those who do not acknowledge it, do not see and think so, because they are unwilling; and thereby they let down their rational principle into the sensual, which derives all its ideas from the luminous principle in which the bodily senses are, and confirms their fallacies urging, 'Do not you see the sun effecting these things by its heat and light? What is that which you do not see?' Is it anything? Those who confirm themselves in favor of the Divine, attend to the wonderful things which are conspicuous in the PRODUCTIONS OF ANIMALS; to mention only what is conspicuous in eggs, that there lies concealed in them a chick in its seed, or first principles of existence, with everything requisite even to the hatching, and likewise to every part of its progress after hatching, until it becomes a bird, or winged animal, in the form of its parent stock. A further attention to the nature and quality of the form cannot fail to cause astonishment in the contemplative mind; to observe in the least as well as in the largest kinds, yea, in the invisible as in the visible, that is, in small insects, as in fowls or great beasts, how they are all endowed with organs of sense, such as seeing, smelling, tasting, touching; and also with organs of motion, such as muscles, for they fly and walk; and likewise with viscera, around the heart and lungs, which are actuated by the brains: that the commonest insects enjoy all these parts of organization is known from their anatomy, as described by some writers, especially SWAMMERDAM in his Books of Nature. Those who ascribe all things to nature do indeed see such things; but they think only that they are so, and say that nature produces them: and this they say in consequence of having averted their minds from thinking about the Divine; and those who have so averted their minds, when they see the wonderful things in nature, cannot think rationally, and still less spiritually; but they think sensually and materially, and in this case they think in and from nature, and not above it, in like manner as those do who are in hell; differing from beasts only in this respect, that they have rational powers, that is, they are capable of understanding, and thereby of thinking otherwise, if only they are willing. Those who have averted themselves from thinking about the Divine, when they see the wonderful things in nature, and thereby become sensual, do not consider that the sight of the eye is so gross that it sees several small insects as one confused mass; when yet each of them is organized to feel and to move itself, consequently is endowed with fibres and vessels, also with a little heart, pulmonary pipes, small viscera, and brains; and that the contexture of these parts consists of the purest principles in nature, and corresponds to some life, by virtue of which their minutest parts are distinctly acted upon. Since the sight of the eye is so gross that several of such insects, with the innumerable things in each, appear to it as a small confused mass, and yet those who are sensual, think and judge from that sight, it is evident how gross their minds are, and consequently in what thick darkness they are respecting spiritual things.

417. "Every one that is willing to do so, may confirm himself in favor of the Divine from the visible things in nature; and he also who thinks of God from the principle of life, does so confirm himself; while, for instance, he observes the fowls of heaven, how each species of them knows its proper food and where it is to be found; how they can distinguish those of their own kind by the sounds they utter and by their external appearance; how also, among other kinds, they can tell which are their friends and which their foes; how they pair together, build their nests with great art, lay therein their eggs, hatch them, know the time of hatching, and at its accomplishment help their young out of the shell, love them most tenderly, cherish them under their wings, feed and nourish them, until they are able to provide for themselves and do the like, and to procreate a family in order to perpetuate their kind. Every one that is willing to think of a divine influx through the spiritual world into the natural, may discern it in these instances, and may also, if he will, say in his heart, 'Such knowledges cannot flow into those animals from the sun by the rays of its light:' for the sun, from which nature derives its birth and its essence, its pure fire, and consequently the rays of its light are altogether dead; and thus they may conclude, that such effects are derived from an influx of divine wisdom into the ultimates of nature.

418. "Every one may confirm himself in favor of the Divine from what is visible in nature, while he observes worms, which from the delight of a certain desire, wish and long after a chang of their earthly state into a state analogous to a heavenly one for this purpose they creep into holes, and cast themselves as it were into a womb that they may be born again, and there become chrysalises, aurelias, nymphs, and at length butterflies; and when they have undergone this change, and according to their species are decked with beautiful wings, they fly into the air as into their heaven, and there indulge in all festive sports, pair together, lay their eggs, and provide for themselves a posterity; and then they are nourished with a sweet and pleasant food, which they extract from flowers. Who that confirms himself in favor of the Divine from what is visible in nature, does not see some image of the earthly state of man in these animals while they are worms, and of his heavenly state in the same when they become butterflies? whereas those who confirm themselves in favor of nature, see indeed such things; but as they have rejected from their

minds all thought of man's heavenly state, they call them mere instincts of nature.

419. "Again, every one may confirm himself in favor of the Divine from what is visible in nature, while he attends to the discoveries made respecting bees,—how they have the art to gather wax and suck honey from herbs and flowers, and build cells like small houses, and arrange them into the form of a city with streets, through which they come in and go out; and how they can smell flowers and herbs at a distance, from which they may collect wax for their home and honey for their food; and how, when laden with these treasures, they can trace their way back in a right direction to their hive; thus they provide for themselves food and habitation against the approaching winter, as if they were acquainted with and foresaw its coming. They also set over themselves a mistress as a queen, to be the parent of a future race, and for her they build as it were a palace in an elevated situation, and appoint guards about her; and when the time comes for her to become a mother, she goes from cell to cell and lays her eggs, which her attendants cover with a sort of ointment to prevent their receiving injury from the air; hence arises a new generation, which, when old enough to provide in like manner for itself, is driven out from home; and when driven out, it flies forth to seek a new habitation, not however till it has first collected itself into a swarm to prevent dissociation. About autumn also the useless drones are brought forth and deprived of their wings, lest they should return and consume the provision which they had taken no pains to collect; not to mention many other circumstances; from which it may appear evident, that on account of the use which they afford to mankind, they have by influx from the spiritual world a form of government, such as prevails among men in the world, yea, among angels in the heavens. What man of uncorrupted reason does not see that such instincts are not communicated to bees from the natural world? What has the sun, in which nature originates, in common with a form of government which vies with and is similar to a heavenly one? From these and similar circumstances respecting brute animals, the confessor and worshiper of nature confirms himself in favor of nature, while the confessor and worshiper of God, from the same circumstances, confirms himself in favor o the Divine: for the spiritual man sees spiritual things therein, and the natural man natural; thus every one according to his quality. In regard to myself, such circumstances have been to me testimonies of an influx of what is spiritual into what is natural, or of an influx of the spiritual world into the natural world; thus of an influx from the divine wisdom of the Lord. Consider also, whether you can think analytically of any form of government, any civil law, any moral virtue, or any spiritual

truth, unless the Divine flows in from his wisdom through the spiritual world: for my own part, I never did, and still feel it to be impossible; for I have perceptibly and sensibly observed such influx now [1768] for twenty-five years continually: I therefore speak this from experience.

420. "Can nature, let me ask, regard use as an end, and dispose uses into orders and forms? This is in the power of none but a wise being; and none but God, who is infinitely wise, can so order and form the universe. Who else can foresee and provide for mankind all the things necessary for their food and clothing, producing them from the fruits of the earth and from animals? It is surely a wonderful consideration among many others, that those common insects, called silk-worms, should supply with splendid clothing all ranks of persons, from kings and queens even to the lowest servants; and that those common insects the bees, should supply wax to enlighten both our temples and palaces. These, with several other similar considerations, are standing proofs, that the Lord by an operation from himself through the spiritual world, effects whatever is done in nature.

421. It may be expedient here to add, that I have seen in the spiritual world those who had confirmed themselves in favor of nature by what is visible in this world, so as to become atheists, and that their understanding in spiritual light appeared open beneath but closed above, because with their thinking faculty they had looked downwards to the earth and not upwards to heaven. The super-sensual principle, which is the lowest principle of the understanding, appeared as a veil, in some cases sparkling from infernal fire, in some black as soot, and in some pale and livid as a corpse. Let every one therefore beware of confirmation in favor of nature, and let him confirm himself in favor of the Divine; for which confirmation there is no want of materials.

422. "Some indeed are to be excused for ascribing certain visible effects to nature, because they have had no knowledge respecting the sun of the spiritual world, where the Lord is, and of influx thence; neither have they known any thing about that world and its state, nor yet of its presence with man; and consequently they could think no other than that the spiritual principle was a purer natural principle; and thus that angels were either in the ether or in the stars; also that the devil was either man's evil, or, if he actually existed, that he was either in the air or in the deep; also that the souls of men after death were either in the inmost part of the earth, or in some place of confinement till the day of judgement; not to mention other like conceits, which sprung from ignorance of the spiritual world and its sun. This is the reason why those are to be excused, who have believed that the visible productions of nature are the effect

of some principle implanted in her from creation: nevertheless those who have made themselves atheists by confirmations in favor of nature, are not to be excused, because they might have confirmed themselves in favor of the Divine. Ignorance inded excuses, but does not take away the false principle which is confirmed; for this false principle agrees with evil, and evil with hell."

ADULTEROUS LOVE AND ITS SINFUL PLEASURES.

ON THE OPPOSITION OF ADULTEROUS LOVE AND CONJUGIAL LOVE.

423. At the entrance upon our subject, it may be expedient to declare what we mean in this chapter by adulterous love. By adulterous love we do not mean fornicatory love, which precedes marriage, or which follows it after the death of a married partner; neither do we mean concubinage, which is engaged in from causes legitimate, just, and excusatory; nor do we mean either the mild or the grievous kinds of adultery, whereof a man actually repents; for the latter become not opposite, and the former are not opposite, to conjugial love, as will be seen in the following pages, where each is treated of. But by adulterous love, opposite to conjugial love, we here mean the love of adultery, so long as it is such as not to be regarded as sin, or as evil, and dishonorable, and contrary to reason, but as allowable with reason. This adulterous love not only makes conjugial love the same with itself, but also overthrows, destroys, and at length nauseates it. The opposition of this love to conjugial love is the subject treated of in this chapter. That no other love is treated of [as being in such opposition], may be evident from what follows concerning fornication, concubinage, and the various kinds of adultery. But in order that this opposition may be made manifest to the rational sight, it may be expedient to demonstrate it in the following series : I. *It is not known what adulterous love is, unless it be known what conjugial love is.* II. *Adulterous love is opposed to conjugial love.* III. *Adulterous love is opposed to conjugial love, as the natural man viewed in himself is opposed to the spiritual man.* IV. *Adulterous love is opposed to conjugial love, as the connubial connection of what is evil and false is opposed to the marriage of good and truth.* V. *Hence adulterous love is opposed to conjugial love, as hell is opposed to heaven.* VI. *The impurity of hell is from adulterous love, and the purity of heaven*

from conjugial love. VII. *The impurity and the purity in the church are similarly circumstanced.* VIII. *Adulterous love more and more makes a man not a man* (homo), *and not a man* (vir), *and conjugial love makes a man more and more a man* (homo), *and a man* (vir). IX. *There are a sphere of adulterous love and a sphere of conjugial love.* X. *The sphere of adulterous love ascends from hell, and the sphere of conjugial love descends from heaven.* XI. *Those two spheres mutually meet each other in each world; but they do not unite.* XII. *Between those two spheres there is an equilibrium, and man is in it.* XIII. *A man is able to turn himself to whichever he pleases; but so far as he turns himself to the one, so far he turns himself from the other.* XIV. *Each sphere brings with it delights.* XV. *The delights of adulterous love commence from the flesh and are of the flesh even in the spirit; but the delights of conjugial love commence in the spirit, and are of the spirit even in the flesh.* XVI. *The delights of adulterous love are the pleasures of insanity; but the delights of conjugial love are the delights of wisdom.* We proceed to an explanation of each article.

424. I. IT IS NOT KNOWN WHAT ADULTEROUS LOVE IS, UNLESS IT BE KNOWN WHAT CONJUGIAL LOVE IS. By adulterous love we mean the love of adultery, which destroys conjugial love, as above, n. 423. That it is not known what adulterous love is, unless it be known what conjugial love is, needs no demonstration, but only illustration by similitudes: as for example; who can know what is evil and false, unless he know what is good and true? and who knows what is unchaste, dishonorable, unbecoming, and ugly, unless he knows what is chaste, honorable, becoming, and beautiful? and who can discern the various kinds of insanity, but he that is wise, or that knows what wisdom is? also, who can rightly perceive discordant and grating sounds, but he that is well versed in the doctrine and study of harmonious numbers? in like manner, who can clearly discern what is the quality of adultery, unless he has first clearly discerned what is the quality of marriage? and who can make a just estimate of the filthiness of the pleasures of adulterous love, but he that has first made a just estimate of the purity of conjugial love? As I have now completed the treatise ON CONJUGIAL LOVE AND ITS CHASTE DELIGHTS, I am enabled, from the intelligence I thence acquired, to describe the pleasures respecting adulterous love.

425. II. ADULTEROUS LOVE IS OPPOSED TO CONJUGIAL LOVE. Every thing in the universe has its opposite; and opposites, in regard to each other, are not relatives, but contraries. Relatives are what exist between the greatest and the least of the same thing; whereas contraries arise from an opposite in contrariety thereto; and the latter are relatives in regard to each other, as the former are in their regard one to another; wherefore also the relations themselves are opposites. That all things have their

opposites, is evident from light, heat, the times of the world, affections, perceptions, sensations, and several other things. The opposite of light is darkness; the opposite of heat is cold; of the times of the world the opposites are day and night, summer and winter; of affections the opposites are joys and mourning, also gladnesses and sadnesses; of perceptions the opposites are goods and evils, also truths and falses; and of sensations the opposites are things delightful and things undelightful. Hence it may be evidently concluded, that conjugial love has its opposite; this opposite is adultery, as every one may see, if he be so disposed, from all the dictates of sound reason. Tell, if you can, what else is its opposite. It is an additional evidence in favor of this position, that as sound reason was enabled to see the truth of it by her own light, therefore she has enacted laws, which are called laws of civil justice, in favor of marriages and against adulteries. That the truth of this position may appear yet more manifest, I may relate what I have very often seen in the spiritual world. When those who in the natural world have been confirmed adulterers, perceive a sphere of conjugial love flowing down from heaven, they instantly either flee away into caverns and hide themselves, or, if they persist obstinately in contrariety to it, they grow fierce with rage, and become like furies. The reason why they are so affected is, because all things of the affections, whether delightful or undelightful, are perceived in that world, and on some occasions as clearly as an odor is perceived by the sense of smelling; for the inhabitants of that world have not a material body, which absorbs such things. The reason why the opposition of adulterous love and conjugial love is unknown to many in the world, is owing to the delights of the flesh, which, in the extremes, seem to imitate the delights of conjugial love; and those who are in delights only, do not know anything respecting that opposition; and I can venture to say, that should you assert, that everything has its opposite, and should conclude that conjugial love also has its opposite, adulterers will reply, that that love has not an opposite, because adulterous love cannot be distinguished from it; from which circumstance it is further manifest, that he that does not know what conjugial love is, does not know what adulterous love is; and moreover, that from adulterous love it is not known what conjugial love is, but from conjugial love it is known what adulterous love is. No one knows good from evil, but evil from good; for evil is in darkness, whereas good is in light.

426. III. ADULTEROUS LOVE IS OPPOSED TO CONJUGIAL LOVE, AS THE NATURAL MAN VIEWED IN HIMSELF IS OPPOSED TO THE SPIRITUAL MAN. That the natural man and the spiritual are opposed to each other, so that the one does not will what the other wills, yea, that they are at strife together, is well known in the church; but still it has not heretofore been explained.

We will therefore shew what is the ground of discrimination between the spiritual man and the natural, and what excites the latter against the former. The natural man is that into which every one is first introduced as he grows up, which is effected by sciences and knowledges, and by rational principles of the understanding; but the spiritual man is that into which he is introduced by the love of doing uses, which love is also called charity: wherefore so far as any one is in charity, so far he is spiritual; but so far as he is not in charity, so far he is natural, even supposing him to be ever so quick-sighted in genius, and wise in judgement. That the latter, the natural man, separate from the spiritual, notwithstanding all his elevation into the light of reason, still gives himself without restraint to the government of his lusts, and is devoted to them, is manifest from his genius alone, in that he is void of charity; and whoever is void of charity, gives loose to all the lasciviousness of adulterous love: wherefore, when he is told, that this wanton love is opposed to chaste conjugial love, and is asked to consult his rational *lumen*, he still does not consult it, except in conjunction with the delight of evil implanted from birth in the natural man; in consequence whereof he concludes, that his reason does not see anything contrary to the pleasing sensual allurements of the body; and when he has confirmed himself in those allurements, his reason is in amazement at all those pleasures which are proclaimed respecting conjugial love; yea, as was said above, he fights against them, and conquers, and, like a conqueror after the enemy's overthrow, he utterly destroys the camp of conjugial love in himself. These things are done by the natural man from the impulse of his adulterous love. We mention these circumstances, in order that it may be known, what is the true ground of the opposition of those two loves; for, as has been abundantly shewn above, conjugial love viewed in itself is spiritual love, and adulterous love viewed in itself is natural love.

427. IV. ADULTEROUS LOVE IS OPPOSED TO CONJUGIAL LOVE, AS THE CONNUBIAL CONNECTION OF WHAT IS EVIL AND FALSE IS OPPOSED TO THE MARRIAGE OF GOOD AND TRUTH. That the origin of conjugial love is from the marriage of good and truth, was demonstrated above in its proper chapter, from n. 83—102; hence it follows, that the origin of adulterous love is from the connubial connection of what is evil and false, and that hence they are opposite loves, as evil is opposed to good, and the false of evil to the truth of good. It is the delights of each love which are thus opposed; for love without its delight is not anything. That these delights are thus opposed to each other, does not at all appear: the reason why it does not appear is, because the delight of the love of evil in externals assumes a semblance of the delight of the love of good; but in internals the delight of the love of evil consists of mere concupiscences of evil, evil itself

being the conglobated mass [or glome] of those concupiscences: whereas the delight of the love of good consists of innumerable affections of good, good itself being the co-united bundle of those affections. This bundle and that glome are felt by man only as one delight; and as the delight of evil in externals assumes a semblance of the delight of good, as we have said, therefore also the delight of adultery assumes a semblance of the delight of marriage; but after death, when every one lays aside externals, and the internals are laid bare, then it manifestly appears, that the evil of adultery is a glome of the concupiscences of evil, and the good of marriage is a bundle of the affections of good: thus that they are entirely opposed to each other.

428. In reference to the connubial connection of what is evil and false, it is to be observed, that evil loves the false, and desires that it may be a one with itself, and they also unite; in like manner as good loves truth, and desires that it may be a one with itself, and they also unite: from which consideration it is evident, that as the spiritual origin of marriage is the marriage of good and truth, so the spiritual origin of adultery is the connubial connection of what is evil and false. Hence, this connubial connection is meant by adulteries, whoredoms, and fornications, in the spiritual sense of the Word; see the APOCALYPSE REVEALED, n. 134. It is from this principle, that he that is in evil, and connects himself connubially with what is false, and he that is in what is false, and draws evil into a partnership of his chamber, from the joint covenant confirms adultery, and commits it so far as he dares and has the opportunity; he confirms it from evil by what is false, and he commits it from what is false by evil: and also on the other hand, that he that is in good, and marries truth, or he that is in truth, and brings good into partnership of the chamber with himself, confirms himself against adultery, and in favor of marriage, and attains to a happy conjugial life.

429. V. HENCE ADULTEROUS LOVE IS OPPOSED TO CONJUGIAL LOVE AS HELL IS OPPOSED TO HEAVEN. All who are in hell are in the connubial connection of what is evil and false, and all who are in heaven are in the marriage of good and truth; and as the connubial connection of what is evil and false is also adultery, as was shewn just above, n. 427, 428, hell is also that connubial connection. Hence all who are in hell are in the lust, lasciviousness, and immodesty of adulterous love, and shun and dread the chastity and modesty of conjugial love; see above, n. 428. From these considerations it may be seen, that those two loves, adulterous and conjugial, are opposed to each other, as hell is to heaven, and heaven to hell.

430. VI. THE IMPURITY OF HELL IS FROM ADULTEROUS LOVE, AND THE PURITY OF HEAVEN FROM CONJUGIAL LOVE. All hell abounds with impurities, all of which originate in immo-

dest and obscene adulterous love, the delights of that love being changed into such impurities. Who can believe, that in the spiritual world, every delight of love is presented to the sight under various appearances, to the sense under various odors, and to the view under various forms of beasts and birds? The appearances under which in hell the lascivious delights of adulterous love are presented to the sight, are dunghills and mire; the odors by which they are presented to the sense, are stinks and stenches; and the forms of beasts and birds under which they are presented to the view, are hogs, serpents, and the birds called ochim and tziim. The case is reversed in regard to the chaste delights of conjugial love in heaven. The appearances under which those delights are presented to the sight, are gardens and flowery fields; the odors whereby they are presented to the sense, are the perfumes arising from fruits and the fragrancies from flowers; and the forms of animals under which they are presented to the view are lambs, kids, turtle-doves, and birds of paradise. The reason why the delights of love are changed into such and similar things is, because all things which exist in the spiritual world are correspondences: into these correspondences the internals of the minds of the inhabitants are changed, while they pass away and become external before the senses. But it is to be observed, that there are innumerable varieties of impurities, into which the lasciviousnesses of whoredoms are changed, while they pass off into their correspondences: these varieties are according to the genera and species of those lasciviousnesses, as may be seen in the following pages, where adulteries and their degrees are treated of: such impurities however do not proceed from the delights of the love of those who have repented; because they have been washed from them during their abode in the world.

431. VII. THE IMPURITY AND THE PURITY IN THE CHURCH ARE SIMILARLY CIRCUMSTANCED. The reason of this is, because the church is the Lord's kingdom in the world, corresponding to his kingdom in the heavens; and also the Lord conjoins them together, that they may make a one; for he distinguishes those who are in the world, as he distinguishes heaven and hell, according to their loves. Those who are in the immodest and obscene delights of adulterous love, associate to themselves similar spirits from hell: whereas those who are in the modest and chaste delights of conjugial love, are associated by the Lord to similar angels from heaven. While these their angels, in their attendance on man, are stationed near to confirmed and determined adulterers, they are made sensible of the direful stenches mentioned above, n. 430, and recede a little. On account of the correspondence of filthy loves with dunghills and bogs, it was commanded the sons of Israel, " That they should carry with them a paddle with which to cover their excrement, lest Jehovah God walking in the midst of their camp should see the nakedness of

the thing, and should return," Deut. xxiii. 13, 14. This was commanded, because the camp of the sons of Israel represented the church, and those unclean things corresponded to the lascivious principles of whoredoms, and by Jehovah God's walking in the midst of their camp was signified his presence with the angels. The reason why they were to cover it was, because all those places in hell, where troops of such spirits have their abode, were covered and closed up, on which account also it is said, "lest he see the nakedness of the thing." It has been granted me to see that all those places in hell are closed up, and also that when they were opened, as was the case when a new demon entered, such a horrid stench issued from them, that it infested my belly with its noisomeness; and what is wonderful, those stenches are to the inhabitants as delightful as dunghills are to swine. From these considerations it is evident, how it is to be understood, that the impurity in the church is from adulterous love, and its purity from conjugial love.

432. VIII. ADULTEROUS LOVE MORE AND MORE MAKES A MAN (*homo*) NOT A MAN (*homo*), AND A MAN (*vir*) NOT A MAN (*vir*), AND CONJUGIAL LOVE MAKES A MAN (*homo*) MORE AND MORE A MAN (*homo*), AND A MAN (*vir*). That conjugial love makes a man (*homo*) is illustrated and confirmed by all the considerations which were clearly and rationally demonstrated in the first part of this work, concerning love and the delights of its wisdom; as 1. That he that is principled in love truly conjugial, becomes more and more spiritual; and in proportion as any one is more spiritual, in the same proportion he is more a man (*homo*). 2. That he becomes more and more wise; and the wiser any one is, so much the more is he a man (*homo*). 3. That with such a one the interiors of the mind are more and more opened, insomuch that he sees or intuitively acknowledges the Lord; and the more any one is in the sight or acknowledgement, the more he is a man. 4. That he becomes more and more moral and civil, inasmuch as a spiritual soul is in his morality and civility; and the more any one is morally civil, the more he is a man. 5. That also after death he becomes an angel of heaven; and an angel is in essence and form a man; and also the genuine human principle in his face shines forth from his conversation and manners: from these considerations it is manifest, that conjugial love makes a man (*homo*) more and more a man (*homo*). That the contrary is the case with adulterers, follows as a consequence from the opposition of adultery and marriage, which is the subject treated of in this chapter; as, 1. That they are not spiritual but in the highest degree natural; and the natural man separate from the spiritual man, is a man only as to the understanding, but not as to the will: this he immerses in the body and the concupiscences of the flesh, and at those times the understanding also accompanies it. That such a

one is but half a man (*homo*), he himself may see from the reason of his understanding, in case he elevates it. 2. That adulterers are not wise, except in their conversation and behaviour, when they are in the company of such as are in high station, or as are distinguished for their learning or their morals; but that when alone with themselves they are insane, setting at nought the divine and holy things of the church, and defiling the morals of life with immodest and unchaste principles, will be shewn in the chapter concerning adulteries. Who does not see that such gesticulators are men only as to external figure, and not as to internal form? 3. That adulterers become more and more not men, has been abundantly confirmed to me by what I have myself been eye-witness to respecting them in hell: for there they are demons, and when seen in the light of heaven, appear to have their faces full of pimples, their bodies bunched out, their voice rough, and their gestures antic. But it is to be observed, that such are determined and confirmed adulterers, but not nondeliberate adulterers: for in the chapter concerning adulteries and their degrees, four kinds are treated of. Determined adulterers are those who are so from the lust of the will; confirmed adulterers are those who are so from the persuasion of the understanding; deliberate adulterers are those who are so from the allurements of the senses; and non deliberate adulterers are those who have not the faculty or the liberty of consulting the understanding. The two former kinds of adulterers are those who become more and more not men; whereas the two latter kinds become men as they recede from those errors, and afterwards become wise.

433. That conjugial love makes a man (*homo*) more a man (*vir*), is also illustrated by what was adduced in the preceding part concerning conjugial love and its delights; as, 1. That the virile faculty and power accompanies wisdom, as this is animated from the spiritual things of the church, and that hence it resides in conjugial love; and that the wisdom of this love opens a vein from its fountain in the soul, and thereby invigorates, and also blesses with permanence, to the intellectual life, which is the very essential masculine life. 2. That hence it is, that the angels of heaven are in this permanence to eternity, according to their own declarations in the MEMORABLE RELATION, n. 355, 356. That the most ancient men in the golden and silver ages, were in permanent efficacy, because they loved the caresses of their wives, and abhorred the caresses of harlots, I have heard from their own mouths; see the MEMORABLE RELATIONS, n. 75, 76. That that spiritual sufficiency is also in the natural principle, and will not be wanting to those at this day, who come to the Lord, and abominate adulteries as infernal, has been told me from heaven. But the contrary befalls determined and confirmed adulterers who are treated of above, n. 432. That the virile faculty and

power with such is weakened even till it ceases; and that after this there commences cold towards the sex; and that cold is succeeded by a kind of fastidiousness approaching to loathing, is well known, although but little talked of. That this is the case with such adulterers in hell, I have heard at a distance, from the sirens, who are obsolete venereal lusts, and also from the harlots there. From these considerations it follows, that adulterous love makes a man (*homo*) more and more not a man (*homo*) and not a man (*vir*) and that conjugial love makes a man more and more a man (*homo*) and a man (*vir*).

434. IX. THERE ARE A SPHERE OF ADULTEROUS LOVE AND A SPHERE OF CONJUGIAL LOVE. What is meant by spheres, and that they are various, and that those which are of love and wisdom proceed from the Lord, and through the angelic heavens descend into the world, and pervade it even to its ultimates, was shewn above, n. 222—225; and n. 386—397. That every thing in the universe has its opposites, may be seen above, n. 425: hence it follows, that whereas there is a sphere of conjugial love, there is also a sphere opposite to it, which is called a sphere of adulterous love; for those spheres are opposed to each other, as the love of adultery is opposed the love of marriage. This opposition has been treated of in the preceding parts of this chapter.

435. X. THE SPHERE OF ADULTEROUS LOVE ASCENDS FROM HELL, AND THE SPHERE OF CONJUGIAL LOVE DESCENDS FROM HEAVEN. That the sphere of conjugial love descends from heaven, was shewn in the places cited just above, n. 434; but the reason why the sphere of adulterous love ascends from hell, is, because this love is from thence, see n. 429. That sphere ascends thence from the impurities into which the delights of adultery are changed with those who are of each sex there; concerning which delight see above, n. 430, 431.

436. XI. THOSE TWO SPHERES MEET EACH OTHER IN EACH WORLD; BUT THEY DO NOT UNITE. By each world is meant the spiritual world and the natural world. In the spiritual world those spheres meet each other in the world of spirits, because this is the medium between heaven and hell; but in the natural world they meet each other in the rational plane appertaining to man, which also is the medium between heaven and hell: for the marriage of good and truth flows into it from above, and the marriage of evil and the false flows into it from beneath. The latter marriage flows in through the world, but the former through heaven. Hence it is, that the human rational principle can turn itself to either side as it pleases, and receive influx. If it turns to good, it receives it from above; and in this case the man's rational principle is formed more and more to the reception of heaven; but if it turns itself to evil, it receives that influx from beneath; and in this case the man's rational principle is formed more and more to the reception of hell. The reason why those two spheres

do not unite, is, because they are opposites; and an opposite acts upon an opposite like enemies, one of whom, burning with deadly hatred, furiously assaults the other, while the other is in no hatred, but only endeavours to defend himself. From these considerations it is evident, that those two spheres only meet each other, but do not unite. The middle interstice, which they make, is on the one part from the evil not of the false, and from the false not of the evil, and on the other part from good not of truth, and from truth not of good; which two may indeed touch each other, but still they do not unite.

437. XII. BETWEEN THOSE TWO SPHERES THERE IS AN EQUILIBRIUM, AND MAN IS IN IT. The equilibrium between them is a spiritual equilibrium, because it is between good and evil; from this equilibrium a man has free will, in and by which he thinks and wills, and hence speaks and acts as from himself. His rational principle consists in his having the option to receive either good or evil; consequently, whether he will freely and rationally dispose himself to conjugial love, or to adulterous love; if to the latter, he turns the hinder part of the head, and the back to the Lord; if to the former, he turns the fore part of the head and the breast to the Lord; if to the Lord, his rationality and liberty are led by himself; but if backwards from the Lord, his rationality and liberty are led by hell.

438. XIII. A MAN CAN TURN HIMSELF TO WHICHEVER SPHERE HE PLEASES; BUT SO FAR AS HE TURNS HIMSELF TO THE ONE, SO FAR HE TURNS HIMSELF FROM THE OTHER. Man was created so that he may do whatever he does freely, according to reason, and altogether as from himself: without these two faculties he would not be a man but a beast; for he would not receive any thing flowing from heaven, and appropriate it to himself as his own, and consequently it would not be possible for anything of eternal life to be inscribed on him; for this must be inscribed on him as his, in order that it may be his own; and whereas there is no freedom on the one part, unless there be also a like freedom on the other, as it would be impossible to weigh a thing, unless the scales from an equilibrium could incline to either side: so, unless a man had liberty from reason to draw near also to evil, thus to turn from the right to the left, and from the left to the right, in like manner to the infernal sphere, which is that of adultery, as to the celestial sphere, which is that of marriage, [it would be impossible for him to receive any thing flowing from heaven, and to appropriate it to himself.*]

439. XIV. EACH SPHERE BRINGS WITH IT DELIGHTS; that is, both the sphere of adulterous love which ascends from hell, and the sphere of conjugial love which descends from heaven, affects the recipient man (*homo*) with delights; because the ultimate

---

* The part within the brackets is inserted to supply what appears to be an omission in the original.

plane, in which the delights of each love terminate, and where they fill and complete themselves, and which exhibits them in their own proper sensory, is the same. Hence, in the extremes, adulterous caresses and conjugial caresses are perceived as similar, although in internals they are altogether dissimilar; that hence they are also dissimilar in the extremes, is a point not decided from any sense of discrimination; for dissimilitudes are not made sensible from their discriminations in the extremes, to any others than those who are principled in love truly conjugial; for evil is known from good, but not good from evil; so neither is a sweet scent perceived by the nose when a disagreeable one is present in it. I have heard from the angels, that they distinguish in the extremes what is lascivious from what is not, as any one distinguishes the fire of a dunghill or of burnt horn by its bad smell, from the fire of spices or of burnt cinnamon by its sweet smell; and that this arises from their distinction of the internal delights which enter into the external and compose them.

440. XV. THE DELIGHTS OF ADULTEROUS LOVE COMMENCE FROM THE FLESH AND ARE OF THE FLESH EVEN IN THE SPIRIT; BUT THE DELIGHTS OF CONJUGIAL LOVE COMMENCE IN THE SPIRIT AND ARE OF THE SPIRIT EVEN IN THE FLESH. The reason why the delights of adulterous love commence from the flesh is, because the stimulant heats of the flesh are their beginnings. The reason why they infect the spirit and are of the flesh even in the spirit, is, because the spirit, and not the flesh, is sensible of those things which happen in the flesh. The case is the same with this sense as with the rest: as that the eye does not see and discern various particulars in objects, but they are seen and discerned by the spirit; neither does the ear hear and discern the harmonies of tunes in singing, and the concordances of the articulation of sounds in speech, but they are heard and discerned by the spirit; moreover, the spirit is sensible of every thing according to its elevation in wisdom. The spirit that is not elevated above the sensual things of the body, and thereby adheres to them, is not sensible of any other delights than those which flow in from the flesh and the world through the senses of the body: these delights it seizes upon, is delighted with, and makes its own. Now, since the beginnings of adulterous love are only the stimulant fires and itchings of the flesh, it is evident, that these things in the spirit are filthy allurements, which, as they ascend and descend, and reciprocate, so they excite and inflame. In general the cupidities of the flesh are nothing but the accumulated concupiscences of what is evil and false: hence comes this truth in the church, that the flesh lusts against the spirit, that is, against the spiritual man; wherefore it follows, that the delights of the flesh, as to the delights of adulterous love, are nothing but the effervescences of lusts, which in the spirit become the ebullitions of immodesty.

441. But the delights of conjugial love have nothing in common with the filthy delights of adulterous love: the latter indeed are in the spirit of every man; but they are separated and removed, as the man's spirit is elevated above the sensual things of the body, and from its elevation sees their appearances and fallacies beneath: in this case it perceives fleshly delights, first as apparent and fallacious, afterwards as libidinous and lascivious, which ought to be shunned, and successively as damnable and hurtful to the soul, and at length it has a sense of them as being undelightful, disagreeable, and nauseous; and in the degree that it thus perceives and is sensible of these delights, in the same degree also it perceives the delights of conjugial love as innocent and chaste, and at length as delicious and blessed. The reason why the delights of conjugial love become also delights of the spirit in the flesh, is, because after the delights of adulterous love are removed, as was just said above, the spirit being loosed from them enters chaste into the body, and fills the breasts with the delights of its blessedness, and from the breasts fills also the ultimates of that love in the body; in consequence whereof, the spirit with these ultimates, and these ultimates with the spirits, afterwards act in full communion.

442. XVI. THE DELIGHTS OF ADULTEROUS LOVE ARE THE PLEASURES OF INSANITY; BUT THE DELIGHTS OF CONJUGIAL LOVE ARE THE DELIGHTS OF WISDOM. The reason why the delights of adulterous love are the pleasures of insanity is, because none but natural men are in that love, and the natural man is insane in spiritual things, for he is contrary to them, and therefore he embraces only natural, sensual, and corporeal delights. It is said that he embraces natural, sensual, and corporeal delights, because the natural principle is distinguished into three degrees: in the supreme degree are those natural men who from rational sight see insanities, and are still carried away by the delights thereof, as boats by the stream of a river; in a lower degree are the natural men who only see and judge from the senses of the body, despising and rejecting, as of no account, the rational principles which are contrary to appearances and fallacies; in the lowest degree are the natural men who without judgement are carried away by the alluring stimulant heats of the body. These last are called natural-corporeal, the former are called natural-sensual, but the first natural. With these men, adulterous love and its insanities and pleasures are of similar degrees.

443. The reason why the delights of conjugial love are the delights of wisdom is, because none but spiritual men are in that love, and the spiritual man is in wisdom; and hence he embraces no delights but such as agree with spiritual wisdom. The respective qualities of the delights of adulterous and of conjugial love, may be elucidated by a comparison with houses: the delights of adulterous love by comparison with a house whose

walls glitter outwardly like sea shells, or like transparent stones, called selenites, of a gold color; whereas in the apartments within the walls, are all kinds of filth and nastiness: but the delights of conjugial love may be compared to a house, the walls of which are refulgent as with sterling gold, and the apartments within are resplendent as with cabinets full of various precious stones.

* * * * * * *

444. To the above I shall add the following MEMORABLE RELATION. After I had concluded the meditations on conjugial love, and had begun those on adulterous love, on a sudden two angels presented themselves, and said, "We have perceived and understood what you have heretofore meditated upon; but the things upon which you are now meditating pass away, and we do not perceive them. Say nothing about them, for they are of no value." But I replied, "This love, on which I am now meditating, is not of no value; because it exists." But they said, "How can there be any love, which is not from creation? Is not conjugial love from creation; and does not this love exist between two who are capable of becoming one? How can there be a love which divides and separates? What youth can love any other maiden than the one who loves him in return? Must not the love of the one know and acknowledge the love of the other, so that when they meet they may unite of themselves? Who can love what is not love? Is not conjugial love alone mutual and reciprocal? If it be not reciprocal, does it not rebound and become nothing?" On hearing this, I asked the two angels from what society of heaven they were? They said, "We are from the heaven of innocence; we came infants into this heavenly world, and were educated under the Lord's auspices; and when I became a young man, and my wife, who is here with me, marriageable, we were betrothed and entered into a contract, and were joined under the first favorable impressions; and as we were unacquainted with any other love than what is truly nuptial and conjugial, therefore, when we were made acquainted with the ideas of your thought concerning a strange love directly opposed to our love, we could not at all comprehend it; and we have descended in order to ask you, why you meditate on things that cannot be understood? Tell us, therefore, how a love, which not only is not from creation, but is also contrary to creation, could possibly exist? We regard things opposite to creation as objects of no value." As they said this, I rejoiced in heart that I was permitted to converse with angels of such innocence, as to be entirely ignorant of the nature and meaning of adultery: wherefore I was free to converse with them, and I instructed them as follows: "Do you not know, that there exist both good and evil, and that good is from creation, but not evil; and still that evil viewed in itself is not

nothing, although it is nothing of good? From creation there exists good, and also good in the greatest degree and in the least; and when this least becomes nothing, there rises up on the other side evil: wherefore there is no relation or progression of good to evil, but a relation and progression of good to a greater and less good, and of evil to a greater and less evil; for in all things there are opposites. And since good and evil are opposites, there is an intermediate, and in it an equilibrium, in which evil acts against good; but as it does not prevail, it stops in a *conatus*. Every man is educated in this equilibrium, which, because it is between good and evil, or, what is the same, between heaven and hell, is a spiritual equilibrium, which, with those who are in it, produces a state of freedom. From this equilibrium, the Lord draws all to himself; and if a man freely follows, he leads him out of evil into good, and thereby into heaven. The case is the same with love, especially with conjugial love and adultery: the latter love is evil, but the former good. Every man that hears the voice of the Lord, and freely follows, is introduced by the Lord into conjugial love and all its delights and satisfactions; but he that does not hear and follow, introduces himself into adulterous love, first into its delights, afterwards into what is undelightful, and lastly into what is unsatisfactory." When I had thus spoken, the two angels asked me, "How could evil exist, when nothing but good had existed from creation? The existence of anything implies that it must have an origin. Good could not be the origin of evil, because evil is nothing of good, being privative and destructive of good; nevertheless, since it exists and is sensibly felt, it is not nothing, but something; tell us therefore whence this something existed after nothing." To this I replied, "This arcanum cannot be explained, unless it be known that no one is good but God alone, and that there is not anything good, which in itself is good, but from God; wherefore he that looks to God, and wishes to be led by God, is in good; but he that turns himself from God, and wishes to be led by himself, is not in good; for the good which he does, is for the sake either of himself or of the world; thus it is either meritorious, or pretended, or hypocritical: from which considerations it is evident, that man himself is the origin of evil; not that that origin was implanted in him by creation; but that he, by turning from God to himself, implanted it in himself. That origin of evil was not in Adam and his wife; but when the serpent said, " In the day that ye shall eat of the tree of the knowledge of good and evil, ye shall be as God" (Gen. iii. 5), they then made in themselves the origin of evil, because they turned themselves from God, and turned to themselves, as to God. *To eat of that tree, signifies to believe that they knew good and evil, and were wise, from themselves, and not from God.*" But the two angels then asked, "How could man turn himself from God, and turn to himself, when yet he cannot will, think, and thence do anything but from God? Why did God permit this?" I replied, "Man was so created, that whatever he wills, thinks, and does, appears to him as in himself, and thereby from himself: without this appearance a man would not be a man; for he would be incapable of receiving, retaining, and as it were appropriating to himself anything of good and truth, or of love and wisdom: whence it follows, that without such appearance, as a living appearance, a man would not have conjunction with God, and consequently neither would he have eternal life. But if from this appearance he induces in himself a belief that he wills, thinks, and thence does good from himself, and not from the Lord, although in all appearance as from himself, he turns good into evil with himself, and thereby makes in himself the origin of evil. This was the sin of Adam. But I will explain this matter somewhat more clearly. The Lord looks at every man in the forepart of his head, and this inspection passes into the hinder part of his head. Beneath the forepart is the *cerebrum*, and beneath the hinder part is the *cerebellum;* the latter was designed for love and the goods thereof, and the former for wisdom and the truths thereof; wherefore he that looks with the face to the Lord receives from him wisdom, and by wisdom love; but he that looks backward from the Lord receives love and not wisdom; and love without wisdom, is love from man and not from the Lord; and this love, since it conjoins itself with falses, does not acknowledge God, but acknowledges itself for God, and confirms this tacitly by the faculty of understanding and growing wise implanted in it from creation as from itself; wherefore this love is the origin of evil. That this is the case, will admit of ocular demonstration. I will call hither some wicked spirit who turns himself from God, and will speak to him from behind, or into the hinder part of the head, and you will see that the things which are said are turned into their contraries." I called such a spirit and he presented himself, and I spoke to him from behind and said, " Do you know anything about hell, damnation, and torment in hell?" And presently, when he was turned to me, I asked him what he heard? He said, "I heard, 'Do you know anything concerning heaven, salvation, and happiness in heaven?'" and afterwards when the latter words were said to him from behind, he said that he heard the former. It was next said to him from behind, "Do you know that those who are in hell are insane from falses?" and when I asked him concerning these words what he heard, he said, " I heard, ' Do you know that those who are in heaven are wise from truths?'" and when the latter words were spoken to him from behind, he said tha he heard, "Do you know that those who are in hell, are insan from falses? and so in other instances: from which it evidently appears, that when the mind turns itself from the Lord, it turns to itself, and then it perceives things contrary. This, as you know, is the reason why, in this spiritual world, no one is allowed to stand behind another, and to speak to him; for thereby there is inspired into him a love, which his own intelligence favors and obeys for the sake of its delight; but since it is from man, and not from God, it is a love of evil, or a love of the false. In addition to the above, I will relate to you another similar circumstance. On certain occasions I have heard goods and truths let down from heaven into hell; and in hell they were progressively turned into their opposites, good into evil, and truth into the false; the cause of this, the same as above, because all in hell turn themselves from the Lord,." On hearing these two things the two angels thanked me, and said, "As you are now meditating and writing concerning a love opposite to our conjugial love, and the opposite to that love makes our minds sad, we will depart;" and when they said, "Peace be unto you," I besought them not to mention that love to their brethren and sisters in heaven, because it would hurt their innocence. I can positively assert that those who die infants, grow up in heaven, and when they attain the stature which is common to young men of eighteen years old in the world, and to maidens of fifteen years, they remain of that stature; and further, that both before marriage and after it, they are entirely ignorant what adultery is, and that such a thing can exist.

ON FORNICATION.

444.* FORNICATION means the lust of a grown up man or youth with a woman, a harlot, before marriage; but lust with a woman, not a harlot, that is, with a maiden or with another's wife, is not fornication; with a maiden it is the act of deflowering, and with another's wife it is adultery. In what manner these two differ from fornication, cannot be seen by any rational being unless he takes a clear view of the love of the sex in its degrees and diversities, and of its chaste principles on the one part, and of its unchaste principles on the other, arranging each part into genera and species, and thereby distinguishing them. Without such a view and arrangement, it is impossible there should exist in any one's idea a discrimination between the chaste principle as to more and less, and between the unchaste principle as to more and less; and without these distinctions all relation perishes, and therewith all perspicacity in matters of judgement, and the understanding is involved in such a shade, that it does not know how to distinguish fornication from adultery, and still less the milder kinds of fornication from the more grievous, and in like manner of adultery; thus it mixes evils, and of different evils makes one pottage, and of different goods one paste. In order therefore that the love of the sex may be distinctly known as to that part by which it inclines and makes advances to adulterous love altogether opposite to conjugial love, it is expedient to examine its beginning, which is fornication; and this we will do in the following series: I. *Fornication is of the love of the sex.* II. *This love commences when a youth begins to think and act from his own understanding, and his voice to be masculine.* III. *Fornication is of the natural man.* IV. *Fornication is lust, but not the lust of adultery.* V. *With some men the love of the sex cannot without hurt be totally checked from going forth into fornication.* VI. *Therefore in populous cities public stews are tolerated.* VII. *The lust of fornication is light, so far as it looks to conjugial love, and gives this love the preference.* VIII. *The lust of fornication is grievous, so far as it looks to adultery.* IX. *The lust of fornication is more grievous, as it verges to the desire of varieties and of defloration.* X. *The sphere of the lust of fornication, such as it is in the beginning, is a middle sphere between the sphere of adulterous love and the sphere of conjugial love, and makes an equilibrium.* XI. *Care is to be taken, lest, by inordinate and immoderate fornications, conjugial love be destroyed.* XII. *Inasmuch as the conjugial principle of one man with one wife is the jewel of human life and the reservoir of the Christian religion.* XIII. *With those who, from various reasons, cannot as yet enter into marriage, and from their passion for the sex, cannot restrain their lusts, this conjugial principle may be preserved, if the vague love of the sex be confined to one mistress.* XIV. *Keeping a mistress is preferable to vague amours, if only one is kept, and she be neither a maiden nor a married woman, and the love of the mistress be kept separate from conjugial love.* We proceed to an explanation of each article.

445. I. FORNICATION IS OF THE LOVE OF THE SEX. We say that fornication is of the love of the sex, because it is not the love of the sex but is derived from it. The love of the sex is like a fountain, from which both conjugial and adulterous love may be derived; they may also be derived by means of fornication, and also without it: for the love of the sex is in every man (*homo*), and either does or does not put itself forth: if it puts itself forth before marriage with a harlot, it is called fornication; if not until with a wife, it is called marriage; if after marriage with another woman, it is called adultery: wherefore, as we have said, the love of the sex is like a fountain, from which may flow both chaste and unchaste love: but with what caution and prudence chaste conjugial love can proceed by fornication, yet from what imprudence unchaste or adulterous love can proceed thereby, we will explain in what follows. Who can draw

the conclusion, that he that has committed fornication cannot be more chaste in marriage?

446. II. THE LOVE OF THE SEX, FROM WHICH FORNICATION IS DERIVED, COMMENCES WHEN A YOUTH BEGINS TO THINK AND ACT FROM HIS OWN UNDERSTANDING, AND HIS VOICE TO BE MASCULINE. This article is adduced to the intent, that the birth of the love of the sex, and thence of fornication, may be known, as taking place when the understanding begins of itself to become rational, or from its own reason to discern and provide such things as are of emolument and use, whereto in such case what has been implanted in the memory from parents and masters, serves as a plane. At that time a change takes place in the mind; it before thought only from things introduced into the memory, by meditating upon and obeying them; it afterwards thinks from reason exercised upon them, and then, under the guidance of the love, it arranges into a new order the things seated in the memory, and in agreement with that order it disposes its own life, and successively thinks more and more according to its own reason, and wills from its own freedom. It is well known that the love of the sex follows the commencement of a man's own understanding, and advances according to its vigor; and this is a proof that that love ascends and descends as the understanding ascends and descends: by ascending we mean into wisdom, and by descending, into insanity; and wisdom consists in restraining the love of the sex, and insanity in allowing it a wide range: if it be allowed to run into fornication, which is the beginning of its activity, it ought to be moderated from principles of honor and morality implanted in the memory and thence in the reason, and afterwards to be implanted in the reason and in the memory. The reason why the voice also begins to be masculine, together with the commencement of a man's own understanding, is, because the understanding thinks, and by thought speaks; which is a proof that the understanding constitutes the man (*vir*), and also his male principle; consequently, that as his understanding is elevated, so he becomes a man-man (*homo vir*), and also a male man (*masculus vir*); see above, n. 432, 433.

447. III. FORNICATION IS OF THE NATURAL MAN, in like manner as the love of the sex, which, if it becomes active before marriage, is called fornication. Every man (*homo*) is born corporeal, becomes sensual, afterwards natural, and successively rational; and, if in this case he does not stop in his progress, he becomes spiritual. The reason why he thus advances step by step, is, in order that planes may be formed, on which superior principles may rest and find support, as a palace on its foundations: the ultimate plane, with those that are formed upon it, may also be compared to ground, in which, when prepared, noble seeds are sown. As to what specifically regards the love of the

sex, it also is first corporeal, for it commences from the flesh: next it becomes sensual, for the five senses receive delight from its common principle; afterwards it becomes natural like the same love with other animals, because it is a vague love of the sex; but as a man was born to become spiritual, it becomes afterwards natural-rational, and from natural-rational spiritual, and lastly spiritual-natural; and in this case, that love made spiritual flows into and acts upon rational love, and through this flows into and acts upon sensual love, and lastly through this flows into and acts upon that love in the body and the flesh; and as this is its ultimate plane, it acts upon it spiritually, and at the same time rationally and sensually; and it flows in and acts thus successively while the man is meditating upon it, but simultaneously while he is in its ultimate. The reason why fornication is of the natural man, is, because it proceeds proximately from the natural love of the sex; and it may become natural-rational, but not spiritual, because the love of the sex cannot become spiritual, until it becomes conjugial; and the love of the sex from natural becomes spiritual, when a man recedes from vague lust, and devotes himself to one of the sex, to whose soul he unites his own.

448. IV. FORNICATION IS LUST, BUT NOT THE LUST OF ADULTERY. The reasons why fornication is lust are, 1. Because it proceeds from the natural man, and in everything which proceeds from the natural man, there is concupiscence and lust; for the natural man is nothing but an abode and receptacle of concupiscences and lust, since all the criminal propensities inherited from the parents reside therein. 2. Because the fornicator has a vague and promiscuous regard to the sex, and does not as yet confine his attention to one of the sex; and so long as he is in this state, he is prompted by lust to do what he does; but in proportion as he confines his attention to one of the sex, and loves to conjoin his life with hers, concupiscence becomes a chaste affection, and lust becomes human love.

449. That the lust of fornication is not the lust of adultery, every one sees clearly from common perception. What law and what judge imputes a like criminality to the fornicator as to the adulterer? The reason why this is seen from common perception is, because fornication is not opposed to conjugial love as adultery is. In fornication conjugial love may lie stored up within, as what is spiritual may lie stored up in what is natural; yea, what is spiritual is also actually disengaged from what is natural; and when the spiritual is disengaged, then the natural encompasses it, as bark does its wood, and a scabbard its sword and also serves the spiritual as a defence against violence. From these considerations it is evident, that natural love, which is love to the sex, precedes spiritual love which is love to one of the sex; but if fornication comes into effect from the natural love of the sex, it may also be wiped away, provided conjugial love be regarded,

desired, and sought, as the chief good. It is altogether otherwise with the libidinous and obscene love of adultery, which we have shewn to be opposite to conjugial love, and destructive thereof, in the foregoing chapter concerning the opposition of adulterous and conjugial love: wherefore if a confirmed and determined adulterer for various reasons enters into a conjugial engagement, the above case is inverted, since a natural principle lies concealed within its lascivious and obscene things, and a spiritual appearance covers it externally. From these considerations reason may see, that the lust of limited fornication is, in respect to the lust of adultery, as the first warmth is to the cold of mid-winter in northern countries.

450. V. WITH SOME MEN THE LOVE OF THE SEX CANNOT WITHOUT HURT BE TOTALLY CHECKED FROM GOING FORTH INTO FORNICATION. It is needless to recount the mischiefs which may be caused and produced by too great a check of the love of the sex, with such persons as labor under a superabundant venereal heat; from this source are to be traced the origins of certain diseases of the body and distempers of the mind, not to mention unknown evils, which are not to be named; it is otherwise with those whose love of the sex is so scanty that they can resist the sallies of its lust; also with those who are at liberty to introduce themselves into a legitimate partnership of the bed while they are young, without doing injury to their worldly fortunes, thus under the first favorable impressions. As this is the case in heaven with infants, when they have grown up to conjugial age, therefore it is unknown there what fornication is: but the case is different in the world where matrimonial engagements cannot be contracted till the season of youth is past, and where, during that season, the generality live within forms of government, where a length of time is required to perform duties, and to acquire the property necessary to support a house and family, and then first a suitable wife is to be courted*.

451. VI. THEREFORE IN POPULOUS CITIES PUBLIC STEWS ARE TOLERATED. This is adduced as a confirmation of the preceding article. It is well known that they are tolerated by kings, magistrates, and thence by judges, inquisitors, and the people, at London, Amsterdam, Paris, Vienna, Venice, Naples, and even at Rome, besides many other places: among the reasons of this toleration are those also above mentioned.

452. VII. FORNICATION IS [COMPARATIVELY] LIGHT SO FAR AS IT LOOKS TO CONJUGIAL LOVE AND GIVES THIS LOVE THE PREFERENCE. There are degrees of the qualities of evil, as there are

---

* This, like some other of the author's remarks, is not so applicable to English laws and customs as to those of several of the continental states, especially Germany, where men are not allowed to marry till they have attained a certain age, or can show that they possess the means of supporting a wife and family.

degrees of the qualities of good; wherefore every evil is lighter and more grievous, as every good is better and more excellent. The case is the same with fornication; which, as being a lust, and a lust of the natural man not yet purified, is an evil; but as every man (*homo*) is capable of being purified, therefore so far as it approaches a purified state, so far that evil becomes lighter, for so far it is wiped away; thus so far as fornication approaches conjugial love, which is a purified state of the love of the sex, [so far it becomes a lighter evil]: that the evil of fornication is more grievous, so far as it approaches the love of adultery, will be seen in the following article. The reason why fornication is light so far as it looks to conjugial love, is, because it then looks from the unchaste state wherein it is, to a chaste state; and so far as it gives a preference to the latter, so far also it is in it as to the understanding; and so far as it not only prefers it, but also pre-loves it, so far also it is in it as to the will, thus as to the internal man; and in this case fornication, if the man nevertheless persists in it, is to him a necessity, the causes whereof he well examines in himself. There are two reasons which render fornication light with those who prefer and pre-love the conjugial state; the first is, that conjugial life is their purpose, intention, or end, the other is, that they separate good from evil with themselves. In regard to the FIRST,—that conjugial life is their purpose, intention, or end, it has the above effect, inasmuch as every man is such as he is in his purpose, intention, or end, and is also such before the Lord and the angels; yea, he is likewise regarded as such by the wise in the world; for intention is the soul of all actions, and causes innocence and guilt in the world, and after death imputation. In regard to the OTHER reason,—that those who prefer conjugial love to the lust of fornication, separate evil from good, thus what is unchaste from what is chaste, it has the above effect, inasmuch as those who separate those two principles by perception and intention, before they are in good or the chaste principle, are also separated and purified from the evil of that lust, when they come into the conjugial state. That this is not the case with those who in fornication look to adultery, will be seen in the next article.

453. VIII. THE LUST OF FORNICATION IS GRIEVOUS, SO FAR AS IT LOOKS TO ADULTERY. In the lust of fornication all those look to adultery who do not believe adulteries to be sins, and who think similarly of marriage and of adulteries, only with the distinction of what is allowed and what is not; these also make one evil out of all evils, and mix them together, like dirt with eatable food in one dish, and like things vile and refuse with wine in one cup, and thus eat and drink: in this manner they act with the love of the sex, fornication and keeping a mistress, with adultery of a milder sort, of a grievous sort, and of a more grievous sort, yea with ravishing or defloration: moreover, they not only

mingle all those things, but also mix them in marriages, and defile the latter with a like notion; but where it is the case, that the latter are not distinguished from the former, such persons, after their vague commerce with the sex, are overtaken by colds, loathings, and nauseousness, at first in regard to a married partner, next in regard to women in other characters, and lastly in regard to the sex. It is self-evident that with such persons there is no purpose, intention, or end, of what is good or chaste, that they may be exculpated, and no separation of evil from good, or of what is unchaste from what is chaste, that they may be purified, as in the case of those who from fornication look to conjugial love, and give the latter the preference, (concerning whom, see the foregoing article, n. 452). The above observations I am allowed to confirm by this new information from heaven: I have met with several, who in the world had lived outwardly like others, wearing rich apparel, feasting daintily, trading like others with money, borrowed upon interest, frequenting stage exhibitions, conversing jocosely on love affairs as from wantonness, besides other similar things: and yet the angels charged those things upon some as evils of sin, and upon others as not evils, and declared the latter guiltless, but the former guilty; and on being questioned why they did so, when the deeds were alike, they replied, that they regard all from purpose, intention, or end, and distinguish accordingly; and that on this account they excuse and condemn those whom the end excuses and condemns, since all in heaven are influenced by a good end, and all in hell by an evil end; and that this, and nothing else, is meant by the Lord's words, *Judge not, that ye be not judged,* Matt. vii. 1.

454. IX. THE LUST OF FORNICATION IS MORE GRIEVOUS AS IT VERGES TO THE DESIRE OF VARIETIES AND OF DEFLORATION. The reason of this is, because these two desires are accessories of adulteries, and thus aggravations of it: for there are mild adulteries, grievous adulteries, and most grievous; and each kind is estimated according to its opposition to, and consequent destruction of, conjugial love. That the desire of varieties and the desire of defloration, strengthened by being brought into act, destroy conjugial love, and drown it as it were in the bottom of the sea, will be seen presently, when those subjects come to be treated of.

455. X. THE SPHERE OF THE LUST OF FORNICATION, SUCH AS IT IS IN THE BEGINNING, IS A MIDDLE SPHERE BETWEEN THE SPHERE OF ADULTEROUS LOVE AND THE SPHERE OF CONJUGIAL LOVE, AND MAKES AN EQUILIBRIUM. The two spheres, of adulterous love and conjugial love, were treated of in the foregoing chapter, where it was shewn that the sphere of adulterous love ascends from hell, and the sphere of conjugial love descends from heaven, n. 435; that those two spheres meet each other in each world, but do not unite, n. 436; that between those two spheres there is an equilibrium, and that man is in it, n. 437;

that a man can turn himself to whichever sphere he pleases; but that so far as he turns himself to the one, so far he turns himself from the other, n. 438 : for the meaning of spheres, see n. 434, and the passages there cited. The reason why the sphere of the lust of fornication is a middle sphere between those two spheres, and makes an equilibrium, is, because while any one is in it, he can turn himself to the sphere of conjugial love, that is, to this love, and also to the sphere of the love of adultery, that is, to the love of adultery; but if he turns himself to conjugial love, he turns himself to heaven; if to the love of adultery, he turns himself to hell : each is in the man's free determination, good pleasure, and will, to the intent that he may act freely according to reason, and not from instinct : consequently that he may be a man, and appropriate to himself influx, and not a beast, which appropriates nothing thereof to itself. It is said the lust of fornication such as it is in the beginning, because at that time it is in a middle state. Who does not know that whatever a man does in the beginning, is from concupiscence, because from the natural man? And who does not know that that concupiscence is not imputed, while from natural he is becoming spiritual? The case is similar in regard to the lust of fornication, while a man's love is becoming conjugial.

456. XI. CARE IS TO BE TAKEN LEST, BY IMMODERATE AND INORDINATE FORNICATIONS, CONJUGIAL LOVE BE DESTROYED. By immoderate and inordinate fornications, whereby conjugial love is destroyed, we mean fornications by which not only the strength is enervated, but also all the delicacies of conjugial love are taken away; for from unbridled indulgence in such fornications, not only weakness and consequent wants, but also impurities and immodesties are occasioned, by reason of which conjugial love cannot be perceived and felt in its purity and chastity, and thus neither in its sweetness and the delights of its prime; not to mention the mischiefs occasioned to both the body and the mind, and also the disavowed allurements, which not only deprive conjugial love of its blessed delights, but also take it away, and change it into cold, and thereby into loathing. Such fornications are the violent excesses whereby conjugial sports are changed into tragic scenes : for immoderate and inordinate fornications are like burning flames which, arising out of ultimates, consume the body, parch the fibres, defile the blood, and vitiate the rational principles of the mind; for they burst forth like a fire from the foundation into the house, which consumes the whole. To prevent these mischiefs is the duty of parents; for a grown up youth, inflamed with lust, cannot as yet from reason impose restraint upon himself.

457. XII. INASMUCH AS THE CONJUGIAL PRINCIPLE OF ONE MAN WITH ONE WIFE IS THE JEWEL OF HUMAN LIFE AND THE RESERVOIR OF THE CHRISTIAN RELIGION These two points have

been demonstrated universally and singularly in the whole preceding part of Conjugial Love and its Chaste Delights. The reason why it is the jewel of human life is, because the quality of a man's life is according to the quality of that love with him; since that love constitutes the inmost of his life; for it is the life of wisdom dwelling with its love, and of love dwelling with its wisdom, and hence it is the life of the delights of each; in a word, a man is a soul living by means of that love: hence, the conjugial tie of one man with one wife is called the jewel of human life. This is confirmed from the following articles adduced above: only with one wife there exists truly conjugial friendship, confidence, and potency, because there is a union of minds, n. 333, 334: in and from a union with one wife there exist celestial blessednesses, spiritual satisfactions, and thence natural delights, which from the beginning have been provided for those who are in love truly conjugial, n. 335. That it is the fundamental love of all celestial, spiritual, and derivative natural loves, and that into that love are collected all joys and delights from first to last, n. 65—69: and that viewed in its origin, it is the sport of wisdom and love, has been fully demonstrated in the Conjugial Love and its Chaste Delights, which constitutes the first part of this work.

458. The reason why that love is the reservoir of the Christian religion is, because this religion unites and dwells with that love; for it was shewn, that none come into that love, and can be in it, but those who approach the Lord, and do the truths of his church and its goods; n. 70, 71: that that love is from the only Lord, and that hence its exists with those who are of the Christian religion; n. 131, 335, 336: that that love is according to the state of the church, because it is according to the state of wisdom with man; n. 130. That these things are so, was fully confirmed in the chapter on the correspondence of that love with the marriage of the Lord and the church; n. 116, 131; and in the chapter on the origin of that love from the marriage of good and truth; n. 83—102.

459. XIII. With those who, from various reasons, cannot as yet enter into marriage, and from their passion for the sex, cannot moderate their lusts, this conjugial principle may be preserved, if the vague love of the sex be confined to one mistress. That immoderate and inordinate lust cannot be entirely checked by those who have a strong passion for the sex, is what reason sees and experience proves: with a view therefore that such lust may be restrained, in the case of one whose passions are thus violent, and who for several reasons cannot precipitately enter into marriage, and that it may be rendered somewhat moderate and ordinate, there seems to be no other refuge, and as it were asylum, than the keeping of a woman, who in French is called *maîtresse* It is well known, that

in kingdoms, where certain forms and orders are to be observed, matrimonial engagements cannot be contracted by many till the season of youth is past; for duties are first to be performed, and property to be acquired for the support of a house and family, and then first a suitable wife is to be courted; and yet in the previous season of youth few are able to keep the springing fountain of manliness closed, and reserved for a wife: it is better indeed that it should be reserved; but if this cannot be done on account of the unbridled power of lust, a question occurs, whether there may not be an intermediate means, by which conjugial love may be prevented from perishing in the mean time. That keeping a mistress is such a means appears reasonable from the following considerations: 1. That by this means promiscuous inordinate fornications are restrained and limited, and thus a less disorderly state is induced, which more resembles conjugial life. II. That the ardor of venereal propensities, which in the beginning is boiling hot, and as it were burning, is appeased and mitigated; and thereby the lascivious passion for the sex, which is filthy, is tempered by somewhat analogous to marriage. III. By this means too the strength is not cast away, neither are weaknesses contracted, as by vague and unlimited amours. IV. By this means also disease of the body and insanity of mind are avoided. V. In like manner by this means adulteries, which are whoredoms with wives, and debaucheries, which are violations of maidens, are guarded against; to say nothing of such criminal acts as are not to be named; for a stripling does not think that adulteries and debaucheries are different from fornications; thus he conceives that the one is the same with the other; nor is he able from reason to resist the enticements of some of the sex, who are proficients in meretricious arts: but in keeping a mistress, which is a more ordinate and safer fornication, he can learn and see the above distinctions. VI. By keeping a mistress, also no entrance is afforded to the four kinds of lusts, which are in the highest degree destructive of conjugial love,—the lust of defloration, the lust of varieties, the lust of violation, and the lust of seducing innocences, which are treated of in the following pages. These observations, however, are not intended for those who can check the tide of lust; nor for those who can enter into marriage during the season of youth, and offer and impart to their wives the first fruits of their manliness.

460. XIV. KEEPING A MISTRESS IS PREFERABLE TO VAGUE AMOURS, PROVIDED ONLY ONE IS KEPT AND SHE BE NEITHER A MAIDEN NOR A MARRIED WOMAN, AND THE LOVE OF THE MISTRESS BE KEPT SEPARATE FROM CONJUGIAL LOVE. At what time and with what persons keeping a mistress is preferable to vague amours, has been pointed out just above. I. The reason why only one mistress is to be kept, is, because if more than one be kept, a polygamical principle gains influence, which induces in

a man a merely natural state, and thrusts him down into a sensual state, so much so that he cannot be elevated into a spiritual state, in which conjugial love must be; see n. 338, 339. II. The reason why this mistress must not be a maiden, is because conjugial love with women acts in unity with their virginity, and hence constitutes the chastity, purity, and sanctity of that love; wherefore when a woman makes an engagement and allotment of her virginity to any man, it is the same thing as giving him a certificate that she will love him to eternity: on this account a maiden cannot, from any rational consent, barter away her virginity, unless when entering into the conjugial covenant: it is also the crown of her honor: wherefore to seize it without a covenant of marriage, and afterwards to discard her, is to make a courtezan of a maiden, who might have been a bride or a chaste wife, or to defraud some man; and each of these is hurtful. Therefore whoever takes a maiden and unites her to himself as a mistress, may indeed dwell with her, and thereby initiate her into the friendship of love, but still with a constant intention, if he does not play the whoremaster, that she shall be or become his wife. III. That the kept mistress must not be a married woman, because this is adultery, is evident. IV. The reason why the love of a mistress is to be kept separate from conjugial love, is because those loves are distinct, and therefore ought not to be mixed together: for the love of a mistress is an unchaste, natural, and external love; whereas the love of marriage is chaste, spiritual, and internal. The love of a mistress keeps the souls of two persons distinct, and unites only the sensual principles of the body; but the love of marriage unites souls, and from their union conjoins also the sensual principles of the body, until from two they become as one, which is one flesh. V. The love of a mistress enters only into the understanding and the things which depend on it; but the love of marriage enters also into the will and the things which depend on it, consequently into every thing appertaining to man (*homo*); wherefore if the love of a mistress becomes the love of marriage, a man cannot retract from any principle of right, and without violating the conjugial union; and if he retracts and marries another woman, conjugial love perishes in consequence of the breach thereof. It is to be observed, that the love of a mistress is kept separate from conjugial love by this condition, that no engagement of marriage be made with the mistress, and that she be not induced to form any such expectation. Nevertheless it is far better that the torch of the love of the sex be first lighted with a wife.

* * * * * * *

461. To the above I shall add the following MEMORABLE RELATION. I was once conversing with a novitiate spirit who, during his abode in the world, had meditated much about heaven and hell. (Novitiate spirits are men newly deceased, who are

called spirits, because they are then spiritual men.) As soon as he entered into the spiritual world he began to meditate in like manner about heaven and hell, and seemed to himself, when meditating about heaven, to be in joy, and when about hell, in sorrow. When he observed that he was in the spiritual world, he immediately asked where heaven and hell were, and also their nature and quality? And he was answered, "Heaven is above your head, and hell beneath your feet; for you are now in the world of spirits, which is immediate between heaven and hell; but what are their nature and quality we cannot describe in a few words." At that instant, as he was very desirous of knowing, he fell upon his knees, and prayed devoutly to God that he might be instructed; and lo! an angel appeared at his right hand, and having raised him, said, "You have prayed to be instructed concerning heaven and hell; INQUIRE AND LEARN WHAT DELIGHT IS, AND YOU WILL KNOW;" and having said this, the angel was taken up. Then the novitiate spirit said within himself, "*What does this mean, Inquire and learn what delight is, and you will know the nature and quality of heaven and hell?*" And leaving that place, he wandered about, and accosting those he met, said, "Tell me, if you please, what delight is?" Some said, "What a strange question! Who does not know what delight is? Is it not joy and gladness? Wherefore delight is delight; one delight is like another; we know no distinction." Others said, that delight was the laughter of the mind; for when the mind laughs, the countenance is cheerful, the discourse is jocular, the behaviour sportive, and the whole man is in delight. But some said, "Delight consists in nothing but feasting, and delicate eating and drinking, and in getting intoxicated with generous wine, and then in conversing on various subjects, especially on the sports of Venus and Cupid." On hearing these relations, the novitiate spirit being indignant, said to himself; "These are the answers of clowns, and not of well-bred men: these delights are neither heaven nor hell; I wish I could meet with the wise." He then took his leave of them, and inquired where he might find the wise? At that instant he was seen by a certain angelic spirit, who said, "I perceive that you have a strong desire to know what is the universal of heaven and of hell; and since this is DELIGHT, I will conduct you up a hill, where there is every day an assembly of those who scrutinize effects, of those who investigate causes, and of those who explore ends. There are three companies; those who scrutinize effects are called spirits of knowledges, and abstractedly knowledges; those who investigate causes are called spirits of intelligence, and abstractedly intelligences; and those who explore ends are called spirits of wisdom, and abstractedly wisdoms. Directly above them in heaven are angels, who from ends see causes, and from causes effects; from these angels those three companies are enlightened." The angelic spirit then taking the novitiate spirit by the hand, led him up the hill to the company which consisted of those who explore ends, and are called wisdoms. To these the novitiate spirit said, "Pardon me for having ascended to you: the reason is, because from my childhood I have meditated about heaven and hell, and lately came into this world, where I was told by some who accompanied me, that here heaven was above my head, and hell beneath my feet; but they did not tell me the nature and quality of either; wherefore, becoming anxious from my thoughts being constantly employed on the subject, I prayed to God; and instantly an angel presented itself, and said, '*Inquire and learn what delight is, and you will know.*' I have inquired, but hitherto in vain: I request therefore that you will teach me, if you please, what delight is." To this the wisdoms replied, "Delight is the all of life to all in heaven and all in hell: those in delight have the delight of good and truth, but those in hell have the delight of what is evil and false; for all delight is of love, and love is the *esse* of a man's life; therefore as a man is a man according to the quality of his love, so also is he according to the quality of his delight. The activity of love makes the sense of delight; its activity in heaven is with wisdom, and in hell with insanity; each in its objects presents delight: but the heavens and the hells are in opposite delights, because in opposite loves; the heavens in the love and thence in the delight of doing good, but the hells in the love and thence in the delight of doing evil; if therefore you know what delight is, you will know the nature and quality of heaven and hell. But inquire and learn further what delight is from those who investigate causes, and are called intelligences: they are to the right from hence." He departed, and came to them, and told them the reason of his coming, and requested that they would teach him what delight is? And they, rejoicing at the question, said, "It is true that he that knows what delight is, knows the nature and quality of heaven and hell. The will-principle, by virtue whereof a man is a man, cannot be moved at all but by delight; for the will-principle, considered in itself, is nothing but an affect and effect of some love, thus of some delight; for it is somewhat pleasing, engaging, and pleasurable, which constitutes the principle of willing; and since the will moves the understanding to think, there does not exist the least idea of thought but from the influent delight of the will. The reason of this is, because the Lord by influx from himself actuates all things of the soul and the mind with angels, spirits, and men; which he does by an influx of love and wisdom; and this influx is the essential activity from which comes all delight, which in its origin is called blessed, satisfactory, and happy, and in its derivation is called delightful, pleasant, and pleasurable, and in a universal sense, GOOD. But the spirits of hell invert all things with themselves; thus they turn good into evil, and the true into the false, their delights continually remaining: for without the continuance of delight, they would have neither will nor sensation, thus no life. From these considerations may be seen the nature and origin of the delight of hell, and also the nature and origin of the delight of heaven." Having heard this, he was conducted to the third company, consisting of those who scrutinize effects, and are called knowledges. These said, "Descend to the inferior earth, and ascend to the superior earth: in the latter you will perceive and be made sensible of the delights of the angels of heaven, and in the former of the delights of the spirits of hell." But lo! at that instant, at a distance from them, the ground cleft asunder, and through the cleft there ascended three devils, who appeared on fire from the delight of their love; and as those who accompanied the novitiate spirit perceived that the three ascended out of hell by *proviso*, they said to them, "Do not come nearer; but from the place where you are, give some account of your delights." Whereupon they said, "Know, then, that every one, whether he be good or evil, is in his own delight; the good in the delight of his good, and the evil in the delight of his evil." They were then asked, "What is your delight?" They said, "The delight of whoring, stealing, defrauding, and blaspheming." Again they were asked, "What is the quality of those delights?" They said, "To the senses of others they are like the stinks arising from dunghills, the stenches from dead bodies, and the scents from stale urine." And it was asked them, "Are those things delightful to you?" They said, "Most delightful." And reply was made, "Then you are like unclean beasts which wallow in such things." To which they answered, "If we are, we are: but such things are the delights of our nostrils." And on being asked, "What further account can you give?" they said, "Every one is allowed to be in his delight, even the most unclean, as it is called, provided he does not infest good spirits and angels; but since, from our delight, we cannot do otherwise than infest them, therefore we are cast together into workhouses, where we suffer direfully. The witholding and keeping back our delights in those houses is what is called hell-torments: it is also interior pain." It was then asked them, "Why have you infested the good?" They replied, that they could not do otherwise: "It is," said they, "as if we were seized with rage when we see any angel, and are made sensible of the divine sphere about him." It was then said to them, "Herein also you are like wild beasts." And presently, when they saw the novitiate spirit with the angel, they were overpowered with rage, which appeared like the fire of hatred; wherefore, in order to prevent their doing mischief, they were sent back to hell. After these things, appeared the angels who from ends see causes, and by causes effects, who were in the heaven above those three companies. They were seen in a bright cloud, which rolling itself downwards by spiral flexures, brought with it a circular garland of flowers, and placed it on the head of the novitiate spirit; and instantly a voice said to him from thence, "This wreath is given you because from your childhood you have meditated on heaven and hell."

ON CONCUBINAGE.

462. IN the preceding chapter, in treating on fornication, we treated also on keeping a mistress; by which was understood the connection of an unmarried man with a woman under stipulated conditions: but by concubinage we here mean the connection of a married man with a woman in like manner under stipulated conditions. Those who do not distinguish genera, use the two terms promiscuously, as if they had one meaning, and thence one signification: but as they are two genera, and the term keeping a mistress is suitable to the former, because a kept mistress is a courtezan, and the term concubinage to the latter, because a concubine is a substituted partner of the bed, therefore for the sake of distinction, ante-nuptial stipulation with a woman is signified by keeping a mistress, and post-nuptial by concubinage. Concubinage is here treated of for the sake of order; for from order it is discovered what is the quality of marriage on the one part, and of adultery on the other. That marriage and adultery are opposites has already been shewn in the chapter concerning their opposition; and the quantity and quality of their opposition cannot be learnt but from their intermediates, of which concubinage is one; but as there are two kinds of concubinage, which are to be carefully distinguished, therefore this section, like the foregoing, shall be arranged into its distinct parts as follows: I. *There are two kinds of concubinage, which differ exceedingly from each other, the one conjointly with a wife, the other apart from a wife.* II. *Concubinage conjointly with a wife, is altogether unlawful for Christians, and detestable.* III. *That it is polygamy which has been condemned, and is to be condemned, by the Christian world.* IV. *It is an adultery whereby the conjugial principle, which is the most precious jewel of the Christian life, is destroyed.* V. *Concubinage apart from a wife, when it is engaged in from causes legitimate, just, and truly excusatory, is not unlawful.* VI. *The legitimate causes of this concubinage are the legitimate causes of divorce, while the wife is nevertheless retained at home.* VII. *The just causes of this concubinage are the just causes of separation from the bed.* VIII. *Of the excusatory causes of this concubinage some are real and some not.* IX. *The really excusatory causes are such as are grounded in what is just.* X. *The excusatory causes which are not real are such as are not*

grounded in what is just, although in the appearance of what is just. XI. *Those who from causes legitimate, just, and really excusatory, are engaged in this concubinage, may at the same time be principled in conjugial love.* XII. *While this concubinage continues, actual connection with a wife is not allowable.* We proceed to an explanation of each article.

463. I. THERE ARE TWO KINDS OF CONCUBINAGE, WHICH DIFFER EXCEEDINGLY FROM EACH OTHER, THE ONE CONJOINTLY WITH A WIFE, THE OTHER APART FROM A WIFE. That there are two kinds of concubinage, which differ exceedingly from each other, and that the one kind consists in taking a substituted partner to the bed, and living conjointly and at the same time with her and with a wife; and that the other kind is when, after a legitimate and just separation from a wife, a man engages a woman in her stead as a bed-fellow; also that these two kinds of concubinage differ as much from each other as dirty linen from clean, may be seen by those who take a clear and distinct view of things, but not by those whose view of things is confused and indistinct: yea, it may be seen by those who are in conjugial love, but not by those who are in the love of adultery. The latter are in obscurity respecting all the derivations of the love of the sex, whereas the former are enlightened respecting them: nevertheless, those who are in adultery, can see those derivations and their distinctions, not indeed in and from themselves, but from others when they hear them: for an adulterer has a similar faculty with a chaste husband of elevating his understanding; but an adulterer, after he has acknowledged the distinctions which he has heard from others, nevertheless forgets them, when he immerses his understanding in his filthy pleasure; for the chaste and the unchaste principles, and the sane and the insane, cannot dwell together; but, when separated, they may be distinguished by the understanding. I once inquired of those in the spiritual world who did not regard adulteries as sins, whether they knew a single distinction between fornication, keeping a mistress, the two kinds of concubinage, and the several degrees of adultery? They said they were all alike. I then asked them whether marriage was distinguishable? Upon this they looked around to see whether any of the clergy were present, and as there were not, they said, that in itself it is like the rest. The case was otherwise with those who in the ideas of their thought regarded adulteries as sins: these said, that in their interior ideas, which are of the perception, they saw distinctions, but had not yet studied to discern and know them asunder. This I can assert as a fact, that those distinctions are perceived by the angels in heaven as to their minutiæ. In order therefore that it may be seen, that there are two kinds of concubinage opposite to each other, one whereby conjugial love is destroyed, the other whereby it is not, we will first describe the kind which is condemnatory, and afterwards that which is not

464. II. CONCUBINAGE CONJOINTLY WITH A WIFE IS ALTOGETHER UNLAWFUL FOR CHRISTIANS, AND DETESTABLE. It is unlawful, because it is contrary to the conjugial covenant; and it is detestable, because it is contrary to religion; and what is contrary to religion, and at the same time to the conjugial covenant, is contrary to the Lord: wherefore, as soon as any one, without a really conscientious cause, adjoins a concubine to a wife, heaven is closed to him; and by the angels he is no longer numbered among Christians. From that time also he despises the things of the church and of religion, and afterwards does not lift his face above nature, but turns himself to her as a deity, who favors his lust, from whose influx his spirit thenceforward receives animation. The interior cause of this apostasy will be explained in what follows. That this concubinage is detestable is not seen by the man himself who is guilty of it; because after the closing of heaven he becomes a spiritual insanity: but a chaste wife has a clear view of it, because she is a conjugial love, and this love nauseates such concubinage; wherefore also many such wives refuse actual connection with their husbands afterwards, as that which would defile their chastity by the contagion of lust adhering to the men from their courtezans.

465. III. IT IS POLYGAMY WHICH HAS BEEN CONDEMNED, AND IS TO BE CONDEMNED, BY THE CHRISTIAN WORLD. That simultaneous concubinage, or concubinage conjoined with a wife, is polygamy, although not acknowledged to be such, because it is not so declared, and thus not so called by any law, must be evident to every person of common discernment; for a woman taken into keeping, and made partaker of the conjugial bed is like a wife. That polygamy has been condemned, and is to be condemned by the Christian world, has been shewn in the chapter on polygamy, especially from these articles therein:—A Christian is not allowed to marry more than one wife; n. 338: If a Christian marries several wives, he commits not only natural, but also spiritual adultery; n. 339: The Israelitish nation was permitted to marry several wives, because the Christian church was not with them; n. 349. From these considerations it is evident, that to adjoin a concubine to a wife, and to make each a partner of the bed, is filthy polygamy.

466. IV. IT IS AN ADULTERY WHEREBY THE CONJUGIAL PRINCIPLE, WHICH IS THE MOST PRECIOUS JEWEL OF THE CHRISTIAN LIFE IS DESTROYED. That it is more opposed to conjugial love than simple adultery; and that it is a deprivation of every faculty and inclination to conjugial life, which is implanted in Christians from birth, may be evinced by arguments which will have great weight with the reason of a wise man. In regard to the FIRST POSITION,—that simultaneous concubinage, or concubinage conjoined with a wife, is more opposed to conjugial love than simple adultery, it may be seen from these considerations:

that in simple adultery there is not a love analogous to conjugial love; for it is only a heat of the flesh, which presently cools, and sometimes does not leave any trace of love behind it towards its object; wherefore this effervescing lasciviousness, if it is not from a purposed or confirmed principle, and if the person guilty of it repents, detracts but little from conjugial love. It is otherwise in the case of polygamical adultery: herein there is a love analogous to conjugial love; for it does not cool and disperse, or pass off into nothing after being excited, like the foregoing; but it remains, renews and strengthens itself, and so far takes away from love to the wife, and in the place thereof induces cold towards her; for in such case it regards the concubine courtezan as lovely from a freedom of the will, in that it can retract if it pleases; which freedom is begotten in the natural man: and because this freedom is thence grateful, it supports that love; and moreover, with a concubine the unition with allurements is nearer than with a wife; but on the other hand it does not regard a wife as lovely, by reason of the duty of living with her enjoined by the covenant of life, which it then perceives as far more constrained in consequence of the freedom enjoyed with another woman. It is plain that love for a wife grows cold, and she herself grows vile, in the same degree that love for a courtezan grows warm, and she is held in estimation. In regard to the SECOND POSITION—that simultaneous concubinage, or concubinage conjoined with a wife, deprives a man of all faculty and inclination to conjugial life, which is implanted in Christians from birth, it may be seen from the following considerations: that so far as love to a wife is changed into love to a concubine, so far the former love is rent, exhausted, and emptied, as has been shewn just above: that this is effected by a closing of the interiors of the natural mind, and an opening of its inferior principles, may appear from the seat of the inclination with Christians to love one of the sex, as being in the inmost principles, and that this seat may be closed, but cannot be destroyed. The reason why an inclination to love one of the sex, and also a faculty to receive that love, is implanted in Christians from birth, is, because that love is from the Lord alone, and is esteemed religious, and in Christendom the Lord's divine is acknowledged and worshipped, and religion is from his Word; hence there is a grafting, and also a transplanting thereof, from generation to generation. We have said, that the above Christian conjugial principle perishes by polygamical adultery: we thereby mean, that with the Christian polygamist it is closed and intercepted; but still it is capable of being revived in his posterity, as is the case with the likeness of a grandfather or a great-grandfather returning in a grandson or a great-grandson. Hence, that conjugial principle is called the most precious jewel of the Christian life, and (see above, n. 457, 458,) the storehouse of human life, and the reservoir of the Christian religion. That that conjugial principle is destroyed with the Christian who practises polygamical adultery, is manifest from this consideration; that he cannot like a Mahometan polygamist, love a concubine and a wife equally; but so far as he loves a concubine, or is warm towards her, so far he does not love his wife, but is cold towards her; and, what is yet more detestable, so far he also in heart acknowledges the Lord only as a natural man, and the son of Mary, and not at the same time as the Son of God, and likewise so far he makes light of religion. It is, however, well to be noted, that this is the case with those who add a concubine to a wife, and connect themselves actually with each; but it is not at all the case with those, who from legitimate, just, and trully excusatory causes, separate themselves, and keep apart from a wife as to actual love, and have a woman in keeping. We now proceed to treat of this kind of concubinage.

467. V. CONCUBINAGE APART FROM A WIFE, WHEN IT IS ENGAGED IN FROM CAUSES LEGITIMATE, JUST, AND TRULY EXCUSATORY, IS NOT UNLAWFUL. What causes we mean by legitimate, what by just, and what by truly excusatory, shall be shown in their order: the bare mention of the causes is here premised, that this concubinage, which we are about to treat of, may be distinguished from that which we have previously described.*

468. VI. THE LEGITIMATE CAUSES OF THIS CONCUBINAGE ARE THE LEGITIMATE CAUSES OF DIVORCE, WHILE THE WIFE IS NEVERTHELESS RETAINED AT HOME. By divorce is meant the annulling of the conjugial covenant, and thence an entire separation, and after this a full liberty to marry another wife. The one only cause of this total separation or divorce, is adultery, according to the Lord's precept, Matt. xix. 9. To the same cause are to be referred manifest obscenities, which bid defiance to the restraints of modesty, and fill and infest the house with flagitious practices of lewdness, giving birth to adulterous immodesty, and rendering the whole mind abandoned. To these things may be added malicious desertion, which involves adultery, and causes a wife to commit whoredom, and thereby to be divorced, Matt. v. 32. These three causes, being legitimate causes of divorce,—the first and third before a public judge, and the middle one before the man himself, as judge, are also legitimate causes of concubinage, when the adulterous wife is retained at home. The reason why adultery is the one only cause of divorce is, because it is diametrically opposite to the life of conjugial love, and totally destroys and annihilates it; see above, n. 255.

469. The reasons why, by the generality of men, the adulterous wife is still retained at home, are, 1. Because the man is

* See note to No. 450, and the Preliminary note.

afraid to produce witnesses in a court of justice against his wife, to accuse her of adultery, and thereby to make the crime public; for unless eye-witnesses, or evidences to the same amount, were produced to convict her, he would be secretly reproached in companies of men, and openly in companies of women. 2. He is afraid also lest his adulteress should have the cunning to clear her conduct, and likewise lest the judges should show favor to her, and thus his name suffer in the public esteem. 3. Moreover, there may be domestic reasons, which may make separation from the house unadvisable: as in case there are children, towards whom also the adulteress has natural love; in case they are bound together by mutual services which cannot be put an end to; in case the wife is connected with and dependent upon her relatives, whether on the father's or mother's side, and there is a hope of receiving an increase of fortune from them; in case he lived with her in the beginning in habits of agreeable intimacy; and in case she, after she became meretricious, has the skill to soothe the man with engaging pleasantry and pretended civility, to prevent blame being imputed to herself; not to mention other cases, which, as in themselves they are legitimate causes of divorce, are also legitimate causes of concubinage; for the causes of retaining the wife at home do not take away the cause of divorce, supposing her guilty of adultery. Who, but a person of vile character, can fulfil the duties of the conjugial bed, and at the same time have commerce with a strumpet? If instances of this sort are occasionally to be met with, no favorable conclusions are to be drawn from them.

470. VII. THE JUST CAUSES OF THIS CONCUBINAGE ARE THE JUST CAUSES OF SEPARATION FROM THE BED. There are legitimate causes of separation, and there are just causes: legitimate causes are enforced by the decisions of judges, and just causes by the decisions come to by the man alone. The causes both legitimate and just of separation from the bed, and also from the house, were briefly enumerated above, n. 252, 253; among which are VITIATED STATES OF THE BODY, including diseases whereby the whole body is so far infected, that the contagion may prove fatal: of this nature are malignant and pestilential fevers, leprosies, the venereal disease, cancers; also diseases whereby the whole body is so far weighed down, as to admit of no sociability, and from which exhale dangerous effluvia and noxious vapors, whether from the surface of the body, or from its inward parts, in particular from the stomach and the lungs: from the surface of the body proceed malignant pocks, warts, pustules, scorbutic pthisis, virulent scab, especially if the face is disfigured by it; from the stomach proceed foul, stinking, and rank eructations; from the lungs, filthy and putrid exhalations arising from imposthumes, ulcers or abscesses, or from vitiated blood or serum. Besides these there are also other various diseases; as *lipothamia*, which

is a total faintness of body, and defect of strength; *paralysis*, which is a loosening and relaxation of the membranes and ligaments which serve for motion; epilepsy; permanent infirmity arising from apoplexy; certain chronical diseases; the iliac passion; rupture; besides other diseases, which the science of pathology teaches. VITIATED STATES OF THE MIND, which are just causes of separation from the bed and the house, are madness, frenzy, furious wildness, actual foolishness and idiocy, loss of memory, and the like. That these are just causes of concubinage, since they are just causes of separation, reason sees without the help of a judge.

471. VIII. OF THE EXCUSATORY CAUSES OF THIS CONCUBINAGE SOME ARE REAL AND SOME ARE NOT. Since besides the just causes which are just causes of separation, and thence become just causes of concubinage, there are also excusatory causes, which depend on judgement and justice with the man, therefore these also are to be mentioned: but as the judgements of justice may be perverted and be converted by confirmations into the appearances of what is just, therefore these excusatory causes are distinguished into real and not real, and are separately described.

472. IX. THE REALLY EXCUSATORY CAUSES AND SUCH AS ARE GROUNDED IN WHAT IS JUST. To know these causes, it may be sufficient to mention some of them; such as having no natural affection towards the children, and a consequent rejection of them, intemperance, drunkenness, uncleanliness, immodesty, a desire of divulging family secrets, of disputing, of striking, of taking revenge, of doing evil, of stealing, of deceiving; internal dissimilitude, whence comes antipathy; a froward requirement of the conjugial debt, whence the man becomes as cold as a stone; being addicted to magic and witchcraft; an extreme degree of impiety; and other similar evils.

473. There are also milder causes, which are really excusatory and which separate from the bed, and yet not from the house; as a cessation of prolification on the part of the wife, in consequence of advanced age, and thence a reluctance and opposition to actual love, while the ardor thereof still continues with the man; besides similar cases in which rational judgement sees what is just, and which do not hurt the conscience.

474. X. THE EXCUSATORY CAUSES WHICH ARE NOT REAL ARE SUCH AS ARE NOT GROUNDED IN WHAT IS JUST, ALTHOUGH IN THE APPEARANCE OF WHAT IS JUST. These are known from the really excusatory causes above mentioned, and, if not rightly examined, may appear to be just, and yet are unjust; as that times of abstinence are required after the bringing forth of children, the transitory sicknesses of wives, from these and other causes a check to prolification, polygamy permitted to the Israelites, and other like causes of no weight as grounded in

justice. These are fabricated by the men after they have become cold, when unchaste lusts have deprived them of conjugial love, and have infatuated them with the idea of its likeness to adulterous love. When such men engage in concubinage, they, in order to prevent defamation, assign such spurious and fallacious causes as real and genuine,—and very frequently also falsely charge them against their wives, their companions often favorably assenting and applauding them.

475. XI. THOSE WHO FROM CAUSES LEGITIMATE, JUST, AND REALLY EXCUSATORY, ARE ENGAGED IN THIS CONCUBINAGE, MAY AT THE SAME TIME BE PRINCIPLED IN CONJUGIAL LOVE. We say that such may at the same time be principled in conjugial love; and we thereby mean, that they may keep this love stored up in themselves; for this love, in the subject in which it is, does not perish, but is quiescent. The reasons why conjugial love is preserved with those who prefer marriage to concubinage, and enter into the latter from the causes above mentioned, are these; that this concubinage is not repugnant to conjugial love; that it is not a separation from it; that it is only a clothing encompassing it; that this clothing is taken away from them after death. 1. That this concubinage is not repugnant to conjugial love, follows from what was proved above; that such concubinage, when engaged in from causes legitimate, just, and really excusatory, is not unlawful, n. 467—473. 2. That this concubinage is not a separation from conjugial love; for when causes legitimate, or just, or really excusatory, arise, and persuade and compel a man, then, conjugial love with marriage is not separated, but only interrupted; and love interrupted, and not separated, remains in the subject. The case in this respect is like that of a person, who, being engaged in a business which he likes, is detained from it by company, by public sights, or by a journey; still he does not cease to like his business: it is also like that of a person who is fond of generous wine, and who, when he drinks wine of an inferior quality, does not lose his taste and appetite for that which is generous. 3. The reason why the above concubinage is only a clothing of conjugial love encompassing it, is, because the love of concubinage is natural, and the love of marriage spiritual; and natural love is a veil or covering to spiritual, when the latter is interrupted: that this is the case, is unknown to the lover; because spiritual love is not made sensible of itself, but by natural love, and it is made sensible as delight, in which there is blessedness from heaven: but natural love by itself is made sensible only as delight. 4. The reason why this veil is taken away after death, is, because then a man from natural becomes spiritual, and instead of a material body enjoys a substantial one, wherein natural delight grounded in spiritual is made sensible in its perfection. That this is the case, I have heard from communication with some in the spiritual world, even from kings there, who in the

natural world had engaged in concubinage from really excusatory causes.

476. XII. WHILE THIS CONCUBINAGE CONTINUES, ACTUAL CONNECTION WITH A WIFE IS NOT ALLOWABLE. The reason of this is, because in such case conjugial love, which in itself is spiritual, chaste, pure, and holy, becomes natural, is defiled and disregarded, and thereby perishes; wherefore in order that this love may be preserved, it is expedient that concubingage grounded in really excusatory causes, n. 472, 473, be engaged in with one only, and not with two at the same time.

* * * * * *

477. To the above I will add the following MEMORABLE RELATION. I heard a certain spirit, a youth, recently deceased, boasting of his libertinism, and eager to establish his reputation as a man of superior masculine powers; and in the insolence of his boasting he thus expressed himself: "What is more dismal than for a man to imprison his love, and to confine himself to one woman? and what is more delightful than to set the love at liberty? Who does not grow tired of one? and who is not revived by several? What is sweeter than promiscuous liberty, variety, deflorations, schemes to deceive husbands, and plans of adulterous hypocrisy? Do not those things which are obtained by cunning, deceit, and theft, delight the inmost principles of the mind?" On hearing these things, the by-standers said, "Speak not in such terms; you know not where and with whom you are; you are but lately come hither. Hell is beneath your feet, and heaven over your head; you are now in the world which is between those two, and is called the world of spirits. All who depart out of the world, come here, and being assembled are examined as to their quality; and here they are prepared, the wicked for hell, and the good for heaven. Possibly you still retain what you have heard from priests in the world, that whoremongers and adulterers are cast down into hell, and that chaste married partners are raised to heaven." At this the novitiate laughed, saying, "What are heaven and hell? Is it not heaven where any one is free; and is not he free who is allowed to love as many as he pleases? and is not it hell where any one is a servant: and is not he a servant who is obliged to keep to one?" But a certain angel, looking down from heaven, heard what he said, and broke off the conversation, lest it should proceed further and profane marriages; and he said to him, "Come up here, and I will clearly shew you what heaven and hell are, and what the quality of the latter is to confirmed adulterers." He then shewed him the way, and he ascended: after he was admitted he was led first into the paradisiacal garden, where were fruit-trees and flowers, which from their beauty, pleasantness and fragrance, filled the mind with the delights of life. When he saw these things, he admired them exceedingly; but he was then in external vision,

such as he had enjoyed in the world when he saw similar objects, and in this vision he was rational; but in the internal vision, in which adultery was the principal agent, and occupied every point of thought, he was not rational; wherefore the external vision was closed, and the internal opened; and when the latter was opened, he said, " What do I see now? is it not straw and dry wood? and what do I smell now? is it not a stench? What is become of those paradisiacal objects?" The angel said, " They are near at hand and are present; but they do not appear before your internal sight, which is adulterous, for it turns celestial things into infernal, and sees only opposites. Every man has an internal and an external mind, thus an internal and an external sight: with the wicked the internal mind is insane, and the external wise; but with the good the internal mind is wise, and from this also the external; and such as the mind is, so a man in the spiritual world sees objects." After this the angel, from the power which was given him, closed his internal sight, and opened the external, and led him away through gates towards the middle point of the habitations: there he saw magnificent palaces of alabaster, marble, and various precious stones, and near them porticos, and round about pillars overlaid and encompassed with wonderful ornaments and decorations. When he saw these things, he was amazed, and said, " What do I see? I see magnificent objects in their own real magnificence, and architectonic objects in their own real art." At that instant the angel again closed his external sight, and opened the internal, which was evil because filthily adulterous: hereupon he exclaimed, " What do I now see? Where am I? What is become of those palaces and magnificent objects? I see only confused heaps, rubbish, and places full of caverns." But presently he was brought back again to his external sight, and introduced into one of the palaces; and he saw the decorations of the gates, the windows, the walls, and the ceilings, and especially of the utensils, over and round about which were celestial forms of gold and precious stones, which cannot be described by any language, or delineated by any art; for they surpassed the ideas of language and the notions of art. On seeing these things he again exclaimed, " These are the very essence of whatever is wonderful, such as no eye had ever seen." But instantly, as before, his internal sight was opened, the external being closed, and he was asked what he then saw? He replied, " Nothing but decayed piles of bulrushes in this place, of straw in that, and of fire brands in a third." Once again he was brought into an external state of mind, and some maidens were introduced, who were extremely beautiful, being images of celestial affection; and they, with the sweet voice of their affection, addressed him; and instantly, on seeing and hearing them, his countenance changed, and he returned of himself into his internals, which were adulterous; and since such internals cannot endure any thing of celestial love, and neither on the other hand can they be endured by celestial love, therefore both parties vanished,—the maidens out of sight of the man, and the man out of sight of the maidens. After this, the angel informed him concerning the ground and origin of the changes of the state of his sights; saying, "I perceive that in the world, from which you are come, you have been two-fold, in internals having been quite a different man from what you were in externals; in externals you have been a civil, moral, and rational man; whereas in internals, you have been neither civil, moral, nor rational, because a libertine and an adulterer: and such men, when they are allowed to ascend into heaven, and are there kept in their externals, can see the heavenly things contained therein; but when their internals are opened, instead of heavenly things they see infernal. Know, however, that with every one in this world, externals are successively closed, and internals are opened, and thereby they are prepared for heaven or hell; and as the evil of adultery defiles the internals of the mind above every other evil, you must needs be conveyed down to the defiled principles of your love, and these are in the hells, where the caverns are full of stench arising from dunghills. Who cannot know from reason, that an unchaste and lascivious principle in the world of spirits, is impure and unclean, and thus that nothing more pollutes and defiles a man, and induces in him an infernal principle? Wherefore take heed how you boast any longer of your whoredoms, as possessing masculine powers therein above other men. I advertise you before hand, that you will become feeble, so that you will scarce know where your masculine power is. Such is the lot which awaits those who boast of their adulterous ability." On hearing these words he descended, and returned into the world of spirits, to his former companions, and converse with them modestly and chastely, but not for any considerable length of time.

ON ADULTERIES AND THEIR GENERA AND DEGREES.

478. NONE can know that there is any evil in adultery, who judge of it only from its externals; for in these it resembles marriage. Such external judges, when they hear of internals, and are told that externals thence derive their good or their evil, say with themselves, "What are internals? Who sees them? Is not this climbing above the sphere of every one's intelligence?" Such persons are like those who accept all pretended good as genuine voluntary good, and who decide upon a man's wisdom from the elegance of his conversation; or who respect the man

himself from the richness of his dress and the magnificence of his equipage, and not from his internal habit, which is that of judgement grounded in the affection of good. This also is like judging of the fruit of a tree, and of any other eatable thing, from the sight and touch only, and not of its goodness from a knowledge of its flavor: such is the conduct of all those who are unwilling to perceive any thing respecting man's internal. Hence comes the wild infatuation of many at this day, who see no evil in adulteries, yea, who unite marriages with them in the same chamber, that is, who make them altogether alike; and this only on account of their apparent resemblance in externals. That this is the case, was shewn me by this experimental proof: on a certain time, the angels assembled from Europe some hundreds of those who were distinguished for their genius, their erudition, and their wisdom, and questioned them concerning the distinction between marriage and adultery, and intreated them to consult the rational powers of their understandings: and after consultation, all, except ten, replied, that the judicial law constitutes the only distinction, for the sake of some advantage; which distinction may indeed be known, but still be accommodated by civil prudence. They were next asked, Whether they saw any good in marriage, and any evil in adultery? They returned for answer, that they did not see any rational evil and good. Being questioned whether they saw any sin in it? they said, "Where is the sin? Is not the act alike?" At these answers the angels were amazed, and exclaimed, "Oh, the gross stupidity of the age! Who can measure its quality and quantity?" On hearing this exclamation, the hundreds of the wise ones turned themselves, and said one among another with loud laughter, "Is this gross stupidity? Is there any wisdom that can bring conviction that to love another person's wife merits eternal damnation?" But that adultery is spiritual evil, and thence moral and civil evil, and diametrically contrary to the wisdom of reason; also that the love of adultery is from hell and returns to hell, and the love of marriage is from heaven and returns to heaven, has been demonstrated in the first chapter of this part, concerning the opposition of adulterous and conjugial love. But since all evils, like all goods, partake of latitude and altitude, and according to latitude have their genera, and according to altitude their degrees, therefore, in order that adulteries may be known as to each dimension, they shall first be arranged into their genera, and afterwards into their degrees; and this shall be done in the following series: 1. *There are three genera of adulteries,—simple, duplicate, and triplicate.* II. *Simple adultery is that of an unmarried man with another's wife, or of an unmarried woman with another's husband.* III. *Duplicate adultery is that of a husband with another's wife, or of a wife with another's husband.* IV. *Triplicate adultery is with relations by blood.* V. *There are four degrees of adulteries, according to* which they have their predications, their charges of blame, and after death their imputations. VI. *Adulteries of the first degree are adulteries of ignorance, which are committed by those who cannot as yet, or cannot at all, consult the understanding, and thence check them.* VII. *In such cases adulteries are mild.* VIII. *Adulteries of the second degree are adulteries of lust, which are committed by those who indeed are able to consult the understanding, but from accidental causes at the moment are not able.* IX. *Adulteries committed by such persons are imputatory, according as the understanding afterwards favors them or not.* X. *Adulteries of the third degree are adulteries of the reason, which are committed by those who with the understanding confirm themselves in the persuasion that they are not evils of sin.* XI. *The adulteries committed by such persons are grievous, and are imputed to them according to confirmations.* XII. *Adulteries of the fourth degree are adulteries of the will, which are committed by those who make them lawful and pleasing, and who do not think them of importance enough to consult the understanding respecting them.* XIII. *The adulteries committed by these persons are exceedingly grievous, and are imputed to them as evils of purpose, and remain with them as guilt.* XIV. *Adulteries of the third and fourth degrees are evils of sin, according to the quantity and quality of understanding and will in them, whether they are actually committed or not.* XV. *Adulteries grounded in purpose of the will, and adulteries grounded in confirmation of the understanding render men natural, sensual, and corporeal.* XVI. *And this to such a degree, that at length they reject from themselves all things of the church and of religion.* XVII. *Nevertheless they have the powers of human rationality like other men.* XVIII. *But they use that rationality while they are in externals, but abuse it while in their internals.* We proceed to an explanation of each article.

479. I. THERE ARE THREE GENERA OF ADULTERIES,— SIMPLE, DUPLICATE, AND TRIPLICATE. The Creator of the universe has distinguished all the things which he has created into genera, and each genus into species, and has distinguished each species, and each distinction in like manner, and so forth, to the end that an image of what is infinite may exist in a perpetual variety of qualities. Thus the Creator of the universe has distinguished goods and their truths, and in like manner evils and their falses, after they arose. That he has distinguished all things in the spiritual world into genera, species, and differences, and has collected together into heaven all goods and truths, and into hell all evils and falses, and has arranged the latter in an order diametrically opposite to the former, may appear from what is explained in a work concerning HEAVEN AND HELL, published in London in the year 1758. That in the natural world he has also thus distinguished and does distinguish goods and truths, and likewise evils and falses, appertaining to men, and thereby

men themselves, may be known from their lot after death, in that the good enter into heaven, and the evil into hell. Now, since all things relating to good, and all things relating to evil, are distinguished into genera, species, and so forth, therefore marriages are distinguished into the same, and so are their opposites, which are adulteries.

480. II. SIMPLE ADULTERY IS THAT OF AN UNMARRIED MAN WITH ANOTHER'S WIFE, OR AN UNMARRIED WOMAN WITH ANOTHER'S HUSBAND. By adultery here and in the following pages we mean the adultery which is opposite to marriage; it is opposite because it violates the covenant of life contracted between married partners: it rends asunder their love, and defiles it, and closes the union which was begun at the time of betrothing, and strengthened in the beginning of marriage: for the conjugial love of one man with one wife, after engagement and covenant, unites their souls. Adultery does not dissolve this union, because it cannot be dissolved; but it closes it, as he that stops up a fountain at its source, and thence obstructs its stream, and fills the cistern with filthy and stinking waters: in like manner conjugial love, the origin of which is a union of souls, is daubed with mud and covered by adultery; and when it is so daubed with mud there arises from beneath the love of adultery; and as this love increases, it becomes fleshly, and rises in insurrection against conjugial love, and destroys it. Hence comes the opposition of adultery and marriage.

481. That it may be further known how gross is the stupidity of this age, in that those who have the reputation of wisdom do not see any sin in adultery, as was discovered by the angels (see just above, n. 478), I will here add the following MEMORABLE RELATION. There were certain spirits who, from a habit they had acquired in the life of the body, infested me with peculiar cunning, and this they did by a softish and as it were waving influx, such as is usual with well-disposed spirits; but I perceived that they employed craftiness and similar means, to the intent that they might engage attention and deceive. At length I entered into conversation with one of them who, it was told me, had while he lived in the world been the general of an army: and as I perceived that in the ideas of his thought there was a lascivious principle, I conversed with him by representatives in the spiritual language which fully expresses what is intended to be said, and even several things in a moment. He said that, in the life of the body in the former world, he had made no account of adulteries: but it was granted me to tell him, that adulteries are wicked, although from the delight attending them, and from the persuasion thence resulting, they appear to the adulterer as not wicked but allowable; which also he might know from this consideration, that marriages are the seminaries of the human race, and thence also the seminaries of the heavenly king

dom, and therefore that they ought not to be violated, but to be accounted holy; also from this consideration, that he ought know, as being in the spiritual world, and in a state of perception, that conjugial love descends from the Lord through heaven, and that from that love, as a parent, is derived mutual love, which is the main support of heaven; and further from this consideration, that adulterers, whenever they only approach the heavenly societies, are made sensible of their own stench, and throw themselves headlong thence towards hell: at least he might know, that to violate marriages is contrary to the divine laws, to the civil laws of all kingdoms, also to the genuine light of reason, and thereby to the right of nations, because contrary to order both divine and human; not to mention other considerations. But he replied, that he entertained no such thoughts in the former life: he wished to reason whether the case was so or not; but he was told that truth does not admit of reasonings, since they favor the delights of the flesh against those of the spirit, the quality of which latter delights he was ignorant of; and that he ought first to think about the things which I had told him, because they are true; or to think from the well-known maxim, that no one should do to another what he is unwilling another should do to him; and thus, if any one had in such a manner violated his wife, whom he had loved, as is the case in the beginning of every marriage, and he had then been in a state of wrath, and had spoken from that state, whether he himself also would not then have detested adulteries, and being a man of strong parts, would not have confirmed himself against them more than other men, even to condemning them to hell; and being the general of an army, and having brave companions, whether he would not, in order to prevent disgrace, either have put the adulterer to death, or have driven the adulteress from his house.

482. III. DUPLICATE ADULTERY IS THAT OF A HUSBAND WITH ANOTHER'S WIFE, OR OF A WIFE WITH ANOTHER'S HUSBAND. This adultery is called duplicate, because it is committed by two, and on each side the marriage-covenant is violated; wherefore also it is twofold more grievous than the former. It was said above, n. 480, that the conjugial love of one man with one wife, after engagement and covenant, unites their souls, and that such union is that very love in its origin; and that this origin is closed and stopped up by adultery, as the source and stream of a fountain. That the souls of two unite themselves together, when love to the sex is confined to one of the sex, which is the case when a maiden engages herself wholly to a youth, and on the other hand a youth engages himself wholly to a maiden, is clearly manifest from this consideration, that the lives of both unite themselves, consequently their souls, because souls are the first principles of life. This union of souls can only take place in monogamical marriages, or those of one man with one wife, but

not in polygamical marriages, or those of one man with several wives; because in the latter case the love is divided, in the former it is united. The reason why conjugial love in its supreme abode is spiritual, holy, and pure, is because the soul of every man from its origin is celestial; wherefore it receives influx immediately from the Lord, for it receives from him the marriage of love and wisdom, or of good and truth; and this influx makes him a man, and distinguishes him from the beasts. From this union of souls, conjugial love, which is there in its spiritual sanctity and purity, flows down into the life of the whole body, and fills with blessed delights, so long as its channel remains open; which is the case with those who are made spiritual by the Lord. That nothing but adultery closes and stops up this abode of conjugial love, thus its origin or fountain and its channel, is evident from the Lord's words, that it is not lawful to put away a wife and marry another, except on account of adultery: Matt. xix. 3—9; and also from what is said in the same passage, that he that marries her that is put away commits adultery, verse 9. When therefore, as was said above, that pure and holy fountain is stopped up, it is clogged about with filthiness of sundry kinds, as a jewel with ordure, or bread with vomit; which things are altogether opposite to the purity and sanctity of that fountain, or of conjugial love: from which opposition comes conjugial cold, and according to this cold is the lascivious voluptuousness of adulterous love, which consumes itself of its own accord. The reason why this is an evil of sin is, because the holy principle is covered, and thereby its channel into the body is obstructed, and in the place thereof a profane principle succeeds, and its channel into the body is opened, whence a man from celestial becomes infernal.

483. To the above I will add some particulars from the spiritual world, which are worthy to be recorded. I have been informed in that world, that some married men are inflamed with the lust of committing whoredom with maidens or virgins; some with those who are not maidens but harlots; some with married women or wives; some with women of the above description who are of noble descent; and some with such as are not of noble descent: that this is the case, was confirmed to me by several instances from the various kingdoms in that world. While I was meditating concerning the variety of such lusts, I asked whether there are any who find all their delight with the wives of others, and none with unmarried women? Wherefore to convince me that there are some such spirits, several were brought to me from a certain kingdom, who were obliged to speak according to their libidinous principles. These declared that it was, and still is, their sole pleasure and delight to commit whoredom with the wives of others; and that they look out for such as are beautiful, and hire them for themselves at a great price according to their

wealth, and in general bargain about the price with the wife alone. I asked, why they do not hire for themselves unmarried women? They said, that they consider this would be cheap and worthless, and therefore undelightful to them. I asked also, whether those wives afterwards return to their husbands and live with them? They replied, that they either do not return, or they return cold, having become courtezans. Afterwards I asked them seriously, whether they ever thought, or now think, that this is twofold adultery, because they commit this at the time they have wives of their own, and that such adultery deprives a man of all spiritual good? But at this several who were present laughed, saying, "What is spiritual good?" Nevertheless I was still urgent, and said, "What is more detestable than for a man to mix his soul with the soul of a husband in his wife? Do you not know, that the soul of a man is in his seed?" Hereupon they turned themselves away and muttered, "What harm can this do her?" At length I said, "Although you do not fear divine laws, do you not fear civil laws?" They replied, "No; we only fear certain of the ecclesiastical order; but we conceal this in their presence; and if we cannot conceal it, we keep upon good terms with them." I afterwards saw the former divided into companies, and some of the latter cast into hell.

484. IV. TRIPLICATE ADULTERY IS WITH RELATIONS BY BLOOD. This adultery is called triplicate, because it is threefold more grievous than the two former. The relations, or remains of the flesh, which are not to be approached, are mentioned in Levit. xviii. 6—18. There are internal and external reasons why these adulteries are threefold more grievous than the two above-mentioned: the internal reasons are grounded in the correspondence of those adulteries with the violation of spiritual marriage, which is that of the Lord and the church, and thence of good and truth; and the external reasons are for the sake of guards, to prevent a man's becoming a beast. We have not leisure, however, to proceed to the further disclosure of these reasons.

485. V. THERE ARE FOUR DEGREES OF ADULTERIES, ACCORDING TO WHICH THEY HAVE THEIR PREDICATIONS, THEIR CHARGES OF BLAME, AND AFTER DEATH THEIR IMPUTATIONS. These degrees are not genera, but enter into each genus, and cause its distinctions between more and less evil or good; in the present case, deciding whether adultery of every genus from the nature of the circumstances and contingencies, is to be considered milder or more grievous. That circumstances and contingencies vary every thing is well known. Nevertheless things are considered in one way by a man from his rational light, in another by a judge from the law, and in another by the Lord from the state of a man's mind: wherefore we mention predications, charges of blame, and after death imputations; for predications

are made by a man according to his rational light, charges of blame are made by a judge according to the law, and imputations are made by the Lord according to the state of the man's mind. That these three differ exceedingly from each other, may be seen without explanation : for a man, from rational conviction according to circumstances and contingencies, may acquit a person, whom a judge, when he sits in judgement, cannot acquit from the law : and also a judge may acquit a person, who after death is condemned. The reason of this is, because a judge gives sentence according to the actions done, whereas after death every one is judged according to the intentions of the will and thence of the understanding, and according to the confirmations of the understanding and thence of the will. These intentions and confirmations a judge does not see; nevertheless each judgement is just; the one for the sake of the good of civil society, the other for the sake of the good of heavenly society.

486. VI. ADULTERIES OF THE FIRST DEGREE ARE ADULTERIES OF IGNORANCE, WHICH ARE COMMITTED BY THOSE WHO CANNOT AS YET, OR CANNOT AT ALL, CONSULT THE UNDERSTANDING, AND THENCE CHECK THEM. All evils, and thus also all adulteries, viewed in themselves, are at once of the internal and the external man; the internal intends them, and the external does them; such therefore as the internal man is in the deeds done by the external, such are the deeds viewed in themselves: but since the internal man with his intention, does not appear before man, every one must be judged in a human court from deeds and words according to the law in force and its provisions: the interior sense of the law is also to be regarded by the judge. But to illustrate the case by example: if adultery be committed by a youth, who does not as yet know that adultery is a greater evil than fornication; if the like be committed by a very simple man; if it be committed by a person who is deprived by disease of the full powers of judgement; or by a person, as is sometimes the case, who is delirious by fits, and is at the time in a state of actual delirium; yet further, if it be committed in a fit of insane drunkenness, and so forth, it is evident, that in such cases, the internal man, or mind, is not present in the external, scarcely any otherwise than in an irrational person. Adulteries in these instances are predicated by a rational man according to the above circumstances; nevertheless the perpetrator is charged with blame by the same rational man as a judge, and is punished by the law; but after death those adulteries are imputed according to the presence, quality, and faculty of understanding in the will of the perpetrators.

487. VII. IN SUCH CASES ADULTERIES ARE MILD. This i manifest from what was said just above, n. 486, without furthe confirmation; for it is well known that the quality of every deed and in general the quality of every thing, depends upon circum

stances, and which mitigate or aggravate it; but adulteries of this degree are mild at the first times of their commission; and also remain mild so far as the offending party of either sex, in the future course of life, abstains from them for these reasons;—because they are evils against God, or against the neighbour, or against the goods of the state, and because, in consequence of their being such evils, they are evils against reason; but on the other hand, if they are not abstained from for one of the abovementioned reasons, they are reckoned amongst grievous adulteries; thus it is according to the divine law, Ezek. xviii, 21, 22, 24, and in other places: but they cannot, from the above circumstances, be pronounced either blameless or culpable, or be predicated and judged as mild or grievous, because they do not appear before man, neither are they within the province of his judgement; wherefore it is meant, that after death they are so accounted or imputed.

488. VIII. ADULTERIES OF THE SECOND DEGREE ARE ADULTERIES OF LUST, WHICH ARE COMMITTED BY THOSE WHO INDEED ARE ABLE TO CONSULT THE UNDERSTANDING, BUT FROM ACCIDENTAL CAUSES AT THE MOMENT ARE NOT ABLE. There are two things which, in the beginning, with every man who from natural is made spiritual, are at strife together, which are commonly called the spirit and the flesh; and since the love of marriage is of the spirit, and the love of adultery is of the flesh, in such case there is also a combat between those loves. If the love of marriage conquers, it gains dominion over and subjugates the love of adultery, which is effected by its removal; but if it happens that the lust of the flesh is excited to a heat greater than what the spirit can control from reason, it follows that the state is inverted, and the heat of lust infuses allurements into the spirit, to such a degree, that it is no longer master of its reason, and thence of itself: this is meant by adulteries of the second degree, which are committed by those who indeed are able to consult the understanding, but by reason of accidental causes at the moment are not able. But the matter may be illustrated by particular cases; as in case a meretricious wife by her craftiness captivates a man's mind (*animum*), enticing him into her chamber, and inflaming his passions to such a degree as to leave him no longer master of his judgement; and especially if, at the same time, she also threatens to expose him if he does not consent: in like manner, in case any meretricious wife is skilled in deceitful allurements, or by powerful stimulants inflames the man to such a degree, that the raging lust of the flesh deprives the understanding of the free use of reason: in like manner, in case a man, by powerful enticements, so far works upon another's wife, as to leave her no longer mistress of herself, by reason of the fire kindled in her will; besides other like cases. That these and similar accidental circumstances lessen the grievousness of adultery, and give a milder turn to the predications of the blame

thereof in favor of the party seduced, is agreeable to the dictates and conclusions of reason. The imputation of this degree of adultery comes next to be treated of.

489. IX. ADULTERIES COMMITTED BY SUCH PERSONS ARE IMPUTATORY, ACCORDING AS THE UNDERSTANDING AFTERWARDS FAVORS THEM OR NOT. So far as the understanding favors evils, so far a man appropriates them to himself and makes them his own. Favor implies consent; and consent induces in the mind a state of the love of them: the case is the same with adulteries, which in the beginning were committed without the consent of the understanding, and are favored: the contrary comes to pass if they are not favored. The reason of this is, because evils or adulteries, which are committed in the blindness of the understanding, are committed from the concupiscence of the body; and such evils or adulteries have a near resemblance to the instincts of beasts: with man (*homo*) indeed the understanding is present, while they are committing, but in a passive or dead potency and not in active and living potency. From these considerations it follows of course, that such things are not imputed, except so far as they are afterwards favored or not. By imputation we here mean, accusation after death, and hence judication, which takes place according to the state of a man's spirit: but we do not mean inculpation by a man before a judge; for this does not take place according to the state of a man's spirit, but of his body in the deed; and unless there was a difference herein, those would be acquitted after death who are acquitted in the world, and those would be condemned who are condemned in the world; and thus the latter would be without any hope of salvation.

490. X. ADULTERIES OF THE THIRD DEGREE ARE ADULTERIES OF THE REASON, WHICH ARE COMMITTED BY THOSE WHO WITH THE UNDERSTANDING CONFIRM THEMSELVES IN THE PERSUASION THAT THEY ARE NOT EVILS OF SIN. Every man knows that there exist such principles as the will and the understanding; for in his common speaking he says, "This I will, and this I understand;" but still he does not distinguish them, but makes the one the same as the other; because he only reflects upon the things which belong to the thought grounded in the understanding, and not upon those which belong to the love grounded in the will; for the latter do not appear in light as the former. Nevertheless, he that does not distingush between the will and the understanding, cannot distinguish between evils and goods, and consequently he must remain in entire ignorance concerning the blame of sin. But who does not know that good and truth are two distinct principles, like love and wisdom? and who cannot hence conclude, while he is in rational illumination, that there are two faculties in man, which distinctly receive and appropriate to themselves those principles, and that the one is the will and the other the understanding, by reason that what the

will receives and reproduces is called good, and what the understanding receives is called truth; for what the will loves and does, is called truth, and what the understanding perceives and thinks, is called truth? Now as the marriage of good and truth was treated of in the first part of this work, and in the same place several considerations were adduced concerning the will and the understanding, and the various attributes and predicates of each, which, as I imagine, are also perceived by those who had not thought at all distinctly concerning the understanding and the will, (for human reason is such, that it understands truths from the light thereof, although it has not heretofore distinguished them;) therefore, in order that the distinctions of the understanding and the will may be more clearly perceived, I will here mention some particulars on the subject, that it may be known what is the quality of adulteries of the reason and the understanding, and afterwards what is the quality of adulteries of the will. The following points may serve to illustrate the subject: 1. That the will of itself does nothing; but whatever it does, it does by the understanding. 2. On the other hand also, that the understanding alone of itself does nothing; but whatever it does, it does from the will. 3. That the will flows into the understanding but not the understanding into the will; yet that the understanding teaches what is good and evil, and consults with the will, that out of those two principles it may choose and do what is pleasing to it. 4. That after this there is effected a twofold conjunction; one, in which the will acts from within, and the understanding from without; the other in which the understanding acts from within, and the will from without: thus are distinguished the adulteries of the reason, which are here treated of, from the adulteries of the will, which are next to be treated of. They are distinguished, because one is more grievous than the other; for the adultery of the reason is less grievous than that of the will; because in adultery of the reason, the understanding acts from within, and the will from without; whereas in adultery of the will, the will acts from within, and the understanding from without; and the will is the man himself, and the understanding is the man as grounded in the will; and that which acts within has dominion over that which acts without.

491. XI. THE ADULTERIES COMMITTED BY SUCH PERSONS ARE GRIEVOUS, AND ARE IMPUTED TO THEM ACCORDING TO CONFIRMATIONS. It is the understanding alone that confirms, and when it confirms, it engages the will to its party, and sets it about itself, and thus compels it to compliance. Confirmations are affected by reasonings, which the mind seizes for its use, deriving them either from its superior region or from its inferior; if from the superior region, which communicates with heaven, it confirms marriages and condemns adulteries; but if from the

inferior region, which communicates with the world, it confirms adulteries and makes light of marriages. Every one can confirm evil just as well as good; in like manner what is false and what is true; and the confirmation of evil is perceived with more delight than the confirmation of good, and the confirmation of what is false appears with greater lucidity than the confirmation of what is true. The reason of this is, because the confirmation of what is evil and false derives its reasonings from the delights, the pleasures, the appearances, and the fallacies of the bodily senses; whereas the confirmation of what is good and true derives its reasons from the region above the sensual principles of the body. Now, since evils and falses can be confirmed just as well as goods and truths, and since the confirming understanding draws the will to its party, and the will together with the understanding forms the mind, it follows that the form of the human mind is according to confirmations, being turned to heaven if its confirmations are in favor of marriage, but to hell if they are in favor of adulteries; and such as the form of a man's mind is such is his spirit; consequently such is the man. From these considerations then it is evident, that adulteries of this degree after death are imputed according to confirmations.

492. XII. THE ADULTERIES OF THE FOURTH DEGREE ARE ADULTERIES OF THE WILL WHICH ARE COMMITTED BY THOSE WHO MAKE THEM LAWFUL AND PLEASING, AND WHO DO NOT THINK THEM OF IMPORTANCE ENOUGH TO CONSULT THE UNDERSTANDING RESPECTING THEM. These adulteries are distinguished from the foregoing from their origins. The origin of these adulteries is from the depraved will connate to man, or from hereditary evil, which a man blindly obeys after he is capable of exercising his own judgement, not at all considering whether they are evils or not; wherefore it is said, that he does not think them of importance enough to consult the understanding respecting them: but the origin of the adulteries which are called adulteries of reason, is from a perverse understanding; and these adulteries are committed by those who confirm themselves in the persuasion that they are not evils of sin. With the latter adulterers, the understanding is the principal agent; with the former the will. The distinctions in these two cases do not appear to any man in the natural world; but they appear plainly to the angels in the spiritual world. In the latter world all are in general distinguished according to the evils which originate in the will and in the understanding, and which are accepted and appropriated: they are also separated in hell according to those evils: those who are in evil from the understanding, dwell there in front, and are called satans; but those who are in evil from the will, dwell at the back, and are called devils. It is on account of this universal distinction that mention is made in the Word of satan and the devil. With those wicked ones, and also those adulterers, who are called

satans, the understanding is the principal agent; but with those who are called devils, the will is the principal agent. It is not however possible to explain these distinctions, so as to render them visible to the understanding, unless the distinctions of the will and the understanding be first known; and also unless a description be given of the formation of the mind from the will by the understanding, and of its formation from the understanding by the will. The knowledge of these subjects is necessary, before the distinctions above-mentioned can be seen by reason; but to express this knowledge on paper would require a volume.

493. XIII. THE ADULTERIES COMMITTED BY THESE PERSONS ARE EXCEEDINGLY GRIEVOUS, AND ARE IMPUTED TO THEM AS EVILS OF PURPOSE, AND REMAIN IN THEM AS GUILT. The reason why they are exceedingly grievous, and more grievous than the foregoing, is, because in them the will is the principal agent, whereas in the foregoing the understanding is the principal agent, and a man's life essentially is his will, and formally is his understanding: the reason of this is, because the will acts in unity with the love, and love is the essence of a man's life, and forms itself in the understanding by such things as are in agreement with it: wherefore the understanding viewed in itself is nothing but a form of the will; and since love is of the will, and wisdom of the understanding, therefore wisdom is nothing but a form of love; in like manner truth is nothing but a form of good. That which flows from the very essence of a man's life, thus which flows from his will or his love, is principally called purpose; but that which flows from the form of his life, thus from the understanding and its thought is called intention. Guilt also is principally predicated of the will: hence comes the common observation, that every one has the guilt of evil from inheritance, but that the evil is from the man. Hence these adulteries of the fourth degree are imputed as evils of purpose, and remain in as guilt.

494. XIV. ADULTERIES OF THE THIRD AND FOURTH DEGREES ARE EVILS OF SIN, ACCORDING TO THE QUANTITY AND QUALITY OF UNDERSTANDING AND WILL IN THEM, WHETHER THEY ARE ACTUALLY COMMITTED OR NOT. That adulteries of the reason or the understanding, which are of the third degree, and adulteries of the will, which are of the fourth, are grievous, consequently evils of sin, according to the quality of the understanding and of the will in them, may be seen from the comment above concerning them, n. 490—493. The reason of this is, because a man (*homo*) is a man by virtue of the will and the understanding; for from these two principles exist not only all the things which are done in the mind, but also all those which are done in the body. Who does not know, that the body does not act of itself, but the will by the body? also that the mouth does not speak of itself, but the thought by the mouth? Wherefore if the will were to be taken away, action would instantly be at a stand, and if thought were

to be taken away, the speech of the mouth would instantly cease. Hence it is clearly manifest, that adulteries which are actually committed, are grievous according to the quantity and quality of the understanding of the will in them. That they are in like manner grievous, if the same are not actually committed, appears from the Lord's words: *It was said by them of old time, Thou shalt not commit adultery; but I say unto you, that if any one hath looked at another's woman, to lust after her, he hath already committed adultery with her in heart;* Matt. v. 27, 28: to commit adultery in the heart is to commit it in the will. There are many reasons which operate to prevent an adulterer's being an adulterer in act, while he is still so in will and understanding: for there are some who abstain from adulteries as to act through fear of the cival law and its penalties; through fear of the loss of reputation and thence of honor; through fear of disease thence arising; through fear of quarrels at home on the part of a wife, and the consequent loss of tranquillity; through fear of revenge on the part of the husband and the next of kin; thus also through fear of being beaten by the servants; through poverty or avarice; through imbecility arising from disease, from abuse, from age, or from impotence, and consequent shame: if any one restrains himself from actual adulteries, under the influence of these and like reasons, and yet favors them in his will and understanding, he is still an adulterer: for he believes nevertheless that they are not sins, and he does not make them unlawful before God in his spirit; and thus he commits them in spirit, although not in body before the world; wherefore after death, when he becomes a spirit, he speaks openly in favor of them.

495. XV. Adulteries grounded in purpose of the will, and adulteries grounded in confirmation of the understanding, render men natural, sensual, and corporeal. A man (*homo*) is a man, and is distinguished from the beasts, by this circumstance, that his mind is distinguished into three regions, as many as the heavens are distinguished into: and that he is capable of being elevated out of the lowest region into the next above it, and also from this into the highest, and thus of becoming an angel of one heaven, and even of the third: for this end, there has been given to man a faculty of elevating the understanding thitherto; but if the love of his will is not elevated at the same time, he does not become spiritual, but remains natural: nevertheless he retains the faculty of elevating the understanding. The reason why he retains this faculty is, that he may be reformed; for he is reformed by the understanding: and this is effected by the knowledges of good and truth, and by a rational intuition grounded therein. If he views those knowledges rationally, and lives according to them, then the love of the will is elevated at the same time, and in that degree the human principle is perfected, and the man becomes more and more a man.

It is otherwise if he does not live according to the knowledges of good and truth: in this case the love of his will remains natural, and his understanding by turns becomes spiritual: for it raises itself upwards alternately, like an eagle, and looks down upon what is of its love beneath; and when it sees this, it flies down to it, and conjoins itself with it: if therefore it loves the concupiscences of the flesh, it lets itself down to these from its height, and in conjunction with them, derives delight to itself from their delights; and again in quest of reputation, that it may be believed wise, it lifts itself on high, and thus rises and sinks by turns, as was just now observed. The reason why adulterers of the third and fourth degree, who are such as from purpose of the will and confirmation of the understanding have made themselves adulterers, are absolutely natural, and progressively become sensual and corporeal, is, because they have immersed the love of their will, and together with it their understanding, in the impurities of adulterous love, and are delighted therewith, as unclean birds and beasts are with stinking and dunghill filth as with dainties and delicacies: for the effluvia arising from their flesh fill the recesses of the mind with their dregs, and cause that the will perceives nothing more dainty and desirable. It is these who after death become corporeal spirits, and from whom flow the unclean things of hell and the church, spoken of above n. 430, 431.

496. There are three degrees of the natural man: in the first degree are those who love only the world, placing their heart on wealth; these are properly meant by the natural: in the second degree are those who love only the delights of the senses, placing their heart on every kind of luxury and pleasure; these are properly meant by the sensual: in the third degree are those who love only themselves, placing their heart on the quest of honor; these are properly meant by the corporeal, because they immerse all things of the will, and consequently of the understanding, in the body, and look backward at themselves from others, and love only what belongs to themselves: but the sensual immerse all things of the will and consequently of the understanding in the allurements and fallacies of the senses, indulging in these alone; whereas the natural pour forth into the world all things of the will and understanding, covetously and fraudulently acquiring wealth, and regarding no other use therein and thence but that of possession. The above-mentioned adulteries change men in these degenerate degrees, one into this, another into that, each according to his favorite taste for what is pleasurable, in which taste his peculiar genius is grounded.

497. XVI. AND THIS TO SUCH A DEGREE THAT AT LENGTH THEY REJECT FROM THEMSELVES ALL THINGS OF THE CHURCH AND OF RELIGION. The reason why determined and confirmed adulterers reject from themselves all things of the church and religion is, because the love of marriage and the love of adultery are

opposite, n. 425, and the love of marriage acts in unity with the church and religion; see n. 130, and throughout the former part; hence the love of adultery, as being opposite, acts in unity with those things which are contrary to the church. A further reason why those adulterers reject from themselves all things of the church and of religion, is, because the love of marriage and the love of adultery are opposite, as the marriage of good and truth is opposite to the connection of evil and the false: see n. 427, 428; and the marriage of good and truth constitutes the church, whereas the connection of evil and the false constitutes the anti-church. A further reason why those adulterers reject from themselves all things of the church and of religion, is because the love of marriage and the love of adultery are as opposite as heaven and hell, n. 429; and in heaven there is the love of all things of the church, whereas in hell there is hatred against them. A further reason why those adulterers reject from themselves all things of the church and of religion, is, because their delights commence from the flesh, and are of the flesh also in the spirit, n. 440, 441; and the flesh is contrary to the spirit, that is, contrary to the spiritual things of the church; hence also the delights of adulterous love are called the pleasures of insanity. If you desire demonstration in this case, go, I pray, to those whom you know to be such adulterers, and ask them privately, what they think concerning God, the church, and eternal life, and you will hear. The genuine reason is, because as conjugial love opens the interiors of the mind; and thereby elevates them above the sensual principles of the body, even into the light and heat of heaven, so, on the other hand, the love of adultery closes the interiors of the mind, and thrusts down the mind itself, as to its will, into the body, even into all things which its flesh lusts after; and the deeper it is so thrust down, the further it is removed and set at a distance from heaven.

498. XVII. NEVERTHELESS THEY HAVE THE POWERS OF HUMAN RATIONALITY LIKE OTHER MEN. That the natural man, the sensual, and the corporeal, is equally rational, in regard to understanding, as the spiritual man, has been proved to me from satans and devils arising by leave out of hell, and conversing with angelic spirits in the world of spirits; concerning whom, see the MEMORABLE RELATIONS throughout; but as the love of the will makes the man, and this love draws the understanding into consent, therefore such are not rational except in a state removed from the love of the will; when they return again into this love, they are more dreadfully insane than wild beasts. But a man, without the faculty of elevating the understanding above the love of the will, would not be a man but a beast; for a beast does not enjoy that faculty; consequently neither would he be able to choose any thing, and from choice to do what is good and expedient, and thus he would not be in a capacity to be

reformed, and to be led to heaven, and to live for ever. Hence it is, that determined and confirmed adulterers, although they are merely natural, sensual, and corporeal, still enjoy, like other men, the powers of understanding or rationality: but when they are in the lust of adultery, and think and speak from that lust concerning it, they do not enjoy that rationality; because then the flesh acts on the spirit, and not the spirit on the flesh. It is however to be observed, that these at length after death become stupid; not that the faculty of growing wise is taken away from them, but that they are unwilling to grow wise, because wisdom is undelightful to them.

499. XVIII. BUT THEY USE THAT RATIONALITY WHILE THEY ARE IN EXTERNALS, BUT ABUSE IT WHILE THEY ARE IN INTERNALS. They are in externals when they converse abroad and in company, but in their internals when at home or with themselves. If you wish, make the experiment; bring some person of this character, as, for example, one of the order called jesuits, and cause him to speak in company, or to teach in a temple, concerning God, the holy things of the church, and heaven and hell, and you will hear him a more rational zealot than any other; perhaps also he will force you to sighs and tears for your salvation; but take him into your house, praise him excessively, call him the father of wisdom, and make yourself his friend, until he opens his heart, and you will hear what he will then preach concerning God, the holy things of the church, and heaven and hell,—that they are mere fancies and delusions, and thus bonds invented for souls, whereby great and small, rich and poor, may be caught and bound, and kept under the yoke of their dominion. Let these observations suffice for illustration of what is meant by natural men, even to corporeal, enjoying the powers of human rationality like others, and using it when they are in externals, but abusing it when in their internals. The conclusion to be hence deduced is, that no one is to be judged of from the wisdom of his conversation, but of his life in union therewith.

* * * * * *

500. To the above I will add the following MEMORABLE RELATION. On a certain time in the spiritual world I heard a great tumult: there were some thousands of people gathered together, who cried out, LET THEM BE PUNISHED, LET THEM BE PUNISHED: I went nearer, and asked what the cry meant? A person that was separate from the crowd, said to me, "They are enraged against three priests, who go about and preach every where against adulterers, saying, that adulterers have no acknowledgement of God, and that heaven is closed to them and hell open; and that in hell they are filthy devils, because they appear there at a distance like swine wallowing in mire, and that the angels of heaven abominate them." I inquired, "Where are the priests? and why is there such a vociferation on that account?" He re-

plied, "The three priests are in the midst of them, guarded by attendants; and those who are gathered together are of those who believe adulteries not to be sins, and who say, that adulterers have an acknowledgement of God equally with those who keep to their wives. They are all of them from the Christian world; and the angels have been to see how many there were there who believe adulteries to be sins; and out of a thousand they did not find a hundred." He then told me that the nine hundred say concerning adulteries, "Who does not know that the delight of adultery is superior to the delight of marriage; that adulterers are in continual heat, and thence in alacrity, industry, and active life, superior to those who live with only one woman; and that on the other hand, love with a married partner grows cold, and sometimes to such a degree, that at length scarce a single expression or act of fellowship with her is alive; that it is otherwise with harlots; that the mortification of life with a wife, arising from defect of ability, is recruited and vivified by adulteries; and is not that which recruits and vivifies of more consequence than that which mortifies? What is marriage but allowed adultery? Who knows any distinction between them? Can love be forced? and yet love with a wife is forced by a covenant and laws. Is not love with a married partner the love of the sex, which is so universal that it exists even among birds and beasts? What is conjugial love but the love of the sex? and the love of the sex is free with every woman. The reason why civil laws are against adulteries is, because lawgivers have believed that to prohibit adultery was connected with the public good; and yet lawgivers and judges sometimes commmit adultery, and say among themselves, 'Let him that is without sin cast the first stone.' Who does not know that the simple and religious alone believe adulteries to be sins, and that the intelligent think otherwise, who like us view them by the light of nature? Are not adulteries as prolific as marriages? Are not illegitimate children as alert and qualified for the discharge of offices and employments as the legitimate? Moreover families, otherwise barren, are provided with offspring; and is not this an advantage and not a loss? What harm can come to a wife from admitting several rivals? And what harm can come to a man? To say that it brings disgrace upon a man, is a frivolous idea grounded in mere fancy. The reason why adultery is against the laws and statutes of the church, is owing to the ecclesiastic order for the sake of power; but what have theological and spiritual things to do with a delight merely corporeal and carnal? Are not there instances of adulterous presbyters and monks? and are they incapable on that account of acknowledging and worshipping God? Why therefore do those three priests preach that adulterers have no acknowledgement of God? We cannot endure such blasphemies; wherefore let them be judged and punished." Afterwards

I saw that they called judges, whom they requested to pass sentence of punishment upon them: but the judges said, "This is no part of our jurisdiction; for the point in question is concerning the acknowledgement of God, and concerning sin, and thus concerning salvation and damnation; and sentence in these cases must come from heaven: but we will suggest a method to you, whereby you may know whether these three priests have preached truths. There are three places which we judges know, where such points are examined and revealed in a singular manner: ONE place is, where a way into heaven is open to all; but when they come into heaven, they themselves perceive their own quality as to the acknowledgement of God: the SECOND is, where also a way is open into heaven; but no one can enter into that way unless he has heaven in himself: and the THIRD is where there is a way to hell; and those who love infernal things enter that way of their own accord, because from delight. We judges charge all to go to those places who require judgement from us concerning heaven and hell." On hearing this, those who were gathered together, said, "Let us go to those places;" and while they were going to the first, where a way into heaven is open to all, it suddenly became dark; wherefore some of them lighted torches and carried them before. The judges who were with them said, "This happens to all who go to the first place; as they approach, the fire of the torches becomes more dim, and is extinguished in that place by the light of heaven flowing in, which is a sign that they are there; the reason of this is, because at first heaven is closed to them, and afterwards is opened." They then came to that place, and when the torches were extinguished of themselves, they saw a way tending obliquely upwards into heaven: this those entered who were enraged against the priests; among the first, those who were determined adulterers, after them those who were confirmed adulterers; and as they ascended, the first cried out, "Follow;" and those who followed cried out, "Make haste;" and they pressed forward. After near an hour, when they were all within in the heavenly society, there appeared a gulph between them and the angels; and the light of heaven above the gulph flowing into their eyes, opened the interiors of their minds, whereby they were bound to speak as they interiorly thought; and then they were asked by the angels, whether they acknowledged that God is? The first, who were determined adulterers, replied, "What is God?" And they looked at each other, and said, "Which of you has seen him?" The second, who were confirmed adulterers, said, "Are not all things of nature? What is there above nature but the sun?" And instantly the angels said to them, "Depart from us; now you yourselves perceive that you have no acknowledgement of God: when you descend, the interiors of your mind will be closed and its exteriors opened, and then you can speak against the interiors, and say that God is. Be assured that as soon as a man actually becomes an adulterer, heaven is closed to him; and when heaven is closed, God is not acknowledged. Hear the reason; every filthy principle of hell is from adulterers, and it stinks in heaven like putrid mire of the streets." On hearing these things they turned themselves and descended by three ways; and when they were below, the first and second groups conversing together said, "The priests have conquered there; but we know that we can speak of God equally with them: and when we say that he is, do we not acknowledge him? The interiors and exteriors of the mind, of which the angels told us, are devised fictions. But let us go to the second place pointed out by the judges, where a way is open into heaven to those who have heaven in themselves, thus to those who are about to come into heaven." When they were come thither, a voice proceeded from that heaven, saying, "Shut the gates; there are adulterers at hand." Then suddenly the gates were shut, and the keepers with sticks in their hands drove them away; and they delivered the three priests, against whom they had been tumultuous, from the hands of their keepers, and introduced them into heaven: and instantly, when the gates were open for the priests, there issued from heaven upon the rebels the delightful principle of marriage, which, from its being chaste and pure, almost deprived them of animation; wherefore, for fear of fainting away through suffocation, they hastened to the third place, concerning which the judges said, that thence there was a way to hell; and instantly there issued from thence the delight of adultery, whereby those who were either determined or confirmed adulterers, were so vivified, that they descended as it were dancing, and there like swine immersed themselves in filth.

ON THE LUST OF DEFLORATION.

501. THE lusts treated of in the four following chapters, are not only lusts of adultery, but are more grievous than those since they exist only from adulteries, being taken to after adulteries are become loathsome; as the lust of defloration, which is first treated of, and which cannot previously exist with any one; in like manner the lust of varieties, the lust of violation, and the lust of seducing innocencies, which are afterwards treated of. They are called lusts, because according to the quantity and quality of the lust for those things, such and so great is their appropriation. In reference specifically to the lust of defloration, its infamous villany shall be made manifest from the following considerations: I. *The state of a maiden or undeflowered woman*

before and after marriage. II. *Virginity is the crown of chastity, and the certificate of conjugial love.* III. *Defloration, without a view to marriage as an end, is the villany of a robber* IV. *The lot of those who have confirmed themselves in the persuasion that the lust of defloration is not an evil of sin, after death is grievous.* We proceed to explain them.

502. I. THE STATE OF A MAIDEN OR UNDEFLOWERED WOMAN BEFORE AND AFTER MARRIAGE. What is the quality of the state of a maiden, before she has been instructed concerning the various particulars of the conjugial torch, has been made known to me by wives in the spiritual world, who have departed out of the natural world in their infancy, and have been educated in heaven. They said, that when they arrived at a marriageable state, from seeing conjugial partners they began to love the conjugial life, but only for the end that they might be called wives, and might maintain friendly and confidential society with one man; and also, that being removed from the house of obedience, they might become their own mistresses: they also said, that they thought of marriage only from the blessedness of mutual friendship and confidence with a husband, and not at all from the delight of any flame; but that their maiden state after marriage was changed into a new one, of which they previously had not the least knowledge: and they declared, that this was a state of the expansion of all things of the life of their body from first principles to last, to receive the gifts of their husband, and to unite these gifts to their own life, that thus they might become his love and his wife; and that this state commenced from the moment of defloration, and that after this the flame of love burned to the husband alone, and that they were sensible of the heavenly delights of that expansion; and further, that as each wife was introduced into this state by her own husband, and as it is from him, and thereby his in herself, it is altogether impossible for her to love any other than him alone. From this account it was made manifest what is the quality of the state of maidens before and after marriage in heaven. That the state of maidens and wives on earth, whose first attachments prove successful, is similar to this of the maidens in heaven, is no secret. What maiden can know that new state before she is in it? Inquire, and you will hear. The case is different with those who before marriage catch allurement from being taught.

503. II. VIRGINITY IS THE CROWN OF CHASTITY AND THE CERTIFICATE OF CONJUGIAL LOVE. Virginity is called the crown of chastity, because it crowns the chastity of marriage: it is also the badge of chastity; wherefore the bride at the nuptials wears a crown on her head: it is also a badge of the sanctity of marriage; for the bride, after the maiden flower, gives and devotes herself wholly to the bridegroom, at that time the husband, and the husband in his turn gives and devotes himself wholly to the

bride, at that time the wife. Virginity is also called the certificate of conjugial love, because a certificate has relation to a covenant; and the covenant is, that love may unite them into one man, or into one flesh. The men themselves also before marriage regard the virginity of the bride as a crown of her chastity, and as a certificate of conjugial love, and as the very dainty from which the delights of that love are about to commence and to be perpetuated. From these and the foregoing considerations, it is manifest, that after the zone is taken away, and the virginity is sipped, a maiden becomes a wife, and if not a wife, she becomes a harlot; for the new state into which she is then introduced, is a state of love for her husband, and if not for her husband, it is a state of lust.

504. III. DEFLORATION, WITHOUT A VIEW TO MARRIAGE AS AN END, IS THE VILLANY OF A ROBBER. Some adulterers are impelled by the cupidity of deflowering maidens, and thence also of deflowering young girls in their state of innocence: the enticements offered are either persuasions suggested by pimps, or presents made by the men, or promises of marriage; and those men after defloration leave them, and continually seek for others: moreover, they are not delighted with the objects they have left, but with a continual supply of new ones; and this lust increases even till it becomes the chief of the delights of their flesh. They add also to the above this abominable deed, that by various cunning artifices they entice maidens about to be married or immediately after marriage, to offer them the first-fruits of marriage, which also they thus filthily defile. I have heard also, that when that heat with its potency has failed, they glory in the number of virginities, as in so many golden fleeces of Jason. This villany, which is that of committing a rape, since it was begun in an age of strength, and afterwards confirmed by boastings, remains rooted in, and thereby infixed after death. What the quality of this villany is, appears from what was said above, that virginity is the crown of chastity, the certificate of future conjugial love, and that a maiden devotes her soul and life to him to whom she devotes it; conjugial friendship and the confidence thereof are also founded upon it. A woman likewise, deflowered by a man of the above description, after this door of conjugial love is broken through, loses all shame, and becomes a harlot, which is likewise to be imputed to the robber as the cause. Such robbers, if, after having run through a course of lewdness and profanation of chastity, they apply their minds (*animus*) to marriage, have no other object in their mind (*mens*) than the virginity of her who is to be their married partner; and when they have attained this object, they loathe both bed and chamber, yea also the whole female sex, except young girls: and whereas such are violators of marriage, and despisers of the female sex, and thereby spiritual robbers, it is evident that the divine Nemesis pursues them.

505. IV. THE LOT OF THOSE WHO HAVE CONFIRMED THEM-SELVES IN THE PERSUASION THAT THE LUST OF DEFLORATION IS NOT AN EVIL OF SIN, AFTER DEATH IS GRIEVOUS. Their lot is this: after they have passed the first time of their stay in the spiritual world, which is a time of modesty and morality, because spent in company with angelic spirits, they are next, from their externals, led into their internals, and in this case into the concupiscences with which they had been ensnared in the world, and the angelic spirits into theirs, to the intent that it may appear in what degree they had been ensnared; and if a lesser degree, that after they have been let into them, they may be let out again, and may be covered with shame. But those who had been principled in this malignant lust to such a degree as to be made sensible of its eminent delight, and to make a boast of those thefts as of the choicest spoils, do not suffer themselves to be drawn away from it; wherefore they are let into their freedom, and then they instantly wander about, and inquire after brothels, and also enter them when they are pointed out; (these brothels are on the sides of hell:) but when they meet with none but prostitutes there, they go away, and inquire where there are maidens; and then they are carried to harlots, who by phantasy can assume supereminent beauty, and a florid girlish complexion, and boast themselves of being maidens; and on seeing these they burn with desire towards them as they did in the world: wherefore they bargain with them; but when they are about to enjoy the bargain, the phantasy induced from heaven is taken away, and then those pretended maidens appear in their own deformity, monstrous and dark, to whom nevertheless they are compelled to cleave for a time: those harlots are called sirens. But if by such fascinations they do not suffer themselves to be draw away from that wild lust, they are cast down into the hell lying to the south and west, beneath the hell of the crafty courtezans, and there they are associated with their companions. I have also been permitted to see them in that hell, and have been told that many of noble descent, and the more opulent, are therein; but as they had been such in the world, all remembrance of their descent and of the dignity derived from their opulence is taken from them, and a persuasion is induced on them that they have been vile slaves, and thence were unworthy of all honor. Among themselves indeed they appear as men: but when seen by others, who are allowed to look in thither, they appear as apes, with a stern look instead of a courteous one, and a horrid countenance instead of one of pleasantry. They walk with their loins contracted, and thereby bent, the upper part of the body hanging forward in front, as if they were ready to fall, and they emit a disagreeable smell. They loathe the sex, and turn away from those they see; for they have no desire towards them. Such they appear when seen near

at hand; but when viewed from afar, they appear like dogs of indulgences, or whelps of delight; and there is also heard somewhat like barking in the tone of their speech.

ON THE LUST OF VARIETIES.

506. THE lust of varieties here treated of, does not mean the lust of fornication, which was treated of above in its proper chapter: the latter lust, notwithstanding its being usually promiscuous and vague, still does not occasion the lust of varieties, unless when it is immoderate, and the fornicator looks to number, and boasts thereof from a principle of cupidity. This idea causes a beginning of this lust; but what its quality is as it advances, cannot be distinctly perceived, unless in some such series as the following: I. *By the lust of varieties is meant the entirely dissolute lust of adultery.* II. *That lust is love and at the same time loathing in regard to the sex.* III. *That lust altogether annihilates conjugial love appertaining to itself.* IV. *The lot of those [who have been addicted to that lust], after death, is miserable, since they have not the inmost principle of life.* We proceed to an explanation of each article.

507. I. BY THE LUST OF VARIETIES IS MEANT THE ENTIRELY DISSOLUTE LUST OF ADULTERY. This lust insinuates itself with those who in youth have relaxed the bonds of modesty, and have had opportunities of association with many loose women, especially if they have not wanted the means of satisfying their pecuniary demands. They implant and root this lust in themselves by immoderate and unlimited adulteries, and by shameless thoughts concerning the love of the female sex, and by confirming themselves in the idea that adulteries are not evils, and not at all sins. This lust increases with them as it advances, so much so that they desire all the women in the world, and wish for whole troops, and a fresh one every day. Whereas this love separates itself from the common love of the sex implanted in every man, and altogether from the love of one of the sex, which is conjugial love, and inserts itself into the exteriors of the heart as a delight of love separate from those loves, and yet derived from them; therefore it is so thoroughly rooted in the cuticles, that it remains in the touch when the powers are decayed. Persons addicted to this lust make light of adulteries; wherefore they think of the whole female sex as of a common harlot, and of marriage as of a common harlotry, and thereby mix immodesty in modesty, and from the mixture grow insane. From these considerations it is evident what is here meant by the lust of varieties, that it is the lust of entirely dissolute adultery.

508. II. THAT LUST IS LOVE AND AT THE SAME TIME LOATH

ING IN REGARD TC THE SEX. Persons addicted to that lust have a love for the sex, because they derive variety from the sex; and they have a loathing for the sex, because after enjoying a woman they reject her and lust after others. This obscene lust burns towards a fresh woman, and after burning, it grows cold towards her; and cold is loathing. That this lust is love and at the same time loathing in regard to the sex, may be illustrated as follows: set on the left side a company of the women whom they have enjoyed, and on the right side a company of those whom they have not; would not they look at the latter company from love, but at the former from loathing? and yet each company is the sex.

509. III. THAT LUST ALTOGETHER ANNIHILATES CONJUGIAL LOVE APPERTAINING TO ITSELF. The reason of this is, because that lust is altogether opposite to conjugial love, and so opposite, that it not only rends it asunder, but as it were grinds it to powder, and thereby annihilates it: for conjugial love is confined to one of the sex; whereas that lust does not stop at one, but within an hour or a day is as intensely cold as it was before hot towards her; and since cold is loathing, the latter by forced cohabitation and dwelling together is so accumulated as to become nauseous, and thus conjugial love is consumed to such a degree that nothing of it is left. From these considerations it may be seen, that this lust is fatal to conjugial love; and as conjugial love constitutes the inmost principle of life with man, that it is fatal to his life; and that that lust, by successive interceptions and closings of the interiors of the mind, at length becomes cuticular, and thus merely alluring; while the faculty of understanding or rationality still remains.

510. IV. THE LOT OF THOSE [WHO HAVE BEEN ADDICTED TO THAT LUST] AFTER DEATH IS MISERABLE, SINCE THEY HAVE NOT THE INMOST PRINCIPLE OF LIFE. Every one has excellence of life according to his conjugial love; for that excellence conjoins itself with the life of the wife, and by conjunction exalts itself; but as with those of whom we are speaking there does not remain the least principle of conjugial love, and consequently not anything of the inmost principle of life, therefore their lot after death is miserable. After passing a certain period of time in their externals, in which they converse rationally and act civilly, they are let into their internals, and in this case into a similar lust and its delights, in the same degree as in the world: for every one after death is let into the same state of life which he had appropriated to himself, to the intent that he may be withdrawn from it; for no one can be withdrawn from this evil, unless he has first been led into it; if he were not to be led into it, the evil would conceal itself, and defile the interiors of the mind, and spread itself as a plague, and would next burst through all barriers and destroy the external principles of the body. For this end there are opened to them brothels, which are on the side of hell.

where there are harlots with whom they have an opportunity of varying their lusts; but this is granted with the restriction to one harlot in a day, and under a penalty in case of communication with more than one on the same day. Afterwards, when from examination it appears that that lust is so inbred that they cannot be withdrawn from it, they are conveyed to a certain place which is next above the hell assigned for them, and then they appear to themselves as if they fall into a swoon, and to others as if they fall down with the face upward; and also the ground beneath their backs is actually opened, and they are absorbed, and sink down into hell among their like; thus they are gathered to their own. I have been permitted to see them there, and likewise to converse with them. Among themselves they appear as men, which is granted them lest they should be a terror to their companions; but at a certain distance they seem to have white faces consisting only of skin, and this because they have no spiritual life in them, which every one has according to the conjugial principle sown in him. Their speech is dry, parched, and sorrowful: when they are hungry, they lament; and their lamentations are heard as a peculiar clashing noise. Their garments are tattered, and their lower garments are drawn above the belly round about the breast; because they have no loins, but their ankles commence from the region of the bottom of the belly: the reason of this is, because the loins with men (*homines*) correspond to conjugial love, and they are void of this love. They said that they loathe the sex on account of their having no potency. Nevertheless, among themselves they can reason as from rationality; but since they are cutaneous, they reason from the fallacies of the senses. This hell is in the western quarter towards the north. These same persons, when seen from afar, appear not as men or as monsters, but as frozen substances. It is however to be observed, that those become of this description who have indulged in the above lust to such a degree as to rend and annihilate in themselves the conjugial human principle.

ON THE LUST OF VIOLATION.

511. THE lust of violation does not mean the lust of defloration, which is the violation of virginities, but not of maidens when it is effected from consent; whereas the lust of violation, which is here treated of, retreats in consequence of consent, and is sharpened in consequence of refusal; and it is the passion of violating all women whatever, who altogether refuse, and violently resist, whether they be maidens, or widows, or wives. Persons addicted to this lust are like robbers and pirates, who are delighted

with spoil and plunder, and not with what is given and justly acquired; and they are like malefactors, who covet what is disallowed and forbidden, and despise what is allowed and granted. These violators are altogether averse to consent, and are set on fire by resistance, which if they observe to be not internal, the ardor of their lust is instantly extinguished, as fire is by water thrown upon it. It is well known, that wives do not spontaneously submit themselves to the disposal of their husbands as to the ultimate effects of love, and that from prudence they resist as they would resist violation, to the end that they may take away from their husbands the cold arising from the consideration of enjoyments being cheap in consequence of being continually allowed, and also in consequence of an idea of lasciviousness on their part. These repugnancies, although they enkindle, still are not the causes, but only the beginnings of this lust: its cause is, that after conjugial love and also adulterous love have grown insipid by practice, they are willing, in order that those loves may be repaired, to be set on fire by absolute repugnances. This lust thus begun, afterwards increases, and as it increases it despises and breaks through all bounds of the love of the sex, and exterminates itself, and from a lascivious, corporeal, and fleshly love, becomes cartilaginous and bony; and then, from the periosteums, which have an acute feeling, it becomes acute. Nevertheless this lust is rare, because it exists only with those who had entered into the married state, and then had lived in the practice of adulteries until they became insipid. Besides this natural cause of this lust, there is also a spiritual cause, of which something will be said in what follows.

512. The lot of persons of this character after death is as follows: these violators then separate themselves from those who are in the limited love of the sex, and altogether from those who are in conjugial love, thus from heaven: afterwards they are sent to the most cunning harlots, who not only by persuasion, but also by imitation perfectly like that of a stage-player, can feign and represent as if they were chastity itself. These harlots clearly discern those who are principled in the above lust: in their presence they speak of chastity and its value; and when the violator comes near and touches them, they are full of wrath, and fly away as through terror into a closet, where there is a couch and a bed, and slightly close the door after them, and recline themselves: and hence by their art they inspire the violator with an ungovernable desire of breaking down the door, of rushing in, and attacking them; and when this is effected, the harlot raising herself erect with the violator begins to fight with her hands and nails, tearing his face, rending his clothes, and with a furious voice crying to the harlots her companions, as to her female servants, for assistance, and opening the window with a loud outcry of thief, robber, and murderer; and when the violator is at hand,

she bemoans herself and weeps: and after violation she prostrates herself, howls, and calls out that she is undone, and at the same time threatens in a serious tone, that unless he expiates the violation by paying a considerable sum, she will attempt his destruction. While they are engaged in these venereal scenes, they appear at a distance like cats, which nearly in like manner before their conjunctions combat together, run forward, and make an outcry. After some such brothel-contests, they are taken away, and conveyed into a cavern, where they are forced to some work: but as their smell is offensive, in consequence of having rent asunder the conjugial principle, which is the chief jewel of human life, they are sent to the borders of the western quarters, where at a certain distance they appear lean, as if consisting of bones covered over with skin only; but when seen at a distance they appear like panthers. When I was permitted to see them nearer, I was surprised that some of them held books in their hands, and were reading; and I was told that this is the case, because in the world they said various things concerning the spiritual things of the church, and yet defiled them by adulteries, even to their extremities, and that such was the correspondence of this lust with the violation of spiritual marriage. But it is to be observed, that the instances of those who are principled in this lust are rare: certain it is, that women, because it is unbecoming for them to prostitute love, are repugnant thereto, and that repugnance enervates; nevertheless this is not from any lust of violation.

ON THE LUST OF SEDUCING INNOCENCIES.

513. THE lust of seducing innocencies is neither the lust of defloration, nor the lust of violation, but is peculiar and singular by itself; it prevails more especially with the deceitful. The women, who appear to them as innocencies, are such as regard the evil of adultery as an enormous sin, and who therefore highly prize chastity, and at the same time piety: these women are the objects which set them on fire. In Roman Catholic countries there are maidens devoted to the monastic life; and because they believe these maidens to be pious innocencies above the rest of their sex, they view them as the dainties and delicacies of their lust. With a view of seducing either the latter or the former because they are deceitful, they first devise arts, and next, when they have well digested them, without receiving any check from shame, they practise them as from nature. These arts are principally pretences of innocence, love, chastity, and piety; by these and other cunning stratagems, they enter into the interior friendship of such women, and thence into their love, which they change

from spiritual into natural by various persuasions and at the same time by insinuations, and afterwards into corporeal-carnal by irritations, and then they take possession of them at pleasure; and when they have attained this end, they rejoice in heart, and make a mock of those whom they have violated.

514. The lot of these seducers after death is sad, since such seduction is not only impiety, but also malignity. After they have passed through their first period in the spiritual world, which is in externals, wherein they excel many others in the elegance of their manners and the courteousness of their speech, they are reduced to another period of their life, which is in internals, wherein their lust is set at liberty, and commences its sport; and then they are first conveyed to women who had made vows of chastity, and with these they are examined as to the quality of their malignant concupiscence, to the intent that they may not be judged except on conviction: when they are made sensible of the chastity of those women, their deceit begins to act, and to attempt its crafty arts; but as this is to no purpose, they depart from them. They are afterwards introduced to women of genuine innocence; and when they attempt to deceive these in like manner, by virtue of a power given to those women, they are heavily fined; for they occasion in their hands and feet a grievous numbness; likewise in their necks, and at length make them feel as it were a swoon; and when they have inflicted this punishment, they run away and escape from the sufferers. After this there is a way opened to them to a certain company of courtezans, who have been versed in the art of cunningly feigning innocence: and these first expose them to laughter among themselves, and at length after various engagements suffer themselves to be violated. After some such scenes, a third period takes place, which is that of judgement; and in this case, being convicted, they sink down, and are gathered to their like in the hell which is in the northern quarter, and there they appear at a distance like weasels; but if they have allured by deceit, they are conveyed down from this hell to that of the deceitful, which is in the western quarter at a depth to the back; in this hell they appear at a distance like serpents of various kinds; and the most deceitful like vipers: but in the hell into which I was permitted to look, they appeared to me as if they were ghastly pale, with faces of chalk: and as they are mere concupiscences, they do not like to speak: and if they do speak, they only mutter and stammer various things, which are understood by none but their companions who are near them; but presently, as they sit or stand, they make themselves unseen, and fly about in the cavern like phantoms; for on this occasion they are in phantasy, and phantasy appears to fly: after flying they rest themselves, and then, what is wonderful, one does not know another; the cause of this is, because they are principled in deceit, and deceit does not believe another, and thereby with-

draws itself. When they are made sensible of any thing proceeding from conjugial love, they fly away into hiding places and conceal themselves. They are also void of all love of the sex, and are real impotencies, and are called infernal genii.

ON THE CORRESPONDENCE OF ADULTERIES WITH THE VIOLATION OF SPIRITUAL MARRIAGE.

515. I SHOULD here say something, in the way of preface, concerning correspondence; but the subject does not properly belong to the present work. The nature and meaning of correspondence may be seen in a brief summary above, n. 76, and n. 342; and fully in the APOCALYPSE REVEALED, from beginning to end, that it is between the natural sense of the Word and the spiritual sense. That in the Word there is a natural and a spiritual sense, and a correspondence between them, has been demonstrated in the DOCTRINE OF THE NEW JERUSALEM CONCERNING THE SACRED SCRIPTURE, and especially, n. 5—26.

516. The spiritual marriage means the marriage of the Lord and the church, spoken of above, n. 116—131; and hence also the marriage of good and truth, likewise spoken of above, n. 83—102; and as this marriage of the Lord and the church, and the consequent marriage of good and truth, is in every thing of the Word, it is the violation of this which is here meant by the violation of the spiritual marriage; for the church is from the Word, and the Word is the Lord: for the Lord is the Word, because he is divine good and divine truth therein. That the Word is that marriage, may be seen fully confirmed in the DOCTRINE OF THE NEW JERUSALEM CONCERNING THE SACRED SCRIPTURE, n. 80—90.

517. Since therefore the violation of the spiritual marriage is the violation of the Word, it is evident that this violation is the adulteration of good and the falsification of truth, for the spiritual marriage is the marriage of good and truth; whence it follows, that when the good of the Word is adulterated, and its truth falsified, the above marriage is violated. How this violation is effected, and by whom, is in some measure evident from what follows.

518. Above, in treating of the marriage of the Lord and the church, n. 116, and the following numbers, and in treating of the marriage of good and truth, n. 83, and the following numbers, it was shewn, that that marriage corresponds to marriages in the world: hence it follows, that the violation of that marriage corresponds to whoredoms and adulteries. That this is the case, is very manifest from the Word itself, in that whoredoms and adulteries there signify the falsifications of truth and the adulterations

of good, as may be plainly seen from numerous passages adduced out of the Word in the APOCALYPSE REVEALED, n. 134.

519. The Word is violated by those in the Christian church who adulterate its goods and truths; and those do this who separate truth from good and good from truth; also, who assume and confirm appearances of truth and fallacies for genuine truths; and likewise, who know truths of doctrine derived from the Word, and live evil lives; not to mention other like cases. These violations of the Word and the church correspond to the prohibited degrees, mentioned in Levit., chap. xviii.

520. As the natural principle and the spiritual appertaining to every man (*homo*), cohere as soul and body, (for a man without the spiritual principle which flows into and vivifies his natural principle, is not a man), it hence follows, that whoever is in spiritual marriage is also in happy natural marriage; and on the contrary, that whoever is in spiritual adultery is also in natural adultery, and whoever is in natural adultery is also in spiritual adultery. Now since all who are in hell are in the nuptial connection of evil and the false, and this is essential spiritual adultery; and all who are in heaven are in the marriage of good and truth, and this is esential marriage; therefore hell in the total is called adultery, and heaven in the total is called marriage.

* * * * *

521. To the above shall be added this MEMORABLE RELATION. My sight being opened, I saw a shady forest, and therein a crowd of satyrs: the satyrs as to their breasts were rough and hairy, and as to their feet some were like calves, some like panthers, and some like wolves, and they had beasts' claws instead of toes. These were running to and fro like wild beasts, crying out, "Where are the women?" and instantly I saw some harlots who were expecting them, and who in various ways were monstrous. The satyrs ran towards them, and laid hold of them, dragging them into a cavern, which was in the midst of the forest deep beneath the earth; and upon the ground round about the cavern lay a great serpent in spiral foldings, breathing poison into the cavern: in the branches of the forest above the serpent dismal birds of night croaked and screeched. But the satyrs and harlots did not see these things, because they were the correspondences of their lasciviousnesses, and therefore their usual appearances at a distance. Afterwards they came out of the cavern, and entered a certain low cottage, which was a brothel; and then being separated from the harlots they talked together, and I listened; for conversation in the spiritual world may be heard by a distant person as if he was present, the extent of space in that world being only an appearance. They talked about marriages, nature, and religion. Those who as to the feet appeared like calves, spoke concerning MARRIAGES, and said, "What are marriages but licit adulteries? and what is sweeter than adulterous hypocrisies, and the making

fools of husbands?" At this the rest clapped their hands with a loud laugh. The satyrs who as to the feet appeared as panthers, spoke concerning NATURE, and said, "What is there but nature? What distinction is there between a man and a beast, except that a man can speak articulately and a beast sonorously? Does not each derive life from heat, and understanding from light, by the operation of nature?" Hereupon the rest exclaimed, "Admirable! you speak from judgement." Those who as to the feet appeared like wolves, spoke concerning RELIGION, saying, "What is God or a divine principle, but the inmost principles of nature in action? What is religion but a device to catch and bind the vulgar?" Hereupon the rest vociferated, "Bravo!" After a few minutes they rushed forth, and in so doing they saw me at a distance looking attentively at them. Being provoked at this, they ran out from the forest, and with a threatening countenance directed their course hastily towards me, and said, "What are you doing here, listening to our whispers?" I replied, "Why should I not? what is to hinder me? you were only talking together:" and I related what I had heard from them. Hereupon their minds (*animi*) were appeased, which was through fear lest their sentiments should be divulged; and then they began to speak modestly and to act bashfully; from which circumstance I knew that they were not of mean descent but of honorable birth; and then I told them, how I saw them in the forest as satyrs, twenty as calf-satyrs, six as panther-satyrs, and four as wolf-satyrs; they were thirty in number. They were surprised at this, because they saw themselves there as men, and nothing else, in like manner as they saw themselves here with me. I then taught them, that the reason of their so appearing was from their adulterous lust, and that this satyr-like form was a form of dissolute adultery, and not a form of a person. This happened, I said, because every evil concupiscence presents a likeness of itself in some form, which is not perceived by those who are in the concupiscence, but by those who are at a distance: I also said, "To convince you of it, send some from among you into that forest, and do you remain here, and look at them." They did so, and sent away two; and viewing them from near the above brothel-cottage, they saw them altogether as satyrs; and when they returned, they saluted those satyrs, and said, "Oh what ridiculous figures!" While they were laughing, I jested a good deal with them, and told them that I had also seen adulterers as hogs; and then I recollected the fable of Ulysses and the Circe, how she sprinkled the companions and servants of Ulysses with poisonous herbs, and touched them with a magic wand, and turned them into hogs,—perhaps into adulterers, because she could not by any art turn any one into a hog. After they had made themselves exceedingly merry on this and other like subjects, I asked them whether they then knew to what kingdoms in the world they had belonged? They said, they had belonged to various kingdoms, and they named Italy, Poland, Germany, England, Sweden; and I enquired, whether they had seen any one from Holland of their party? And they said, Not one. After this I gave the conversation a serious turn, and asked them, whether they had ever thought that adultery is sin? They replied, "What is sin? we do not know what it means." I then inquired, whether they ever remembered that adultery was contrary to the sixth* commandment of the Decalogue. They replied, "What is the Decalogue? Is not it the catechism? What have we men to do with that childish pamphlet? I asked them, whether they had ever thought at all about hell. They replied, "Who ever came up thence to give us information?" I asked, whether they had ever thought at all in the world about a life after death. They said, "Just as much as about the future life of beasts, and at times as about phantoms, which exhale from dead bodies and float about." I further asked them, whether they had heard any thing from the priests on any of these subjects. They replied, that they had attended only to the sound of their voices, and not to the matter: and what is it? Being astonished at these answers, I said to them, "Turn your faces, and direct your eyes to the midst of the forest, where the cavern is in which you have been:" and they turned themselves, and saw that great serpent around the cavern in spiral foldings, breathing poison, and also the doleful birds in the branches over the serpents. I then asked them, "What do you see?" But being much terrified, they did not answer: and I said, "Do you see the dreadful sight? Know then that this is a representative of adultery in the baseness of its lust." Suddenly at that instant an angel presented himself, who was a priest, and opened the hell in the western quarter into which such spirits are at length collected; and he said, "Look thither:" and they saw that firy lake, and knew there some of their friends in the world, who invited them to themselves. Having seen and heard these things, they turned themselves away, and rushed out of my sight, and retired from the forest; but I observed their steps, that they only pretended to retire, and that by winding ways they returned into the forest.

522. After this I returned home, and the next day, from a recollection of these sad scenes, I looked to the same forest, and saw that it had disappeared, and in its place there was a sandy plain, and in the midst thereof a lake, in which were some red serpents. But some weeks after when I was looking thither again, I saw on its right side some fallow land, and upon it some husbandmen: and again, after some weeks I saw springing out of that fallow land some tilled land surrounded with shrubs: and I then heard a voice from heaven, "Enter into your cham-

---

* According to the division of the commandments adopted by the Church of England, it is the *seventh* that is here referred to.

ber, and shut the door, and apply to the work begun on the Apocalypse, and finish it within two years."

ON THE IMPUTATION OF EACH LOVE, ADULTEROUS AND CONJUGIAL.

523. THE Lord saith, JUDGE NOT, THAT YE BE NOT CONDEMNED, Matt. vii. 1; which cannot in any wise mean judgement respecting any one's moral and civil life in the world, but respecting his spiritual and celestial life. Who does not see, that unless a man was allowed to judge respecting the moral life of those who live with him in the world, society would perish? What would society be if there were no public judicature, and if every one did not exercise his judgement respecting another? But to judge what is the quality of the interior mind, or soul, thus what is the quality of any one's spiritual state, and thence what his lot is after death, is not allowed; for that is known only to the Lord: neither does the Lord reveal this till after the person's decease, to the intent that every one may act freely in whatever he does, and thereby that good or evil may be from him, and thus be in him, and that thence he may live to himself and live his own to eternity. The reason why the interiors of the mind, which are kept hid in the world, are revealed after death is, because this is of importance and advantage to the societies into which the man then comes; for in them all are spiritual. That those interiors are then revealed, is plain from these words of the Lord: *There is nothing concealed, which shall not be revealed, or hidden, which shall not be known: therefore whatsoever things ye have said in darkness, shall be heard in light; and that which ye have spoken into the ear in closets shall be preached on the house-tops*, Luke xii. 2, 3. A common judgement, as this for instance,—" If you are such in internals as you appear to be in externals, you will be saved or condemned," is allowed; but a particular judgement, as this, for instance,—" You are such in internals, therefore you will be saved or condemned," is not allowed. Judgement concerning the spiritual life of a man, or the internal life of the soul, is meant by the imputation which is here treated of. Can any human being know and decide who is in heart an adulterer, and who a conjugial partner? And yet the thoughts of the heart, which are the purposes of the will, judge every one. But we will explain this subject in the following order: 1. *The evil in which every one is principled, is imputed to him after death; and so also the good.* II. *The transference of the good of one person into another is impossible.* III. *Imputation, if by it is meant such transference, is a frivolous term.* IV. *Evil is imputed to every one according to the quality of his will and his understanding; in like manner good.* V. *Thus adulterous love is*

imputed to every one. **VI.** *In like manner conjugial love.* We proceed to the explanation of each article.

524. I. THE EVIL IN WHICH EVERY ONE IS PRINCIPLED, IS IMPUTED TO HIM AFTER DEATH; AND SO ALSO THE GOOD. To make this proposition in some degree evident, it shall be considered according to the following arrangement: 1. That every one has a life peculiar to himself. 2. That every one's life remains with him after death. 3. That to an evil person is then imputed the evil of his life, and to a good person the good of his life. As to the first point,—that every one has a life peculiar to himself, thus distinct from that of another, it is well known; for there is a perpetual variety, and there is not any thing the same as another, consequently every one has his own peculiar principle. This is evident from men's faces, the faces of no two persons being absolutely alike, nor can there be two alike to eternity: the reason of this is, because there are no two minds (*animi*) alike, and faces are derived from minds; for the face, as it is said, is a type of the mind, and the mind derives its origin and form from the life. Unless a man (*homo*) had a life peculiar to himself, as he has a mind and a face peculiar to himself, he would not have any life after death, separate from that of another; yea, neither would there be a heaven, for heaven consists of perpetual varieties; its form is derived solely from the varieties of souls and minds arranged into such an order as **to** make a one; and they make a one from the One, whose life is in every thing therein as the soul is in a man: unless this was the case, heaven would be dispersed, because form would be dissolved. The One from whom all things have life, and from whom form coheres, is the Lord. In general every form consists of various things, and is such as is their harmonic co-ordination and arrangement to a one: such is the human form; and hence it is that a man, consisting of so many members, viscera, and organs, is not sensible of any thing in himself and from himself but as of a one. As to the SECOND point,—that every one's life remains with him after death, it is known in the church from these passages of the Word: *The Son of Man will come and will then render to every one according to his deeds,* Matt. xvi. 27. *I saw the books open; and all were judged according to their works,* Rev. xx. 12. *In the day of judgement God will render to every one according to his works,* Rom. ii. 6; 2 Cor. v. 10. The works, according to which it will be rendered to every one, are the life, because the life does the works, and they are according to the life. As I have been permitted for several years to be associated with angels, and to converse with the deceased, I can testify for certain, that every one is then examined as to the quality of the life which he has led, and that the life which he has contracted in the world abides with him to eternity. I have conversed with those who lived ages ago, whose life I have been acquainted with from history.

and I have known it to be like the description given of it; and I have heard from the angels, that no one's life after death can be changed, because it is organized according to his love and consequent works; and that if it were changed the organization would be rent asunder, which cannot be done in any case; also that a change of organization can only be effected in the material body, and is utterly impossible in the spiritual body, after the former has been laid aside. In regard to the THIRD point—that to an evil person is then imputed the evil of his life, and to a good person the good of his life, it is to be observed, that the imputation of evil is not accusation, inculpation, and judication, as in the world, but evil itself produces this effect; for the evil freely separate themselves from the good, since they cannot remain together. The delights of the love of evil are different from those of the love of good; and delights exhale from every one, as odors do from every vegetable in the world; for they are not absorbed and concealed by the material body as heretofore, but flow freely from their loves into the spiritual *aura;* and as evil is there made sensible as in its odor, it is in this which accuses, fixes blame, and judges,—not before any judge, but before every one who is principled in good; and this is what is meant by imputation. Moreover, an evil person chooses companions with whom he may live in his delights; and because he is averse from the delight of good, he spontaneously betakes himself to his own in hell. The imputation of good is effected in like manner, and takes place with those who in the world have acknowledged that all good in them is from the Lord, and nothing from themselves. These, after they have been prepared, are let into the interior delights of good, and then there is opened to them a way into heaven, to the society where its homogeneous delights are: this is effected by the Lord.

525. II. THE TRANSFERENCE OF THE GOOD OF ONE PERSON TO ANOTHER IS IMPOSSIBLE. The evidence of this proposition may also be seen from the following points: 1. That every man is born in evil. 2. That he is led into good by regeneration from the Lord. 3. That this is effected by a life according to his precepts. 4. Wherefore good, when it is thus implanted, cannot be transferred. The FIRST point,—that every man is born in evil, is well known in the church. It is generally said that this evil is derived hereditarily from Adam; but it is from a man's parents. Every one derives from his parents his peculiar temper, which is his inclination. That this is the case, is evinced both by reason and experience; for the likenesses of parents as to face, genius, and manners, appear extant in their immediate offspring and in their posterity; hence families are known by many, and a judgement is also formed concerning their minds (*animi*); wherefore the evils which parents themselves have contracted, and which they have transmitted to their offspring, are the evils

in which men are born. The reason why it is believed that the guilt of Adam is inscribed on all the human race, is, because few reflect upon any evil with themselves, and thence know it; wherefore they suppose that it is so deeply hid as to appear only in the sight of God. In regard to the SECOND point,—that a man is led into good by regeneration from the Lord, it is to be observed that there is such a thing as regeneration, and that unless a person be regenerated, he cannot enter into heaven, as appears clearly from the Lord's words in John iii. 3, 5. The regeneration consists in purification from evils, and thereby renovation of life, cannot be unknown in the Christian world; for reason also sees this when it acknowledges that every one is born in evil, and that evil cannot be washed and wiped away like filth by soap and water, but by repentance. As to the THIRD point,—that a man is led into good by the Lord, by a life according to his precepts, it is plain from this consideration, that there are five precepts of regeneration; see above, n. 82; among which are these,—that evils are to be shunned, because they are of and from the devil, and that goods are to be done, because they are of and from God; and that men ought to go to the Lord, in order that he may lead them to do the latter. Let any one consult himself and consider, whether a man derives good from any other source; and if he has not good, he has not salvation. In regard to the FOURTH point,—that good, when it is thus implanted, cannot be transferred, (that is, the good of one person into another,) it is evident from what has been already said; for from that it follows, that a man by regeneration is made altogether new as to his spirit, which is effected by a life according to the Lord's precepts. Who does not see that this renewing can only be effected from time to time, in nearly the same manner as a tree successively takes root and grows from a seed, and is perfected? Those who have other perceptions of regeneration, do not know any thing about the state of man, or about evil and good, which two are altogether opposite, and that good can only be implanted so far as evil is removed; nor do they know, that so long as any one is in evil, he is averse from the good which in itself is good; wherefore if the good of one should be transferred into any one who is in evil, it would be as if a lamb should be cast before a wolf, or as if a pearl should be tied to a swine's snout: from which considerations it is evident, that any such transfer is impossible.

526. III. IMPUTATION, IF BY IT IS MEANT SUCH TRANSFERENCE, IS A FRIVOLOUS TERM. That the evil in which every one is principled, is imputed to him after death, and so also the good, was proved above, n. 524; hence it is evident what is meant by imputation: but if by imputation is meant the tranference of good into any one that is in evil, it is a frivolous term, because any such transference is impossible, as was also proved above, n. 525. In the world, merits may as it were be transferred by men;

that is, good may be done to children for the sake of their parents, or to the friends of any client out of favor; but the good of merit cannot be inscribed on their souls, but only be externally adjoined. The like is not possible with men as to their spiritual life: this, as was shewn above, must be implanted; and if it is not implanted by a life according to the Lord's precepts, as above-mentioned, a man remains in the evil in which he was born. Before such implantation, it is impossible for any good to reach him, or if it reaches him, it is instantly struck back and rebounds like an elastic ball falling upon a rock, or it is absorbed like a diamond thrown into a bog. A man not reformed as to the spirit, is like a panther or an owl, and may be compared to a bramble and a nettle; but a man regenerated is like a sheep or a dove, and may be compared to an olive and a vine. Consider, I pray, if you are so disposed, how can a man-panther be changed into a man-sheep, or an owl into a dove, or a bramble into an olive, or a nettle into a vine, by any imputation, if by it is meant transference? In order that such a change may be effected is it not necessary that the ferine principle of the panther and the owl, or the noxious principle of the bramble and the nettle, be first taken away, and thereby the truly human and innocent principle be implanted? How this is effected, the Lord also teaches in John, chap. xv. 1—7.

527. IV. EVIL OR GOOD IS IMPUTED TO EVERY ONE ACCORD-ING TO THE QUALITY OF HIS WILL AND HIS UNDERSTANING. It is well known that there are two principles which make a man's life, the will and the understanding; and that all things which a man does, are done from his will and his understanding; and that without these acting principles he would have neither action nor speech other than as a machine; hence it is evident, that such as are a man's will and understanding, such is the man; and further, that a man's action in itself is such as is the affection of his will which produces it, and that a man's conversation in itself is such as is the thought of his understanding which produces it: wherefore several men may act and speak alike, and yet they act and speak differently: one from a depraved will and thought, the other from an upright will and thought. From these considera-tions it is evident that by the deeds or works according to which every one will be judged, are meant the will and the understand-ing; consequently that evil works means the works of an evil will, whatever has been their appearance in externals, and that good works mean the works of a good will, although in externals they have appeared like the works done by an evil man. All things which are done from a man's interior will, are done from purpose, since that will proposes to itself what it acts by its intention; and all things which are done from the understanding, are done from confirmation, since the understanding confirms. From these con-siderations it may appear, that evil or good is imputed to every

one according to the quality of his will therein, and of his understanding concerning them. These observations I am allowed to confirm by the following relation: In the spiritual world I have met several who in the natural world had lived like others, being sumptuous in their dress, giving costly entertainments, frequenting the exhibitions of the stage, jesting loosely on love topics, with other similar practices; and yet the angels accounted those things as evils of sin to some, and not to others, declaring the latter guiltless, and the former guilty. Being questioned why they did so, when all had done alike, they replied that they regard all from their purpose, intention, or end, and distinguish accordingly; and that therefore they excuse or condemn those whom the end either excuses or condemns, since an end of good influences all in heaven, and an end of evil all in hell.

528. To the above I will add the following observation: it is said in the church that no one can fulfil the law, and the less so, because he that offends against one precept of the decalogue, offends against all: but this form of speaking is not such as it sounds; for it is to be understood thus, that he who, from purpose or confirmation, acts against one precept, acts against the rest; since to act so from purpose or confirmation is to deny that it is a sin; and he who denies that it is a sin, makes nothing of acting against the rest of the precepts. Who does not know, that he that is an adulterer is not on that account a murderer, a thief, and a false witness, or wishes to be so? But he that is a determined and confirmed adulterer makes no account of anything respecting religion, thus neither does he make any account of murder, theft, and false witness; and he abstains from these evils, not because they are sins, but because he is afraid of the law and of the loss of reputation. That determined and confirmed adulterers make no account of the holy things of the church and religion, may be seen above, n. 490—493, and in the two MEMORABLE RELATIONS, n. 500, 521, 522: it is a similar case, if any one, from purpose or confirmation, acts against any other precept of the decalogue; he also acts against the rest because he does not regard anything as sin.

529. The case is similar with those who are principled in good from the Lord: if these from will and understanding, or from purpose and confirmation, abstain from any one evil because it is a sin, they abstain from all evil, and the more so still if they abstain from several; for as soon as any one, from purpose or confirmation, abstains from any evil because it is a sin, he is kept by the Lord in the purpose of abstaining from the rest: wherefore, if unwittingly, or from any prevailing bodily concupiscence, he does evil, still this is not imputed to him, because he did not purpose it to himself, and does not confirm it with himself. A man comes into this purpose, if once or twice in a year he examines himself, and repents of the evils which he discovers in himself: it

is otherwise with him who never examines himself. From these considerations it evidently appears to whom sin is not imputed, and to whom it is.

530. V. THUS ADULTEROUS LOVE IS IMPUTED TO EVERY ONE ;—not according to his deeds, such as they appear externally before men, nor either such as they appear before a judge, but such as they appear internally before the Lord, and from him before the angels, which is according to the quality of a man's will and of his understanding therein. Various circumstances exist in the world which mitigate and excuse crimes, also which aggravate and charge them upon the perpetrator: nevertheless, imputations after death take place, not according to the external circumstances of the deed, but according to the internal circumstances of the mind; and these are viewed according to the state of the church with every one: as for example, a man impious in will and understanding, that is, who has no fear of God or love of his neighbour, and consequently no reverence for any sanctity of the church,—he, after death, becomes guilty of all the crimes which he did in the body; nor is there any remembrance of his good actions, since his heart, from whence as from a fountain those things flowed, was averse from heaven, and turned to hell; and deeds flow from the place of the habitation of every one's heart. In order that this may be understood, I will mention an arcanum: Heaven is distinguished into innumerable societies, and so is hell, from an opposite principle; and the mind of every man, according to his will and consequent understanding, actually dwells in one society, and intends and thinks like those who compose the society. If the mind be in any society of heaven, it then intends and thinks like those who compose that society; if it be in any society of hell, it intends and thinks like those who are in the same society; but so long as a man lives in the world, so long he wanders from one society to another, according to the changes of the affections of his will and of the consequent thoughts of his mind: but after death his wanderings are collected into one, and a place is accordingly allotted him, in hell if he is evil, in heaven if he is good. Now since all in hell are influenced by a will of evil, all there are viewed from that will; and since all in heaven are influenced by will of good, all there are viewed from that will; wherefore imputations after death take place according to the quality of every one's will and understanding. The case is similar with adulteries, whether they be fornications, whoredoms, concubinages, or adulteries; for those things are imputed to every one, not according to the deeds themselves, but according to the state of the mind in the deeds; for deeds follow the body into the tomb, whereas the mind rises again.

531. VI. THUS CONJUGIAL LOVE IS IMPUTED TO EVERY ONE There are marriages in which conjugial love does not appear, and yet is; and there are marriages in which conjugial love appears

and yet is not: there are several causes in both cases, which may be known in part from what was related concerning love truly conjugial, n. 57—73; concerning the cause of colds and separations, n. 234—260; and concerning the causes of apparent love and friendship in marriages, n. 271—292: but external appearances decide nothing concerning imputation; the only thing which decides is the conjugial principle, which abides in every one's will, and is guarded, in whatever state of marriage a man is. The conjugial principle is like a scale, in which that love is weighed; for the conjugial principle of one man with one wife is the storehouse of human life, and the reservoir of the Christian religion, as was shewn above, n. 457, 458; and this being the case, it is possible that that love may exist with one married partner, and not at the same time with the other; and that it may lie deeper hid than that the man (*homo*) himself can observe any thing concerning it; and also it may be inscribed in a successive progress of the life. The reason of this is, because that love in its progress accompanies religion, and religion, as it is the marriage of the Lord and the church, is the beginning and inoculation of that love; wherefore conjugial love is imputed to every one after death according to his spiritual rational life; and for him to whom that love is imputed, a marriage in heaven is provided after his decease, whatever has been his marriage in the world. From these considerations then results this short concluding observation, that no inference is to be drawn concerning any one, from appearances of marriages or of adulteries, whereby to decide that he has conjugial love, or not; wherefore *Judge not, lest ye be condemned*, Matt. vii. 1.

* * * * * *

532. To the above I will add the following MEMORABLE RELATION. I was once raised, as to my spirit, into one of the societies of the angelic heaven; and instantly some of the wise men of the society came to me, and said, " What news from the earth?" I replied, "This is new; the Lord has revealed arcana which in point of excellence surpass all the arcana heretofore revealed since the beginning of the church." They asked, "What are they?" I said, "The following: 1. That in every part of the Word there is a spiritual sense corresponding to the natural sense; and that by means of the former sense the men of the church have conjunction with the Lord and consociation with angels; and that the sanctity of the Word resides therein. 2. That the correspondences are discovered of which the spiritual sense of the Word consists." The angels asked, " Have the inhabitants of the earth had no previous knowledge respecting correspondences?" I said, "None at all;" and that the doctrine of correspondences had been concealed for some thousands of years, ever since the time of Job; and that with those who lived at that time, and before it, the science of correspondences was

their chief science, whence they derived wisdom, because they derived knowledge respecting the spiritual things of heaven and the church; but that this science, on account of its being made idolatrous, was so extirpated and destroyed by the divine providence of the Lord that no visible traces of it were left remaining; that nevertheless at this time it has been again discovered by the Lord, in order that the men of the church may have conjunction with him, and consociation with the angels; which purposes are effected by the Word, in which all things are correspondences. The angels rejoiced exceedingly to hear that it has pleased the Lord to reveal this great arcanum, which had lain so deeply hid for some thousands of years; and they said it was done in order that the Christian church, which is founded on the Word, and is now at its end, may again revive and draw breath through heaven from the Lord. They inquired whether by that science it is at this day discovered what are signified by baptism and the holy supper, which have heretofore given birth to so many various conjectures about their true meaning. I replied, that it is. 3. I said further, that a revelation has been made at this day by the Lord concerning the life of man after death? The angels said, "What concerning the life after death? Who does not know that a man lives after death? I replied, "They know it, and they do not know it: they say that it is not the man that lives after death, but his soul, and that this lives a spirit; and the idea they have of a spirit is as of wind or ether, and that it does not live a man till after the day of the last judgement, at which time the corporeal parts, which had been left in the world, will be recollected and again fitted together into a body, notwithstanding their having been eaten by worms, mice, and fish; and that thus men will rise again." The angels said, "What a notion is this! Who does not know that a man lives a man after death, with this difference alone, that he then lives a spiritual man, and that a spiritual man sees a spiritual man, as a material man sees a material man, and that they know no distinction, except that they are in a more perfect state?" 4. The angels inquired, "What do they know concerning our world, and concerning heaven and hell?" I said, "Nothing at all; but at this day it has been revealed by the Lord, what is the nature and quality of the world in which angels and spirits live, thus what is the quality of heaven and of hell; and further, that angels and spirits are in conjunction with men; besides many wonderful things respecting them." The angels were glad to hear that it has pleased the Lord to reveal such things, that men may no longer be in doubt through ignorance respecting their immortality. 5. I further said, that at this day it has been revealed from the Lord, that in your world there is a sun, different from that of our world, and that the sun of your world is pure love, and the sun of our world is pure fire; and that on this account, whatever proceeds from your sun, since it is pure love, partakes of life, and whatever proceeds from our sun, since it is pure fire, does not partake of life; and that hence is the difference between spiritual and natural, which difference, heretofore unknown, has been also revealed: hereby also is made known the source of the light which enlightens the human understanding with wisdom, and the source of the heat which kindles the human will with heat. 6. It has been further discovered, that there are three degrees of life, and that hence there are three heavens; and that the human mind is distinguished into those degrees, and that hence man (*homo*) corresponds to the three heavens. The angels said, "Did not they know this heretofore?" I answered, "They were acquainted with a distinction of degrees in relation to greater and less, but not in relation to prior and posterior." 7. The angels inquired whether any other things have been revealed? I replied "Several; namely, concerning the last judgement: concerning the Lord, that he is God of heaven and earth; that God is one both in person and essence, in whom there is a divine trinity; and that he is the Lord: also concerning the new church to be established by him, and concerning the doctrine of that church; concerning the sanctity of the sacred scripture; that the Apocalypse also has been revealed, which could not be revealed even as to a single verse except by the Lord; moreover concerning the inhabitants of the planets, and the earths in the universe; besides several memorable and wonderful relations from the spiritual world, whereby several things relating to wisdom have been revealed from heaven."

533. The angels were exceedingly rejoiced at this information; but they perceived that I was sorrowful, and asked the cause of my sorrow. I said, because the above arcana, at this day revealed by the Lord, although in excellence and worth exceeding all the knowledges heretofore published, are yet considered on earth as of no value. The angels wondered at this, and besought the Lord that they might be allowed to look down into the world: they did so, and lo! mere darkness was therein: and they were told, that those arcana should be written on a paper, which should be let down to the earth, and they would see a prodigy: and it was done so; and lo! the paper on which those arcana were written, was let down from heaven, and in its progress, while it was in the world of spirits, it shone as a bright star; but when it descended into the natural world, the light disappeared, and it was darkened in the degree to which it fell: and while it was let down by the angels into companies consisting of men of learning and erudition, both clergy and laity, there was heard a murmur from many, in which were these expressions, "What have we here? Is it any thing or nothing? What matters it whether we know these things or not? Are they not mere creatures of the brain?" And it appeared as if some of them took the paper and

folded it, rolling and unrolling it with their fingers, that they might deface the writing; and it appeared as if some tore it in pieces, and some were desirous to trample it under their feet: but they were prevented by the Lord from proceeding to such enormity, and charge was given to the angels to draw it back and secure it: and as the angels were affected with sadness, and thought with themselves how long this was to be the case, it was said, *For a time, and times, and half a time*, Rev. xii. 14.

534. After this I conversed with the angels, informing them that somewhat further is revealed in the world by the Lord. They asked, "What?" I said, "Concerning love truly conjugial and its heavenly delights." The angels said, "Who does not know that the delights of conjugial love exceed those of all other loves? and who cannot see, that into some love are collected all the blessednesses, satisfactions, and delights, which can possibly be conferred by the Lord, and that the receptacle thereof is love truly conjugial, which is capable of receiving and perceiving them fully and sensibly?" I replied, "They do not know this, because they have not come to the Lord, and lived according to his precepts, by shunning evils as sins and doing goods; and love truly conjugial with its delights is solely from the Lord, and is given to those who live according to his precepts; thus it is given to those who are received into the Lord's new church, which is meant in the Apocalypse by the New Jerusalem." To this I added, "I am in doubt whether in the world at this day they are willing to believe that this love in itself is a spiritual love, and hence grounded in religion, because they entertain only a corporeal idea respecting it." Then they said to me, "Write respecting it, and follow revelation; and afterwards the book written respecting it shall be sent down from us out of heaven, and we shall see whether the things contained in it are received; and at the same time whether they are willing to acknowledge, that that love is according to the state of religion with man, spiritual with the spiritual, natural with the natural, and merely carnal with adulterers."

535. After this I heard an outrageous murmur from below, and at the same time these words, "Do miracles; and we will believe you." And I asked, "Are not the things above-mentioned miracles?" Answer was made, "They are not." I again asked, "What miracles then do you mean?" And it was said, "Disclose and reveal things to come; and we will have faith." But I replied, "Such disclosures and revelation are not granted from heaven; since in proportion as a man knows things to come, in the same proportion his reason and understanding, together with his wisdom and prudence, fall into an indolence of inexertion, grow torpid, and decay." Again I asked, "What other miracles shall I do?" And a cry was made, "Do such miracles as Moses did in Egypt." To this I answered, "Possibly you

may harden your hearts against them as Pharaoh and the Egyptians did." And reply was made, "We will not." But again I said, " Assure me of a certainty, that you will not dance about a golden calf and adore it, as the posterity of Jacob did within a month after they had seen the whole Mount Sinai on fire, and heard Jehovah himself speaking out of the fire, thus after the greatest of all miracles;" (a golden calf in the spiritual sense denotes the pleasure of the flesh;) and reply was made from below, " We will not be like the posterity of Jacob." But at that instant I heard it said to them from heaven, "If ye believe not Moses and the prophets,—that is, the Word of the Lord, ye will not believe from miracles, any more than the sons of Jacob did in the wilderness, nor any more than they believed when they saw with their own eyes the miracles done by the Lord himself, while he was in the world."

GENERAL INDEX.

PART THE FIRST.

PRELIMINARY RELATIONS RESPECTING THE JOYS OF HEAVEN AND NUPTIALS THERE, n. 1—26.

ON MARRIAGES IN HEAVEN, n. 27—41.

A MAN lives a man after death, n. 28—31. In this case a male is a male, and a female a female, n. 32, 33. Every one's peculiar love remains with him after death, n. 34—36. The love of the sex especially remains; and with those who go to heaven, which is the case with all who become spiritual here on earth, conjugial love remains, n. 37, 38. These things fully confirmed by ocular demonstration, n. 39. Consequently there are marriages in heaven, n. 40. Spiritual nuptials are to be understood by the Lord's words, "After the resurrection they are not given in marriage," n. 41.

ON THE STATE OF MARRIED PARTNERS AFTER DEATH, n. 45—54.

THE love of the sex remains with every man after death, according to its interior quality; that is, such as it had been in his interior will and thought in the world, n. 46, 47. Conjugial love in like manner remains such as it has been anterior.y; that is, such as it had been in the man's interior will and thought in the world, n. 48. Married partners most commonly meet after death, know each other, again associate, and for a time live together: this is the case in the first state, thus while they are in externals as in the world, n, 47.* But successively, as they put off their externals and enter into their internals, they perceive what had been the quality of their love and inclination for each other, and consequently whether they can live together or not, n. 48.* If they can live together, they remain married partners; but if they cannot, they separate, sometimes the husband from the wife, sometimes the wife from the husband, and sometimes each from the other, n. 49. In this case there is given to the man a suitable wife, and to the woman a suitable husband, n. 50. Married pairs enjoy similar communications with each other as in the world, but more delightful and blessed, yet without prolification; in the place of which they experience spiritual prolification, which is that of love and wisdom, n. 51, 52. This is the case with those who go to heaven; but i is otherwise with those who go to hell, n. 53, 54.

ON LOVE TRULY CONJUGIAL, n. 57—73.

There exists a love truly conjugial, which at this day is so rare, that it is not known what is its quality, and scarcely that it exists, n. 58, 59. This love originates in the marriage of good and truth, n. 60, 61. There is a correspondence of this love with the marriage of the Lord and the church, n. 62, 63. This love, from its origin and correspondence, is celestial, spiritual, holy, pure, and clean, above every other love imparted by the Lord to the angels of heaven and the men of the church, n. 64. It is also the foundation love of all celestial and spiritual loves, and thence of all natural loves, n. 65—67. Into this love are collected all joys and delights from first to last, n. 68, 69. None, however, come into this love, and can remain in it, but those who approach the Lord, and love the truths of the church, and practise its goods, n. 70—72. This love was the love of loves with the ancients, who lived in the golden, silver, and copper ages, n. 73.

ON THE ORIGIN OF CONJUGIAL LOVE AS GROUNDED IN THE MARRIAGE OF GOOD AND TRUTH n. 83—102.

Good and truth are the universals of creation, and thence are in all created things; but they are in created subjects according to the form of each, n. 84—86. There is neither solitary good nor solitary truth; but in all cases they are conjoined, n. 87. There is the truth of good, and from this the good of truth; or truth grounded in good, and good grounded in that truth; and in those two principles is implanted from creation an inclination to join themselves together into a one, n. 88, 89. In the subjects of the animal kingdom, the truth of good, or truth grounded in good, is male (or masculine); and the good of that truth, or good grounded in that truth, is female (or feminine), n. 90, 91. From the influx of the marriage of good and truth from the Lord, the love of the sex and conjugial love are derived, n. 92, 93. The love of the sex belongs to the external or natural man; and hence it is common to every animal, n. 94. But conjugial love belongs to the internal or spiritual man; and hence this love is peculiar to man, n. 95, 96. With man conjugial love is in the love of the sex as a gem in its matrix, n. 97. The love of the sex with man is not the origin of conjugial love, but its first rudiment; thus it is like an external natural principle, in which an internal spiritual principle is implanted, n. 98. During the implantation of conjugial love, the love of the sex inverts itself, and becomes the chaste love of the sex, n. 99. The male and the female were created to be the essential form of the marriage of good and truth, n. 100. Married partners are that form in their inmost principles, and thence in what is derived from those principles, in proportion as the interiors of their minds are opened, n. 101, 102.

ON THE MARRIAGE OF THE LORD AND THE CHURCH, AND ITS CORRESPONDENCE, n. 116—131.

The Lord in the Word is called the Bridegroom and Husband, and the church the bride and wife; and the conjunction of the Lord with the church, and the reciprocal conjunction of the church with the Lord, is called a marriage, n. 117. The Lord is also called a Father, and the church, a mother, n. 118, 119. The offspring derived from the Lord as a husband and father, and from the church as a wife and mother, are all spiritual; and in the spiritual sense of the Word are understood by sons and daughters, brothers and sisters, sons-in-law and daughters-in-law, and by other names of relations, n. 120. The spiritual offspring which are born from the Lord's marriage with the church, are truths and goods; truths, from which are derived understanding, perception, and all thought; and goods, from which are derived love, charity, and all affection, n. 121. From the marriage of good and truth, which proceeds from the Lord in the way of influx, man receives truth, and the Lord conjoins good thereto; and thus the church is formed by the Lord with man, n. 122—124. The husband does not represent the Lord, and the wife the church; because both together, the husband and the wife, constitute the church, n. 125. Therefore there is not a correspondence of the husband with the Lord, and of the wife with the church, in the marriages of the angels in the heavens, and of men on earth, n. 126. But there is a correspondence with conjugial love, semination, prolification, the love of infants, and similar things which exist in marriages and are derived from them, n. 127. The Word is the medium of conjunction, because it is from the Lord, and thereby is the Lord, n. 128. The church is from the Lord, and exists with those who come to him and live according to his precepts, n. 129. Conjugial love is according to the state of the church, because it is according to the state of wisdom with man, n. 130. And as the church is from the Lord, conjugial love is also from him, n. 131.

ON THE CHASTE PRINCIPLE AND THE NON-CHASTE, n. 138—156.

The chaste principle and the non-chaste are predicated only of marriages and of such things as relate to marriages, n. 139, 140. The chaste principle is predicated only of monogamical marriages, or of the marriage of one man with one wife, n. 141. The Christian conjugial principle alone is chaste, n. 142. Love truly conjugial is essential chastity, n. 143. All the delights of love truly conjugial, even the ultimate, are chaste, n. 144. With those who are made spiritual by the Lord, conjugial love is more and more purified and rendered chaste, n. 145, 146. The chastity of marriage exists by a total renunciation of whoredoms from a principle of religion, n. 147—149. Chastity cannot be predicated of infants, or of boys and girls, or of young men and maidens before they feel in themselves a love of the sex, n. 150. Chastity cannot be predicated of eunuchs so made, n. 151. Chastity cannot be predicated of those who do not believe adulteries to be evils in regard to religion; and still less of those who do not believe them to be hurtful to society, n. 152. Chastity cannot be predicated of those who abstain from adulteries only for various external reasons, n. 153. Chastity cannot be predicated of those who believe marriages to be unchaste, n. 154. Chastity cannot be predicated of those who have renounced marriage by vows of perpetual celibacy, unless there be and remain in them the love of a life truly conjugial, n. 155. A state of marriage is to be preferred to a state of celibacy, n. 156.

ON THE CONJUNCTION OF SOULS AND MINDS BY MARRIAGE, WHICH IS MEANT BY THE LORD'S WORDS,—THEY ARE NO LONGER TWO BUT ONE FLESH. n 156*—181.

From creation there is implanted in each sex a faculty and inclination, whereby they are able and willing to be joined together as it were into a one, n. 157. Conjugial love conjoins two souls, and thence two minds, into a one, n. 158. The will of the wife conjoins itself with the understanding of the man, and thence the understanding of the man with the will of the wife, n. 159. The inclination to unite the man to herself is constant and perpetual with the wife, but inconstant and alternate with the man, n. 160. Conjunction is inspired into the man from the wife according to her love, and is received by the man according to his wisdom, n. 161. This conjunction is effected successively from the first days of marriage: and with those who are principled in love truly conjugial, it is effected more and more thoroughly to eternity, n. 162. The conjunction of the wife with the rational wisdom of the husband is effected from within, but with his moral wisdom from without, n. 163—165. For the sake of this conjunction as an end, the wife has a perception of the affections of her husband, and also the utmost prudence in moderating them, n. 166. Wives conceal this perception with themselves, and hide it from their husbands for reasons of necessity, in order that conjugial love, friendship, and confidence, and thereby the blessedness of dwelling together, and the happiness of life may be secured, n. 167. This perception is the wisdom of the wife, and is not communicable to the man; neither is the rational wisdom of the man communicable to the wife, n. 168. The wife from a principle of love is continually thinking about the man's inclination to her, with the purpose of joining him to herself; it is otherwise with the man, n. 169. The wife conjoins herself to the man by applications to the desires of his will, n. 170. The wife is conjoined to her husband by the sphere of her life flowing from the love of him, n. 171. The wife is conjoined to the husband by the appropriation of the powers of his virtue; which however is effected according to their mutual spiritual love, n. 172. Thus the wife receives in herself the image of her husband, and thence perceives, sees, and is sensible of his affections, n. 173. There are duties proper to the husband, and others proper to the wife; and the wife cannot enter into the duties proper to the husband, nor the husband into the duties proper to the wife, so as to perform them aright, n. 174, 175. These duties also, according to mutual aid, conjoin the two into a one, and at the same time constitute one house, n. 176. Married partners, according to these conjunctions, become one man more and more, n. 177. Those who are principled in love truly conjugial, are sensible of their being a united man, as it were one flesh, n. 178. Love truly conjugial, considered in itself, is a union of souls, a conjunction of minds, and an endeavour towards conjunction in the bosoms, and thence in the body, n. 179. The states of this love are innocence, peace, tranquillity, inmost friendship, full confidence, and a mutual desire of mind and heart to do every good to each other; and the states derived from these are blessedness, satisfaction, delight, and pleasure; and from the eternal enjoyment of these is derived heavenly felicity, n. 180. These things can only exist in the marriage of one man with one wife, n. 181.

ON THE CHANGE OF THE STATE OF LIFE WHICH TAKES PLACE WITH MEN AND WOMEN BY MARRIAGE, n. 184—206.

The state of a man's life, from infancy even to the end of his life, and afterwards to eternity, is continually changing, n. 185. In like manner a man's internal form, which is that of his spirit, is continually changing n. 186. These changes differ in the case of men and of women; since men from creation are forms of knowledge, intelligence, and wisdom, and women are forms of the love of those principles as existing with men, 187. With men there is an elevation of the mind into superior light, and with women an elevation of the mind into superior heat; and the woman is made sensible of the delights of her heat in the man's light, n. 188, 189. With both men and women, the states of life before marriage are different from what they are afterwards, n. 190. With married partners the states of life after marriage are changed, and succeed each other according to the conjunctions of their minds by conjugial love, n. 191. Marriage also induces other forms in the souls and minds of married partners, n. 192. The woman is actually formed into a wife, according to the description in the book of creation, n. 193. This formation is effected on the part of the wife by secret means: and this is meant by the woman's being created while the man slept, n. 194. This formation on the part of the wife, is effected by the conjunction of her own will with the internal will of the man, n. 195. The end herein is, that the will of both may become one, and that thus both may become one man, n. 196. This formation [on the part of the wife] is effected by an appropriation of the affections of the husband, n. 197. This formation [on the part of the wife] is effected by a reception of the propagations of the soul of the husband, with the delight arising from her desire to be the love of her husband's wisdom, n. 198. Thus a maiden is formed into a wife, and a youth into a husband, n. 199. In the marriage of one man with one wife, between whom there exists love truly conjugial, the wife becomes more and more a wife, and the husband more and more a husband, n. 200. Thus also their forms are successively perfected and ennobled from within, n. 201. Children born of parents who are principled in love truly conjugial, derive from them the conjugial principle of good and truth, whence they have an inclination and faculty, if sons, to perceive the things relating to wisdom; and if daughters, to love those things which wisdom teaches, n. 202—205. The reason of this is, because the soul of the offspring is from the father, and its clothing from the mother, n. 206.

UNIVERSALS RESPECTING MARRIAGES, n. 209—230.

The sense proper to conjugial love is the sense of touch, n. 210. With those who are in love truly conjugial, the faculty of growing wise increases; but with those who are not, it decreases, n. 211, 212. With those who are in love truly conjugial, the happiness of dwelling together increases; but with those who are not, it decreases, n. 213. With those who are in love truly conjugial, conjunction of minds increases, and therewith friendship; but with those who are not, they both decrease, n. 214. Those who are in love truly conjugial, continually desire to be one man; but those who are not in conjugial love, desire to be two, n. 215. Those who are in love truly conjugial, in marriage have respect to what is eternal; but with those who are not, the case is reversed, n. 216. Conjugial love resides with chaste wives; but still their love depends on the husbands, n. 216.* Wives love the bonds of marriage, if the men do, n. 217. The intelligence of women is in itself modest, elegant, pacific, yielding, soft, tender; but the intelligence of men is in itself grave, harsh, hard, daring, fond of licentiousness, n. 218. Wives are in no excitation as men are; but they have a state of preparation for reception, n. 219. Men have abundant store according to the love of propagating the truths of wisdom, and to the love of doing uses, n, 220. Determination is in the good pleasure of the husband, n. 221. The conjugial sphere flows from the Lord through heaven into everything in the universe, even to its ultimates, n. 222. This sphere is received by the female sex, and through that is transferred to the male sex, n. 223. Where there is love truly conjugial, this sphere is received by the wife, and only through her by the husband, n. 224. Where there is love not conjugial, this sphere is received indeed by the wife, but not by the husband through her, n. 225. Love truly conjugial may exist with one of the married partners, and not at the same time with the other, n. 226. There are various similitudes and dissimilitudes, both internal and external, with married partners, n. 227. Various similitudes can be conjoined, but not with dissimilitudes, n. 228. The Lord provides similitudes for those who desire love truly conjugial, and if not on earth he yet provides them in heaven, n. 229. A man, according to the deficiency and loss of conjugial love, approaches to the nature of a beast, n. 230.

ON THE CAUSES OF COLDNESS, SEPARATION, AND DIVORCE IN MARRIAGES, n. 234—260.

THERE are spiritual heat and spiritual cold; and spiritual heat is love, and spiritual cold is the privation thereof, n. 235. Spiritual cold in marriages is a disunion of souls and a disjunction of minds, whence come indifference, discord, contempt, disdain, and aversion; from which, in several cases, at length comes separation as to bed, chamber, and house, n. 236. There are several successive causes of cold, some internal, some external, and some accidental, n. 237. Internal causes of cold are from religion, n. 238, 239. Of internal causes of cold the first is the rejection of religion by each of the parties, n. 240. Of internal causes of cold the second is that one of the parties has religion and not the other, n. 241. Of internal causes of cold the third is, that one of the parties is of one religion and the other of another, n. 242. Of internal causes of cold the fourth is, the falsity of the religion, n. 243. With many, the above-mentioned are causes of internal cold, but not at the same time of external, n. 244, 245. There are also several external causes of cold, the first of which is dissimilitude of minds and manner, n. 246. Of external causes of cold the second is, that conjugial love is believed to be the same as adulterous love, only that the latter is not allowed by law, but the former is, n. 247. Of external causes of cold the third is, a striving for preeminence between married partners, n. 248. Of external causes of cold the fourth is, a want of determination to any employment or business, whence comes wandering passion, n. 249. Of external causes of cold the fifth is, inequality of external rank and condition, n. 250. There are also causes of separation, n. 251. The first cause of legitimate separation is a vitiated state of mind, n. 252. The second cause of legitimate separation is a vitiated state of body, n. 253. The third cause of legitimate separation is impotence before marriage, n. 254. Adultery is the cause of divorce, n. 255. There are also several accidental causes of cold; the first of which is, that enjoyment is common (or cheap), because continually allowed, n. 256. Of accidental causes of cold the second is, that living with a married partner, from a covenant and contract, seems forced and not free, n. 257. Of accidental causes of cold the third is, affirmation on the part of the wife, and her talking incessantly about love, n. 258. Of accidental causes of cold the fourth is, the man's continually thinking that his wife is willing, and on the other hand, the wife's thinking that the man is not willing, n. 259. As cold is in the mind, it is also in the body; and according to the increase of that cold, the externals also of the body are closed, n. 260.

ON THE CAUSES OF APPARENT LOVE, FRIENDSHIP, AND FAVOR IN MARRIAGES, n. 271—292.

IN the natural world almost all are capable of being joined together as to external, but not as to internal affections, if these disagree and are apparent, n. 272. In the spiritual world all are conjoined according to internal, but not according to external affections, unless these act in unity with the internal, n. 273. It is the external affections, according to which matrimony is generally contracted in the world, n. 274. But in case they are not influenced by internal affections which conjoin minds, the bonds of matrimony are loosed in the house, n. 275. Nevertheless those bonds must continue in the world till the decease of one of the parties, n. 276

In cases of matrimony, in which the internal affections do not conjoin, there are external affections, which assume a semblance of the internal, and tend to consociate, n. 277. Thence come apparent love, friendship, and favor between married partners, n. 278. These appearances are assumed conjugial semblances, and they are commendable, because useful and necessary, n. 279. These assumed conjugial semblances, in the case of a spiritual man conjoined to a natural, are founded in justice and judgement, n. 280. For various reasons, these assumed conjugial semblances with natural men are founded in prudence, n. 281. They are for the sake of amendment and accommodation, n. 282. They are for the sake of preserving order in domestic affairs, and for the sake of mutual aid, n. 283. They are for the sake of unanimity in the care of infants and the education of children, n. 284. They are for the sake of peace in the house, n. 285. They are for the sake of reputation out of the house, n. 286. They are for the sake of various favors expected from the married partner, or from his or her relations, and thus from the fear of losing such favors, n. 287. They are for the sake of having blemishes excused, and thereby of avoiding disgrace, n. 288. They are for the sake of reconciliations, n. 289. In case favor does not cease with the wife, when faculty ceases with the man, there may exist a friendship resembling conjugial friendship when the parties grow old, n. 290. There are various species of apparent love and friendship between married partners, one of whom is brought under the yoke, and therefore is subject to the other, n. 291. In the world there are infernal marriages between persons who interiorly are the most inveterate enemies, and exteriorly are as the closest friends, n. 292.

ON BETROTHINGS AND NUPTIALS, n. 295—314.

THE right of choice belongs to the man, and not to the woman, n. 296. The man ought to court and intreat the woman respecting marriage with him, and not the woman the man, n. 297. The woman ought to consult her parents, or those who are in the place of parents, and then deliberate with herself before she consents, n. 298, 299. After a declaration of consent, pledges are to be given, n. 300. Consent is to be secured and established by solemn betrothing, n. 301. By betrothing, each party is prepared for conjugial love, n. 302. By betrothing, the mind of the one is united to the mind of the other, so as to effect a marriage of the spirit previous to a marriage of the body, n. 303. This is the case with those who think chastely of marriages; but it is otherwise with those who think unchastely of them, n. 304. Within the time of betrothing it is not allowable to be connected corporeally, n. 305. When the time of betrothing is completed, the nuptials ought to take place, n. 306. Previous to the celebration of the nuptials, the conjugial covenant is to be ratified in the presence of witnesses, n. 307. Marriage is to be consecrated by a priest, n. 308. The nuptials are to be celebrated with festivity, n. 309. After the nuptials, the marriage of the spirit is made also the marriage of the body, and thereby a full marriage, n. 310. Such is the order of conjugial love with its modes, from its first heat to its first torch, n. 311. Conjugial love precipitated without order and the modes thereof, burns up the marrows, and is consumed, n. 312. The states of the minds of each of the parties proceeding in successive order, flow into the state of marriage; nevertheless in one manner with the spiritual and in another with the natural, n. 313. There are successive and simultaneous order, and the latter is from the former and according to it, n. 314.

ON REPEATED MARRIAGES, n. 317—355.

AFTER the death of a married partner, again to contract wedlock, depends on the preceding conjugial love, n. 318. After the death of a married part-ter, again to contract wedLock, depends also on the state of marriage in which the parties had lived, n. 319. With those who have not been in love truly conjugial, there is no obstacle or hindrance to their again contracting wedlock, n. 320. Those who had lived together in love truly conjugial, are unwilling to marry again, except for reasons separate from conjugial love, n. 321. The state of a marriage of a youth with a maiden differs from that of a youth with a widow, n. 322. Also the state of marriage of a widower with a maiden differs from that of a widower with a widow, n. 323. The varieties and diversities of these marriages, as to love and its attributes, are innumerable, n. 324. The state of a widow is more grievous that that of a widower n. 325.

ON POLYGAMY, n. 332—352.

LOVE truly conjugial can only exis twith one wife, consequently neither can friendship, confidence, ability truly conjugial, and such a conjunction of minds that two may be one flesh, n. 333, 334. Thus celestial blessedness, spiritual-satisfactions, and natural delights, which from the beginning were provided for those who are in love truly conjugial, can only exist with one wife, n. 335. All those things can only exist from the Lord alone; and they do not exist with any but those who come to him alone, and live according to his commandments, n. 336. Consequently love truly conjugial with its felicities can only exist with those who are of the Christian church, n. 337. Therefore a Christian is not allowed to marry more than one wife, n. 338. If a Christian marries several wives, he commits not only natural but also spiritual adultery, n. 339. The Israelitish nation was permitted to marry several wives, because they had not the Christian church, and consequently love truly conjugial could not exist with them, n. 340. At this day the Mahometans are permitted to marry several wives, because they do not acknowledge the Lord Jesus Christ to be one with Jehovah the Father, and thereby to be the God of heaven and earth, and hence cannot receive love truly conjugial, n. 341. The Mahometan heaven is out of the Christian heaven, and is divided into two heavens, the inferior and the superior; and only those are elevated into their superior heaven, who renounce concubines, and live with one wife, and acknowledge our Lord as equal to God the Father, to whom is given dominion over heaven and earth, n. 342—344. Polygamy is lasciviousness, n. 345. Conjugial chastity, purity, and sanctity, cannot exist with polygamists, n. 346. A polygamist, so long as he remains such, cannot become spiritual, n. 347. Polygamy is not sin with those who live in it from a religious notion, n. 348. Polygamy is not sin with those who are in ignorance respecting the Lord, n. 349, 350. Of these, although polygamists, such are saved as acknowledge a God, and from a religious notion live according to the civil laws of justice, n. 351. But none either of the latter or of the former can be associated with the angels in the Christian heavens, n. 352.

ON JEALOUSY, n. 357—379.

ZEAL considered in itself is like the ardent fire of love, n. 358. The burning or flame of that love, which is zeal, is a spiritual burning or flame, arising from an infestation and assault of the love, n. 356—361. The quality of a man's zeal is according to the quality of his love; thus it differs according as the love is good or evil, n. 362. The zeal of a good love and the zeal of an evil love, are alike in externals, but altogether different in internals, n. 363, 364. The zeal of a good love in its internals contains a hidden store of love and friendship: but the zeal of an evil love in its internals contains a hidden store of hatred and revenge, n. 365, 366. The zeal of conjugial love is called jealousy, n. 367. Jealousy is like an ardent fire against those who infest love exercised towards a married partner, and like a terrible fear for the loss of that love, n. 368. There is spiritual jealousy with monogamists, and natural with polygamists, n. 369, 370. Jealousy with those married partners who tenderly love each other, is a just grief grounded in sound reason, lest conjugial love should be divided, and should thereby perish, n. 371, 372. Jealousy, with married partners who do not love each other, is grounded in several causes; arising in some instances from various mental weaknesses, n. 373—375. In some instances there is not any jealousy; and this also from various causes, n. 376. There is a jealousy also in regard to concubines, but not such as in regard to wives, n. 377. Jealousy likewise exists among beasts and birds, n. 378. The jealousy of men and husbands is different from that of women and wives, n. 379.

ON THE CONJUNCTION OF CONJUGIAL LOVE WITH THE LOVE OF INFANTS, n. 385—414.

Two universal spheres proceed from the Lord to preserve the universe in its created state; of which the one is the sphere of procreating, and the other the sphere of protecting the things procreated, n. 386. These two universal spheres make a one with the sphere of conjugial love and the sphere of the love of infants, n. 387. These two spheres universally and singularly flow into all things of heaven and all things of the world, from first to last, n. 388—390. The sphere of the love of infants is a sphere of protection and support of those who cannot protect and support themselves, n. 391. This sphere affects both the evil and the good, and disposes every one to love, protect, and support his offspring from his own love, n. 392. This sphere principally affects the female sex, thus mothers; and the male sex, or fathers, by derivation from them, n. 393. This sphere is also a sphere of innocence and peace [from the Lord,] n. 394. The sphere of innocence flows into infants, and through them into the parents, and affects them, n. 395. It also flows into the souls of the parents, and unites with the same sphere with the infants; and it is principally insinuated by means of the touch, n. 396, 397. In the degree in which innocence retires from infants, affection and conjunction also abate, and this successively, even to separation, n. 398. A state of rational innocence and peace with parents towards infants, is grounded in the circumstance, that they know nothing and can do nothing from themselves, but from others, especially from the father and mother; and this state successively retires, in proportion as they know and have ability from themselves, and not from others, n. 399. The sphere of the love of procreating advances in order from the end through causes into effects, and makes periods; whereby creation is preserved in the state foreseen and provided for, n. 400, 401. The love of infants descends, and does not ascend, n. 402. Wives have one state of love before conception, and another state after, even to the birth, n. 403. With parents conjugial love is conjoined with the love of infants by spiritual causes, and thence by natural, n. 404. The love of infants and children is different with spiritual married partners from what it is with natural, n. 405—407. With the spiritual, that love is from what is interior or prior, but with the natural, from what is exterior or posterior, n. 408. In consequence hereof that love prevails with married partners who mutually love each other, and also with those who do not at all love each other, n. 409. The love of infants remains after death, especially with women, n. 410. Infants are educated under the Lord's auspices by such women, and grow in stature and intelligence as in the world, n. 411, 412. It is there provided by the Lord, that with those infants the innocence of infancy becomes the innocence of wisdom, [and thus they become angels] n. 413, 414.

PART THE SECOND.

PRELIMINARY NOTE BY THE EDITOR.

ON THE OPPOSITION OF ADULTEROUS LOVE AND CONJUGIAL LOVE, n. 423—443.

It is not known what adulterous love is, unless it be known what conjugial love is, n. 424. Adulterous love is opposed to conjugial love, n. 425. Adulterous love is opposed to conjugial love, as the natural man viewed in himself is opposed to the spiritual man, n. 426. Adulterous love is opposed to conjugial love, as the connubial connection of what is evil and false is opposed to the marriage of good and truth, n. 427, 428. Hence adulterous love is opposed to conjugial love as hell is to heaven, n. 429. The impurity of hell is from adulterous love, and the purity of heaven from conjugial love. n. 430. In the church, the impurity and the purity are similarly circumstanced, n. 431. Adulterous love more and more makes a man (*homo*) not a man (*homo*), and a man (*vir*) not a man (*vir*); and conjugial love makes a man (*homo*) more and more a man (*homo*) and a man (*vir*), n. 432, 433. There are a sphere of adulterous love and a sphere of conjugial love, n. 434. The sphere of adulterous love ascends from hell, and the sphere of conjugial love descends from heaven, n. 435. In each world those two spheres meet, but do not unite, n. 436. Between those two spheres there is an equilibrium, and man is in it, n. 437. A man can turn himself to whichever sphere he pleases; but so far as he turns himself to the one, so far he turns himself from the other, n. 438. Each sphere brings with it delights, n. 439. The delights of adulterous love commence from the flesh, and are of the flesh even in the spirit; but the delights of conjugial love commence in the spirit, and are of the spirit even in the flesh, n. 440, 441. The delights of adulterous love are the pleasures of insanity; but the delights of conjugial love are the delights of wisdom, n. 442, 443.

ON FORNICATION, n. 444*—460.

Fornication is of the love of the sex, n. 445. The love of the sex, from which fornication is derived, commences when a youth begins to think and act from his own understanding, and his voice to be masculine, n. 446. Fornication is of the natural man, n. 447. Fornication is lust, but not the lust of adultery, n. 448, 449. With some men, the love of the sex cannot without hurt be totally checked from going forth into fornication, n. 450. Therefore in populous cities public stews are tolerated, n. 451. Fornication is light, so far as it looks to conjugial love, and gives this love the preference, n. 452. The lust of fornication is grievous, so far as it looks to adultery, n. 453. The lust of fornication is more grievous as it verges to the desire of varieties and of defloration, n. 454. The sphere of the lust of fornication, such as it is in the beginning, is a middle sphere between the sphere of adulterous love and the sphere of conjugial love, and makes an equilibrium, n. 455. Care is to be taken, lest by immoderate and inordinate fornications conjugial love be destroyed, n. 456. Inasmuch as the conjugial principle of one man with one wife is the jewel of human life, and the reservoir of the Christian religion, n. 457, 458. With those who, from various reasons, cannot as yet enter into marriage, and from their passion for the sex, cannot moderate their lusts, this conjugial principle may be preserved, if the vague love of the sex be confined to one mistress, n. 459. Keeping a mistress is preferable to vague amours, provided only one be kept, and she be neither a maiden nor a married woman, and the love of the mistress be kept separate from conjugial love, n. 460.

ON CONCUBINAGE, n. 462—476.

THERE are two kinds of concubinage, which differ exceedingly from each other, the one conjointly with a wife, the other apart from a wife, n. 463. Concubinage conjointly with a wife, is altogether unlawful for Christians, and detestable, n. 464. It is polygamy, which has been condemned, and is to be condemned by the Christian world, n. 465. It is an adultery whereby the conjugial principle, which is the most precious jewel of the Christian life, is destroyed, n. 466. Concubinage apart from a wife, when it is engaged in from causes legitimate, just, and truly excusatory, is not unlawful, n. 467. The legitimate causes of this concubinage are the legitimate causes of divorce, while the wife is nevertheless retained at home, n. 468, 469. The just causes of this concubinage are the just causes of separation from the bed, n. 470. Of the excusatory causes of this concubinage some are real and some not, n. 471. The really excusatory causes are such as are grounded in what is just, n. 472, 473. The excusatory causes which are not real are such as are not grounded in what is just, although in the appearance of what is just, n. 474. Those who, from causes legitimate, just, and really excusatory, are engaged in this concubinage, may at the same time be principled in conjugial love, n. 475. While this concubinage continues, actual connection with a wife is not allowable, n. 476.

ON ADULTERIES AND THEIR GENERA AND DEGREES, n. 478—499.

THERE are three genera of adulteries,—simple, duplicate, and triplicate, n. 478. Simple adultery is that of an unmarried man with another's wife, or of an unmarried woman with another's husband, n. 480, 481. Duplicate adultery is that of a husband with another's wife, or of a wife with another's husband, n. 482, 483. Triplicate adultery is with relations by blood, n. 484. There are four degrees of adulteries, according to which they have their predications, their charges of blame, and after death their imputation, n. 485. Adulteries of the first degree are adulteries of ignorance, which are committed by those who cannot as yet, or cannot at all, consult the understanding, and thence check them, n. 486. In such cases adulteries are mild, n. 487. Adulteries of the second degree are adulteries of lust, which are committed by those who indeed are able to consult the understanding, but from accidental causes at the moment are not able, n. 488. Adulteries committed by such persons are imputatory, according as the understanding afterwards favors them or not, n. 489. Adulteries of the third degree are adulteries of the reason, which are committed by those who with the understanding confirm themselves in the persuasion that they are not evils of sin, n. 490. The adulteries committed by such persons are grievous, and are imputed to them according to confirmations, n. 491. Adulteries of the fourth degree are adulteries of the will, which are committed by those who make them lawful and pleasing, and who do not think them of importance enough to consult the understanding respecting them, n. 492. The adulteries committed by these persons are exceedingly grievous, and are imputed to them as evils of purpose, and remain in them as guilt, n. 493. Adulteries of the third and fourth degree are evils of sin, according to the quantity and quality of understanding and will in them, whether they are actually committed or not, n. 494. Adulteries grounded in purpose of the will, and adulteries grounded in confirmation of the understanding, render men natural, sensual, and corporeal, n. 495, 496. And this to such a degree, that at length they reject from themselves all things of the church and of religion, n. 497.

Nevertheless they have the powers of human rationality like other men, n. 498. But they use that rationality while they are in externals, but abuse it while they are in externals, n. 499.

ON THE LUST OF DEFLORATION, n. 501—505.

THE state of a virgin or undeflowered woman before and after marriage, n. 502. Virginity is the crown of chastity and the certificate of conjugial love, n. 503. Defloration, without a view to marriage as an end, is the villany of a robber, n. 504. The lot of those who have confirmed themselves in the persuasion that the lust of defloration is not an evil of sin, after death is grievous, n. 505.

ON THE LUST OF VARIETIES, n. 506—510.

BY the lust of varieties is meant the entirely dissolute lust of adultery, n. 507. That lust is love, and at the same time loathing, in regard to the sex, n. 508. The lot of those [who have been addicted to that lust] after death is miserable, since they have not the inmost principle of life, n. 510.

ON THE LUST OF VIOLATION, n. 511, 512.

ON THE LUST OF SEDUCING INNOCENCIES, n. 513, 514.

ON THE CORRESPONDENCE OF ADULTERIES WITH THE VIOLATION OF SPIRITUAL MARRIAGE, n. 515—520.

ON THE IMPUTATION OF EACH LOVE. ADULTEROUS AND CONJUGIAL, n. 523—531.

THE evil in which every one is principled, is imputed to him after death; and so also the good, n. 524. The transference of the good of one person into another is impossible, n. 525. Imputation, if by it is meant such transference, is a frivolous term, n. 526. Evil or good is imputed to every one according to the quality of his will and of his understanding, n. 527—529. Thus adulterous love is imputed to every one, n. 530. Thus also conjugial love is imputed to every one, n. 531.

INDEX

TO THE

MEMORABLE RELATIONS.

CONJUGIAL love seen in its form with two conjugial partners, who were conveyed down from heaven in a chariot, n. 42, 43.
Three novitiates from the world receive information respecting marriages in heaven, n. 44.
On the chaste love of the sex, n. 55.
On the temple of wisdom, where the causes of beauty in the female sex are discussed by wise ones, n. 56.
On conjugial love with those who lived in the golden age, n. 75.
———————— with those who lived in the silver age, n. 76.
———————— with those who lived in the copper age, n. 77.
———————— with those who lived in the iron age, n. 78.
———————— with those who lived after those ages, n. 79, &c.
On the glorification of the Lord by the angels in the heavens, on account of his advent, and of conjugial love, which is to be restored at that time, n. 81.
On the precepts of the New Church, n. 82.
On the origin of conjugial love, and of its virtue or potency, discussed by an assembly of the wise from Europe, n. 103, 104.
On a paper let down from heaven to the earth, on which was written, The marriage of good and truth, n. 115.
What the image and likeness of God is, and what the tree of life, and the tree of the knowledge of good and evil, n. 132—136.
Two angels out of the third heaven give information respecting conjugial love there, n. 137.
On the ancients in Greece, who inquired of strangers, What news from the earth? Also, on men found in the woods, n. 151*—154*.
On the golden shower and hall, where the wives said various things respecting conjugial love, n. 155.
The opinion of the ancient sophi in Greece respecting the life of men after death, n. 182.
On the nuptial garden called Adramandoni, where there was a conversation respecting the influx of conjugial love, n. 183.
A declaration by the ancient sophi in Greece respecting employments in heaven, n. 207.
On the golden shower and hall, where the wives again conversed respecting conjugial love, n. 208.
On the judges who were influenced by friendship, of whom it was exclaimed, O how just! n. 231.

On the reasoners, of whom it was exclaimed, O how learned! n. 232.
On the confirmators, of whom it was exclaimed, O how wise! n. 233.
On those who are in the love of ruling from the love of self, n. 261—266.
On those who are in the love of possessing all things of the world, n. 267, 268.
On Lucifer, n. 269.
On conjugial cold, n. 270.
On the seven wives sitting on a bed of roses, who said various things respecting conjugial love, n. 293.
Observations by the same wives on the prudence of women, n. 294.
A discussion what the soul is, and what is its quality, n. 315.
On the garden, where there was a conversation respecting the divine providence in regard to marriages, n. 316.
On the distinction between what is spiritual and what is natural, n. 326—329.
Discussions, whether a woman who loves herself for her beauty, loves her husband; and whether a man who loves himself for his intelligence, loves his wife, n. 330, 331.
On self-prudence, n. 353.
On the perpetual faculty of loving a wife in heaven, n. 355, 356.
A discussion, whether nature is of life, or life of nature; also respecting the centre and expanse of life and nature, n. 380.
Orators delivering their sentiments on the origin of beauty in the female sex, n. 381—384.
That all things which exist and take place in the natural world, are from the Lord through the spiritual world, n. 415—422.
On the angels who were ignorant of the nature and meaning of adultery, n. 444.
On delight, which is the universal of heaven and hell, n. 461.
On an adulterer who was taken up into heaven, and there saw things inverted n. 477.
On three priests who were accused by adulterers, n. 500.
That determined and confirmed adulterers do not acknowledge anything of heaven and the church, n. 521, 522.
On the new things revealed by the Lord, n. 532.

FINIS.

INDEX

TO

CONJUGIAL LOVE.

The Numbers refer to the Paragraphs, and not to the Pages

ABOMINATION OF DESOLATION, Matt. xxiv. 15, signifies the falsification and deprivation of all truth, 80.

ABSENCE in the spiritual world, its cause, 171.

ACTION.—In all conjunction by love there must be action, reception, and reaction, 293. From the will, which in itself is spiritual, actions flow, 220.

ACTIVITY is one of the moral virtues which respect life, and enter into it, 164. The activity of love makes a sense of delight, 461. The influx of love and wisdom from the Lord is the essential activity from which comes all delight, 461. From conjugial love, as from a fountain, issue the activities and alacrities of life, 249.

ACTORS.—In heaven, out of the cities, are exhibited stage entertainments, wherein the actors represent the various virtues and graces of moral life, 17, 79.

ACTUALLY, 66, 98, 178, &c. *Obs.*—This expression is used to distinguish *Actualiter* from *Realiter*, of which the author also makes use; thus between *actually* and *really*, there is the same distinction as between *actual*, taken in a philosophical sense, and *real*.

ACUTION.—The spiritual purification of conjugial love may be compared with the purification of natural spirits effected by chemists, and called acution, 145.

ADAM.—In what his sin consisted, 444. Error of those who believe that Adam was wise and did good from himself, and that this was his state of integrity, 135. The evil in which each man is born, is not derived hereditarily from Adam, but from his parents, 525. If it is believed that the guilt of Adam is inscribed on all the human race, it is because few reflect on any evil in themselves, and thence know it, 525. Adam and man are one expression in the Hebrew tongue, 156*.

ADJUNCTION.—The union of the soul and mind of one married partner to those of the other, is an actual adjunction, and cannot possibly be dissolved, 321. This adjunction is close and near according to the love, and approaching to contact with those who are principled in love truly conjugial,

158. It may be called spiritual cohabitation, which takes place with married partners who love each other tenderly, however remote their bodies may be from each other, 158.

ADMINISTRATIONS in the spiritual world, 207. The discharge of them is attended with delight, 207.

ADMINISTRATORS.—In the spiritual world there are administrators, 207.

ADORATIONS.—Why the ancients in their adorations turned their faces to the rising sun, 342.

ADRAMANDONI is the name of a garden in the spiritual world; this word signifies the delight of conjugial love, 183.

ADULTERERS.—As soon as a man actually becomes an adulterer, heaven is closed to him, 500. Adulterers become more and more not men, 432. There are four kinds of adulterers:—1st, Adulterers from a purposed principle are those who are so from the lust of the will; 2d, adulterers from a confirmed principle are those who are so from the persuasion of the understanding; 3d, adulterers from a deliberate principle are those who are so from the allurements of the senses; 4th, adulterers from a non-deliberate principle are those who are not in the faculty or not in the liberty of consulting the understanding, 432. Those of the two former kinds become more and more not men, but the two latter kinds become men as they recede from those errors, 432. Reasonings of adulterers, 500. Every unclean principle of hell is from adulterers, 500, 477. Whoever is in spiritual adultery is also in natural adultery, 520.

ADULTERERS from a deliberate principle and from a non-deliberate principle, 432.

ADULTERY, by, is meant scortation opposite to marriage, 480. The horrible nature of adultery, 483. Spiritual adultery is the connection of evil and the false, 520. Adulteries are the complex of all evils, 356. Why hell in the total is called adultery, 520. There are three genera of adulteries, simple, duplicate, and triplicate, 478, 484. There are four degrees of adulteries, according to which they have their predications, their charges of blame, and after death, their imputations, 485-499:—1st, Adulteries of ignorance, &c., 486, 487; 2d, adulteries of lust, 488, 489; 3d, adulteries of the reason or understanding, &c., 490, 491; 4th, adulteries of the will, 492, 493. The distinction between adulteries of the will and those of the understanding, 490. The adultery of the reason is less grievous than the adultery of the will, 490.—Accessories of adultery and aggravations of it, 454. Adultery is the cause of divorce, 255. Representative of adultery in its business, 521.

AFFECT.

Obs.—This word signifies to impress with affection either good or bad.

AFFECTIONS which are merely derivations of the love, form the will, and make and compose it, 197. Every affection of love belongs to the will, for what a man loves, that he also wills, 196. Every affection has its delight, 272. Affections, with the thoughts thence derived, appertain to the mind, and sensations, with the pleasures thence derived, appertain to the body, 273. In the natural world, almost all are capable of being joined together as to external affections, but not as to internal affections, if these disagree and appear, 272. In the spiritual world all are conjoined as to internal affections, but not according to external, unless these act in unity with the internal, 273. The affections according to which wedlock is commonly contracted in the world, are external, 274; but in that case they are not influenced by internal affections, which conjoin minds, the bonds of wedlock are loosed in the house, 275. By internal affections are meant the mutual inclinations which influence the mind of each of the parties from heaven; whereas by external affections are meant the inclinations which influence the mind of each of the parties from the world, 277. The external affections by death follow the body, and are entombed with it, those only remaining which cohere with internal principles, 320. Women were created by the Lord affections of the wisdom of men, 56. Their affection of wisdom is essential beauty, 56. All the angels are affections of love in a human form, 42; the ruling affection itself shines forth from their faces; and from their affection, and according to it, the kind and quality of their raiment is derived and determined, 42.

AFFLICTION, great, Matt. xxiv. 21, signifies the state of the church infested by evils and falses, 80.

AFFLUX, 293.

Obs.—Afflux is that which flows *upon* or *towards*, and remains generally in the external, without penetrating interiorly, *A. C.*, n. 7955. Efflux is that which flows *from*, and is generally predicated of that which proceeds from below upwards. Influx is that which flows *into*, or which penetrates interiorly, provided it meets with no obstacle; it is generally used when speaking of

that which comes from above, thus from heaven, that is, from the Lord through heaven.

AFRICANS more intelligent than the learned of Europe, 114.

AGE.—The common states of a man's life are called infancy, childhood, youth, manhood, and old age, 185. Unequal ages induce coldness in marriage, 250. In the heavens there is no inequality of age, all there are in the flower of youth, and continue therein to eternity, 250. Golden age, 75. Silver age or period, 76. Copper age, 77. Iron age, 78. Age of iron mixed with miry clay, 79. Age of gold, 42, 75; of silver, 76; of copper, 77; of iron, 78; of iron mixed with clay, 79. The ages of gold, silver, and copper are anterior to the time of which we have any historical records, 73. Men of the golden age knew and acknowledged that they were forms receptive of life from God, and that on this account wisdom was inscribed on their souls and hearts, and hence that they saw truth from the light of truth, and by truths perceived good from the delight of the love thereof, 153*. All those who lived in the silver age had intelligence grounded in spiritual truths, and thence in natural truths, 76.

AID, mutual, of husband and wife, 176.

ALACRITY is one of those moral virtues which have respect to life, and enter into it, 164.

ALCOHOL.—Wisdom purified may be compared with alcohol, which is a spirit highly rectified, 145.

ALCORAN, 342.

ALPHA, the, and the Omega.—Why the Lord is so called, 326.

ALPHABET in the spiritual world, each letter of it is significative, 326.

AMBASSADOR in the spiritual world discussing with two priests on the subject of human prudence, 354.

ANCIENTS.—Of marriages among the ancients, and the most ancient, 75, 77. The most ancient people in this world did not acknowledge any other wisdom than the wisdom of life; but the ancient people acknowledged the wisdom of reason as wisdom, 130. Precepts concerning marriages left by the ancient people to their posterity, 77. Angels are men; their form is the human form, 30. They appear to man when the eyes of his spirit are opened, 30. All the angels are affections of love in the human form, 42. Angels who are loves, and thence wisdoms, are called celestial; and with them conjugial love is celestial; angels who are wisdoms, and thence loves, are called spiritual, and similar thereto is their conjugial principle, 64. There are among the angels some of a simple, and some of a wise character, and it is the part of the wise to judge, when the simple, from their simplicity and ignorance, are doubtful about what is just, or through mistake wander from it, 207. Every angel has conjugial love with its virtue, ability, and delights, according to his application to the

INDEX.

genuine use in which he is, 207. Every man has angels associated to him from the Lord, and such is his conjunction with them, that if they were taken away, he would instantly fall to pieces, 404.

ANGER.—Why it is attributed to the Lord, 366.

ANIMALS.—Wonderful things conspicuous in the productions of animals, 416. Every animal is led by the love implanted in his science, as a blind person is led through the streets by a dog, 96. See *Beasts.*

ANIMUS.—By *animus* is meant the affections, and thence the external inclinations, which are principally insinuated after birth by education, social intercourse, and consequent habits of life, 246.

Obs.—These affections and inclinations constitute a sort of inferior mind.

ANTIPATHY.—In the spiritual world, antipathies are not only felt, but also appear in the face, the discourse, and the gesture, 273. It is otherwise in the natural world, where antipathies may be concealed, 272. Among certain married partners in the natural world, there is an antipathy in their internals, and an apparent sympathy in their externals, 292. Antipathy derives its origin from the opposition of spiritual spheres which emanate from subjects, 171.

ANTIQUITY.—Memorable things of antiquity seen in heaven amongst a nation that lived in the copper age, 77.

AORTA, 315.

APES.—Of those in hell who appear like apes, 505.

APOCALYPSE.—A voice from heaven commanded Swedenborg to apply to the work begun in the Apocalypse, and finish it within two years, 522, 532.

APOPLEXY.—Permanent infirmity, arising from apoplexy, a cause of separation, 253, 470.

APPEARANCE.—Spaces in the spiritual world are appearances; distances, also, and presences are appearances, 158. The appearances of distances and presences there, are according to the proximities, relationships, and affinities of love, 158. Those things which, from their origin, are celestial and spiritual, are not in space, but in the appearances of space, 158.

Obs.—Those things which in the spiritual world are present to the sight of spirits and angels are called *appearances;* those things are called appearances, because, corresponding to the interiors of spirits and of angels, they vary according to the states of those interiors. There are real appearances and appearances unreal; the unreal appearances are those which do not correspond to the interiors. See *Heaven and Hell.*

APPROPRIATION of evil, how it is effected, 489.

ARCANA of wisdom respecting conjugial love; it is important that they should be discovered, 43. Arcana of conjugial love concealed with wives, 166, 155*, 293. Arcanum relative to conception, which takes place though the souls of two married partners be disjoined, 245. Arcanum respecting the actual habitation of every man in some society, either of heaven or hell, 530. Arcana known to the ancients, and at this day lost, 220. Arcana revealed, which exceed in excellence all the arcana heretofore revealed since the beginning of the church, 532. These arcana are yet reputed on earth as of no value, 533.

ARCHITECTONIC ART, the, is in its essential perfection in heaven, and hence are derived all the rules of that art in the world, 12.

ARISTIPPUS, 151.*

ARISTOTLE, 151.*

ARMIES of the Lord Jehovih. Thus the most ancient people called themselves, 75.

ARTIFICERS in the spiritual world, 207: wonderful works which they execute there, 207.

AS FROM HIMSELF, 132, 134, 269, 340.

ASSAULT.—How love defends itself when assaulted, 361.

ASSES.—Of those who, in the spiritual world, appear at a distance like asses heavily laden, 232. Blazing ass upon which a pope was seated in hell, 265.

ASSOCIATE, to.—All in the heavens are associated according to affinities and relationships of love, and have habitations accordingly, 50.

ASTRONOMY is one of those sciences by which an entrance is made into things rational, which are the ground of rational wisdom, 163.

ATHEISTS, who are in the glory of reputation arising from self-love, and thence in a high conceit of their own intelligence, enjoy a more sublime rationality than many others; the reason why, 269. Why the understanding of atheists, in spiritual light, appeared open beneath but closed above, 421.

ATHENÆUM, city of, in the spiritual world, 151*, 182, 207. Sports of the Athenæides, 207. These games were spiritual exercises, 207.

ATMOSPHERES.—The world is distinguished into regions as to the atmospheres, the lowest of which is the watery, the next above is the aerial, and still higher is the etherial, above which there is also the highest, 188. The reason why the atmosphere appears of a golden color in the heaven in which the love of uses reigns, 266.

AURA.—Thus the superior atmosphere is named, 145. The aura is the continent of celestial light and heat, or of the wisdom and love in which the angels are principled, 145. See *Atmospheres.*

AUTHORESSES, learned.—Examination of their writings in the spiritual world in their presence, 175.

AVERSION between married partners arises from spiritual cold, 236. Whence arises aversion on the part of the husband towards the wife, 805. Aversion between married partners arises from a disunion of souls and a disjunction of minds, 236.

BACK, the.—The sphere which issues forth from man encompasses him on the back and on the breast, lightly on the back, but more densely on the breast, 171, 224. The effect of this on married partners, who are of different minds and discordant affections, 171.

BALANCE.—Love truly conjugial is like a balance in which the inclinations for iterated marriages are made, 318. The mind is kept balancing to another marriage, according to the degree of love in which it was principled in the former marriage, 318.

BANK of roses, 8, 294.

BATS, in the spiritual world, are correspondences and consequent appearances of the thoughts of confirmators, 233.

BEARS signify those who read the Word in the natural sense, and see truths therein, without understanding, 193. Those who only read the Word, and imbibe thence nothing of doctrine, appear at a distance, in the spiritual world, like boars, 79.

BEASTS are born into natural loves, and thereby into sciences corresponding to them: still they do not know, think, understand, and relish any sciences, but are led through them by their loves, almost as blind persons are led through the streets by dogs, 134. Beasts are born into all the sciences of their loves, thus into all that concerns their nourishment, habitation, love of the sex, and the education of their young, 133. Difference between man and beasts, 133, 134. Every beast corresponds to some quality, either good or evil, 76. Beasts in the spiritual world are representative, but in the natural world they are real, 133. Wild beasts in the spiritual world are correspondences, and thus representatives of the lusts in which the spirits are, 79. The state of men compared with that of beasts, 151*. Men like beasts, found in the forests, 151*. Beast-men, 233.

BEAUTY.—The affection of wisdom is essential beauty, 56. Cause of beauty in the female sex, 56. Women have a two-fold beauty, one natural, which is that of the face and the body, and the other spiritual, which is that of the love and manners, 330. Beauty in the spiritual world is the form of the love and manners, 330. Discussion on the beauty of woman, 330. Origin of that beauty, 382-384. Ineffable beauty of a wife in the third heaven, 42.

BEES.—Their wonderful instinct, 419.

BEHIND.—In the spiritual world, it is not allowed any one to stand behind another, and speak to him, 444.

BEINGS.—The desire to continue in its form is implanted by creation in all living beings, 361.

BENEVOLENCE is one of those virtues which have respect to life and enter into it, 164.

BETROTHINGS, cf. 295-314. Reasons of betrothings, 301. By betrothing each party is prepared for conjugial love, 302. By betrothing, the mind of one is conjoined to the mind of the other, so as to effect a marriage of the spirit, previous to marriage, 303, 305. Of betrothings in heaven, 20, 21.

BIRDS in the spiritual world are representative forms, 76. Every bird corresponds to some good or bad quality, 76.

BIRDS OF PARADISE.—In heaven the forms under which the chaste delights of conjugial love are presented to the view, are birds of paradise, &c., 430. A pair of birds of paradise represent the middle region of conjugial love, 270.

BLESSEDNESS, 69, 180. Love receives its blessedness from communication by uses with others, 266. The infinity of all blessedness is in the Lord, 335.

BLESSING of marriages by the priests, 308.

BLUE.—What the color blue signifies, 76.

BODY, the material, is composed of watery and earthy elements, and of aerial vapors thence arising, 192. The material body of man is overcharged with lusts, which are in it as dregs that precipitate themselves to the bottom when the must of wine is clarified, 272. Such are the constituent substances of which the bodies of men in the world are composed, 272. The bodies of men viewed interiorly are merely forms of their minds exteriorly organized to effect the purposes of the soul, 310. See Mind. Every thing which is done in the body is from a spiritual origin, 310. All things which are done in the body by man flow in from his spirit, 310. Man when stripped of his body is in his internal affections, which his body had before concealed, 273. What is in the spirit as derived from the body does not long continue, but the love which is in the spirit and is derived from the body does continue, 162, 191. Marriages of the spirit ought to precede marriages of the body, 310.

BOND.—The internal or spiritual bond must keep the external or natural in its order and tenor, 320. Wives love the bonds of marriage if the men do, 217. Unless the external affections are influenced by internal, which conjoin minds, the bonds of wedlock are loosed in the house, 275.

BOOKS.—In heaven, as in the world, there are books, 207.

BORN, to be.—Man is born in total ignorance, 134. Every man by birth is merely corporeal, and from corporeal he becomes natural more and more interiorly, and thus rational, and at length spiritual, 59, 305, 447. He becomes rational in proportion as he loves intelligence, and spiritual if he loves wisdom, 94, 102. Man is not born into any knowledge, and if he does not receive instruction from others, is viler than a beast, 350. Man is born without sciences, to the end that he may receive them all, and he is born into no love, to the intent that he may come into all love, 134. Every man is born for heaven and no one for hell, and every one comes into heaven (by in-

INDEX.

fluence) from the Lord, and into hell (by influence) from self, 350.

BREAST, the, of man signifies wisdom, 193. All things which by derivation from the soul and mind have their determination in the body, first flow into the bosom, 179. The breast is as it were a place of public assembly, and a royal council chamber, and the body is as a populous city around it, 179. The sphere of the man's life encompasses him more densely on the breast, but lightly on the back, 171, 224. See *Back*.

BRETHREN.—The Lord calls those brethren and sisters who are of his church, 120.

BRIDE.—The church in the Word is called the bride and wife, 117. Clothing of a bride in heaven, 20.

BRIDEGROOM.—The Lord in the Word is called the bridegroom and husband, 117. Clothing of a bridegroom in heaven, 20.

BRIMSTONE signifies the love of what is false, 80. Lakes of fire and brimstone, 79, 80.

CABINET of antiquities in the spiritual world, 77.

CALF, a golden, signifies the pleasure of the flesh, 535.

CAP, a, signifies intelligence, 293. Turreted cap, 78.

CAROTID ARTERIES, 315.

CASTIGATION.—The spiritual purification of conjugial love may be compared with the purification of natural spirits effected by chemists, and named castigation, 145.

CATS.—Comparison concerning them, 512.

CAUSE.—See *End*. To speak from causes is the speech of wisdom, 75. Causes of coldness, separations, and divorces in marriages, 234-260. Causes of concubinage, 467-474.

CAUSES, the various, of legitimate separation, 253, 470.

CELEBRATION of the Lord from the Word, 81.

CELESTIAL.—In proportion as a man loves his wife he becomes celestial and internal, 77.

CELIBACY ought not to be preferred to marriage, 156. Chastity cannot be predicated of those who have renounced marriage by vows of perpetual celibacy, unless there be and remain in them the love of a life truly conjugial, 155. The sphere of perpetual celibacy infests the sphere of conjugial love, which is the very essential sphere of heaven, 54. Those who live in celibacy, if they are spiritual, are on the side of heaven, 54. Those who in the world have lived a single life, and have altogether alienated their minds from marriage, in case they be spiritual, remain single; but if natural, they become whoremongers, 54. For those who in their single state have desired marriage, and have solicited it without success, if they are spiritual, blessed marriages are provided, but not until they come into heaven, 54.

CENTRE of nature and of life, 380.

CERBERUS, 79.

CEREBELLUM, the, is beneath the hinder part of the head, and is designed for love and the goods thereof, 444.

CEREBRUM, the, is beneath the anterior and upper part of the head, and is designed for wisdom and the truths thereof, 444.

CHANGE, the, of the state of life which takes place with men and with women by marriage, 184-206. By changes of the state of life are meant changes of quality as to the things appertaining to the understanding, and as to those appertaining to the will, 184. The changes which take place in man's internal principles are more perfectly continuous than those which take place in his external principles, 185. The changes which take place in internal principles are changes of the state of the will as to affections, and changes of the state of the understanding as to thoughts, 185. The changes of these two faculties are perpetual with man from infancy even to the end of his life, and afterwards to eternity, 185. These changes differ in the case of men and in the case of women, 187.

CHARGES of blame are made by a judge according to the law, 485. Difference between predications, charges of blame, and imputations, 485.

CHARIOT, a, signifies the doctrine of truth, 76.

CHARITY is love, 10.

CHARITY AND FAITH.—Good has relation to charity, and truth to faith, 115, 124. To live well is charity, and to believe well is faith, 283. Charity and faith are the life of God in man, 135.

CHASTE PRINCIPLE, concerning the, and the non-chaste, 138-156. The chaste principle and the non-chaste are predicated solely of marriages, and of such things as relate to marriages, 139. The Christian conjugial principle alone is chaste, 142. See *Conjugial*.

CHASTITY OF MARRIAGE, 138, and following. See *Contents*. The chastity of marriage exists by a total abdication of what is opposed to it from a principle of religion, 147-149. The purity of conjugial love is what is called chastity, 139. Love truly conjugial is essential chastity, 139, 143. Non-chastity is a removal of what is unchaste from what is chaste, 138.

CHEMISTRY is one of the sciences by which, as by doors, an entrance is made into things rational, which are the ground of rational wisdom, 163.

CHEMISTS.—Spiritual purification compared to the natural purification of spirits effected by chemists, 145.

CHILDREN born of parents who are principled in love truly conjugial, derive from their parents the conjugial principle of good and truth, 202-205. Infants in heaven become men of stature and comeliness, according to the increments of intelligence with them; it is otherwise with infants on earth, 187. When they have attained the stature of young men of eighteen, and young girls of fifteen years of age, in this world, then marriages are provided by the Lord for them, 444. The love of infants remains after death, especially with women, 410. Infants are educated under the Lord's auspices by such women, 411. Little children in the Word signify those who are in innocence, 414. The love of infants corresponds to the defence of good and truth, 127.

CHRIST.—The kingdom of Christ, which is heaven, is a kingdom of uses, 7. To reign with Christ signifies to be wise, and to perform uses, 7.

CHRISTIAN.—Love truly conjugial with its delights can only exist among those who are of the Christian church, 337. Not a single person throughout the Christian world is acquainted with the true nature of heavenly joy and eternal happiness, 4.

CHRYSALISES, 418.

CHURCH, the, is from the Lord, and exists with those who come to Him, and live according to His precepts, 129. The church is the Lord's kingdom in the world, corresponding to his kingdom in the heavens; and also the Lord conjoins them together, that they may make a one, 431. The church in general and in particular is a marriage of good and of truth, 115. The church with man is formed by the Lord by means of truths to which good is adjoined, 122-124. The church with its goods and truths can never exist but with those who live in love truly conjugial with one wife, 76. The church is of both sexes, 21. The husband and wife together are the church; with these the church first implanted in the man and by the man in the wife, 125. How the church is formed by the Lord with two married partners, and how conjugial love is formed thereby, 63. The origin of the church and of conjugial love are in one place of abode, 238.

CIRCE, 521.

CIRCLE.—What circles round the head represent in the spiritual life, 269. Circle and increasing progression of conjugial love, 78.

CIRCUMSTANCES and contingencies vary every thing, 485. The quality of every deed, and in general the quality of every thing, depends upon circumstances, 487.

CIVIL things have relation to the world, they are statutes, laws, and rules, which bind men, so that a civil society and state may be composed of them in a well-connected order, 130. Civil things with man reside beneath spiritual things, and above natural things, 130.

CIVILITY is one of the moral virtues which have respect to life, and enter into it, 164. In heaven they show each other every token of civility, 16.

CLAY mixed with iron, 79.

COHABIT, to.—When married partners have lived in love truly conjugial, the spirit of the deceased cohabits continually with that of the survivor, and this even to the death of the latter, 321.

COHABITATION, spiritual, takes place with married partners who love each other tenderly, however remote their bodies may be from each other, 158. See *Adjunction*. Internal and external cohabitation, 322. With those who are principled in love truly conjugial the happiness of cohabitation increases, but it decreases with those who are not principled in conjugial love, 213.

COHOBATION.—The spiritual purification of conjugial love may be compared to the purification of natural spirits, as effected by chemists, and called cohobation, 145.

COLD.—Spirits merely natural grow intensely cold while they apply themselves to the side of some angel, who is in a state of love, 235. Spiritual cold in marriages is a disunion of souls, 236. Causes of cold in marriages, 237-250. Cold arises from various causes, internal, external, and accidental, all of which originate in a dissimilitude of internal inclinations, 275. Spiritual cold is the privation of spiritual heat, 235. Whence it arises, 235. Whence conjugial cold arises, 294. Every one who is insane in spiritual things is cold towards his wife, and warm towards harlots, 294.

COLUMN.—Comparison of successive and simultaneous order to a column of steps, which, when it subsides, becomes a body cohering in a plane, 314.

COMMUNICATIONS.—After death, married pairs enjoy similar communications with each other as in the world, 51.

CONATUS is the very essence of motion, 215. From the endeavor of the two principles of good and truth to join themselves together into one, conjugial love exists by derivation, 238.

CONCEPTIONS. — Between the disjoined souls of married partners there is effected conjunction in a middle love, otherwise there would be no conceptions, 245.

CONCERTS of music and singing in the heavens, 17.

CONCLUDE, to, from an interior and prior principle, is to conclude from ends and causes to effects, which is according to order; but to conclude from an exterior or posterior principle, is to conclude from effects to causes and ends, which is contrary to order, 408.

CONCUBINAGE, 462-476. Difference between concubinage and pellicacy, 462. See *Pellicacy*. There are two kinds of concubinage which differ exceedingly from each other, the one conjointly with a wife, the other apart from a wife, 463. Concubinage conjointly with a wife is illicit to Christians and detestable, 464. See also 467, 476.

CONCUBINE, 462.

CONCUPISCENCE, concerning, 267. Every one is by truth interiorly in concupiscence, but by education exteriorly in intelligence, 267. Interesting particulars concerning concupiscence not visionary or fantastic, in which all men are born, 269. All the concupiscences of evil reside in the lowest region of the mind, which is called the natural; but in the region above, which is called the spiritual, there are not any concupiscences of evil, 305. In every thing that proceeds from the natural man there is concupiscence, 448. Imputation of concupiscence, 455. In the spiritual world every evil concupiscence presents a likeness of itself in some form, which is not perceived by those who are in the concupiscence, but by those who are at a distance, 521.

CONFIDENCE, full, is in conjugial love, and is derived from it, 180. Full confidence relates to the heart, 180.

CONFINES OF HEAVEN.—Those who enter into extra-conjugial life are sent to their like, on the confines of heaven, 155.

CONFIRM, to.—The understanding alone confirms, and when it confirms it engages the will to its party, 491. Every one can confirm evil equally as well as good, in like manner what is false as well as what is true. The reason why the confirmation of evil is perceived with more delight than the confirmation of good, and the confirmation of what is false with greater lucidity than the confirmation of what is true, 491. Intelligence does not consist in being able to confirm whatever a man pleases, but in being able to see that what is true is true, and that what is false is false, 233. Every one may confirm himself in favor of the divine principle or Being, by the visible things of nature, 416-419. Those who confirm themselves in favor of a divine principle or Being, attend to the wonderful things which are conspicuous in the productions both of vegetables and animals, 416. Those who had confirmed themselves in favor of nature, by what is visible in this world, so as to become atheists, appeared in spiritual light with the understanding open beneath, but closed above, 421.

CONFIRMATIONS are effected by reasonings, which the mind seizes for its use, deriving them either from its superior region or its inferior, 491. The form of the human mind is according to confirmations turned towards heaven, if its confirmations are in favor of marriages, but turned to hell, if they are in favor of adulteries, 491. Confirmations of falsities, so as to make them appear like truths, are represented in the spiritual world under the forms of birds of night, 233. See *To Confirm.*

CONFIRMATORS.—They are called such in the spiritual world who cannot at all see whether truth be truth, but yet can make whatever they will to be truth, 233. Their fate in the other life, 233.

CONJUGIAL PAIRS.—It is provided by the Lord that conjugial pairs be born, and that these pairs be continually educated for marriage, neither the maiden nor the youth knowing any thing of the matter, 316.

CONJUGIAL PRINCIPLE, the, of good and truth is implanted from creation in every soul, and also in the principles derived from the soul, 204. The conjugial principle fills the universe from first principles to last, and from a man even to a worm,

204. It is inscribed on the soul, to the end that soul may be propagated from soul, 236. It is inscribed on both sexes from inmost principles to ultimates, and a man's quality as to his thoughts and affections, and consequently as to his bodily actions and behavior, is according to that principle, 140. In every substance, even the smallest, there is a conjugial principle, 316. In the minutest things with man, both male and female, there is a conjugial principle: still the conjugial principle with the male is different from what it is with the female, 316. There is implanted in every man from creation, and consequently from his birth, an internal conjugial principle, and an external conjugial principle; man comes first into the latter, and as he becomes spiritual he comes into the former, 148, 188. Children derive from their parents the conjugial principle of good and truth, for it is that principle which flows into man from the Lord, and constitutes his human life, 203. The conjugial human principle ever goes hand in hand with religion, 80. This conjugial principle is the desire of living with one wife, and every Christian has this desire according to his religion, 80. The Christian conjugial principle alone is chaste, 142. By the Christian conjugial principle is meant the marriage of one man with one wife, 142. The conjugial principle of one man with one wife, is the storehouse of human life, and the reservoir of the Christian religion, 457, 458. The conjugial principle is like a scale in which conjugial love is weighed, 531.

CONJUNCTION.—In every part, and even in every particular, there is a principle tending to conjunction, 33, 37; it was implanted from creation, and thence remains perpetually, 37. The conjunctive principle lies concealed in every part of the male, and in every part of the female, 37, 46. In the male conjugial principle there is what is conjunctive with the female conjugial principle, and *vice versa*, even in the minutest things, 316.

CONJUNCTION of souls and minds by marriage, so that they are no longer two but one flesh, 156*, 161. Spiritual conjunction cannot possibly be dissolved, 321. How there is a conjunction of the created universe with its Creator, and by conjunction everlasting conservation, 85. There is conjunction with the Lord by a life according to his commandments, 341. There is no conjunction unless it be reciprocal, for conjunction on one part, and not on the other in its turn, is dissolved of itself, 61.

CONNECTION, the connubial, of what is evil and false is the spiritual origin of adultery, 428, 520. It is the anti-church, 497. In hell all are in this *connubium*, 520.

CONNUBIAL PRINCIPLE, the, of what is evil and false, is the opposite of the conjugial principle of good and truth, 203. Beneath heaven there are only nuptial connections which are tied and loosed, 192.

CONSCIENCE is a spiritual virtue which

flows from love towards God, and love towards the neighbor, 164. See *To Flow.*
CONSCIENTIOUSNESS in regard to marriage, 271.
CONSECRATION of marriages, 308.
CONSENT constitutes marriage and initiates the spirit into conjugial love, 299. Consent against the will, or extorted, does not initiate the spirit, 299.
CONSOCIATION, 45, 153*.
CONSUMMATION of the Age, signifies the last time or end of the church, 80.
CONTEMPT between married partners springs from disunion of souls, 236.
CONTINGENCIES and circumstances vary every thing, 485, 488.
CONTRARIES arise from an opposite principle in contrariety thereto, 425.
CONVICTION of the spirit of man, how it is effected, 295. Those things in which the spirit is convinced, obtain a place above those which, without consulting reason, enter from authority, and from the faith of authority, 295.
COPPER, the, signifies natural good, 77. The age or period of copper, 77.
CORPORA STRIATA, 315.
CORPOREAL PRINCIPLE, the, is like ground wherein things natural, rational, and spiritual, are implanted in their order, 59. Man is born corporeal as a worm, and he remains corporeal, unless he learns to know, to understand, and to be wise from others, 133. Every man by birth is merely corporeal, and from corporeal he becomes natural more and more interiorly, and thus rational, and at length spiritual, 59, 143. By corporeal men are properly meant those who love only themselves, placing their heart in the quest of honor, 496; they immerse all things of the will, and consequently of the understanding in the body, and look backward at themselves from others, and love only what is proper to themselves, 496. Corporeal spirits, 495.
CORRESPONDENCES, 76, 127, 342, 532. Concerning the correspondence of the marriage of the Lord and the church, 116. There is a correspondence of conjugial love with the marriage of the Lord and the church, 62. Of the correspondence of the opposite with the violation of spiritual marriage, 515. See *Science of Correspondences.*
CORTICAL substance of the brain, 315.
COURAGE is one of the moral virtues which have respect to life and enter into it, 164.
COVENANT signifies conjunction, 128. As the Word is the medium of conjunction, it is therefore called the old and the new covenant, 128. The covenant between Jehovah and the heavens, 75.
CRAB, the.—What it is to think as a crab walks, 295.
CREATE, to.—Why man was so created that whatever he wills, thinks, and does, appears to him as in himself, and thereby from himself, 444. How man, created a form of God, could be changed into a form of the devil, 153*.

CREATION cannot be from any other source than from divine love, by divine wisdom in divine use, 183. All fructifications, propagations, and prolifications, are continuations of creation, 183. The creation returns to the Creator, through the angelic heaven which is composed of the human race, 85. Creation of man for conjugial love, 66.
CROCODILES, in the spiritual world, represent the deceit and cunning of the inhabitants, 79.
CROWNS of flowers on the head, 153. The crown of chastity, 508.
CUPIDITIES, the, of the flesh are nothing but the conglomerated concupiscences of what is evil and false, 440.
CUSTOMARY RITES, there are, which are merely formal, and there are others which at the same time are also essential; among the latter are the nuptials, 306. Nuptials are to be reckoned among essentials, 306.

DANES, the, 108, 111.
DARKNESS of the north signifies dulness of mind and ignorance of truth, 77.
DAUGHTERS-IN-LAW. — What daughters and sons-in-law signify in the Word, 120.
DAUGHTERS, in the Word, signifies the goods of the church, 120, 220.
DEATH.—Man after death is perfectly a man, yea, more perfectly a man than before in the world, 182.
DECALOGUE, why the, was promulgated by Jehovah God upon Mount Sinai with a stupendous miracle, 351.
DECANTATION.—The purification of conjugial love may be compared with the purification of natural spirits, as effected by the chemists, and called decantation, 145.
DECEASED.—When married partners have lived in love truly conjugial, the spirit of the deceased cohabits continually with that of the survivor, and this even to the death of the latter, 321.
DECLARATION, the, of love belongs to the men, 296.
DEFECATION.—The purification of conjugial love may be compared with the purification of natural spirits, as effected by the chemists, and called defecation, 145.
DEGREES.—There are three degrees of life, and hence there are three heavens, and the human mind is distinguished into those degrees, hence man corresponds to the three heavens, 532. Heretofore the distinction of degrees in relation to greater and less has been known, but not in relation to prior and posterior, 532. There are three degrees of the natural man: the first degree is that properly meant by the natural, the second the sensual, and the third the corporeal, 496. Adulteries change men into these degenerate degrees, 496. Four degrees of adulteries, 485–494. Violations of the Word and the church correspond to the prohibited degrees enumerated in Levit., ch. xviii., 519.
DELIGHTS, all, whatever, of which man has any sensation, are delights of his love,

68. By delights love manifests itself, yea, exists and lives, 68. Delights follow use, and are also communicated to man according to the love thereof, 68. The love of use derives its essence from love, and its existence from wisdom. The love of use, which derives its origin from love by wisdom, is the love and life of all celestial joys, 68. The activity of love makes the sense of delight: its activity in heaven is with wisdom, its activity in hell is with insanity: each in its objects presents delights, 461. Delight is the all of life to all in heaven, and to all in hell, 461. Delights are exalted in the same degree that love is exalted, and als· in the degree that the incident affec:.ions touch the ruling love more nearly, 68. Every delight of love, in the spiritual world, is presented to the sight under various appearances, to the sense under various odors, and to the view under various forms of beasts and birds, 430. Delights of love truly conjugial, 68.

DELIGHTS, external, without internal have no soul, 8. Every delight without its corresponding soul continually grows more and more languid and dull, and fatigues the mind (*animus*) more than labor, 8. The delight of the soul is derived from love and wisdom proceeding from the Lord, 8. This delight enters into the soul by influx from the Lord, and descends through the superior and inferior regions of the mind into all the senses of the body, and in them is complete and full, 8. In conjugial love are collated all joys and delights from first to last, 68, 69. The delights of conjugial love are the same with the delights of wisdom, 293, 294. They proceed from the Lord, and flow thence into the souls of men (*homines*), and through their souls into their minds, and there into the interior affections and thoughts, and thence into the body, 183, 69, 144, 155*, 193. As good is one with truth in spiritual marriage, so wives desire to be one with their husband; and hence arise conjugial delights with them, 198. Paradisineal delights, 8. The delights of conjugial love ascend to the highest heaven, and in the way thither, and there, join themselves with the delights of all heavenly loves, and thereby enter into their happiness, and endure forever, 294.

DELIRIUM.—An eminent degree of delirium is occasioned by truths which are falsified until they are believed to be wisdom, 212. Delirium in which those are, in the spiritual world, who have been in the unrestrained love of self and the world, 267.

DEMOCRITUS, 182.
DEMOSTHENES, 182.

DEVILS.—Those are called devils who have lived wickedly, and thereby rejected all acknowledgment of God from their hearts, 380. See *Satans*. With adulterers who are called devils, the will is the principal agent, and with those who are called satans, the understanding is the principal agent, 492. Devil of a frightful form, 263.

DIFFERENCE between the spiritual and the natural, 326-329.

DIGNITIES, concerning, in heaven, 7, 266, there they do not prefer dignity to use but the excellence of use to dignity, 250.
DIOGENES, 182.

DISCIPLES, the twelve, together represented the church as to all its constituent principles, 119. Who they are who are called disciples of the Lord in the spiritual world, 261.

DISCORD between married partners arises from spiritual cold, 236.

DISCOURSE, man's, in itself is such as is the thought of his understanding which produces it, 527. Discourse itself is grounded in the thought of the understanding, and the tone of the voice is grounded in the will affection, 140. Speech which is said to flow from the thought, flows not from the thought, but from the affection through the thought, 86. Spiritual language with representatives fully expresses what is intended to be said, and many things in a moment, 481. Conversation in the spiritual world may be heard by a distant person as if he were present, 521. Frequent discourse from the memory and from recollection, and not at the same time from thought and intelligence, induces a kind of faith, 415.

DISJUNCTION, all, derives its origin from the opposition of spiritual spheres, which emanate from their subjects, 171.

DISSIMILITUDES in the spiritual world are separated, 273. See *Likeness*.

DISTANCES.—Spheres cause distances in the spiritual world, 171. Distances in the spiritual world are appearances according to the states of mind, 78.

DISTINCTION, characteristic, of the woman and the man, 217.

DIVERSITIES.—Distinction between varieties and diversities. There are varieties between those things which are of one genus, or of one species, also between the genera and species; but there is a diversity between those things which are in the opposite principle, 324. In heaven there is infinite variety, and in hell infinite diversity, 324.

DIVIDED.—Every thing divided is more and more multiple, and not more and more simple, because what is continually divided approaches nearer and nearer to the Infinite, in which all things are infinitely, 329.

DIVINE GOOD AND TRUTH.—The divine good is the *esse* of the divine substance, and the divine truth is the *existere* of the divine substance, 115. The divine good and truth proceed as one from the Lord, 87. The Lord God, the Creator, is essential divine good, and essential divine truth, 84. The divine truth in the Word is united to the divine good, 129. All divine truth in the heavens gives forth light, 77.

DIVINE ESSENCE, the, is composed of love, wisdom, and use, 183. Nothing but what is of the divine essence can proceed from the Lord, and flow into the inmost principle of man, 183. There is not any essence without a form, nor any form without an essence, 87.

DIVINE LOVE AND WISDOM.—In the Lord God, the Creator, there are divine love and Divine Wisdom, 84.

DIVISIBLE.—Every grain of thought, and every drop of affection, is divisible *ad infinitum:* in proportion as his ideas are divisible man is wise, 829. Every thing is divisible *in infinitum*, 185.

DIVORCE, by, is meant the abolition of the conjugial covenant, and thence a pecuniary separation, and after this an entire liberty to marry another wife, 468. The only cause of divorce is adultery, according to the Lord's precept. Matt. xix. 9, 255, 468.

DOCTRINALS of the New Church in five precepts, 82.

Does in the spiritual world represent the lusts in which the inhabitants are principled, 79. Who those are who appear like dogs of indulgences, 505.

DOVES, turtle.—In heaven, the appearances under which the chaste delights of conjugial love are presented to the view, are turtle-doves, &c., 430. A pair of turtle-doves represents conjugial love of the highest region, 270.

DRAGONS in the spiritual world represent the falsities and depraved inclinations of the inhabitants to those things which appertain to idolatrous worship, 79.

DRESS of a bridegroom and bride during their marriage in heaven, 20, 21.

DRINK, to, water from the fountain signifies to be instructed concerning truths, and by truths concerning goods, and thereby to grow wise, 182.

DRINKS.—In the heaven as well as in the world there are drinks, 6. See *Food*.

DRUNKENNESS, 252, 472.

DURA-MATER, 315.

DUTIES.—There are duties proper to the man, and duties proper to the wife, 174. In the duties proper to the men, the primary agent is understanding, thought, and wisdom; whereas in the duties proper to the wives, the primary agent is will, affection, and love, 175.

EAR, the, does not hear and discern the harmonies of tunes in singing, and the concordances of the articulation of sounds in discourse, but the spirit, 440. In heaven the right ear is the good of hearing, and the left the truth thereof, 316.

EARTH, the, or ground is the common mother of all vegetables, 206, 397; and of all minerals, 397.

EARTH, the lower, in the spiritual world, is next above hell, 231.

EARTH, or country, 13, 27, 37, 49, 69, 71, 144, 320, &c.

EASE, by, and sloth the mind grows stupid and the body torpid, and the whole man becomes insensible to every vital love, especially to conjugial love, 249.

EAST, the.—The Lord is the East, because he is in the sun there, 261.

EAT, to, of the tree of life, in a spiritual sense, is to be intelligent and wise from the Lord; and to eat of the tree of knowledge of good and evil, signifies to be intelligent and wise from self, 353. To eat of the tree of life, is to receive eternal life; to eat of the tree of knowledge of good and evil, is to receive damnation, 135, 444.

ECCLESIASTICAL ORDER, the, on the earth minister those things which appertain to the Lord's priestly character, 308. What is the nature of ecclesiastical self-love, 264. They aspire to be gods, so far as that love is unrestrained, 264.

EDEN.—See *Garden*.

EDUCATION of children in the spiritual world, 411–413.

EFFECT.—See *End*.

EFFIGY.—Two married partners, between or in whom conjugial love subsists, are an effigy and form of it, 65. In the spiritual world the faces of spirits become the effigies of their internal affections, 273.

ELECTION belongs to the man and not to the woman, 296. The women have the right of election of one of their suitors, 296.

ELEVATION.—With men there is an elevation of the mind into superior light, and with women elevation of the mind into superior heat, 188. Elevation into superior light with men is elevation into superior intelligence, and thence into wisdom, in which also there are ascending degrees of elevation, 188. The elevation into superior heat with women is an elevation into chaster and purer conjugial love, and continually towards the conjugial principle, which from creation lies concealed in their inmost principles, 188. These elevations considered in themselves are openings of the mind, 188.

ELYSIAN FIELDS, 182.

EMPLOYMENTS in the spiritual world, 207.

END of this Work, 295.

END, the, and the cause, in what is to be effected and in effects, act in unity because they act together, 387. The end, cause, and effect successively progress as three things, but in the effect itself they make one, 401. Every end considered in itself is a love, 212. Every end appertains to the will, every cause to the understanding, and every effect to action, 400. The end, unless the intended effect is seen together with it, is not any thing, neither does each become any thing, unless the cause supports, contrives, and conjoins, 400. All operations in the universe have a progression from ends, through causes into effects, 400. Ends advance in a series, one after the other, and in their progress the last end becomes first, 387. Ends make progression in nature through times without time, but they cannot come forth and manifest themselves, until the effect or use exists and becomes a subject, 401. The end of marriage is the procreation of children, 254. All in heaven are influenced by an end of good, and all in hell by an end of evil, 453, 527.

INDEX.

ENGLAND, 380
ENGLISH, 103, .07, 326.
ENUNCIATIONS, the.—The name of the prophetic books of the Word that was given to the inhabitants of Asia, before the Israelitish Word, 77.
EPICURUS, 182.
EQUILIBRIUM, there is an, between the sphere of conjugial love, and between the sphere of its opposite, and man is kept in this equilibrium, 437. This equilibrium is a spiritual equilibrium, 437. Spiritua. equilibrium is that which exists between good and evil, or between heaven and hell, 444. This equilibrium produces a free principle, 444. See *Freedom*.
ERUDITE, the pretended, in the spiritual world, 232.
ERUDITION appertains to rational wisdom, 163.
ERUDITION is one of the principles constituent of rational wisdom, 163.
ESSE and EXISTERE.—The esse of the substance of God is Divine good, and the existere of the substance of God is Divine truth, 115.
ESSENTIALS.—Love, wisdom, and use, are three essentials, together constituting one divine essence, 183. These three essentials flow into the souls of men, 183.
ETERNITY is the infinity of time, 185.
ETHICS is one of those sciences by which an entrance is made into things rational, which are the ground of rational wisdom, 168.
EUNUCHS. — Of those who are born eunuchs, or of eunuchs so made, 151. Who are understood by the eunuchs who make themselves eunuchs for the kingdom of heaven's sake, Matt. xix. 12, 156.
EVIL is not from creation; nothing but good exists from creation, 444. Man himself is the origin of evil, not that that origin was implanted in him by creation, but that he, by turning from God to himself, implanted it in himself, 444. Love without wisdom is love from man, and this love is the origin of evil, 444. No one can be withdrawn from evil unless he has been first led into it, 510. So far as any one removes evil, so far a capacity is given for good to succeed in its place, 147. So far as evil is hated, so far good is loved, 147. Evils and falses, after they arose, were distinguished into genera, species, and differences, 479. All evils are together of the external and internal man; the internal intends them, and the external does them, 486. So far as the understanding favors evils, so far a man appropriates them to himself, and makes them his own, 489. See *Hereditary*.
EXTENSION cannot be predicated of things spiritual, 158. The reason why, 389.
EXTERNALS derive from their internals their good or evil, 478. Of the external derived from the internal, and of the external separate from the internal, 148. How man after death puts off externals, and puts on internals, 48*.

EYE, the, does not see and discern various particulars in objects, but they are seen and discerned by the spirit, 440. In heaven the right eye is the good of vision, and the left the truth thereof, 316.
EYES, when the, of the spirit are opened, angels appear in their proper form, which is the human, 30.

FABLES.—Things which are called fables at this day, were correspondences agreeable to the primeval method of speaking, 182.
FACE, the, depends on the mind (*animus*), and is its type, 524. The countenance is a type of the love, 35. The variety of countenances is infinite, 35. There are not two human faces which are exactly alike, 186. The faces of no two persons are absolutely alike, nor can there be two faces alike to eternity, 524.
FACULTY.—Man is born faculty and inclination; faculty to know, and inclination to love, 134. The faculty of understanding and growing wise as of himself, was implanted in man by creation, 444. The faculty of knowing, of understanding, and of growing wise, receives truths, whereby it has science, intelligence, and wisdom, 122. Man has the faculty of elevating his understanding into the light of wisdom, and his will into the heat of celestial love; these two faculties are never taken away from any man, 230. The faculty of becoming wise increases with those who are in love truly conjugial, 211.
FAITH is truth, 10, 24. Saving faith is to believe on the Lord Jesus Christ, 82.
FALLACIES of the senses are the darkness of truths, 152*.
FALSES, all, have been collated into hell, 479. See *Evils*.
FALSIFICATIONS of truth are spiritual whoredoms, 77, 80.
FATHER.—The Lord in the Word is called Father, 118. Most fathers, when they come into another life, recollect their children who have died before them, and they are also presented to, and mutually acknowledge, each other, 406. In what manner spiritual and natural fathers act, 406. By father and mother, whom man is to leave, Matt. xix. 4, 5, in a spiritual sense, is meant his *proprium* (self-hood) of will, and *proprium* of understanding, 194. See *Proprium*.
FAVOR, causes of, between married partners, 278, 287, 290.
FEAR.—In love truly conjugial there is a fear of loss, 318. This fear resides in the very inmost principles of the mind, 318.
FEASTS.—There are in heaven, as in the world, both feasts and repasts, 6.
FEMALE.—See *Male* and *Female*. The female principle is derived from the male, or, the woman was taken out of the man, 32. The female principle cannot be changed into the male principle, nor the male into the female, 32. The difference between the essential feminine and masculine principle, 32, 168. The good of truth, or truth from

445

g[l], .he female principle, 61, 88, 90. The female principle consists in perceiving from love, 168, 220.

FEVERS, malignant and pestilential, 253, 470.

FIRE in heaven represents good, 326.

FIRE in the spiritual sense signifies love, 380. The fire of the angelic sun is divine love, 84. The fire of the altar and of the candlestick in the tabernacle among the Israelites, represented divine love, 380. The fire of the natural sun has existed from no other source than from the fire of the spiritual sun, which is divine love, 380. The fires of the west signify the delusive loves of evil, 77.

FISH, in the spiritual world fishes are representative forms, 76. Every fish corresponds to some quality, 76.

FLAME.—Celestial love with the angels of heaven appears at a distance as flame; and thus also infernal love appears with the spirits of hell, 359. Flame in the spiritual world does not burn like flame in the natural world, 359. Celestial flame in no case bursts out against another, but only defends itself, and defends itself against an evil person, as when he rushes into the fire and is burnt, 365.

FLESH, the, is contrary to the spirit, that is, contrary to the spiritual things of the church, 497. Combat between the flesh and the spirit, 488. The flesh is ignorant of the delights of the spirit, 481. The flesh is not sensible of those things which happen in the flesh, but the spirit perceives them, 440. What is signified by the words of our Lord, "They are no more twain but one flesh," 50, 156*, 178, 321. By "all flesh," in the Word, is signified every man, 156*.

FLOW FROM, to.—All that which flows from a subject, and encompasses and environs it, is named a sphere, 386.

FLOW IN, to.—Every thing which flows in from the Lord into man, flows into his inmost principle, which is the soul, and descends thence into his middle principle, which is the mind, and through this into his ultimate principle, which is the body, 101. The marriage of good and truth flows thus from the Lord with man, immediately into his soul, and thence proceeds to the principles next succeeding, and through these to the extreme or outermost, 101.

FLOWERS.—The delights of conjugial love are represented in heaven by the flowers with which the cloaks and tunics of married partners are embroidered, 137.

FLOWERY FIELDS.—In heaven there are flowery fields which are the appearances under which the chaste pleasures of conjugial love are presented to the sight, 430.

FOOD, heavenly, in its essence is nothing but love, wisdom, and use, united together; that is, use effected by wisdom, and derived from love, 6. Food for the body is given to every one in heaven, according to the use which he performs, 6.

FORM.—There is nothing that exists but in a form, 186. There is no substance without a form, 66. Every form consists of various things, and is such as is the harmonic co-ordination thereof and arrangement to one, 524. All a man's affections and thoughts are in forms, and thence from forms, 186. The form of heaven is derived solely from varieties of souls and minds arranged into such an order as to make a one, 524. Truth is the form of good, 198. The human form in its inmost principles is from creation a form of love and wisdom, 361. Men from creation are forms of science, intelligence, and wisdom; and women are forms of the love of those principles as existing with men, 187. Form of the marriage of good and truth, 100. Two married partners are that form in their inmost principles, and thence in what is derived from those principles, in proportion as the interiors of their mind are opened, 101, 102. Two married partners are the very forms of love and wisdom, or of good and truth, 66. The internal form of man is that of his spirit, 186. The woman is a form of wisdom inspired with love-affection, 56. The male form is the intellectual form, and the female is the voluntary, 223. The most perfect and most noble human form results from the conjunction of two forms by marriage, so as to become one form, 201. How man, created a form of God, could be changed into a form of the devil, 153*. The desire to continue in its form is implanted from creation in all living things, 361. See Substance.

FORMATION.—As to formation, the masculine soul, as being intellectual, is thus truth, 220. Formation of the woman into a wife according to the description in the Book of Creation, 193-198.

FOUNTAIN, a, signifies the truth of wisdom, 293. Fountain of Parnassus, 182. See Water.

FOWLS.—Wonderful things conspicuous respecting fowls, 417.

FRANCE, 380, 381.

FREEDOM originates in the spiritual equilibrium which exists between heaven and hell, or between good and evil, and in which man is educated, 444. The freedom of love truly conjugial is most free, 257. The Lord wills that the male man (*homo*) should act from principle according to reason, 208, 438. Without freedom and reason man would not be a man, but a beast, 438.

FRENCH, the, 103, 110, 326.

FRENSY, or furious wildness, a legitimate cause of separation, 252, 470.

FRIENDS meet after death, and recollect their friendships in the former world; but when their consociation is only from external affections, a separation ensues, and they no longer see or know each other, 278.

FRIENDSHIP is one of the moral virtues which have respect to life, and enter into it, 164. Friendship increases with those who are principled in love truly conjugial, 214. Inmost friendship is in love truly

INDEX.

conjugial, and is derived from it, 180. Inmost friendship is seated in the breast, 180. Friendship from conjugial love differs greatly from the friendship of every other love, 214. Apparent friendship between married partners is a consequence of the conjugial covenant being ratified for the term of life, 278. There are various species of apparent friendship between married partners, one of whom is brought under the yoke, and therefore subject to the other, 291. Difference between conjugial friendship and servile friendship in marriages, 248. Under what circumstances there may exist between married partners, when old, a friendship resembling that of conjugial love, 290.

FROZEN SUBSTANCES, 510.

FRUCTIFICATION, all, is originally derived from the influx of love, wisdom, and use from the Lord; from an immediate influx into the souls of men; from a mediate influx into the souls of animals; and from an influx still more mediate into the inmost principles of vegetables, 183. Fructifications are continuations of creation, 183. Fructification in the heavens, 44, 355.

FUTURE, the.—The Lord does not permit any man to know the future, because in proportion as he does so, in the same degree his reason and understanding, with his prudence and wisdom, become inactive, are swallowed up and destroyed, 535.

GALLERY, open, 208.
GANGRENES, 253.
GARDENS.—In heaven the appearances under which the chaste delights of conjugial love are presented, are gardens and flowery fields, 430. The garden of Eden signifies the wisdom of love, 135. Nuptial gardens, 316. Paradisiacal gardens, 8. Description of the garden of the prince of a heavenly society, 13.

GARLAND OF ROSES, a, in heaven signifies the delights of intelligence, 293.

GARLANDS in heaven represent the delights of conjugial love, 137, 293.

GENERA.—Distinction of all things into genera, species, and discriminations; the reason why, 479. There are three genera of adulteries, simple, duplicate, and triplicate, 479, 484.

GENERAL of an army, 481.
GENERALS cannot enter into particulars, 328.

GENEROSITY is one of those moral virtues which have respect to life, and enter into it, 164.

GENII.—Who those are who, in the spiritual world, are called infernal genii, 514.

GENITAL region, 183.

GENTILES.—Why there is no communication between the Christian heaven, and the heaven of the Gentiles, 352.

GEOMETRY is one of the sciences by which an entrance is made into things rational, which are the ground of rational wisdom, 163.

GERMANS, 103, 109.
GERMANY, 380.

GESTURES.—In the spiritual world the internal affections appear even in the gestures, 273.

GIANTS, abode of, 77.
GLAND, pineal, 315.

GLORIFICATION of the Lord by the angels of the heavens on account of his coming, 81.

GLORIFYING, by, God is meant the discharging of all the duties of our callings with faithfulness, sincerity, and diligence; hereby God is glorified, as well as by acts of worship at stated times, succeeding these duties, 9.

GLORY, the, of the love of self, elevates the understanding even into the light of heaven, 269. The glory of honor with men induces, exalts, and sharpens jealousy, 378.

GOD, the, of heaven is the Lord, 78. There is only one God, in whom there is a divine trinity, and He is the Lord Jesus Christ, 82, 532. God is love itself, and wisdom itself, 132. The *esse* of the substance of God is divine good, and the *existere* of His substance is divine truth, 115. See *Lord, obs.*

GOOD and TRUTH.—What the will loves and does is called good, and what the understanding perceives and thinks is called true, 490. All those things which pertain to the love are called good, and all those things which pertain to wisdom are called truths, 60. All things in the universe have relation to good and truth, 60. Good and truth are the universals of creation, and thence are in all created things, 84. Good has relation to love, and truth to wisdom, 84. By truths, man has understanding, perception, and all thought; and by goods, love, charity, and all affection, 121. Man receives truth as his own, and appropriates it as his own, for he thinks what is true as from himself, 122; but he cannot take good as of himself, it being no object of his sight, 123. The truth of faith constitutes the Lord's presence, and the good of life according to the truths of faith constitutes conjunction with Him, 72. The truth of faith constitutes the Lord's presence, because it relates to light; and the good of life constitutes conjunction, because it relates to heat, 72. In all things in the universe, good is conjoined with truth, and truth with good, 60. There is not any truth without good, nor good without truth, 87. Good is not good, only so far as it is united with truth; and truth is not truth, only so far as it is united with good, 87. Relations of good and truth to their objects, and their conjunction with them, 87. The good which joins itself with the truth belonging to the man is from the Lord immediately, but the good of the wife, which joins itself with the truth belonging to the man, is from the Lord mediately through the wife, 100. See *Marriage of Good and Truth.*

GOVERNMENT.—In heaven there are governments and forms of government, 7.

447

GOVERNMENTS.—There are in heaven, as on the earths, distinctions of dignity and governments, 7.
GRAPES, good, and bad grapes, what they represent in the spiritual world, 294, 76.
GROUND.—Man at his first birth is as a ground in which no seeds are implanted, but which nevertheless is capable of receiving all seeds, and of bringing them forth and fructifying them, 184.
GROVES, 76, 132, 183, 316.
GUILT, *Reatus*, is principally predicated of the will, 493.
GYMNASIA in the spiritual world, 151*, 207, 315, 380.
GYMNASIA, Olympic, in the spiritual world, where the ancient *sophi* and many of their disciples met together, 151*.

HABITATIONS.—How men have ceased to be habitations of God, 153*.
HAND.—In heaven the right hand is the good of man's ability, and the left the truth thereof, 316. If, in the Word, mention is made of a thing's being inscribed on the hands, it is because the hands are the ultimates of man, wherein the deliberations and conclusions of his mind terminate, and there constitute what is simultaneous, 314. The angels can see in a man's hand all the thoughts and intentions of his mind, 314. Whatever a man examines intellectually, appears to the angels as if inscribed on his hands, 261.
HAPPINESS, concerning eternal, 2 and following. Happiness ought to be within external joys, and to flow from them, 6. This happiness abiding in external joys, makes them joys, it enriches them, and prevents their becoming loathsome and disgusting; and this happiness is derived to every angel from the use he performs in his function, 6. From the reception of the love of uses, springs heavenly happiness, which is the life of joys, 6. Heavenly happiness results from the eternal enjoyment of different states derived from conjugial love, 180. The delights of the soul, with the thoughts of the mind and the sensations of the body, constitute heavenly happiness, 16. The happiness which results from the sensations of the body alone, is not eternal, but soon passes away, and in some cases becomes unhappiness, 16. Eternal happiness does not arise from the place, but from the state of the life of man (*homo*), 16.
HAPPINESS, the, of cohabitation increases with those who are principled in love truly conjugial, 213.
HEALING of the sick by the touch, 396.
HEARING, natural, is grounded in spiritual hearing, which is attention of the understanding, and at the same time accommodation of the will, 220. The love of hearing grounded in the love of hearkening to and obeying has the sense of hearing, and the gratifications proper to it are the various kinds of harmony, 210. The perception of a thing imbibed by hearing only flows in indeed, but does not remain unless the hearer also thinks of it from himself, and asks questions concerning it 183.
HEART, the, signifies love, 75. The heart has relation to good, 87. The heart rules by the blood in every part of the body, 179.
HEAT, spiritual, is love, 235. This heat is from no other source than the sun of the spiritual world, 235. Heat is felt, and not seen, 123. When the heat of conjugial love removes and rejects the heat of adulterous love, conjugial love begins to acquire a pleasant warmth, 147. The quality of the heat of conjugial love with polygamists, 344.
HEAT and LIGHT.—In heaven heat is love, and the light with which heat is united, is wisdom, 137. Natural heat corresponds to spiritual heat, which is love, and natural light corresponds to spiritual light, which is wisdom, 145. Heavenly light acts in unity with wisdom, and heavenly heat with love, 145. Those things which have relation to light are seen, and those which have relation to heat are felt, 163. The delight of spiritual heat with spiritual light is perceivable in human forms, in which this heat is conjugial love, and this light is wisdom, 189.
HEAVEN.—The angelic heaven is formed from the human race, 156. There are three heavens, the first or ultimate heaven, the second or middle heaven, and the third or highest heaven, 42. The universal heaven is arranged in order according to all the varieties of the affections of the love of good, 36. In heaven human forms are altogether similar to those in the natural world. Nothing is wanting in the male, and nothing in the female, 44. The heaven of infants, its situation, 410. Heaven of innocence, 444. Heaven of Mahometans, 342-344.
HELICON, 151*, 182.
HELICONIDES, sports of the, in the spiritual world, 207. These sports were spiritual exercises and trials of skill, 207.
HELL.—The universal hell is arranged in order according to the affections of the love of evil, 36. Those who are in evil from the understanding dwell there in front and are called satans, but those who are in evil from the will dwell to the back and are called devils, 492. Hell of the deceitful, 514.
HERACLITUS, 182.
HEREDITARY evil is not from Adam, but from a man's parents, 525. Whence it springs, 245.
HETEROGENEITES in the spiritual world are not only felt, but also appear in the face, the discourse, and the gesture, 273.
HETEROGENEOUS or DISCORDANT, what is, causes disjunction and absence in the spiritual world, 171.
HIEROGLYPHICS, the, of the Egyptians derive their origin from the science of correspondences and representations, 76, 342.

HISTORY is one of the sciences by which an entrance is made into things rational, which are the ground of rational wisdom, 163.

HOGS.—In hell, the forms of beasts under which the lascivious delights of adulterous love are presented to the view are hogs, &c., 430. Companions of Ulysses changed into hogs, 521.

HOLLAND, 360.

HOLLANDERS or Dutchmen, 103, 105.

HOMOGENEITES, in the spiritual world, are not only felt, but also appear in the face, language, and gesture, 273.

HOMOGENEOUS or CONCORDANT, what is, causes conjunction and presence, 171.

HONORS.—In heaven the angels feel that the honors of the dignities are out of themselves, and are as the garments with which they are clothed, 266.

HOOF, by the, of the horse Pegasus is understood experiences whereby comes natural intelligence, 182.

HORSE, the, signifies the understanding of truths, 76. See *Pegasus*.

HOUSE.—In heaven no one can dwell but in his own house, which is provided for him, and assigned to him, according to the quality of his love, 50.

HUMAN PRINCIPLE, the, consists in desiring to grow wise, and in loving whatever appertains to wisdom, 52.

HUNCH-BACKED.—When the love of the world constitutes the head, a man is not a man otherwise than as hunch-backed, 269.

HUSBAND.—How with young men the youthful principle is changed into that of a husband, 199.

HUSBAND, the, does not represent the Lord, and the wife the church, because both together, the husband and the wife, constitute the church, 125. The husband represents wisdom, and the wife represents the love of the wisdom of the husband, 21. The husband is truth, and the wife the good thereof, 76. A state receptible of love, and perceptible of wisdom, makes a youth into a husband, 321. See *Wife*.

HYPOCRITE.—Every man who is not interiorly led by the Lord is a hypocrite, and thereby an apparent man, and yet not a man, 267.

IDEA, every, of man's, however sublimated, is substantial—that is, affixed to substances, 66. To every idea of natural thought there adheres something derived from space and time, which is not the case with any spiritual idea, 328. Spiritual ideas, compared with natural, are ideas of ideas, 326. There is not any idea of natural thought adequate to any idea of spiritual thought, 326. Spiritual ideas are supernatural, inexpressible, ineffable, and incomprehensible to the natural man, 326. One natural idea contains innumerable spiritual ideas, and one spiritual idea contains innumerable celestial ideas, 329.

IDENTITY.—No absolute identity of two things exist, still less of several, 186.

IDOLATERS, ancient, in the spiritual world, 78.

IDOLATRY.—Its origin, 78, 342.

IJIM, the, in hell represent the images of the phantasies of the infernals, 264. See *Phantasy*.

ILLUSTRATE, to, 42, 43*, 130, 134, &c.

Obs.—In the writings of the Author, to illustrate is generally used in the sense of to enlighten.

ILLUSTRATION.—In the Word there is illustration concerning eternal life, 28.

Obs.—Illustration is an actual opening of the interiors which pertain to the mind, and also an elevation into the light of heaven, *H. D.*, 256.

IMAGE.—What are the image and likeness of God into which man was created, 132, 134. Image of the husband in the wife, 173.

IMAGINATION, 4, 7. See *Phantasy*

IMMODESTY, 252, 472. All in hell are in the immodesty of adulterous love, 429.

IMMORTALITY.—Man may no longer be in doubt through ignorance respecting his immortality, after the discoveries which it has pleased the Lord to make, 532.

IMPLANT, to.—That which is implanted in souls by creation, and respects propagation, is indelible, and not to be extirpated, 409. Good cannot be implanted, only so far as evil is removed, 525.

IMPLETION.—The soul is a spiritual substance, which is not a subject of extension, but of impletion, 220.

IMPOSITION OF HANDS.—Whence it has originated, 396.

IMPURE.—To the impure every thing is impure, 140.

IMPURITY, the, of hell is from adulterous love, 430, 495. In like manner the impurity in the church, 431, 495. There are innumerable varieties of impurities; all hell overflows with impurities, 430.

IMPUTATION, the, of evil in the other life is not accusation, incusation, inculpation, and judication, as in the world, 524; evil is there made sensible as in its odor; it is this which accuses, incuses, fixes blame, and judges, not before any judge, but before every one who is principled in good, and this is what is meant by imputation, 524. Imputation of adulterous love, and imputation of conjugial love, 523–531. Imputation of adulteries after death, how effected, 485, 489, 493; these imputations take place after death, not according to circumstances, which are external of the deed, but according to internal circumstances of the mind, 530. Imputation of good, how it is effected, 524. If by imputation is meant the transcription of good into any one who is in evil, it is a frivolous term, 526.

IMPUTE, to.—The evil in which every one is, is imputed to him after death; in like manner the good, 524, 530, 531. Evil or good is imputed to every one after death, according to the quality of his will and of his understanding, 527. Who it is to whom sin is not imputed, and who to whom it is imputed. 529, 527.

INACTIVITY or SLOTH occasions a universal languor, dulness, stupor, and drowsiness of the mind, and thence of the body, 207. In consequence of sloth the mind grows stupid and the body torpid, and the whole man becomes insensible to every vital love, especially to conjugial love, 249.

INCLINATION.—In the truth of good, and in the good of truth, there is implanted from creation an inclination to join themselves together into one, 88, 100; the reason why, 89. The conjunctive inclination, which is conjugial love, is in the same degree with the conjunction of good and truth, which is the church, 63. Every one derives from his parents his peculiar temper, which is his inclination, 525. Children are born with inclinations to such things as their parents were inclined to, 202; but it is of the Divine Providence that perverse inclinations may be rectified, 202. Inclinations of married partners towards each other, 171. Husbands know nothing at all of the inclinations and affections of their own love, but wives are well acquainted with those principles in their husbands, 208. Inclination of the wife towards the husband, 160. Dissimilitude of internal inclinations is the origin and cause of cold, 275. External inclinations, whence they arise, 246.

INDIFFERENCE with married partners comes from a disunion of souls and disjunction of minds, 236, 256.

INDUSTRY is one of the moral virtues which have respect to life, and enter into it, 164.

INEQUALITY of external rank and condition is one of the external causes of cold, 250. There are many inequalities of rank and condition which put an end to the conjugial love commenced before marriage, 250.

INFANCY is the appearance of innocence, 75.

INFLUX.—What is meant by influx, 313. There is an immediate influx from the Lord into the souls of men, a mediate influx into the souls of animals, and an influx still more mediate into the inmost principles of vegetables, 183. Every subject receives influx according to its form, 86. The subject does not perceive the influx, 392. The influx is alike into all; but the reception, which is according to the form, causes every species to continue a particular species, 86. The influx of love and wisdom from the Lord is the essential activity from which comes all delight, 461. Influx of conjugial love, 183, 208, 355.

INHERENT, 23, 217, 410, 422.

Obs.—That is called inherent which proceeds from a common influx, A. E., 955. Common influx is a continual effort proceeding from the Lord through all heaven, into each of the things which pertain to the life of man. See A. E., 6214. What is inherent is as a graft.

INHERENT, to be, 32, 51, 93, 221, 422, 426.

INMOST principles of the mind, and inmost principles of the body; 69. The highest things of successive order become the inmost of simultaneous order, 314. The inmost principle of man is his soul, 183.

INNOCENCE is the esse of every good; good is only so far good as innocence is in it, 394, 414. The Lord is innocence itself, 394. Innocence is to be led by the Lord, 414. The innocence of infants flows in from the Lord, 395. The sphere of innocence flows into infants, and through them into parents, and affects them, 395, 396. What is the innocence of infants which flows into parents, 395. The innocence of infancy is the cause of the love called storge, 395. Innocence corresponds to infancy, and also to nakedness, 413. The innocence of childhood is external innocence, and the innocence of wisdom internal innocence, 413. The innocence of wisdom is the end of all instruction and progression with infants in the spiritual world, 413. When they come to the innocence of wisdom, the innocence of infancy is adjoined to them, which in the mean time had served them as a plane, 413. Innocence is in conjugial love, and pertains to the soul, 180. Innocence is one of the spiritual virtues which flow from love to God and love towards the neighbor, 164.

INSANITY, 212.—Insanity, a vitiated state of the mind, is a legitimate cause of separation, 252, 470.

INSCRIBED ON THE HANDS.—Why this form of expression is used in the Word, 314. See Hand.

INSTRUCTION of children in heaven, 411-413. Places of instruction in the spiritual world, 261.

INTEGRITY, state of, 185, 155.

INTELLECTUAL, the, principle is nothing but truth, 220. Man's intellectual principle is the inmost principle of the woman, 195.

INTELLIGENCE is a principle of reason, 130. There is no end to intelligence, 185. Every one is in intelligence, not by birth, but exteriorly by education, 267. The intelligence of women is in itself modest, elegant, pacific, yielding, soft, tender; and the intelligence of men in itself is grave, harsh, hard, daring, fond of licentiousness, 218. Circles around the head represent intelligence, 269.

INTEMPERANCE, 252, 472.

INTENTION.—That which flows forth from the form of a man's life, thus from the understanding and its thought, is called intention; but that which flows forth from the essence of a man's life, thus that which flows forth from his will or his love, is principally called purpose, 493. The intention which pertains to the will is principally regarded by the Lord, 71, 146. Intention is as an act before determination; hence it is that, by a wise man and also by the Lord, intention is accepted as an act, 400, 452.

INDEX.

Intention is the soul of all actions, and causes blamableness and unblamableness in the world, and after death imputation, 452.

INTERCOURSE.—In heaven there are frequent occasions of cheerful intercourse and conversation, whereby the internal minds (*mentes*) of the angels are exhilarated, their external minds (*animi*) entertained, their bosoms delighted, and their bodies refreshed, but such occasions do not occur till they have fulfilled their appointed uses in the discharge of their respective business and functions, 5.

INTERIORS, the, form the exteriors to their own likeness, 33. The opening of the interiors cannot be fully effected except with those who have been prepared by the Lord to receive the things which are of spiritual wisdom, 39. These interiors, which in themselves are spiritual, are opened by the Lord alone, 340, 341.

INTERNAL PRINCIPLES, man's, by which are meant the things appertaining to his mind or spirit, are elevated in a superior degree above his external principles, 185.

INTREPIDITY is one of the moral virtues which have respect to life, and enter into it, 164.

IRON.—Age of iron, 78.

ISRAELITISH NATION.—Why it was permitted to the Israelitish nation to marry a plurality of wives, 340.

ITALIANS, 103, 106. Italian eunuchs, 156.

JAMES, the Apostle, represented charity, 119.

JEALOUSY, concerning, 357–379. The zeal of conjugial love is called jealousy, 367. Jealousy is like a burning fire against those who infest love exercised towards a married partner, and it is a horrid fear for the loss of that love, 368. There is a spiritual jealousy with monogamists, and natural with polygamists, 369, 370. Jealousy with those married partners who tenderly love each other is a just grief grounded in sound reason lest conjugial love should be divided, and should thereby perish, 371, 372. Jealousy with married partners who do not love each other is grounded in several causes, proceeding in some instances from various mental sickness, 373, 375. Jealousy with men resides in the understanding, 372. In some instances there is not any jealousy, and this also from various causes, 376. There is a jealousy also in regard to concubines, but not such as in regard to wives, 377. Jealousy likewise exists among beasts and birds, 378. The jealousy prevalent with men and husbands is different from what is prevalent with women and wives, 379.

JEHOVAH.—The Lord is Jehovah from eternity, 29. Why Jehovah is said to be jealous, 366.

JERUSALEM, the New, signifies the new church of the Lord, 43, 534.

JESUIT, 499.

JESUS CHRIST.—The divine trinity is in Jesus Christ, in whom dwells all the fulness of the Godhead bodily, 24. See *God, Lord*.

JEW, a, may be recognized by his look, 262.

JOB.—The doctrine of correspondences, of which the spiritual sense of the Word is composed, has been concealed now for some thousands of years, namely, since the time of Job, 532.

JOHN, the Apostle, represented the works of charity, 119. He represented the church as to the goods of charity, John xix. 26, 27, 119.

JOY, heavenly, 2, and following. Heavenly joy consists in the delight of doing something that is useful to ourselves and others, which delight derives its essence from love, and its existence from wisdom, 5. The delight of being useful, originating in love and operating by wisdom, is the very soul and life of all heavenly joys, 5.

JUDGE, a, gives sentence according to actions done, but every one after death is judged according to the intentions; thus a judge may absolve a person, who after death is condemned, and *vice versa*, 455, 527. Unjust judges, their fate in the other life, 231.

JUDGE, to.—It is permitted to every one to judge of the moral and civil life of another in the world, but to judge what is the quality of his interior mind or soul, thus what is the quality of any one's spiritual state, and thence what is his lot after death, is not allowed, 523. No one is to be judged of from the wisdom of his conversation, but of his life in union therewith, 499. After death every one is judged according to the intentions of the will, and thence of the understanding; and according to the confirmations of the understanding, and thence of the will, 435.

JUDGMENT.—Difference between corporeal judgment, and judgment of the mind, 57. By corporeal judgment is meant the judgment of the mind according to the external senses, which judgment is gross and dull, 57. See *Justice and Judgment*.

JUDICIAL PROCEEDINGS.—In heaven there are judicial proceedings, 207, 231.

JURISPRUDENCE is one of the sciences by which, as by doors, an entrance is made into things rational, which are the ground of rational wisdom, 164.

JUSTICE, Divine.—It is contrary to Divine justice to condemn those who acknowledge a God and from a principle of religion practise the laws of justice, which consist in shunning evils because they are contrary to God, and doing what is good because it is agreeable to God, 351.

JUSTICE and JUDGMENT.—Justice has relation to moral wisdom, and judgment to rational wisdom, 164. The spiritual man in all he does acts from justice and judgment, 280.

KIDS.—In heaven, the forms of animals under which the chaste delights of conju-

451

gial love are presented to view are kids, &c., 430.

KINGDOM, the, of Christ, which is heaven, is a kingdom of uses, 7.

LABYRINTH, paradisiacal, 8.

LAKES signify falsifications of truth, 80. Lakes of fire and brimstone, 79, 80.

LAMBS in the spiritual world are representative forms of the state of innocence and peace of the inhabitants, 75. The forms of animals under which the chaste delights of conjugial love are there presented to the view, are lambs, &c., 430. The Lord from innocence is called a lamb, 394.

LAMPS signify truth, 44.

LANGUAGE.—All in the spiritual world have the spiritual language, which has in it nothing common to any natural language, 326. Every man comes of himself into the use of that language after his decease, 326. Every spirit and angel, when conversing with a man, speaks his proper language. 326. The sound of spiritual language differs so far from the sound of natural language, that a spiritual sound, though loud, could not at all be heard by a natural man, nor a natural sound by a spiritual man, 326.

LASCIVIOUS.—Angels discern in the extremes what is lascivious from what is not lascivious, 439. The external principle separated from the internal, is lascivious in the whole and in every part, 149. The lascivious mind acts lasciviously, and the chaste mind chastely; and the latter arranges the body, whereas the former is arranged by the body, 191.

LASCIVIOUSNESS, in its spiritual origin, is insanity, 212. In the lowest region of the mind, which is called the natural, reside all the concupiscences of lasciviousness, but in the superior region, which is called the spiritual, there are not any concupiscences, 305. All in hell are in lasciviousness, 429. A sphere of lasciviousness issues forth from the unchaste, 140.

LATITUDE.—All goods and evils partake of latitude and altitude, and according to latitude have their genera, and according to altitude their degrees, 478.

LAW.—Divine law and rational are one law, 276. How the declaration, that no one can fulfil the law, is to be understood, 528.

LEAVE his father and mother, to, Gen. ii. 4; Matt. xix. 45, signifies to divest himself of the proprium of the will and of the understanding, 194.

LEFT, the, signifies truth, 316.

LEOPARDS in the spiritual world represent the falsities and depraved inclinations of the inhabitants to those things which pertain to idolatrous worship, 79. Those who only read the Word, and imbibe thence nothing of doctrine, but confirm false principles, appear like leopards, 78.

LEPROSY, 253, 470.

LIBERALITY is one of those virtues which have respect to life, and enter into it, 164.

LIBERTY.—See *Rationality* and *Liberty.*

LIBRARIES in the spiritual world, 207.

LIFE.—The life of man essentially is his will, and formally is his understanding, 493. Every one has excellence of life according to his conjugial love, 510.

LIGHT.—In heaven, the light with which warmth is united is wisdom, 137. In heaven there is perpetual light, and on no occasion do the shades of evening prevail; still less is there darkness, because the sun does not set, 137. Heavenly light is above the rational principle with man, and rational light is below it, 233. If heavenly light does not flow into natural light, a man does not see whether any thing true is true, and neither does he see that any thing false is false, 233. False and delusive lights, 77. See *Heat* and *Light.*

LIGHTNING.—In the spiritual world, the vibration of light, like lightning, is a correspondence and consequent appearance of the conflict of arguments, 415.

LIKE.—There is not one angel of heaven absolutely like another, nor any spirit of hell, neither can there be to eternity, 362. There are not two human faces exactly alike, 186.

LIKENESS or SIMILITUDE.—The likeness of children to their parents, 525. Man is a likeness of God from this circumstance, that he feels in himself that the things which are of God are in him as his, 132, 134. Similitudes and dissimilitudes between married partners in general originate from connate inclinations, varied by education, connections, and imbibed persuasions, 227. . There are both internal and external similitudes and dissimilitudes; the internal derive their origin from religion, and the external from education, 246. The varieties of similitudes are very numerous, and differ more or less from each other, 228. Various similitudes can be conjoined, but not with dissimilitudes, 228. The Lord provides similitudes for those who desire love truly conjugial; and if they are not given in the earths, he provides them in the heavens, 229. In the spiritual world, similitudes are joined, and dissimilitudes separated, 273.

LIPOTHAMIA, 253, 470.

LIVE, to, for others is to perform uses, 18.

LOINS, the, with men correspond to conjugial love, 510.

LOOK, to.—The Lord looks at every man in the fore front of his head, and this aspect passes into the hinder part of his head, 444. In heaven it is impossible to look at the wife of another from an unchaste principle, 75.

LORD, the, is the God of heaven and earth, 129. The Lord is essential good and essential truth; and these in Him are not two, but one, 121. The Lord loves every one, and desires to do good to every one, 7. He promotes good or use by the mediation of angels in heaven, and of men on earth, 7. From the Lord, the creator and conservator of the universe, there continually proceed love, wisdom, and use, and these three as one, 400.

Obs.—In all the writings of the Author, by the *Lord*, is signified the Saviour of the world, Jesus Christ, who is the One only God, because in Him dwelleth the Trinity of Father, Son, and Holy Spirit.

LOT.—Such as a man's life has been in the world, such is his lot after death, 46. Lot of those who have abandoned themselves to various lusts, 505, 510, 512, 514. Happy lot of those who wished for dominion from the love of uses, 266.

LOVE, to.—Whether it be possible for a woman to love her husband, who constantly loves her own beauty, 330. Whether a man who loves himself from his intelligence can love a wife, 331.

LOVE is the *esse* or essence of a man's life, 36, 46, 358. It is the man himself, 36. It is the heat of the life of man, or his vital heat, 34, 359. Love is the essential active principle of life, 183; it is kept alive by delight, 18. Each love has its delight, 18. All love is of such a nature that it bursts out into indignation and anger, yea, into fury, whenever it is disturbed in its delights, 358. Love, without its delights, is not any thing, 427. Love is spiritual heat, 235. Love is spiritual heat originating in the fire of the angelic sun, which is pure love, 358. Spiritual heat living in subjects is felt as love, 235. Love resides in man's will; in the will it is like fire, and in the understanding like flame, 360. Love cannot do otherwise than love, and unite itself, in order that it may be loved in return, 160. It is such, that it desires to communicate with another whom it loves from the heart, yea, to confer joys upon him, and thence to derive its own joys, 180. The love of man is his very life, not only the common life of his whole body, and the common life of all his thoughts, but also the life of all the particulars thereof, 34. A man is such as his love is, and not such as his understanding is, since the love easily draws over the understanding to its side, and enslaves it, 269. It is not possible that any love should become perfect either with men or with angels, 71, 146.

LOVE, conjugial, is the foundation love of all celestial and spiritual loves, and thence of all natural loves, 65, 143, 240. It is as a parent, and all other loves are as the offspring, 65. Conjugial love essentially consists in the desire of two to become one, that is, their desire that two lives may become one life, 215, 37. It is the conjunction of love and wisdom, 65. The very origin of this love resides in the inmost principles appertaining to man, that is, his soul, 238, 466. This origin springs from the marriage of good and truth, 60, 83-102, 103, 148. This love is celestial, spiritual, and holy, because derived from a celestial, spiritual, and holy origin, 61. The love of the sex with man is not the origin of conjugial love, but is its first rudiment, 98. Conjugial love in its origin is the sport of wisdom and love, 75. It is called celestial, as appertaining to the angels of the highest heaven, and spiritual, as appertaining to the angels beneath that heaven, 64. Every angel has conjugial love with its virtue, ability, and delights, according to his application to the genuine use in which he is, 207. Into conjugial love are collated all joys and delights from first to last, 68. Whence arise the delights of conjugial love, which are innumerable and ineffable, 183. This love belongs to the internal or spiritual man, and hence is peculiar to man, 95, 96. Conjugial love corresponds to the affection of truth, its chastity, purity, and sanctity, 127. It is according to the state of wisdom with man, 130. It remains with man after death such as it had been interiorly, that is, in the interior will and thought, 48. The purity of heaven is from conjugial love, 430. The delights of conjugial love commence in the spirit, and are of the spirit even in the flesh, 440. These delights are the delights of wisdom, 442. What are the delights of conjugial love, 69. How conjugial love is formed, 162. It corresponds to the marriage of the Lord with the church, 62, 148. Conjugial love is according to the state of the church, because it is according to the state of wisdom with man, 130. The states of this love are, innocence, peace, tranquillity, inmost friendship, full confidence, &c., 180. Conjugial love is of infinite variety, 57. Experience testifies that conjugial love exceeds self-love, the love of the world, and even the love of life, 333. Conjugial love is so rare at this day, that its quality is not known, and scarcely its existence, 69. Conjugial love, such as it was with the ancients, will be raised again by the Lord, 78, 81. Conjugial love is according to religion with man, spiritual with the spiritual, natural with the natural, and merely carnal with adulterers, 534. Of the conjunction of conjugial love with the love of infants, 385-414. Of the imputation of conjugial love, 523-531. Of love truly conjugial, 57-78. Considered in itself, love truly conjugial is a union of souls, a conjunction of minds, and an endeavor towards conjunction in the bosoms, and thence in the body, 179. It was the love of loves with the ancients who lived in the golden, silver, and copper ages, 73. Considered in its origin and correspondence, it is celestial, spiritual, holy, pure, and clean, 71. Love truly conjugial is only with those who desire wisdom, and who consequently advance more and more into wisdom, 98. So far as a man loves wisdom from the love thereof, or truth from good, so far he is in love truly conjugial, and in its attendant virtue, 355. So far as man becomes spiritual, so far he is in love truly conjugial, 130. This love with its delights is solely from the Lord, and is given to those who live according to his precepts, 534. Love truly conjugial may exist with one of the married partners, and not at the same time with the other, 226. How love truly conjugial is distinguished from spurious, false, and cold conjugial love, 224. Difference between love truly conjugial and vulgar love, which is also called conjugial, and which with some is merely the limited love of the sex, 98.

LOVE OF THE BODY, the.—Dignities and honors are peculiarly the objects of the love of the body; besides these, there are also various enticing allurements, such as beauty and an external polish of manners, sometimes even an unchasteness of character, 49.

LOVE OF CHILDREN, the, with the mother and the father, conjoin themselves as the heart and lungs in the breast, 284. The love of infants corresponds to the defence of truth and good, 127. Why the love of infants descends and does not ascend, 402. The love of infants and of children is different with spiritual married partners from what it is with natural, 405. The love of infants remains after death, especially with women, 410. Of the conjunction of conjugial love with the love of infants, 395-414.

LOVE OF DOMINION, the, grounded in the love of self, and the love of dominion grounded in the love of uses, 262. The love of dominion grounded in the love of self, is the first universal love of hell; it is in the highest degree infernal, 262. The love of dominion grounded in the love of uses is the universal love of heaven; it is in the highest degree celestial, 262, 266. When the ruling love is touched, there ensues an emotion of the mind (*animus*), and if the touch hurts, there ensues wrath, 358.

LOVE OF THE NEIGHBOR, the, is also the love of doing uses, 269. The love of the neighbor, or of doing uses, is a spiritual love, 269.

LOVE, polygamical, is connubial, and at the same time adulterous, 78. It is the love of the sex, limited to a number, 345. It is the love of the external or natural man, and thus is not conjugial love, 345. It is inscribed on the natural man, 345.

LOVE OF SELF, the, is also the love of bearing rule over others, 269. The love of self, or the love of bearing rule over others, is a corporeal love, 269.

LOVE OF THE SEX, the, is a love directed to several, and contracted with several of the sex, 48. The love of the sex exists with the natural man, but conjugial love with the spiritual man, 38. The love of the sex with man is not the origin of conjugial love, but is its first rudiment; thus it is like an external natural principle, in which an internal spiritual principle is implanted, 98. It is the first in respect to time, but not in respect to end, 98. The love of the sex is the universal of all loves, being implanted from creation in the heart of man, and is for the sake of the propagation of the human race, 46. What the chaste love of the sex is, and whence derived, 55, 99. The love of the sex belongs to the external or natural man, and hence is common to every animal, 94. It is in itself natural, 141. Origin of the love of the sex, 446. It is at first corporeal, next it becomes sensual, afterwards it becomes natural, like the same love with other animals; but afterwards it may become natural-rational, and from natural-rational, spiritual, and lastly spiritual-natural, 447. The nature of the love of the sex if it becomes active before marriage, 447. The results of checking such love, 450. Tho love of the sex remains with man after death, 37. It remains such as it was in its interior quality, that is, such as it had been in his interior will and thought, 46.

LOVE OF USES, the, is from the Lord, 262, 266, 305. So far as we do uses from the love thereof, so far that love increases, 266. The love of doing uses is also neighborly love, 269.

LOVE OF THE WORLD, the, is also the love of possessing wealth, 269. The love of the world, or the love of possessing wealth, is a material love, 269.

LOVE, the ruling, is the head of all the rest, 46. The reason why this love remains with man to eternity, 46.

LOVES.—There are three universal loves which form the constituents of every man by creation, neighborly love, the love of the world, and the love of self, 269. A man is a man if these loves are subordinate in that degree that the first constitutes the head, the second the body, and the third the feet, 269. Natural, spiritual, and celestial loves; natural loves relate to the loves of self and the world, spiritual loves to love towards the neighbor, and celestial loves to love towards the Lord, 67. When natural loves flow from spiritual loves, and spiritual from celestial; then the natural loves live from the spiritual, and the spiritual from the celestial; and all in this order live from the Lord, in whom they originate, 67. Apparent loves between married partners are a consequence of the conjugial covenant being ratified for the term of life, 278. The loves of animals are altogether united with their connate science, 96. See *Beasts*.

LOVE, adulterous.—Concerning the opposition of adulterous love to conjugial love, 423-443. By adulterous love opposite to conjugial love, is meant the love of adultery, so long as it is such as not to be reputed as sin, nor as evil and dishonorable, contrary to reason, but as allowable with reason, 423. The quality of adulterous love is not known, unless it be known what is the quality of conjugial love, 424. The impurity of hell is from adulterous love, 430. The delights of adulterous love commence from the flesh, and are of the flesh even in the spirit, 440. The origin of adulterous love is from the connection (*connubium*) of what is evil and false, 427. Of the imputation of adulterous love, 523-531.

LOVE and WISDOM constitute the marriage of the Lord and the church, 21. The Lord is love, and the church is wisdom,

21. Love and wisdom are the same thing as good and truth, 84. Love consists of goods, and wisdom of truths, 84.

Lowest, the, things of successive order become the outermost of simultaneous order, 314.

Lucifer, 269.

Lungs, the, signify wisdom, 75. The lungs rule by respiration in every part of the body, 179.

Lust.—The natural man is nothing but an abode and receptacle of concupiscences and lust, 448. In all that proceeds from the natural man, there is concupiscence and lust, 440. Concerning the unchaste love of the sex with the young, 98. With the married, 483. Concerning various lusts, 444*–460, 448; 501–505, 460, 506–510, 511, 512, 513, 514.

Luxury, 252.

Lymphs of the brain, 315.

Madness is a vitiated state of the mind, and a legitimate cause of separation, 252.

Mahomet, 342, 344.

Mahometan Religion, 341. How it originated, 342. It was raised up of the Lord's divine providence, to the end that it might destroy the idolatries of many nations, 342.

Mahometans.—Why it is permitted the Mahometans to marry a plurality of wives, 341. The Mahometan heaven is out of the Christian heaven, and is divided into two heavens, the one inferior and the other superior, 342.

Male and Female.—Man (*homo*) is male and female, 32, 100. The male and female were created to be the essential form of the marriage of good and truth, 100 and following. The male was created to be the understanding of truth, thus truth in form; and the female was created to be the will of good, thus good in form, 100, 220. The male is born intellectual, or in the affection of knowing, of understanding, and growing wise; and the female partakes more of the will principle, or is born into the love of conjoining herself with the affection in the male, 33. Therefore, the male and female differ as to the face, tone of the voice, and form, 33, 218. Distinct affections, applications, manners, and forms of the male and female, 90, 91. The male is the wisdom of love, and the female the love of that wisdom, 32. After death the male lives a male, and the female a female, each being a spiritual man, 32, 100; neither is there any thing wanting, 51.

Male Principle, the, consists in perceiving from the understanding, 168. The truth of good, or truth grounded in good, is in the male principle, 61, 88, 90. In what the male principle essentially consists, 32. See *Female Principle.*

Man is born in a state of greater ignorance than the beasts, 152*. Without instruction he is neither a man nor a beast, but he is a form which is capable of receiving in itself that which constitutes a man, thus he is not born a man but he is made a man, 152*. Man is man by virtue of the will and the understanding, 404. He is a man from this circumstance, that he can will good, and understand truth, altogether as from himself, and yet know and believe that it is from God, 132. A man is a man, and is distinguished from the beasts by this circumstance, that his mind is distinguished into three regions, as many as the heavens are distinguished into, and that he is capable of being elevated out of the lowest region into the next above it, and also from this into the highest, and thus of becoming an angel of heaven, even of the third, 495. There are three things of which every man consists, the soul, the mind, and the body; his inmost principle is the soul, his middle is the mind, and his ultimate is the body, 101. As the soul is man's inmost principle, it is from its origin celestial; as the mind is his middle principle, it is from its origin spiritual; and as the body is his ultimate principle, it is from its origin natural, 158. The supreme principles in man are turned upwards to God, the middle principles outwards to the world, and the lowest principles downwards to self, 269. In man are all the affections of love, and thence all the perceptions of wisdom, compounded in the most perfect order, so as to make together what is unanimous, and thereby a one, 361. Man, as to the affections and thoughts of his mind, is in the midst of angels and spirits, and is so consociated with them, that were he to be plucked asunder from them, he would instantly die, 28. Man was created for uses, 249. Man is male and female, 32. The male man and the female man were so created, that from two they may become as it were one man, or one flesh; and when they become one, then, taken together, they are a man (*homo*) in his fulness; but without such conjunctions they are two, and each is a divided or half man, 37. Man was born to be wisdom, and the woman to be the love of the man's wisdom, 75. Man is such as his love is, and not such as his understanding is, 269. The natural man, separate from the spiritual, is only man as to the understanding, and not as to the will; such a one is only half man, 432. A spiritual man is sensible of, and perceives spiritual delight, which is a thousand times superior to natural delight, 29. Man lives a man after death, 28. Man after death is not a natural man, but a spiritual or substantial man, 31. A spiritual or substantial man sees a spiritual or substantial man, as a natural or material man sees a natural or material man, 31. Man after death puts off every thing which does not agree with his love, yea, he successively puts on the countenance, the tone of voice, the speech, the gestures, and the manners of the love proper to his life, 36; instead of a material body he enjoys a substantial one, wherein natural delight grounded in spiritual is made sensible in its eminence, 475. Men left in the forests when they were about two or three years old, 151*, 152*. Difference between men and beasts, 133, 134, 493.

MARRIAGE-APARTMENT of the will and understanding, 270.

MARRIAGE is the fulness of man (*homo*), for by it a man becomes a full man, 156; thus a state of marriage is preferable to a state of celibacy, 156. Consent is the essential of marriage, and all succeeding ceremonies are its formalities, 21. The covenant of marriage is for life, 276. Marriages in themselves are spiritual, and thence holy, 53. Marriages are the seminaries of the human race, and thence also the seminaries of the heavenly kingdom, 481. Marriages made in the world are for the most part external, and not at the same time internal, when yet it is the internal conjunction, or conjunction of souls, which constitutes a real marriage, 49, 274. Marriages interiorly conjunctive can hardly be entered into in the world, the reason why, 320, 49. Of reiterated marriages, 317–325. There are in the world infernal marriages between married partners, who interiorly are the most inveterate enemies, and exteriorly are as the closest friends, 292. Of marriages in heaven, 27–41. How in heaven marriages from love truly conjugial are provided by the Lord, 229, 316. Spiritual prolification of love and wisdom from marriages in heaven, 52. Beneath heaven there are no marriages (*conjugia*), 192. Concerning the marriage of the Lord and the church, and the correspondence thereof, 116-131.

MARRIAGE, the, of God and truth, 83, 115. The reason why it has been heretofore unknown, 83. How it takes place with man, 122, 123. It is the church with man, and is the same thing as the marriage of charity and faith, 62. The marriage of good and truth is in every thing of the Word, 516; from this marriage proceed all the loves which constitute heaven and the church with man, 65. The marriage of good and truth flows into every thing of the universe, 220, 84. To be given in marriage signifies to enter heaven, where the marriage of good and truth takes place, 44.

MARRIED PARTNERS, two, who are principled in love truly conjugial, are actually forms of the marriage of good and truth, or of love and wisdom, 66, 101, 102. The will of the wife conjoins itself with the understanding of the man, and thence the understanding of the man with the will of the wife, 159, 160. Love is inspired into the man by his wife, 161. The conjunction of the wife with the man's rational principle is from within, 165. The wife is conjoined to her husband by the sphere of her life flowing forth from the love of him, 171–173. There are duties proper to the man, and duties proper to the wife; the wife cannot enter into the duties proper to the man, nor can the man enter into the duties proper to the wife, so as to perform them aright, 174, 175. Marriage induces other forms in the souls and minds of married partners, 192. The woman is actually formed into a wife according to the description in the book of creation, Gen. ii. 21, 22, 23, 193. Two married partners in heaven are called, not two angels, but one angel, 50. Two married partners most commonly meet after death, know each other, again associate, &c., 49. If they can live together, they remain married partners, but if they cannot, they separate themselves, 49, 51, 52.

MARROW, spinal, 315.—The marrows represent the interiors of the mind and of the body, 312.

MARRY, to.—When a man marries he becomes a fuller man, because he is joined with a consort, with whom he acts as one man, 59. See *Marriage*.

MARY signifies the church, 119.

MATERIALS.—Substantials are the beginnings of materials, 328. Natural things, which are material, cannot enter into spiritual things, which are substantial, 328. Material things originate in substantial, 207.

MATERIAL things derive their origin from things substantial, 207.

MECHANICS is one of the sciences by which an entrance is made into things rational, which are the ground of rational wisdom, 163.

MEATS.—There are in heaven, as in the world, both meats and drinks, 6. See *Food*.

MEDIUMS are conducive to what is first in itself, 98.

MEDIUM, the, of conjunction of the Lord with man, is the Word, 128.

MEDULLARY substance of the brain, 315.

METEOR in the spiritual world, 315.

MIND, the, is intermediate between the soul and the body, 178; although it appears to be in the head, it is actually in the whole body, 178, 260. The human mind is distinguished into regions, as the world is distinguished into regions as to the atmospheres, 188, 270; the supreme region of the mind is called celestial, the middle region spiritual, and the lowest region natural, 270, 305. The mind is successively opened from infancy even to extreme old age, 102. As a man advances from science into intelligence, and from intelligence into wisdom, so also his mind changes its form, 94. With some, the mind is closed from beneath, and is sometimes twisted as a spire into the adverse principle; with others that principle is not closed, but remains half open above, and with some open, 203. With men there is an elevation of the mind into superior light, and with women there is an elevation of the mind into superior heat, 188. The mind of every man, according to his will and consequent understanding, actually dwells in one society of the spiritual world, and intends and thinks in like manner with those who compose the society, 530. The lower principles of the mind are unchaste, but its higher principles chaste, 302. Every man has an internal and an external mind, with the wicked the internal mind is insane, and the external is wise; but with the good the internal mind is wise, and from this also the external, 477. With the ancients, the science of correspondences conjoined the sensual things of the body with the perceptions of the mind, and procured intelligence, 76.

Obs.—The mind is composed of two faculties which make man to be man, namely, the will and the understanding. The mind composed of the spiritual will and of the spiritual understanding, is the internal man; it incloses the inmost man or soul (*anima*), and it is inclosed by the natural mind or external man, composed of the natural will and understanding. This natural mind, together with a sort of mind still more exterior, called the *animus*, which is formed by the external affections and inclinations resulting from education, society, and custom, is the external mind. The whole organized in a perfect human form, is called spirit (*spiritus*). The spirit in our world is covered with a terrestrial body, which renders it invisible; but, freed from this body by natural death, it enters the spiritual world, where its spiritual body is perfectly visible and tactile.

MIRACLES.—Why there are none in the present day, 585.

MIRE.—In hell lascivious delights are represented under the appearance of mire, &c., 430.

MISTRESS, 459.

MODESTY is one of those virtues which have respect to life, and enter into it, 164.

MONASTERIES.—What becomes in the other life of those who have been shut up in monasteries, 54, 155. Virgins devoted to the monastic life, 513.

MONOGAMISTS.—All in heaven live married to one wife, 77.

MONOGAMICAL marriages, 70, 77, 141. They correspond to the marriage of the Lord and the church, and originate in the marriages of good and truth, 70.

MONOGAMY.—Why monogamy exists with Christian nations, 337-339.

MOTH.—Wonderful things respecting it, 329.

MOTHER.—The church in the world is called mother, 118, 119.

MORALITY, genuine, is the wisdom of life, 363. Spiritual morality is the result of a life from the Lord according to the truths of the Word, 293.

MULTIPLICABLE.—Every thing is multiplicable *in infinitum*, 185.

MUNIFICENCE is one of those virtues which have respect to life, and enter into it, 164.

MUSES, nine, in the Word, represent knowledges and sciences of every kind, 182.

NAKEDNESS signifies innocence, 413.

NATURAL, the, derives its origin from the spiritual, 320. Difference between the natural and spiritual, 326-329. The natural principle is distinguished into three degrees; the so-called natural, the natural-sensual, and the natural-corporeal, 442. The natural man is nothing but an abode and receptacle of concupiscences and lusts, 448. There are three degrees of the natural man, 496. Those who love only the world, placing their heart in wealth, are properly meant by the natural, 496; they pour forth into the world all things of the will and understanding, covetously and fraudulently acquiring wealth, and regarding no other use therein, and thence but that of possession, 496.

NATURE is the recipient whereby love and wisdom produce their effects or uses, 380; thus nature is derived from life, and not life from nature, 380. All the parts of nature derive their subsistence and existence from the sun, 380. Nature is in all time, in time, and in all space, in space, 328. Nature, with her time and space, must of necessity have a beginning and a birth, 328. Wherefore nature is from God, not from eternity, but in time, that is, together with her time and space, 328.

NECESSITY for apparent love and friendship in marriages, for the sake of order being preserved in houses, 271, and following, 283.

NEMESIS, 504.

NOVITIATES, 182.—Novitiate spirit, 461. See *Spirits*.

NUPTIALS celebrated in heaven, 19-25 There are nuptials in the heavens as in the earths, but only with those in the heavens who are in the marriage of good and truth; nor are any others angels, 44. By the words of the Lord, "Those who shall be accounted worthy to attain another age, neither marry nor are given in marriage," no other nuptials are meant than spiritual nuptials, and by spiritual nuptials is meant conjunction with the Lord, 41. These spiritual nuptials take place in the earths, but not after departure thence, thus not in the heavens, 44. To celebrate nuptials signifies to be joined with the Lord, 41. To enter into nuptials is to be received into heaven by the Lord, 41. Why nuptials in the world are essential solemnities, 306.

OBSTRUCTIONS of inmost life, whence they proceed, 313.

OCCIPUT, 267, 444.

OCHIM, the, in hell, represent the images of the phantasies of the infernals, 264, 430.

ODE sung by virgins in the spiritual world, 207.

ODORS, the, whereby the chaste pleasures of conjugial love are presented to the senses in the spiritual world, are the perfumes arising from fruits, and the fragrances from flowers, 430.

OFFENSIVE appearances, odors, and forms, under which unchaste delights are presented to the view in hell, 430.

OFFICES and employments in the spiritual world, 207.

OFFSPRINGS, the, derived from the Lord as a husband and father, and from the church as a wife and mother, are all spiritual, 120. The spiritual offsprings which are born from the Lord's marriage with the church are truths and goods, 121. From the marriages of the angels in the heavens are generated spiritual offsprings, which are those of love and wisdom, or of good and truth, 65. Spiritual offsprings, which are produced from the marriages of the angels, are such things as are of wisdom from the father, and of love from the mother, 211. See *Storge.*

OIL signifies good, 44.

OLD men, decrepit, and infirm old women are restored by the Lord to the power of their age, when from a religious principle they have shunned adulteries as enormous sins, 187.

OLIVE-TREES in the spiritual world represent conjugial love in the highest region, 270.

ONE, the, from whom all things have life and from whom form coheres, is the Lord, 524. In heaven two married partners are called two when they are named husband and wife, but one when they are named angels, 177. When the will of two married partners become one, they become one man (*homo*), 196.

OPERATIONS, all, in the universe have a progression from ends through causes into effects, 400.

OPINIONS on celestial joys and eternal happiness, 3.

OPPOSITE.—There is not any thing in the universe which has not its opposite, 425. Opposites, in regard to each other, are not relatives, but contraries, 425. When an opposite acts upon an opposite, one destroys the other even to the last spark of its life, 255. Marriages and adulteries are diametrically opposite to each other, 255.

OPPOSITION of adulterous love and conjugial love, 423-443.

OPULENCE in heaven is the faculty of growing wise, according to which faculty wealth is given in abundance, 250.

ORCHESTRA, 315.

ORDER, all, proceeds from first principles to last, and the last becomes the first of some following order, 311. All things of a middle order are the last of a prior order, 311. There is successive order and simultaneous order; the latter is from the former and according to it, 314. In successive order, one thing follows after another from what is highest to what is lowest, 314. In simultaneous order, one thing is next to another from what is inmost to what is outermost, 314. Successive order is like a column with steps from the highest to the lowest, 314. Simultaneous order is like a work cohering from the centre to the superficies, 314. Successive order becomes simultaneous in the ultimate, the highest things of successive order become the inmost of simultaneous order, and the lowest things of successive order become the outermost of simultaneous order, 314. Successive order of conjugial love, 305, 311.

ORGANIZATION, the, of the life of man according to his love, cannot be changed after death, 524. A change of organization cannot possibly be effected, except in the material body, and is utterly impossible in the spiritual body after the former has been rejected, 524.

ORGANS.—Such as conjugial love is in the minds or spirits of two persons, such is it interiorly in its organs, 310. In these organs are terminated the forms of the mind with those who are principled in conjugial love, 310.

ORIGIN of evil, 444. Origin of conjugial love, 60, 61, 83, 103-114, 183, 239. Origin of the Mahometan religion, 342. Origin of the beauty of the female sex, 381-384.

OUTERMOST, the, lowest things of successive order become the outermost of simultaneous order, 314.

Obs.—The outermost is predicated of what is most exterior, in opposition to the inmost, or that which is most interior.

OWLS in the spiritual world are correspondences and consequent appearances of the thoughts of confirmators, 233.

PAGANS, the, who acknowledge a God and live according to the civil laws of justice, are saved, 351.

PALACE representative of conjugial love, 270. Small palace inhabited by two novitiate conjugial partners, 316. Description of the palace of a celestial society, 12.

PALLADIUM, 151*.

PALM-TREES, in the spiritual world, represent conjugial love of the middle region, 270,

PALMS OF THE HANDS, in the, resides with wives a sixth sense, which is a sense of all the delights of the conjugial love of the husband, 151*.

PAPER on which was written arcana at this day revealed by the Lord, 533. Paper bearing this inscription, "The marriage of Good and Truth," 115.

PARADISE, spiritually understood, is intelligence, 353. Paradise on the confines of heaven, 8.

PARALYSIS, 253, 470.

PARCHMENT IN HEAVEN.—Roll of parchment containing arcana of wisdom concerning conjugial love, 43. Sheet of parchment, on which were the rules of the people of the first age, 77.

PARNASSIDES, sports of the, in the spiritual world, 207. These sports were spiritual exercises and trials of skill, 207.

PARNASSUS, 151*, 182, 207.

PARTICULARS are in universals as parts in a whole, 261. Whoever knows universals, may afterwards comprehend particulars, 261.

Obs.—Particulars taken together are called universals.

PARTNER.—Those who have lived in love truly conjugial, after the death of their married partners, are unwilling to enter into iterated marriages, the reason why, 321 See *Married Partners.*

PATHOLOGY, 253.

PEACE is the blessed principle of every delight which is of good, 394. Peace, because it proceeds immediately from the Lord, is one of the two inmost principles of heaven, 394. Peace in their homes gives serenity to the minds of husbands, and disposes them to receive agreeably the kindnesses offered by their wives, 285. Peace is in conjugial love, and relates to the soul, 180.

PEGASUS.—By the winged horse Pegasus the ancients meant the understanding of truth, by which comes wisdom; by the hoofs of his feet they understood experiences, whereby comes natural intelligence, 182. See *Horse*.

PELLICACY, 459, 460, 462.

PERCEPTION, common, is the same thing as influx from heaven into the interiors of the mind, 28. By virtue of this perception, man inwardly in himself perceives truths, and as it were sees them, 28. All have not common perception, 147. There is an internal perception of love, and an external perception, which sometimes hides the internal, 49. The external perception of love originates in those things which regard the love of the world, and of the body, 49.

Obs.—Perception is a sensation derived from the Lord alone, and has relation to the good and true, *A. C.* 104. Perception consists in seeing that a truth is true, and that a good is good; also that an evil is evil, and a false is false, *A. C.*, 7680. Its opposite is phantasy. See *Phantasy*, *obs.*

PEREGRINATIONS of man in the societies of the spiritual world, during his life in the natural world, 530.

PERIODS whereby creation is preserved in the state foreseen and provided for, 400, 401.

PERIOSTEUMS, 511.

PETER, the Apostle, represented truth and faith, 119.

PHANTASY, 267.—Those are in the phantasy of their respective concupiscences who think interiorly in themselves, and too much indulge their imagination by discoursing with themselves; for these separate their spirit almost from connection with the body, and by vision overflow the understanding, 267. What is the fate of those after death who have given themselves up to their phantasy, 268, 514. Errors which phantasy has introduced through ignorance of the spiritual world, and of its sun, 422.

Obs.—Phantasy is an appearance of perception: it consists in seeing what is true as false, and what is good as evil; and what is evil as good, and what is false as true, *A. C.*, 7680.

PHANTOMS.—Who those are who in the other life appear as phantoms, 514.

PHILOSOPHERS, difference between, and *Sophi*, 180. The ancient people, who acknowledged the wisdom of reason as wisdom, were called philosophers, 180. See *Sophi*.

PHILOSOPHICAL considerations concerning the abstract substance, form, subject, &c., 66, 186.

PHILOSOPHY is one of those sciences by which an entrance is made into things rational, which are the grounds of rational wisdom, 163.

PHYSICS is one of the sciences by which an entrance is made into things rational, which are the ground of rational wisdom, 163.

PLACE.—In the spiritual world there are places as in the natural world, otherwise there could be no habitations and distinct abodes, 10. Nevertheless place is not place, but an appearance of place, according to the state of love and wisdom, 10. Places of instruction in the spiritual world, 261.

PLACES, public, in the spiritual world, 17, 79.

PLANES successive, formed in man, on which superior principles may rest and find support, 447. The ultimate plane in which the sphere of conjugial love and its opposite terminate is the same, 439. The rational plane, with man, is the medium between heaven and hell; the marriage of good and truth flows into this plane from above, and the marriage of evil and false flows into it from beneath, 436.

PLANETS.—Revelations made at the present day concerning the inhabitants of the planets, 532. See Treatise by the Author on *The Earths in the Universe*.

PLASTIC force in animals and vegetables, whence it proceeds, 238.

PLATO, 151*.

PLATONIST, 153*.—Arcana unfolded by a Platonist, 153*.

PLEASURES.—Sensations, with the pleasures thence derived, appertain to the body, 278. The delights of adulterous love are the pleasures of insanity, 442, 497.

PLEDGES.—After a declaration of consent, pledges are to be given, 300. These pledges are continual visible witnesses of mutual love, hence also they are memorials thereof, 300.

POLAND, 521.

POLES, 103, 108.

POLITICAL SELF-LOVE, its nature and quality, 264. It would make its votaries desirous of being emperors if left without restraint, 264.

POLITICS is one of those sciences by which an entrance is made into things rational, which are the ground of rational wisdom, 163.

POLYGAMICAL love is the love of the external, or natural man, 345. In this love there is neither chastity, purity, nor sanctity, 346.

POLYGAMIST, no, so long as he remains such, is capable of being made spiritual, 347. Conjugial chastity, purity, and sanctity cannot exist with polygamists, 346.

POLYGAMY, of, 332-352. Whence it originates, 349. Polygamy is lasciviousness,

845. Polygamy is not a sin with those who live in it from a religious principle, as did the Israelites, 848. Why polygamy was permitted to the Israelitish nation, 840.

POPES.—Dreadful fate of two popes who had compelled emperors to resign their dominions, and had behaved ill to them, both in word and deed, at Rome, whither they came to supplicate and adore them, 265.

PORTICO of palm-trees and laurels, 56.

POSTERIOR, the, is derived from the prior, as the effect from its cause, 326. That which is posterior exists from what is prior, as it exists from what is prior, 380. Between prior and posterior, there is no determinate proportion, 326.

POWER, active or living, and passive or dead, 489. Whence proceeds the propagative, or plastic force, in seeds of the vegetable kingdom, 238.

PRECEPT.—He who from purpose or confirmation acts against one precept, acts against the rest, 528. The precepts of regeneration are five, see No. 82: among which are these, that evils ought to be shunned, because they are of the devil, and from the devil; that goods are to be done, because they are of God, and from God; and that men ought to go to the Lord, in order that He may lead them to do the latter, 525.

PREDICATES.—A subject without predicates is also an entity which has no existence in reason (ens nullius rationis), 66.

PREDICATIONS are made by a man according to his rational light, 485. Predications of four degrees of adulteries, 485 and following. Difference between predications, charges of blame, and imputations, 485.

PRELATES, why the, of the church have given the pre-eminence to faith, which is of truth, above charity, which is of good, 126.

PREPARATION for heaven or for hell, in the world of spirits, has for its end that the internal and external may agree together and make one, and not disagree and make two, 48*.

PRESENCE.—The origin or cause of presence in the spiritual world, 171. Man is receptible of the Lord's presence, and of conjunction with Him. To come to Him, causes presence, and to live according to His commandments, causes conjunction, 341. His presence alone is without reception, but presence and conjunction together are with reception, 341. The truth of faith constitutes the Lord's presence, 72.

PRESERVATION is perpetual creation, 86. Whence arises perpetual preservation, 85.

PRETENDER.—Every man who is not interiorly led by the Lord is a pretender, a sycophant, a hypocrite, and thereby an apparent man, and yet not a man, 267.

PRIEST, chief, of a society in heaven, 266.

PRIMARY.—What is first in respect to end, is first in the mind and its intention, because it is regarded as primary, 98. Things primary exist, subsist, and persist, from things ultimate, 44.

PRIMEVAL.—In the world, at the present day, nothing is known of the primeval state of man, which is called a state of integrity, 355. What the primeval state of creation was, and how man is led back to it by the Lord, 355.

PRINCE of a society in heaven, 14 and following, 266.

PRINCIPLE, the primary, of the church is the good of charity, and not the truth of faith, 126.

PRINCIPLES and PRINCIPIATES, 328.

Obs.—Principiates derive their essence from principles, T. C. R., 177. All things of the body are principiates, that is, are compositions of fibres, from principles which are receptacles of love and wisdom, D. L. and W., 369.

PROBITY is one of those virtues which have respect to life, and enter into it, 164.

PROBLEM concerning the soul, 315.

PROCEED, to.—All things which proceed from the Lord, are in an instant from first principles in last, 389.

PROCREATION, sphere of the love of, 400.

PROGRESSION.—There is no progression of good to evil, but a progression of good to a greater and less good, and evil to a greater and less evil, 444. A progression from ends through causes into effects is inscribed on every man in general, and in every particular, 400, 401. Decreasing progression of conjugial love, 78.

PROLIFICATION corresponds to the propagation of truth, 127. Spiritual prolification is that of love and wisdom, 51, 52. Origin of natural prolifications, 115. The sphere of prolification is the same as the universal sphere of the marriage of good and truth, which proceeds from the Lord, 92. All prolification is originally derived from the influx of love, wisdom, and use from the Lord, from an immediate influx into the souls of men, from a mediate influx into the souls of animals, and from an influx still more mediate into the inmost principles of vegetables, 183. Prolifications are continuations of creation, 183. The principle of prolification is derived from the intellect alone, 90. In the principle of prolification of the husband is the soul, and also his mind as to its interiors, which are conjoined to the soul, 172. Its state with husbands, if married pairs were in the marriage of good and truth, 115.

PROMULGATION, cause of the, of the decalogue by Jehovah God upon Mount Sinai, 351.

PROPAGATE, to.—Love and wisdom, with use, not only constitute man (homo), but also are man, and propagate man, 183. A feminine principle is propagated from intellectual good, 220.

PROPAGATION, all, is originally derived from the influx of love, wisdom, and use from the Lord, from an immediate influx into the souls of men, from a mediate in-

INDEX.

flux into the souls of animals, and from an influx still more mediate into the inmost principles of vegetables, 133. Propagations are continuations of creation, 183. Propagation of the soul, 220, 236, 238, 245, 321. The propagation of the human race, and thence of the angelic heaven, was the chief end of creation, 68.

PROPAGATIVE, or plastic force of vegetables and animals, whence it originated, 133.

PROPRIUM, man's, from his birth is essentially evil, 262. The *proprium* of man's (*homo*) will, is to love himself, and the *proprium* of his understanding is to love his own wisdom, 194. These two propriums are deadly evils to man, if they remain with him, 194. The love of these two propriums is changed into conjugial love, so far as man cleaves to his wife, that is, receives her love, 194.

PROVIDENCE, the Divine, of the Lord extends to every thing, even to the minutest particulars concerning marriages, and in marriages, 229, 316. The operations of uses, by the Lord, by the spheres which proceed from Him, are the Divine Providence, 386, 391.

Obs.—The Divine Providence is the same as the mediate and immediate influx from the Lord, *A. C.*, 6480. See the *Treatise on the Divine Providence*, by the Author.

PRUDENCE is one of the moral virtues which have respect to life, and enter into it, 164. Nothing of prudence can possibly exist but from God, 354. Prudence of wives in concealing their love, 294. This prudence is innate, 187. It was implanted in women from creation, and consequently by birth, 194. Of self-derived prudence, 354.

PULPIT in a temple in the spiritual world, 23.

PU, or PAU, 28, 29, 182.

Obs.—This is the Greek word πoῦ, written in ordinary characters; the Author gives the Latin translation at No. 28. (In quodam pu seu ubi.) This word expresses the uncertainty in which philosophers and theologians are on the subject of the soul.

PURE.—It is not possible that any love should become absolutely pure, with men or with angels, 71, 146. To the pure all things are pure, but to them that are defiled, nothing is pure, 149.

PURIFICATION the spiritual, of conjugial love may be compared to the purification of natural spirits, as effected by the chemists, 145. Wisdom purified may be compared with alcohol, which is a spirit highly rectified, 145.

PURITY, the, of heaven is from conjugial love, 430. In like manner the purity of the church, 431.

PURPLE, the, color from its correspondence signifies the conjugial love of the wife, 76.

PURPOSE.—That which flows forth from the very essence of a man's life, thus which flows forth from his will or his love, is principally called purpose, 493. As soon as any one from purpose or confirmation abstains from any evil because it is sin, he is kept by the Lord in the purpose of abstaining from the rest, 529.

PUSTULES, 253, 470.

PUT AWAY, to.—Putting away on account of adultery is a plenary separation of minds, which is called divorce, 255. Other kinds of putting away, grounded in their particular causes, are separations, 255.

PUT OFF, to.—Man after death puts off every thing which does not agree with his love, 36. How a man after death puts off externals and puts on internals, 48*.

PYTHAGORAS, 151*.

PYTHAGOREANS, 153*.

QUALITY of the love of the sex in heaven, 44. The quality of every deed, and in general the quality of every thing depends upon the circumstances which mitigate or aggravate it, 487.

RAINBOW painted on a wall in the spiritual world, 76.

RATIONAL principle, the, is the medium between heaven and the world, 145. Above the rational principle is heavenly light, and below the rational principle is natural light, 233. The rational principle is formed more and more to the reception of heaven or of hell, according as man turns himself towards good or evil, 436.

Obs.—The rational principle of man partakes of the spiritual and natural, or is a medium between them, *A. C.*, 268.

RATIONALITY, spiritual, comes by means of the Word, and of preachings derived therefrom, 293. Natural, sensual, and corporeal men enjoy, like other men, the powers of rationality, but they use it while they are in externals, and abuse it while in their internals, 498, 499. Rationality, with devils, proceeds from the glory of the love of self, 269, and also with atheists, who enjoy a more sublime rationality than many others, 269.

RATIONALITY and LIBERTY.—When man turns himself to the Lord, his rationality and liberty are led by the Lord; but if backwards, from the Lord, his rationality and liberty are led by hell, 437.

REACTION.—In all conjunction by love there must be action, reception, and reaction, 293.

READ, to.—While man reads the Word, and collects truths out of it, the Lord adjoins good, 128; but this takes place interiorly with those only who read the Word to the end that they may become wise, 128.

REAL.—Love and wisdom are collected together in use, and therein become one principle, which is called real, 183.

REASON, human, is such that it understands truths from the light thereof, although it has not heretofore distinguished them, 490.

REASONERS.—They are named such who never conclude any thing, and make whatever they hear a matter of argument and dispute whether it be so, with perpetual contradiction, 232. What their fate is in the other life, 232.

REASONINGS, the, of the generality commence merely from effects, and from effects proceed to some consequences thence resulting, and do not commence from causes, and from causes proceed analytically to effects, 385. Truth does not admit of reasonings, 481. They favor the delights of the flesh against those of the spirit, 481.

RECEPTION is according to religion, 352. Without conjunction there is no reception, 341. See *Reaction.*

RECIPIENT.—Man is a recipient of God, and consequently a recipient of love and wisdom from Him, 132. A recipient becomes an image of God according to reception, 132.

RECIPROCAL principle, the, of conjunction with God, is, that a man should love God, and relish the things which are of God, as from himself, and yet believe that they are of God, 132, 122. Without such a reciprocal principle conjunction is impossible, 132.

RECTIFICATION.—The purification of conjugial love may be compared to the purification of natural spirits, effected by chemists, and called rectification, 145.

REFORMED, to be.—Man is reformed by the understanding, and this is effected by the knowledges of good and truth, and by a rational intuition grounded therein, 495.

REGENERATION is a successive separation from the evils to which man is naturally inclined, 146. Regeneration is purification from evils, and thereby renovation of life, 525. The precepts of regeneration are five, 525. See *Precepts.* By regeneration a man is made altogether new as to his spirit, and this is effected by a life according to the Lord's precepts, 525.

REGIONS of the mind.—In human minds there are three regions, of which the highest is called the celestial, the middle the spiritual, and the lowest the natural, 305. In the lowest man is born; he ascends into the next above it by a life according to the truths of religion, and into the highest by the marriage of love and wisdom, 305. In the lowest region dwells natural love, in the superior spiritual love, and in the supreme celestial love, 270. In each region there is a marriage of love and wisdom, 270. The pleasantnesses of conjugial love in the highest region are perceived as blessednesses, in the middle region as satisfactions, and in the lowest region as delights, 335. In the lowest region reside all the concupiscences of evil and of lasciviousness; in the superior region there are not a ny concupiscences of evil and of lasciviousness, for man is introduced into this region by the Lord when he is reborn; in the supreme region is conjugial chastity in its love, into this region man is elevated by the love of uses, 305.

REIGN, to, with Christ is to be wise, and perform uses, 7.

RELATION, there is no, of good to evil, but a relation of good to a greater and less good, and of evil to a greater and less evil, 444. What is signified by the expression, for the sake of relatives, 17.

RELATIVES subsist between the greatest and the least of the same thing, 425, 17.

RELIGION constitutes the state of the church with man, 238. Religion is implanted in souls, and by souls is transmitted from parents to their offspring, as the supreme inclination, 246. With Christians it is formed by the good of life, agreeable to the truth of doctrine, 115. Conjugial love is grounded in religion, 238. Where there is not religion, neither is there conjugial love, 239. There is no religion without the truths of religion; what is religion without truths, 239. Religion, as it is the marriage of the Lord and the church, is the initiament and inoculation of conjugial love, 531. That love in its progress accompanies religion, 531. The first internal cause of cold in marriages is the rejection of religion by each of the parties, 240. The second cause is, that one has religion and not the other, 241. The third is, that one of the parties is of one religion, and the other of another, 242. The fourth is the falsity of religion, 243.

Obs.—There is a difference which it is important to bear in mind, between religion and the church; the church of the Lord, it is true, is universal, and is with all those who acknowledge a Divine Being, and live in charity whatever else may be their creed; but the church is especially where the Word is, and where by means of the Word the Lord is known. In the countries where the Word does not exist, or is withdrawn from the people and replaced by human decisions, as among the Roman Catholics, there is religion alone, but there is, to speak correctly, no church. Among Protestants, there is both religion and a church, but this church has come to an end, because it has perverted the Word.

RENEW, to.—Every part of man, both interior and exterior, renews itself, and this is effected by solutions and repurations, 171.

RENUNCIATION of whoredoms, whence exists the chastity of marriage, how it is effected, 148.

REPASTS.—In heaven, as in the world, there are repasts, 6.

REPRESENTATIONS.—Among the ancients the study of their bodily senses consisted in representations of truths in forms, 76.

REPRESENTATIVE.—To those who are in the third heaven, every representative of love and wisdom becomes real, 270.

RESPIRATION OF THE LUNGS, the, has relation to truth, 87.

INDEX.

REST.—What is the meaning of eternal rest, 207.
RETAIN, to —In whatever state man is he retains the faculty of elevating the understanding, 495.
REVELATIONS made at the present day by the Lord, 532.
RIB, by a, of the breast is signified, in the spiritual sense, natural truth, 193.
RIGHT, the, signifies good, 316. It also signifies power, 21.
RITES. customary.—There are customary rites which are merely formal, and there are others which, at the same time, are also essential, 306.
RIVALSHIP or emulation between married parties respecting right and power, 291. Emulation of prominence between married partners is one of the external causes of cold, 248.
RULES of life concerning marriages, 77. Universal rule, 147, 313.

SABBATH, the.—The life of heaven from the worship of God, is called a perpetual Sabbath, 9. Celebration of the Sabbath in a heavenly society, 23, 24.
SACRILEGE.—See *Sacrimony*.
SACRIMONY.—In heaven, marriage with one wife is called sacrimony, but if it took place with more than one it would be called sacrilege, 76.
SAGACITY is one of the principles constituent of natural wisdom, 163.
SANCTITIES.—The marriage of the Lord and the church, and the marriage of good and truth, are essential sanctities, 64. Sanctity of the Holy Scriptures, 24.
SANCTUARY of the tabernacle of worship amongst the most ancient in heaven, 75.
SATANS.—They are called satans who have confirmed themselves in favor of nature to the denial of God, 380. Those who are evil from the understanding dwell in the front in hell, and here are called satans, but those who are in evil from the will, dwell to the back and are called devils, 492. See *Devils*. Satan wishing to demonstrate that nature is God, 415.
Obs.—In the Word, by the devil is understood that' her' which is to the back, and in which are the most wicked, called evil genii; and by satan, that hell in which dwell those who are not so wicked, who are called evil spirits, *H. and H.*, 544.
SATISFACTION.—In love truly conjugial exists a state of satisfaction, 180.
SATURNINE or golden age, 153*.
SATYRS.—In the spiritual world the satyr-like form is the form of dissolute adultery, 521.
SAVED, to be.—All in the universe who acknowledge a God, and, from a religious principle, shun evil as sins against Him, are saved, 343.
SCIENCE is a principle of knowledges, 130. There is no end to science, 195. Man is not born into the science of any love, but beasts and birds are born into the science of all their loves, 133. Man is born without sciences, to the end that he may receive them all; whereas, supposing him to be born into sciences, he could not receive any but those into which he was born. 134. Science and love are undivided companions, 134.
SCIENCE OF CORRESPONDENCES, the, was among the ancients the science of sciences, 532. It was the knowledge concerning the spiritual things of heaven and the church, and thence they derived wisdom, 532. It conjoined the sensual things of their bodies with the perceptions of their minds, and procured to them intelligence, 76. This science having been turned into idolatrous science, was so obliterated and destroyed by the divine providence of the Lord, that no visible traces of it were left remaining, 532. Nevertheless, it has been again discovered by the Lord, in order that the men of the church may again have conjunction with Him, and consociation with the angels; which purposes are effected by the Word, in which all things are correspondences, 532. See *Correspondences*.
SCORBUTIC PHTHISIC, 253, 470.
SCRIPTURE, the sacred, which proceeded immediately from the Lord, is, in general and in particular, a marriage of good and truth, 115.
SEAT, the, of jealousy is in the understanding of the husband, 372.
SEDUCERS.—Their sad lot after death, 514.
SEE, to, that what is true is true, and that what is false is false, is to see from heavenly light in natural light, 233.
SEEDS spiritually understood are truths, 220. By the seed of man, whereby iron shall be mixed with clay, and still they shall not cohere, is meant the truth of the Word falsified, 79. Formation of seed, 220, 245, 183.
SELF-CONCEIT, or SELF-DERIVED INTELLIGENCE.—The love of wisdom, if it remains with man, and is not transcribed into the woman, is an evil love, and is called self-conceit, or the love of his own intelligence, 88, 353. The wife continually attracts to herself her husband's conceit of his own intelligence, and extinguishes it in him, and verifies it in herself, 353. He who, from a principle of self-love, is vain of his own intelligence, cannot possibly love his wife with true conjugial love, 193.
SEMBLANCES, conjugial, 279-289.
SEMINATION corresponds to the potency of truth, 127. It has a spiritual origin, and proceeds from the truths of which the understanding consists, 220.
SENSATIONS with the pleasures thence derived appertain to the body, and affections with the thoughts thence derived appertain to the mind, 273.
SENSE.—Every love has its own proper sense, 210. Spiritual origin of the natural senses, 220. See *Taste*, *Smell*, *Hearing*, *Touch*, *Sight*. Each of these senses has its

delights, with variations according to the specific uses of each, 68. The sense proper to conjugial love is the sense of touch, 210. The use of this sense is the complex of all other uses, 68. Wives have a sixth sense, and which is a sense of all the delights of the conjugial love of the husband, and this sense they have in the palms of their hands, 155*.

SENSUAL.—Natural men who love only the delights of the senses, placing their heart in every kind of luxury and pleasure, are properly meant by the sensual, 496. The sensual immerse all things of the will, and consequently of the understanding, in the allurements and fallacies of the senses, indulging in these alone, 496.

SEPARATIONS of married partners. Legitimate causes thereof, 251–254.

SERENE, principle of peace, 155*.

SERIES.—All those things which precede in minds form series, which collect themselves together, one near another, and one after another, and these together, compose a last or ultimate, in which they co-exist, 313. The series of the love of infants, from its greatest to its least, thus to the boundary in which it subsists or ceases, is retrograde, the reason why, 401.

SERPENT, the, signifies the love of self-intelligence, 353. By the serpent, Gen. iii. 1, is meant the devil, as to the conceit of self-love and self-intelligence, 135. In hell, the forms of beasts, under which the lascivious delights of adulterous love are presented to the sight, are serpents, &c., 430.

SEX.—The love of the male sex differs from that of the female sex, 382. Origin of the beauty of the female sex, 381–384. Cause of the beauty of the female sex, 56.

SHEEP, in the spiritual world, are the representative forms of the state of innocence and peace of the inhabitants, 75.

SHEEPFOLD signifies the church, 129.

SHOWER, golden, 155*, 208.

SIGHT.—There is in man an internal and an external sight, 477. Natural sight is grounded in spiritual sight, which is that of the understanding, 220. The love of seeing, grounded in the love of understanding, has the sense of seeing; and the gratifications proper to it are the various kinds of symmetry and beauty, 210. How gross the sight of the eye is, 416.

SILVER signifies intelligence in spiritual truths, and thence in natural truths, 76. The silver age, 76.

SIMPLE.—Every thing divided is more and more multiple, and not more and more simple, 329.

SIMULTANEOUS.—There is simultaneous order and successive order, 314. That simultaneous order is grounded in successive, and is according to it, is not known, 314.

SIN.—All that which is contrary to religion is believed to be sin, because it is contrary to God; and, on the other hand, all that which agrees with religion is believed not to be sin, because it agrees with God, 348.

SINCERITY is one of those virtues which have respect to life, and enter into it, 164.

SINCIPUT, 267.

SINGING in heaven, 55, 155*.

SIRENS, fantastic beauty of, in the spiritual world, 505.

SISTERS.—The Lord calls those brethren and sisters who are of his church, 120.

SIX.—The number six signifies all and what is complete, 21.

SLEEP, the, into which Adam fell, when the woman was created, signifies man's entire ignorance that the wife is formed, and, as it were, created from him, 194.

SLEEP, to, Gen. ii. 21, signifies to be in ignorance, 194. Sleep in heaven, 19.

SLOTHFUL, to the, in the spiritual world, food is not given, 6.

SMALL-POX, 253, 470.

SMELLING, natural, is grounded in spiritual smelling, which is perception, 220. The love of knowing those things which float about in the air, grounded in the love of perceiving, is the sense of smelling; and the gratifications proper to it are the various kinds of fragrance, 210.

SOBRIETY is one of those virtues which have respect to life, and enter into it, 164.

SOCIETY, every, in heaven may be considered as one common body, and the constituent angels as the similar parts thereof, from which the common body exists, 10.

SOCRATES, 151*.

SOCRATICS, 153*.

SOLITARY, there is neither good nor solitary truth, but in all cases they are conjoined, 87.

SOLUTIONS and reparations by which every part of man, both interior and exterior, renews itself, 171.

SOMNAMBULISTS act from the impulse of a blind science, the understanding being asleep, 134.

SONS in the Word signify truths conceived in the spiritual man, and born in the natural, 120, 220. Those who are regenerated by the Lord are called in the Word sons of God, sons of the kingdom, 120.

SONS-IN-LAW, what, and daughters-in-law signify in the Word, 120.

SONGS in heaven, 17, 19. Heavenly songs are in reality sonorous affections, or affections expressed and modified by sounds, 55. Singing in heaven is an affection of the mind, which is let forth through the mouth as a tune, 155*. Affections are expressed by songs, as thoughts are by discourse, 55.

SOPHI.—The most ancient people did not acknowledge any other wisdom than the wisdom of life, and this was the wisdom of those who were formerly called *sophi*, 130.

SOUL, the, is the inmost principle of man, 101, 158, 206. It is not life, but the proximate receptacle of life from God, and thereby the habitation of God, 315. It is a form of all things relating to love, and of all things relating to wisdom, 315. It is a form from which the smallest thing cannot be taken away, and to which the smallest thing cannot be added, and it is the inmost of all the forms of the whole body, 315. Propagation of the soul, 220, 245. The soul of the offspring is from the father, and its clothing from the mother, 206, 238. The principle of truth in the soul is the origin of seed, in which is the soul of man, 220, 483. It is in a perfect human form, covered with substances from the purest principles of nature, whereof a body is formed in the womb of the mother, 183. The soul of man, and of every animal, from an implanted tendency to self-propagation, forms itself, clothes itself, and becomes seed, 220; because the soul is a spiritual substance, which is not a subject of extension but of impletion, and from which no part can be taken away, but the whole may be produced without any loss thereof, hence it is that it is as fully present in the smallest receptacles, which are seeds, as in its greatest receptacle, the body, 220. The soul of every man, by its origin, is celestial, wherefore it receives influx immediately from the Lord, 482. The soul and the mind are the man, since both constitute the spirit which lives after death, and which is in a perfect human form, 260. The soul constitutes the inmost principles not only of the head, but also of the body, 178. The soul and mind adjoin themselves closely to the flesh of the body, to operate and produce their effects, 178. A masculine soul, 220. How a feminine principle is produced from a male soul, 220. How a union of the souls of married partners is effected, 172. See *Mind, obs.*

SPACE.—Those things which, from their origin, are celestial and spiritual, are not in space, but in the appearances of space, 158. The soul of man being celestial, and his mind spiritual, are not in space, 158.

SPANIARDS, 103, 104.

SPECIES.—Why the Creator has distinguished all things into genera, species, and discriminations, 479.

SPEECH, the, of wisdom is to speak from causes, 75. From the thought, which also is spiritual, speech flows, 220.

SPHERE.—All that which flows from a subject, and encompasses and surrounds it, is named a sphere, 386. From the Lord, by the spiritual sun, proceeds a sphere of heat and light, or of love and wisdom, to operate ends which are uses, 386. The universal sphere of generating and propagating the celestial things, which are of love, and the spiritual things, which are of wisdom, and thence the natural things, which are of offspring, proceeds from the Lord, and fills the universal heaven and the universal world, 355. The divine sphere which looks to the preservation of the universe in its created state by successive generations, is called the sphere of procreating, 386. The divine sphere which looks to the preservation of generations in their beginnings, and afterwards in their progressions, is called the sphere of protecting the things created, 386. There are several other divine spheres, which are named according to uses, as the sphere of defence of good and truth against evil and false, the sphere of reformation and regeneration, the sphere of innocence and peace, the sphere of mercy and grace, &c., 222, 386. But the universal of all is the conjugial sphere, because this is the supereminent sphere of conservation of the created universe, 222. This sphere fills the universe, and pervades all things from first to last, 222; thus from angels even to worms, 92. Why it is more universal than the sphere of heat and light which proceed from the sun, 222. In its origin, the conjugial sphere, flowing into the universe, is divine; in its progress in heaven with the angels, it is celestial and spiritual; with men it is natural; with beasts and birds, animal; with worms merely corporeal; with vegetables, it is void of life; and, moreover, in all its subjects it is varied according to their forms, 225. This sphere is received immediately by the female sex, and mediately by the male, 225. The sphere of conjugial love is the very essential sphere of heaven, because it descends from the heavenly marriage of the Lord and the church, 54. Whereas there is a sphere of conjugial love, there is also a sphere opposite to it, which is called a sphere of adulterous love, 434. This sphere ascends from hell, and the sphere of conjugial love descends from heaven, 435, 455. These spheres meet each other in each world, but do not conjoin, 436, 455. Between these two spheres there is equilibrium, and man is in it, 437, 455. Man can turn himself to whichever sphere he pleases; but so far as he turns himself to the one, so far he turns himself from the other, 438, 455. A sphere of love from the wife, and of understanding from the man, is continually flowing forth, and unites them, 321. A natural sphere is continually flowing forth, not only from man, but also from beasts—yea, from trees, fruits, flowers, and also from metals, 171. There flows forth—yea, overflows from every man (*homo*)—a spiritual sphere, derived from the affections of his love, which encompasses him, and infuses itself into the natural sphere derived from the body, so that these two spheres are conjoined, 171. Every one, both man and woman, is encompassed by his own sphere of life, densely on the breast, and less densely on the back, 224.

SPIRE.—With whom the mind is closed from beneath, and sometimes twisted as a spire into the adverse principle, 203.

SPIRIT, the.—There are two principles which, in the beginning, with every man, who from natural is made spiritual, are at strife together, which are commonly called the spirit and the flesh, 453. The love of marriage is of the spirit, and the love of adultery is of the flesh, 455. See *Flesh.*

SPIRITS.—See *Mind, obs.* By novitiate

spirits are meant men newly deceased, who are called spirits because they are then spiritual men, 461. Who those are, who, after death, become corporeal spirits, 495.

SPIRITUAL.—The difference between what is spiritual and natural is like that between prior and posterior, which bear no determinate proportion to each other, 326. Spiritual principles without natural, which are their continent, have no consistence, 52. Spiritual principles considered in themselves have relation to love and wisdom, 52. The things relating to the church, which are called spiritual things, reside in the inmost principles with man, 130. By the spiritual is meant he who loves spiritual things, and thereby is wise from the Lord, 281. A man (*homo*) without religion is not spiritual, but remains natural, 149. To become spiritual is to be elevated out of the natural principle, that is, out of the light and heat of the world into the light and heat of heaven, 347. Man becomes spiritual in proportion as his rational principle begins to derive a soul from influx out of heaven, which is the case so far as it is affected and delighted with wisdom, 145.

SPIRITUALLY, to think, is to think abstractedly from space and time, 329.

SPORTS of wisdom in the heavens, 132. Literary sports, 207. Conjugial love in its origin is the sport of wisdom and love, 75, 183. Games and shows, in the heavens, 17. The sixth sense in the female sex is called in the heavens the sport of wisdom with its love, and of love with its wisdom, 155*.

SPRING.—In heaven the heat and light proceeding from the sun cause perpetual spring, 137. In heaven, with conjugial partners, there is spring in its perpetual conatus, 355. All who come into heaven return into their vernal youth, and into the powers appertaining to that age, 44.

STABLES signify instructions, 76.

STAGE entertainments. See *Actors*.

STATES.—The state of a man's life is his quality as to the understanding and the will, 184. The state of a man's life from infancy, even to the end of life, is continually changing, 185. The common states of a man's life are called infancy, childhood, youth, manhood, and old age, 185. No subsequent state of life is the same as a preceding one, 186. The last state is such as the successive order is, from which it is formed and exists, 313. What was the primeval state, which is called a state of integrity, 355. Of the state of married partners after death, 45–54. There are two states into which a man enters after death—an external and an internal state; he comes first into his external state, and afterwards into his internal, 47*.

STATUE, the, which Nebuchadnezzar saw in a dream represented the ages of gold, silver, copper, and iron, 78.

STONES signify natural truths, and precious stones spiritual truths, 76.

STORE, abundant, 220, 221.

STOREHOUSE.—The conjugial principle of one man with one wife is the storehouse of human life, 457.

STORGE.—The love called *storge* is the love of infants, 392. This love prevails equally with the evil and the good, and, in like manner, with tame and wild beasts; it is even in some cases stronger and more ardent with evil men, and also with wild beasts, 392. The innocence of infancy is the cause of the love called *storge*, 395. Spiritual storge, 211.

STUDY, what was the, of the men who lived in the silver age, 76. Study of sciences in the spiritual world, 207.

STUPIDITY of the age, 431.

SUBLIMATION.—The purification of conjugial love may be compared to the purification of natural spirits, as effected by chemists, and called sublimation, 145.

SUBJECT, every, receives influx according to its form, 86. All a man's affections and thoughts are in forms, and thence from forms, for forms are their subjects, 186. A subject without predicates is an entity which has no existence in reason, 66. See *Substance*.

SUBSISTENCE is perpetual existence, 86.

SUBSTANCE.—There is no substance without a form, an unformed substance not being any thing, 66. There is not any good or truth which is not in a substance as in its subject, 66. Every idea of man's, however sublimated, is substantial, that is, affixed to substance, 66. Material things derive their origin from things substantial, 207. In man, all the affections of love, and all the perceptions of wisdom, are rendered substantial, for substances are their subjects, 361. See *Form*.

SUBSTANTIAL.—The difference between what is substantial and what is material is like the difference between what is prior and what is posterior, 81. Spiritual things are substantials, 328. Spirits and angels are in substantials and not in materials, 328. Man after death is a substantial man, because this substantial man lay inwardly concealed in the natural or material man, 31. The substantial man sees the substantial man, as the material man sees the material man, 31. All things in the spiritual world are substantial and not material, whence it is that there are in their perfection in that world, all things which are in the natural world, and many things besides, 207. Every idea of man's, however sublimated, is substantial, that is, attached to substances, 66.

SUCCESSIVE.—There is a successive order and a simultaneous order, and there is an influx of successive order into simultaneous order, 314. See *Order*.

SUMMARY of the Lord's commandments, 340, 82.

SUN.—There is a sun of the spiritual world as there is a sun of the natural world, 380. The sun of the spiritual world proceeds immediately from the Lord, who is in the midst of 't, 235. That sun is pure

INDEX.

.ove 235, 880, 582. It appears fiery before the angels, altogether as the sun of our world appears before men, 235. It does not set nor rise, but stands constantly between the zenith and the horizon, that is, at the elevation of 45 degrees, 137. The spiritual sun is pure love, and the natural sun is pure fire, 182, 532. Whatever proceeds from the spiritual sun partakes of life, since it is pure love; whatever proceeds from the natural sun partakes nothing of life, since it is pure fire, 532. The spiritual sun is in the centre of the universe, and its operation, being without space and time, is instant and present from first principles in last, 391. For what end the sun of the natural world was created, 235. The fire of the natural sun exists from no other source than from the fire of the spiritual sun, which is divine love, 380.
SUPPERS.—In heaven, as in the world, there are suppers, 19.
SURVIVOR, 321.—See *Deceased*.
SWAMMERDAM, 416.
SWANS, in the spiritual world, signify conjugial love in the lowest region of the mind, 270.
SWEDENBORG.—He protests in truth that the memorable relations annexed to the chapters in this work are not fictions, but were truly done and seen; not seen in any state of the mind asleep, but in a state of full wakefulness, 1. That it had pleased the Lord to manifest Himself unto him, and send him to teach the things relating to the New Church, 1. That the interiors of his mind and spirit were opened by the Lord, and that thence it was granted him to be in the spiritual world with angels, and at the same time in the natural world with men, 1, 39, 326. State of anxiety into which he fell when once he thought of the essence and omnipresence of God from eternity, that is, of God before the creation of the world, 328. The angels, as well as himself, did not know the differences between spiritual and natural, because there had never before been an opportunity of comparing them together by any person's existing at the same time in both worlds; and without such comparison and reference those differences were not ascertainable, 327. On a certain time, as he was wandering through the streets of a great city inquiring for a lodging, he entered a house inhabited by married partners of a different religion; the angels instantly accosted him, and told him they could not on that account remain with him there, 242. He had observed for twenty-five years continually, from an influx perceptible and sensible, that it is impossible to think analytically concerning any form of government, civil law, moral virtue, or any spiritual truth, unless the divine principle flows in from the Lord's wisdom through the spiritual world, 419. He declares, that having related a thousand particulars respecting departed spirits, he has never heard any one object, how can such be their lot when they are not yet risen from their sepulchres, the last judgment not being yet accomplished? 28.
SWEDES, 103, 112.
SWEETNESS.—In heaven, the chaste love of the sex is called heavenly sweetness, 55.
SYMPATHIES.—In the spiritual world sympathies are not only felt, but also appear in the face, the discourse, and gesture, 273. With some married partners in the natural world, there is antipathy in internals, combined with apparent sympathy in their externals, 292. Sympathy derives its origin from the concordance of spiritual spheres, which emanate from subjects, 171.

TABERNACLE.—In heaven, the most ancient people dwell in tabernacles, because, whilst in the world, they lived in tabernacles, 75. Tabernacle of their worship exactly similar to the tabernacle of which the form was showed to Moses on Mount Sinai, 75.
TABLES of wood and stone on which were the writings of the most ancient people, 77. Tablet with this inscription, "The covenant between Jehovah and the Heavens," 75.
TARTARUS, 75.—Shades of Tartarus, 75.
TARTARY.—The ante-Mosaic Word, at this day lost, is reserved only in Great Tartary, 77.
TASTE, sense of.—The love of self-nourishment, grounded in the love of imbibing goods, is the sense of tasting, and the delights proper to it are the various kinds of delicate foods, 210.
TEMPERANCE is one of those moral virtues which have respect to life and enter into it, 164.
TEMPLE, description of a, in heaven, 23. Temple of wisdom, where the causes of the beauty of the female sex were discussed, 56.
TEMPORAL.—Idea of what is temporal in regard to marriages, effect that it produced on two married partners from heaven present with Swedenborg, 216.
THEATRES in the heavens, 17.—See *Actors*.
THING, every, created by the Lord is representative, 294.
THINK, to, spiritually is to think abstractedly from space and time, and to think naturally is to think in conjunction with space and time, 328. To think and conclude from an interior and prior principle is to think and conclude from ends and causes to effects, but to think and conclude from an exterior or posterior principle, is to think and conclude from effects to causes and ends, 408. The spiritual man thinks of things incomprehensible and ineffable to the natural man, 826.
THOUGHT is the *existere*, or existence of a man's life, from the *esse* or essence, which is love, 36. Spiritual thoughts, compared with natural, are thoughts of thoughts, 326. Spiritual thoughts are the begin-

467

nings and origins of natural thoughts, 826. Spiritual thought so far exceeds natural thought as to be respectively ineffable, 826.

THUNDER.—Clapping of the air like thunder is a correspondence and consequent appearance of the conflict and collision of arguments amongst spirits, 415.

TONES, discordant, brought into harmony, 243.

TOUCH, to.—This sense is common to all the other senses, and hence borrows somewhat from them, 210. It is the sense proper to conjugial love, 210. The love of knowing objects, grounded on the love of circumspection and self-preservation, is the sense of touching, and the gratifications proper to it are the various kinds of titillation, 210. The innocence of parents and the innocence of children meet each other by the touch, especially of the hands, 396. See *Sense.*

TRADES.—In the spiritual world there are trades, 207.

TRANQUILLITY is in conjugial love, and relates to the mind, 180.

TRANSCRIBED, to be.—Whereas every man (*homo*) by birth inclined to love himself, it was provided from creation, to prevent man's perishing by self-love, and the conceit of his own intelligence, that that love of the man (*vir*) should be transcribed into the wife, 353, 88, 193, 293.

TRANSCRIPTION, the, of the good of one person into another is impossible, 525.

TREE, a, signifies man, 185. The tree of life signifies man living from God, or God living in man, 135. To eat of this tree signifies to receive eternal life, 135. The tree of the knowledge of good and evil, signifies the belief that life for man is not God, but self, 135. By eating thereof signifies damnation, 135.

TRINITY, the Divine, is in Jesus Christ, in whom dwells all the fulness of the Godhead bodily, 24.

TRUTH.—What the understanding perceives and thinks is called truth, 490. Truth is the form of good, 193, 493. There is the truth of good, and from this the good of truth, or truth grounded in good, and good grounded in that truth; and in these two principles is implanted from creation an inclination to join themselves together into one, 88. The truth of good, or truth grounded in good, is male (or masculine), and the good of truth, or good grounded in truth, is female (or feminine), 61, 88. See *Good and Truth.*

TRUTH does not admit of reasonings, 481.

TRUTHS pertain to the understanding, 128.

Two.—In every part of the body where there are not two, they are divided into two, 316.

TZIIM.—In hell, the forms of birds, and under which the lascivious delights of adulterous love are presented to the view, are birds called tziim, 480.

ULCERS, 253.

ULTIMATE.—It is a universal law that things primary exist, subsist, and persist from things ultimate, 44. That the ultimate state is such as the successive order is, from which it is formed and exists, is a canon which, from its truth, must be acknowledged in the learned world, 318.

ULYSSES, companions of, changed into hogs, 521.

UNCHASTITY, difference between, and what is not chaste, 139. Unchastity is entirely opposed to chastity, 139. There is a conjugial love which is not chaste, and yet is not unchastity, 189. The love opposite to conjugial love is essential unchastity, 189. If the renunciations of whoredoms be not made from a principle of religion, unchastity lies inwardly concealed like corrupt matter in a wound only outwardly healed, 149.

UNCLEAN or FILTHY, every, principle of hell is from adulterers, 500.

UNCLEANNESS, 252, 472.

UNDERSTANDING, the.—Man has understanding from heavenly light, 233. The understanding considered in itself is merely the ministering and serving principle of the will, 196. It is only the form of the will, 493. Man is capable of elevating his intellect above his natural loves, 96. See *Will and Understanding.*

UNION.—Spiritual union of two married partners is the actual adjunction of the soul and mind of the one to the soul and mind of the other, 321. Conjugial love is the union of souls, 179, 480, 482. Union between two married partners in heaven is like that of the two tents in the breast, which are called the heart and the lungs, 75.

UNITY, the, of souls between two married partners in heaven is seen in their faces; the life of the husband is in the wife, and the life of the wife is in the husband—they are two bodies but one soul, 75,

UNIVERSALS.—Whoever knows universals may afterwards comprehend particulars, because the latter are in the former as parts in a whole, 261. Good and truth are the universals of creation, 84, 92. There are three universals of heaven and three universals of hell, 261. A universal principle exists from, and consists of singulars, 388. If we take away singulars, a universal is a mere name, and is like somewhat superficial, which has no contents within, 388. A universal truth is acknowledged by every intelligent man, 60. Every universal truth is acknowledged as soon as it is heard, in consequence of the Lord's influx and at the same time of the confirmation of heaven, 62.

UNIVERSE.—The universe, with all its created subjects, is from the divine love, by the divine wisdom, or what is the same thing, from the divine good, by the divine truth, 87. All things which proceed from the Lord, or from the sun, which is from him, and in which he is, pervade the created universe, even to the last of all its prin ciples, 389. All things in the universe have relation to good and truth, 60. In every thing in the universe good is conjoined with truth, and truth with good, 60. USE is essential good, 183, 77. Use in doing good from love by wisdom, 183. Creation can only be from divine love by divine wisdom, in divine use, 183. All things in the universe are procreated and formed from use, in use, and for use, 183. All use is from the Lord, and is effected by angels and men, as of themselves, 7. Uses are the bonds of society; there are as many bonds as there are uses, and the number of uses is infinite, 18. There are spiritual uses, such as regard love towards God, and love towards our neighbor, 18. There are moral and civil uses, such as regard the love of the society and state to which a man belongs, and of his fellow-citizens among whom he lives, 18. There are natural uses, which regard the love of the world and its necessities, 18; and there are corporeal uses, such as regard the love of self-preservation with a view to superior uses, 18. The delight of the love of uses is a heavenly delight, which enters into succeeding delights in their order, and according to the order of succession exalts them and makes them eternal, 18. Delights follow use, and are also communicated to man according to the love thereof, 68. The delight of being useful derives its essence from love, and its existence from wisdom, 5. This delight, originating in love and operating by wisdom, is the very soul and life of all heavenly joys, 5. Those who are only in natural and corporeal uses are satans, loving only the world and themselves, for the sake of the world; and those who are only in corporeal uses are devils, because they live to themselves alone, and to others only for the sake of themselves, 18. Happiness is derived to every angel from the use he performs in his function, 6. The public good requires that every individual, being a member of the common body, should be an instrument of use in the society to which he belongs, 7. To such as faithfully perform uses, the Lord gives the love thereof, 7. So far as uses are done from the love thereof, so far that love increases, 266. The use of conjugial love is the most excellent of all uses, 183, 305. Conjugial love is according to the love of growing wise, for the sake of uses from the Lord, 183. How can any one know whether he performs uses from self-love, or from the love of uses? 266. Every one who believes in the Lord, and shuns evils as sins, performs uses from the Lord; but every one who neither believes in the Lord, nor shuns evils as sins, does uses from self, and for the sake of self, 266. All good uses in the heavens are splendid and refulgent, 266. Blessed lot of those who are desirous to have dominion from the love of uses, 266.

Obs.—Use consists in fulfilling faithfully, sincerely, and carefully, the duties of our functions, *T. C. R.*, 744. Those things are called *uses* which, proceeding from the Lord, are by creation in order, *D. L. and W.*, 298.

USES of apparent love and friendship between married partners, for the sake of preserving order in domestic affairs, 271, and following, 283.

UTILITY of apparent love and apparent friendship between married partners, for the sake of preserving order in domestic affairs, 271, and following, 283.

VAPOR.—From reason it may be seen that the soul of man after death is not a mere vapor, 29.

VARIETY.—There is a perpetual variety, and there is not any thing the same with another thing, 524. Heaven consists of perpetual varieties, 524. Distinction between varieties and diversities, 324. See *Diversities.*

VEGETABLES.—Wonders in the productions of vegetables, 416.

VEIN.—There is a certain vein latent in the affection of the will of every angel which attracts his mind to the execution of some purpose, 6. Vein of conjugial love, 44, 68, 183, 293, 313, 433, 482.

VENTRICLES of the brain, 315.

VERNAL, the, principle exists only where warmth is equally united to light, 137. With men (*homines*) there is a perpetual influx of vernal warmth from the Lord, it is otherwise with animals, 137. In heaven, where there is vernal warmth, there is love truly conjugial, 137.

VIOLATION of spiritual marriage, 515-520. Violation of spiritual marriage is violation of the Word, 516. Violation of the Word is adulteration of good, and falsification of truth, 517. This violation of the Word corresponds to scortations and adulteries, 518. By whom, in the Christian church, violation of the Word is committed, 519.

VIRGINITY.— Fate of those who have vowed perpetual virginity, 155, 460, 503.

VIRGINS, 21, 22, 293, 321, 502, 511. The affection of truth is called a virgin, 293. The virgins (Matt. xxv. 1) signify the church, 21. Quality of the state of virgins before and after marriage in heaven, 502. Virgins of the fountain, 207, 293. The nine virgins, or muses, signify knowledge and science of every kind, 182. How a virgin is formed into a wife, 199.

VIRTUES, moral, and spiritual virtues, 164. Various graces and virtues of moral life represented in theatres in heaven, 17. Manly virtue, 433, 355.

VISIBLE.—Every one may confirm himself in favor of a divine principle or being, from what is visible in nature, 416-421.

VISION, posterior, 233.

VITIATED states of mind and body which are legitimate causes of separation, 252, 253.

WARS, the, of Jehovah. The name of the historical books of the ante Mosaic Word, 77.

WATER FROM THE FOUNTAIN, to drink, signifies to be instructed concerning truths, and by truths concerning goods, and thereby to grow wise, 182.

WEASELS.—Who they are who appear at a distance in the spiritual world like weasels, 514.

WHIRLPOOLS which are in the borders of the worlds, 389.

WHITE, the color, signifies intelligence, 76.

WHITE, what is, in heaven is truth, 316.

WHOREDOM, spiritual, is the falsification of truth, which acts in unity with that which is natural, because they cohere, 80. Whoredoms in the spiritual sense of the word signify the connubial connection of what is evil and false, 423. They signify the falsification of truth, 518. Whoredom is the destruction of society, 345. They are imputed to every one after death, not according to the deeds themselves, but according to the state of the minds in the deeds, 530.

WHOREDOMS in the spiritual sense signify the connection (*connubium*) of evil and false, 423. Toleration of such evils in populous cities, 451.

WIDOW.—Why the state of a widow is more grievous than that of a widower, 325.

WIFE, a, is the love of a wise man's wisdom, 56. She represents the love of her husband's wisdom, 21. The wife signifies the good of truth, 76. In heaven, the wife is the love of her husband's wisdom, and the husband is the wisdom of her love, 75. The wife perceives, sees, and is sensible of the things which are in her husband, in herself, and thence as it were herself in him, 173. There is with wives a sixth sense, which is the sense of all the delights of the conjugial love of the husband, and this sense is in the palms of the hands, 155*. Conjugial love resides with chaste wives, but still their love depends on the husband's, 216*. Wives love the bonds of marriage if the men do, 217. Wives seated on a bed of roses, 293. In a rosary, 294. Acts which certain wives employ to subject their husbands to their own authority, 292. See *Woman, Married Partners.*

WILL, the, is the receptacle of love, for what a man loves that he wills, 347. Will principle, considered in itself, is nothing but an affect and effect of some love, 461. Whoever conjoins to himself the will of a man, conjoins to himself the whole man, 196. The will acts by the body, wherefore, if the will were to be taken away, action would be instantly at a stand, 494.

WILL and UNDERSTANDING.—The will is the man himself, and the understanding is the man as grounded in the will, 490. The life of man essentially is his will, and formally is his understanding, 493. The will is the receptacle of good, and the understanding is the receptacle of truth, 121. Love, charity, and affection, belong to the will, and perception and thought to the understanding, 121. All things which are done by a man are done from his will and understanding, and without these acting principles a man would not have either action or speech, otherwise than as a machine, 527. Whoever conjoins to himself the will of another, conjoins also to himself his understanding, 196. The understanding is not so constant in its thoughts as the will is in its affections, 221. He that does not discriminate between will and understanding, cannot discriminate between evils and goods, 490. The will alone of itself acts nothing, but whatever it acts, it acts by the understanding, and the understanding alone of itself acts nothing, but whatever it acts, it acts from the will, 490. With every man the understanding is capable of being elevated according to knowledges, but the will only by a life according to the truths of the church, 269. The natural man can elevate his understanding into the light of heaven, and think and discourse spiritually, but if the will at the same time does not follow the understanding, he is still not elevated, for he does not remain in that elevation, but in a short time he lets himself down to his will, and there fixes his station, 347, 495. The will flows into the understanding, but not the understanding into the will, yet the understanding teaches what is good and evil, and consults with the will, that out of those two principles it may choose, and do what is agreeable to it, 490. The will of the wife conjoins itself with the understanding of the man, and thence the understanding of the man with the will of the wife, 159. In adultery of the reason, the understanding acts from within, and the will from without, but in adultery of the will, the will acts from within, and the understanding from without, 490.

WISDOM is nothing but a form of love, 493. It is a principle of life, 130. Wisdom, considered in its fulness, is a principle, at the same time, of knowledges, of reason, and of life, 130. What wisdom is as a principle of life, 130, 293. Wisdom consists of truths, 84. The understanding is the receptacle of wisdom, 400. The abode of wisdom is in use, 18. Wisdom cannot exist with a man but by means of the love of growing wise, 88. Wisdom with men is twofold, rational and moral; their rational wisdom is of the understanding alone, and their moral wisdom is of the understanding and life together, 163, 293. Rational wisdom regards the truths and goods which appear inwardly in man, not as its own, but as flowing in from the Lord, 102. Moral wisdom shuns evils and falses as leprosies, especially the evils of lasciviousness, which contaminate its conjugial love, 102. The things which relate to rational wisdom constitute man's understanding, and those which relate to moral wisdom constitute his will, 195. Wisdom of wives, 208. The perception, which is the wisdom of the wife, is not communicable to the man, neither is the rational wisdom

470

of the man communicable to the wife, 168, 208. The moral wisdom of the man is not communicable to women, so far as it partakes of rational wisdom, 168. Wisdom and conjugial love are inseparable companions, 98. The Lord provides conjugial love for those who desire wisdom, and who consequently advance more and more into wisdom, 98. There is no end to wisdom, 185. Temple of wisdom, 56. Sports of wisdom, 132, 151*. See *Love and Wisdom.*

WISE.—A wise one is not a wise one without a woman, or without love, a wife being the love of a wise man's wisdom, 56.

WOMAN, the, was created and born to become the love of the understanding of a man, 55, 91. Woman was created out of the man, hence she has an inclination to unite, and, as it were, reunite herself with the man, 173. Conjugial love is implanted in every woman from creation, 409. Woman is actually formed into a wife, according to the description in the book of creation, 193. In the universe nothing was created more perfect than a woman of a beautiful countenance and becoming manners, 56. The woman receives from the man the truth of the church, 125. Woman, by a peculiar property with which she is gifted from her birth, draws back the internal affections into the inner recesses of her mind, 274. Affection, application, manners, and form of woman, 91, 218. Women were created by the Lord affections of the wisdom of men, 56. They are created forms of the love of the understanding of men, 187. Women have an interior perception of love, and men only an exterior, 47*. In assemblies where the conversation of the men turns on subjects proper to rational wisdom, women are silent, listen only, the reason why, 165. Intelligence of wisdom, 218. Women cannot enter into the duties proper to men, 175. Difference between females, women, and wives, 199. See *Wife.*

WONDERS conspicuous in eggs, 416.

WOOD signifies natural good, 77. Woods of palm-trees, and of rose-trees, 77.

WORD, the ancient, at this day is lost, and is only reserved in Great Tartary, 77. The historical books of this Word are called the Wars of Jehovah, and the prophetic books The Enunciations, 77.

WORD, the, with the most ancient, and with the ancient people, 77.

WORD, the, is the Lord, 516. In every thing of the Word there is the marriage of good and truth, 516. The Word is the medium of conjunction of the Lord with man, and of man with the Lord, 128. In its essence it is divine truth united to divine good, and divine good united to divine truth, 128. It is the perfect marriage of good and truth, 128. In every part of the Word there is a spiritual sense corresponding to the natural sense, and by means of the former sense the men of the church have conjunction with the Lord, and consociation with angels, 532. The sanctity of the Word resides in this sense, 532. While man reads the Word, and collects truths out of it, the Lord adjoins good, 128.

WORKHOUSES, infernal, 264. See also 54, 80, 461.

WORKS are good or bad, according as they proceed from an upright will and thought, or from a depraved will and thought, whatever may be their appearance in externals, 527. Good works are uses, 10.

WORLD OF SPIRITS, the, is intermediate between heaven and hell, and there the good are prepared for heaven, and the wicked for hell, 48*, 436, 461, 477. It is in the world of spirits that all men are first collected after their departure out of the natural world, 2, 477. The good are there prepared for heaven, and the wicked for hell; and after such preparation, they discover ways open for them to societies of their like, with whom they are to live eternally, 10, 477.

WORLD, the, natural, subsists from its sun, which is pure fire, 380. There is not any thing in the natural world which is not also in the spiritual world, 182, 207. In the natural world, almost all are capable of being joined together as to external affections, but not as to internal affections, if these disagree and appear, 272.

WORLD, the spiritual, subsists from its sun, which is pure love, as the natural world subsists from its sun, 380. In the spiritual world there are not spaces, but appearances of spaces, and these appearances are according to the states of life of the inhabitants, 50. All things there appear according to correspondences, 76. All who, from the beginning of creation have departed by death out of the natural world, are in the spiritual world, and as to their loves, resemble what they were when alive in the natural world, and continue such to eternity, 78. In the spiritual world there are all such things there as there are on earth, and those things in the heavens are infinitely more perfect, 182.

Obs.—The spiritual world in general comprehends heaven, the world of spirits, and hell.

WORMS.—Wonders concerning them, 418. Silk-worms, 420.

WORSHIP, the, of God in heaven returns at stated periods, and lasts about two hours, 23.

WRATH.—If love, especially the ruling love, be touched, there ensues an emotion of the mind (*animus*); if the touch hurts, there ensues wrath, 358.

WRITERS.—The most ancient writers, whose works remain to us, do not go back beyond the iron age, 73. See *Writings.*

WRITINGS, the, of the most ancient and of the ancient people are not extant; the writings which exist are those of authors who lived after the ages of gold, silver, and iron, 73. Writings of some learned authoresses, examined in the spiritual world in the presence of those authoresses, 175. The writings, which proceed from ingenui-

471

ty and wit, on account of the elegance and neatness of the style in which they are written, have the appearance of sublimity and erudition, but only in the eyes of those who call all ingenuity by the name of wisdom, 175. Writing in the heavens, 182, 326.

XENOPHON, 151*.

YOUTH.—In heaven, all are in the flower of youth, and continue therein to eternity, 250. All who come into heaven return into their vernal youth, and into the powers appertaining to that age, and thus continue to eternity, 44. Infants in heaven do not grow up beyond their first age, and there they stop, and remain therein to eternity, 411, 444; and that when they attain the stature which is common to youths of eighteen years old in the word, and to virgins of fifteen, 444.

YOUTH.—In heaven they remain forever in a state of youth, 355. See *Age*.

YOUTH, A.—The state of marriage of a youth with a widow, 322. How a youth formed into a husband, 199.

YOUTHFUL.—With men, the youthful principle is changed into that of a husband, 199.

ZEAL is of love, 358. Zeal is a spiritual burning or flame, 359. Zeal is not the highest degree of love, but it is burning love, 358. The quality of a man's zeal is according to the quality of his love, 362. There are the zeal of a good love and the zeal of an evil love, 862. These two zeals are alike in externals, but altogether unlike in internals, 363. The zeal of a good love in its internals contains a hidden store of love and friendship; but the zeal of an evil love in its internals contains a hidden store of hatred and revenge, 365. The zeal of conjugial love is called jealousy, 367. Wives are, as it were, burning zeals for the preservation of friendship and conjugial confidence, 155*.

ZEALOUS (*Zelotes*).—Why Jehovah in the Word is called zealous, 366.

www.ingramcontent.com/pod-product-compliance
Lightning Source LLC
Chambersburg PA
CBHW022104300426
44117CB00007B/579